Praise for *The Crusade Years, 1933-1955*

"*The Crusade Years* fills a crucial gap in the literary legacy left by our thirty-first president in the years after he left the White House. Another important piece of the Hoover puzzle, it complements *Freedom Betrayed*, posthumously plugging gaps in domestic policy as the earlier book did for foreign policy. Beyond the political wars, it illuminates the human side of Hoover: his family and hobbies, love of fishing, of people, and of his alma mater. The orphan's heart also lingered long over the plight of America's children, demonstrated by his contributions to the Boys' Clubs of America. Editor George H. Nash provides an introductory analysis of Hoover's life, establishes the historical context for the evolution of the manuscript, and elucidates Hoover's motives and methodology. This long-delayed, scrupulously edited book is essential to understanding our most active and tenacious ex-president, a cornerstone in the written legacy compiled by this prolific statesman and his most indefatigable historian."

> —GLEN JEANSONNE is professor of history, University of Wisconsin–
> Milwaukee, and author of *The Life of Herbert Hoover: Fighting Quaker, 1928–*
> *1933.*

"Herbert Hoover, self-styled crusader, is in full flower in these pages—part memoirist, part polemicist, coupling intimate portraiture with a public history that is profoundly relevant. Once again George Nash demonstrates an encyclopedic knowledge of all things Hoover, while assembling the former president's intellectual brief against the New Deal in a style that is both highly readable and faithful to its author's sometimes quirky standards. Together with its companion volume, *Freedom Betrayed*, *The Crusade Years* completes at last the sprawling work of revisionism Hoover called 'my Roosevelt book.' It is, in fact, much more than that. It is hard to imagine any comprehensive account of those tumultuous years that fails to incorporate the evidence compiled by Hoover and made accessible to modern Americans by his foremost interpreter."

> —RICHARD NORTON SMITH is a presidential historian and author, former
> director of several presidential libraries, and current scholar-in-residence at
> George Mason University.

"Superbly introduced and edited by acclaimed Herbert Hoover biographer George H. Nash, *The Crusade Years* is far more than a simple apologia pro vita sua. It offers touching glimpses into Hoover's rich personal life and a trenchant critique of the post–New Deal American social contract that amounts to nothing less than the cornerstone of modern conservatism. By turns intimate, humorous, and combative—even occasionally petulant—this last volume of Hoover's memoirs will interest historians and general readers alike."

> —DAVID KENNEDY is professor of history emeritus at Stanford University and
> the author of *Freedom from Fear: The American People in Depression and War,*
> *1929–1945.*

"George Nash, always the curious academic detective, has discovered and published the private thoughts of Hoover on the New Deal. This excellent memoir edition reminds us that Hoover (1) was the chief original crusader against New Deal collectivism, (2) argued that the New Deal could be rolled back, and (3) showed what it took to be the first activist ex-president in American politics. Well done, very timely, and with a helpful introduction."

> —GORDON LLOYD is professor of public policy at the School of Public Policy, Pepperdine University.

"For many years Herbert Hoover worked on a memoir of his post presidential years, almost until his death at ninety. Now George Nash, the premier historian of American conservatism, has unearthed this vast work from the Hoover Institution Archives and has edited it for publication. Nash has also provided an illuminating introduction to this fine contribution to the historical record."

> —MICHAEL BARONE is senior political analyst at the *Washington Examiner*, resident fellow at the American Enterprise Institute, and coauthor of *The Almanac of American Politics*.

"Herbert Hoover's life, despite his difficult presidency, was followed by his many humanitarian works. After World War II, he worked to provide food for the new Germany. Hoover helped provide 40,000 tons of food for more than three million children. Few people, both before and after his presidency, have done more to help so many people."

> —ALAN BRINKLEY is Allan Nevins Professor of History and provost emeritus at Columbia University, and author of *Franklin Delano Roosevelt* and *The Publisher: Henry Luce and his American Century*.

"Through tenacious and persistent scholarship coupled with artful editing, George H. Nash, the dean of Hoover scholars, has admirably reconstructed Hoover's last literary effort, a missing link long unknown to scholars. In *The Crusade Years* the guarded, enigmatic ex-president candidly discusses his personal and family life and clearly articulates his objections to collectivism while forcefully arguing for a realist political philosophy based on individualism and volunteerism. *The Crusade Years* establishes Hoover as one of the preeminent political thinkers of the last century, a man who developed a 'political yardstick' useful in analyzing today's topsy-turvy politics."

> —HAL ELLIOTT WERT is professor of history, Kansas City Art Institute, and author of *Hoover, the Fishing President: Portrait of the Private Man and His Life Outdoors*.

"With unparalleled and meticulous scholarship, editor George Nash reveals the Herbert Hoover we never knew: the prophet. It is striking how powerful Hoover's warnings against statist progressivism remain—how easily these pages could be turned into blogposts as conservatives battle 'progressives' in our own day."

> —AMITY SHLAES, author, *Coolidge* and *The Forgotten Man: A New History of the Depression*

The Crusade Years

Herbert Hoover on the eve of his 85th birthday, August 6, 1959.

THE
CRUSADE YEARS
1933 – 1955

Herbert Hoover's
Lost Memoir *of the* New Deal Era
and Its Aftermath

Edited with an Introduction by

George H. Nash

HOOVER INSTITUTION PRESS
Stanford University ◆ Stanford, California
2013

www.hoover.org

Hoover Institution Press Publication No. 641

Hoover Institution at Leland Stanford Junior University,
    Stanford, California, 94305-6010

First printing 2013
20 19 18 17 16 15 14 13   8 7 6 5 4 3 2 1

Manufactured in the United States of America

The paper used in this publication meets the minimum Requirements of The American National Standard for Information Sciences—Permanence of Paper for Printed Library Materials, ANSI/NISO Z39.48-1992. ∞

Cataloging-in-Publication Data is available from the Library of Congress.
ISBN 978-0-8179-1674-9 (cloth. : alk. paper)
ISBN 978-0-8179-1676-3 (e-book)
ISBN 978-0-8179-1677-0 (mobi)
ISBN 978-0-8179-1678-7 (PDF)

The world has survived error in ideas and confusion before. And men have grown in soul and safety because some groups of them have stood solid. They stood fast not because they knew the solutions to all the confusions, not even because they had the power to find the solution. They stood firm and they held up the light until the furies passed because they held certain sacred principles of life, of morals, and of spiritual values. I could at least do that.

—Herbert Hoover, April 1950

CONTENTS

[*Illustrations follow pages 56 and 344.*]

EDITOR'S ACKNOWLEDGMENTS

It is a pleasure to acknowledge and thank the Herbert Hoover Foundation for authorizing publication of *The Crusade Years* and for its grant support to the Hoover Institution on War, Revolution and Peace for my work as editor. At the Hoover Institution itself, the director, John Raisian, and his colleagues David Davenport, Jeffrey Jones, Stephen Langlois, and Richard Sousa have enthusiastically encouraged my efforts. At the Hoover Institution Archives, where most of the relevant papers for this project are housed, I spent part of the summer of 2012 as a visiting fellow and benefited once again from the expertise and courteous assistance of the archival staff. My thanks to one and all, particularly Linda Bernard, Carol Leadenham, Dale Reed, and Nicholas Siekierski for their efficient and helpful responses to my many queries. I am grateful also to Deborah Ventura and Celeste Szeto of the Hoover Institution for again facilitating my use of Stanford University's academic resources during my weeks in residence.

Whenever I visit Stanford it is a special pleasure to call on the retired director of the Hoover Institution Archives, Charles Palm, and his wife, Miriam, whose friendship and hospitality now stretch back many years. Warm thanks to Charles for again sharing his great knowledge of Herbert Hoover's papers and the history of the Hoover Institution and to Miriam for sharing her own substantial knowledge of the history of the university that was home to the Hoovers for so many years.

The Herbert Hoover Presidential Library in West Branch, Iowa, is another repository on whose resources I drew repeatedly while editing this volume. Although I no longer live in its vicinity, the members of the library staff, led by its director, Thomas Schwartz, continue to be my "neighbors" in cyberspace. My thanks especially to Matt Schaefer for his expert answers to my many reference questions and to his colleagues Jim Detlefsen, Spencer Howard, Lynn Smith, and Craig Wright for their able assistance as well.

In western Massachusetts, where I now reside, Charlotte Slocum Patriquin and her colleagues in the library of Mount Holyoke College readily and competently facilitated my research on many occasions, as did the reference librarians at my alma mater, Amherst College. At the public library in my hometown of South Hadley, the resourceful adult services librarian, Desirée Smelcer, repeatedly located elusive books and articles that I needed to consult.

To all these librarians and archivists, near and far, I offer appreciative thanks.

In steering *The Crusade Years* to publication I have had the pleasure of working with a team of talented and conscientious individuals at the Hoover Institution Press and the Hoover Institution's media relations office, including: Jennifer Presley, Marshall Blanchard, Sarah Bielecki, Scott Harrison, Jennifer Navarrette, Laura Somers, and Erin Witcher. The Press's designated copy editor, Kathy Swain, carried out her large task with commendable care and precision.

For proofreading assistance I am grateful to Jennifer Holloway and Betsy Dietrich. My thanks to Cynthia Swanson for preparing the index.

I am also grateful to Jerry Fleagle, Delene McConnaha, and the Herbert Hoover Presidential Library Association for permission to quote from an oral history copyrighted by the association and for permission to adapt and incorporate into the editor's introduction certain previously published writings of mine to which the association holds copyright. I also thank Martin Scrivener of Scrivener Publishing for permission to adapt and incorporate into the editor's introduction a few paragraphs from my foreword to *The Two Faces of Liberalism*, edited by Gordon Lloyd and published in 2006 by M & M Scrivener Press.

For most of my career the life of Herbert Hoover has been at the center of my scholarship, and my sister Nancy, a writer herself, has heard me discourse about it often. Her encouragement has been unstinting. This is also an appropriate moment to acknowledge the hearty support of Andrew, Jean, and Margaret Hoover for *The Crusade Years* publication project.

Finally, and for the second time in three years, I have the genuine pleasure of thanking Jennifer Holloway, who typed virtually every word of this volume, assisted with the proofreading, and guided the manuscript past various technical shoals. As always, she carried out her tasks with high efficiency and good cheer.

EDITOR'S INTRODUCTION

The Crusader

Prelude: Success and Rejection

On a cool October morning in 1964, Herbert Hoover died in New York City at the age of ninety. He had lived a phenomenally productive life, including more than half a century in one form or another of public service. It was a record that in sheer scope and duration may be without parallel in American history.

His life had begun in humble circumstances in 1874 in a little Iowa farming community as the son of the village blacksmith and of a mother who became a recorded minister in the Society of Friends. Orphaned before he was ten, Hoover managed to enter Stanford University when it opened its doors in 1891. Four years later he graduated as a member of the "pioneer" class, with a degree in geology and a determination to become a mining engineer.

From then on, Hoover's rise in the world was meteoric. By the time he was twenty-four, he was superintendent of a gold mine in the desolate outback of Western Australia. By the age of twenty-seven, he had managed a gigantic coal mining enterprise in northern China and had survived a harrowing brush with death in the Boxer Rebellion. By 1914, at the age of forty, Hoover was an internationally acclaimed and extraordinarily successful mining engineer who had traveled around the world five times and had business interests on every continent except Antarctica.

During World War I, Hoover, residing in London, rose to prominence as the founder and director of the Commission for Relief in Belgium, an institution that provided desperately needed food supplies to more than nine million Belgian and French citizens trapped between the German army of occupation and the British naval blockade. His emergency relief mission in 1914 quickly evolved into a gigantic humanitarian enterprise without precedent in world history. By 1917 he was an international hero, the embodiment of a new force in global politics: American benevolence.

When America declared war on Germany in 1917, Hoover returned home and became head of the United States Food Administration, a specially created wartime agency of the federal government. "Food Will Win the War" became his slogan. As the architect and implementer of America's food policies, he was one of the nation's most important wartime leaders.

At the conflict's victorious close in 1918, President Woodrow Wilson dispatched Hoover to Europe to organize food distribution to a continent careening toward disaster. There, for ten grueling months, he directed American-led efforts to combat famine and disease, establish stable postwar economies, and in the process check the advance of Bolshevik revolution from the East. It was a herculean undertaking, entailing the purchase and shipping of food from all over the earth and then the distribution of it in more than twenty strife-torn nations.

A little later, between 1921 and 1923, Hoover's American Relief Administration administered a massive emergency relief operation in the interior of Soviet Russia, where a catastrophic famine—Europe's worst since the Middle Ages—had broken out. He did so at the request of Russia's anxious but suspicious Communist leaders, who wanted his help but feared his militant anticommunism. Millions died before Hoover's food shipments and aid workers could reach all of the starving, but millions more survived thanks to Hoover's provision. At its peak of operations, his organization fed upward of ten million Russian citizens a day.

All in all, between 1914 and 1923 the American-born engineer-turned-humanitarian directed, financed, or assisted a multitude of international relief endeavors without parallel in the history of mankind. Nearly thirty-four million metric tons of food were delivered to the lands and peoples imperiled by World War I and its aftermath. The monetary value of this sustenance exceeded $5,234,000,000—a figure that, in today's currency, would easily top $60 billion. For most of this incredible undertaking, Herbert Hoover had high administrative responsibility.

No one can say precisely how many people owed their lives to his exertions. By one possibly conservative estimate, prepared by this author some years ago, between 1914 and 1923 more than eighty-three million men, women, and children in more than twenty countries received food allotments for which Hoover and his associates were at least partially responsible. This figure does not include the belligerent populations of America's principal wartime allies (Great Britain, France, and Italy)—120,000,000 people—who received critically needed foodstuffs from the United States in 1917–18: a form of "foreign aid" that cannot be considered humanitarian assistance in the ordinary sense of the term.

Eighty-three million people—it is a staggering figure. But whether this estimate is high or low, Hoover's standing in the annals of humanitarianism is incontestable. As someone remarked a number of years ago, Herbert Hoover was responsible for saving more lives than any other person in history.

In 1919 the "food regulator for the world" (as General John J. Pershing called him) returned from Europe an international luminary.[1] He became known as the "Great Humanitarian" and was hailed as the "Napoleon of Mercy."[2] Just forty-five years old, he was at the threshold of political stardom in his native land.

During the Roaring Twenties Hoover ascended still higher on the ladder of public esteem. As secretary of commerce under Presidents Warren Harding and Calvin Coolidge, he quickly became one of the three or four most influential men in the U.S. government—and in all of American public life. He seemed ubiquitous: it was said of him that he was secretary of commerce and undersecretary of every other department. He took time in 1922 to write a book titled *American Individualism* in which he expounded his understanding of the American sociopolitical system and its undergirding principles. In 1927, with President Coolidge's blessing, he orchestrated a relief operation for more than six hundred thousand displaced victims of the great Mississippi River flood in the lower South—the worst natural disaster in American history. His success added even more luster to his humanitarian reputation. The next year, the "master of emergencies" (as admirers called him) was elected president of the United States in a landslide—without ever having held an elective public office.

Then came the crash of 1929 and the most severe economic trauma this nation has ever experienced. During his tormented presidency, Hoover strained without stint to return his country to prosperity while safeguarding its political moorings. His labors—even now misunderstood—seemed unavailing, and in the election of 1932 his fellow citizens' verdict was harsh.

Before his single term as chief executive, Hoover's career trajectory had curved unbrokenly upward. Now it headed pitifully down. "Democracy is not a polite employer," he later wrote of his defeat at the polls. This was putting it gently. On March 4, 1933, he left office a virtual pariah, maligned and hated like no other American in his lifetime.

And then, astonishingly, like a phoenix, he slowly rose from the ashes of his political immolation. Now came the final phase of Hoover's career: his remarkable ex-presidency. For the next thirty-one and one-half years, in fair political weather and foul, the former chief executive became, in his self-image, a crusader—a tireless and very visible castigator of the dominant political trends of his day.

Now all modern former presidents engage to some degree in ritualistic political activity, such as addressing their party's nominating conventions, campaigning for like-minded candidates, and working the so-called mashed potato circuit. But for Hoover this activity was never ritualistic. He behaved as a committed ideological warrior more persistently and more fervently than any other former president in our history.

Why? Partly, one suspects, because of what he himself once called his "naturally combative disposition" and partly because of the searing circumstances of his repudiation at the polls and rivalry with the man who defeated him. But most of all, it was because Hoover perceived in the New Deal of Franklin Roosevelt not a moderate and pragmatic response to economic distress but something more sinister: a revolutionary transformation in America's political economy and constitutional order.

Having espied the unpalatable future, Hoover could not bring himself to acquiesce. For him, unlike his successors, the New Deal did not seem irreversible. He therefore could not content himself with conventional, above-the-fray elder statesmanship. More than any other former president to date, he chose to be both partisan and nonpartisan simultaneously.

It is this eventful period in Hoover's career—and, more specifically, his life as a political pugilist from 1933 to 1955—that is the main subject of the volume before you. *The Crusade Years* is a previously unknown memoir that Hoover composed and revised during the 1940s and 1950s—and then, surprisingly, set aside. Placed in storage by his heirs after his death, the manuscript (in its various versions) lay sequestered—its existence unsuspected by scholars—until 2009, when it was discovered among the files of another hitherto inaccessible Hoover manuscript being readied for posthumous publication.

This other tome, known informally as the Magnum Opus, addressed American foreign policy in the 1930s and 1940s. Part memoir, part diplomatic history, part polemic, it was a scathing indictment of what Hoover termed Franklin Roosevelt's "lost statesmanship" during World War II. Hoover ultimately titled the book *Freedom Betrayed*. It was published in 2011 by the Hoover Institution Press.

The Crusade Years—a companion volume of sorts to the Magnum Opus— covers much the same time period on the American home front. More fully a memoir than *Freedom Betrayed*, it recounts Hoover's family life after March 4, 1933, his myriad philanthropic interests, and, most of all, his unrelenting "crusade against collectivism" in American life. Rescued from obscurity, this nearly forgotten manuscript is published here—and its contents made available to scholars—for the first time.

The Road Back: Crusading against Collectivism

To appreciate *The Crusade Years* as a historical document, one needs to understand the contours of Hoover's ex-presidency: the stormy context in which this memoir took form.

When Hoover left the White House in 1933, he was not yet fifty-nine years old, a comparatively young age for a former president. Temperamentally incapable of extended repose, he had no intention of receding mutely into the shadows.

Not that retirement lacked appeal after the travails of his embattled presidency. Happily married since 1899 to his wife, Lou, blessed with two grown sons and grandchildren, and possessed of financial resources sufficient to ride out the Depression, Hoover and his wife returned in 1933 to Palo Alto, California, and to the magnificent home they had built in 1919–20 on the campus of their beloved alma mater. Years earlier, as a mining engineer toiling in Australia, Hoover had written wistfully that "Stanford is the best place in the world."[3] So it seemed in the summer of 1933 as he surveyed the placid campus from his home atop San Juan Hill. In his first speech since leaving the White House, he told friends: "I get up fairly early and take a look from the Palo Alto place into Santa Clara Valley. It's very pleasant. Then I have breakfast and a walk. Then I get my mail and look over the newspapers. Then I take another long look at the valley, thanking Providence I'm in California. Then I sit down and think things over and spend the rest of the day laughing and laughing and laughing."[4]

Nevertheless, there was very little that Hoover found amusing in the news streaming out of the nation's capital that summer. Despite his mounting anguish and displeasure—recorded in countless letters to his friends—in 1933 and 1934 Hoover maintained a deliberate public silence about the new man in the White House and his shimmering New Deal. The ex-president did not wish, by any premature, partisan outburst, to jeopardize or appear to jeopardize economic recovery during the national emergency. He doubted that any comments of his would do much good in the current public atmosphere, poisoned as he considered it to be by the incessant "smearing" of his record by the opposition. He hoped also that, as New Deal measures failed (which he expected them to do), the American people would learn from disillusioning experience and return to their traditional values.

But if Hoover stayed aloof from the hullabaloo in Washington for tactical reasons, he was far from indifferent to what he observed. At the climax of the bitter election campaign of 1932, he had portrayed the decision facing the American electorate as more than a choice between two men and two parties. It was a "contest between two philosophies of government," an election that would determine the nation's course for "over a century to come."[5] The proposed New Deal, he had warned, was nothing less than a form of collectivism that would destroy the very foundations of the American system of life.[6] Everything that had happened since had reinforced this conviction. In September 1933 he told a close friend: "The impending battle in this country obviously will be between a properly regulated individualism (which I have always expounded as 'American Individualism') and sheer socialism. That, directly or indirectly, is likely to be the great political battle for some years to come."[7]

Although Hoover continued to use the term "American Individualism" (and even considered reissuing his 1922 book of that title in 1933),[8] increasingly he invoked another word to describe his social philosophy. That word was liberalism. Liberalism, he said late in 1933, "is an intangible, imponderable thing. It is the freedom of men's minds and spirits. It was born with the Renaissance, was re-enforced with the Reformation, was brought to reality by the American revolution, and has survived by much suffering down to the corruption of the great war [World War I]. Today we are engaged in creating regimented men, not free men, both in spirit and in economic life."[9]

Hoover contended that the progress of American civilization had come from "its fidelity to true liberalism." To be sure, our economic system had "often bred autocracies and privilege which in themselves tended to stifle freedom." But, he insisted, until March 4, 1933 (the day of President Roosevelt's inauguration), America had "kept the lamp of liberalism alight by reform and not by revolution."[10]

For Hoover the fundamentals of historic liberalism were embodied in the Constitution and above all in the Bill of Rights. Increasingly, in 1933–34, the Bill of Rights—that charter (in his words) of "ordered individual liberty"—was on his mind. "The discouraging thing," he lamented privately, "is that for some fancied economic boom the American people are prepared to sacrifice their most fundamental possession."[11] Events in Europe, where Adolf Hitler and Benito Mussolini were on the march, added a somber dimension to his concerns. Everywhere, it seemed, the noxious forces of statism were recrudescent. By the end of 1933, as vast New Deal programs such as the National Recovery Administration (NRA) proliferated, the profoundly worried former president believed that the policies of the Roosevelt administration were "driving more clearly to Fascism and Nazism than even towards socialism."[12]

Hoover now responded as he would respond so often to adversity in the years ahead: by firmly putting his pencil to paper. By early 1934 "the Chief" (as his close friends called him) was hard at work on a book manuscript that would confront the ascendant statist ideologies on the terrain where he believed they must be fought: the terrain of philosophy and principle. He solicited comments from a number of old friends, notably the advertising executive Bruce Barton and the editor of the *Woman's Home Companion*, Gertrude Lane.[13] Hoover was not interested in making money on his literary riposte; he told a friend that what did matter was the conveyance of his message to the public in his own manner and idiom.[14] He turned down a chance to publish two articles based on the book in *American Magazine* for $25,000, preferring instead to publish them in the more influential *Saturday Evening Post* for $10,000.[15] Nor was he interested (he said) in the book's possible political reverberations. It was not intended for the 1934 congressional election campaign, he asserted in June, "as I have no interest in its party effect. The Old Guard are not likely to approve it any more than will the Republican Progressives."[16]

For a time Hoover was apparently uncertain whether to publish his book before the election at all.[17] But by early summer he had determined to bring his book out in September.[18] "The time is getting short if this book is to be of service," he told Barton.[19] He later remarked to a friend that if he had held off until after the election, his fellow Republicans could legitimately accuse him of "shirking my responsibility." "In any event," he added, "the campaign itself may enliven a discussion of the question, and that we have to have."[20]

Throughout the summer Hoover prepared to unleash his salvo with as much effect as possible. He arranged for the *Saturday Evening Post* to print two excerpts just prior to publication. He considered a plan to distribute twenty-five thousand copies of his book to political workers (presumably Republicans).[21] He conceived the idea of asking "friendly college professors" to prepare a manifesto defending it against "the deluge of mud which may be coming." After all, he tartly recalled, thirteen hundred professors had publicly petitioned him not to sign the Smoot-Hawley tariff bill in 1930. "I do not see why they should not make a declaration on Liberty itself apropos of this book."[22]

The prospects for wide circulation were enhanced during the summer when the prestigious Book-of-the-Month Club adopted Hoover's volume for October distribution. But to his annoyance the club decided to offer it conjointly with a defense of the New Deal written by Secretary of Agriculture Henry A. Wallace: a book with the alluring title *New Frontiers*. The Chief would have to share the spotlight with a political enemy. To Hoover the club "would never have dreamed of buying [Wallace's book] if it had not been from a desire to appear to be so terribly unbiased." He added: "I am perhaps over-suspicious these days, but when an old and reliable newspaper friend informs me this morning that he has just had an offer of $2,000 from quarters which unquestionably represent the opposition if he would secretely [*sic–ed.*] get copies of the text, and when my mail is tampered with, . . . I begin to think that this is no longer a Republic."[23]

As the moment of publication approached, Hoover's excitement intensified. He hoped that the book's publisher, Charles Scribner's Sons, would keep an advance copy out of the hands of the New Dealers, "as they have no scruples as to the methods which they use."[24] On August 10, his sixtieth birthday, he disclosed to a Republican senator that he would soon "bust loose into print." "I hope that it will do some good," he added. "At least it will relieve my pent up feelings."[25] A few days later he told another friend that his "conscience would not stand further suppression despite much contrary advice from friends."[26]

At times that summer Hoover seemed on the verge of succumbing to despair. On July 9 he told Gertrude Lane that his book was "my last shot at public service." The Chief admitted that he did not "over-estimate the book's usefulness; but it clears my own conscience and does what I can for people groping in the dark. Privately, I have no expectation that a nation which has once cut loose from its moorings to definite human rights and places them at the disposal of the State will ever return to them. History does not move that way, and those who cling to such a philosophy are just part of the wreckage. We can nevertheless yell 'help, help.'"[27] At other times he allowed himself a modest measure of hope. On August 12 he informed Barton that in the past month the country had "turned definitely against the New Deal"[28]—a development that made the need for his book even more compelling. For when the revulsion against the New Deal comes, he wrote in September, "we will have laid such foundations that will make the revulsion to the right instead of to the left. That, in fact, is one of the major objectives of the book."[29]

If Hoover's mood appeared occasionally apocalyptic, it no doubt reflected the incredible ordeal he had been through. Striving conscientiously throughout his presidency against the worst economic calamity in American history, he had found himself relentlessly caricatured as a cold and heartless leader. Shantytowns of the homeless had been derisively named "Hoovervilles";

across the land millions of Americans had seemed to hold him personally responsible for the loss of their homes, their farms, their jobs. Rejection at the polls in 1932 had brought not catharsis but the collapse of the nation's banks during the last days of his presidency—a debacle deliberately precipitated, he believed, by President-elect Roosevelt's refusal to cooperate with the outgoing administration. Nor had the advent of the New Deal led to a ceasefire from his foes. As recently as February 1934, Roosevelt's acerbic secretary of the interior, Harold Ickes, had publicly derided Hoover as "the champion of that ruthless exploiting individualism that was in the main responsible for the terrible economic situation in which we found ourselves."[30] No wonder his regimen of silence was proving difficult to bear.

As Hoover prepared to reenter the public arena, he was especially anxious to counter an expected "deluge of defamation" that his book was the creed of a reactionary. He therefore asked the nationally respected liberal Republican editor, William Allen White, to issue a laudatory review to the press on the day of publication. In this way Hoover hoped to neutralize some of the negative stereotyping sure to ensue.[31]

On September 28, 1934, Hoover's cri de coeur at last appeared. Although initially he had titled his manuscript *American Liberalism*,[32] the book as published bore the more militant title *The Challenge to Liberty*. According to Hoover, the American system of liberty, a system infused by the philosophy of historic liberalism, was under fundamental assault. Where liberalism championed the individual as master of the state and possessor of inalienable rights, alternative philosophies were now boldly advocating "the idea of the servitude of the individual to the state."[33] Among these philosophies—all sharing this fundamental premise—were Nazism, fascism, socialism, communism, and "regimentation" (his term for Franklin Roosevelt's New Deal).

Hoover freely admitted that the American regime of liberty had at times been abused. Repeatedly in his book he expatiated on the need for reform and emphasized that America's traditional social philosophy was not one of unfettered laissez-faire. But the former president insisted that the flaws in the American system were "marginal," corrigible, and far less pernicious than the "bureaucratic tyranny" that would inevitably accompany the collectivist alternatives. In a powerful conclusion the statesman-turned-political-philosopher drew the line:

> We cannot extend the mastery of government over the daily life of a people without somewhere making it master of the people's souls and thoughts. That is going on today. It is part of all regimentation.

Even if the government conduct of business could give us the maximum of efficiency instead of least efficiency, it would be purchased at the cost of freedom. It would increase rather than decrease abuse and corruption, stifle initiative and invention, undermine the development of leadership, cripple the mental and spiritual energies of our people, extinguish equality of opportunity, and dry up the spirit of liberty and the forces which make progress.

It is a false Liberalism that interprets itself into government dictation, or operation of commerce, industry and agriculture. Every move in that direction poisons the very springs of true Liberalism. It poisons political equality, free thought, free press, and equality of opportunity. It is the road not to liberty but to less liberty. True Liberalism is found not in striving to spread bureaucracy, but in striving to set bounds to it. Liberalism is a force proceeding from the deep realization that economic freedom cannot be sacrificed if political freedom is to be preserved. True Liberalism seeks all legitimate freedom first in the confident belief that without such freedom the pursuit of other blessings is in vain.[34]

To Hoover, this was nearly sacred truth. Only partly in jest, he privately referred to his book as "the gospel according to Palo Alto."[35]

The Challenge to Liberty was Hoover's first major public statement after he left the White House, and as he had anticipated, its appearance was an "event." By early October the volume was the best-selling nonfiction book in New York City and was on the best-seller list in nine of the principal book markets of the country.[36] By March 1935, six months after its publication, more than 100,000 copies had been distributed, including 29,600 through the "trade" and 31,000 through the Book-of-the-Month Club.[37] In the grim Depression years of 1934–35 this was a credible showing indeed.

Hoover and his allies labored assiduously to distribute the book far and wide. Nearly eleven thousand copies were sent to libraries throughout the United States, twenty-five hundred to editorialists, and eighty-five hundred to an anti–New Deal organization known as the Crusaders. Seven hundred were shipped to selected preachers. Hoover personally took thirteen thousand copies, which he then gave to Republican Party county chairmen, delegates to the 1932 Republican national convention, former associates in his humanitarian relief organizations, and many others.[38] In all likelihood much of the cost of this immense effort was borne, directly or indirectly, by Hoover himself.[39]

Reviewing *The Challenge to Liberty* and *New Frontiers* in the *Saturday Review of Literature*, the historian Allan Nevins described the two books as "opening guns in a great battle" that would "rage with increasing fury" until after the election of 1936.[40] In the weeks that followed, much of the response to Hoover's work in fact bore a partisan hue. To ardent New Dealers his book was dull, doctrinaire, and abstract.[41] Interior Secretary Ickes, as usual, was caustic. Hoover, he asserted, wanted "liberty of privilege": "Mr. Hoover and those who think along with him don't seem to be concerned with the masses of the people who want decent living conditions and jobs with fair wages. They emphasize the right of those with property to be free from disturbance of any one."[42] Hoover must have wondered whether Ickes understood his argument.

The former president was particularly incensed by the critical review in the *New York Times* by its daily book reviewer, John Chamberlain, a left-leaning journalist who in later years became a libertarian conservative. Not only was Chamberlain a nonentity, Hoover complained; the *Times* itself was suffering from "a complex of humiliation from having betrayed American institutions by their support of Roosevelt for election after having denounced him as a dangerous man to the country before nomination."[43] He took solace in the knowledge that outside the nation's "pink and sophisticated areas" the nation's press was giving his book "a good run."[44]

Not all the commentary, by any means, was hostile. In a nationally circulated appraisal William Allen White acclaimed *The Challenge to Liberty* as "an honest man's patriotic protest against shortcuts to economic security." According to White, Hoover was not a "hard and fast enemy" of the New Deal's "objectives"—only of its "methods." The "object" of the New Deal, claimed White, was a "readjustment of our national income," guaranteeing both economic security to the "average man of no acquisitive talents" and a "chance to rise" to "the man with talents." According to White, Hoover also believed in "some such fundamental reconstruction of the American economic system."[45]

It is not known how Hoover reacted to White's bold assertion that he disagreed only with the New Deal's methods. But in his review the Kansas editor quoted from a letter that Hoover had recently written to him:

I hope some day our people will learn that property rights are not the foundation of human liberty. Those foundations lie in the other rights which free the spirit of men—free conscience, worship, thought, opinion, expression, creativeness, security of home, family and justice. . . .

When governments take or destroy property rights they not only extinguish these motivations [toward enterprise and creativity] but they invariably use economic power to stifle the other rights, and they employ a lot of bureaucrats to rub it in. But unrestrained use of property rights by the individual can also abuse, dominate and extinguish the more precious liberties and securities. Therefore governments must enact laws against abuse and domination and must umpire these matters. The activities of governments must be limited to that.

This, said Hoover, was the difference between "real liberalism" and its enemies: "reaction and radicalism."[46]

Perhaps the most dispassionate review of *The Challenge to Liberty* came from a longtime friend, Professor Wesley C. Mitchell of Columbia University. "To call [Hoover] a reactionary or conservative," wrote Mitchell, "is as wrong as to call him a radical. He occupies a middle ground and wages a war on two fronts. Hence he is exposed more than most public men to misrepresentations."[47] Hoover was warmly grateful for Mitchell's comments.[48]

But as the former president now realized with trepidation, the "middle ground" he had once tried to occupy was not holding. Not so long ago, in 1920, he had been a hero to many of the nation's progressives. Franklin Roosevelt had been his friend and had urged him to run for president that year as a Democrat—as Woodrow Wilson's political heir. Now, in the turbulent mid-1930s, Roosevelt himself was in the White House, his friendship with Hoover had dissolved into bitter antagonism, and the country was veering sharply to the left. Anxious, in the new political world, to clarify his own position, Hoover increasingly identified his political philosophy as "historic liberalism," in contrast to what he scorned as the regimenting "false liberalism" of the New Deal. In 1937 he declared: "The New Deal having corrupted the label of liberalism for collectivism, coercion [and] concentration of political power, it seems 'Historic Liberalism' must be conservatism in contrast."[49]

With these words of recognition, Hoover's political odyssey was complete. The Bull Moose Progressive Republican of 1912, the Wilsonian food regulator of World War I and its aftermath, the self-described "independent progressive" of early 1920, the assertive and reformist secretary of commerce whom Old Guard Republicans tried to block from the party's presidential nomination in 1928: he, Herbert Hoover, had become a man of the Right.

The publication in 1934 of *The Challenge to Liberty* marked Hoover's emergence from a year and a half of political exile. More important, it announced his postpresidential debut as a crusader-prophet, a role he did not relinquish until his death. Fresh from his recent success with the printed word, in 1935 he took to the nation's public forums and airwaves. Although public speaking before large gatherings had never come easily to him, he did not flinch from its demands. Crisscrossing the country in the mid- and late 1930s, he delivered an unceasing barrage of verbal fusillades against the New Deal and its defenders. In the process he became the Republican Party's intellectual leader and President Roosevelt's most formidable critic from the Right.

In 1938, with financial support from the breakfast cereals magnate W. K. Kellogg, Hoover published a collection of his principal speeches and public writings since 1933, under the title *Addresses upon the American Road.*[50] Seven more such volumes appeared before his death.[51] These periodic and widely disseminated compilations were further evidence of his unflagging determination to rescue America from the abyss. The books also became convenient reference works for him when it came time to organize *The Crusade Years.*

Hoover's conspicuous hammerings at Rooseveltian liberalism evoked cheers among conservative Republicans, nervousness among GOP leaders (who worried that he had become a political albatross), and puzzlement among pundits and journalists alike. His spectacular return to the political stage was nearly unprecedented for a former president (only Theodore Roosevelt had shown similar verve), and inevitably the question arose: What did Hoover want? Was the ex-president seeking a political comeback and a rematch against Roosevelt at the polls?

Although Hoover himself never publicly admitted it (not even in the memoir at hand), from 1934 on (if not sooner) he began to hanker for a return to the Oval Office.[52] Particularly during late 1939 and 1940, he covertly maneuvered to orchestrate a "spontaneous" draft of himself as the presidential nominee of what he expected would be a deadlocked Republican national convention. He hoped, by a powerful speech to the convention delegates, to establish himself as the party's giant among pygmies and to stampede the excited delegates into nominating him. His strategy and best-laid plans were upended by the meteoric rise of a man named Wendell Willkie and by some suspicious happenings at the convention, as readers of *The Crusade Years* will discover.[53] For Hoover it was a keen disappointment whose sting he did not conceal from his friends. To a few he confided in elegiac tones: "There are things in this world that cannot be brought about. There are mistakes that cannot be repaired." He thanked them for giving him "the most precious possessions a man can have": "loyalty and friendship."[54]

Denied another chance for vindication at the polls, Hoover did not retreat from the public eye. Indeed, if Willkie had defeated Franklin Roosevelt in the election of 1940, the Chief intended to move back to Washington, where he and his wife still owned a home at 2300 S Street in which they had lived while he was secretary of commerce in the 1920s. There, presumably, he would have tried with characteristic tenacity to guide the course of the Willkie administration. Instead, with FDR ensconced in the White House for another four years, Hoover decided to uproot himself from California (where he felt increasingly marooned) and make New York City—the nation's intellectual and communications capital—his principal residence. On December 3, 1940, he and his wife forsook Palo Alto (except for periodic visits, mostly in the summertime) and moved into Suite 31-A in the Waldorf Towers of the Waldorf-Astoria Hotel in midtown Manhattan.[55] For the rest of his life it would be his base of operations in his tireless pursuit of influence on the nation's destiny.

Hoover's fight to save America from the curse of collectivism forms the centerpiece of *The Crusade Years*. In its pages readers will find fresh and sometimes caustic accounts of the great election contests of the New Deal era and of such upheavals as the Republican national convention of 1940. We shall see Hoover returning to public esteem as chairman of two commissions to reorganize the executive branch of the federal government under Presidents Truman and Eisenhower. Here also (and in the documents assembled in Appendix II) we will read candid appraisals of Alf Landon, Wendell Willkie, Thomas Dewey, Harry Truman, and others with whom he crossed paths (and sometimes swords). Nor will readers be at a loss to learn what Hoover thought of Franklin Roosevelt and of the swarm of "leftwingers" (as Hoover called them) who honeycombed New Deal Washington, to his dismay.

Politics, then, predominates as the subject of *The Crusade Years*. This is, after all, the portion of Hoover's memoirs devoted primarily to his "crusade against collectivism" after he ceased to be president.

But the book before you is not exclusively about politics. Much as Hoover craved political vindication after 1932, much as he cherished the roles of political evangelist and crusader, much as he ached to turn his country back onto the right path, politics never totally defined his place in the American public square. Part of the value of *The Crusade Years* is that it enhances our awareness of the remarkable breadth of Hoover's *nonpolitical* accomplishments during his postpresidential decades. There were, for instance, what he called his "Crusades for Benevolent Institutions," such as the Boys' Clubs of America and the Hoover Institution on War, Revolution and Peace, undertakings in which he invested much time and energy during a period when one might expect that he had no time or energy to spare. In Appendix I of this volume, readers will find four unknown memoirs that he composed in 1955 describing still more of his civic and philanthropic endeavors, including his "Crusade against Waste in the Federal Government, 1921 to 1955." It seems never to have occurred to him to desist.

Yet it would be wrong to think of Hoover as simply a public man, totally consumed by public concerns as he grew older. Perhaps the most charming feature of *The Crusade Years* is his depiction of his private life after his presidency—a side of his existence that he rarely permitted the world to observe. In part I of this volume, readers will discover tender reminiscences of Hoover's wife and sons, of his passion for fishing, and of his membership in the Bohemian Club that gave him surcease from "dull care" for more than fifty years. In these pages one will also find amusing vignettes of his travels by auto in the American West in the 1930s, including the times the former president of the United States was stopped for speeding. In *The Crusade Years* we catch a glimpse of Hoover at peace as well as at "war."

To the end of his days Hoover lived, we may truly say, abundantly. One might suppose that the aging ex-president—absorbed in political strife, in myriad philanthropies, and in the quiet enjoyment of family and friends—would have had little time or inclination to write a mammoth series of memoirs. But he did, and his *Crusade Years* volume was only a fraction of it. To the story of this long unknown memoir we now turn.

The Making of *The Crusade Years*

It is not uncommon for famous men to write their memoirs. Among former American presidents, it has become routine to produce books as big as doorstops about their careers. But in this realm of exertion, as in so many others, Herbert Hoover was no ordinary man. Of all the individuals who have served as president of the United States, none has ever written a set of memoirs as prodigious as his.

Perhaps the most important point to bear in mind about *The Crusade Years* is that it was but a single component in an elaborate literary project that he undertook at the age of sixty-six: a series of memoirs that grew to comprise six substantial volumes (including the aptly named Magnum Opus that became three volumes in one). Although Hoover later claimed that he wrote parts of the first three installments as early as 1915–16, the relevant files in his papers establish that the systematic production of his memoirs began in the summer of 1940, less than a month after he failed to receive the Republican Party's presidential nomination. These two events were almost certainly connected. Hoover's plunge into memoir writing was one of many signs that summer that his life, as he told friends, had reached a "turning point."[56] And, indeed, in one sense it had. For the next twenty-four years the past would vie with the present for his attention.

Readers interested in the labyrinthine history of Hoover's memoirs project should consult the detailed editor's introduction to Hoover's book *Freedom*

Betrayed, published posthumously by the Hoover Institution Press in 2011.[57] Here we shall concentrate on the story of its sister volume, *The Crusade Years*.

Between 1940 and 1944 Hoover wrote and revised what became the first three volumes of his *Memoirs*, the only ones to be released with that designation during his lifetime. They focused on his youth and mining engineer career, his monumental humanitarian achievements during and after World War I, and his government service culminating in the presidency.

By the autumn of 1944 the now seventy-year-old memoirist was ready to take up the story of his postpresidential life and his battle against the foreign and domestic policies of Franklin Roosevelt. In September Hoover scribbled out the first passages of what was in effect the fourth volume of his projected memoirs (see Appendix II, Document 3). He titled it *Twelve Years 1932–1944* (see Appendix II, Document 8). Its subject was to be his crusades in the 1930s against what he labeled "the creeping collectivism of the New Deal."[58]

That same autumn, he composed the first rough chapters of a parallel volume devoted to World War II and his fight to keep the United States out of it. He referred to this segment informally as the "War Book." An early table of contents gave it the title "Volume V: World War II."[59] It was the embryo of what he and his friends came to call the Magnum Opus (*Freedom Betrayed*).

Initially Hoover intended to incorporate in this volume an unvarnished account of his crusade to provide food relief to suffering civilians in Nazi-occupied Europe during World War II — an effort largely thwarted by Franklin Roosevelt and Winston Churchill. Eventually he converted this portion of his manuscript into a separate book.

Hoover's three-pronged literary offensive quickly sped into high gear. As with his earlier memoirs volumes and with other books to come, his modus operandi was unvarying. First, he would write a chapter or a section of his manuscript in longhand and give it to one of his secretaries to type. Then, using his ever-present pencil, he would correct and revise the typescript, which was then retyped and returned to him for still more revisions, a process that might go on for some time. All the while, Hoover would be composing and revising other portions of his manuscript in the same manner. Eventually, when he deemed the process of writing and revision to be well advanced, he would send a large batch of typescript pages to a printer for conversion into page proofs in order (it seems) to give Hoover a sense of how the manuscript would look in print. Then he would proceed to edit and revise the printer's handiwork and eventually send it back for resetting. It was a laborious process and no doubt a costly one, but the perfectionist ex-president did not seem to mind the expense.

Although Hoover employed a team of loyal secretaries and, for seven years, a very able, part-time research assistant named Arthur Kemp,[60] his evolving memoirs were very much his own creation. Every word of his original manuscripts, it appears, he himself composed by hand. And how he worked, with a drive and resolve that amazed his friends and staff. By mid-1947 the "War Book" alone encompassed 1,099 pages in page-proof form.[61]

Meanwhile, the Chief had been assembling—"incidentally," he later claimed[62]—the sections of his memoirs devoted to his private life and other subjects, notably his struggle against the forces of collectivism in the United States. By early 1950 Hoover's manuscript *Twelve Years 1932–1944* had morphed into a two-volume tome titled *Collectivism Comes to America*. The first volume was subtitled *Roosevelt's First Term, 1933–1936*; the second, *Roosevelt's Second Term, 1936–1940*. In page-proof form, the work totaled 538 pages.[63]

In its preface (Appendix II, Document 10) Hoover acknowledged his didactic intent: "First, to prove the follies of our departure from the American system we have steadily builded over 300 years. Second, to strip polluted history of its falsehoods. That is necessary if a people are to be guided by experience and truth. Third, to give the views I held on these questions at the time."

The veteran controversialist admitted that some of his crusades might have been "lost causes at the time." "But with the faith of a crusader to himself," he added, "his cause is never lost." In a revealing, climactic paragraph he gave an inkling of the motivation gripping his soul: "The world has survived error in ideas and confusion before. And men have grown in soul and safety because some groups of them have stood solid. They stood fast not because they knew the solutions to all the confusions, not even because they had the power to find the solution. They stood firm and they held up the light until the furies passed because they held certain sacred principles of life, of morals, and of spiritual values. I could at least do that."

Now, however, Hoover was obliged to confront the consequences of his zeal. In a letter to a close friend in 1950 (Appendix II, Document 11), he confided that his entire set of memoirs, upon which he had been working, on and off, for nearly a decade, had grown to include eight distinct components. (The accumulated page proofs probably exceeded three thousand printed pages.) In what order, he wondered, should he arrange and publish this mountain of material?

In 1951–52 the former president solved part of his problem by publishing *The Memoirs of Herbert Hoover* in three volumes, covering his life from birth through 1932. The Macmillan Company of New York City was the publisher. In the final section (called "The Aftermath") of volume III, he drew heavily on the first half of his *Collectivism Comes to America* manuscript to mount a stinging critique of the New Deal and its failure to end the Great Depression.

In the meantime, Hoover had taken another look at the rest of what he had written and had decided that it needed to be revamped. Early in 1950 he began to condense the "War Book" or Magnum Opus and gave it the title *Lost Statesmanship*. In 1950–51 he reworked the unpublished parts of *Collectivism Comes to America* into a new text called *The Crusade against Collectivism*. He planned to incorporate it—and several other unpublished units of his memoirs—into a four-part volume to be titled *The Years as Crusader*.

Early in 1951 *The Years as Crusader* was put into page proofs. As Hoover explained in its introduction (Appendix II, Document 12), the volume would cover not only his family life and his "Seventeen Years' Crusade against Collectivism in America" but also many foreign policy subjects, including a 215-page segment on his "crusades on behalf of starving people" during and after the Second World War. He called this section *The Four Horsemen in World War II*.

Although *The Years as Crusader* now gave the appearance of being ready for publication, its meticulous author declined to let it go.[64] A year earlier Hoover had told a friend that his "Collectivism" manuscript, Magnum Opus manuscript, and "Four Horsemen" manuscript "should not be released for some years in any event"[65]—probably because of their explosive character and perhaps for fear of offending living persons. His caution did not, however, cause him to stop tinkering with his texts. Soon after the 1952 election he completed another updating of *Lost Statesmanship*; it now totaled 1,001 printed pages in proofs.[66] A few months later he finished revising and reorganizing his 1951 manuscript *The Years as Crusader*. To the new edition he gave the title *The Crusade Years* (see Appendix II, Document 15). As thus reconfigured, it comprised 564 pages in page proofs.

At this point it would be easy to conclude that since moving to the Waldorf-Astoria a dozen years earlier, Hoover had been a virtual hermit, doing little else than write (and rewrite) his memoirs. Such an inference, though plausible, would be wrong. His burgeoning writing project developed in the 1940s and 1950s amid a regimen of public speaking, travel, charitable work, and government service that showed little sign of slacking off. In 1946, for instance, at President Truman's invitation, Hoover conducted a survey of postwar food and famine conditions on five continents. He visited thirty-eight countries and traveled more than fifty thousand miles. In 1947 Truman invited him to chair the newly created federal Commission on Organization of the Executive Branch of the Government. It speedily became known to the press and public as the Hoover Commission. For the next year and a half, he directed its deliberations at a pace that would have exhausted men half his age. No sooner did he finish than he launched an elaborate publicity campaign to induce the president and Congress to implement the commission's recommendations.

In 1950–51 Hoover participated prominently in the heated nationwide "Great Debate" over American policy toward Europe as the Cold War turned hot in Korea. In 1952 he worked assiduously behind the scenes to help his friend and ideological soul mate, Senator Robert Taft, win the Republican presidential nomination (see Appendix II, Document 14).

Then, in 1953, came another summons to public service that the Chief could not refuse. That summer the U.S. Congress voted to create a second prestigious Commission on Organization of the Executive Branch of the Government, and President Dwight Eisenhower invited Hoover to chair it. For the aging foe of nearly all things Rooseveltian, it was an opportunity for vindication on a new and heroic scale: a chance to devise and promote an agenda to curtail the federal bureaucracy, stop the growth of "creeping Socialism," and crown his twenty-year "crusade against collectivism" with success. For the next two years he immersed himself in the duties of what friend and foe alike called the Second Hoover Commission—so commanding was his presence and domination of its proceedings. In the midst of these grueling labors, in 1954, he turned eighty years old.

When the Second Hoover Commission wrapped up its work a year later, its indefatigable chairman turned back to his private affairs and a nagging piece of unfinished business: What should he do about the remainder of his memoirs? In the summer and autumn of 1955, Hoover took a fresh look at the 1953 page-proof edition of *The Crusade Years* and promptly launched another round of revision.[67] As he did so, he decided to break down the massive *Crusade Years* manuscript into separate components and to augment them by writing still more segments covering still more of his crusades.[68] By mid-December he had produced at least four additional autobiographical essays describing, among other subjects, his "Crusade for American Children" and "My Crusade against Collectivism" (which covered the years 1919–32). (See the editorial note for Appendix I.)

It is uncertain how Hoover planned to integrate these mini-memoirs into the unfinished architecture of his *Crusade* project (they are published here in Appendix I), for scarcely had he ventured in this new direction than he abruptly changed course. At the end of 1955 he put his collection of *Crusade* manuscripts aside and (with one exception) never worked on them again.

What happened? Although the record is not completely explicit, it seems that another literary venture had begun to take priority in his mind, a project to which he gave the title *The Crusade against Famine*.[69] Sometime in 1955 the octogenarian elder statesman resolved to prepare a detailed chronicle of his Commission for Relief in Belgium (CRB) in World War I and of his gigantic food distribution efforts in Europe after that calamity (subjects he had already addressed, though not exhaustively, in volume I of his published *Memoirs*). He apparently planned to couple the CRB book with his "Four Horsemen" manuscript about World War II. Originally, Hoover intended to prepare two volumes (presumably one for each war). They soon became three and then four: a comprehensive history of American "enterprises in compassion" (primarily *his* enterprises) that saved literally millions of lives from famine and disease during and after both world wars. He eventually gave this series the title *An American Epic*.

In the last installment of the *Epic* Hoover revealed the inside history of his largely frustrated "crusade against famine" during World War II. To tell this story, he substantially revised and condensed the "Four Horsemen" memoir he had completed in 1950 and 1951 and had once intended to publish as part of *The Crusade Years*. In effect, the final volume of *An American Epic* was volume VI of his *Memoirs*. The long-projected volumes IV and V—the *Crusade* book and the foreign policy Magnum Opus—still awaited his decision to release them.

In 1957, while he was laboring on the *American Epic*, Hoover's memoir writing took another impulsive turn. He decided to expand a chapter he was then writing about the Paris peace conference of 1919 into a spin-off book about Woodrow Wilson's experience at the conclave, where Hoover had been one of his ablest associates. In short order the Chief churned it out. Part memoir, part historical narrative, *The Ordeal of Woodrow Wilson* was published in 1958.[70] It proved to be one of Hoover's most admired publications.[71]

In August 1959 Hoover celebrated his eighty-fifth birthday. He told an interviewer that he felt like he was sixty-eight.[72] Rising daily around five thirty in the morning, he was at his desk by six. His awed secretaries kept statistics about his lifestyle. Between 1946 and 1959, they reported, he delivered 185 major speeches and published seven books.[73] From August 1959 to August 1960 he delivered five major speeches, attended thirty-five public functions, answered 21,195 letters, and traveled more than fourteen thousand miles.[74] And still—despite growing health problems—he pushed on.

Between 1959 and 1964 Hoover published seven more books: *An American Epic* (in four volumes), a collection of his letters to children titled *On Growing Up*, a book called *Fishing for Fun—And to Wash Your Soul*, and the eighth volume of his *Addresses upon the American Road*. It was an astounding feat: seven books, published between the ages of eighty-five and ninety.

But not yet *The Crusade Years*, nor the manuscript that now mattered to him most: the Magnum Opus, to which, in 1962, he affixed its final title, *Freedom Betrayed*. He considered its compilation to be "the most important job of my remaining years."[75] He informed a friend that he hoped to leave behind the tome "as a sort of 'will and testament'" to the American people.[76] He wanted it to stand as the definitive critique of the "lost statesmanship" of World War II—the unshakeable indictment before the bar of history of the feckless foreign policy of Franklin Roosevelt.

With *The Crusade Years* manuscript now indefinitely in limbo, Hoover strained every nerve in his final years to revise and perfect *Freedom Betrayed*. In September 1963 he told a friend that it was essentially finished.[77] But before his staff could complete what he called its "overhaul" (meticulous fact-checking), Hoover died in the Waldorf-Astoria in 1964.

Under the terms of his will, ownership of his "memorabilia, documents, personal papers and books" was bequeathed to a family foundation, whose directors included his two sons and a few other relatives and friends. It would be up to the foundation to decide what to do about the Magnum Opus.

Evidently concerned that its release soon after Hoover's death might reopen old political wounds and ignite unseemly controversies, the foundation did not proceed to publication. Instead, it placed the Magnum Opus and related papers in storage at the Hoover Institution, where they remained out of public view for many years. (These files are now open to researchers.) Perhaps without realizing it, Hoover's heirs included among the transferred documents several boxes of manuscripts and supporting materials pertaining to Hoover's *other* "opus"—*The Crusade Years*—which had lain dormant since he set it aside late in 1955. There—buried, as it were, among the files for the Magnum Opus—the *Crusade* manuscripts remained for more than fifty years, apparently forgotten by the handful of people who had known of their existence.

In 2009 the Herbert Hoover Foundation authorized the editing of *Freedom Betrayed* for publication, and the Hoover Institution invited me to perform the task. While conducting research in the pertinent papers (more than two hundred boxes) at the Hoover Institution Archives, I discovered several boxes containing the drafts of the *Crusade* book and its offshoots. With the permission of the Herbert Hoover Foundation, and at the invitation of the Hoover Institution, I have edited this memoir for publication.

Hoover's most advanced edition of it—revised for the final time in 1955—is included in the main text of the present volume. Appendix I contains the most advanced versions of four collateral mini-memoirs that he prepared in that same year. In Appendix II I have assembled a collection of documents from his papers that elucidate the *Crusade* book's purposes and development.

Concluding Reflections

What do we learn from the pages of the volume at hand? Aside from its often spicy account of Hoover's political activities during the Roosevelt/Truman era, and its window on Hoover's private life and campaigns for good causes, *The Crusade Years* invites us to reflect on the factors that made possible his extraordinarily fruitful postpresidential years. As least as much as Theodore Roosevelt, he came to personify the activist ex-presidency; some historians have even argued that he invented it. If Hoover was indeed the paradigmatic modern former president, what were the essential sources of his achievement?

The first requirement for a successful ex-presidency is clearly longevity, and here Hoover was supremely successful. Between 1933 and 1964 he lived longer as a former president than any other occupant of the White House, before or since, until Jimmy Carter. During these years Hoover not only outlived most of his political adversaries but also witnessed an abatement of the storms spawned in the 1930s. He further benefited from the human tendency to confer honorific status on any public figure who attains an advanced age. After elder statesmen turn eighty, he once remarked wryly, they are politically "harmless."[78]

A second trait that made Hoover's productive "twilight" years possible was his remarkably robust constitution. For nearly all his life the engineer-turned-statesman was blessed with exceptionally good health and a phenomenal capacity for work. And when in later years an occasional illness did strike, he refused to let it encumber him. Hence, in 1947, he launched the first Hoover Commission while suffering a tormenting case of shingles that lasted for months. Similarly, in 1958, less than three months after a gall bladder operation that some did not expect him to survive, he flew to Belgium as President Eisenhower's personal envoy to the Brussels World Fair. Even in his mid-eighties he worked eight to twelve hours a day. Sinclair Lewis once observed that the secret of success is to "make the seat of your pants adhere to the seat of your chair for long enough." This was one of Hoover's secrets also.

But there was more to his physical makeup than simple good health and stamina. Hoover was endowed with an extraordinary amount of nervous energy. One of his closest friends, Will Irwin, asserted in 1916 that Hoover did not need to exercise to control his weight. At times, Irwin wrote, Hoover "fairly thinks himself thin."[79] A man who worked with him at the U.S. Food Administration in 1917 claimed that Hoover's pulse always exceeded 100 beats a minute—and sometimes went up to 125.[80] This observer may or may not have been correct, but Hoover did have a number of habits—such as jingling the change in his pocket—that revealed an inwardly nervous disposition. Only while fishing did he appear fully to relax, but one suspects that even then his thoughts were often elsewhere.

Hoover's mind, in fact, "was never still," one of his grandchildren once observed. Often, in his last years in Suite 31-A in the Waldorf Towers, he would awaken at two o'clock in the morning and go to work. On these occasions he would open a can of soup, heat it, gulp it down, and then proceed to write until four in the morning.

A third key to Hoover's productivity was his financial security. Living largely before the days of the subsidized ex-presidency,[81] he possessed a comfortable income derived ultimately from his pre-1914 success as a mining engineer and investor. Although not especially imposing by today's standards, his savings nevertheless enabled him to devote himself unceasingly to public service. They also permitted him to maximize his influence in a variety of ways. Maintaining a residence at the Waldorf-Astoria, for instance, along with a staff of secretaries and research assistants, must have cost him thousands—eventually tens of thousands—of dollars a year. But Hoover very deliberately assumed this expense as the price of being where he wanted to be: at the epicenter of American political and intellectual life. Similarly, in 1934, when *The Challenge to Liberty* was published, he and his associates (as we have seen) donated more than thirty thousand copies to libraries, opinion leaders, and politically active individuals. It was a practice that he repeated with every book he subsequently published—a deliberate form of influence building that only a man of some means could afford.

Hoover's customary writing practices for *The Crusade Years* and other books further illustrate this point. Not only did he repeatedly revise the typed drafts that his secretaries supplied him; he showed no hesitation about marking up the voluminous page proofs that came back from the printer—and then returning them for fresh resetting. The seemingly compulsive reviser could not have done this had he not possessed the financial resources to be a perfectionist.

A fourth reason that the defeated president was able to recover from the obloquy of 1932 lay in his astonishing array of friendships. From his earliest days as a mining engineer and mine manager, he displayed an uncanny ability to select men of talent and turn them into loyalists for life. Why was he able to engender such boundless devotion? One source of his appeal was his personal example of self-sacrifice and total dedication. From his days as head of Belgian relief through his days as president, he refused to accept a salary for his work—or, if required by law to do so, gave the money away to charities or as income supplements to his staff. Another source of bonding was a management style that encouraged subordinates to take the initiative and do all they could for their leader. Still another source—and a potent one indeed—was the altruistic character of the humanitarian relief efforts that made him famous. For many who worked with him in these undertakings (and they numbered in the thousands), the experience was the most exhilarating one of their lives. Some, such as Senator Robert Taft and Admiral Lewis Strauss, held him in almost filial esteem.

An unbreakable cord of idealism drew these and other Hooverites to the man they revered as "the Chief." They provided him an independent political base in the 1920s and a personal following and nationwide intelligence network after 1932. In nearly every major city in America in the thirties and forties there were "Hoover men" eager to distribute his books, arrange for local radio stations to carry his nationally broadcast speeches, defend him in letters to the press, and otherwise rally to his side. Of no other former president, with the exception, perhaps, of Theodore Roosevelt, could the same be said. Like the hero of San Juan Hill, Hoover in his years of "retirement" commanded a following based in part on his *non*political and *pre*political achievements. It helped to ensure his presence in what he once called the "big game" of public life.

Yet longevity, good health, driving energy, wealth, and admiring friends do not alone explain the Hoover phenomenon. In a sense these were only preconditions for his success: necessary but not sufficient. Three additional factors— *volitional* factors—gave his ex-presidency its singular intensity. First, more than any other chief executive in our history, Hoover, after he left the White House, felt impelled to defend his previous conduct as a public servant. The quest for vindication was perhaps the dominant theme of his later life. It found expression in his crusade against the New Deal, his campaign for presidential renomination in 1940, his attempt to have himself appointed senator from California when Hiram Johnson died in 1945, his assistance to scholars engaged in revisionist history, and, above all, his unending series of books. Hoover was never content to leave the judgment of his legacy to historians. Like another contemporary who experienced both political triumph and rejection—Winston Churchill—the former president became his own biographer.

If all this seems a trifle quixotic, remember: Hoover left office repudiated and scorned by his fellow citizens during America's greatest domestic emergency since the Civil War. Remember, too, that *before* his presidency he had never truly experienced defeat. These circumstances, combined with his own unique temperament, forged in him an unbending determination—a will— to clear his name.

Blended in with this profound urge for vindication was a second catalyst of activism: a philosophy of life that exalted practical achievement. If Hoover had spent two terms in the White House and retired to popular acclaim in 1937, it is quite likely that he still would have been an unusually enterprising former president. An autobiographical statement that he composed around the time of World War I helps to explain why. "There is little importance to men's lives," he wrote, "except the accomplishments they leave posterity. . . . When all is said and done, accomplishment is all that counts."[82] For Hoover life was not meant for solipsistic leisure. His physical aversion to passivity was matched by his creed. Moreover, for him the most definable form of accomplishment was the creation or administration of what he called "tangible institutions." Between 1933 and 1964 several became the beneficiaries of his labors, as *The Crusade Years* makes plain. On each he left a perdurable imprint; each in a way conferred on him the secular immortality that he seemed to crave.

In 1920 Hoover remarked that "words without action are the assassins of idealism."[83] This statement reveals the third volitional wellspring of his post-presidential behavior. He ordered his life not only by a philosophy of achievement but by a self-conscious ethic of benefaction. It was not enough for him to do well; from an early point in his life he yearned and strove to do good. As he told a friend before World War I, "Just making money isn't enough."[84] It was one more bar to complacency and quietism. In the 1930s Hoover's brother, Theodore, estimated that Herbert had given away more than one-half of his profits for benevolent purposes over the years.[85] He did not change his ways later on. Thus in 1944 he deeded to Stanford University his beautiful home on campus; the mansion is now the official residence of Stanford's president. Thus he committed countless hours to philanthropic and educational endeavors such as those described in the pages of this volume. Undergirding his ceaseless activity was an impulse to perform good works, a desire raised in his mind to the level of an ethical imperative. One cannot understand his perpetual restlessness without taking this motivation into account.

From Hoover's kaleidoscopic ex-presidency, then, we may adduce this formula. If you wish to be a model of a modern former president, you should live a long life; be blessed with excellent health and superabundant energy; have a source of income that frees you for public service; have a far-flung legion of friends willing to labor on your behalf; feel a passionate need to justify your record before your countrymen and posterity; and have a philosophy of life that imbues in you a consuming desire to achieve, to build great institutions that will survive you, and to serve your fellow men and women unstintingly. And one thing more: you should possess an utter willingness to fade away.

All this Herbert Hoover exemplified.

But Hoover, one suspects, would be much disappointed if we were to read *The Crusade Years* solely for its anecdotes and insights into his career. Although his book has the flavor of an apologia pro vita sua, plainly he intended it to be more.

His chosen title provides the critical clue. "Crusade": how he savored this word as he scribbled away at his desk in the early 1950s. The stirring persona of a crusader, with its connotations of dynamism and idealism, was his cherished self-image at a time when many of his enemies had dismissed him as a curmudgeon whom Roosevelt and history had passed by. Undaunted, Hoover fought on as a man with a mission, seeking not just the recovery of his reputation but the intellectual and spiritual rescue of a nation gone astray.

This transcendent objective helps to explain a somewhat quirky feature of the memoir before you: Hoover's habit of quoting at length speeches that he had delivered years before. As a practical matter, this device had certain advantages. It was a convenient way for an old man in a hurry to organize his narrative. But Hoover's decision to quote his own addresses in extenso also signified something more profound: his awareness that he was not just recording political history but waging an ongoing and fateful battle of ideas.

In the 1930s and 1940s, both Hoover and his archrival Franklin Roosevelt knew that they were engaged in a contest for the American mind and political soul. What had gone wrong since the crash of 1929? Was the Great Depression a crisis of capitalism, a product of Hooverian mismanagement, or a catastrophe brought on by uncontrollable happenings abroad? Was the New Deal a humane and pragmatic reform movement or a muddled and meddlesome experiment in collectivism? Did the traditional "American System" of limited government, private initiative, and volunteerism apotheosized by Hoover fail disastrously in 1929–1932, or did his successor in the White House launch America on an unnecessary and dangerous spiral into socialism? Did the New Deal actually save American capitalism, or did it delay economic recovery and poison the wellsprings of future prosperity? As Hoover foresaw in 1932, the answers to these questions would determine the nation's course for generations to come.

"Who controls the past controls the future: who controls the present controls the past." This was the slogan of the totalitarian Party in *1984*. Hoover probably never read George Orwell's novel, but he understood the force of this sinister slogan as he battled to change America's direction after 1933. Unlike most men in politics then or since, he realized the supreme importance of constructing a compelling narrative of past events as a weapon in the ongoing war of political philosophies. Hence the fervency and persistence of his efforts in *The Crusade Years* and elsewhere to establish what he considered to be the proper narrative of the causes and course of the Great Depression. Hence his anger at Republican politicians who evaded the ideological issues. (His little essay printed in Appendix II, Document 5 is an excellent example.) Unless Americans had a correct understanding of their recent past, he feared, the future would belong to the advocates of statism.

Reading *The Crusade Years*, one is struck by how resonant Hoover's arguments continue to be. As an unapologetic believer in American exceptionalism, he unceasingly resisted what he saw as the insidious "Europeanization" and "collectivization" of American society. To him the American system of ordered liberty was ineffably precious and must be preserved. Today one could easily take passages from *The Crusade Years* and convert them into blog posts and op-ed pieces, so current are the problems of political and economic philosophy that he addressed.

And the issues do not go away. Ever since the Gilded Age (someone has observed) the free market and governmental regulation have defined a polarity in our discourse on public policy: Which is the problem? Which is the solution? In 1981, in his first inaugural address, President Ronald Reagan proclaimed his intention to "curb the size and influence" of the federal government and to make it "stand by our side, not ride on our back." "We are a nation that has a government," he asserted—"not the other way around."

Herbert Hoover was not a pure Reaganite; there was in him too much of the social engineer and temperamental activist for such a label to be affixed to his name. It has been said of Hoover that he was "too progressive for the conservatives and too conservative for the radicals."[86] But in the larger sweep of the twentieth century, Hoover, the unflagging anti–New Dealer, contributed mightily to the critique of ever-aggrandizing statism that has long been integral to American conservatism. It was among the most enduring of his legacies.

To the very end, he strove to preserve it. Late in his life, he told one of his grandchildren: "When you stop wanting to know, then you start to die." Even as the infirmities of age crept up on him, he seemed driven by an urge to know and especially to teach: about his experiences in office, about the meaning of America, and about the threats posed by what he called "pernicious" ideologies to the land he loved.

Just a few weeks before Hoover died in 1964, a young friend named Marie Therese Nichols visited him at the Waldorf-Astoria. The Chief, who had recently turned ninety, was now frail and confined to a wheelchair, but his mind and formidable will were unbowed. As he and his guest drank tea together, he suddenly asked her: "Tell me, child, what do you really want in life?" After pausing for a moment, the young woman replied that she liked her life just as it was and wanted it to go on without change: "I have a nice husband, I have a nice apartment, so the answer is I want a status quo."

Hoover looked at his young visitor with horror. "How can you say a thing like that," he exclaimed, "because *I want more*. I want to write a *better* book, I want to have *more* friends—*I just want more*—and I think you should never sit back and say, 'I want a status quo.'"[87]

Throughout his life journey, and especially during his arduous ex-presidency, Hoover refused to settle for the "status quo." In his multivolume memoirs he attempted to tell why. A few weeks after his conversation with Mrs. Nichols, his race against mortality came to an end, and he never got to write the "better book" of which he still dreamed. But during his life he published more than thirty books, and he left behind the makings of two more. By any standard it was an impressive achievement.

The Crusade Years is the "missing link" in Hoover's memoirs: the final brick in a literary edifice that he began to build in a summer of sorrow nearly seventy-five years ago. In its pages we learn the story of his later life, of his abiding political philosophy, and of his vision of the land of liberty that gave him opportunity for service: a remarkable saga told in his own words, his way.

George H. Nash
South Hadley, Massachusetts
April 2013

NOTES

1. John J. Pershing to Herbert Hoover, December 12, 1918, Herbert Hoover Subject Collection, Hoover Institution Archives (hereinafter HIA), Stanford University.

2. "Sons of the Stanford Red: Hoover—Pioneer," *Stanford Illustrated Review* 21 (December 1919): 140.

3. Herbert Hoover to Harriette Miles, August 5, 1897, extract in "Mining—Australia, Hoover's Accounts of Western Australia," Pre-Commerce Papers, Herbert Hoover Papers, Herbert Hoover Presidential Library (hereinafter HHPL), West Branch, Iowa.

4. Hoover remarks at the Bohemian Grove, summer 1933, quoted in *Time*, August 14, 1933, p. 22.

5. Hoover's presidential campaign address in New York City, October 31, 1932, printed in *Public Papers of the Presidents of the United States: Herbert Hoover, Containing the Public*

Messages, Speeches, and Statements of the President, January 1, 1932 to March 4, 1933 (Washington, DC: U.S. Government Printing Office, 1977), pp. 656–80 (quotations at pp. 656, 657.)

6. Ibid., p. 657.

7. Hoover to Edward Eyre Hunt, September 14, 1933, Post-Presidential Individual Correspondence File (hereinafter PPI), Hoover Papers, HHPL.

8. Ibid.

9. Hoover to Will Irwin, December 16, 1933, PPI, Hoover Papers, HHPL.

10. Ibid.

11. Hoover to Henry J. Allen, November 14, 1933, PPI, Hoover Papers, HHPL.

12. Hoover to Irwin, December 16, 1933.

13. See Hoover correspondence with Bruce Barton and Gertrude Lane, PPI, Hoover Papers, HHPL; also Edgar Rickard diary, June 19 and 21, 1934, HHPL.

14. Rickard diary, July 14, 1934.

15. Ibid.

16. Hoover to Bruce Barton, June 7, 1934, Bruce Barton Papers, State Historical Society of Wisconsin.

17. At least one of his intimate friends, Lewis L. Strauss, initially advised him to wait. See Arch W. Shaw to Hoover, August 8, 1934, PPI, Hoover Papers, HHPL.

18. Hoover to Gertrude Lane, July 3, 1934, PPI, Hoover Papers, HHPL.

19. Hoover to Barton, June 23, 1934, Barton Papers.

20. Hoover to Allen, September 17, 1934, PPI, Hoover Papers, HHPL.

21. Rickard diary, August 3, 6, and 22, 1934.

22. Hoover to Arch W. Shaw, August 22, 1934; copy in Barton Papers.

23. Hoover to Barton, August 22, 1934, Barton Papers.

24. Hoover to Barton, July 31, 1934, Barton Papers.

25. Hoover to Warren Austin, August 10, 1934, PPI, Hoover Papers, HHPL.

26. Hoover to George Akerson, August 14, 1934, PPI, Hoover Papers, HHPL.

27. Hoover to Lane, July 9, 1934, PPI, Hoover Papers, HHPL.

28. Hoover to Barton, August 12, 1934, Barton Papers.

29. Hoover to Allen, September 17, 1934.

30. *New York Times*, February 9, 1934, p. 1.

31. Hoover to Barton, July 20, 30, and August 22, 1934, Barton Papers.

32. Shaw to Hoover, August 8, 1934.

33. Herbert Hoover, *The Challenge to Liberty* (New York: Charles Scribner's Sons, 1934), p. 49.

34. Ibid., pp. 203–4.

35. Hoover to William Allen White, August 23, 1934, William Allen White Papers, Box C215, Library of Congress.

36. Barton to Hoover, October 11, 1934, Barton Papers.

37. H. Meier memorandum, March 22, 1935, "Books by HH: *The Challenge to Liberty*, Printing Arrangements," Post-Presidential Subject File, Hoover Papers, HHPL.

38. See the various memoranda in the file cited in note 37.

39. In a letter to his friend Mark Sullivan in August 1934, Hoover disclosed that the "whole New York group" (evidently Barton and Lane) had "opposed" his book when he had shown them the manuscript. Moreover, the New Yorkers had been "very sarcastic about the whole works." In response Hoover had relayed their criticism to "some friends of mine here" (California) who had reacted by "putting up their money to distribute 30,000 copies for nothing" (Hoover to Mark Sullivan, August 7, 1934, PPI, Hoover Papers, HHPL).

It is difficult to know how literally to interpret Hoover's statements. Sometimes in later years, when he remarked that unspecified friends had contributed financially to projects he favored, it appeared that he was being euphemistic. By "friends" he seems at times to have meant himself and his family. We cannot be sure of the circumstances here, but we know from the memorandum by one of his associates (note 37) that he personally reserved thirteen thousand copies to distribute. Presumably he had to pay to purchase them or some portion of them.

40. Allan Nevins, "The Battle of 1936 Begins," *Saturday Review of Literature*, October 6, 1934, pp. 15, 168, 170, 172.

41. See, for example, the reviews in the *Christian Century*, *Commonweal*, the *Nation*, and the *Times Literary Supplement* in the autumn of 1934.

42. *New York Times*, September 5, 1934, p. 15.

43. Hoover to Lewis L. Strauss, October 1, 1934, PPI, Hoover Papers, HHPL.

44. Hoover to Ashmun Brown, October 17, 1934, PPI, Hoover Papers, HHPL.

45. White's review was circulated by the North American Newspaper Alliance and quoted extensively in the *New York Times*, September 28, 1934, p. 21.

46. Hoover, quoted in White's review and in the *New York Times*, September 28, 1934, p. 21.

47. Wesley C. Mitchell, "Mr. Hoover's 'The Challenge to Liberty,'" *Political Science Quarterly* 49 (December 1934): 599 (full review: 599–614).

48. Hoover to Wesley C. Mitchell, December 17, 1934, PPI, Hoover Papers, HHPL.

49. Hoover to William Allen White, May 11, 1937, PPI, Hoover Papers, HHPL.

50. Herbert Hoover, *Addresses upon the American Road* (New York: Charles Scribner's Sons, 1938).

51. They were published between 1940 and 1964.

52. The evidence on this point is overwhelming. One of the best contemporary sources on Hoover's maneuvering is the diary of his longtime friend and confidant Edgar Rickard, at HHPL. For excellent accounts of Hoover's political activities and ambitions in the 1930s, see Richard Norton Smith, *An Uncommon Man: The Triumph of Herbert Hoover* (New York: Simon and Schuster, 1984) and Gary Dean Best, *The Life of Herbert Hoover: Keeper of the Torch, 1933–1964* (New York: Palgrave Macmillan, 2013).

53. On Hoover's quest for the 1940 Republican presidential nomination, see, in addition to the books by Smith and Best cited above, Steve Neal, *Dark Horse: A Biography of Wendell Willkie* (Garden City, NY: Doubleday & Company, Inc., 1984), pp. 100–102, 111, 112, 119; Charles Peters, *Five Days in Philadelphia* (New York: Public Affairs, 2005), pp. 78–79, 82–84, 87–89.

54. For example, see Hoover to Arthur Hyde and Mark Sullivan, June 28, 1940 (separate letters), PPI, Hoover Papers, HHPL.

55. Rickard diary, November 30 and December 4, 1940. Hoover and his wife kept their home on the Stanford University campus and visited it often. After Mrs. Hoover's death in 1944, Hoover bequeathed the property to the university. Since then it has served as the official residence of the president of the university.

56. Hoover to William Starr Myers, Larry Sullivan, and John Spargo, June 29, 1940 (separate letters), PPI, Hoover Papers, HHPL.

57. See George H. Nash, ed., *Freedom Betrayed: Herbert Hoover's Secret History of the Second World War and Its Aftermath* (Stanford, CA: Hoover Institution Press, 2011), pp. xv–cxiii.

58. Hoover, "Twelve Years 1932–1944: Chapter 1," p. 21 (page-proof version), in "The Aftermath: Twelve Years 1932–1944 Edition Undated," *Memoirs of Herbert Hoover* Book Manuscript File, Box 13, HHPL.

59. Hoover, table of contents of "Volume V: World War II," June 4, 1945, in "Magnum Opus: 1932–44, Vol. V (1)," Magnum Opus Materials, Box 5, HHPL.

60. From 1946 to 1953 Arthur Kemp (1916–2002) worked on an essentially half-time basis for Hoover while teaching at New York University and earning his doctorate there. Kemp also advised Hoover about his unpublished memoirs volumes in the summers of 1954 and 1955. See Arthur Kemp oral history (1968), pp. 5–8, copies at HHPL and HIA.

61. This version of the Magnum Opus is in the Herbert Hoover Papers, Boxes 6 and 7, HIA. (Note: The Herbert Hoover Papers at HIA is an entirely different collection from the Herbert Hoover Papers at HHPL.)

62. See Hoover's introduction to the 1953 version of *The Crusade Years*, printed below in Appendix II, Document 15.

63. A page-proof set of volume I of *Collectivism Comes to America* is in "The Aftermath: 'Collectivism Comes to America—Roosevelt's First Term, 1933–1936,'" *Memoirs of Herbert Hoover* Book Manuscript Material, HHPL. It bears a penciled notation that the proofs were returned by the printer on April 7, 1950. No copy of volume II of *Collectivism Comes to America* has been located. But an eighteen-page, typewritten table of contents of volume II is in the Arthur Kemp Papers, Box 7, folder 5, HIA. What happened to this volume is unknown. A copy of it existed at the Hoover Institution in 1953. See Hazel Lyman Nickel to Bernice Miller, September 25, 1953, "Lost Statesmanship—Condensed Version of the Magnum Opus Correspondence," Magnum Opus Materials, Box 2, HHPL.

64. An excerpt appeared in a popular magazine in 1951. See Herbert Hoover, "The Life of an Ex-President," *Colliers*, March 24, 1951, pp. 30–31, 54–56, 59–60.

65. See Appendix II, Document 11.

66. Many of the page proofs of this version are in the Herbert Hoover Papers, Box 88, HIA.

67. Arthur Kemp gave Hoover some advice about it. See Arthur Kemp memo to Hoover (plus enclosure), August 13, 1955, Herbert Hoover Papers, Box 92, folder 2, HIA.

68. See Loretta Camp to Rita Campbell, August 8, 1964, Hoover Institution Records, Box 2800, Magnum Opus folder, HIA.

69. See ibid. and, in this volume, Appendix I, Document 3, chapter 1, note 1.

70. Herbert Hoover, *The Ordeal of Woodrow Wilson* (New York: McGraw-Hill, Inc., 1958).

71. For an excellent account of this book project, see Timothy Walch, "The Ordeal of a Biographer: Herbert Hoover Writes about Woodrow Wilson," *Prologue* 40 (Fall 2008): 12–19.

72. Herbert Hoover, *Addresses upon the American Road, 1955–1960* (Caldwell, ID: Caxton Printers, 1961), p. 75.

73. "Resumé of Mr. Hoover's Activities, January 1946–April 1959," in "Hoover's Statistics: 1946–1964," Post-Presidential Subject File, Hoover Papers, HHPL.

74. "Statistics, August 7, 1959–August 10, 1960," in "Hoover's Statistics: 1946–1964."

75. Hoover memorandum to Bernice Miller and Loretta Camp, n.d. (circa June 10, 1963), in "War Book (*Freedom Betrayed*): Herbert Hoover Holograph Material," Arthur Kemp Papers, HHPL. (Note: This is a separate collection from the Arthur Kemp Papers at HIA that are cited elsewhere in these notes.)

76. Hoover to Clarence Budington Kelland, January 31, 1963, PPI, Hoover Papers, HHPL.

77. Hoover to George Mardikian, September 26, 1963, PPI, Hoover Papers, HHPL.

78. Hoover to Richard Nixon, January 27, 1961, PPI, Hoover Papers, HHPL.

79. Will Irwin, "The Autocrat of the Dinner Table," *Saturday Evening Post*, June 23, 1917, p. 58.

80. Charles McCarthy, "Some Notes on Hoover's Personality" (typescript, April 23, 1920), Charles McCarthy Papers, Box 41, State Historical Society of Wisconsin.

81. Only in 1958 did the U.S. Congress enact the Former Presidents Act, which provided a pension and other financial perquisites for ex-presidents. For Hoover's reaction to this legislation, see, in this volume, p. 10, note 8.

82. Herbert Hoover, undated autobiographical essay (circa World War I), in "Information for Biographers," Pre-Commerce Papers, Hoover Papers, HHPL.

83. Hoover statement to *New York Tribune*, April 27, 1920, Public Statements File, Hoover Papers, HHPL.

84. Will Irwin, *The Making of a Reporter* (New York: G. P. Putnam's Sons, 1942), pp. 182–83.

85. Theodore Hoover, *Memoranda: Being a Statement by an Engineer* (typescript, Stanford University, 1939), p. 267, copy at HHPL.

86. Herbert Gaylord Warren, *Herbert Hoover and the Great Depression* (New York: Oxford University Press, 1959), p. viii.

87. William I. and Marie Therese Nichols oral history (1968), pp. 10–11, copies at HHPL and HIA.

EDITOR'S NOTE ON SOURCES AND EDITING METHODS

Sources

The Crusade Years is the last-to-be-published component of a multivolume set of memoirs that Herbert Hoover began to write in 1940. Three of his volumes were published in 1951–52 under the title *The Memoirs of Herbert Hoover*. A fourth appeared, in considerably revised form, in 1964 as the concluding volume of Hoover's four-part series *An American Epic*, a history of American humanitarian relief work during and after World Wars I and II. A fifth volume of memoirs evolved into a work known informally as the Magnum Opus and eventually as *Freedom Betrayed*. It did not see publication until 2011. The sixth segment, *The Crusade Years*, is published here for the first time.

Nearly all the documentation relating to *The Crusade Years* reposes in the Hoover Institution Archives at Stanford University. Among the archives's collections are the recently opened and thoroughly processed Herbert Hoover Papers (formerly the Herbert C. Hoover Papers). Most of its 173 boxes contain manuscripts, page proofs, correspondence, printed matter, and other materials relating to foreign and domestic policy during the presidencies of Franklin Roosevelt and Harry Truman and, above all, to Hoover's preparation of his mammoth memoir/history, *Freedom Betrayed*. But also included in this collection are successive drafts and page-proof editions of *The Crusade Years*, as well as several smaller memoir-essays that Hoover wrote in 1955.

Also of value for studying the genesis and development of Hoover's *Crusade* book is a small but significant collection called *The Memoirs of Herbert Hoover* Book Manuscript File at the Herbert Hoover Presidential Library in West Branch, Iowa. Box 13 of this collection holds miscellaneous fragments, dating from the 1940s, of Hoover's early drafts of the portion of his memoirs devoted to his public and private life after leaving office in 1933. Box 13 also contains a complete set of page proofs of volume I of Hoover's manuscript "Collectivism Comes to America," completed in early 1950. Much of this volume—a critical study of President Franklin Roosevelt's first term—was incorporated into the last section of volume III of Hoover's published *Memoirs*. The second volume of "Collectivism Comes to America" has not been located, but a surviving table of contents indicates that its subject was Roosevelt's second term in office. This missing manuscript was undoubtedly the direct antecedent of what became, a little later, *The Crusade Years*.

Virtually all of the contents of this book have been assembled from the Hoover Institution Archives—and, specifically, the Herbert Hoover Papers. During the two decades and more that Hoover labored over his memoirs, he frequently revised them, and multiple versions of most segments have survived. In the case of *The Crusade Years*, and in the absence of any clear directive on Hoover's part, I have chosen to publish the most recent available version of each section of his manuscript. As it happens, the most advanced drafts of Hoover's *Crusade* book and its offshoots all date from the latter half of 1955, the last time he is known to have worked on this portion of his autobiography. These are the texts I have selected for publication here.

Hoover's introduction and part I ("Some Notes on Family Life"), as revised in August 1955, are found in the Herbert Hoover Papers, Box 89, folder 4. The contents of part II ("Crusading for Benevolent Institutions"), as revised in November 1955, are filed in Box 89, folder 4, and Box 90, folder 2. Part III ("The Crusade against Collectivism in American Life"), as returned in page proofs from the printer in November and December 1955, is located in Box 90, folders 3 and 4.

In Appendix I ("Other Crusades"), I have included four previously unknown, spinoff memoirs that Hoover composed in 1955 about certain of his crusades and interests. Their location in the Hoover Papers is duly recorded in my editorial introduction for each.

In Appendix II ("Selected Documents Pertaining to Hoover's Crusade Book Project"), I have printed seventeen items found in the Hoover Institution Archives or the Herbert Hoover Presidential Library. The precise location of these documents is indicated in the editorial notes that accompany them.

In the book at hand, then, we have Hoover's account of his "crusade years" as he entered the ninth decade of his life. He was eighty-one years old when he put this set of manuscripts aside and turned to other, even more ambitious, writing projects.

Editing Methods

The Crusade Years is what historians call a primary source: a document whose author is a direct witness to, or participant in, the events he narrates. In this case, the author was also one of the leading actors on the stage of twentieth century history—a fact that renders his words even more inviolable. Moreover, having died in 1964, he is not here to accept or reject the interventions of a latter-day editor. For all these reasons, I have endeavored to reproduce Hoover's text as nearly as possible as he composed it, well over half a century ago.

The volume at hand is not, however, a mere photostat of the final stage of Hoover's work product. Most of the text printed in this volume exists, in Hoover's files, in the form of page proofs that seem not to have been fully subjected to what he called "clean up"—or what we might call copyediting. From time to time, therefore, I have made minor grammatical and typographical adjustments in his text—such as adding or deleting commas, capitalizing or lowercasing words, and fixing obvious misspellings and typographical errors—in the interest of elementary correctness or clarity. None of this very limited copyediting has altered the substance of Hoover's narrative. In no case have I knowingly altered his meaning or tried to rewrite his text. On the few occasions when it has seemed advisable to modify or clarify his prose by inserting a word or a phrase, I have done so in brackets with the attached abbreviation "ed." In certain instances I have allowed anomalies to remain but have followed them with the bracketed words "sic" and "ed." Brackets that appear in the text without "ed." are Hoover's.

Hoover wrote relatively few footnotes in *The Crusade Years*, and I have left them largely as he composed them, while occasionally adding bracketed words for clarity or consistency of citation. Most of the footnotes in this volume are the editor's own, duly identified as such and enclosed in brackets. Adding such notes, of course, has required me to renumber Hoover's footnotes as needed. Wherever possible I have inserted the useful word *ibid.*, a form of citation that he rarely used.

My aim, then, has been to present Hoover's memoir as he wrote it, with a minimum of editorial screening. In this way, perhaps, we can hear him speak anew, in his own idiom, about a weighty and tempestuous period in his life and times.

THE
CRUSADE YEARS
1933–1955

by

Herbert Hoover

INTRODUCTION

This volume recounts my activities during the 22-year period after leaving the White House in 1932 [1933–ed.] until my 80th birthday in August 1954. The material in this volume was put together incidentally during the work on the three volumes of *Memoirs*, published in 1951–1952,[1] and on the two volumes of *Memoirs* entitled *Foreign Relations of the United States from 1932 to 1954*.[2] Its composition has served to fill in many lonesome hours between public service and occasional periods of recreation.

I have divided this volume into six parts,[3] treating the subjects topically rather than chronologically. Within the sections I have also followed the topical pattern. Although there is, as a result, an overlap in time, much confusion of the various subjects is avoided.

The Parts Are:

Part I   Some Notes on Family Life
Part II   Crusades for Benevolent Institutions
Part III   Crusade against Collectivism in American Life
Part IV   Crusade against American Entry into World War II[4]

---

1. *The Memoirs of Herbert Hoover: Years of Adventure* (Vol. I); *The Cabinet and the Presidency* (Vol. II); *The Great Depression* (Vol. III). All three volumes were published by The Macmillan Company in 1951–1952.

2. To be published at some subsequent date. [*Editor's note*: Hoover is referring here to the portion of his memoirs known informally as the Magnum Opus. It bore different working titles, including the one given here, over a number of years. Hoover ultimately settled on the title *Freedom Betrayed*, under which it was published long after his death. See George H. Nash, ed., *Freedom Betrayed: Herbert Hoover's Secret History of the Second World War and Its Aftermath* (Stanford, CA: Hoover Institution Press, 2011).]

3. [*Editor's note*: Only parts I, II, and III are published in this volume. See notes 4, 5, and 6.]

4. [*Editor's note*: No Hoover manuscript of this title has been found. Hoover may have been referring to his chapters on this topic in volume I of his work *Freedom Betrayed*.]

Part V   The Crusade against the Four Horsemen in World War II[5]
Part VI   Crusade for Less Involvement in Europe.[6]

In this text, wherever possible, I have condensed documents and statements to eliminate repetitions and subordinate matter. My public addresses during this period have been published in full in a series of volumes entitled *Addresses upon the American Road*. The full texts of all other documents referred to are in the War Library[7] at Stanford University.

---

5. [*Editor's note*: Also known as "The Crusade against Famine in World War II." It is not printed here. This was Hoover's account of his humanitarian relief efforts during and after World War II. As he put it in his introduction to the 1951 version of the present volume, this was his "account of my crusades on behalf of starving peoples and my relief activities." In the 1951 manuscript, this section comprised more than 160 pages in page proofs. Hoover published this section, in revised and expanded form, as volume IV of his *American Epic* series. See Herbert Hoover, *An American Epic*, vol. IV: *The Guns Cease Killing and the Saving of Life from Famine Begins, 1939–1963* (Chicago: Henry Regnery Company, 1964).

Hoover's reference to the "Four Horsemen" was an allusion to the Four Horsemen of the Apocalypse in chapter 6 of the Book of Revelation in the Christian Bible. Hoover came to believe that the Four Horsemen were War, Death, Famine, and Revolution. See Herbert Hoover, *Addresses upon the American Road, 1955–1960* (Caldwell, ID: Caxton Printers, 1961), pp. 383–87.]

6. [*Editor's note:* No Hoover manuscript of this title has been located, and it is unlikely that he ever wrote it. Its subject would probably have been his participation in the "Great Debate" over American foreign policy in 1950–1951.]

7. [*Editor's note:* Now known as the Hoover Institution on War, Revolution and Peace. Hoover founded it in 1919.]

PART I

Some Notes on Family Life

CHAPTER 1

Family Life[1]

Having lived for nineteen years, from 1914 to 1933, under the limelight of the curiosity of the public — mostly through the press — into the private life of my family, I had a faint hope that after leaving the White House these lights might be dimmed. But public interest in the innermost sanctuaries of private life of public men never ceases — until sometime after death. Those who enter public life have little right to complain for it is one of the minor safeguards of a free people. This "insatiable curiosity" can be a useful prop of morals and rectitude in wellknown individuals.

In any event, "insatiable curiosity" with its good or evil fables — and even smears — as to our family life continued after leaving the White House. I have decided to devote a few chapters to what I know about myself. And I may well reproduce a part of a chapter in Volume III of my *Memoirs* as bearing on the subject.[2]

Mrs. Hoover and I left the White House for Palo Alto[3] without regrets except that the job of recovery from the depression and some needed national reforms were incomplete. We had no illusions that America would come to an end because we were going back home again. I had now been in almost fulltime public service since 1914 — nineteen years. And during that time we had not lived at home for a total of more than a few scattered months. The mental taste of one's own gadgets and gardens was good.

---

1. [*Editor's note*: In his last known revision (August 1955) of this chapter, Hoover did not give a chapter title. This was probably an oversight. I have entered here the title he used in his 1953 version.]

2. [*Editor's note*: Hoover took the next seven paragraphs in the text from his *Memoirs*, vol. III: *The Great Depression* (New York: The Macmillan Company, 1952), pp. 344–46.]

3. [*Editor's note*: In 1919–20 the Hoovers built a magnificent home on the Stanford University campus. To this home they returned in 1933. After Hoover's wife's death in 1944, he offered their home (on certain conditions) to the university. His offer was accepted. Today the Lou Henry Hoover House, as it is called, is the official residence of Stanford University's president.]

Democracy is not a polite employer. The only way out of elective office is to get sick or die or get kicked out. Otherwise one is subject to the charge of being a coward, afraid to face the electorate. When a President is out he carries no pension, privilege, nor pomp.[4] He does not even carry an honorary title, not even Governor, Judge, or Colonel. He is about the only retiring public official who is just Mister. He stands in line for a seat and for tickets just like other citizens.

When the British Prime Minister is defeated he may if he wishes receive a great title, he automatically draws a great pension, and everybody makes way for his Lordship.[5]

But the American method is better. It emphasizes the equalities of its democracy. And an ex-President is not devoid of honor or advantages. He is naturally recognized everywhere because his picture has appeared in every print every day for years. To his misfortune the pictures are mostly the flashlight sort with their mechanistic absence of flattery and implications of a prison personality. But recognition brings honor. The proof is that an ex-President is high in the seeking of autograph hunters. And their appraisals of his relative importance are definite. One day a youngster demanded three autographs, which seemed to imply a generous compliment. I asked: "Why three?" "It takes two of yours to get one of Babe Ruth's."

The American treatment of an ex-President has other real advantages. He can just be himself. He can go and come without the restraint of representing a class or a symbol. Up to the time of this writing, I have traveled tens of thousands of miles alone or with Mrs. Hoover, have wandered in the slums of a score of cities, bought things in a thousand stores, visited hundreds of industrial works, been entertained in every sort of home from the roadside cottage to the greatest of establishments. And everywhere I received pleasant, often affectionate, greetings, never an offensive word—to my face.

It might be difficult for some families to adjust themselves to the abrupt drop from palace to cottage. And the White House is a palace more comfortable than that of most kings. Our family had long alternated between the luxury of great cities and the primitive living of world frontiers, so that this change was no bump. Indeed Mrs. Hoover and I found abundant compensations from being kicked out of a job after this nearly forty years of

---

4. [*Editor's note*: At the time Hoover wrote these words, there was no provision in the law for pensions for former presidents. The U.S. Congress made such provision in the Former Presidents Act, enacted in 1958.]

5. Some Prime Ministers delay this sign of retirement in order to hold position in the House of Commons, but most accept it—none fail on the pension.

administrative responsibility and those nineteen years of strenuous public service. There came a great sense of release. It was emancipation from a sort of peonage—a revolution back to personal freedom. It was a release not alone from political pressures but from the routines of twelve to fourteen hours of work seven days a week. Even mealtime had to be given over to the discussion of the problems of the day; the nights were haunted by the things that went wrong; the so-called vacations were tied to the telephone and telegraph or to the visitor who knew that now was the time to discuss his problem.

Therefore, for the first time in long memory, neither Mrs. Hoover nor I had to get up in the morning at the summons of a human or mechanical alarm clock with its shock into reality. Breakfast was to be had when we wanted it. We read the papers and listened to the radio after breakfast instead of between bites. We did it with complete detachment, for no longer did events so directly affect us as before. We looked over the hundreds of letters with the feeling that we did not have to answer them at all, or anyway not today. We could walk about and admire the neighbors' flower gardens and lay out our own. There were no scores of visitors to see at fifteen-minute intervals, most of whom wanted something for themselves that they ought not to have. Now we could choose our visitors without fear of injury to the public or party interest. The many whom we met carried good cheer or useful conversation. There were no piles of documents to be signed before noon. There was no compulsion to make disagreeable decisions. We were not chained to the telephone bell nor were we the slaves of a host of secretaries. I was able to walk out the front door, get in an automobile without a chauffeur and just drive away anywhere—to see the country, to fish or to visit. If it were not from a sense of service or ambition, there would be no recruits for public jobs at all. Men can make a living with far more satisfaction and many less wounds to the soul at other callings.[6]

What to do with former Presidents has always been a problem. At least it is a perpetual trouble in the subscribers' columns. It is a problem to their party officials. It is a problem to administrations of the same party. It is of course trouble to opponents.

It is also a financial problem to many former Presidents. The President, unlike the Military, Judicial, Legislative officers and all civil servants of the Federal Government, receives no pension.[7]

---

6. [*Editor's note*: The passage drawn from volume III of Hoover's *Memoirs* ends at this point.]

7. [*Editor's note*: As mentioned in note 4, former U.S. presidents received a government pension beginning in 1958.]

To those who have no former savings, the support of their families is difficult to solve as savings from Presidential salaries are scanty at best. The alternatives are to accept corporation connections with consequent public discredit of advice in matters of state; or to become a columnist and crowd some worthy workman out of the press; or take soap or insurance or pill money for broadcasting news comments and opinions; or to solicit payment for public speaking. Any of these alternatives means more or less exploitation of the office of President. Many former Presidents have been compelled to adopt one or more of these alternatives despite the adverse effect on the dignity of the office.

In later years, I several times proposed that former Presidents should receive pensions but always with the stipulation it would not begin with me.[8] I also urged that former Presidents, except myself, be made ex-officio members of the Senate without a vote. That would bring their experience into use. It would provide staff and a living.

I was more fortunate than most former Presidents. My professional life had been during the period when the income tax was only 1%. However, my savings in this period were greatly depleted by expenditures beyond my income during nearly 40 years of service in and out of government. There were losses from conversion of all investments into "Trustee" securities when I took office as secretary of commerce, together with a foolish resolution to spend no public salaries on myself or family. Yet we had enough left to live on in modest circumstance.

Our financial life did present some embarrassments. The very considerable contributions to charity and public organizations which we had been able to make from official salaries could not be continued. These charitable agencies seemed to think that such sums as had been previously made should be repeated. Further, a popular belief had been established by the opposition that I was very rich. As a matter of fact, my net assets at their top were never one-half the inherited fortune of Mr. Roosevelt.

---

8. [*Editor's note*: When the Former Presidents Act became law in 1958, Hoover publicly applauded it. But he also disclosed that as a successful man before entering public life, he had made it a practice to devote "all personal compensation derived from our government to public service or charity" (in other words, not to himself). He thereupon announced that he would apply the entire "residue" of his new federal pension after income taxes to "such public purposes." (The pension amounted to $25,000 per year.) He did, however, accept the free mailing privilege and monetary "allowances for office rent and secretarial staff" provided by the new law. See *New York Times*, August 28, 1958, p. 25, and *Los Angeles Times*, August 28, 1958, p. 13. The full text of Hoover's press release, dated August 27, 1958, is in the Public Statements File, Herbert Hoover Papers, Herbert Hoover Presidential Library, West Branch, Iowa.]

An incident of private means arose as soon as I was able to review our remaining assets. In 1893 while earning college expenses I worked on certain government surveys in California concerning silting up the rivers by debris from the mines. In that work I had been sent into the great tule swamps in the delta at the junction of the Sacramento and San Joaquin Rivers. It appeared to me that some day these marshes would be reclaimed and would form the richest agricultural land outside of the Nile Valley. I returned to California from an engineering journey to Australia in 1899 with my first $10,000 and a firm intention of buying 1,000 acres of these swamps, then selling at $10 per acre. I engaged a former classmate, then in the real estate business, to buy the land and gave him the $10,000. Two years later, returning from an engineering journey to China, I found my real estate classmate had concluded that my judgment was bad; and with my $10,000 he had opened a bank in Nevada which had already failed. A lawyer classmate finally recovered from the wreck of his affairs a reversionary deed to an eighty-acre farm in Northern Missouri subject to the life interest of his mother. I gave the matter no further thought, except when I recalled that these unreclaimed swamp lands had advanced to $100 an acre, and I had lost a modest fortune.

However, twenty-eight years later, in the midst of the 1928 Presidential campaign, I received a telegram from a county chairman in Missouri saying that upon the death of an old lady in that neighborhood I had been recorded as the owner of an eighty-acre farm. He added that it was the most disreputable looking place in Missouri; that hundreds of people were driving out to see the "Hoover Farm" and that I should at once spend $2,000 to render it respectable. I did so. I tried for years to sell it for the $2,000. Also, I found that absentee ownership of eighty acres was a continuing unprofitable business. Finally, forty years after the original transaction I gave it to a public institution with the thought that in loss of possible profit in the Delta and compounded interest, that gift had cost me about $150,000.

In the years after leaving Washington, my various crusades kept me constantly traveling. In 1934, Mrs. Hoover and I found that we must spend much of the time in the east and therefore we took an apartment at the Waldorf Astoria Towers where we lived during all but the summer months over the succeeding years.[9]

---

9. [*Editor's note*: Between March 1933 and late 1939, Hoover's primary residence was his home on the Stanford University campus in California. During his increasingly frequent trips east to New York City, he stayed at the Waldorf-Astoria Hotel. Between September 1939 and the summer of 1940, he lived there most of the time. After spending much of the summer in California, he returned to New York City—and the Waldorf—in September 1940. If Wendell Willkie had been elected President in

The boys had established their own homes and the Stanford Campus house was no longer their refuge. In fact, their various businesses brought them more often to New York than Palo Alto. Gradually the intervals of our living in California became shorter and shorter. The great importance of these western visits was to give me an opportunity to wash off of my soul the superficialities, the inanities, and the un-American atmosphere too frequent in New York. On looking back, I find that next to living in Washington, our real family headquarters in the aggregate were longer in New York than in any other place in the world.

New York is the place from which a large part of America's intellectual life in transmitted. Here centers the control of much of the magazine, the book and the radio world. Some of its daily papers spread into every other newspaper office in the country. The control of much national charitable and educational institutions center here because of the closeness to "big money." A multitude of political, social and economic, and propaganda organizations infiltrate into the whole of American life from the great city. When one is interested also in the promulgation of ideas, it is more effective to be at the distributing point than at the receiving end.

New York is probably 75 percent first and second generation European. Its ideas are strongly tempered from recent European origins. It steadily recruits its men and women of leadership from the hinterland. Being the financial and business center of the United States it is astonishing to find how few New York–born men occupy its positions of leadership. Out of the living in its slums come the rebellious spirits which dominate left-wing thought in the country. Nor is this any denial of the multitude of good and devoted citizens in its precincts.

New York, outside the slums, is a place of good food, of human comforts. Its museums, its art galleries and its business buildings overtower the whole world. Its fine shopping streets exceed all others—but a step away is the

---

1940, Hoover planned to move back to Washington, D.C., where he still owned the home on S Street in which he had lived while secretary of commerce in the 1920s. When Willkie lost the presidential election of 1940 to Franklin Roosevelt, Hoover quickly decided to lease his Washington, D.C., home to a U.S. senator and take up permanent residence instead in New York City. Anxious to escape California (where he feared that his political influence was waning), Hoover at last decided to rent what a friend called a "homelike suite" in the Waldorf-Astoria Towers. On December 3, 1940, he moved into Suite 31-A, which became his principal residence until his death in 1964. He continued to visit his California home in the summertime. His wife, Lou Henry Hoover, lived with him at the Waldorf from 1940 until her death in 1944.

On Hoover's decision to make the Waldorf-Astoria Towers his permanent, primary home, see Edgar Rickard diary, November 14 and 30 and December 4, 1940, Herbert Hoover Presidential Library.]

sodden life of congested areas. It was these depressing borders that led me to establish the first Federal aid to slum clearance in 1932. And it was in hopes of helping its millions of pavement boys that led me to undertake the Chairmanship of the Boys Clubs of America. The former work has grown apace; the latter at this writing provides character building for some 400,000 pavement boys in our cities.

In these settings and travelings about, I was able to observe the New Deal methods of "making America over" and their method of solving the depression with much detachment. In the next section I give a summary of the "aftermath" which amply confirmed all my warnings in the campaign.[10]

In time, as a matter of convenience, I removed my voting residence to New York. In 1949, Governor Dewey did me the courtesy of offering me the appointment of United States Senator to succeed to the unexpired term from the passing of Senator Robert F. Wagner. I felt it necessary to refuse for several reasons. The period in the United States Senate would be under 60 days and I could not undertake to run for that office. It was in my view desirable to confer the honor on a younger man to whom the office would be an aid in such a campaign. Moreover, I felt my greatest remaining service would be to maintain my independence from political harness.

A Family Grows Up

The real sanctuaries and joys of life are within the family. We had always wanted some daughters. It had not happened. But Herbert and Allan brought to us two daughters whom we would have been proud to have as our own. They established their own homes, as Americans do. In time we were to have grandchildren and great grandchildren, whose association with their grandparents was free of responsibilities for their upbringing and thus unalloyed joy.

After finishing his engineer training, Herbert,[11] entirely on his own initiative, had advanced rapidly in his profession. Over the years his engineering reputation and his field expanded until his professional income had far exceeded that to which I had attained in that profession. He, however, lived in an age when the government took most of it in taxes. One time or another, he was consulting engineer to ten governments in addition to his large private practice. He had the satisfaction of having his laboratories selected for

---

10. [*Editor's note*: Hoover appears to be referring to the introduction to part III, below: "The Crusade against Collectivism in American Life."]

11. [*Editor's note*: Herbert Charles Hoover (1903–69), known as Herbert Hoover Jr.]

development of vital instruments for detection of submarines and the development of aeroplane instruments for the Army and Navy in World War II. The success of these instruments and their contribution to the services were noted by the Army and the Navy by the conferring of their "E."[12]

Finally, after Mr. Roosevelt's time, he was called upon by the United States Government for advice and negotiation of great projects. Among them was the settlement of the oil problem [in Iran—ed.] created by the seizure of the British oil property in that country. From his success in this tangled negotiation upon which hinged the salvation of Iran from Communism, he was in 1954 called to be Under Secretary of State.

Allan,[13] after college, had entered the management field first in farming and mining and later into other industrial enterprises. At one time he managed some 12,000 acres of irrigated farms in the San Joaquin Valley. He was one of the first of the large farmers to recognize the social situation in industrial agriculture and evidenced his concern by the provision of decent wages and housing for workers. And he was to prove that industrial farming could be at least economically better for its workers than the so-called family-sized farm.

At one time Mrs. Roosevelt visited the San Joaquin Valley under a specially conducted tour by her Communist fellow travellers. The local Chamber of Commerce was anxious to demonstrate that their agricultural development had exceptions to John Steinbeck's "Grapes of Wrath."[14] To do so they suggested she visit representative farms. The Chairman of the Chamber informed me that on arriving at Allan's ranch she noticed the sign "Allan Hoover" on the gate. She asked if that was the former President's son Allan. Upon receiving an affirmative answer, she refused to go in.

On one occasion, when visiting Allan, he took me to see his newly-erected village for itinerant harvest workers. He had built in a beautiful grove some forty houses of three rooms and a screened porch, with modern plumbing, a common laundry with modern machinery, a swimming pool, and a meeting-room equipped for movies. The houses had been painted white with blue trimmings and made a most pleasant impression. They had been first occupied the previous season by what Allan called "The Grapes of Wrath"—migrants

---

12. [*Editor's note*: From 1942 to 1945, the U.S. Army and Navy presented the Army-Navy Production Award to plants that had "achieved outstanding performance on war production." The award consisted of pennants and emblems featuring a capital letter "E" (for "excellence"). More than four thousand war production facilities and their employees received the "E" award for their part in winning the war.]

13. [*Editor's note*: Allan Henry Hoover (1907–93).]

14. [*Editor's note*: Hoover is alluding to John Steinbeck's novel *The Grapes of Wrath* (1939) with its controversial portrait of conditions among migrant farm laborers in California in the 1930s.]

from the Southern states who had never lived in such good surroundings. The paint was smeared, the windows broken, the faucets and door knobs stolen, many floor boards ripped up for fuel, the yards a mass of papers, banana and orange peels and rubbish. The laundry machinery was a wreck. While we were contemplating the scene, a man drove up in an automobile. Allan exclaimed, "This is the last straw—here is the State Inspector of Housing." But the man said, "Allan, I hope you will not clean this place up for a month. I want to bring people here to show them the sort of people these heroes of Steinbeck's really are."

Ultimately, Allan concluded that an occupation subject to Government price fixing and dictation of what he should plant and harvest was becoming a precarious business. He sold all his holdings and devoted himself solely to other industries. But the country lost a farmer with a social sense. In 1952 he was engaged as advisor and administrator for one of the largest financial houses in the country.

Neither of these boys ever traded an atom upon my position. Indeed it was at times a handicap to them. I may add to this chapter on family matters by reprinting a letter to Mrs. Hoover which I wrote from London on a journey abroad in 1938, having not been there for nineteen years:

> . . . I sneaked away on a visit of unalloyed sentiment. I stole out of the hotel alone, found a cab, told the driver the old formula—"Kensington, High Street, Horton [Hornton–ed.] Street to the Red House." On the way, my mind traveled over the thousands of times we had driven along Pall Mall, Knightsbridge and High Street, nearly every house of which was still unchanged. We came to High Street, and as always, I had to direct the cabby to take the second turning to the left beyond the church. And the church was the same as when the boys used to attend all weddings as doorstep-observers, returning to tell us if the red carpet or the awning were up—that service being five shillings extra—and how many bridesmaids or how many peals of the bells there were—these being two shillings sixpence each.
>
> I came to the door of the Red House, flooded with memories of the months we had lived there, alternatively with our New York and California homes for nearly twenty years.[15] How we had first come, as a couple, from

---

15. [*Editor's note*: Between 1901 and early 1917, Hoover was based largely in London, first as an international mining engineer and then as director of food relief for Belgium during World War I. Between 1907 and 1917 he and his family leased the Red House on Hornton Street in the Kensington section of London. In 1917 the family returned to the United States, where Hoover soon entered wartime service in the administration of President Woodrow Wilson.]

stays in Australia or China or Russia or Burma, or New York or the Continent; then when we had brought the babies; then when I would return from long journeys to meet you all again.

At the door, even after twenty years, I automatically fumbled in my pocket for the key. I rang the bell. A stiff man-servant answered and I asked if I might see the lady of the house, explaining that I was an American who had lived in this house many years ago, was in London only for a day, and would like to walk through the rooms and the garden again. He seemed nonplussed, but came back after some minutes, and through the partially opened door, announced, "Her Ladyship is not in." I was prepared for this British event with a ten-shilling note, sufficiently exposed, and suggested that perhaps he would let me see any part of the house that was not in use at the moment. To the left was the oak-panelled library with its fine fireplace and its leaded glass bookcases—the same as ever. I imagined again, sitting on the opposite side of the desk from you, with the manuscripts and reference books piled between us, as we worked over the translation of *De Re Metallica*. Again I saw "Pete" at the little table in the corner, making marks and announcing that he was writing a book too; and "Bub" clambering into his mother's lap and demanding to know what the book said. The dining room was the same walnut panelled room and evoked all kinds of memories of the multitude of happy gatherings which had filled it. The living room had been redecorated from its old neutral tints to modern white and was a repellent stranger to me. The century-old mulberry tree, which we had nursed for years with steel eye-beams and which had given character to the garden was gone and replaced by some formal bushes.

Altogether my mind was a maze of revived emotional pictures and some disappointments. But by now the butler was standing on one foot and filled with anxieties—and to finish him, I shook his hand and from his astonishment I guessed no "gentleman" had ever done [this–*ed.*] before.

Your old grim-faced parlor-maid came to Claridge's [hotel]. She timidly inquired of Perrin if she might see me. She asked me to thank "Madame" for sending her a nice card every Christmas and especially for the 'elp you had given her from the White 'ouse in the unemployment times and to inquire after the 'ealth of the "young Masters,"—and her stolid old face softened at every reference to the "young Masters." I suspect in her memory they were still little more than babies.

I thought perhaps she had come for more 'elp, and not wanting to offend her, I remarked that if she got in a tight place again she should write to the "madame." She replied at once: "Oh no, I 'ave a nice place with a family in 'yde Park, but they are not the likes of Madame, and besides when I sent the money back to Madame, she would not take it and told me to put it in the bank in case 'ard times come again and then I 'ave it."

So you will see she has never yet been able to place her H's and I have discovered your secret transactions. I directed one of the secretaries to take her down to the afternoon tea then going on in the hotel with the fashionables of London and to treat her like the real lady she is in her heart. He reported that her major observation was that "these waiters is not trained to serve tea properly." She is part of passing England.[16]

---

16. [*Editor's note*: A slightly variant version of this letter is printed in Hoover's *Memoirs*, vol. I: *Years of Adventure, 1874–1920* (New York: The Macmillan Company, 1951), pp. 128–30.]

CHAPTER 2

Recreation

Even former Presidents deserve recreations. First there came fishing. As I was known to like fishing and Mrs. Hoover liked motoring, we soon had invitations from friends all over the country who had fishing camps or boats. It was thus an inexpensive luxury. Gradually we established a route among these opportunities by plane or automobile. For trout and bass, we visited camps on the streams and lakes in California, Oregon, Washington, Idaho, Montana, Wyoming, Colorado, New Mexico, Wisconsin, Minnesota, British Columbia, Connecticut, Massachusetts, and New Jersey, New Hampshire and Maine. For salmon, to Washington, and New Brunswick. For deep sea big game fish, Florida, Texas and Lower California. To Mrs. Hoover, it was opportunity to do some fishing but mainly to exercise a variety of cameras.

Someone propounded the question to me: "Why have all Presidents in modern times gone fishing?" It seemed to me a worthy investigation, for the habits of Presidents are likely to influence the nation's youth. Some of us had been fishermen from boyhood and required no explanation. But others adopted or greatly expanded their fishing after entering the White House. In examining this national phenomenon, I concluded that the pneumatic hammering of demands on the President's mind had increased in frequency with the rising tide of economic and international complexity. He just had to get away somehow, somewhere, and be alone for a few hours once in awhile. But Presidents must have a convincing explanation for everything they do and everywhere they go. Otherwise their movements are subject to suspicion and espionage. The American people accept without question the statement, "He has gone fishing."

Some years later, and prior to the 1952 Presidential campaign, at a dinner of the Gridiron Club, I elaborated the relationship of fishing to candidates and Presidents, saying:

Tonight, you have occupied yourselves as examiners of the auguries of presidential candidates. In Roman times the people formed their political auguries by observing the flights of birds and the entrails of dead sheep.

I have recently been fishing. In the long time between bites I have come to the firm conclusion that today fish have taken the place of the flight of birds and the entrails of sheep.

Before I start to prove this, I should inform you that over 12,000,000 voters each year pay for a fishing license and most veterans fish for free. (That is a potent part of the electorate.) Both candidates for nomination or election, and even Presidents, seem aware of this fact.

Also, I should inform you that from an augury point of view, there are two kinds of fish. There are the host of species of common or garden fish which are the recreation of the common man.

There are also the rare species of fish sought by the aristocracy of fishermen. They require more equipment and more incantations than merely spitting on the bait. They can be ignored as auguries as they are only landed the hard way and have no appeal to the common man.

Despite the fact that every great human advance has come from the uncommon man, every fish sign points up the validity of Mr. Wallace's assertion that we are firmly chained to the common man.

Now the augury process with fish is conducted by press photographs. A few years ago a press photograph showed my friend Senator Taft awkwardly holding a common fish, taken from many angles for all the common men to see. I knew without other evidence that he was a candidate. Two years ago my friend, General Eisenhower, burst into photographs from all angles, gingerly holding three very common fish. The augury was positive. A month ago General Ike stated that he was coming home to go fishing. Governors Warren and Stassen have not been in press photos with a fish! The augury swells up from 12,000,000 licensed fishermen that they are not likely to be nominated.

The political potency of fish is known to Presidents as well as to candidates.

Now you may think this fishing by Presidents has to do with the 12 million paid license holders. It does not. Presidents have long since learned that the American people respect privacy on only two occasions: fishing and prayer. Some presidents take to fishing.

Three Presidents, including President Cleveland, Theodore Roosevelt and myself, fished from boyhood but we wasted all of our political time upon the uncommon fishes in places where photographers seldom come. However, in modern times all Presidents quickly begin to fish soon after election.

I am told that McKinley, Taft, Wilson and Harding all undertook fishing in a tentative way and for the common fishes.

President Coolidge apparently had not fished before election. Being a fundamentalist in religion, economics and fishing, he began his fish career for common trout with worms. Ten million fly fishermen at once evidenced disturbed minds. Then Mr. Coolidge took to a fly. He gave the Secret Service guards great excitement in dodging his back cast and rescuing flies from trees. There were many photographs. Soon after that he declared he did not choose to run again. President Franklin Roosevelt caught many common fish from the military base of a battleship.

President Truman, prior to his 1948 election, appeared once in a photograph somewhere in a boat gingerly holding a common fish in his arms. An unkind reporter wrote that someone else had caught it. I can find no trace of the letter he must have received from the President. It is reported also that Mr. Truman was one day fishing somewhere north of Key West when his boat was surrounded by sharks. It was decided that it might upset the boat if one were caught. There were no photographs. But sharks are always a bad augury. He subsequently announced he would not run for office again.[1]

But far more important than political auguries are the positive joys of fishing. The break of waves in the sun, the joyous rush of the brook, the contemplation of the eternal flow of the stream, the stretch of forest and mountain in their manifestation of the Maker soothes our troubles, shames our wickedness and inspires us to esteem our fellow men—especially other fishermen.

Fishermen, at least in the Northern States, are mostly Republicans. The drawback for me in this quarter, however, was that the local political leader insisted on sitting on the bank or getting into the boat and pouring out the local frictions or the wastes and injustices of "Planned Economy."

Necessarily, fishermen are gregarious. Otherwise, the mighty deeds of the day or of a year ago or of ten years ago would go unsung. No one else will listen to them. Also, they are an optimistic class or they would not be fishermen. Therefore, as two or three are gathered together, the spiritual vitamins of faith, hope and charity have constant regeneration. And we need all that in these years of creaking civilization, and especially in the years of war tribulation.

---

1. [*Editor's note*: Hoover delivered this address at the Gridiron Club dinner in Washington, D.C., on May 10, 1952. The full text, the "fishing" part of which is quoted here in slightly altered form, is printed in Herbert Hoover, *Addresses upon the American Road, 1950–1955* (Stanford, CA: Stanford University Press, 1955), pp. 323–27.]

The people who have bad "isms" scoff at the game fisherman and demand to know how they get that way. The cause of his itch to go fishing is simple. That is the regeneration which comes to one physically and spiritually.

And I might add in this vein that the human animal originally came from out-of-doors. When spring begins to move in his bones, he just must get out again. One time, in the spring, our grandmothers used to give us nasty brews from herbs to purify our blood of the winter's corruptions. They knew something was the matter with the boys. They could have saved trouble by giving them a pole, a string and a hook. Some wise ones (among them my own) did just that.

There are class distinctions among fishermen. The dry-fly devotees hold themselves a bit superior to the wet-fly; the wet-fly fishermen, superior to the spinner fishermen; and the spinners, superior to the bait fishermen. I have noticed, however, that toward the end of the day when there were no strikes fishermen sometime descend down the scale until they get some fish for supper. This class distinction may perhaps be ignored as any contribution to the collectivist revolution now going on for it is not based on the economic levels.

The swordfish, the tarpon and bone fishermen likewise have some social distinctions on the basis both of the fish and the size of line and reel. The lower-thread line operators are the dukes and earls in that aristocracy. Also, the sailfish and marlin devotees are naturally superior to those who take mere mackerel or amberjacks. The bonefish fishermen claim a little superiority to the tarpon seekers. But again it is not economic or social status that counts so much as knowing what the fish bite. Whatever the class distinction may be among fishermen, from the point of view of the fish all men are equal—and often less efficient than small boys.

Someone reproduced a passage of mine on fishing in beautiful type. From the number of them I was called upon to autograph I judge they hang in every fishing camp in the country.[2]

---

2. [*Editor's note*: At this place in the 1955 version of his text, Hoover interfiled a copy of an undated page from *Sports Illustrated*. It showed a reproduction of a painting of a man fishing and, below it, in large letters, the following quotation by Hoover:

To go fishing is the chance to wash one's soul with pure air, with the rush of the brook, or with the shimmer of the sun on blue water. It brings meekness and inspiration from the decency of nature, charity toward tackle-makers, patience toward fish, a mockery of profits and egos, a quieting of hate, a rejoicing that you do not have to decide a darned thing until next week. And it is discipline in the equality of men—for all men are equal before fish.

Herbert Hoover.]

The Highways and Byways

Our motor trips brought a multitude of touches of America. Stopping over-night in scores of auto camps en route always brought evenings with the carpenter, the plumber and the grocer on holiday with their wives and children. One learned again the depth of family devotion, their understanding, and real patriotism in this America.

Here is a development in our national life that should open a new segment of distinctively American literature. We have a literature on the life in the first Atlantic Coast settlements, on the pioneering migrations to the Midwest, upon the trek to the Pacific Coast in '49, upon the life on the railroads, upon the life on the river steamboats. There could be a whole new set of Canterbury Tales spun upon the life of the newly constructed Western highways. Born of the automobile, here has developed a whole world all of its own—and different. There is a special saga of American life among the roadbuilders, the truckmen, the travelers of serious purpose, and especially the life of the holiday makers. It has an enlivening spirit different from any other phase of American life. There is on the mountain and desert roads the hourly incident of narrow escape from accidents, of changing vistas, of fields, of hills and mountains, of villages, towns, all of which gives it a spirit of adventure. There is the life of the hundreds of thousands who live by the roadside service of supplying food, shelter, gas, and repairs. There are the hot-dog stands, the filling stations, the roadside garages, the auto camps and the camp grounds. Only those who have a spirit of cheerfulness and of hospitality can succeed in those occupations. Probably this necessity in these folks creates a natural selection of the sturdy, the good-humored and the patient varieties of the human animal. Certainly they seem to feel a public responsibility to keep all travelers moving, and happy. As we were mostly on fishing expeditions or just visiting or looking at the scenery, the roadside people, the travelers and the traffic police constantly volunteered not only information but would often take us to their own private spots. And the traffic officers bob up unexpectedly everywhere, and their spirit is helpful. They are tough only to red-handed malefactors who want to argue their misdeed is not so.

The radio keeps all of these people—those who serve the highway and those in cars—in touch with the world. The universality of the telephone along the highways knits them together for business and gossip. They know for miles around of every accident or incident on the road. They go instantly to rescue, whether it is a stalled engine or an injured driver. And they gossip about the road with each other. It always seemed to me that there was an advance courier when I was on the road, for everybody seemed to know I was coming for miles ahead. Once when I had picked up an injured motorist in Colorado, mention was made all about it at filling stations as soon as I arrived.

To every traveler, highways and byways, there rises a dozen Canterbury Tales in a 20th Century garb. Upon one occasion when I was driving alone up the Salinas Valley, I suddenly heard the stern call of the traffic officer's siren. I pulled up at the side of the road with a sinking feeling that I was headed for the Justice of the Peace Court with the inevitable national publicity upon the lawless conduct of a former President. The officer came alongside and said: "Excuse me, sir, but I have wanted to shake hands with you for fifteen years, and I hope you don't mind." My spirits rose to such a degree that I was glad to see him.

On another occasion I stopped at a "dude ranch" over night in Wyoming. Among the guests was a professor of law from an eastern university, looking the dead end of awkwardness in new blue-jeans, top boots, spurs and carrying a 5-gallon hat. He sat down at my table and communicated to me the horror of this, his first experience of life in the West. His especial dislike was being herded every morning to ride a horse. Every item of the life jarred his nerves and stimulated his complaints. The clothes that the proprietor had induced him to buy did not add to his comfort or his self-esteem. He saw no good in the West at all.

He was such a misfit in the place that, for pity of him, I suggested that owing to the inability of a friend to continue with me on our fishing trip, I was returning to the Pacific Coast and I would be glad if he would keep me company, starting early in the morning—provided he did not wear those clothes. He lighted up at once. He became again the kindly and companionable spirit he was. Just at dusk of the next evening, as we were motoring along the strip of cement between the tall trees of the Shoshone Forest, a lady standing lonesomely in the forest beside the road signaled for a ride. We stopped. As the lady climbed into the back seat with the professor who was taking a nap, she said, "The Lord will provide." I thereby knew her profession and suggested to her at once that the professor needed some spiritual help, but that I had to drive. She went to work immediately inquiring as to his spiritual state and delivering sermonettes between questions. I could feel the professor becoming more and more restless and finally as we came into sight of an autocamp, he suggested it would be a good idea for the lady to stay there overnight. I opined that we did not know the character of the place and that we had better take her further and suggested to the lady that I hoped she would not be discouraged, for the professor's skepticism ought to be broken down; that she must renew her efforts. This she did, among moans from the professor who was naturally a polite man. After another hour we came to an autocamp that I thought would do, and we let the lady out. She remarked again, "The Lord will provide"—the greeting word of a group of women evangelists who at that time hitch-hiked along the highways, laboring with travelers and the inhabitants of autocamps. Here was the modern nun of Canterbury Tales who could no doubt relate experiences of her own. The professor was so impressed or depressed that he would not speak to me until after a good breakfast and the gorgeous mountain views had melted his indignation.

One night, Mrs. Hoover and I put up at a small autocamp in Northern Montana. I asked the proprietress if there was any good fishing nearby. She replied that the cook was the fisherman and would come and tell me about it after dinner. To my surprise the cook was a comely woman who said that as soon as she finished the breakfast for the camp she would guide us to her favorite stream. As she turned to go, she said: "You do not fish with bait, do you?" I replied, no, that we were devoted to flies. And then the second surprise was her answer, "I am a dry-fly fisherman." No one will understand that except devoted anglers. She was a woman of fine intelligence and gracious manners and could cast a beautiful dry fly. In the course of the fishing, I learned that she and her husband at one time kept a sporting goods store in St. Paul. Her husband had died, leaving her very little to live on, but with the help of her Ford she got her vacations and fishing by cooking in autocamps.

One time to avoid the heat, Allan and I were driving across the great valleys of California in the night, each taking turns at the wheel while the other slept. It was my turn along the great straight highway in the Salinas Valley when we came to a village with all the lights out and obviously everybody safe in bed. I did not slow down. But just through the village, the call of the siren sprang out of nowhere. I pulled up to the road side. The officer came alongside and asked for my license. I showed it to him. He examined it under his hand lamp; then went and re-examined it under the headlights; coming back the conversation ran:

"Are you that guy?"

"I am the guy."

"Do you get any joy out of driving at 60 miles an hour at four o'clock in the morning?"

"I do."

"Pass on, brother, but look out for my mate, he is camped this side of King City."

Motoring the highways also developed some of the more somber sides of the trials through which the American people were passing.

One day, Mrs. Hoover and I driving through the most gorgeous mountain complex in America—above Ouray, Colorado—stopped over night at a neat looking camp. There were a dozen other overnighters. In the dining room they at once fell to asking national questions of me. One visitor, an obvious New Dealer, repeated the contemptuous reference that "you could not eat the Constitution." Near me sat a grizzly, elderly man and his wife who had taken no part. At once, he rose and delivered the clearest and most inspiring discussion of the relation of the Constitution to the daily life of the "ordinary man"—as he called him—to which I have ever listened. After he had finished, I asked him what his job was. "I am a carpenter," he replied.

CHAPTER 3

The Bohemian Club Encampment

On the lighter side of private life was the annual Bohemian Encampment in the redwoods—the greatest men's party in the world. I had been a member since 1913. My classmates, Ray Lyman Wilbur, Charles Field, Will Irwin, and Shirley Baker (all of whom have now passed on) had kept our camp fire potent in my long absences. In the years after the White House there came a stream of life-long friends to narrate, to argue, to make humor, to make music and to eat—as of old. They were not political friends who ran from the loser as if he were a leper. In time the members' demand for an extemporaneous talk expressing my frank opinion on the state of the world became an annual obligation to the encampment over a period of 20 years. All speeches at this place are "off-the-record" and this has never been violated in seventy-five years, despite the fact that a quarter of the members are from the press. Such a speech seemed very little to contribute compared to the gifts to all of us of the great artists from all over the world who each year gave so much of music, poetry, drama and humor. The world fame of the Encampment and the kindness of the Directors of the Club made it easy for me to bring to California from many countries old friends of my engineering days, of war days, and of Washington days, and thus add to their assembly men of distinction from government, from the press, of literature, of the bench and bar—for here in the redwoods they could, for a fortnight, escape the worried world.

I presided over the club's annual Thanksgiving evening dinner on one occasion. A part of the job was a speech. As it had a tinge of political reminiscence, I give part of it here.[1]

---

1. [*Editor's note*: Hoover delivered these remarks, or a variant of them, at the Bohemian Club in San Francisco on November 22, 1934.]

One outstanding characteristic of Thanksgiving dinners is that they are never infested with after-dinner speeches. This is indeed a surprising fact, but it has been true for the whole three hundred years. I wish to impress this upon you. Here is a powerful statistic. If you multiply 314 annual dinners that have taken place since 1621 by the index number of families in the United States, you will find that there have been 4,221,648,121 dinners without someone wanting to impose his whimsies, his humor, and his inspirational ability upon the public. You would not have believed that was possible. Nevertheless, there is one oratorical effort overshadowing these dinners. That is the President's Thanksgiving Proclamation. This document provides the necessary authority to hold these occasions, but it is not solely an authority, for it tells you in detail what you are to be thankful about. The proclamation does not bubble with humor or spontaneous joy, but without it you could not hold the dinner nor be constructively thankful. It may be that it is the lack of spontaneity or inspirational quality of the Proclamation which dampens the universal instinct for after-dinner remarks.

In the light of all these facts, I inquired of the President of the Club why I had been chosen to preside here. He replied: "You must know all about Thanksgiving Proclamations." I at once acknowledged that I knew all about them, that I had not only issued several myself, but I had served ten years under other Presidents and observed the process fourteen times very intimately. The method is to send a clerk for the form originally drafted by George Washington, and then to fill in the middle between the introduction and the benediction with new and original matter. You do this filling in by directing your secretary to inquire around the Government what we can be thankful for without hurting somebody's feelings. And having received these attenuated items for the body of the Proclamation, then you add a few words about being kind to your neighbors, and put on the Great Seal of the United States at the end.

Now in finding appropriate items for a Proclamation to you on this occasion you can all be unanimously thankful without reservation. But what can be included in the body of this text tonight is not so easy. For bear in mind that the Proclamation tonight must bear the element of constructive joy, which is the essential component of thankfulness. I may illustrate to you the varieties of hurt feelings, of dampening emotions, and spectral thoughts which can arise in this connection.

Like George Washington, I thought the first reference should be to the progress of peace of [in–ed.] the world. Then my resolves were stifled by the morning paper which envisaged the stealthy approach of Japanese aggression and Hitler.

I had considered some expression as to the gratitude for the progress of the Republic. Then the apparitions raised by the new use of the alphabet in Washington[2] fail to give lift to the soul of man so necessary for a setting of grateful ease.

I then ranged around the physical landscape looking for those more usual items which might be included in the body of this Proclamation without hurt to the feelings of any of you. One naturally turned at this season to the abundant products of the harvest. But here again the heat of emotion might arise in the thought of the predestination of those suckling pigs which met an untoward end in collision with the alphabet before they could reach a million Thanksgiving tables.[3]

Then there were the abundant products of labor which deserve our gratitude. But here will arise in some tangled minds the general strike[4] and a consequent falling barometer of thankfulness over some of its by-products.

I even thought we might consider an expression of pleasure at the stability and courage of our financial institutions, but again an unhappy note arises from those souls who have been sacrificed by the high priests of liquidity or it might raise reminiscences of recent devaluation of the currency.[5]

Then I turned to the intellectual harvest of the year as a safe inclusion for gratitude, but that thought was instantly stricken by the depressing visage of that army of brightly colored books written by government officials during the past year.

I felt at one moment safe in including in our list of new blessings the broad advance of scientific discovery in the realms of cosmic rays and revitalizing the dead. But there arose an uneasy feeling that the cosmic rays only added to the things we must some day regulate, and a clammy feeling that resuscitation after one peaceful death only resulted in having to pass that fearsome event twice.

I then thought I might include an inspiring reference to those great invisible spirits who have been present at our hallowed Thanksgiving tables

---

2. [*Editor's note*: Hoover was evidently alluding to the rapid proliferation of new federal agencies during the New Deal—entities with acronyms such as AAA, CCC, and WPA. Critics disparaged these "alphabet" agencies as "alphabet soup."]

3. [*Editor's note*: Hoover is referring here to the slaughter of six million pigs at the behest of the federal government in September 1933, in an effort to drive up what the secretary of agriculture considered to be the "intolerably low" price of hogs. The government purchased the slaughtered animals at packing houses. The aim was to make hog raising more profitable in the future.]

4. [*Editor's note*: Probably a reference to the San Francisco general strike of July 1934.]

5. [*Editor's note*: In Hoover's earlier drafts, which evidently quoted his Bohemian Club speech more accurately, he had ended this sentence with the words "recent repudiation." Probably for clarity, he altered this phrase in 1955 to read: "recent devaluation of the currency."]

through three centuries of American life. There was the grim Governor Bradford who stood with bowed head before that meager board at Plymouth and gave thanks to the Almighty for the new land which had welcomed them with the products of its soil; which had opened to them visions of a mighty nation; a nation in which their children and their children's children should build the bulwarks of human freedom and hold upon it a banner inscribed to human liberty. I had thought of the great voice of Washington, who drew the first national Proclamation and whose diction and strength yearly appear in the formulation of each President's bidding of the Nation to a feast of thankfulness. I thought of Lincoln, who added great tenderness to its tones. I thought of Longfellow, of Whittier, of Oliver Wendell Holmes, of Hawthorne, of Walt Whitman, and of James Whitcomb Riley, who implanted its sentiment in American prose and poetry. But then a deflating thought came to me that alongside this inspiring orchestra of the past, I detected today the notes of the New Deal, the revival of P. T. Barnum, and of Dr. Coué, the spread of jazz, of cubist art, of technocracy, of Bolshevism, of ballyhoo, and many assistant professors.

For all these blessings I proclaim your thankfulness.

While on the subject of the Bohemian Club, I might include two other occasions which illustrate this atmosphere of companionship at this the greatest men's party in the world. In March 1953 I had reached my 40th year of membership. The several members of the Club in New York, together with the Club officials in San Francisco, decided to put on a simultaneous dinner in each city, perfectly interconnected by the magic of electronics. The Club Symphony Orchestra in San Francisco played interspersed parts of the overtures of the great dramas written for the Encampment by the members of my camp — Will Irwin, Charles Field and Budington Kelland. For New York, the Club had shipped carloads of redwoods to decorate the Waldorf dining room. Members Vice President Richard Nixon and Justice of the Supreme Court [Robert H. Jackson–*ed.*] made the appropriate kindly remarks as did the President of the Club who, with other members, came especially from California.

In August 1955 [1954–*ed.*] I reached my 80th birthday and the Encampment of that year in the Club's Redwood Grove put on a celebration.[6] Neither the Club members nor I had any desire for long oratory. The 1500 members assembled in the Club's dining room at one o'clock. Even including speeches,

---

6. [*Editor's note*: The celebration at the Bohemian Grove occurred on July 31, while Hoover was attending the encampment. His birthday was August 10.]

the Club orchestra, the Club chorus and lunch, we finished in one hour. I may be pardoned for reproducing the Club President's remarks, prepared by Budington Kelland, for they indicate the personal relationships of the place. As the Club subsequently published them, they are not "off-the-record."

To Herbert Hoover, good companion, cherished friend, upon his completion of his eightieth year of a life well lived.

The Members of the Bohemian Club reaffirm their affection and esteem for you, in whom have been gathered all those qualities of integrity, leadership, wisdom, love of country and of mankind which Bohemia most reveres.

By your courage in adversity and your modesty in triumph, you have erected in our hearts a monument more enduring than granite. You have molded our minds to right thinking, and you have pointed out the paths of wisdom to this nation.

Even those who have opposed you have been compelled to call you to high service.

You have earned the gratitude of hungry millions in foreign lands.

With each added year the appreciation of your fellow citizens for your contributions to their happiness and security has grown; until today you are the most beloved of all Americans.

We, who have walked beneath these ancient trees with you in intimacy, can find no words to say as apt as these: "Well done, thou good and faithful servant."

Clarence Budington Kelland[7]

---

7. [*Editor's note*: Kelland's tribute to Hoover on July 31, 1954, is not filed with Hoover's memoir. However, the tribute was later printed in elegant, diploma-like form. Hoover's copy, from which the words in the text are taken, is in the Herbert Hoover Subject Collection, Box 327, Hoover Institution Archives, Stanford University.]

CHAPTER 4

The Passing of Mrs. Hoover

Mrs. Hoover passed away in the evening of the 7th of January, 1944 in our apartment at the Waldorf Towers. She had been out to a concert with my secretary, Miss Miller, in the afternoon, [and–*ed.*] had walked part way home. Saying that she felt a little tired they took a cab, arriving at just 6:30 o'clock. She came to the door of the room in which I was working, smiled, waved her hand and went to her room. A little later, two friends came to escort me to a public dinner for men. Before starting, I stepped to her room to bid her good-night, but found her on the floor unconscious. She passed away at seven o'clock—in the few minutes before the doctor could arrive—from heart failure. We took her to California.

She had aged greatly since the war began in 1941. She had lived and worked in the first World War and its aftermaths. She knew well its hideous injustices, its tragedies, its suffering and its human wreckage. She took almost with bitterness the refusal of Churchill and Roosevelt to allow the feeding of European children.[1] "They have never seen children suffer."

President Wilbur presided over the memorial service for her at Stanford.[2] He had been her friend of fifty years—since their school days together. He drew so tender a picture of her that it may well be reproduced here.

Our country was built from almost nothing to its present state by American women as much as by American men. Throughout our whole pioneer background the explorer, hunter, and trapper were soon followed by settlers and

---

1. [*Editor's note*: In 1940–41 Hoover attempted to establish humanitarian food relief operations in several European countries under German occupation. Fearing that his effort would benefit the Nazi enemy, Prime Minister Winston Churchill and President Franklin Roosevelt stymied Hoover's plans.]

2. [*Editor's note*: Ray Lyman Wilbur (1875–1949) was president of Stanford University for many years and was one of the Hoovers' closest friends.]

their vigorous, patient, industrious, intelligent, home-building, home-loving, and God-fearing women. These women took conditions as they found them and molded them for a better future. Above all, they sought for the right conditions for their children.

Lou Henry Hoover was such a woman. She could have fitted equally well into any stage of our American development from the log cabin with its loop-holes for a rifle to the most modern dwelling in the largest of our modern cities.

A chain of circumstances brought her into marriage with one of the great world figures of this period and took her all over the world. Her experiences varied from being under fire in Tientsin to entertaining the great scientists, statesmen, authors, and government officials of this and other countries in her own home and at the White House. Wherever she went she made a home for her husband and children. She had great skill in making domes-tic things simple, in welcoming and entertaining guests, and in providing a background of comfort for the household, particularly for her husband. His friends and associates became at once her friends and associates.

Lou Henry Hoover could deal as understandingly and sympathetically with a gardener as with the head of a world conference. Her mind was scien-tific, her training good, her mental discipline excellent. These qualities were invaluable to her husband. She was capable of sustained work, and needed to be so in order to keep up with her family job.

I knew Lou Henry when she was an out-of-doors high-school girl. We became friends then and have been ever since. It happened that Herbert Hoover graduated from Stanford in '95, I in '96, and Lou Henry in '98. In our student lives we covered the early period of the University's his-tory. Throughout all the years since, Lou Henry has been to us and to this community that fine, inquiring, well-balanced American girl whose range constantly increased but whose qualities and loyalties remained the same. She was just as interested in the smallest Girl Scout as in the biggest eco-nomic or political person. A fine book, a good painting, a lovely concert, a good speech, a rare geological specimen, a research project, always held her attention. . . .

Here in her home community, Lou Henry Hoover had a unique position. She was known to all, and loved by all who knew her. Just a few weeks ago she went East, full of life and vigor and radiating friendship. It is hard for us to realize that she is not to be with us again. With our sorrow goes the feeling that she went as she would have liked—with her work largely done, without suffering, and near the one she loved beyond all others.

I could write much more. For I had lived with the loyalty and tender affection of an indomitable soul almost fifty years. Hers were those qualities which make a real lady: loyalty and gentle consideration for the rights and needs of others, no matter who. And these qualities brought her great loyalty in return. Her many secretaries were eternally getting married and in after years bringing their children to visit. Loyalties came to her from her classmates and the many women of favored positions in life. She had headed innumerable committees and institutions carrying service, especially to the women and children. She had contributed more to the building of the Girl Scouts than any other woman. Her labors for others were unending.

These loyalties included servants over many years and of many nationalities. Ours was a home without servant trouble, and above all, one of peace and good will with everybody. The servants seldom changed—and then only because of marriage, or death, or our moving away, or such. And they never willfully failed in their duties. Their very names make up a League of Nations. Quah and Troi, who stayed with us during the siege of Tientsin[3] when all other servants fled the Settlement, and who during their lives afterward never failed to send some trifle and inquiry to her every Chinese New Year. Then the English women, "Lovell the Parlor Maid," "Judith the Cook," "Amy the Nurse," "Player the Chauffeur," and "Jenkins the Gardener," were fixed parts of the London house—which they kept open for our periodic sojourns from America and elsewhere for fifteen years. They too "corresponded" regularly afterwards. Abdul the Arab and his multitudinous family in Burma were always inquiring when she would be coming back. The colored servants in Washington were the same for fourteen years. One of the touching things of her funeral was the fact that Ellis and Leon came up from Washington to New York to attend the services. And in California there were Kosta Boris, the Serbian; Mary Gianelli, the Italian; Marie and Frank Franquet, the Belgians; Perry, the gardener; and Lee, the Chinese cook, who was always there.

When World War I came we divided our accumulated savings in order to simplify things that might result from her and my dangerous occupations. I knew little—and wanted to know nothing—of her personal expenditures. But in settling the taxes for her estate, we had to go back over many years of her carefully kept accounts. And there we learned that she, over the twenty-five years since that division, had given away most of her possessions, and this largely in helping out individuals in trouble or in aiding the education of a

---

3. [*Editor's note*: In 1900 Hoover and his wife survived the siege of Tientsin during the Boxer Rebellion in China.]

multitude of boys and girls. There were in her files many thousand dollars in checks to her order which she had never cashed. They were all repayments of "loans" which she had turned into gifts by so simple a device as not depositing them in a bank. And not even I knew many of the persons who had been the beneficiaries.

She had wanted our home on the Campus at Stanford to go ultimately to the University for a President's House. As she had not provided for this in her will, I purchased it from our sons, who were her heirs, and presented it to the Trustees, subject to their making a substantial contribution to the Memorial Fund which her friends in the university had established.

She left the sweetest compliment ever given to men when in her simple letter of a will addressed to her sons she wrote: "You have been lucky boys to have had such a father and I am a lucky woman to have had my life's trail alongside the paths of three such men and boys."

PART II

Crusades for Benevolent Institutions

CHAPTER 5

Crusading for Benevolent Institutions

I realize that former Presidents are a kind of menace chiefly because people must at times listen to them talk on public questions. I relate that sort of activity elsewhere, and will for the moment deal with extra-curricular occupations, equally serious but less painful to the public. In all our history, former Presidents have been incessantly and usefully called upon to aid in management and to crusade for a multitude of charitable institutions and movements.

After leaving the White House, I at once resumed active participation in the management of a number of benevolent organizations with which I had been actively connected before the Presidency. In various capacities as trustee, director and chairman, I had taken part in the work of Stanford University, the Huntington Library, Mills College, the Carnegie Institute, the Boys' Clubs of America, the American Children's Fund, the Belgian-American Educational Foundation, the American Child Health Association and "Better Homes for America." In addition to resuming these duties I accumulated a host of other boards and committees devoted to public service.

In these institutions there were substantial endowments (a total of over $100,000,000). My first effort after leaving the White House was to secure the investment of part of such funds in common stocks instead of all in bonds and prior lien securities. I was confident that sooner or later the inevitable consequence of "Planned Economy" with its managed money and credit would decrease the purchasing power of the dollar and thus a decrease in the real income of prior lien securities. While common stocks were no guarantee that income would grow as purchasing value decreased, yet they at least had a chance. In the case of Stanford University it was necessary to secure an amendment to the trust deed through the courts before we could acquire other than prior lien securities. The institutions with which I was connected ultimately converted from 40% to 60% of their funds into equities.

In every single case both their income and capital greatly profited by the conversion.

It was necessary for me to devote a good deal of time to crusades for funds for these and other various scientific, educational, public welfare and relief institutions. During the years I made hundreds of speeches or statements supporting all sorts of universities, colleges, relief agencies, hospitals, character-building agencies, Community Chests, the Salvation Army, Boys' Clubs, Boy Scouts and what not. Directly and indirectly I must have taken part in raising 200 to 300 million dollars for such purposes after leaving the White House.

The point of view which I often expressed in the urgent need to maintain our voluntary charitable institutions was summarized in a short address in the '50ties [1950s–ed.] before a fund-raising audience in New York City, I said:

We have a steady expansion of government into welfare activities. I am not here criticizing the expansion of those agencies. They have a place in American life—provided the cloak of welfare is not used as a disguise for Karl Marx. But parallel with this expansion, we have stupendous taxation to support the hot and cold wars. That makes it difficult for the citizens to support the voluntary welfare agencies. It requires more personal sacrifice than ever before.

Many citizens ask themselves: For what reasons must we continue to support the voluntary agencies? Why not let the Government do it all?

The first short answer to this question is that you cannot retire from the voluntary field if you wish our American civilization to survive. The essence of our self-government lies by cooperation in self-government outside of political government. Ours is a voluntary cooperative society. The fabric of American life is woven around our tens of thousands of voluntary associations. That is, around our churches, our professional societies, our women's organizations, our businesses, our labor and farmers' associations—and not least, our charitable institutions. That is the very nature of American life. The inspirations of progress spring from these voluntary agencies, not from bureaucracy. If these voluntary activities were to be absorbed by government bureaus, this civilization would be over. Something neither free nor noble would take its place.

The second answer to this question is that it is our privately-supported and managed hospitals and educational institutions that establish the standards for similar governmental agencies. It is the voluntary institutions which are the spur to official progress. Without them our governmental healing and educational agencies will lag and will degenerate.

The third answer to this question is that morals do not come from government. No government agency can create and sustain a system of morals. You perhaps are not working specifically in the religious field, but your works confirm religious faith and morals. You do support the development of sports in our youth. The ethics of good sportsmanship are second only to religious ethics.

There is a fourth answer. Governments and bureaucracies cannot build character in our youth. With the brutalization which is inevitable from war, revitalized character-building has never been as necessary as it is today.

There is a fifth answer. The greatest and, in fact, the only impulse to social progress is the spark of altruism in the individual human being. "And the greatest of these is charity" has been a religious precept from which no civilized people can depart without losing its soul. If governments practice charity, then it is solely because it rises from that spark in the hearts of the people. The day when altruism in the individual dies from lack of opportunity for personal expression, it will die in the government. At best, charity by government must be formal, statistical and mechanistic. Yours is charity in its real sense—not obligatory but from the heart.

There is a sixth reason. The world is in the grip of a death struggle between the philosophy of Christ and that of Hegel and Marx. The philosophy of Christ is a philosophy of compassion. The outstanding spiritual distinction of our civilization from all others is compassion. With us, it is the noblest expression of man. Those who serve receive an untold spiritual benefit. The day when we decide that the Government is our brother's keeper, that is the day the spirit of compassion has been lost. If you fail somewhere we have lost something that is vital to moral and spiritual welfare.

But a simpler answer than all this lies in the Parable of the Good Samaritan. He did not enter into governmental or philosophic discussion. It is said when he saw the helpless man "he had compassion on him . . . he bound his wounds . . . and took care of him."

That is your mission.[1]

In addition to what service I could be generally in these directions I carried an administrative responsibility in several of the charitable agencies. Of these, one of the most interesting was the Boys' Clubs.

---

1. [*Editor's note*: This address is very similar to one Hoover delivered in Washington, D.C., on September 22, 1954, at a rally of Community Chest campaign workers in the federal government (*Washington Post*, September 23, 1954, p. 1). His speech on that occasion is printed in full in Herbert Hoover, *Addresses upon the American Road, 1950–1955* (Stanford, CA: Stanford University Press, 1955), pp. 299–300.

The Boys' Clubs

After leaving the White House I served for over twenty years as Chairman of the National Board of the Boys' Clubs of America. I visited many of the Boys' Clubs and crusaded in a number of cities to stimulate their creation and support. I can give no better indication of the importance and work of this institution than some quotations from annual addresses to its National Convention:

This convention is dealing with the Public Relations of boys. We do not exclude their sisters—if anything, our sentiment for them is even more tender. But we are here engaged with the business of boys.

This evening I wish to examine the nature of the animal.

To explore what civilization has done to some of them.

To relate an experiment.

To lay before you a proposition which involves $7,000,000.

To give the reasons for it all.

And finally to wind up with the peroration. And to do it all in fifteen minutes. . . .[2]

The Boys' Clubs are a great school. They might even be called the University of the Pavements, for our purpose is mostly directed to the pavement boys in our congested areas.

Here are linked together over 325 institutions with 300,000 to 350,000 boys, with an equipment that $60 million could not replace and with an annual budget of $7 million. There were 24 building projects nearly completed in 1949 and 18 more are underway, costing a total of about $5 million. All these great sums are made possible by generous people who love boys.

If you need some more statistics, I may tell you that there are 35,000 adults giving generously of their time to the Boys' Clubs as boards of directors or auxiliary organizations. The Clubs are guided by over six thousand trained adult leaders who are the "faculty."

This education includes self-organization and their own discipline in the conduct of their clubs. It includes testing out their natural bents in shops, crafts, music and the professions. It includes medical inspection and training in health. It involves every known indoor and outdoor game and sport except horseracing and golf. It even includes the flying trapeze.

---

2. [*Editor's note:* Hoover's quotation up to this point is taken from his address to the Boys' Club of America in New York City on May 13, 1937. See Herbert Hoover, *Addresses upon the American Road, 1933–1938* (New York: Charles Scribner's Sons, 1938), p. 237 (and pp. 237–42 for the full text).]

There is no discrimination as to religion or race. Theirs is that equality which is the foundation of free men. The greatest moral training except for religious faith comes from training these boys in team work and sportsmanship.

We do not claim that the Boys' Clubs substitute for either Mother or the public schools. We are concerned with the kid from the hour when school is out until he goes to bed or when he gets a holiday. When a boy is inside our doors, Mother has no worry. The police have no worry from some of his primitive instincts.

We have a right to brag a little. We have produced some major league ball players and some great editors and artists. In the war draft the total number of rejects among our graduates was less than 5% as against the national average of over 30%. I could tell you of districts where we have reduced delinquency by 75%. Over the years we have brought joy into the lives of millions of boys.

You will anticipate my next remark. We need more money and lots of it, for there are 2,000,000 of these pavement boys whom we have not taken care of.

His Rights, Characteristics, Environment, and Hopes

The work of the Boys' Clubs is geared to certain ideas.

First. When the founding fathers announced the unalienable rights, they laid proper emphasis on the pursuit of happiness. I have no doubt any lawyer would construe that as especially intended to include boys. However, we are not so worried at the moment with his unalienable rights to the pursuit of happiness as we are with his processes in the pursuit.

Second. In pursuit of happiness, the boy has two jobs. One is being a boy and the other is training to be a man.

When the Boys' Clubs contemplate his jobs, we take into account certain characteristics of the animal and his environment. Some years ago I made some observations on these essentials. I have combined them with some further observations to bring you up to date in this important matter.

Together with his sister, the boy is our most precious possession. But he presents not only joys and hopes, but also paradoxes. He strains our nerves, yet he is a complex of cells teeming with affection. He is a periodic nuisance, yet he is a joy forever. He is a part-time incarnation of destruction, yet he radiates sunlight to all the world. He at times gives evidence of being the child of iniquity, yet his idealism can make a great nation. He is filled with curiosity as to every mortal thing. He is an illuminated interrogation point, yet he is the most entertaining animal that is.

The whole world is new to him. He must discover it all over again. All its corners and things must be explored or taken apart. Therefore his should be a life of discovery, of adventure, of great undertakings. He must spend much time in the land of make-believe, if he is to expand his soul. One of the sad things in the world is that he must grow up into the land of taxpayers.

He is endowed with a dynamic energy and an impelling desire to take exercise on all occasions. He is a complete self-starter, and therefore wisdom in dealing with him consists mostly in what to do with him next. His primary instinct is to hunt in a pack and that multiplies his devices. He and his pack can go on the hunt either for good or evil. Our first problem is to find him constructive joy, instead of destructive glee.

To complicate this problem, this civilization has gone and built up great cities. We have increased the number of boys per acre. We have paved all this part of the land with cement and cobblestones. Of these human organisms, perhaps two and a half million must find their outdoor life on these pavements and confined by brick walls. Much of their life is concerned with stairs, light switches, alleys, fire escapes, bells and cobblestones, and a chance to get run over by a truck. Thus these boys are today separated from Mother Earth and all her works, except the weather. In the days before our civilization became so perfectly paved with cement, he matched his wits with the birds, the bees and the fish. But the outlet of his energies in exploring the streams and the fields is closed to him. The mysteries of the birds and bees and fish are mostly denied to him.

The normal boy is a primitive animal and takes to competition and battle. If he doesn't have much of a chance to contend with nature, and unless he is given something else to do, he is likely to take on contention with a policeman.

I dislike to refer to these boys as "underprivileged." That is only a part-truth. He has better facilities for education and better protection of health than boys in any other country in the world. He suffers less from mumps and measles than his grandfather did; more quickly do we heal his broken bones. He will live longer, and if his start is blighted, the nation will have to board him longer in jail.

He has other gains. The electric light has banished the former curse of all boys, of cleaning lamps and everlastingly carrying them about. The light switch has driven away the goblins that lived in dark corners and under the bed. It clothes drab streets with gaiety and cheer by night. And it is the attraction of these bright lights that increases our problem.

But we are concerned with the privileges which all these bricks and cement have taken away from him. The particular ones with which we are concerned bear on his character and moral stature. This brick and cement foundation of life is a hard soil for his growths. Somebody will say morals are the job of parents. But the best of parents cannot keep him indoors all the time. And the world in the streets is a distorted and dangerous world, which the parents cannot make or unmake. So it becomes a job of public relations.

But there is more than that. The fine qualities of loyalty to the pack are not so good on the pavements. For here the pack turns to the gang, where his superabundant vitality leads him to depredation. And here we make gangsters and feed jails. The way to stop crime is to stop the manufacture of criminals.

This is only a marginal problem to the total boys in the United States. If we can start this marginal group right on the road to character, we will have done more to cure our national ills than either subsidies or so-called security.

And there is more to this than even exercise and morals. There is the job of stretching his vision of life. The right to glimpse into constructive joy, the right to discover an occupation fitted to his inclinations and talents, and the right to develop his personality. The priceless treasure of boyhood is his endless enthusiasm, his high store of idealism, his affections, and his hopes. When we preserve these with character, we have made men. We have made citizens and we have made Americans.[3]

Since the time of that address the movement has continued to expand until at the time of this writing there are over 450 thriving clubs with nearly half a million boys and equipment that could not be replaced for $125,000,000.

As an illustration of the value of these institutions, I may cite an experience in the slums of one of our large cities. The magistrate in one of those areas came to me to urge that we build a Boys' Club in his district. He stated that he had to deal with 85% of delinquency in all the boys in his jurisdiction. That is, 85% of the boys were at one time or another during each year in the hands of the police. We succeeded in building the Club. Various individuals and organizations provided $300,000 to erect it. Five years later this judge informed me that delinquency in his district was then under 15%.

Over 1,500,000 boys passed through the Clubs during the period of my chairmanship. They are better citizens. This movement in building character is the answer to the delinquency which thrives and breeds crime in our slums. But there are still a million of these boys which it does not reach.

---

3. [*Editor's note*: This passage (beginning at "The Boys' Clubs are a great school") is drawn from Hoover's address before the annual convention of the Boys' Clubs of America, held in Washington, D.C., on May 18, 1950. The text appears also in Herbert Hoover, *Addresses upon the American Road, 1948–1950* (Stanford, CA: Stanford University Press, 1951), pp. 195–99.]

The Belgian American Educational Foundation

This institution had its foundation in some left-over funds after the liquidation of the billion dollar expenditure of the Belgian Relief Commission during the first World War, the circumstances of which I have related in previous memoirs.[4] Its endowment amounted to about $2,500,000 and its purpose was intellectual exchanges between the United States and Belgium. The Foundation was, for 35 years, directed at all times by former Commission for Relief in Belgium men, with Edgar Rickard, Hallam Tuck, Millar Shaler, John White, Sidney Mitchell, Lewis Strauss, and that fine product of American life, Perrin Galpin, for many years its active President. Except while in the White House, I participated mostly as Chairman. The Foundation has brought a constant stream of Belgian youth to America for graduate work, Belgian professors to lecture in our American Universities, and we have sent a constant stream of American students to Belgian universities, together with our best American professors to lecture at their institutions. So careful has been the selection of Belgian students that at times as many as five of the twelve members of the Belgian Cabinet, and over one-third of the faculties of Belgian universities, had done post-graduate work in the United States under our auspices. The loyalties of the Belgian and American people to each other have been greatly sustained by this work.

The American Children's Fund

Another of the agencies in which I had administrative responsibilities was the American Children's Fund where I was chairman or director for about thirty years.[5] It was formed from the residues after the liquidation of all liabilities of the very large relief activities for European children which were conducted under my direction from 1918 to 1923. The total funds raised and used in those operations amounted to an excess of $325,000,000. In 1923, as there was no further imperative call for these foreign activities, I secured the approval of the various state committees and foundations (which had been active in raising these funds) that we devote the residues to American institutions, chiefly for children. The recoveries from insurance losses, etc., took several years and, chiefly by Edgar Rickard's nursing of the investments, they

---

4. [*Editor's note*: See Herbert Hoover, *The Memoirs of Herbert Hoover*, vol. I: *Years of Adventure, 1874–1920* (New York: The Macmillan Company, 1951), pp. 228–31.]

5. [*Editor's note*: It was first known as the ARA Children's Fund. Established in 1923, it eventually changed its name to the American Children's Fund.]

ultimately realized $7,260,000. The directors, in addition to Mr. Rickard, were mostly the same men as those of the Belgian Educational Foundation. We distributed these funds over the years to support the Boy Scouts, the Girl Scouts, the Boys' Clubs, the [American–*ed.*] Child Health Association, various southern mountain educational institutions, and other activities devoted to the upbuilding of youth. We finally wound it up in 1947.

The War Library at Stanford University

I can give no better account of this institution than an address I made at the University.[6] I said:

Soon after the outbreak of the [First–*ed.*] World War I happened to read some remarks by President Andrew D. White of Cornell on the difficulty he experienced in the study of the French Revolution because of the disappearance of contemporaneous documents and fugitive literature. The position I held at that time required regular visits to several belligerent countries. It seemed to me to offer a unique opportunity to collect and preserve such records. I therefore established centers for such collections in each country and enlisted the aid of others who believed in the importance of this work. [. . .–*ed.*]

On my return to the United States to participate in the war administration, I was able to expand further these collections on the American side and to secure material from the many agencies of the European governments.

Immediately after the Armistice I returned to Europe to become the executive head of the Supreme Economic Council. This body had to do with the economic rehabilitation of Europe in general and of the former enemy countries in particular. Our duty was to further the rehabilitation of railroads and canals, the opening of ports and the reduction of blockade, to supervise the proper utilization of coal in Central Europe, and to foster the restoration of trade relations generally. It included the food relief of 150,000,000 people in some twenty-three countries of Central and Eastern Europe and the establishment of refuges and special relief for 10,000,000 children. We furnished expert advisers on finance, railroads, and other public activities in some twelve new governments. For the administration of this work I recruited from the American Army about 1,500 officers (previously civilians) and established them in all parts of Europe.

---

6. August 30, 1939; [Herbert Hoover,] *Further Addresses* [*up*]*on the American Road, 1938–1940* [New York: Charles Scribner's Sons, 1940], pp. 215–218.

All this brought a very much enlarged opportunity for collecting histori-cal material. I was able to interest all these men in the job. I was also able to enlist the heads of governments, many of their Cabinet officers, and offi-cials of some twenty-five countries in furnishing us with copies of their own records of the war and especially their interdepartmental and public docu-ments bearing on economic and social as well as military questions. We also secured complete files of periodicals and newspapers issued in the belliger-ent countries during the war.

In order to organize this work effectively, I requested President Ray Lyman Wilbur to permit Professor Ephraim Adams of the Stanford Univer-sity Department of History to come to Europe and take charge of the work. I placed under him some fifteen professors and students of history whom I had recruited out of the American Army, and Professor Adams assigned to them the detailed tasks involved in the different countries.

We established co-operation in Paris with the various delegations to the Peace Conference and secured from them their publications. Documents of the Supreme Council and of other Allied bodies were also acquired. We also established relations with the war propaganda agencies of the Allied and enemy governments, securing from them material which they had used dur-ing the war. These records, together with the entire files of the Commission for Relief in Belgium, and those of the various agencies which were estab-lished during the Armistice, including the Supreme Economic Council, the American Relief Administration, the Coal Mission, and the various railway, blockade and other technical commissions, were all dispatched to the Uni-versity. I might mention here an incidental contribution of great importance, in that the United States Shipping Board and some of the private shipping agencies gave free transportation of this enormous amount of material to San Francisco.

Soon after the war I became impressed with the fact that the most impor-tant aspect of the century was perhaps not the war, so much as the conse-quences of the war, that is, the social, economic, and political currents which had sprung from it. The rise of democracy in Europe after the war and its collapse into Communism, Fascism, and National Socialism have contrib-uted to make one of the greatest human crises in history. Therefore, instead of limiting the new Library to purely war material, I determined that the work of collecting should be continued and should be directed especially to securing records of these movements. In the building up of these collec-tions the Library has had the cooperation of many governments and a great many individuals, and it now bids to possess one of the largest collections on

Communism, Fascism, and National Socialism, outside of the countries in which these movements originated. . . .

I am confident we have established an institution of primary value to the American people. This period of world-wide experimentation in social, economic and political institutions will be of importance for a thousand years to come. The work of collection will not be complete until these social and economic currents have run their course and have reached again some common elements of stability.

At the dedication of the beautiful new building on June 20, 1941, I said:[7]

I suppose some one will wonder why all this trouble and expense to preserve these records. They embrace the campaigns of armies, the negotiations of statesmen. They tell the great drama of superlative sacrifice, of glory, of victory, of death, of sorrow, of frustration and defeat. If we assume that humanity is going to abandon the lessons of its own experience, the whole of this collection is useless, except to the casual visitor. But sometimes the voice of experience does call out to stop, look and listen. And sometimes peoples respond to that call. [. . .–ed.]

And there are the records of the world's effort to make peace. Here are the proofs of the highest idealism. And here are the records of selfishness and the lowest trickery. Here can be found the record of the ideas and forces which made for failure of the last peace and the ideas and forces which might have made its success. Out of these files the world can get great warning of what not to do and what to do when it next assembles around the peace table. True, there must be brought to that table a concept of new human relations, a concept that substitutes peace for war. But if the world is to have long peace, that concept must find its origins in human experience and its inspiration in human idealism.

And here are the documents which record the suffering, the self-denial, the devotion, the heroic deeds of men. Surely from these records there can be help to mankind in its confusions and perplexities, and its yearnings for peace.

As to the importance of the Library I give this quotation from a statement of the professor of history at Harvard, Sidney B. Faye [Fay–ed.]:[8]

---

7. [Herbert Hoover,] Addresses [up]on the American Road, 1940–1941 [New York: Charles Scribner's Sons, 1941], pp. 196–198.

8. Dedication of the Hoover Library on War, Revolution and Peace (Stanford University Press, 1941), pp. 5–15. [Editor's note: In the quotation that follows, I have deleted (at its beginning) three sentences

... It gives me [...–*ed.*] pleasure ... to express my great gratitude for the aid which the Hoover War Library so kindly gave me when I was writing my books on *The Origins of the World War.* The library had some manuscript minutes of the proceedings of the Russian Councils of Ministers in the crisis of July, 1914 which, I believe, existed nowhere else in the world but which were of priceless value to me in determining Russia's actions. . . .

. . . There are only two libraries of importance in the world of this kind[9] that can be compared with the Hoover Library.

The first of these is the German Weltkriegsbucherei at Schloss Rosenstein near Stuttgart. . . .

The other War Library is the French Bibliothèque et Musée de la Guerre at Vincennes. . . .

. . . They are of great interest and value to historical scholars . . . but [...–*ed.*] by comparison with them it will be seen how greatly the Hoover Library excels them in breadth of scope and in usefulness to scholars and students. . . .

The French, British and German libraries of this character were practically destroyed by World War II. Stanford alone has these records.

After the second World War we again expanded hugely into the collection of materials of economic, social and political order from every part of the world. The collections on Communist Russia, Naziism, the Vichy regime, the development of Communism in China and Asia, the political developments of Japan, India and all Asia in this period are unique to this institution.

The Library contributed in a minor way to winning World War II by its being America's major source of vital military material from World War I. Whether it will contribute to winning the peace is more problematical. Military men are avid for the lessons of experience. Politicians want to create the impression of inventing something "new."

I spent much time over the years crusading for funds for its support. Through over ten thousand contributors we secured an amount exceeding $4,000,000. A half thousand friends under the leadership of Edgar Rickard, Jeremiah Milbank, Fred A. Wickett and Arch W. Shaw have aided in this movement.[10] The

---

delivered by Hoover that he inadvertently attributed to Fay. I have also inserted a couple of words that appear in the cited source but were evidently lost in transcription. Fay's own words quoted here appear on pp. 5, 6, 8, 9, and 11.]

9. [*Editor's note:* Fay was referring to what he called "specialized" libraries on "the First World War, its causes, course, and multifarious consequences" (ibid., pp. 8–9).]

10. [*Editor's note:* Edgar Rickard (1874–1951) was Hoover's longtime friend, confidant, and adviser in financial matters. Jeremiah Milbank (1887–1972) was a prominent businessman, philanthropist, and longtime friend of Hoover. Fred A. Wickett (1879–1970) was a California businessman and

collection, however, comes more largely from gifts of material than from purchase. Today, over 100 graduate and research students are on its rolls. The Army and Navy have officers constantly in its stacks. Those stacks contain probably 20 million items.

There are incidents in its collection which would fill volumes of interesting tales.

One of our zealous youngsters walked into the deserted headquarters of Bela Kun after the Communist Hungarian revolution during the Armistice of 1918—which I relate in a previous volume[11]—and, gathering up all the papers, shipped them to Trieste. Years afterward, at the request of the Hungarian Ambassador, I gave the originals back to the Hungarian Government. We retained copies.

Dr. Kellogg[12] one day during the Armistice after the first World War informed President Ebert of the German Republic, that I had an important personal matter in which I would like his co-operation. Kellogg informed me that Ebert seemed to brace himself for the worst. But when Dr. Kellogg explained that it was the collection of material for the War Library, Ebert cheered up. And he co-operated to the extent of several carloads of papers, the duplicates of which cannot be found in Germany today. Among other things, this collection included a copy of the minutes and reports of the German Supreme War Council for the whole period of the First World War down to the Armistice. To Ebert they belonged to an age that was past forever, but a few years later the German Ambassador asked me for their return. We compromised by my agreement to allow him to take photostats and my agreement to lock up the collection for a period of years in order not to embarrass living men.

Another example of acquisition was the gift to us of the important Ministry of Foreign Affairs files of the Czarist regime by a member of the Kerensky government who had escaped to Finland with them.

Hundreds of nuggets of this kind covering governmental action, revolutionary action, economic action were ours for the asking. All governments seemed eager to co-operate with me.

This collection now ranks not only as the most complete in the world, but it is unique in the world. And from it will come not only a rewriting of much false history but many lessons in statesmanship.

---

friend who often assisted in Hoover's projects at Stanford University. Arch W. Shaw (1876–1972) was a Chicago business executive, publisher, and longtime friend and confidant of Hoover.]

11. [*Editor's note*: Hoover, *Years of Adventure*, pp. 398–404.]

12. [*Editor's note*: Vernon L. Kellogg (1867–1937), a distinguished biologist, was a friend and close associate of Hoover in relief work during and after World War I.]

PART III

The Crusade against Collectivism in American Life

INTRODUCTION

During all the years after 1934, in addition to crusades for American charities and crusades for relief of famine, and crusades against being involved in war, I was engaged in a constant crusade against the attempt to collectivize.

In Volume III of my *Memoirs* in the chapters devoted to "The Aftermath" I have given in detail the attempts, the progress and the failures of the New Dealers in collectivizing America.[1]

The titles of the chapters in that account are indicative of these activities:

Building the Trojan Horse of Emergency

The Recognition of Russia and the World Economic Conference in 1933

Usurpation of Power: Collectivizing the Legislative Arm, Packing
the Supreme Court, The Purge, Power Via Bureaucracy, [. . .–*ed.*][2]
Roosevelt's Own Ideas of Personal Power

Collectivism Comes to the Currency—and Its Consequences:
Abandonment of the Gold Standard, Devaluation, Silver Realizes
Bryan's Dream,[3] [Some–*ed.*] Subsequent Economic History of
Devaluation, Shifts in Property Ownership, Relative Value of Our
Currency to Foreign Currencies, Gold Movement to the United States,
Subsidizing Speculators, Devaluation Increased the Tariffs

Fascism Comes to Agriculture

---

1. [*Editor's note*: See Herbert Hoover, *The Memoirs of Herbert Hoover*, vol. III: *The Great Depression, 1929–1941* (New York: The Macmillan Company, *1952*), pp. 350–485.]

2. [*Editor's note*: Here Hoover omitted the following subtitles: "Reorganization of the Executive Branch, Political Use of Relief Funds." Whether these omissions (and others noted below) were intentional or inadvertent cannot be determined.]

3. [*Editor's note*: Here Hoover omitted the following words: "—and More."]

Fascism Comes to Business—With Dire Consequences: [. . .–ed.][4]
Dictation in the Coal Industry, Dictation to the Railroads

Fascism Comes to Labor—With Consequences

Introduction to Socialism Through Electrical Power [. . .–ed.][5]

Collectivism by Thought Control and Smear:
The American Liberty League, Boulder Dam, The Attempted
Conviction of Andrew Mellon [. . .–ed.][6]

Increasing National Debt[7]

The Expenditures, Accounting and Statistics: Index Numbers

The Consequences: The Numbers on Relief, Comparison with Other
Countries, Causes of the United States' Failure to Recover [. . .–ed.][8]

As a restorative of employment, these measures were an utter failure. In 1940, after eight years of the New Deal, unemployment and the number of families on relief were about the same as the day Roosevelt was elected. However, within two years after his election, the great non-Socialist nations had fully recovered from the depression. As a corruptor of American Freedom and the American spirit, it was a success.

As shown by my addresses in the campaign of 1932 I was fully aware of, and warned against, the import and character of the New Deal "Planned Economy," although the public could not or would not then believe it.

Nationally broadcast addresses by a former President were certain to reach the front page and editorial columns of every important newspaper. I, therefore, had a great audience. No one except the President had such an audience. It seemed to me therefore an obligation to make a fight to save the moral, spiritual, economic and political values of America.

The crusade against this New Deal mixture of European collectivism into our American system involved not only constant direct attack but also the participation in Republican organization. The one hope to defeat these

---

4. [*Editor's note*: Here Hoover omitted the first subtitle: "Dictation in the Oil Industry."]
5. [*Editor's note*: Here Hoover omitted the next chapter title: "Direct Relief and Public Works."]
6. [*Editor's note*: Here Hoover omitted the next chapter title and its subtitles: "Some Good Actions: Further Relief from Mortgage Pressures, Export-Import Bank of Washington, Social Security Acts, Business Regulation, Unregulated Business, The American System of Regulation."]
7. [*Editor's note*: This chapter title did not appear in the table of contents for volume III of Hoover's memoirs. Why Hoover added this title is unknown.]
8. [*Editor's note*: Here Hoover omitted the final subtitle: "Mr. Roosevelt's Comforting Optimism."]

forces lay in holding the Republican Party in opposition and forthrightness for free men. Therefore, the cumulative points of action were the Congressional and Presidential elections. The progress of the battle can best be described in connection with these events. Between election campaigns it was obviously a job of public education, but to be effective it had to be defeated at the ballot box.

I do not claim that my multitude of activities were more than a contribution to those many who also fought in this vital battle. But our successes in strengthening a Republican Congress in 1938, in electing a majority in 1948 [1946–ed.], and in winning the Presidential campaign in 1952, certainly saved America from completely eliminating the safeguards of free men.

The Hoover family at Herbert and Lou Henry Hoover's home in Palo Alto, California, on Christmas Eve, 1933. Front row (left to right): the grandchildren: Herbert III; Joan; Peggy Ann. The adults: Herbert Hoover, Jr.; Margaret Hoover (his wife); Lou Henry Hoover; Allan Hoover; Herbert Hoover.

Above: Herbert and Lou Henry Hoover at the Army–Notre Dame football game at Yankee Stadium, November 16, 1935.

Right: Lou Henry Hoover in her Girl Scout uniform, with "Weegie," ca. 1937.

Herbert Hoover in Barnard, Vermont, practicing his favorite avocation, June 8, 1935 (with Garfield Miller, oarsman).

Hoover relaxing after fishing in the McKenzie River near Blue River, Oregon, July 8, 1953.

Herbert Hoover delivering his annual Lakeside Talk, at the Bohemian Grove, California, 1948.

Hoover visiting a Boys' Club, May 1940.

Hoover autographing photos for Boys' Club members after receiving a gold medal on the Boys' Clubs of America's fiftieth anniversary, April 1956.

Herbert Hoover at the Bohemian Grove, 1953.

The Hoover Institution building (285 feet high), towering over the Stanford University campus, 1941 (the year of the tower's completion and dedication).

CHAPTER 6

The Crusade against Collectivism to the Presidential Campaign of 1936

During the three years after Mr. Roosevelt took office in 1933, the American people were carried away by the promise of Utopia and the propaganda and glitter.

I took no part in the Congressional campaign of 1934, as the so-called Republican leaders considered I was a political leper. That election resulted in a loss of 15 Republican seats in the House and 10 seats in the Senate, leaving the Party with only 102 House members and only 25 members in the Senate.

One day at Stanford, after I left the White House, I asked Professor Robinson,[1] Dean of the History Department, to send me a list of books of required reading by all students in a course on "Citizenship." I found about one hundred books listed, of which some thirty were objective descriptives of the machinery of our civil government and over sixty devoted, directly or indirectly, to the favorable discussion at least in part of ideas embraced either by the Socialists, Fascists, and even Communists, accompanied by innuendo or direct attacks upon the American system of free men. There was only one book that attempted to expound our American ideology.

I determined to contribute a book on our American philosophy of government, and in 1934 I published *The Challenge to Liberty*.[2]

The purpose of this book is thus stated in its introduction:

> For the first time in two generations the American people are faced with the primary issue of humanity and all government—the issue of human liberty.

---

1. [*Editor's note*: Edgar Eugene Robinson (1887–1977), a professor of history at Stanford University for many years. He was chairman of the History Department from 1935 to 1952.]

2. [*Editor's note*: The publisher was Charles Scribner's Sons in New York City.]

Not only in the United States, but throughout the world, the whole philosophy of individual liberty is under attack. In haste to bring under control the sweeping social forces unleashed by the political and economic dislocations of the World War, by the tremendous advances in productive technology during the last quarter-century, by the failure to march with a growing sense of justice, peoples and governments are blindly wounding, even destroying those fundamental human liberties which have been the foundation and the inspiration of progress since the Middle Ages.

The great question before the American people is not whether these dislocations and abuses can be mastered and these new and powerful forces organized and directed to human welfare, but whether they can be organized by free men. We have to determine now whether, under the pressures of the hour, we must cripple or abandon the heritage of liberty for some new philosophy which must mark the passing of freedom. [. . .–*ed.*]

In every generation men and women of many nations have died that the human spirit may be thus free. In our race, at Plymouth Rock, at Lexington, at Valley Forge, at Yorktown, at New Orleans, at every step of the Western frontier, at Gettysburg, at San Juan Hill, in the Argonne, are the graves of Americans who died for this purpose.

From these sacrifices and in the consummation of these liberties there grew a great philosophy of society [—Liberalism–*ed.*].[3] The high tenet of this philosophy is that Liberty is an endowment from the Creator of every individual man and woman upon which no power, whether economic or political, can encroach, and that not even the government may deny. And herein it challenges all other philosophies of society and government; for all others, both before and since, insist that the individual has no such inalienable rights, that he is but the servant of the state. [. . .–*ed.*][4] All others insist that Liberty is not a God-given right; that the state is the master of the man. Herein is the widest divergence of social and governmental concepts known to mankind. No man long holds his freedom under a government which claims men's liberties. That government cannot exist or continue unless it end in [be of–*ed.*] despotic powers. The whole of human experience has shown that. [. . .–*ed.*]

---

3. [*Editor's note*: This word appears in the text of *The Challenge to Liberty* on page 3. Why Hoover omitted it here is unknown. For accuracy, I have inserted it as shown.]

4. [*Editor's note*: Here Hoover omitted, without so indicating, the following sentence in *The Challenge to Liberty*: "Liberalism holds that man is master of the state, not the servant; that the sole purpose of government is to nurture and assure these liberties." Whether Hoover's omission of this sentence was deliberate or accidental is unknown. Possibly, in the 1950s, he thought that its reference to "Liberalism" might be confusing, given the changing usage of the term since publication of *The Challenge to Liberty* in 1934.]

From the creativeness of mankind's liberated mind and spirit has come the host of ideas, discoveries, and inventions with their freight of comforts and opportunities. And with all of them has come a burden of difficult problems to Liberty. Today, these complexities, added to the aftermaths of war, loom large, and the voices of discouragement join with the voices of other social faiths to assert that an irreconcilable conflict has arisen in which Liberty must be sacrificed upon the altar of the Machine Age. But Liberty is a living force, expanding to every new vision of humanity, and from its very dynamic freedom of mind and thought comes the conquest of its ceaseless problems. [. . .–ed.]

It is now claimed by large and vocal groups, both in and out of government, that Liberty has failed; that emergency encroachments upon its principles should be made permanent. Thereby are created the most urgent issues: first, whether we must submit to some other system by which the fundamentals of Liberty are sacrificed; and second, whether, even if we make these sacrifices, we shall not defeat the hope and progress of humanity. These are not partisan issues. They are the greatest issues of American life.

It is my hope to show that to resume the path of Liberty is not to go backward; it is definitely to choose the sole path of progress instead of following the will-o'-the-wisps which lead either to the swamps of primitive greed or to political tyranny. The hope of America and the world is to regenerate Liberty with its responsibilities and its obligations—not to abandon it. [. . .–ed.]

Over a period of twenty years I have been honored by my country with positions where contention with the forces of social disintegration was my continued duty. I should be untrue to that service did I not raise my voice in protest . . . at the threat of the eclipse of Liberty.[5]

In the text I reviewed our American heritage; the utility of and ideals of economic freedom and its accomplishments. I discussed the various collectivist systems; the collectivist course of the New Deal and its consequences. I reviewed the constructive courses which liberty required, its abuses, and I concluded with this paragraph:

It is as true today as when first uttered that "the condition upon which God hath given liberty to man is eternal vigilance." We have in our lifetime seen the subjection of Liberty in one nation after another. It has been defeated by the untruth that some form of dictation by government alone can overcome

---

5. [*Editor's note*: The passages quoted by Hoover are in *The Challenge to Liberty*, pp. 1–2, 3–4, 5–6, 7, 10. I have corrected a couple of minor transcription errors in Hoover's manuscript.]

immediate difficulties and can assure entry into economic perfection. America must not succumb to that lure. That is the issue of our generation, not a partisan issue but the issue of human liberty.[6]

The book had an unusual circulation (135,000 were printed). The normal circulation of a philosophic book is usually under 10,000. But the book was before its time, for a large majority of the public were still incredulous of such danger. The left-wingers were quick to appreciate the import of the book and their reviews were vociferous in denunciation. As the sales of all books are greatly influenced by the book reviewers in New York, the violence of their efforts should have utterly destroyed it. I soon learned that the reviewers of the *New York Times*, the *New York Herald Tribune*, the *Saturday Review* and of other journals of review in New York kept in touch to determine in what manner they should destroy books which were not to their liking. They did their best on this book. The journals west of the Hudson River gave it much more favorable treatment.

Early in 1935, George Horace Lorimer, Editor of the *Saturday Evening Post*, indignant at the misrepresentation of my administration by Roosevelt and his cohorts, asked if he could publish a narrative, with the documentation, covering the period from the election of 1932 to March 3, 1933—the purpose being to show the truth of who created the wholly unnecessary bank panic and bank closures. He secured Walter Newton, who had been the White House Secretary,[7] and associated with him the historian William Starr Myers of Princeton University, to prepare four articles, with much hitherto unknown material on that period. The articles appeared in the *Saturday Evening Post* issues of June 8, 15, 22 and 29, 1935.

Newton and Myers had concluded, in working up this material, that the public record and understanding needed a complete account of my administration. They prepared a book, *The Hoover Administration*.[8] This book had considerable circulation and at least put the truth on the shelves of the public libraries of the country. The book, however, being a chronological account, did not pull together the policies of the Administration in concrete form. Soon afterwards, former Secretary of the Interior Ray Lyman Wilbur and former Secretary of Agriculture Arthur M. Hyde agreed that the public should

---

6. [*Editor's note*: Hoover, *Challenge to Liberty*, p. 205.]

7. [*Editor's note*: Walter H. Newton (1880–1941) served as one of President Hoover's senior secretaries (administrative assistants) between 1929 and 1933.]

8. Published by Charles Scribner's Sons, New York, 1936. [*Editor's note*: The full title was *The Hoover Administration: A Documented Narrative*.]

have a more concrete exposition of the policies of the Hoover Administration and they published a book entitled *The Hoover Policies*[9] in 1937.

The Presidential Campaign of 1936

The Presidential campaign of 1936 of necessity began in 1935. By this time we had many exhibits of the collectivist drive of the New Dealers. They had destroyed the World Economic Conference [in mid-1933–*ed.*] which I had called and which could have established stability in the international currencies and lessened trade barriers in the world; they had given world respect to the Communist Government in Russia[10]; they had increased the Federal deficit of about a billion (if recoverable loans be taken into account) to over three billions; they had devalued the currency; they had reduced Congress to a rubber stamp for a long sequence of "must" legislation. And by 1936 the Supreme Court had declared many of their acts as unconstitutional.

In the meantime, a great underground conspiracy against the American people had [been–*ed.*] begun by Communist Russia as a result of the recognition.

In 1934, the Communists organized the "Ware" cell among important policy-making heads of Federal employees. The original cell contained such persons as Harry Dexter White, Assistant Secretary of the Treasury, Alger Hiss of the State Department, Lee Pressman, and others in the Department of Agriculture. From this beginning, they infiltrated all parts of the Administration.[11]

In March 1935, I concluded to take to the public platform and delivered a number of nationally broadcast addresses. I found, however, that not having much research assistance, I could not collect the necessary information and formulate more than eight or ten comprehensive speeches during a year. These were interspersed with short extemporaneous and "off-the-record" addresses. I had hoped that by the time of the national election of 1936 we might create a more effective opposition. I give paragraphs from them which illuminate the New Deal policies of that era.[12]

---

9. Published by Charles Scribner's Sons, New York, 1937.

10. [*Editor's note*: A probable reference to the U.S. government's diplomatic recognition of the Soviet Union in November 1933.]

11. Before the tide turned over 250 Communists held important posts and eventually some 2,000 persons had to be removed as "bad risks." These persons had a profound influence upon the policies of the Roosevelt and Truman Administrations. If they did not originate New Deal measures they certainly expanded them under the disciplines exacted from Moscow.

12. The full text of all these addresses can be found under their dates in the volumes entitled *Addresses upon the American Road* by Herbert Hoover.

I started with an address at Sacramento, California, on March 22, 1935, which concluded:

> To the young men and women it is vital that their opportunity in life shall be preserved; that the frontiers of initiative and enterprise shall not be closed; that their future shall not be burdened by unbearable debt for our follies; that their lives and opportunities shall not be circumscribed and limited; that they shall have the right to make their homes and careers and achieve their own position in the world. . . . The first condition . . . is orderly individual liberty and responsible constitutional government as opposed to un-American regimentation and bureaucratic domination.[13]

The NRA [National Recovery Administration–*ed.*]being before Congress for further expansion, my first public attack was against this proposal in May 1935 when I replied to a press question in part as follows:

> In reply to your question, the one right answer by the House of Representatives to the Senate's action is to abolish the NRA entirely.
>
> This whole idea of ruling business through code authorities made of committees with delegated powers of law is un-American in principle and a proved failure in practice. The codes are retarding recovery. They are a cloak for conspiracy against the public interest. They are and will continue to be a weapon of bureaucracy, a device for intimidation of decent citizens.
>
> . . . I suggest that the only substitute for an action that rests on definite and proved economic error is to abandon it. We do not construct new buildings on false foundations, and we cannot build a Nation's economy on a fundamental error. . . .
>
> The multitude of code administrators, agents or committees has spread into every hamlet, and, whether authorized or not, they have engaged in the coercion and intimidation of presumably free citizens. People have been sent to jail, but far more have been threatened with jail. Direct and indirect boycotts have been organized by the bureaucracy itself. Many are being used today. Claiming to cure immoral business practices, the codes have increased them a thousandfold. . . . They have deprived the public of the benefits of fair competition.
>
> This whole NRA scheme has saddled the American people with the worst era of monopolies we have ever experienced. However monopoly is defined, its objective is to fix prices or to limit production or to stifle competition. . . .These

---

13. [*Editor's note:* Herbert Hoover, *Addresses upon the American Road, 1933–1938* (New York: Charles Scribner's Sons, 1938), pp. 43–44.]

have been the very aim of certain business elements ever since Queen Elizabeth. Most of the 700 NRA codes effect those very purposes.

Exactly such schemes to avoid competition in business were rejected by my Administration. . . .

NRA codes have been crushing the life out of small business, and they are crushing the life out of the very heart of the local community body. . . .

The codes are preventing new enterprises. In this they deprive America's youth of the opportunity and the liberty to start and build their independence. . . .

The whole concept of NRA is rooted in a regimented "economy of scarcity"—an idea that increased costs, restricted production and hampered enterprise will enrich a Nation. That notion may enrich a few individuals and help a few businesses, but it will impoverish the nation. . . .

[. . .–ed.] If we subtract the persons temporarily employed by the coded industries as the direct result of the enormous Government expenditures, we find that the numbers being employed are not materially greater than when the project was enacted. NRA's pretended promises to labor . . . have only promoted conflict without establishing real rights. . . .

Some business interests already have established advantages out of the codes, and therefore seek the perpetuation of NRA. Even these interests should recognize that in the end they . . . will become either the pawns of a bureaucracy. . . .[14]

On June 16, 1935, I made a nation-wide broadcast of the Commencement Address at Stanford University. I analyzed the principles of individualism as the major social security, without direct attack on the New Deal.[15]

Some years ago I marched up, as you do to receive the diploma of this University. Like some of you here present, my occasion was somewhat distracted by the sinking realization of a shortage of cash working capital and the necessity to find an immediate job. Put into economic terms, I was earnestly wishing some person with a profit motive would allow me to try to earn him a profit. At the risk of seeming counterrevolutionary or as a defender of evil, I am going to suggest that basis of test for a job has some advantages. . . . It does not require qualifications as to either ancestry, religion, good looks, or ability to get votes.

14. [*Editor's note*: Here, for unknown reasons, Hoover omitted the following words: "or the instruments of a bureaucracy the American people do not want." The lengthy passage quoted here is in ibid., pp. 45, 46, 47.]

15. *Addresses upon the American Road, 1933–1938*, pp. [48–49, 50, 51–52, 53, 54, 55, 56, 57–*ed.*]

I did not immediately succeed in impressing any of the profit or loss takers with the high profit potentialities of my diploma. The white-collar possibilities having been eliminated, my first serious entrance into the economic world was by manual labor. But somehow, both in the stages of manual labor and professional work, I missed the discovery that I was a wage slave. I at least had the feeling that it was my option that if I did not like that particular profit taker I could find another one somewhere. But what mainly interests you is the fact that I found them a cheery and helpful lot of folk who took an enormous interest in helping young people to get a start and get along in life. And you will find that is the case today. Indeed human helpfulness has improved rather than deteriorated in this generation. You will find many friendly hands. Moreover, as our world has become more intricate, special training has become more respected. They will give more credence to your diploma.

There has indeed been great change in our American world since that time. Our huge surge forward in the conquest of science and of mechanical power has brought new visions and a new vista of further advance in social justice and the general welfare among our people. As we have nearly doubled in numbers we jostle our elbows more. We must have more rules of the road. In the midst of this changing scene there has been injected the inflation and destruction of the greatest war of history. Its shivering instabilities still remain with us. Surplus production is pitted against mass poverty. Under these pressures every weakness of the system has come to the surface. The wounds of war are made to appear as the result of organic disease of the system. New systems of life are urged as a cure for all human ills. Our economic and governmental system is slow to adjust itself to these changes and aspirations. There is great confusion of thought and ideals.

Such periods of confused thought are not new in the world. You will find an uncanny parallel in England during the period following the Napoleonic Wars. . . .

Our standards of life have immensely increased since Napoleonic times. Then the Englishman had less than 100 mechanical horsepower at his command for each thousand adults. Today we command 6,000 mechanical horsepower for each thousand adults. And this does not include the . . . automobiles. At that period a skilled mechanic with his whole week's wages could purchase less than 200 pounds of the fixings from which bread and butter are made. Today he can purchase 500 pounds, if he were disposed to take all his week's wages in that form. . . .

[. . .–ed.] The new surge forward in our productivity of this last generation has for the first time in history given us the possibility and the vision that we can raise our whole people to higher standards of living.... We want to be secure against unemployment, old age, and misfortune, so that fear of poverty will be driven from among us....

The first of social securities is freedom.... Freedom is a spiritual need and a spiritual right of man. We can get security in food, shelter, education, leisure, music, books, and what not, in some jails. But we don't get freedom. Those who scoff that individual liberty is of no consequence to the under-privileged and the unemployed are grossly ignorant of the primary fact that it is through the creative impulses of liberty that the redemption of these suf-ferings and that social security must come.

The second of social securities is the capacity to produce a plenty of goods and services with which to give economic security to the whole of us. Scientific discovery ... vast technology ... initiative, and enterprise are the dynamic forces of civilization. They thrive alone among free men and women....

Any system which curtails these freedoms or stimulants to men destroys the possibility of ... production.... Social security will never be attained by an economy of scarcity. That is the economy of fear.... [Only] out of abun-dance can society make provision for all its members and support the un-employed, the sick, the aged, and the orphan. That is the economy of hope.

The hope of social security can be destroyed both from the right and the left. From the right come the abuses of monopoly, economic tyranny, ex-ploitation of labor, or of consumers or investors. From the left come power-seeking, job-holding bureaucracies, which bleed our productive strength with taxes and destroy confidence and enterprise with their tyrannies and their interferences. The concentration of economic power and the concen-tration of political power are equally destructive. The weeds of abuse will always grow among the fine blossoms of free initiative and free enterprise.... [We must] dig them out....

If we are to attain social security we must find remedy or mitigation of inter-ruptions and dislocations in the economic system.... War and its long dread-ful aftermaths ... is the first and worst of these interruptions.... We should not blame the social and economic system for injuries produced by war....

Having the vast majority economically secure when the system is stable, our job is not to pull down this great majority but to build up those who lag. And herein lies a great area of unclarified national thought. Here America has, however, developed one new idea—that wages are linked to ability to consume goods; that the highest possible real wage is the necessary accom-paniment of mass production. No one denies today that the road to higher consumption of goods and services is lower costs, lower prices, and thus higher real wages and incomes.

Theoretically, the end of that road would be complete economic security. But there is and will be a segment of the dislocated, the less fortunate, the misused and the less wise. . . .

Universal social security cannot be had by sudden inspiration of panaceas. There are no short cuts. . . .

Social security must be builded upon a cult of work, not a cult of leisure. The judgment on Adam has not yet been reversed. . . .

[. . .–ed.] Our sympathetic thought properly drives to consideration of the twenty-five percent of the less fortunate. It is right that it should be so. But let us not forget that the seventy-five per cent need consideration also. They alone can carry the burden of the twenty-five per cent. . . . If they be harassed, coerced, intimidated, discouraged, unduly taxed, the whole fabric will fall. The times demand a determined spirit whose faith is not dulled by the mere aftermaths of a great war, a vicious business cycle, or the sudden triumphs of science.[16]

None of these attainments is beyond America's capacity to realize. They can be realized in the pure air of orderly liberty. . . .

Having been asked to take part in a nation-wide broadcast symposium in celebration of Constitution Day, I spoke from San Diego on September 17, 1935. I said in part:

Today the Constitution is indeed under more vivid [attack] than at any time since the years before the Civil War. . . . Today this issue is the rights of the individual. . . . This discussion has been forced upon us because new philosophies and new theories of government have arisen in the world which militantly deny the validity of our principles.

Our Constitution is not alone the working plan of a great Federation of States under representative government. There is embedded in it also the vital principles of the American system of liberty. That system is based upon certain inalienable freedoms and protections which not even the government may infringe and which we call the Bill of Rights. It does not require a lawyer to interpret those provisions. They are as clear as the Ten Commandments. . . .

---

16. [*Editor's note*: This paragraph actually precedes the previous paragraph ("Social security must be builded") in Hoover's *Addresses . . . 1933–1938*, pp. 56, 57. I have let the incorrect sequence stand. Why Hoover, in the volume at hand, altered the paragraph order is unknown.]

Even in America, where liberty blazed brightest and by its glow shed light on all the others ... many, in honest belief, hold that we cannot longer accommodate the growth of science, [and] technology ... to the Bill of Rights and our form of government. With that I do not agree. ...

Nor is respect for the Bill of Rights a fetter upon progress. It has been no dead hand that has carried the living principles of liberty over these centuries. ... We have amended the Constitution many times in the past century to meet the problems of growing civilization. ... Always groups of audacious men in government or out will attempt to consolidate privilege against their fellows. New invention and new ideas require the constant remolding. ...

Liberty comes alone and lives alone where the hard-won rights of men are held inalienable ... where governments are indeed but the mechanisms to protect and sustain these principles. It was this concept for which America's sons have died on a hundred battlefields.[17]

On October 5, 1935, I delivered a nationally broadcast address in Oakland, California, on New Deal spending and administrative methods.

Three years ago I warned[18] America against the consequences of the adoption of the ideas ... which have since been forced upon us. You have now had nearly three years in which these ideas ... have dominated the nation. They are no longer glowing promises of the more abundant life. ... Now they can be examined and appraised in the cold light of daily experience.

... We have need to awake from the spell of hypnotic slogans. Phrases can be made to scintillate like the aurora borealis ... [but–*ed.*] the issue of America is not a battle of phrases, but a battle between straight and crooked thinking. ... This gigantic spending and this unbalanced budget is the most subtle and one of the most powerful dangers which has been set in motion by this administration. If it be continued, its result ... is as inexorable as an avalanche. ...

... Expenditures are now running over $8,000,000,000 a year. The annual deficit is running nearly three and a half billions. ...

[The national debt] at the end of [four years of] Roosevelt's administration will exceed $35,000,000,000. ... Outside of recoverable loans ... [their] spending will exceed the Hoover administration by from $14,000,000,000 to $15,000,000,000. ... But the important thing is that the Republican administration genuinely endeavored to balance the whole government budget. ...

---

17. [*Editor's note*: Hoover, *Addresses ... 1933–1938*, pp. 58, 60, 61–62.]
18. [*Editor's note*: In the original quoted text: "we were warning."]

That in the year 1931 the Democratic Congress was urged by the Republican administration to enact additional revenues of $1,200,000,000 and to cooperate in a cut of $600,000,000 of less pressing expenditures. Only a part of this revenue was wrung from the Democratic Congress after nearly six months of fighting . . . obstruction, punctuated by vetoes of pork-barrel appropriations. Even then over half of the recommended decreases in expenditures were rejected. Again in 1932, $700,000,000 of additional revenues and $300,000,000 of additional reductions in expenditures were urged, [but] again, after months of delay, were refused altogether. . . .

I do not need recall the promises . . . that they [Hoover's Democratic opponents in 1932–ed.] would balance the budget and reduce expenditures by one billion a year. . . . Our opponents in 1932 would have received far less votes had they disclosed to the country their intention to increase the expenditures by $14,000,000,000 in four years; or . . . that they would maintain a deficit of three and a half billion per annum; that they would increase the number of the government bureaucracy by 160,000 persons and create five thousand paid committees and commissions. They would have lost still more votes had they informed us that they would abandon the gold standard; that they would devalue the dollar by 41 per cent; . . . that they would seek to circumvent the Constitution; that they would attempt to socialize and regiment Americans. . . .

[. . .–ed.] According to the reports of the Civil Service Commission, there were about 573,000 civilian employees in the Federal Government at the end of the Coolidge administration. There were about 565,000 at the end of the Hoover administration. There are 730,000 today. And this does not include some 100,000 part-time paid members of some 5,000 committees . . . or another who all spend money. . . . This . . . constitutes the most gigantic spoils raid in our history. Even Andrew Jackson appointed less than ten thousand. . . .

[. . .–ed.] When we protest at those expenditures we are met with the sneer, "Would you let the people starve?" . . . A Republican administration . . . in 1930 announced that no American should go hungry or cold through no fault of his own. It organized the relief so effectively . . . the public health actually improved during that whole period. . . . The presumed purpose of this spending has been to secure recovery. . . . We may well inquire what has been accomplished toward finding real jobs . . . by this roaring torrent of Federal spending and deficit. . . . I take the date of the election of November, 1932, for this test. For months prior to that election unemployment had been steadily decreasing . . . prior to the election, there were 11,585,000 people out of work, according to the American Federation of Labor. Sixty days ago, two years and eight months after the election, after all this gigantic spending, there were still 10,900,000 unemployed, according to the same authority, or a decrease of only 700,000. . . .

[. . .–*ed.*] The New Deal form of repudiation [of the national debt] is devaluation. [. . .–*ed.*] Devaluation is a modern and polite term for clipping the coin. Rome relied upon this method during its decline. If devaluation has the inflationary effect that the New Deal claims, then in the long run it raises the prices of everything we buy and the cost of living goes up to everybody, farmer and worker alike. . . . The returns from your insurance policy, your savings account . . . for your children, your veteran's allowance, and your old-age pension, are . . . depleted in purchasing power. Who then pays? It is the same economic middle class and the poor. That would still be true if the rich were taxed to the whole amount of their fortunes. . . .

[. . .–*ed.*] You may put it down both economically and historically . . . every continued government deficit has led to inflation in some form. That is the implacable avenger of profligate spending in government. . . . There is a place on that road where there lurks an appalling national peril. We have not reached these extremes, but that is the road we are traveling. The administration may not know where they are going, but they are taking us with them.

[. . .–*ed.*] If the history of the last hundred years teaches anything, it is that inflation is more dangerous to a people than war. It has been the abyss into which democracy has fallen in these recent years. It has been the cradle of tyranny in a dozen countries. . . .

In the coming months the Republican Party will meet in convention. . . . Theirs is the duty to enunciate great principles. . . . Minor issues, petty opposition, sectional interest, group ideas, and every shred of personal ambition must be dumped. . . . None of these things must count in the fate of the nation. . . .[19]

On November 16, 1935, I spoke in New York City with a national broadcast, saying in part:[20]

I recently made an address upon the New Deal Spending, Debts, and their Consequences. I purpose [*sic*–*ed.*] on this occasion to discuss what the New Deal calls "National Planning." . . . You might think that meant blueprints. But this sort of "National Planning" includes political management of money, credit,

19. [*Editor's note: Addresses . . . 1933–1938*, pp. 63, 64, 65–66, 67, 68–69, 70–71, 72, 74.]
20. Ibid., pp. [75–76, 77, 78–79, 80–81, 85–86–*ed.*]

farming, industry, morals, and the more abundant life. Two years ago the phrase more frequently used was "Planned Economy." . . . Even "National Planning" is threatened with ejection by a still more glittering phrase, the "Third Economy." I trust it is not so expensive as the others.

. . . "Planned Economy" is the American name for the European diseases which have infected us for the past three years. . . . These catchwords cloak that incarnate passion for power, the insidious end of which is the destruction of liberty and the rise of the regimented state.

. . . "National Planning" is an attempt of a collegiate oligarchy to sanctify by a phrase a muddle of unco-ordinated reckless adventures in government—flavored with unctuous claims to monopoly in devotion to their fellow men.

. . . I will not take your time to enumerate all the alphabetical agencies. I may say, however, there are only four letters of the alphabet not now in use by the Administration in Washington. When we establish the Quick Loans Corporation for Xylophones, Yachts, and Zithers, the alphabet of our fathers will be exhausted. But of course the . . . Russian alphabet has thirty-four letters. [. . .–ed.]

There is one consistency in all this . . . "National Planning," or "Planned Economy," or "Third Economy." Every branch of these plans has the habit of carefree scattering of public money. They are haunted by no old ghost of a balanced budget. . . .

The new "National Planning" of relief shifted its administration from local and state authorities to a political bureaucracy centralized in Washington. . . . It[21] has added nothing to the security and care of those deserving in distress except—expense. [. . .–ed.]

. . . It is not a more abundant life. It erodes the purchasing power of wages. It gives birth to strikes and inflames class conflict. During the depression years of the last Administration the loss of man days from strikes and lockouts averaged about 5,000,000 per year. During this Administration it has averaged a loss of about 18,000,000 man days per year. These gigantic losses appear in the worker's budget, not in the treasury.

. . . "Economic Planning" . . . raises somber questions of government morals and honor. In any event it devalued the dollar by 41 percent. It gave us the gift of "Managed Currency." . . . The stock market is already peeking into that Bluebeard's cave. [. . .–ed.]

There is the folly of buying foreign silver. I could at least see some reason for spending ten to fifteen million a year to subsidize employment in our

---

21. [*Editor's note*: In the original quoted text: "That."]

Western silver mines by buying their product at a profitable price. But what earthly reason we have for buying vast amounts of foreign silver will take generations of politicians to explain. If we are to have managed currency, we do not require any metallic base. . . .

[. . .–ed.] We have joyfully subsidized every foreign speculator in silver. We have also subsidized every silver mine in Australia, India, Mexico, and Peru. We have stirred up currency troubles in China and other silver currency countries. [. . .–ed.]

Another result of "Economic Planning" has been the attraction of billions of gold—over two billions in two years. [. . .–ed.] We ought to have had goods instead. Apparently "Planned Economy" aims to become a bimetallic Midas.

. . . We devalued the dollar 41 per cent under the hypnosis that if we reduced the length of a yard to 21.2 inches we would have more cloth in the bolt. One result is that the foreigner is shipping us more gold every day to buy our good domestic assets for the price of 21.2 inches to the yard. . . .

[. . .–ed.] Of course if . . . [devaluation] worked it would increase the cost of living by 41 per cent. Thus it would reduce the living to be obtained from all life insurance policies, college endowments, pensions, wages and salaries, and. . . . Here we again enter higher economics . . . if you explore it thoroughly you will find that the 10,000,000 stockholders of corporations, including the wicked power companies, profit at the expense of the 65,000,000 insurance policy holders. The sum of all these shifts does not make the poor any richer. [. . .–ed.]

In any event, so long as "managed currency" lasts, the purchasing value of the dollar lies at the whim of political government. . . .

. . . Do you wish a constructive fiscal program?

The waste of taxpayers' money on unnecessary public works should end.

The administration of relief should be turned over to local authorities. [. . .–ed.]

This horde of political bureaucracy should be rooted out.

The provision of the Constitution requiring that expenditures shall only be in accordance with appropriations actually made by law should be obeyed. [. . .–ed.]

The budget should be balanced, not by more taxes, but by reduction of follies.

The futile purchases of foreign silver should be stopped.

The gold standard should be re-established, even on the new basis.

The act authorizing the President to inflate the currency should be repealed. . . .

These matters are no abstractions. . . . They are the invisible forces which surround every American fireside. They determine the happiness of every American home. . . .

I delivered a nationally broadcast address at St. Louis on December 16, 1935, devoted to exposing the history of the bank panic and Roosevelt's financial policies.

I have recently discussed the New Deal at Oakland and again at New York. Since then President Roosevelt at Atlanta has entered the debate in defense of the New Deal—particularly its spending, deficits, and debts. I propose to debate so much of that statement as time permits.

You will not be astonished if we do not agree.

There recently have been some premonitions of change. In that aspect I find a newspaper dispatch dated November 28 from Los Angeles . . . announcing the naming of a new street as New Deal Avenue. . . . "Because New Deal Avenue comes to a dead end the county supervisors will arrange ample room . . . to turn around." [. . .–ed.]

Three years ago, speaking in New York City, I said, "This . . . is a contest between two philosophies of government. The expressions our opponents use must refer to important changes in our . . . system . . . otherwise they are nothing but vacuous words. . . . They are proposing changes which would destroy the very foundations. . . ." That warning was denied by our opponents.

We have now had three years of it. . . .

In speaking at Atlanta two weeks ago the President's first basis of defense for his gigantic spending, deficits, and debts was the assertion that "The mechanics of civilization came to a dead stop on March 3, 1933."

What happened on March 3, 1933, was an induced hysteria of bank depositors. The banking structure at large subsequently proved to be sound. That is scarcely a dead stop to civilization.

. . . The newspapers are one of the mechanisms of civilization. They did not quit. At that time I saw no headlines that the farmer had ceased to till the fields. Most of you did not detect that the delivery of food to your doors had stopped. Railway managers apparently did not know that their trains had stalled. Somebody failed to inform us that the hum of our factories was silent. We still had to jump out of the way of the twenty-three million automobiles. Our churches, schools, and courts are a part of the mechanics of civilization. They did not close. And the Supreme Court seemed to be functioning yet. If civilization came to a dead stop the press missed a great piece of news that day. [. . .–ed.]

The truth is that the world-wide depression was turned in June–July, 1932, all over the world. That was before the election of the New Deal. That is supported by scores of leading American economists, business men, and public leaders. It is supported by the economic publications throughout the world.

That turning was aided by the measures of our Republican government. These measures were within the Constitution of the United States. They were not that futile financial juggling which has violated economic law, morals, the Constitution, and the structure of American liberty. . . . Every commercial country, including the United States, surged forward. Prices rose, employment increased, the whole agricultural, financial and business structure grew in strength. After the election of the New Deal we began a retreat. Only in the United States was there an interruption. We were the strongest and should have led the van. And we lagged behind. . . . The other countries of the world went forward without interruption. They adopted no New Deal. Apparently those nations did not hear that the mechanics of civilization came to a dead stop on March 3, 1933.

It did not come to a stop even in the United States. It was meddled with. . . . But why did we have a panic of bank depositors in 1933? Because they were scared. We had no bank panic from the crash of the boom in 1929. We had no panic at the financial collapse in Europe in 1931. We had no panic at the most dangerous point in the depression when our banks were weakest in the spring of 1932. There was no panic before the election of November, 1932. When did they become frightened? They became scared a few weeks before the inauguration of the New Deal on March 4, 1933.

What[22] were they frightened of? They could not have been scared by the outgoing administration which had only a few days to run. They were frightened at the incoming New Deal. Why were they scared at the New Deal? Because soon after the election large numbers of people awoke to the fact that promises given in the campaign would be violated. . . . It gradually spread that the gold standard would be abandoned . . . [23] that the currency would be tinkered with. It was evident that a wholesale orgy of spending of public money would be undertaken. Business slackened its energies. Shrewd speculators shipped their money abroad at fabulous profits. Bankers tried to protect themselves. The public in blind fear demanded gold and the "covenants" of the United States which called for gold. Some of them were

---

22. [*Editor's note*: In the original quoted text: "But what."]
23. [*Editor's note*: Here Hoover omitted the word "or."]

scared at the banks by the destructive publication of RFC loans. The banking structure was not insolvent. After the banks were closed it was found that the solvent banks, measured by deposits, comprised 92 percent of the banking strength of the country. The President himself stated they were sound. Subsequently more banks were found sound and reopened. And beyond this, important banks wrongfully closed by the New Deal, such as in the Detroit area, are now paying out 100 percent to the depositors. It was the most political and the most unnecessary bank panic in all our history. It could have been prevented. It could have been cured by simple co-operation with us. [. . .–ed.]

The breakdown in confidence which sounded the advent of the New Deal is of course a helpful statistical point when they want to show how good they have been to us.

I have no desire to waste time over historical discussion. But correction of distortion which is used to justify destructive national policies and this high piling up of debt and taxes is imperative. . . .

But now we come to the President's major defense for this gigantic spending and unpaid bills. That is the need to relieve the unemployed. . . .

Let me say one thing right at the outset. There is no disagreement upon the public obligation to relieve distress which flows from national calamity. The support of that comes from the conscience of a people. It comes from their fidelity to the Sermon on the Mount. The American people know that the genuine sufferers on relief are not slackers. They know the weary days of tramping the streets in search for a chance to work. They know the discouragement and despair which have stalked those homes. There is not a real man or woman whose heart does not warm to them, who will not sacrifice for them.

Some five years ago I stated that, "as a nation we must prevent hunger and cold to those of our people who are in honest difficulties." I have never heard a disagreement with that. . . . There is no humor in relief. It is grim human tragedy.

I believe I can without egotism claim to have had some special experience in relief. At one time or another it became my task to organize and administer relief to over three hundred and fifty million people at home and abroad, who had been reduced to destitution by war or by famine or by flood. I gave some years to that service in the aspiration to save life, to allay suffering, to restore courage and faith.[24]

---

24. [*Editor's note*: Here Hoover omitted the words "in humanity."]

It also became my duty in 1930 to see that relief was organized for our unemployed. [. . .–*ed.*] It therefore fell to me and my colleagues to pioneer in methods for America. . . .[25]

We held[26] that relief was an emergency operation, not a social experiment; that the object was to serve the people in genuine distress and nobody else. We held[27] that the dreamers cannot effectually conduct the grinding tasks of relief; that politics must be shunned as a plague. . . . We held[28] that we must mobilize on a voluntary basis the best hearts and brains of every community to serve their neighbors. We held[29] that there must be complete decentralization to them of both authority and administration. We did not have to learn that local self-government and local responsibility was the basis of American life.

In 1930 by co-operation with the States, we secured the creation of State committees of leading citizens. With them we secured the creation of similar committees in every city, town and county where relief was needed. These committees had no politics. They were men and women experienced in large affairs, sympathetic, understanding of the needs of their neighbors in distress. And they served without pay. In those days one did not enter into relief of his countrymen through the portals of a payroll. American men and women of such stature cannot be had as a paid bureaucracy, yet they will serve voluntarily all hours of the day and defer their own affairs to night. . . . Their stewardship was under the limelight of their own community. They gave spiritual aid and encouragement.

At the start the relief in 1930 had depended upon private giving. As times became more difficult, the committees co-operated in the use of county and municipal funds; and as it became still more difficult many of the State governments provided them with funds. Finally, as State resources weakened, we provided Federal Government funds to be distributed to the State governments and by them redistributed to the local organizations. [. . .–*ed.*] We built up no bureaucracy. . . . That form of organization expressed in its noblest form the whole American ideal of local self-government, local responsibility, national cooperation, and the voluntary spirit of human service.

There was no important failure to provide for those in real need. There was no substantial complaint or suggestion of waste, politics, or corruption.

---

25. [*Editor's note*: The words "for America" are not in the text as printed in Hoover's *Addresses*. He evidently added the words for clarity.]

26. [*Editor's note*: In the original quoted text: "learned."]

27. [*Editor's note*: In the original quoted text: "learned."]

28. [*Editor's note*: In the original quoted text: "learned."]

29. [*Editor's note*: In the original quoted text: "learned."]

Neither the Republican Party nor any of its agencies ever asked for votes or claimed that its administration reserved votes for it. That idea was repugnant to every decent sense of Americanism.

However all this was forgotten on March 3, 1933. We may accept that the date of Creation was moved to March 4, and we may examine what sort of a world has been made. [. . .–ed.]

The whole relief work was promptly centralized from Washington. State and local organizations were dismissed. . . . A paid bureaucracy was spread over the land. The history of the last two and one-half years shows the floundering of this Administration. That needs no more proof than the buffeting of those in distress from FERA or PWA or its subsidiaries to EPW, then to SERA, then to CWA, partly to FRSC, then back to FERA, and over to WPA. It has been a sort of rain-maker's cabalistic dance. As each of these alphabetical organizations flares up in folly and waste, its victims and its accounts have been buried by juggling of the alphabet. When they are all buried their spirit will live on as IOU. . . .

We may compare the most of these two forms of administration—the one founded on local self-government under the glare of its local public opinion; the other being run by a political bureaucracy from Washington.

Statistics are dry subjects, but just now figures are the most important thing in our national life. The entire cost of relief to unemployment during the last year of the Republican Administration was about $1,100,000,000. That includes Federal, State, municipal, county and private giving. It includes Federal public works above normal and does not include relief to agriculture. The Federal overhead was not over $250,000 a year. The total number of paid Federal employees was less than two hundred.

Now let us examine . . . these two periods. The average of the monthly figures of the American Federation of Labor shows 11,600,000 unemployed during the last year of the Hoover Administration. During the year of the New Deal ending this October the unemployed have averaged about 11,100,000. That was a decrease of the unemployment load by about five per cent.

[. . .–ed.] Judging from Treasury and other statements the expenditures on all relief alphabets in the year ending last October for Federal, State, and local were over $3,500,000,000. This also includes Federal Public Works over normal, but does not include relief to agriculture. There were over 140,000 officials on the Federal payroll, not including the people on relief. The salaries of these officials alone must come to about $300,000,000 a year. It is easy to detect another $200,000,000 in pencils, typewriters, offices, automobiles, Pullman fares, etc., not to mention press releases. That is an overhead of four or five hundred million per annum. Some increase in relief was necessary, but an increase of 300 per cent in costs in the face of a five percent decrease in unemployment load is significant. And the overhead amounts to nearly one-half the whole cost of relief three years ago. [. . .–ed.]

We may well wonder why[30] relief . . . has been shifted to a Federal bureaucracy at Washington. . . . Jobs have been thereby found for over 140,000 new Federal officials. . . . You know and I know and the people know that this horde of officials has been appointed by the advice and consent of Democratic politicians.

. . . The administration of relief needs reform right now.[31]

In a nation-wide broadcast from Lincoln, Nebraska, on January 16, 1936, I discussed New Deal Agricultural Policies and their collectivist nature:[32]

I have recently debated various realities of the New Deal at Oakland, New York, and St. Louis. I propose now to explore . . . its agricultural policies. . . .

The New Deal has developed a new technique in debate. They set up a glorious ideal to which we all agree unanimously. Then they drive somewhere else or into the ditch. When we protest they blackguard us for opposing the glorious ideal. And they announce that all protestors are the tools of Satan or Wall Street. When we summon common sense and facts they weep aloud over their martyrdom for the ideal.

The New Deal [published] explanations of their agricultural policies exceed thirty million words. You will not expect me to turn the light into every dark corner in thirty minutes. Some of the rugged prima donnas who have directed these policies have resigned and said worse things than I would say. One quality of the old . . . Individualists was team work.

. . . There is an agricultural problem. It concerns the entire nation. It concerns the happiness of 7,000,000 homes. Our country will not have reached either full moral or economic stature until confidence and hope shine in these homes. The problem is still unsolved.

. . . The urgent need of farm relief has been used as a cover to impose the New Deal philosophy upon the American people. . . . Government by individuals in place of a government of laws. . . . Goosestepping the people under this pinkish banner of Planned Economy. That was tried under the NRA but the Supreme Court halted it early. It has had a longer march under the AAA. Step by step the New Deal Agricultural Policies advanced from cajolery with

---

30. [Editor's note: Here Hoover omitted the words "local organization of."]
31. [Editor's note: The full text of this speech is printed in Hoover's Addresses . . . 1933–1938, pp. 87–100. The excerpts quoted here appear on pp. 87, 88, 89–91, 92–95, 96–97, 98.]
32. Full text in [ibid.–ed.], pp. 101–113.

a gentle rain of checks to open coercion. Men who planted on their own farms and sold in their own way the product which God and their own labor give them could have been sent to jail for doing just that. That is not liberty. That is collectivism.

. . . Those ideas of production control revolve upon planned scarcity instead of the plenty upon which America alone has made progress. To stop the production of 50,000,000 fertile acres is not progress. . . . Civilization has made progress solely through producing more and more of varied things. . . . In this plan of scarcity we are surrendering the very foundations of human hope. . . .

The difficulties of our agriculture came mainly from the war and its hectic aftermaths. Wars always do that to the farmer. Demoralization lasted twenty years after the Napoleonic wars and a dozen years after our own Civil War.

I am glad that the President at last admits that the war had something to do with the farm depression. At Chicago, on December 9, 1935, he says, in referring to farm prosperity in the period before the war: "They were the last years before the world-wide disturbance, caused by the World War, took place in our economic life." I had been told so often by the New Deal that I did it that I had given up hope of salvation. I feel better.

The dislocation of wars and slumps hits the farmer harder than any other group. Farm prices are more sensitive to these shocks than wages and industrial prices. All parts of the economic system inevitably come back into balance with time. But farm recovery is longer drawn out. [. . .–ed.]

When the world depression was turned, in June and July, 1932, agricultural prices rose in a start toward equality with industrial prices. The farmer's dollar improved more than 20 per cent. Prices were moving into a natural relation again.

. . . About one-quarter of the $14,000,000,000 of probable increased New Deal debt will rest on the farm as a super-mortgage. Blessed are the young, for they shall inherit the national debt. . . .

The largest justification [of New Deal farm policy–ed.] has been [devaluation] that it has raised prices. . . . The *Chicago Tribune* is authority for the statement that the farmer's income from many uncontrolled commodities has been greater in proportion than from those which have had the attention of the New Deal. President Roosevelt on May 30, 1935, prophesied that "if we abandon crop control wheat will immediately drop to 36 cents a bushel and cotton to five cents a pound." He felt the same about hogs. I do not know how long a time there is in "immediately." They did not drop, they rose.[33] . . .

---

33. [*Editor's note*: In the original text this sentence does not appear. Instead Hoover wrote: "It is more than a week."]

Another principle of the New Deal was to lift wages and industrial prices. The sum of these . . . principles is that the farmer has less to sell and pays more for what he buys. . . . By this device we have got the Economic Dog running around in circles chasing his tail. [. . .–*ed.*]

We may explore what these New Deal principles did to our export and import market. You will remember that 1932 was the year when "it could not be worse." So we will take that worst year and compare it with the New Deal year of 1935. From that worst year exports of cotton have decreased 4,250,000 bales; our grain 93,000,000 bushels; our animal products by 500,000,000 pounds. This is estimated to be the product of about 20,000,000 acres. But, worse than that, this greatest food-producing country on earth has imported this year about 100,000,000 bushels of grain, 700,000,000 pounds of animal products, and increased its imports of vegetable oils to be used as substitutes by another 700,000,000 pounds. It would take another probable 15,000,000 acres to produce these imports. . . .

From all this . . . the farmer has lost the market for more acres than the whole New Deal curtailment of 50,000,000 fertile acres. Is that not the principle of the Economic Dog chasing his tail?

On January 10 President Roosevelt declared himself in opposition to "shipping our soil fertility to foreign nations." The logical conclusion of all that is to stop exports altogether. There is a futility here somewhere. The idea is that we encourage imports of industrial products and create unemployment at home. We are told we must do this in order that the farmer may export his products. Now we are told that it is not to our advantage to export farm products at all. He overlooks the fact that we can manufacture synthetic fertilizers to any amount necessary to cover export of "soil fertility." [. . .–*ed.*]

We must explore as to where we get to when we start controlling crops. This principle of scarcity gets scarcer and scarcer. The moment one farm product was regimented, another had to be mobilized to prevent the farmers' energy from going into that. So we marched from seven controlled commodities in May, 1933, to five more in April, 1934, another in May, 1934, and finally we come to potatoes in 1935. Moreover, these measures are moving steadily to more and more coercion . . . as witness the Cotton and the Potato Acts. As I read further and further into the 6,250 verboten words of the potato law, I realized that one of the impulses to cheerfulness was about to be mashed out of American life. The potato yielded not only food, but it had radiated humor to our daily conversation. It was once the happiest of all the vegetables. Its life would have been saddened by the bootlegger, the passive resister, and the Federal inspectors. Confined to a package by law, its eyes would have been dimmed by the alphabetical revenue stamps it must bear.

... One would think in the thunders of idealism that have accompanied Planned Agriculture it would be clean of politics. I have but one comment. That is to read two lines from a letter I hold written by a high officer in the AAA to a gentleman who spent his life in scientific work for the farmer and who was accepted for appointment in that service. It says, ". . . it will be necessary [for you] to secure political clearance, which means a letter of approval from the Democratic National Committee in California." The Department of Agriculture was wholly under merit service before this sort of idealist got it. . . .

We may explore the effect of this economy of scarcity and crop control upon employment. For instance, the reduction of cotton by ten million acres is producing a hideous poverty in the share croppers of the South. It is creating unemployment all over the nation of some hundreds of thousands of agricultural laborers, railway men, and others who formerly lived by producing and handling the 20 million tons of agricultural products that could come from the acres forced to idleness.

And above all other consequences, the whole notion of regimenting the farmer under bureaucracy was the negation of the free American spirit. The system of scarcity was being applied to human freedom. [. . .–ed.]

Finally—Does anybody believe that this flimsy structure under agriculture, of regimenting men, of putting fertile acres out of action, of giving American markets to foreigners, and levying its cost on the poor would not have fallen of its own weight, even without the Supreme Court? [. . .–ed.]

We shall be less than intelligent, and we shall be heartless of the farmers' problems if we do not distill from this wreckage of these experiments some lessons in truth. [. . .–ed.] The first group of these aids [to recovery–ed.] is: Increase consumption of food by restoration of employment. That can come only with a balanced budget, stable currency and credit. Give the farmer our own home market. Adopt such sane national policies as will again restore reasonable export markets. Out of this group of policies we can restore demand to many millions of fertile acres.

The second group of policies is: To retire submarginal lands where people cannot make a living. Do it in the more effective and humane way proposed by Secretary Hyde in 1932. Retard new reclamation projects until the land can be used.

... Instead of ... paying the farmer to curtail a crop, we should endeavor to expand another crop which can be marketed or which would improve the fertility of the soil. We import vast quantities of vegetable oils, sugars and other commodities. There are industrial products that could be introduced by the American farmer. We need to replenish our soils with legumes and restore coverages. . . . We would be able to employ more than all the acres put out of action by the New Deal. We would reverse this economy of scarcity to an economy of plenty.

. . . In order to secure these objectives I believe we must be prepared to subsidize directly such special crops until agriculture has again been brought into balance. At the end of such a road we could hope for a balanced agriculture in full production and increased fertility in our soils. [. . .–*ed*.]

Somebody will shy at the blunt word "subsidy." And, in fact, the American people have been going all around Robin Hood's barn, rather than use it. Over a century ago we began it in canals and turnpikes, since then we have kept it up. Railroads, highways, ships and aviation, and silver mines and land reclamation—agriculture—we usually do it under some other name than subsidy. We had better begin to use straight words and we will act straight. A subsidy is a burden on the taxpayer, but it does not regiment or destroy the initiative or freedom of the receiver—it is to stimulate that.

In conclusion may I offer a word of personal emotion? It lies far beyond the land of economics. I have spent years in public service in many countries during this most fateful period of human history. I saw as few men the backwash of war. . . . I saw at first hand revolution creeping in under promises of relief from the agonies of war destruction. I have seen the insidious destruction of liberty by propaganda. I have seen suffering humanity sacrifice that liberty, the greatest of all human achievements, for an illusion of security. The farmers of Russia supported the Bolsheviki against the new-born Democracy on the promise of the land. Today they have the choice of Siberia or the collectivist farms. I have seen freedom, the most priceless heritage, torn from children that this generation might escape its responsibilities. I wish to say to you unhesitatingly that our country has been following step by step the road through which these millions of people in foreign countries lost their liberties. Our farmers have had that blessing of individual liberty in greater fullness in their lives than any other part of even our own people. It was the farmers who fired the first shot at Lexington. It must be the farmers of America who defend that heritage. I ask you to stop, look, and listen.

President Roosevelt had delivered one of his typical speeches in January 1936. I replied to him in a broadcast address at Portland, Oregon, on February 12, 1936:[34]

---

34. [Hoover, *Addresses . . . 1933–1938*], pp. 114–115.

There has lately been a new avalanche of oratory on behalf of the "common man," the "average man," the "economic middle class," and the "rank and file." That is right. These are the people for whom America was made. They carry the burdens of America. They make its moral fiber. They are the people whose interest needs defense right now. Mr. Lincoln said the Lord must have loved them because he created so many of them. There are others who love their votes. [. . .–*ed.*]

The issue is the attempt to fasten upon the American people some sort of a system of personal government for a government of laws; a system of centralization under a political bureaucracy; a system of debts; a system of inflation; a system which would stifle the freedom and liberty of men. And it can be examined in the cold light of three years' experience.

I then analyzed the New Deal's damage to American ideals:[35]

Ten of the assaults upon liberty have already cracked against the Constitution of the United States. And has there been public outcry at their loss? There has been a lift to the soul of the Nation. Millions of average men and women have given thanks to the Almighty that the forethought of great Americans has saved for them freedom itself.

But the Court cannot deal with all the assaults upon the spirit of American liberty. . . . The undermining of local government by centralization at Washington, the spoils system, the reduction of Congress to a rubber stamp, these monetary policies—what of these?

One of the constants of Roosevelt's and all New Dealers' speeches and propaganda was the assertion that they alone were humane; that I and all others would trample upon all human progress; that we would return to "laissez faire"; that we were wicked individualists; that we were "reactionaries" with no heart or soul. I resolved to deal with this whole gamut of thought and to define American individualism and the relation of Government to economic life. I delivered this address to a convention of Young Republicans at Colorado Springs on March 7, 1936. I said in part:[36]

My remarks tonight are addressed in large measure to the younger generation. . . . Our immense objectives upon which depend the welfare of mankind require the faith, the idealism, the courage of youth that they shall not fail. . . .

---

35. Ibid., p. 124.
36. Ibid., pp. 128, 130–2, [133–36, 138–40–*ed.*].

American young men and women should have the right to plan, to live their own lives with just one limitation—that they shall not injure their neighbors. What they want of government is to keep the channels of opportunity open and equal, not to block them and then charge them for doing it. They want rewards to the winners in the race. They do not want to be planed down to a pattern. To red-blooded men and women there is joy of work and joy in the battle of competition. There is the daily joy of doing something worth while, of proving one's own worth, of telling every evil person where he can go. There is the joy of championing justice to the weak and downtrodden. These are the battles which create the national fiber of self-reliance and self-respect. That is what made America. If you concentrate all adventure in the government it does not leave much constructive joy for the governed. . . .

And at once we came to the relation of government to economic life. . . .

We have three alternatives.

First: Unregulated business.

Second: Government-regulated business, which I believe is the American system.

Third: Government-dictated business, whether by dictation to business or by government in business. This is the New Deal choice. These ideas are dipped from cauldrons of European Fascism or Socialism.

While some gentlemen may not agree, we may dismiss any system of unregulated business. We know from experience that the vast tools of technology and mechanical power can be seized for purposes of oppression. They have been used to limit production and to strangle competition and opportunity. We can no more have economic power without checks and balances than we can have political power without checks and balances. Either one leads to tyranny.

And there must be regulation of the traffic even when it is honest. . . .

I am one who believes that the only system which will preserve liberty and hold open the doors of opportunity is government-regulated business. And this is as far from government-dictated business as the two poles. Democracy can regulate its citizens through law and judicial bodies. No democracy can dictate and survive as a democracy. The only way to preserve individual initiative and enterprise is for the government to make the same rules for everybody and act as umpire.

But if we are to preserve freedom we must face the fact that ours is a regulatory system.

And let us be definite once and for all as to what we mean by a system of regulation. It looms up more clearly against the past three years.

1. A great area of business will regulate its own prices and profits through competition. Competition is also the restless pillow of progress. But we must compel honest competition through prevention of monopolies and unfair practices. That is indirect regulation.

2. The semi- yet natural monopolies, such as railways and utilities, must be directly regulated as to rates to prevent the misuse of their privilege.

3. Banking, finance, public markets, and other functions of trust must be regulated to prevent abuse and misuse of trust.

The failure of the States, particularly New York, to do their part during the boom years has necessitated an extension of Federal action. The New Deal regulations of stock and security promotion in various aspects have the right objectives. They were hastily and poorly formed without proper consideration by Congress. But they point right.

4. Certain groups must be appropriately regulated to prevent waste of natural resources.

5. Labor must have the right to free collective bargaining. But it must have responsibilities as well as rights.

6. At one time we relied upon the theory of "shirt sleeves to shirt sleeves in three generations" to regulate over-accumulations of wealth. This is now guaranteed by our income and inheritance taxes. Some people feel these taxes take the shirt also.

But there are certain principles that must run through these methods.

1. The first principle of regulation is the least regulation that will preserve equality of opportunity and liberty itself. We cannot afford to stifle a thousand honest men in order to smother one evil person.

2. To preserve Liberty the major burden of regulation must fall upon the States and local government. But where the States hopelessly fail or when the problem grows beyond their powers we should call upon the Federal government. Or we should invoke the machinery of interstate compacts.

3. Regulation should be by specific law, that all who run may read. That alone holds open the doors of the courts to the citizen. This must be "a government of laws and not of men."

4. And the American System of Liberty will not function solely through traffic policemen. The fundamental regulation of the nation is the Ten Commandments and the Sermon on the Mount. [. . .–ed.]

There are certain humanities which run through all business. As we become more experienced, more humane, as conditions change, we recognize things as abuses which we once passed over. There are the abuses of slums, child-labor, sweated hours, and sweated wages. They have been diminishing for decades before the New Deal. They have not been solved yet. They must be solved. We must not be afraid to use the powers of government to eliminate them.

There will be periodic unemployment in any system. It is even so in the self-declared economic heavens of Socialism and Fascism. With common sense we could provide insurance programs against it. We could go further and prevent many causes of depressions.

Out of medical and public-health discoveries we have in eighty years increased the number of people over sixty years of age from four percent to eight percent. That imposes another problem upon us.

This American System has sprung from the spirit of our people. It has been developing progressively over many generations. However grave its faults may be they are but marginal to a great area of human well-being. The test of a system is its comparative results with others and whether it has the impulses within to cure its faults. This system based on ordered liberty alone answers these tests.

The doors of opportunity cannot be held open by inaction. That is an ideal that must be incessantly fought for.

These doors are partly closed by every gentleman who hatches some special privilege. They are closed to somebody by every betrayal of trust. But because brickbats can be used for murder we do not need stop building houses. These doors are partly shut by every needless bureaucrat. And there is the tax collector. He stands today right in the door.

Every new invention, every new idea, every new war shifts and changes our economic life. That greatest instrument of American joy, the automobile, has in twenty years shifted regulation in a hundred directions.

Many obstructions and abuses have been added by the New Deal. . . . While the inspiration to reform comes from the human heart, it is achieved only by the intellect. Enthusiastic hearts have flooded us with illusions. Ideals without illusions are good. Ideals with illusions are no good. You may remember that youth with a banner of strange device. Was it "Excelsior" or was it "Planned Economy"? He froze to death.

Government-Dictated Economic Life

Young men and women have grave need to look into this New Deal alternative to our American system.

If any one does not believe there is a bite in that innocent term "Planned Economy," he might reread this paragraph from one of the leading New Deal spokesmen:

"It is . . . a logical impossibility to have a *planned economy* and to *have business operating its industries,* just as it is also impossible to have one within our present *constitutional* and *statutory structure.* Modifications in both, so serious as to mean *destruction* and *rebeginning,* are required."

That is involved language but if it means anything it means that both private business and the Constitution must be modified so seriously as to mean destruction. . . .[37]

The President, far from repudiating these ideas, has continuously supported "Planned Economy." On one occasion he said, ". . . All of the proposals and all of the legislation since the fourth of March have not been just a collection of haphazard schemes but rather the orderly component parts of a connected and logical whole."

The Supreme Court has removed some ten of these component parts. And rather than have the score raised to thirteen before an election we have seen three more quietly removed. However, if the New Deal is re-elected they will be found to have a lot of spare parts.

Do not mistake. The choice is still yours. But the New Deal has no choice. The New Deal is committed to drive ahead for government dictation of our economic life. It is committed by a thousand statements, by a thousand actions. It is committed by the supporters upon whom it is dependent. . . .

We hear much as to who is a Tory, a Reactionary, a Conservative, a Liberal, or a Radical. These terms when used honestly reflect an attitude of mind. The political use of them was imported from England. They do not fit well in America. However, they have certain advantages. You can elect yourself to any one of these groups if you say it often enough. If you do not like anybody you can consign him to the one which is most hated by your listener. [. . .–*ed.*]

Today, however, the term Liberal is claimed by every sect that would limit human freedom and stagnate the human soul whether they be Fascists, Socialists, Communists, Epics,[38] or New Dealers.

This misuse of English political terms is used to cover the confusion of thought that pumps from the New Deal. Yet our American problems cut squarely across such muddy classifications.

If an open mind, free to search for the truth and apply it in government, is liberal, then you should be liberal.

---

37. [*Editor's note:* Here Hoover omitted the words "and rebeginning." Ibid., p. 136.]

38. [*Editor's note:* "Epics" was a term for supporters of the socialist Upton Sinclair's End Poverty in America (EPIC) movement in 1934. Sinclair was the California Democratic Party's unsuccessful candidate for governor that year.]

If belief in open opportunity and equal opportunity has become conservative, then you should be conservative.

If belief that this can be held only in a society of orderly individual initiative and enterprise is conservative, then you should be conservative.

If opposition to those things which abuse and limit equal opportunity, such as privilege, monopolies, exploitation, or oppression whether in business or in government, is liberal, then you should be liberal.

If opposition to managed economy whether of the Socialist, Fascist, or New Deal pattern is Tory, then you should be Tory.

If the humane action to eliminate such abominations as slum squalor, child labor, and sweated labor, to give greater protection from unemployment and old age is radical, then you should be radical.

If the use of all the powers of the government to relieve our people from hunger and cold in calamity is radical, then you should be radical.

If belief in the old-fashioned virtues of self-reliance, thrift, government economy, of a balanced budget, of a stable currency, of fidelity of government to its obligations is reactionary, then you should be reactionary.

If holding to the Bill of Rights with its safeguards of the balance of powers and local government is Tory, then you should be Tory.

If demand that change in the Constitution be by open submission to the people and not by subterfuge constitutes reaction, then again you should be reactionary. . . .

As a matter of fact, science and invention during even these troubled years since the war have given us further mighty powers of progress. These inventions will create a thousand new frontiers. You have the blood and the urge of your American forebears. You are as good stuff as they. You are better trained and equipped than they were. I have no doubt of your character and your resolution. I know American youth is champing at the bit to take advantage of an opening world. From that, if we preserve the American System of Liberty, we could have a century of glorious opportunity to every young man and woman. We could have a century of unparalleled progress to the nation.

Nationally broadcast, it brought to me thousands of telegrams and letters of approval, as did each of these addresses. One was a letter from William Allen White as follows:

Dear Mr. Hoover:
     . . . You and I will agree in our definition of liberalism. No economic benefits that seriously restrict the liberties guaranteed in the Bill of Rights may be

honestly called liberal measures. . . . Which brings me down to your Colorado speech. . . . By that sign we can conquer. . . .

In a few days when I get straightened around I'll try to take a flyer on the reorganization under the Colorado speech. There, as the old song says, we can raise our Ebenezer.

Sincerely yours,

(s) W. A. White[39]

On April 4, 1936, I delivered a nation-wide broadcast to a large and enthusiastic audience at Fort Wayne, Indiana. Much of it was a reiteration of [an–*ed.*] attack on collectivism of the New Deal in new terms.[40]

On May 14, 1936, a month before the Republican Convention, I addressed an audience of 10,000 under the auspices of an organization of women in Philadelphia. I had hopes of casting the Republican Platform into a higher mould. Some parts of this address were:[41]

During the past year I have devoted myself to debate and the exposure of the New Deal for what it really is. I have done so solely because the republic is in great peril. These men have set forces in motion which unless they be stopped will lessen the living and happiness in every cottage. They will shrink the chance in life of every boy and girl.

I have offered constructive American alternatives. The President recently in addressing the youth of our nation advised them "to dream dreams and see visions." I have advised them to wake up. [. . .–*ed.*]

. . . The Republican Party is the only available instrumentality through which an aroused people can act. The Democratic Party is imprisoned by the New Deal. We should dismiss all factional issues and invite those Democrats who feel as we do to join us in faith that we have but one purpose—that is to place the republic on the road to safety. The platform must be more than a party platform. It must be a platform for the American people. Upon the determinations of the Convention will depend the fate of a generation.

The bare planks in the platform can be composed on a sheet of paper. They should be composed in the fighting words which the times demand.

---

39. [*Editor's note*: White's letter, written more than a year later (May 15, 1937), is in the Post-Presidential Individual Correspondence File, Herbert Hoover Papers, Herbert Hoover Presidential Library, West Branch, Iowa. In a separate letter to Hoover on May 4, 1937, White declared that Hoover's "Colorado Springs speech a year ago . . . stands up as the most important pronouncement that has been made by a first grade public man for four years." This letter is in the William Allen White Papers, Series C, Box 268, Library of Congress.]

40. *Addresses upon the American Road, 1933–1938*, pp. 142–158.

41. Ibid., pp. 159–160, [161–62, 164, 165–66, 167–70, 171, 172–*ed.*].

But behind these words must be the determination to restore American liberty and to revitalize American life. [. . .–*ed.*]

It would be far better that the party go down to defeat with the banner of principle flying than to win by pussyfooting.

The grim danger that confronts America is the destruction of human freedom. . . .

There are five horsemen of this new Apocalypse. They are Profligacy, Propaganda, Patronage, Politics, and Power. Their other names are Pork-barrel, Poppy-cock, Privilege, Panaceas, and Poverty.

As a result, after three years the number of unemployed is about as great as it was at election day in 1932. The agricultural problem is still unsolved. The business world has little confidence in the good intentions, or the sanity, or the integrity of our government. [. . .–*ed.*]

There are a multitude of . . . economic and social questions. . . .

I have discussed many of these questions elsewhere. There are three which are of special interest to women to which I might refer again.

Every decent American agrees upon the abolition of child labor. Republican Presidents have progressively mobilized opinion against it. We did in twenty years decrease the number of children under sixteen . . . outside of farming, from about 900,000 to less than 200,000 at the . . . census report in 1930. That was a decrease in proportion of about 70 per cent in twenty years. The President said that under the codes child labor went out in a flash. It was mostly a flash in the pan. [. . .–*ed.*]

Many states under normally Republican governments have given old age pensions for years. We should approve of Federal subsidy to the states to strengthen and unify their efforts. The contributory pension part of the social security acts will require radical revision. It covers only 50 percent of the people. . . . The Republicans must find a sane plan of old age pensions.

I have for years been promoting better housing. The last Republican administration established the Home Loan Bank system and the R.F.C. provisions for slum clearance. That was the first governmental effort to better the financing of home building. The whole New Deal housing set-up needs reorganization. We must get the government out of the home mortgage foreclosing and house-renting business and give a genuine impulse to better homes. . . .

If I were writing a bill of rights for women I should include something about her rights as a consumer. The woman does most of the buying. She has to make things go around. She has to do most of the saving. She has to protect the future. . . .

What of those women who must eke out the reduced buying power of these magic formulas?

Doctor Kemmerer,[42] speaking in New York City a month ago, said: "We have already set into operation powerful inflationary forces which when they have ultimately worked out their influence on commodity prices will probably result in giving us a cost of living approximately double what it is today."

Over 40,000,000 women are the beneficiaries of life-insurance policies alone. Sixty-five per cent of all savings accounts are in the names of women. . . . We have been accused of a few forgotten men, but the New Deal has forgotten all the women. Lincoln said, "Don't swap horses in the middle of the stream." A school for Democratic ladies is repeating that advice. They should be sure it is a horse. My belief is that it is a white rabbit.

Moral Regeneration in Government

The Republican Party must face tasks beyond economic and social regeneration. These are tasks of moral regeneration. The Republican Party was born to meet a moral issue.

A nation is great not by its riches or buildings or automobiles but through the character of its people. The fibres of that are work, thrift, piety, truth, honesty, honor and fidelity to trust. I emphasize this before a group of American women because it is at the knees of American womanhood that the men of America have generation by generation learned these standards.

. . . But there is apparently a New Deal in virtue.

Honor in public life begins with political parties. The people must depend upon political parties to carry out their will. When men are elected to high office on certain promises and those promises are cynically broken, how may we expect a citizen to feel the obligation of a promise and good faith?

There are standards of intellectual honesty in government. Framed propaganda and perverted figures mislead the thinking of the people. . . . That is salesmanship, not statesmanship.

There are standards of gentlemen in government. The seizure by the government of the communications of persons not charged with wrong-doing justifies the immoral conduct of every snooper.

There are standards of financial honor in government. The New Deal devalued the dollar. Thus it repudiated the covenants of the government to those

---

42. [*Editor's note*: Edwin W. Kemmerer (1875–1945), a noted economist, defender of the gold standard, and professor at Princeton University.]

who had entrusted it with their savings. Senator Carter Glass on April 27, 1933, rightly said: "To me it means dishonor; in my conception it is immoral." If a private citizen had repudiated 41 per cent of his debt to the grocer by just telling him it was off, at least he would be removed from his church. He also would be expelled from Wall Street. . . . Do such transactions build character in a people?

The New Deal administration ordered every citizen to bring in his gold coin and receive $20.00 an ounce for it under penalty of jail. . . . If a private person were to coerce his neighbor into selling him something for less than it was worth, he would be sent to jail. If financial honor does not rest in the government, can we expect it in the people?

The Republican Party has never dishonored the government promise to pay. . . .

The Spoils System
[. . .–ed.]

Recently I had opportunity to observe comparative morals in the spoils systems by a contrast between Tammany Hall and the New Deal. In a Tammany-dominated borough in New York in early 1933 before the New Deal, there were about 11,000 persons on relief. Tammany had appointed about 270 additional officials under their particular spoils system to manage a relief at a cost of under $30,000 a month for the officials. This job was taken away from wicked Tammany influence and directly administered by the New Deal. At a recent date there were in the same borough 2000 Federal officials appointed under the New Deal spoils system at a cost of $300,000 per month for salaries to manage 16,000 persons on relief. Tammany may learn something new in the spoils system. It was only 10 percent efficient. And the same thing is going on all over the country and you know it.

Can the American people be bought with their own money? [. . .–ed.]

Does it improve national morals and character in our people when they see huge sums being rushed into politically important districts two jumps ahead of an election? [. . .–ed.]

When the New Dealers' Convention meets near Independence Hall they will no doubt summon with powerful oratory the shades of that heroic Continental Congress. I trust at that moment the American people will remember what the New Deal has done to the Congress of the United States in these recent years. . . .

If we examine the fate of wrecked republics the world over and through all history, we will find first comes a weakening of the legislative arm. It is in the legislative halls that liberty has committed suicide. For two hundred years the Roman Senate lingered on a social distinction and as a scene of noisy prattle after it had surrendered its real responsibilities to personal government. [. . .–ed.]

Our trouble today is moral as well as economic. Is it not time we jerk ourselves out of this, and clean out the high priests of these heresies? Should we not defy a few Brain Trusts and restore the national virtues of thrift and honor and hard work?

Then the greatness of America will shine again.

I made a short address in New York on September 23, 1936 on the organization of relief, saying in part:

The only remedy lies in nonpolitical direction. It lies in completed decentralization of administration into the hands of the leading men and women of each State and community.

That basis of quick and effective local nonpolitical administration exists in America to a greater degree than anywhere else in the world. . . .

This was the basis of organization for three years—1930, 1931, and 1932. At that time when it was my duty to see that relief to unemployment was assured, we spread over the country a network of local volunteer committees free from political domination. As the need of relief increased, the number and authority of these committees were extended until there were over 3000 of them. They were co-ordinated under existing organizations and the local authorities. This committee structure hired such paid staff as they required. The committees received no pay. Citizens of the type needed for such administration require no pay. They did the work with a minimum of administrative machinery and a maximum of volunteer service. They found jobs for the unemployed. They created a spirit in the community that held people from being discharged. They co-ordinated municipal, county, State and Federal, and private funds. They knew their own people and the needs of their localities. . . . They gave particular solicitude to children. They gave encouragement and hope. They were doing neither politics nor social reform. They were taking care of distress.

From 1933, that organization was replaced or reduced to a façade by Federal centralization. We have now had time to measure the relative merits of the two methods.

There is the question of comparative costs. . . .

The unemployed today are . . . about the same as in 1932. The relief numbers are about the same today as they were [in–ed.] 1932. The 1932 abnormal

Federal, State, and local expenditures for unemployment relief and Federal public works totaled about $1,100,000,000. . . . But the cost of the various present branches of relief is now somewhere near $3,500,000,000 yearly. . . . The total . . .[43] Federal staff then cost less than $250,000 per annum. Today, the overhead is between three and four hundred million dollars. . . .[44]

. . . Undernourishment and cold are at once expressed in terms of increased disease and mortality. A study . . . will show the surprising result that the population was in better physical health in 1932 than even during the boom year of 1928. . . . That the infant mortality has been rising since the relief was taken from local administration and centralized under political Washington is shown in the public Health indexes: [. . .–ed.]

1932   5760 deaths per 100,000
1933   5810 deaths per 100,000
1934   5990 deaths per 100,000.[45]

---

43. [*Editor's note*: Here Hoover omitted the words "increase in."]
44. [*Editor's note*: Here Hoover omitted the words "for all kinds of relief activities."]
45. [*Editor's note*: See Hoover, *Addresses . . . 1933–1938*, pp. 188–91, for the full text of the speech quoted here.]

CHAPTER 7

The Crusade against
Collectivism — Continued

The Party Conventions and Campaign of 1936

The Democratic Side

Roosevelt really began his campaign for re-election in 1936 during the year and [*sic–ed.*] prior to the election. In this period he made over 120 speeches great and small of intended effect upon the election. The basis of his campaign was simple, direct and effective. He used four methods. Sometimes all of them were used in one speech, sometimes only one of them:

1. He erected straw men whose ideas he attacked as those of the most hideous villains. They are mostly business men or "reactionaries." This technique appears in 24 different speeches.
2. He implied promises of future good to each pressure group or section. He was careful in this campaign seldom to use the word "promise" and thereby avoided bad reminiscence from his campaign in 1932. This technique appears in some 14 speeches.
3. He made the vociferous announcement of great strides in recovery from the depression. He used this technique 26 times although there were about as many unemployed and as many on relief as on the day he was elected.
4. He continued his successful tactic of 1932 by direct or implied attack upon my administration as responsible for the depression. He was most effective in painting the sufferings of the depression. He invariably used the induced panic of bank depositors in March 1933 as the statistical date of salvation. He naturally made no mention of the recovery already in motion before the election, which was set back by his own actions.

One of the most sizzling of his political speeches was a "State of the Union" speech of January 3, 1936. Concerning this speech, Raymond Moley, who soon afterwards left his administration, says:[1]

When I next saw Roosevelt—on December 20, 1935—he announced that he wanted a "fighting speech" for his annual message.

"Whom are you going to fight? And for what?" I asked. . . .

[. . .–ed.] He was concerned about keeping his left-wing supporters satisfied. What was more, he wanted the speech to be a kind of prelude to the presidential campaign, a "keynote" speech. . . .

He got it. I was the technician again. His "fighting speech" excoriated "entrenched greed," "our resplendent economic autocracy," those who sought "the restoration of their selfish power," those who would "gang up" against the people's liberties. It was passionate, stirring. As he came to the peroration and spoke the words, "I cannot better end this message on the 'State of the Union' . . ." a spontaneous guffaw went up from the Republican ranks on the floor of the House. [. . .–ed.]

[. . .–ed.] Delivered at a new pitch of emotional intensity, its invective; its cries of defiance ("Let them no longer hide their dissent in a cowardly cloak of generality"); its oversimplified appeals . . . its talk of "great crises," of "unceasing warfare," of "new instrumentalities of public power" which, "in the hands of political puppets of an economic autocracy . . . would provide shackles for the liberties of the people"—all this caught, held, and swayed most of its listeners.

Infinitely more serious, it seemed to have caught, held, and swayed its speaker.

I was not unfamiliar with the practice of politics. But never until the moment that I heard Roosevelt deliver that speech on the night of January 3, 1936, did I realize the extent to which verbal excesses can intoxicate not only those who hear them but those who speak them. [. . .–ed.] I alternately excused and loathed myself for doing it.

The next day I decided that, technician or no technician, I couldn't square things with myself. There was such a thing as paying too high a price for the privilege of service. So far as my participation was concerned, the incident would never be repeated.

---

1. Raymond Moley, *After Seven Years* (Harper and Brothers, Publishers, New York, 1939), pp. 330–331 [332–*ed.*].

Another bitter speech was his acceptance of the nomination from the Democratic Convention at Philadelphia on June 27, 1936. Moley says of this speech:[2]

Friday morning, June 26, the President turned again to his acceptance speech, which I'd over-optimistically thought, the preceding afternoon, was finished. He decided, cheerfully, that there was not enough "fire" in the speech. And so he revised it—eliminating a long passage on coopera- tion and inserting in its place a diatribe about "economic royalists," "new economic dynasties, thirsting for power," "economic tyranny," "the resolute enemy within our gates," the Revolution, the Minute Men, et cetera. An examination of the text of this speech as finally delivered will show the almost ludicrous juxtaposition of these fulminations and the invocation to Faith, Hope, and Charity. It was Friday morning that this oratorical Gry- phon emerged.

Farley writes of this convention:[3]

The Democratic convention at Philadelphia was more of a family reunion than anything else. We could have completed our work in one day and gone home. The convention's crescendo of Democratic enthusiasm came the night of Saturday, June 27, ... Millions throughout the country heard his fighting denunciation of "economic royalists."

Prior to, and after the convention Roosevelt took extended trips over the country with special trains, at government expense, which purported to be non-political "inspections." Upon these trips he made dozens of speeches, often two or three a day.

James A. Farley says:[4]

On May 19, 1936, the President ... said he thought he ... might follow the inspection pattern in other states.

"And, of course, there won't be anything political about the inspection trips." He gave me a broad wink and threw back his head and laughed.

For the first time in American history a President accepted campaign gifts of a huge sum of money for campaign expenses from a labor union. Single campaign gifts had been limited by law to $5000. Lest I should be charged

---

2. Ibid., pp. 347–8.
3. James A. Farley, *Jim Farley's Story* (McGraw-Hill Book Company, New York 1948), p. 62.
4. Ibid., pp. 61–62.

with over-statement, I give George Creel's account. He was intimately in and out of the White House at the time.

Under John [L.–ed.] Lewis, the United Mine Workers had passed a resolution endorsing Roosevelt.

Creel says:[5]

The high command of the UMWA[6] met soon afterward and decided that a contribution of $250,000 would be more than generous in view of the fact that F.D.R. was a hundred-to-one choice over Alf Landon. In due course, therefore, President Lewis called at the White House, flanked by Vice-President Philip Murray and Thomas Kennedy, the treasurer. The resolution was read, and after a brief exchange of speeches the UMW officials presented the check and asked President Roosevelt if he would be kind enough to let a photographer record the historic scene.

"No, John," the President replied, beaming affectionately, "I don't want your check, much as I appreciate the thought. Just keep it, and I'll call on you if and when any small need arises."

As the group left the White House, Mr. Lewis remarked, somewhat gloomily, that they had been "outsmarted," for now there was no limit to the amount that could be asked. The others took a more cheerful view, holding that Democratic victory was so sure that a large part of the $250,000 might be saved. "You don't know politicians," was the Lewis retort. "They stay under the golden drip from the honey barrel until no drop is left."

Time confirmed his fears. . . . Cannily enough, John Lewis adopted a fixed pattern of procedure at the start. As each petitioner presented himself, he intoned this ritual: "Sir, I know you well and favorably, of course, and have no doubt as to your authority. My arrangement, however, was with the President, and I must ask that you bring me his written order."

. . . Slowly at first, but then faster and faster the appeals poured in, and eventually this steady suction exhausted the $250,000. Mr. Lewis then called his Policy Committee together and asked for instructions. All of the members, while unhappy, insisted that since their good money was on the board, the bet must be protected. Surely, they argued, not many more contributions would be asked, as everybody conceded Roosevelt's re-election.

For a second time Mr. Lewis expressed doubt, and again had the poor satisfaction of saying, "I told you so." Requests continued to pour in, each

5. George Creel, *Rebel at Large* (G. P. Putnam's Sons, New York, 1947), pp. 301–302.

6. [*Editor's note:* The United Mine Workers of America, a labor union led at that time by John L. Lewis (1880–1969).]

backed by an order or telephone call from the President, and when election day came around at last, the treasury of the UMW had been nicked for $469,668.91. To this amount was added the sum of $14,119.64 turned in by local unions, and $2,500 worth of tickets for the inaugural parade, making a total of $486,288.55. A large part of this huge sum was plainly earmarked as loans, but only $50,000, secured by the Democratic National Committee's note, was ever repaid.

Through some of the labor leaders began the first entry of avowed Communists into important political action in the United States.

Benjamin Gitlow, a repentant Communist, says:[7]

The Communist party carried out its dualistic political policy by nominating Browder for president and Ford, a Negro, for vice-president, to run on the Communist party ticket. After he was nominated, Browder declared: "The only way to force Roosevelt to fight and put up any resistance is to have a strong force to the left of him." And that was precisely what the communists did in the 1936 campaign. Their staff of competent organizers, expending hundreds of thousands of dollars, got a strong force to the left of him securely entrenched in the New Deal political machine. Thus communists, and those who followed the Party line, were in a position first, to exert pressure upon the New Deal administration and second, to become recipients of political plums in the government.

Farley related another variation in campaign organization in which he quotes Roosevelt as saying:[8]

"I also think it would be a good idea to have speeches made by the Ministers and Ambassadors who are or will be in the country," Roosevelt said. "They could speak effectively in cities where there are a goodly number of inhabitants from the countries they represent abroad. . . ."

Farley comments on this strategy:

This employment of envoys to unite various groups of nationals behind the New Deal, although most effective in both the 1940 and 1944 campaigns, was a mistake. For men charged with representing this nation in foreign lands should not run political errands. I said so at the time.[9]

---

7. [Benjamin Gitlow,] *The Whole of Their Lives* (Charles Scribner's Sons, New York, 1948), [p]p. 262[-263-ed.].
8. Farley, *Jim Farley's Story*, p. 63.
9. [*Editor's note*: Ibid.]

That relief money was used to influence the vote in this campaign was not alone a charge of the Republicans. It has been confirmed by Henry Morgenthau in his published *Diaries*:[10]

Harry Hopkins and I got along well basically during our years in Washington, though we had occasional sharp differences. One such occasion was when he confused need with politics.

During the 1936 Presidential campaigns, relief rolls increased. After the election Hopkins insisted that he could drop 150,000 relief workers. The President was out of Washington at the time, but I sent word to him that I thought the cuts were too drastic. He replied that he agreed. Soon afterward I met at the White House with Hopkins, Bell and William H. McReynolds, my executive assistant. Marvin McIntyre of the White House secretariat represented the President.

"If you can find 150,000 people now on the relief rolls who you say are not in need of relief," I asked Harry, "how are you going to answer the charge that you must have known, before the November election, that these people were not in need of relief? How can you explain in the month of December, two weeks before Christmas, that you can find 150,000 not in need of relief when you could not discover this excess on your rolls a month earlier?"

"The President," Hopkins said, "does not have to take the heat on this until he gets back. . . . The place where the budget is unbalanced is in my shop."

"There is no way you can take the responsibility," McIntyre told him. "The President will have to take it."

"What I wanted to do was to clear the relief rolls as far as possible of all cases not meriting relief," Hopkins explained, "so that I can walk into this session of Congress with a conviction in my own mind that there is actual need in every case of persons on the rolls."

Senator Glass, in November, 1936, said:[11]

[. . .–*ed.*] The election[s–*ed.*] would have been much closer had my party not had a four billion, eight hundred million dollar relief bill as campaign fodder.

There can be no challenge to Mr. Roosevelt's superb ability at political manipulation in the 1936 campaign. What history will say of it in the cold light of intellectual and public morals is something else. He had with great

---

10. Henry Morgenthau, Jr., "The Morgenthau Diaries," *Collier's*, September, 1947, p. 81.

11. Rixey Smith and Norman Beasley, *Carter Glass* (Longmans, Green and Company, New York, 1939), p. 370.

political adroitness made an amalgam of (a) the most corrupt sort of local political bosses—Kelly of Chicago, Hague of Jersey City, Crump of Memphis, Tammany of New York, Flynn of the Bronx, Lawrence of Pittsburgh, and others; and (b) the labor politicians; (c) the left-wing intellectuals, Socialists and Communists; (d) the ultraconservative Southern Democrats who liked the local spending and patronage; (e) young men and women of inherited wealth attracted by their mania for social recognition through public office; (f) certain strong voting racial groups, such as the Jews and Poles; (g) the use of labor organizations and left-wingers as a poison squad for his opponents.

It required an abundance of patronage, and billions from pork-barrel to make the amalgam which held them to the ballot box. The Republican candidate Alf Landon had none of the amalgam.

Mr. Roosevelt's vivid portrayal of the miseries of the depression and Republican "Do-Nothing" policies was most effective. It was the more effective because the Republicans refused to defend their own party or even to take the high advantage of exposing the dishonesty of such statements. He quickly detected their [these?–ed.]weakness in his opponents. As the campaign proceeded he drove this misrepresentation ceaselessly, aided by an infamous train of smear from his subordinates.

He secured the most sweeping victory ever known in American political history.

On the Republican Side

The Republican Convention of 1936 was called for Cleveland, Ohio, on June 9th. I had been mentioned as a candidate but at every start of a "club" or activity in the primaries or the Convention I squashed out such action. I was resolved not to take the nomination even if it were possible and with the attitude of the Republican Old Guard leaders, it was not possible.

As indicating my actions, the New York delegation held a meeting at once after reaching Cleveland and a motion was made that it cast its vote for me. Being already apprised of this possibility, I secured that former Secretary of the Treasury, Ogden Mills, who was its dominant member, should prevent it, which he did. Ogden Mills was obviously the ablest man in the Republican Party, both in intelligence, information, character and courage. But as he had been classed with me as a political leper by the politicians, his nomination was impossible. He refused to have his name proposed although he could have had the support of the New York delegation.

As to my own possible nomination I felt that overriding all other consider-ations was Roosevelt's amalgam of corrupt city machines, the solid South, the left wing, his rain of checks to the farmers, his use of relief funds for votes, his immense increase in the Federal bureaucracy, and his poison squad, would win the election in any event.

Moreover, I would be under the same ceaseless smear and misrepresenta-tion of the campaign of 1932 and as on that occasion I would have little sup-port from the Republican leaders for any adequate defense and counterattack. Therefore, I came to the firm conclusion that with a second defeat, any fur-ther value of my voice in the country would be extinguished. My real friends agreed with me and employed themselves in squashing out the number of incipient movements for my nomination.[12]

The question had arisen as to whether I should be asked to address the Convention. It was violently opposed by some of the Old Guard, but my friends insisted upon it. I wanted to make the address in the hope that the Republican party would fight on the fundamental principle of opposition to collectivism and thus leave us in [a–ed.] stronger position for the future even if we lost. Even after the invitation was extended to me the Convention

---

12. The statement of Vice President John Garner in his authorized biography, as follows, is a political curio of the times:

"The Republican used to do the politically smart thing most of the time. If they get back the knack I would imagine they will give Herbert Hoover a Grover Cleveland try. [Cleveland had been renominated by the Democrats in 1892 after being defeated by Harrison in 1888.] He couldn't win, but he would carry more states than anyone else they can put up. From an organization standpoint in a year when they have little chance, Hoover would be their best nominee, because even though he would lose, he might carry a number of other Republican candidates to victory." When Landon was nominated, he said: "The Republicans have set the stage for a party debacle."

Garner was a friendly enemy as evidenced by another passage in his Memoirs:

"[On some things–ed.] I fought him [President Hoover–ed.] with everything I had, under Marquis of Queensberry, London Prize Ring and catch-as-catch-can rules. But I always fought according to rules. My judgment may have been frail as to the proper solution of the vexing problems, but my course from 1931 to 1933, while I was Speaker, as in all of my public career, put public welfare above partisan advantage. I thought my party had a better program for national recovery than Mr. Hoover and his party.

"I never reflected on the personal character or integrity of Herbert Hoover. I never doubted his probity or his patriotism. In many ways he was superbly equipped for the Presi-dency. If he had become President in 1921 or 1937, he might have ranked with the greatest Presidents. [...–ed.] I think Herbert Hoover today is the wisest statesman on world affairs in America. He may be on domestic affairs, too."

[Editor's note: The quoted passages in this footnote are found in Bascom N. Timmons, Garner of Texas: A Personal History (New York: Harper & Brothers Publishers, 1948), pp. 209, 279–80. I have corrected Hoover's transcription in several places.]

manager tried to arrange my address on an afternoon when, due to Committee sessions, few would be present and the radio audience at its lowest. However, due largely to Lawrence Richey[13] and my own refusal to agree, it was fixed at a good evening hour. I delivered an address entitled "The Road to Freedom" to an immediate audience of 20,000 and a radio audience of many millions who were tuned it [in–*ed.*] at home. I said:

> In this room rests the greatest responsibility that has come to a body of Americans in three generations. In the lesser sense this is a convention of a great political party. But in the larger sense it is a convention of Americans to determine the fate of those ideals for which this nation was founded. That far transcends all partisanship.
>
> There is a moral purpose in the universe. There are elemental currents which make or break the fate of nations. Those forces which affect the vitality and the soul of a people will control its destinies. They far transcend the importance of transitory . . . issues of national life.

The New Deal Creeping Collectivism

I have given about four years to research into the New Deal, trying to determine . . . what sort of a system it is imposing on this country.

To some people it appears to be a strange interlude in American history in that it has no philosophy, that it is sheer opportunism, that it is a muddle of a spoils system, of emotional economics, of reckless adventure, of unctuous claims to a monopoly of human sympathy, of greed for power, of a desire for popular acclaim, and an aspiration to make the front pages of the newspapers. That is the most charitable view.

To other people it appears to be a cold-blooded attempt by starry-eyed boys to infect the American people by a mixture of European ideas, flavored with our native predilection to get something for nothing.

You can choose either one you like best. But the first is the road of chaos which leads to the second. Both of these roads lead over the same grim precipice that is the crippling and possibly the destruction of the freedom of men.

I then pointed out the analogies to the decadence of liberty abroad by chapter and verse quotations from foreign leaders. I sketched the march of Roosevelt actions, and continued:

---

13. [*Editor's note:* Lawrence Richey (1885–1959), Hoover's longtime confidential secretary and troubleshooter.]

... We have seen repeated violation of morals and honor in government. Do I need recall the repudiation of obligations, the clipping of the coin, the violation of trust to guard the Constitution and the coercion of the voter? When the standards of honor and morals fail in government they fail in the people.

There are some moral laws written in a Great Book. Over all there is the gospel of brotherhood. For the first time in the history of America we have heard the gospel of class hatred preached from the White House. That is human poison far more deadly than fear. Every reader of the history of democracy knows that is the final rock upon which all democracies have been wrecked. [. . .–ed.]

... The New Deal has brought that which George Washington called "alterations which may impair the energy of the system and thus overthrow that which cannot be directly overthrown."

Republicans! After a hundred and fifty years, we have arrived at that hour.

The New Deal may be a revolutionary design to replace the American System with despotism. It may be dream stuff of a false liberalism. It may be the valor of muddle. Their relationship to each other, however, is exactly the sistership of the witches who brewed the cauldron of powerful trouble for Macbeth. Their product is the poisoning of Americanism. [. . .–ed.]

The Republican Party must be a party which accepts the challenge. . . . We welcome change when it will produce fairer, more just, and satisfying civilization. But change which destroys the safeguards of free men and women is only apples of Sodom.

... Design of the structure of betterment . . . can only be builded by using the mold of justice, by laying brick upon brick from the materials of scientific research; by the painstaking sifting of truth from the collection of fact and experience. Any other mold is distorted; any other bricks are without straw; any other foundations are sand. That great structure of human progress can be built only by free men and women. [. . .–ed.]

Does this issue not transcend all other issues? Is it not alone the ground of Republican unity but unity beyond all partisanship? [. . .–ed.]

There are principles which neither tricks of organization, nor the rigors of depression, nor the march of time, nor New Dealers, nor Socialists, nor Fascists can change. There are some principles which came into the universe along with the shooting stars of which worlds are made, and they have always been and ever will be true. Such are laws of mathematics, the law of gravitation, the existence of God, and the ceaseless struggle of humankind to be free. [. . .–ed.]

... For this the best and bravest of earth have fought and died. To embody human liberty in workable government, America was born. Shall we keep that faith? Must we condemn the unborn generations to fight again and to die for the right to be free?

Less than twenty years ago we accepted those ideals as the air we breathed. We fought a great war for their protection. . . . We buried our sons in foreign soil. But in this score of years we have seen the advance of collectivism and its inevitable tyranny in more than half the civilized world. In this thundering era of world crisis distracted America stands confused and uncertain.

The Whig Party temporized, compromised upon the issue of slavery for the black man. That party disappeared. It deserved to disappear. Shall the Republican Party deserve or receive any better fate if it compromises upon the issue of freedom for all men, white as well as black? [. . .–ed.]

There's something vastly bigger than payrolls, than economics, than materialism, at issue in this campaign. The free spirit of men is the source of self-respect, of sturdiness, of moral and spiritual progress. . . . Nations die when these weaken no matter what their material prosperity.

Fundamental American liberties are at stake. Is the Republican Party ready for the issue? Are you willing to cast your all upon the issue, or would you falter and look back? Will you, for expediency's sake, also offer will-o'-the-wisps which beguile the people? Or have you determined to enter in a holy crusade for liberty which shall determine the future and the perpetuity of a nation of free men? That star shell fired today over the no man's land of world despair would illuminate the world with hope. [. . .–ed.]

. . . This is your call. Stop the retreat. In the chaos of doubt, confusion, and fear, yours is the task to command. . . . turning the eyes of your fellow Americans to the sunlight of freedom, lead the attack to retake, recapture, and retain the citadels of liberty. . . .Thus can the opportunity, the inheritance, and the spiritual future of your children be guaranteed. And thus you will win the gratitude of posterity, and the blessing of Almighty God.[14]

The address received a great ovation from the convention. Although I left the Hall after half an hour of acknowledging applause and although the Chairman vainly tried to adjourn the session, the demonstration continued for a half hour after I had left the hall. Several of the demonstrators wished my nomination and tried to move a suspension of the rules and proposed it by acclaim. My friends, however, stopped any such movement.

---

14. [*Editor's note*: Hoover delivered this address at the Republican national convention in Cleveland, Ohio, on June 10, 1936. The full text is reprinted in Herbert Hoover, *Addresses upon the American Road, 1933–1938* (New York: Charles Scribner's Sons, 1938), pp. 173–83.]

There were no strong Republican candidates in the field. Governor Alf Landon of Kansas, Frank Knox of Chicago, Senator William E. Borah and Senator Arthur H. Vandenburg were "receptive" candidates.

Landon was not a "left-winger." He had made a good Governor of Kansas. But his experience had never extended to the national field, much less the foreign field.

By the time of the Convention, Borah had done badly in the primaries, Knox had failed to secure much support. Vandenburg was generally ignored. Landon's nomination was brought about by the skillful management of John Hamilton.

The party platform was not strong on what I deemed was the real issue. Among other things, at Governor Landon's request, it omitted any reference to the reestablishment of the gold standard and used only the New Deal phrase "sound money." After reaching New York, the Chairman of the Resolutions Committee wired me, asking my opinion in the matter. I replied:

> ... There are some things on currency that must be remembered.
>
> The term "sound money" was polluted by its being used to mislead the people by the New Deal. It is a weasel word.
>
> So-called managed currencies will be managed by politicians and subject to pressures of demagoguery or special interest. There can be no economic stability in that quarter. [...–ed.]
>
> A large part of our unemployment is due to lack of long-term confidence and consequently long-term capital for new enterprise and permanent improvement. These people cannot be returned to work and the farmers given a full market until that confidence is restored....
>
> ... It seems to me the course to pursue is:
>
> (a) Repeal all Presidential powers over currency.
> (b) Guarantee that there will be no further devaluation.
> (c) Seek international agreement to stabilize currencies.
> (d) Resolutely determine to restore gold convertibility of the currency, either in coin or bullion....[15]

The Landon forces refused to accept the idea. I then informed the Chairman that I would not support the ticket unless that idea was adopted. We settled this question by Landon agreeing to make a public statement confirming the gold standard as the meaning of "sound" money, which he did.

---

15. [*Editor's note*: Printed in Hoover's *Addresses . . . 1933–1938*, pp. 184–85.]

Governor Landon and his immediate advisors designed the strategy of his campaign as based upon:

1. His known integrity and wise Governorship of his State.
2. That the conservative Republicans must vote for him anyway.
3. That he could attract the so-called liberals by incorporating much of the New Deal program, insisting he could do it cheaper.
4. Avoiding any reference to or defense of my Administration.
5. Allowing it to be known that he considered myself and such as "reactionary."
6. Complete avoidance of the issues which I had been raising.

Landon was probably politically wise in his strategy of the campaign and his judgment that I was still crying in the wilderness. He could not have been elected on any strategy.

Early in the campaign, John Hamilton, Chairman of the National Committee, made a speech in Chicago, eulogizing my Administration. Landon at once severely reprimanded him and my Administration was not again mentioned by him or the Republican speakers. Being informed of this I promptly checked it with Hamilton, as I naturally wanted to know where I stood in the campaign. The Democrats, observing this weakness, concentrated their campaign of attack upon me instead of Landon, whom they mostly ignored.

The Governor was necessarily unfamiliar with the witches' cauldron in Europe and the fumes from it which were infecting the Roosevelt Administration and spreading over the United States.

From lack of extensive knowledge of the American scene, he was compelled to rely almost wholly on ghost writers for his many speeches.

All this brought several half ludicrous incidents in the campaign.

During the latter end of the campaign some of the Landon supporters, particularly my friend Roy Roberts, publisher of the *Kansas City Star*, becoming alarmed concluded that I should be brought into the campaign. He and John Hamilton urged that I call upon Governor Landon at Topeka. In view of Landon's strategy, I did not wish to force myself on him or embarrass him and without a strong defense of my Administration I could be of little use to him. I therefore refused to go to Topeka unless I was publicly invited by the Governor. The men immediately around Landon were adamant that no invitation be issued and, of course, my old press friends promptly so advised me. After long delay the Governor did issue and publicized such an invitation and received me very graciously.

Landon's shyness of the Hoover Administration was amusingly illustrated on an occasion when Ogden Mills sought to visit him. The men around Landon insisted that Mills be taken from the train at a station before Topeka and brought secretly into his headquarters so that the press would not know of this leprous association. Mills was more deeply offended by this act than by anything that had happened in his long and useful life.

When I visited him [Landon–ed.] at Topeka I strongly urged him to take up the major issue of collectivism. I also suggested that he speak infrequently and then only upon subjects with which he had some knowledge by experience and to prepare the speeches himself. I told him that his sincerity and native common sense were his greatest assets; that he could not carry conviction with ghost-written speeches. However, he made nearly a hundred speeches during the campaign, most of which—certainly those made over the radio—were ghost-written. A whole battery of people of diverse views were put to work on this job. Some were written by a New York committee under Ogden Mills, some by a Midwest committee, most by his Topeka staff. And like all ghost-written stuff, sooner or later the people smelled it out and lost all interest.

An amusing incident concerning these ghost-written speeches was related to me during the campaign. Landon was given five prepared speeches on the same five subjects from the two different committees. He could not decide which ones to deliver. He requested one of his aides to call a jury of six Republican news men to decide, without disclosing the origins. They voted for speeches drafted by a committee under Ogden Mills, but Landon had fears that my philosophy, through Mills, would not do and asked that a compound be made of the two versions leaning to those of a Topeka group who were more "liberal."

Becoming still more desperate, Hamilton insisted that I make some speeches in the campaign and so arranged it with Landon. It was, however, too near the election to do any good, even if good could be done. However, I agreed to make two speeches.

My first address was at Philadelphia on October 16, 1936. It was an analysis of New Deal fraudulent accounting and the wastefulness of their expenditures. Anyone interested in the comedy and deceit of this New Deal operation might read it.[16]

My other address was at Denver on October 30, 1936, where I returned to the major issue of the American people. I said in part:

---

16. Ibid., pp. [201–15–ed.]

These issues are too great and the stakes too large for us to examine these questions in any mean or smearing fashion. . . . The only field which the opposition[17] have not entered in this debate is the field of sportsmanship. . . .

If the Republic is to head in the right direction we must get at the real issues. We must dismiss the shadow boxing of a political campaign. . . . We must strip our problems down to the great issue before the country.[18]

I recalled the prophetic speech I had made in 1932 where I said:

"The spirit of liberalism is to create free men; it is not the regimentation of men."[19] . . . Freedom does not die from frontal attack. It dies because men in power no longer believe in a system based upon Liberty.[20]

I then recited the invasions of liberty during the previous four years and continued:[21]

Does Mr. Roosevelt not admit all this in his last report on the state of the Union: "We have built up new instruments of public power" which he admits could "provide shackles for the liberties of the people." Does freedom permit any man or any government any such power? Have the people ever voted for these shackles? [. . .–ed.]

You might think that reform and change . . . are discoveries of the New Deal. . . . We have been reforming and changing ever since George Washington. Democracy is not static. It is a living force. Every new idea, every new invention offers opportunity for both good and evil.

We are in need of reform every day in the week as long as men are greedy for money or power. We need a whole list of reforms right now, including the reform of these people who have created a gigantic spoils system as a method of seizing political power.

Many of the problems discussed in this campaign concern our material welfare. That is right. But there are things far more important to a nation than material welfare. It is possible to have a prosperous country under a dictatorship. . . . No great question will ever be settled in dollars and cents. Great questions must be settled on moral grounds and the tests of what makes free men. What is the nation profited if it shall gain the whole world and lose its own soul? [. . .–ed.]

---

17. [*Editor's note:* In the original text of his speech, Hoover had written "we" instead of "the opposition." Why he changed his wording here is unknown.]

18. [*Editor's note:* Hoover, *Addresses . . . 1933–1938*, pp. 216–17.]

19. [*Editor's note:* Hoover here quoted a line from his campaign address in Madison Square Garden on October 31, 1932.]

20. [*Editor's note:* Hoover, *Addresses . . . 1933–1938*, pp. 217, 218.]

21. Ibid., pp. 220, 225–227.

The transcendent issue before us today is free men and women. [. . .–*ed.*]

The conviction of our fathers was that all these freedoms come from the Creator. . . [and–*ed.*] they[22] can be denied by no man or no government or no New Deal. They were spiritual rights of men. The prime purpose of liberal government is to enlarge and not to destroy these freedoms. . . .

And again I repeat that statement of four years ago—"This campaign is more than a contest between two men. It is a contest between two philosophies of government."

Whatever the outcome of this election that issue is set. We shall battle it out until the soul of America is saved.

I am afraid these ideas were not too much help for Governor Landon.

At this time I urged Hamilton to secure that the Governor come out strongly for the major issue in order to leave the Party with a great issue. Hamilton was unable to bring this about. The Governor's failure in the election was probably greater than would have been the case had he done so. He gained no democratic votes, even from their conservative wing. Through the failure to meet the real issue he was deserted at the ballot box by hundreds of thousands of disappointed Republicans. This large desertion is proved by the fact that his vote was nearly a million behind the votes for Republican state and local candidates. Presidential candidates usually run ahead of their ticket because many people vote for the President only.

The election left the Republican party thoroughly demoralized. We carried only two states and elected the lowest representation in the Senate and House in the entire history of the Republican Party. Fourteen seats were lost in the House and nine in the Senate, leaving us with only 16 Senators, 88 Congressmen and 6 Governors—the lowest in the 70 years of Republican history.

When, in after years, Landon attained a deeper understanding, he became most effective in exposition of the fundamental issue at stake. He gained a great deal of knowledge of national affairs during this campaign and with more maturity in subsequent years, he developed sound and courageous attitudes in these matters.

Just an Observation

In the subsequent campaign of 1940 [1944–*ed.*] the Republican nominee, Governor Thomas E. Dewey, followed the Landon tactics in respect to myself but

---

22. [*Editor's note*: In the original quoted text, Hoover wrote: "Creator and that they."]

more consistently and I had no contacts with him and made no speeches, it being his judgment that Landon had been wrong in even belatedly bringing me in.

Upon this whole subject, a leading Democratic journalist, Mr. Frank Kent, of the *Baltimore Sun*, said of these tactics of the Republicans:[23]

[...–*ed.*] The President himself [Franklin Roosevelt–*ed.*] frequently used the word "falsifications." . . .

The fact is that the biggest falsification of the whole campaign emanated from his own side, and it had its origin back in the early days of his first campaign. It consisted of the charge that the depression of 1930–32 was caused by the Republican party; that the Republicans did nothing about it; that the people were allowed to starve and were forced to sell apples; that the country was in ruins and that Mr. Roosevelt rescued it from the complete wreck.

So successful was the smear campaign between 1930 and 1932 that these allegations became deeply impressed upon a vast number of unthinking and uninformed people. They were promulgated in a thousand speeches, in millions of scurrilous pamphlets and circulars. They became a fundamental New Deal conviction. Mr. Roosevelt himself has given currency to them and has often referred to apple selling. He did in the last campaign. In fact, the Democrats started at their convention to recreate this picture and to yell "apple selling" and "Hoover." One might almost have gathered from the speeches that the Republicans had nominated Mr. Hoover instead of Mr. Dewey. And they kept it up for three months. It was part of their basic campaign strategy. Before stating the facts it is proper to point out that in 1930 Mr. Roosevelt, then a candidate for President, was Governor of New York, the richest State in the Union; that the Democratic party was in control of the richest city in the world, and that he could have met any relief needed and could have stopped apple dealers from exploiting people's sympathy by marketing their wares in this fashion.

The broader facts, which history will record, are that the depression was world-wide; that its major origins were in Europe; that it swept in on the

---

23. The *Baltimore Sun*, November 12, 1944. [*Editor's note*: Kent's syndicated column was widely commented on. It was printed in the *Congressional Record* 90 (November 14, 1944): A4377. What neither Kent nor Hoover divulged was that Hoover largely ghostwrote Kent's column. In early November 1944, Hoover sent a two-paged typewritten essay to Kent and other friends on the "lie" that the Depression of 1930–32 had been caused by the Republican Party, that the Republicans had done nothing about it, and that Franklin Roosevelt had rescued America from "complete wreck." Kent took Hoover's blast, revised it in a few places, and published it under Kent's name in his syndicated column on November 13. Thus in quoting Kent's column here in his memoir, Hoover was mostly quoting himself.

For Hoover's original text, see Appendix II, Document 5 in this volume.]

United States like a hurricane; that it originated from the backwash of World War I; that by action of the Republican Administration 18,000,000 people were under organized relief; that no one starved and that the Hoover Administration took drastic steps to protect the people's savings by creating the RFC and the Home Land Banks and by expanding agricultural credit institutions. The bank failures were mostly in State banks not under Federal control.

It is likely, too, that history will record that in June and July of 1932 we were on our way out of the depression, with employment increasing, but that recovery was halted when business confidence was shaken by the impending election of the New Deal; that with the election, the whole country further hesitated, awaiting the new policies; that rumors quickly spread that Mr. Roosevelt would devalue the currency; that, in consequence, people tried to get their money out of the banks and that speculators tried to ship it out of the country; that Mr. Roosevelt refused Mr. Hoover's request to reaffirm the promise he had made the night before election not to tinker with the currency; that Mr. Roosevelt refused to cooperate in other directions with Mr. Hoover; that the closing of the banks was not from fear of a retiring administration and could have been averted had Mr. Roosevelt been willing to cooperate. Those are the facts. After the banks were reopened, it was found that 98 percent of their deposits were good.

Further, the historical truth is that the rest of the world, not having a "New Deal," went straight out of the depression and recovered its employment by 1934 or 1935; that unemployment here in the United States continued on a large scale for six years and that Governor Dewey told the exact truth when he said it took a war to get us out of it. *The whole story of the 1930–1932 depression as painted by the New Deal publicity agencies beginning in 1932 and continuing straight through the last campaign is about as big and complete a falsification as has been known in American politics.* It shows what can be done by large-scale, skillful and unscrupulous publicity. It is the classic example of what can be done by distortion and suppression of facts. *It probably has deceived more people than any other piece of political fiction in fifty years.* (Italics supplied.)[24]

24. One of the curios of politics was the publication by Mrs. Roosevelt some 12 years later of a disavowal of this sort of charge. Its reversal of her late husband was so complete as to merit a column in the *New York Times* of July 23, 1948. [*Editor's note:* The column, by Arthur Krock, appeared on page 18 of the *New York Times* of that date.]

CHAPTER 8

The Crusade against Collectivism from the Landon Defeat until the Congressional Election of 1938

A Visit to Europe in 1938

To be better equipped for continued battle against New Deal collectivism, and to appraise the rising dangers of war, early in 1938 I spent some months [seven weeks–*ed.*][1] in a journey over Europe visiting many countries. Over the years I had received many invitations from governments to visit them as they wished to show their lasting appreciation for my efforts during the first world war and the Armistice. These invitations gave me an unusual opportunity to study the causes and the steps by which some thirteen countries had abandoned the free institutions which they had set up after the world war and gone collectivist. I believed I could thereby better interpret the meaning of these dangers of collectivism and war if I could see them at work. And, incidentally I wished to learn more about the origins of World Depression. I have given in other volumes of these memoirs a more ample account of the force rumbling for war in Europe but for understanding of the social and economic forces in the United States, they cannot be wholly separated in this account.[2]

I had the fine company of two of my old associates—Perrin Galpin and Paul Smith—who had now grown into important ways. Their sense of humor inspired by the incidents of the journey compensated for otherwise wearisome

---

1. [*Editor's note*: Hoover left New York for Europe on February 9, 1938, and arrived back in New York on March 28, 1938.]

2. [*Editor's note*: Hoover was alluding here to a separate volume of his memoirs on which he was concurrently working: an installment known informally as the Magnum Opus. He essentially completed it shortly before his death in 1964, but it was not published until 2011. See George H. Nash, ed., *Freedom Betrayed: Herbert Hoover's Secret History of the Second World War and Its Aftermath* (Stanford, CA: Hoover Institution Press, 2011). *Freedom Betrayed*, pp. 55–105, contains a detailed account of his 1938 journey to Europe. It is similar to the version presented here, but there are significant differences.]

hours. We visited Belgium, France, Switzerland, Austria, Czechoslovakia, Germany, Poland, Latvia, Estonia, Finland, Sweden and England.

This account was written before the Second World War and is produced here as then written.[3] It is of no purpose to record here the multitude of receptions, banquets, University degrees, naming of streets, and even planets, after me.

The important element of the journey was the opportunity for personal discussion with twenty-two Presidents, Kings and Prime Ministers, fifteen Foreign Ministers, a host of Cabinet officers, editors, professors, business and labor leaders, a total of more than 350 such interviews. On my return, I made, on March 30, 1938, a nation-wide broadcast from New York summing up my conclusions, and supplemented this address with others from San Francisco on April 7th and from Oklahoma City on May 5th.

[Belgium–*ed.*]

My first visit was to Belgium. There I had the opportunity for intimate discussion of the European situation with the King, Prime Minister Paul Janson and other Cabinet members, the leaders of the opposition parties, the Rectors and leading professors of the Universities and the leading business men, labor leaders—and our Ambassador Hugh Gibson.

Belgium, occupying as it does a tenuous national existence among conflicting European forces, is naturally one of the best informed centers in Europe. Their willingness and action in furnishing me any information, no matter how confidential, was most helpful. I began here extensive notes on conversations which continued throughout my journey.

The King[4] was a young man but showed great moral strength and understanding of European problems. He spoke very frankly. He opened our conversation by saying that his father, the late King Albert, regarded me as a personal friend and one whose advice he greatly valued. Among other things, he said,

> Of course Hitler and his national socialism with its racialism and aggressiveness is a constant menace. But the French are an equal liability to the peace of Europe.

---

3. [*Editor's note:* There are, however, occasional differences between Hoover's personal notes of conversations with European leaders as quoted here and his notes of the same conversations as quoted in *Freedom Betrayed*. See, for example, notes 5 and 6 below. Hoover's original notes made in 1938 have not been located, and the explanation for the variations is unknown.]

4. [*Editor's note:* Leopold III (1901–83), king of the Belgians from 1934 to 1951.]

I expressed surprise. And he added:

Russia is of course Germany's objective, but Russia's and Britain's ally,[5] France, is so torn by internal dissension, there is such degeneration in its leadership and in political life, that the French are a menace through weakness. A strong France and a strong Britain would be an assurance that Hitler would at least leave the Western Democracies alone, but the Germans have no fear of France.

I asked why Britain had been so complacent in the presence of Hitler's repudiation of the Versailles Treaty, Locarno, re-armament, the occupation of the Rhineland, and the formation of the Berlin-Rome Axis. He replied:

Britain is fearful of the growth of Russia's military power, has lost faith in France. She is engaged in her traditional practice of "balance of power."

I asked him how he accounted for the degeneration in France. He said:

Probably the primary cause is the depletion of the race for a generation as the consequence of being bled white in the last war, but the immediate cause is the disintegrating influence of the Russian Communists and Communistic ideas which reached alarming proportions under Prime Minister Blum.

He said it was so bad that Blum's continuation in office depended upon the Russian Ambassador. He then smiled and added,

Blum was trying to imitate your New Deal. He called it by that name.[6]

Blum's ministry had fallen some months before to be succeeded by Chautemps[7] whom the King said was "insufficient." The King explained the recent termination of the Franco-Belgian military alliance as due to their fear that France with its weakness, its recklessness and its alliance with Russia would involve the Belgians unnecessarily.

The Belgian Prime Minister gave me the same impressions, but expressed his opinions in a more guarded fashion. I asked him what motivating forces

---

5. [*Editor's note*: The words "Russia is of course Germany's objective, but Russia's and Britain's ally" do not appear in Hoover's account of this conversation in *Freedom Betrayed*, p. 59. Why he omitted them there or added them here is unknown.]

6. [*Editor's note*: This paragraph, including the quotation attributed to King Leopold, is not included in Hoover's account of this interview in *Freedom Betrayed*, p. 60. Presumably there should be quotation marks before "Blum" and after "New Deal," but Hoover did not use them, and I have let this line stand as written.]

7. [*Editor's note*: Camille Chautemps (1885–1963), prime minister of France during Hoover's 1938 visit.]

had led eleven or twelve democracies in Europe into more or less dictatorship. (Italy, Germany, Austria, Hungary, Greece, Roumania, Bulgaria, Poland, Lithuania, Latvia, Estonia, Turkey.) His reply was epigrammatic:

> Misery; socialists; Communists, aided by liberals who believed they could have totalitarian economics and maintain personal liberty; spenders; demagogues; too many political parties; weak compromise governments.

He added:

> The movement away from democracy in each country was gradual at the start, but created its own accelerations by frightening business and thus increased disorganization of the economic system and increased unemployment.

He said he had no fear of Belgium going down that slide because the people were hard working, prosperous and individualistic.

Nevertheless, the rise of totalitarianism all around them, the activities of the Fascist, Communist and Socialist groups in their own midst and the ever-present fear of European war were causing their leading men great anxiety.

From the Belgian Prime Minister and several of his Ministers I heard for the first time a new note as to the United States. I was to hear it again and again from leaders in the smaller countries. It came in response to an inquiry of mine designed to provoke discussion. "What do you think the relation of the United States to Europe should be?" The replies were, in summary:

> If war comes again, the United States should keep out. First, because you must maintain at least one great center of social stability, of moral and economic power, around which the world can rally after a war is over; and second, your American ideas of foreign relations and your insistence on freedoms which are not fitted to the European scene. Your ideas introduce cross currents, fan conflicts which can only delay those settlements which Europe must find for itself. If general war comes again, European civilization will be near death; it can only revive if you have preserved it in America from the moral and physical destructions which would come to you from war.

When I asked from which direction war might come, they and others afterward had one constant reply.

> The ultimate and inevitable conflict in Europe is between Germany and Russia, both for ideological and economic and political reasons. The Germans are land people; their military strength is on land; they want land; they will sooner or later clash with Russia for Russia alone has the opportunities they

want. And the Germans want to remove what they consider as their greatest menace, Communism. Russia would have no objection to Germany at war with Britain and western Europe as that would weaken both the Democracies and Germany. If the Germans did overrun western Europe, Russia would only be waiting for German exhaustion to attack her. The greatest folly of all history would be for the western Democracies to cultivate war with Germany. The western powers should not be drawn into conflict with her. It would only demoralize themselves and aid Russia and the spread of Communism in the end.

When I asked when war may come the answer was:

Who knows? Perhaps a year, perhaps two years, perhaps never. The very fear of its coming stirs every peace-anxious statesman to action. But the whole structure of Europe was left unstable by the Treaty of Versailles and the explosives which it laid.

I was to find the same answers from thoughtful men all over Europe.

France

From Belgium I went to Lille and other cities in our former relief territory in Northern France. In those cities I had many conversations with their officials.

I spent some days in Paris. Altogether, in France, I discussed the French and European forces in motion with President [Albert–ed.] Lebrun, Foreign Minister [Georges–ed.] Bonnet, the President of the Bank of France, the Chancellor of the Sorbonne, six permanent French officials of importance, two Senators, four Deputies, two former French Ambassadors to the United States, six mayors of cities, three leading French bankers, two engineers, two editors, two leading economists, two labor leaders, seven educators, one poet, six American correspondents and three American officials—in all, 48 [52–ed.] informed persons. Added to which were incidental persons at lunches and dinners.

The President and the Foreign Minister told me there was but little danger of war in Europe.

Despite these assurances the sum of my conclusions were that as the result of the Blum regime in 1936–1937 (and his New Deal planned economy) France was in great difficulties. The manufacturing productivity of the country had dropped over 40%. The country was unable to maintain its exports, and in consequence they were being drained of exchange to pay for the increase of imports to fill their deficiency in production. There was a considerable flight of capital. The Ministry under Camille Chautemps was struggling to remedy matters but with little success and seemed doomed to fall. The whole moral structure seemed to be sinking.

The defense preparedness was demoralized, the output of planes had dropped to 50 per month when they needed 500 per month.

The multiplicity of parties in the Parliament, the consequent composition of every Ministry on a compromise basis, which permitted only negative instead of positive policies, the growing power of the left-wing group and the general lowering of public morals presented a gloomy picture which seemed to me to mark France for the scene of a totalitarian revolution or the resort of all failing governments—war.

The League of Nations

We spent two days at Geneva. I had sent word ahead, to the American Consul General, Howard Bucknall [Bucknell–ed.], at Geneva, an old friend, asking him to invite the career heads of the League to visit with me. Prime Minister [Neville–ed.] Chamberlain some weeks previously had announced that the League was "impotent" and the British had given a sort of notice that they did not consider they were bound to join in any of its decisions as to economic or military sanctions except so far as the British might agree upon the merits of each case. This straw would have broken the League's back if it had not been broken long before.

My discussions at Geneva, beginning with Joseph Avenol, the French Secretary General, embraced six officials of the League, four American officials and three professors of sociology and economics. The men in the political section of the League seemed utterly discouraged and Avenol had no credible suggestion as to how the peace of Europe could be preserved. He blamed Britain for the armament of Germany and said it was the full return of the "balance of power" theory of peace and that it was pointed at Russia. The men at the heads of divisions of economic and social work were confident that in these fields the League was making substantial accomplishment. But the League was the creation of liberal governments and, with the steady European degeneration of liberalism into totalitarianism, it was dying. As if this were not enough to kill it, the network of military alliances and the daily pressures of power politics and balances of power were steadily sapping its vitality. I concluded, that as a peace agency it was not only dead but overdue for burial and the substitution of something else.

The League officials and some American residents in Geneva laid the failure of the League primarily upon America's original refusal to join. Upon my question as to what America as a member of the League could have done to stem the tide of totalitarianism and the other pressures, their replies were discussions of "moral and economic strength." I asked if they did not consider that the provisions of the Treaty of Versailles had contributed to the degeneration of Europe and if the obligation of the League to enforce these degenerating provisions had anything to do with the failure. They were sure that, had the League been strong enough to enforce the Treaty of Versailles, through American participation, the organization would not have weakened. To which I asked a series of questions:

> Do you think the American people could have been called upon to put troops into Germany to prevent the Nazi revolution or to enforce the stupendous reparations; or into Europe to prevent Russian fifth columns breeding revolution; or to have compelled the succession states from setting up a mass of trade barriers to their internal economic destruction; or to have prevented the network of military alliances and growth of armament; or to prevent the British building up Hitler as a balance of power against Russia on their continued theory of power balances, which had continued from a hundred years before the League was born; or could we have prevented the inflations, imposed balanced budgets on a score of spending governments, or insisted upon the proper treatment of minorities?
>
> As they seemed to think that we could have brought all these things about, I asked: Did we not take a leading part in disarmament which was one of the prime functions of the League and did we not meet with opposition from the leading powers; did we not join fully in the Japanese case only to meet defeat from France and England? What you are really asking for is American domination and support of Europe, economically, socially and politically. Is that not a confession of European moral and political bankruptcy?

But we wandered about for hours in a maze of questions and phrases, nebular ideas and futile searches for somebody to blame.

While in Geneva I called upon my old friend Ignace Paderewski[8] who lived in a village some miles away. He was practically an exile from Poland and spoke at great length upon the failures and weaknesses of the Polish

---

8. [Editor's note: Ignace Paderewski (1860–1941), an internationally acclaimed pianist and composer, and prime minister of newly independent Poland in 1919. He and Hoover were acquainted for many years. See Hoover, Freedom Betrayed, pp. 587–89.]

Government. He was especially indignant at their dalliance with Germany and the ascending totalitarian dictatorship in his country. As to the immediate future of Europe, he was wholly discouraged.

Austria

The Austrian Government did not seem terrorized by the Roosevelt Administration and had sent me a cordial invitation. Arriving at Vienna on March 2nd, we were met at the frontier by officials of the Ministry of Foreign Affairs who accompanied us to Vienna. We were welcomed at the station by the Minister of Education; Dr. Richard Schmitz, the Bourgomaster of Vienna; Dr. Richard Pernter; American Chargé d'Affaires, John C. Wiley; and my old friend, Gardner Richardson, who was still Commercial Attaché. We were installed in the great suite of rooms at the Imperial Hotel by the Government. I was given an official reception by the Bourgomaster, at the City Hall, and a banquet by the Minister of Education, attended by other ministers (except Chancellor [Kurt–ed.] Schuschnigg).

On the occasions of various banquets, conferring of honorary degrees, etc., I had many opportunities for conversation with national leaders. I had such discussions with the President, the Chancellor, Ministers of Foreign Affairs, of Education and Finance, the President of the National Bank, two Bourgomasters, one editor, five University professors, three engineers, two labor leaders and five other Austrian citizens of importance. I also discussed the subjects in which I was interested with three American press representatives and all the American officials.

In a discussion at dinner with Finance Minister [Rudolf–ed.] Neumayer, President [Viktor–ed.] Kienbock of the National Bank and the University economics professors, I asked their views as to the underlying causes of the European economic collapse in 1931 which had been touched off from Vienna. I was certainly interested because the most disastrous of the woes of my administration, the great depression, really had its springboard with the financial collapse of Austria. And I may say here that their views were the same as those expressed by corresponding leaders in all the other countries I visited. In sum, my notes record that the Austrians said:

> There were several primary and a number of secondary causes. The primary
> causes were, first, the weakening of the economic structure of every nation
> in Europe by the war; second, the economic consequences of the Treaty of
> Versailles which had divided the Danube Valley among five states, each of

which had set up trade barriers by tariffs, discriminatory rail rates, quotas, etc., and thus weakened and impoverished the productivity of that whole great area. This had impoverished and paralyzed the great financial and trade center of Vienna with its skills and former resources. Third, the reparations and intergovernmental war debts which distorted all finance and exchange and through pressures had forced the export of goods into unnatural channels. Fourth, the economic isolation of Russia by the Communist destruction of her productivity, thus stopping the flow of food and raw materials into Europe and closing a large part of the market for European manufactured goods in Russia. Fifth, immediately after the Treaty and despite the League, military alliances and power politics had steadily increased armaments with their inevitable unbalanced budgets. Sixth, the rise of the school (the totalitarian liberals) which believed governments could produce employment and increase productivity by bureaucratic control and dictation of business with the consequent fright to business. From this followed hesitation and increasing unemployment. Seventh, the attempts of governments to provide for this unemployment by public works drove budgets into further deficits with a train of foreign and domestic borrowing, kiting of bills and disguised inflation. From all this flowed government controls of imports and exports in an effort to protect currencies and gold reserves, all of which created more unemployment. The whole of the process was an aftermath of the World War and the Treaty of Versailles. If there had been no war, there would have been no world depression.

The crack started at its weakest point, that is, in Austria, and was widened when the French demanded payment of short-term bills as a pressure measure to prevent the proposed economic union with Germany in 1931.

It did not seem to occur to these gentlemen in Europe that I was personally responsible for the world-wide depression as Mr. Roosevelt so repeatedly charged.

The Austrians, of course, laid great emphasis upon the Treaty of Versailles as a cause. Many of us had protested at the time that it would make Vienna the center of poverty in Europe with political and social instability which was bound to radiate woe and disturbance to all Europe. After Versailles the Austrians had tried to commend themselves to the Democracies by a genuine parliamentary government and all the basic freedoms. But misery and ideologies had produced a multitude of political groups which paralyzed parliamentary action. The Austrians had never liked the Germans, but in economic desperation they tried to bring about an economic union with

Germany in 1931, which France and England prevented. Before the time of my visit, Austria had turned to semi-dictatorship and a mild sort of Fascist government.

A few months before my arrival, Hitler had again proposed union. Joining Nazi Germany was, however, different from joining the Weimar Republic as it meant sacrifice of all local government and independence. The Nazis had been constantly stirring revolution in Austria. About two weeks previously, Chancellor Schuschnigg had been summoned to Berchtesgaden, threatened and abused by Hitler. A few days before my arrival he had made his great and courageous speech of defiance with an impressive plea to the Austrians to maintain their independence.

The air everywhere was tense with impending events. I felt we were going through a sort of unreal stage performance in the activities of my reception. I was embarrassed by the exceeding politeness of a people preoccupied with such anxieties and burdens. All this setting necessarily dominated my every conversation with leaders. Those I met—except one group—were anti-Nazi. The one group that I found pro-Nazi, to my surprise, comprised some of the authorities of the University of Vienna where I received an honorary degree. They felt that Austria had been kicked about by the western Democracies for twenty years, and that this attitude made the outlook for Austria hopeless. With Germany there might be some chance. They said that the large majority of Austrians were in favor of the Nazi union. All of the government leaders seemed despondent.

The Chancellor, not being well, excused himself from the various ceremonies and banquets on my behalf. He asked that I call upon him. He did not look ill. With feeling, he spoke of the service of America to Austria after the war in 1919 and my efforts to help them during the financial panic in 1931. He talked at length upon the situation in Europe and said his ministry would resist the Nazi [sic–ed.] as a matter of honor. But he seemed despaired. He was bitter over the treatment of Austria in the Treaty of Versailles and emphatically stated the Treaty would crash in war. He quoted Mr. Chamberlain's speech of ten days before in which the British Prime Minister had called the League of Nations "impotent" and added that it certainly was proving impotent to save Austria from the Nazi now, but had been potent in the destruction of Austria six years before (referring to the League's attitude against the union at that time with democratic Germany). He seemed to like conversing with an outsider and asked me to call again the day I was leaving. On this occasion I asked him about the causes of transition from democracy to partial dictatorship in Austria. In condensation, he said:

Democracy is not fitted to people in misery; it is fitted to peoples in prosperity. Out of misery comes a score of agitations and remedies—Communism, Socialism, Fascism, agrarian and religious blocks and what not—all with their political parties represented in parliament. No group has a majority; no ministry can have stability, strength or last for long. Moreover, political and social chaos creates economic chaos because it destroys the initiative in business. Finally the people themselves welcome strong government—dictatorship, if you wish to call it that. You in America know little of what you have to be thankful for.

I asked him what he thought America's part should be in Europe. He exclaimed:

Keep out of European power politics and wars! Your people do not understand the forces of Europe. You make things worse; your great part is to preserve a sanctuary where civilization can live.

I formed the impression of Mr. Schuschnigg as less than a great statesman, perhaps, but a man of great nobility of character; a student rather than a man of action, but with great moral courage and honesty. The President of Austria, Mr. [Wilhelm–ed.] Miklas, was an amiable nonentity. He invited me to the Palace and insisted upon showing me the exact spot where [Engelbert–ed.] Dollfuss was murdered by the first Nazi "putsch" with all the details. The Chancellor was, of course, the ruling personality.

Eight days later the Germans marched into Vienna. Schuschnigg was imprisoned by Hitler who watched the ecstatic Austrians "Heil" from the same apartment I had occupied at the Imperial Hotel.

Czechoslovakia

Just before leaving Vienna I received from the Hungarian Minister at Vienna a renewed and cordial invitation from his government to visit Budapest. I did not, however, think we should take the time. Hungary had long since turned into a Fascist dictatorship.

We arrived in Prague and were met at the station by Czech Minister of Foreign Affairs Kamil Krofta and my old friend, American Minister Wilbur C. Carr, with whom we stopped. I attended an informal lunch by President Edward [Edvard–ed.] Benes and a long private discussion afterward, a State dinner in the evening with all top Czech officials and a large reception following. The next few days were given to visits for discussion with Prime

Minister Dr. Milan Hodza, the Minister of Foreign Affairs, Dr. Kamil Krofta, the Minister of Education, Dr. Emil Franke and others. Many groups called to pay respects and I attended receptions by various scientific and public institutions where there were opportunities for more learning on current events.

Altogether I had the opportunity for discussion with something over fifty officials and leaders in various fields. I had known President Benes and some of the others from war days. Benes said peace could be preserved if only the western Democracies would be firm enough with the Germans. He blamed the British for building up a military Germany again. He had made a long-standing alliance with France and now had made an alliance with Soviet Russia so that he believed Czechoslovakia was protected. He was very critical of the Polish Government, saying it was a corrupt, reactionary oligarchy constantly conspiring with the Germans.

President Benes gave me no hint of internal tensions, but the Prime Minister spoke bitterly of the opposition being fanned by the Nazi among the Sudeten Germans and the Communist-stimulated agitations in Slovakia stirred up from Moscow. Both he and President Benes referred to the great military strength of their nation. They had a standing army of 400,000 men and 1,000,000 efficiently equipped first reserves, with another 1,000,000 older men who had been trained. I made a mental note that in proportion to the population, this would mean a standing military force for the United States of 4,500,000 men with 9,000,000 more equipped in the first reserves. It did not look much like peace. The Americans in Prague were a great deal less than confident of the stability of the Czech state.

Instead of organizing the state on a cantonal basis, as was expected at Versailles, through which the 2,500,000 Sudeten Germans and 2,000,000 Slovaks would have had a large degree of local self-government, they had organized a centralized state in which the Czechs were in control of all branches. Naturally the Czechs had a bitter recollection of the 150 years of oppression from the Austrian Germans, and were not disposed to trust any German. At the same time there was a considerable expansion of racial egotism among the Czechs. The League had taken them to task for treatment of minorities. Anyway there were disintegrating racial explosive forces smoldering in the country.

I came away impressed with the feeling that they relied a great deal upon power politics and balances of power to solve both external and internal problems. Their military alliances to encircle Germany seemed to me weak, because in Russia there was no fidelity and in France no strength. I did not feel at all confident of their political future.

The Czech people were making steady economic progress; art, music and education had flowered beautifully under their independence. They are a people that compel admiration for their courage and character.

Germany

We motored from Prague, staying overnight at Carlsbad, arriving at Berlin that evening by way of a number of German Government housing projects which I wanted to see. I had not expected to meet any German officials but hoped to get some feeling of what was going on from Americans and some of my old personal friends among the Germans—chiefly former officials, engineers and other professional men. In the morning, however, a high Nazi, Captain Fritz Wiedmann, called at the Adlon, placing a German army officer and two automobiles at our disposal, and informed me that Chancellor [Adolf–ed.] Hitler invited me to call at 12 o'clock with the American Ambassador.[9] I was not enthusiastic as I had long since formed a great prejudice against the whole Nazi faith and its disciples for destroying every foundation of free men. The American Ambassador, Hugh Wilson, however, felt there was no escape; in fact he was delighted, as he had never seen Hitler except in parades. His relations were confined to the Foreign Office officials.

I give here rather an extended account of this interview and that with Field Marshal Goering later on. They give some indications of things to come. We were supposed to be with Hitler for a few moments of a formal call, but he kept us for considerably over the hour. He was aware I had been looking over some of Germany's new housing projects and gave me a very interesting and lucid statement of their experience and conclusions. The latter were, generally, that purchasable detached houses, no matter how small, with gardens and rapid transit were the only satisfactory solution—socially and economically. We ranged over many other economic and social subjects.

My definite impressions were that he was forceful, highly intelligent, had a remarkable and accurate memory, a wide range of information and a capacity for lucid exposition. All this was contrary to my preconceptions based on belittling books—most of which tried to make him out a dummy in front of some group of unknown geniuses. I was soon convinced that this was the boss himself. My adverse reactions to his whole totalitarian aspects were, however, confirmed by minor items which are perhaps unfair weights in judgment. From his clothing and hairdo he was obviously a great deal of an exhibitionist.

---

9. [*Editor's note*: Hoover's meeting with Adolf Hitler occurred on March 8, 1938.]

He seemed to have trigger spots in his mind which set him off when touched like a man in furious anger. The conversation touched on Communism whereupon he exploded and orated. I silently agreed with his conclusions so did not mind. A moment later the discussion spread to democracy, and he began to explode again whereupon I remarked that I could not be expected to agree as I was one of those myself. The subject was dropped and we went on to some less controversial topics.

I of course did not then know that Hitler had already determined upon his barbarous invasion of Austria to take place a few days later. He certainly did not confide in me.

At a lunch given by the American Ambassador I sat next to Count [Konstantin–ed.] von Neurath who had recently been removed as German Minister of Foreign Affairs and [Joachim von–ed.] Ribbentrop substituted. I did not get much out of him.

Field Marshal Herman [Hermann–ed.] Goering had sent word he would like to see me. The American Ambassador was all for it, for he had never seen the No. 2 Nazi either, except in parades. We went to lunch at his hunting lodge, "Karin Hall," some distance outside Berlin. Its only relation to a shooting lodge was the imitation shingles on the roof. It was an immense structure, with rooms as large as a Waldorf dining room crammed with hundreds of thousands of dollars in furniture, paintings and art generally, including two or three busts of Napoleon. Goering came from an impecunious military family and had never legitimately enjoyed more than a general's salary. But this is ahead of my story. When our cars entered the courtyard we were stopped by a sentry for no apparent reason. In a few moments there emerged from a side door twelve or sixteen men dressed as huntsmen and armed with French horns. They played the Huntsman's Call from *Siegfried* the most beautifully I have ever heard. I knew we were certainly in a Wagnerian atmosphere. This being over we pulled up at the entrance and the atmosphere changed again.

Many years ago I had seen a play on the American stage called "The Beggar on Horseback." Its chief impression on my memory was twelve butlers, each with twelve footmen. They were all present here. Perhaps part of those we met were secret service men in livery to prevent visitors doing bodily harm to our host. In any event some of them were always within reach. After some general conversation, Goering asked me into his study where he had a memorandum list of questions, no doubt prepared by some functionary. He was at this time the head of the German Economic Council—the central body busy managing German industry.

He stated that all Germans appreciated the help I had given to Germany during the famine after the last war. And he remarked emphatically that they would never be caught like that again, as they had developed German agriculture to the point where they were practically self-supporting within their own boundaries. I did not believe it. The questions he had in hand mostly related to the general economic situation in the world. In one of them he inquired as to the progress of simplification in American industrial processes initiated under my direction as secretary of commerce which he said they were introducing into Germany. I mentioned that the adoption of such technical standards was necessarily slow because it must be voluntary among manufacturers and others. He replied that "national socialism" has no bothers like that. "If I am given a rationalization (the German term for our word simplification) in the morning, it is in effect by noon." With a prelude that he had been informed of my large engineering practice in Russia before the last war, he asked many questions as to their mineral resources. I restricted my information to facts already well known.

I asked him questions concerning progress upon the now gigantic Herman Goering Iron Works which were being built to treat low-grade Austrian iron ores. I asked particularly about the magnetic processes which I had heard they were using. He told me they were a great success and that it would take about 18 months to complete the works.

He attempted to get into a discussion of American foreign relations, implying that my ideas would no doubt differ from Roosevelt's. I ended these questions by the remark that he would not want any German traveling abroad to take an attitude on foreign relations different from his government's. He laughed. He pushed a button and an illuminated map of Europe appeared on the wall with different brilliant colors for the different countries. He pointed to Czechoslovakia and said, "What does the shape of that country remind you of?" Nothing occurred to me apropos so he continued, "That is a spearhead. It is a spearhead plunged into the German body."

We went out to lunch with a number of young people, each of us attended by at least one butler and a footman. In the middle of the table was a life-sized bust of a lady wearing a string of pearls. Curiosity probably drew my eye to it in contemplation of whether it was brass or gold. Goering noted this and remarked, "My first wife. It's pure gold." His second wife, Emmy, was somewhere in the house.

My net impressions of him, noted at the time, were that he was far more agreeable than Hitler; probably had a clever mind; was utterly ruthless, utterly selfish and probably utterly cruel.

During my stay in Berlin I had a great number of callers. They included Dr. Hjalmar Schacht, former head of the Reichsbank whom I had met in various negotiations in former years; Dr. Bruno Bruhn, former chief engineer of the Krupp Works; Dr. [Theodor–*ed.*] Lewald, former Minister of the Interior in World War I; Dr. Smitz, Food Administrator of Germany after the war; Dr. [Hermann–*ed.*] Schmitz, head of I. G. Farben; and a number of old personal friends, together with American newspaper correspondents. The Reich Minister of Education[10] called and invited me to inspect their various youth movements as he learned I had made some inquiries in respect to them. I did not inspect, but he gave me a full and enthusiastic description of the Government disciplines that began at seven years of age and extended in various stages for about fifteen years thereafter, including their separation of children "gifted in mind" from those "gifted in hand" and the special training of each. He believed they had the formula for developing genius for government and the professions. I did not ask where character came in or the basic freedom of men to choose their own jobs in life.

I noticed that when two or more of my German visitors were in the room together they all talked in banalities. When there was only one he spoke softly, and answered social and economic questions fairly frankly—although only two of them offered any criticism of the Nazis. Dr. Bruhn and Herr Lewald, each whispered to me that Germany was en route to destruction. I had pleasantly dealt with Lewald in connection with Belgian Relief during the first World War.

My greatest illumination on German economic life in these conversations came from a paper manufacturer married to a fine American lady whom I had known before her marriage. Without a word of criticism he described exactly how National Socialism worked in his business, employing 2,000 men. It had denuded him of real control; it had reduced his income to the extent that he had given up his seashore cottage and his Berlin house and was living in a three room apartment. That did not seem to bother him so much as the fact that he had no free will or free judgment left in the conduct of his business and, above all, that Nazi controls had reduced both him and his workmen to a sort of peonage. Wages and promotions were fixed by the government; men could not leave their jobs or be discharged without government approval and every youth was compelled to follow the calling chosen for him.

Germany had long had a most able bureaucracy of non-policy-making officials who really carried on the routine housekeeping of government. They

---

10. [*Editor's note*: Bernard Rust (1883–1945), was Nazi Germany's minister of science, education, and culture from 1934 to 1945.]

had weathered the World War, the postwar revolution and now had mostly weathered the Nazi revolution. I had dealt with them over food supply, transport and other matters during Belgian relief and the relief of Germany and German children after the Armistice in 1918. They were most cooperative after the war and several—some now retired because of age—called to express their appreciation. They told me about great improvements in German agriculture by which Germany should never be reduced to the 1918–1919 situation again.

I, of course, talked at great length to some of my old friends among the American correspondents, particularly Louis Lochner of the Associated Press, and the American professional men in Berlin. The able American Military Attaché, Colonel Truman Smith, gave me a comprehensive account of the arming of Germany. He said that his own and Colonel [Charles–ed.] Lindbergh's investigation indicated they were manufacturing military planes at the rate of 4,800 per annum. His conclusion was that it would take 18 months more to complete their military program up to an initial launching of 2,000,000 men on a battle front. Our Commercial Attaché, Mr. [Douglas–ed.] Miller, one of our old force, gave me a good summary of their industrial program and economic methods in foreign trade which also would seem to require about 18 months for full speed. Something seemed to revolve around 18 months.

One of my inquiries from such sources as I could properly ask was how has Hitler managed to get away with the violations of the Versailles Treaty, re-armament, the occupation of the Ruhr, and other actions without trouble? The invariable answer was "the British are glad to have a military power in Central Europe as a check upon Communist Russia." Nevertheless, I found an almost uncontrollable hate of the British—a survival of World War I.

The Nazi regime with its destruction of personal liberty, its materialistic and militaristic aspects have been fully described elsewhere. My feeling was that no such system could last but that it might cause a world disturbance even if it did not lead to war and would require years to burn itself out. I was convinced it was a structure that would ultimately destroy itself from within. My impressions of Germany are perhaps indicated by the great lift of spirit that came over me the moment we passed over the frontier into Poland. One experienced a sort of indescribable oppression and dread while in Germany. Here was a nation preparing for some aggressive purpose; certainly it was not a system founded on peace. The great theme was "living-space" (*Lebensraum*) for an expanding population. The Nazis were going to expand Germany by peace if possible—by force if necessary. Their fanatical racialism was certainly directed to embracing all Germans in Europe into the German State.

Their expansionist ideas went far beyond that. The only really valuable area was the Balkans and Russia. I was convinced they had no desire for war with the democracies; they saw no profit in it; they were a land people with land armies; they could not cross the sea, and to occupy France, Belgium or the other already overcrowded European countries afforded no opportunity for expansion of German population. To reach Russia, they must crush Czecho-slovakia, Poland or Roumania or obtain a permanent right of way over them. The sum of my view was that an explosion was coming; that they would sooner or later move eastward.

Poland

We were met at the frontier of Poland by Mr. Michael Kwapiszewski of the Polish Foreign Office, who accompanied us throughout our journey. We were greeted at the Posnan [Poznan–*ed.*] station by the Mayor of Posnan [Poznan–*ed.*] with a committee of citizens and a great crowd. The streets were jammed with cheering people waving American flags. A huge reception by thousands of children had been prepared in the public park; a degree was presented to me from the University in the afternoon and a public banquet given by the municipality at the town hall in the evening. On these occasions I discussed the political and economic situation with city officials and university authorities. The latter evidently greatly deplored the drift of Poland toward Fascism and gave me a multitude of pertinent arguments based on their own experience of the greater vitality of individualism.

Accompanied by Polish officials upon a special train, we traveled during the night to Krakow where we arrived on the morning of the 11th. There were great crowds at the station and lining the streets; with schools dismissed, there were children everywhere—vociferous, waving flags, throwing flowers and singing songs. At noon there was a degree conferred by the University with many speeches. The ceremonies were attended by the city authorities whence we adjourned to a long lunch with more speeches. Between events I was able to ask a few questions.

During the two days at Warsaw there was a minute to minute program of receptions, banquets, visits, calls, deputations, degrees and ceremonies of various kinds. At an official luncheon by President Ignace Moscicki, and with the Prime Minister [Felicjan–*ed.*] Slawoj Skladkowski, I had an opportunity to discuss the various questions in which I was interested. I subsequently had about an hour each with the Vice Minister of Foreign Affairs, [Jan–*ed.*] Szembeck [Szembek–*ed.*], the Minister of Education and General [Edward–*ed.*]

Smedly-Ridz [Smigly-Rydz–*ed*.], the "Marshal of Poland" and the real power behind the throne. The American Chargé d'Affaires and American newspaper correspondents called and a banquet was given by joint societies of Poland interested in welfare projects. An official of the American Legation gave me a copy of a "verbal" note from the Polish Foreign Office expressing concern that the reception to me should not cause difficulties with the American government. Obviously they had some fear of Roosevelt's disfavor.

On these occasions in Poland, I had opportunity to converse with over 100 officials, university authorities, our old relief leaders, business and labor leaders. Most of the information poured into me in reply to my questions was obviously colored; many of the opinions guarded, but by check and cross-check certain things stood out.

Compared to the 150 years of degradation before liberation in 1919, the Poles had made astonishing economic, cultural and educational advances. They had in the earlier years made great progress in the redistribution of large land holdings which now had slackened. Despite their progress, however, the picture was still disheartening. Great masses of people were poverty stricken. The country was far behind the rest of the world in the arts of agriculture and manufacturing, relying on sweated labor to compete with other nations in international trade.

[Jozef–*ed*.] Pilsudski had overthrown the democratic regime and instituted a dictatorship with a sort of half Fascist system without German efficiency and then had died. He left a group of Polish colonels in control of the government led by militarists Smedly-Ridz [Smigly-Rydz–*ed*.] and Skladowski. They were a combination of the army and landlord groups. President Moscicki was only a dull dummy. They had driven out the democratic spirits, such as Paderewski and the leaders of the peasant party. The Vice Minister of Foreign Affairs informed me that their real enemy was Russia, that they must depend upon Germany, that the western Democracies were too weak and too far away to be of any help.

I asked the professors of sociology and economics why Poland had turned towards Fascism and a half way dictatorship. The universal answer was that the Communists and socialists were boring from within; that the multiplicity of parties in the parliament made constructive government impossible because the ministries had to compromise on everything to maintain a majority; that the dislocation and unemployment after the depression in 1932, arising from the Austrian collapse, ultimately resulted in practical chaos; that "strong government" had saved the country from Communism. The more frank among them also said that in addition to the abandonment of much of the democratic process and partially completed social measures such as land reform, there was a great deal of corruption.

Enlarging the army had been used as an unemployment remedy—and to take disturbers into discipline. In turn the army certainly now dominated the government. My queries on how far the personal freedoms had been preserved received little illumination. Certainly there was no vigorous opposition press, but there was much more freedom than in Germany. There were no concentration camps or "liquidations." I was told that Pilsudski and his successors promised to protect and restore personal liberty. The whole structure seemed very weak and could not last against any real pressure.

Latvia

On arrival at the Latvian frontier we were met by President [Karlis–ed.] Ulmanis' private car, bringing representatives of the Government and the American Chargé d' Affaires. I was taken directly to the President's Palace in Riga, where I spent some three hours in conversation with him. We had some contacts in 1919 when he led the revolution for Latvian independence.

The President was Latvian born, had been sent to an uncle in the Midwest when 10 years old, had graduated from an American University in economics and had taught in high schools. He had returned to Latvia in 1914 to get his mother and was caught in the war. He of course spoke English in the American idiom and with the great advantage to me that our terms and meanings in political and economic discussion were identical (which is far from the case when talking through an interpreter). After the war he had led in establishing independence and a democratic government in Latvia but a few years later had been defeated by parliamentary vote and retired from office.[11]

He told me that as the country had fallen into complete chaos during the depression he, together with the commander of their army, had dissolved parliament, abolished the supreme court and that he had conducted the

---

11. [*Editor's note*: Hoover's summary of Ulmanis's life is not completely accurate. Born in Latvia (then part of czarist Russia) in 1877, Karlis Ulmanis fled to the United States after participating in the unsuccessful revolution of 1905 against the czar. He graduated from the University of Nebraska in 1909 with a bachelor's degree in agriculture and animal husbandry. He returned to his Latvian homeland in 1913 after Czar Nicholas II granted an amnesty to participants in the 1905 revolution. After Latvia became an independent state in 1918, Ulmanis was elected its first prime minister. He was in and out of office during the 1920s and early 1930s. In 1934, during a period of national crisis, he dissolved parliament and initiated authoritarian rule. When the Soviet Union occupied Latvia in 1940, President Ulmanis was forced to resign. He was soon arrested, deported to the Soviet Union, and imprisoned. He died in the Soviet Union in 1942. In addition to standard reference sources, see Hoover, *Freedom Betrayed*, pp. 76–78.]

government ever since. He said parliamentary government had broken down through multiple parties, the boring from within by the Socialists and the Communists resulting in compromise ministries and inability of a strong government to live; that the government credit and currency had practically collapsed in spending as a cure for unemployment.

He said frankly that he had established an adaptation of Italian Fascism and was acting as a dictator; that he considered it only a passing phase and that later he would be able to restore representative government and the constitutional guarantees.

In reply to my request that he outline the forces and incidents which had led to the revolution, he not only outlined them for Latvia but pointed out the parallels and distinctions in the other twelve European revolutions away from democracy to some form of Fascism. A summary of his statement was:

> There were two roots to revolution and several fertilizers. The first root was that few Continental people are adapted to parliamentary democracy. That form of liberalism conceives at least one majority party. When there are half a dozen, including parties on the extreme right and extreme left, both intent on destroying democracy, it is unworkable. Ministries are then formed by compromise, they are founded mostly on negative action—they cannot last or give strong constructive government.
>
> The second root of revolution was the slow recovery from the impoverishment of war. The financial debacle of 1931, originating in Central Europe, was simply an accumulation of war aftermaths, of which armament, government spending for unemployment, unbalanced budgets, inflation, dislocation of trade channels by the Treaty of Versailles, the dissolution of the economic unit of the Danube Valley, and especially the economic isolation of Russia from the economy of Europe were a part.
>
> The fertilizers were the fifth column operators of the Russian Communist [sic–ed.] boring into labor groups together with the intellectuals who believed in personal liberty but who thought you could have economic totalitarianism and maintain the personal freedoms. This stage with its "Managed Economy" at once curtailed and frightened business from which unemployment and government spending were both increased. Finally it was chaos.

He kept using the word chaos—which was the constant word of explanation of the fall of democratic governments in my discussions in every other country. I said that, if all this was to be the destiny of the United States (which he implied), I would like to know what chaos looked like when it approached. He took me over to the window overlooking the great square at Riga and said:

When you see armed mobs of men in green shirts, red shirts and white shirts coming down different streets, converging into the square, fighting with clubs and firearms, mobs of women and children crowding in and crying for bread, then you know chaos has come.

With the head of the Army I took possession. I thought I could preserve personal liberty by mere restoration of public order, but I quickly discovered that the fundamental cause of chaos arising from the depression was fear—fear in business men, fear in workmen, fear in farmers, fear of currency, fear of the government, all paralyzing economic and moral life. The only way to dissolve fear is more fear. I had to tell men and groups exactly what they had to do and put them in fear of the concentration camps if and when they wouldn't do it; fix prices; fix wages; order employees to start the factories, working men to work and order farmers to bring their products to market; issue new currency, and order people to take it and lock people up if they wouldn't. By and by, the system began to function again; confidence returned and the worst was over. Don't let anyone tell you that personal liberty can survive in totalitarian economics or that preliminary stage called "Managed Economy" can ever stop short of collectivism. Today, Latvia has full employment, remunerative prices and the currency has a sound gold reserve.

He had said that he hoped to restore representative government and the personal liberties. I asked him how he proposed to do it. He said:

The British parliamentary form of democracy based upon territorial representation is a failure. We must establish a fixed executive for a term as in the American form, but our legislative body must be based upon vocational representation. We must realistically accept the fact that we are no longer dealing with a civilization in which individuals are competing with each other for advancement but one in which the competition is by classes and groups.

He was of the opinion that territorial representation had already failed in the United States because representatives were elected by group and class pressures with group and class obligations, and men no longer reflected their own judgments. He mentioned that 500 different groups had offices around our Capitol in Washington to watch their representatives perform. He asserted that it would be better if, for instance, the farmers elected their own representatives than to have some scalawag who promised them the earth. He said, "There would be more integrity, more skill and more responsibility." I opined that I did not entirely agree that America had completely gone into this swamp, but that it would be a valuable experiment for the world if he would try out his plan. He replied:

> America with its "Managed Economy" is well on the road to chaos and the eclipse of democracy; I have been through it and am on the way out.

And with a laugh he added,

> American may need expert advice later on and I will come home—I mean come back—and help.

This slip into the word home echoed in my mind for days, for that was the grip that America takes on men's souls.[12]

We were given a dinner by the American Chargé, Earl Parker, where I was able to learn the views of Latvian Minister of Foreign Affairs, Vilhelms Munters, and the Minister of Finance, Ludwig Elkis. Estonia's President Ulmanis sent us to Estonia by his private car that night. We found on board two officials from the Estonian Foreign Office, Messrs. Edgar Kover and Albert Tatter, to greet and escort us. They had recently served in the Estonian Legation to Russia, and we talked about Russia and their fears of Russian aggression far into the night.

[Estonia-*ed.*]

When we arrived at Tallinin [Tallinn-*ed.*] we were met by the Estonian Minister of Foreign Affairs and the American Minister, Mr. Walter Leonard. We were given a reception at the City Hall although the President of Estonia was ill and could not attend. Various Ministers and the Mayor conducted the affair and I was made an honorary citizen of the city.

The government was mostly Fascist, patterned upon Latvia. The country was prosperous, but the people were haunted by fear of Russia.

That same day Hitler entered Vienna and, as I have said, reviewed the marching crowds from the balcony of the same suite I had occupied two weeks before. The rape of Austria depressed me unspeakably. Weeks had passed since Hitler's threats to Schuschnigg and not a word had come from Britain or France in opposition. Mussolini promptly congratulated Hitler. Britain, France, and Italy had, all of them, intervened to prevent democratic Austria from making a trade agreement with Democratic Germany in 1931. The silence

---

12. I may add here that two years later when Russia violated her treaties and invaded Latvia, Ulmanis was taken prisoner, and a truly great man died or was liquidated in a Russian prison.

of Britain especially impressed me as another link in the proof that they would put up no obstacle to growing German strength and movement eastward.

I found in Estonia as in all the Baltic states that, except for the depression period, the measure of social, economic and cultural progress since 1919 was astonishing. As a matter of fact the standard of living in these states was at the time of my visit higher than any country east of the Rhine.

Finland

We arrived by steamer at Helsinki. There was a crowd of some 30 to 40 thousand upon the pier and neighboring streets who greeted us vociferously. The Prime Minister, Kaarlo Cajander; the Minister of Foreign Affairs, Rudolph [Rudolf–ed.] Holsti; the American Minister and a committee of citizens met us at the dock. During three days every moment from breakfast to midnight was filled with a succession of banquets, speeches, and conferences with officials, leading business men, labor leaders, university officials and finally a degree from the University of Finland. I had opportunities for long discussions with President Kydati [Kyosti–ed.] Kallio; the Prime Minister; the Ministers of Foreign Affairs [Rudolf Holsti–ed.], and Finance, Harold [Väinë–ed.] Tanner; the President of the National Bank, Risto Ryti; also with two former Presidents; the Speaker of the Parliament, Vaino Haklila; the Chancellor of the University, Hugo Suolahti; several professors; publishers of the principal journals and citizens generally. Over eighty serious conversations could be enumerated.

The Finns under freedom had made more economic progress than any other country in Europe. But it was obvious that their officials, at least, lived under the pall of possible Russian aggression. The Finnish people were naturally individualistic and were furiously anti-Communist. They were constitutionally anti-Russian because of hundreds of years of Russian oppression under the Czars. They needed no other lesson against Communism than the contrast between their own land, flowing in milk, honey, meat and white bread, and miserable, hungry Soviet Russia only a few miles away, a deluded, starving, slave-driven people. But this very contrast was one of their dangers, because the Communist leaders of Russia did not like such an exhibit on their very borders. This was true of neighboring Baltic States generally, as well as Poland.

The Finns, as an exception to the rule in Europe, were maintaining successful parliamentary government. I sat with the speaker during one session and gave a short address. The speeches in debate of the measure at hand as translated to me were upon a high level both of oratory and content. When

I asked what the differences were that enabled Finland to hold representative government without an atom of dictation as contrasted to Estonia, Latvia and Lithuania, they said that in Finland, except while suppressed by Russia, they had some form of parliamentary government and personal freedom for 500 years. The other Baltic states have had no background of experience or deep-seated personal rights or representative government. The Communist fifth column had not been able to get as far in Finland as in the other states in carrying their discord and disaster. The Finns would have none of it.

Sweden

At Stockholm we were welcomed by Swedish officials, taken to quarters which were provided by the government and thence to lunch with the Crown Prince—the King being absent. I spent an hour with the Minister of Foreign Affairs, Mr. Rickard Sandler. The American Minister, Frederick Dearing, one of my old associates, provided a dinner where the Ministers [sic–ed.] of Foreign Affairs, together with Dr. Barge Britioth, the leading editor, and Professors [Bertil–ed.] Ohlin and [Gunnar–ed.] Myrdal, economists at Stockholm University, were present. The conclusions on the state of Europe, and the gyrations of the British, Germans and Russians were much the same as elsewhere.

Sweden is often cited as a successful example of "Managed Economy." Nothing creates more resentment in Sweden than the implication that they are collectivists, for their country is a collection of individualists. The confusion arises from their large development of cooperatives. True cooperatives are not Statism; they are a form of capitalism.

Russia

I consolidate here the conclusions I made from the discussion of Russia with scores of statesmen and thoughtful citizens, particularly in the countries near to Russia. They are no doubt tempered by my own views and long experiences with the Russians prior to the World War, during the Armistice, my periods [sic–ed.] as secretary of commerce, and during my Presidency—a period of thirty years. Many of the officials with whom I discussed Russia had recently served as their country's representatives in that country. Moreover, they had intimate information from their mechanics and engineers who were constantly going in and out, engaged at high wages by the Russians.

They were emphatic that Russia was not turning toward "capitalism"—an idea then current in the foreign press at that time. Although workmen were now paid differential and incentive wages, they could not leave their jobs, their wages were fixed by the state, they had no right to strike and if they left their jobs, they left their ration cards behind. The farmers were compelled to work on collective farms and had never more than two free acres (usually less) allotted for truck gardens; they could not leave the farms; they had no voice in prices and they, too, could obtain no food if they left their jobs. There was no right to property or inheritance and, therefore, any savings from wages could be invested only in government bonds and thus reabsorbed by the state.

What was really going on was something very different from a turn to capitalism. Russian society was being restratified onto traditional Russian lines. The members of the Communism Party enjoyed special privileges, larger incomes, opportunity to secure clothing, food and luxuries not available to the great mass. They comprised a new middle class. The more important officials were a higher stratum, already taking on all the pomp and perquisites of the old Russian nobility. The great mass of people were simply serfs to these upper strata under any definition. By any western standards, the country lived in mass poverty. Freedom of religion, speech and of press were nonexistent. The people were kept in complete ignorance of the rest of the world. No one but trusted agents were allowed abroad lest they realize their state of misery. Purported restoration of freedom of worship was an illusion because the churches were being steadily destroyed; or put to other uses. I was given an estimate by a credible source that as places of worship their number had decreased from 46,000 to under 5,000. The people were constantly terrorized by the secret police. "Liquidation" of individuals, groups and classes was commonplace. There were millions of people in concentration work-camps, condemned with no semblance of trial. The number of political convicts under the Czars probably never exceeded 200,000; Stalin had raised the number to over 10,000,000. The execution of "old Bolshevists" had run into the thousands, not the few cases of the Moscow trials. I remarked to a leading statesman in a neighboring country that "Stalin seems to me equally a reincarnation of Ivan the Terrible and Lenin." He replied, "Add to that something of Peter the Great and a large amount of Genghis Khan and you have him."

But above all was the fanatical determination to [communize the world. Every statement of Lenin and Stalin breathed it.][13] The world was faced with an aggressive "Red Imperialism."

---

13. [*Editor's note*: In Hoover's 1955 *Crusade against Collectivism in American Life* manuscript (as returned from the printer on November 30, 1955), this sentence was garbled. I have restored it to its probable wording by taking the words shown in brackets from an earlier version (ca. 1954) of this chapter in the Arthur Kemp Papers, Box 4, Hoover Institution Archives, Stanford University.]

The ten year plan of industrialization was directed far more to military preparedness than to civil supply. The dearth of technical skill due to the original wholesale execution of the middle class has necessitated both the purchase of tools and the hiring of technicians from abroad. A great army was in the making. Two emotions dominated their foreign policies—hate of the Western Democracies and fear of Germany and Japan. To me at that time a curious belief of these surrounding officials was that Russia, out of fear from combined action of Germany and Japan and the ease of collaboration among dictators, would seek co-operation with them rather than with the Western Democracies.

The people in all the Baltic States were in constant terror as to Russia's intentions. She continually preached peace and goodwill toward them and, at the same time, steadily undermined their governments with aggressive fifth columnists directed from Moscow. At the proposal of Stalin all his adjoining states had signed, five years before (in 1932), nonaggression pacts with Russia which had been strengthened again in 1934. These treaties provided against every sort of aggression except 5th columns and bad faith. Despite the documents there was little real belief that they meant much because of the Communist ideology which asserts that no agreements are binding except on the other fellow.

One of their ministers of foreign affairs called my attention to Lenin's statement:

Estonia, Latvia and Lithuania are directly on the road from Russia to Western Europe and are, therefore, a hindrance to our revolution, because they separate Soviet Russia from revolutionary Germany. . . . This separating wall has to be destroyed. . . . The conquest of the Baltic Sea would make it possible for Soviet Russia to agitate in favor of the Soviet Revolution in the Scandinavian countries so that the Baltic Sea would be transformed into the sea of the Soviet Revolution. (*Izvestia*, December 25, 1918.)

One reaction in these states was to lean somewhat on Germany as the lesser of the two evils. The Germans were not carrying on revolutionary ideological penetration; possibly because of their egotism that their system would win on its own merits.[14]

---

14. The subsequent history of Russia's unprovoked attack first upon Finland and then upon the other Baltic States should comprise an unforgettable commentary on treaties with the Communists. Its only parallel in history is the similar morals of the Nazi [*sic–ed.*] and Fascists.

General Conclusion as to the Continent

There could be no doubt that the reaction from Communist penetration had a very large part in all the Fascist revolutions in Europe. The demand for dictatorship and strong government came in part from the demand that the Communist-organized fifth column of destruction be expurgated. There could also be no doubt that one stage in the revolution to some sort of Fascist dictatorship in some part had been due to the intellectuals who, while not favoring Communism, had been infected both from the Communists and the Fascists with the idea that they could maintain a system of personal liberty in combination with totalitarian economics. Their favorite phrase was "Managed or Planned Economy." Their product was the development of increased unemployment.

The belief was universal that the Nazi outcome of national socialism, anti-communism, racialism, militarism and ambition for expansion would result in war with Russia sometime. The German anti–Comintern Pact with Italy and Japan pointed directly to Russia. And such a war meant that the intermediate states would be trampled upon.

What we were witnessing in Germany, Russia and Italy was one of the universal consequences of deep-seated revolutions. In every such revolution new regimes of men come into power. Their constant impulse is to new adventures and new avenues of power. Moreover, such revolutions give birth to a new dynamic spirit in the people. These forces raise high emotions of self-sacrifice, new purpose and new glory, with their impulses for crusade. Sooner or later these pressures take the form of national expansion and military conquest. That was the history of the French Revolution. The American Revolution gave birth to such spirit and such expansion. Fortunately, its dynamic force was able to spend itself in the conquest of a vacant hinterland and not in such conflict with other nations as to produce world war. I was convinced that unless these revolutions in Germany, Russia and Italy took an entirely different course from all others, we should look for trouble.

As I have said, one of the general subjects of my inquiry was concerning the causes of the world-wide depression in 1931, which hurricane swept across the Atlantic and did such damage to us. I was familiar enough with these causes but thought it desirable to secure confirmation. Some of the expressed views I have given already, but I can well sum them up again.

It was not Fascism that caused the economic debacle, for when the depression came in 1931 the only fascist country in Europe was Italy.

If one were to search for the psychological causes, one contribution to the economic debacle was fear and hate. These emotions expressed themselves in a maze of military alliances, increasing armaments, diversion of men from production to armies in every government in Europe.

The Treaty of Versailles had also played a part by the creation of some eight new states without restraint on their erection of trade and transportation barriers which lowered the whole productivity of Europe. Austria had been set in poverty and instability.

General political instability had played a part. Unused to democratic processes the twelve nations who rushed into Parliamentary government of the British type were confronted with a multitude of political parties who were able to agree on only one positive action. That was spending to support unemployment by public works and military establishments. Deficit budgets were universal all over Europe with constant borrowing, inflation and weakening of currencies. These evils in turn drove policies more and more to restriction of imports to protect foreign exchange. More and more government control of internal production and distribution was in course, all of which became a vicious cycle by restricting and frightening free enterprise and thus laying further fuel on the fire of unemployment. And then came the general economic collapse of Europe in 1931–32.

And I may repeat that the effect of Russia's economic isolation should not be overlooked. European economy before the war had been, to some extent, based upon buying large supplies of food and raw materials from Russia and in turn furnishing her with manufactured goods. The Communist Revolution had stifled production and almost ended the surpluses for export and, likewise, destroyed most of Russia's ability to import. In consequence, Europe had been obliged to seek that food and raw material elsewhere and to find new markets for manufactured goods. All this shift served to increase economic instability.

The debacle had started in Vienna, the weakest spot, ten years after the war with the banking and currency collapse amid the instabilities of the rest of Europe. It served in 1930, like Serajevo [sic–ed.] which lighted the fire of war in 1914, to light the fire of world depression. Persons who are unable to connect these events with the economy of the United States need only to remember that following the European panic that continent almost wholly ceased to buy Western Hemisphere exports of wheat, cotton and animal products, thus demoralizing our prices. Under the financial pressure they sold their American securities on our markets, thus demoralizing our security prices. They repudiated or were unable to pay trade and other debts to the United States, thus striking our credit institutions.

There was one other general observation which arose for discussions with University authorities, and was common to all of the states around Germany; that is, Belgium, France, Switzerland, Czechoslovakia, Poland, the Baltic States, and Sweden. With authentic instances and emphasis they agreed that the Nazis had not only destroyed the entire freedom of teaching in the German universities by limiting students to Nazi-approved boys, which had decreased attendance greatly; but of more importance, the limitations on freedom had stifled cultural expansion and research in pure science which was reflected in their scientific publications. These had one time led the world but now were sterile.

Going about over Europe, I was struck with another universal fact. None of the heads of state or their cabinet officers who had conducted their affairs in the World War, either enemy or ally, was retained in office for more than a short time after Versailles, and they never came back. The same applied to the United States. An exception to this generalization sometimes mentioned to me later on was Winston Churchill. He was no real exception for he was ousted from his job in the British Ministry after eighteen months of the war of 1914 and was thus saved from bearing its responsibilities. The lesson involved might be borne in mind by officials cultivating war.

Britain

We planned to remain in London only overnight to catch the "Normandie" home. (It was, however, held up by fog, and we were delayed for five days.) At once some forty British press representatives crowded into our rooms at the hotel demanding to know why I was in England. Upon my reply that I was on my way home after visiting various countries on the Continent, one of them said aside, "The censor has not allowed us to more than barely mention it." I explained I had no other purpose in coming to London than to catch the steamer next day and expected to see no one but some old friends that night for dinner. They then wanted to know what I thought about the possibilities of war. I gave several reasons why I did not think it could possibly happen for at least a year, if ever. In any event, a year would give time for statesmen to stop any such disaster altogether. It was a careful statement of about 600 words delivered from notes and so slowly that every reporter could write it out. The next morning about 200 garbled words appeared. The next day an old friend who was one of the editors of the London *Times* told me that the censor's office had "screened" it. Later on American Ambassador Joseph P. Kennedy called and told me that he could not get even a mimeographed statement or speech into the British press without parts of it being censored out and often the intent greatly distorted. The British evidently were frightened at something.

The first evening I dined with some old friends including Sir Frederick Hamilton. The next morning Lord Walter Runciman came to breakfast with me. Both of these gentlemen were greatly interested in some of my findings and, as I learned later, insisted to Prime Minister [Neville–*ed*.] Chamberlain that he should ask me to call. He made such a request through the American Embassy. The delay of the "Normandie" enabled me to accept his invitation.

I had known Mr. Chamberlain before, but at our last interview in those times we had not been in agreement over some secondary matter. He laughingly referred to that occasion and then abruptly asked for my views as to the political situation on the Continent. I tried to dodge, saying I had been mainly engaged in seeking information on social and economic movements; that I had only hunches as to the political situation; that no doubt the British Government was much better informed than I could possibly be. He laughed and said he had plenty of information but that he would like a hunch. A summary of my statement of which I made a note immediately upon my return to the hotel, follows. Some of it is repetition of my observations already given, but at least it has the merit of summarizing my conclusions at that moment and an indication of British policies. I said:

> The dominant spiritual note of the Continent after the war was hope, confidence, progress and expanding human liberty. The note now, 20 years after, is fear, even despair, and universal continuous restriction of personal liberty—always excepting a few small countries. The explosive centers are Germany and Russia.
>
> The Russians are arming for defense against Germany. They are unceasing in their spread of Communism and the rise of Fascism in many countries has been the antidote. I doubt if the Russians will start anything except revolutions, for the present at least.
>
> The Germans are the most virile people on the Continent. From half a century of internal propaganda they believe they must have more elbow room either through domination of their neighbors or foreign trade and colonies.
>
> Prior to 1914 their face was turned mainly to the seven seas. I believe the face of Germany is today turned east. There are many reasons. They are a land people; they think they must have more land and natural resources to exploit with their own people under their own government. France, Belgium—all Western Europe—is populated. There are no lands or underdeveloped

resources there. The alternative to an eastward land expansion is foreign trade or colonies, for which they would need to become a sea people and enter competition with Britain and America. They have little hope of overseas expansion. Certainly they have not been a sea people since the war. Being a land people the German military strength is land armies. The only great land expanses open to them are in Russia and the Balkans. To this must be added the violent opposition to Communism, as indicated by the anti–Comintern Pact.

Add to pressure toward Russia the dangerous chemicals of desire for revenge, a new stimulation of racialism, national socialism, dictatorship, regenerated militarism, growing armies, the pressure to destroy Communism, and Hitler's unstable character something is bound to explode somewhere. Their egotism and fanned racialism is showing in their absorption of Austria and is the first step in their determination to consolidate all Germans. But beyond that my hunch is that another Armageddon is inevitable and my hope is that if it comes it will be on the Plains of Russia, not on the Frontiers of France.

Western Civilization will be infinitely better off if the Germans fight in the east instead of the west. It would be a disaster to civilization if the western Democracies were dragged down by a war the end of which would be to save the cruel Russian despotism. The net result would at least be a desert of Communism over a large part of Europe if this woe were added to the present weakened condition of most European peoples. My information is that it will take the Germans another eighteen months to complete their plans. After that anything can happen.[15]

These ideas were not discoveries of mine. They were the echo of scores of voices. To my surprise Mr. Chamberlain was outspoken in agreement with this "hunch." He even said these ideas dominated their policies. And then he added:

The weakness of western Europe is France; you have seen it; they are now in alliance with Russia. In consequence Hitler may think he had better polish off the weakest first.

---

15. Although I was unaware of it at that time, Hitler had made a long speech to the top Nazi leaders on November 5, 1937—four months before my visit—in which he outlined Nazi policies to gain "living space." He discussed three alternatives: (1) "autarchy," which he found wanting for lack of raw materials; (2) participation in a world economy, which he considered blocked by other sea powers for many years; and (3) a rapid expansion eastward to annex Austria and Czechoslovakia and dominate Poland. He discounted the possibility of dangerous interference from France and Britain, and therefore favored the third alternative. In stating the problem, Hitler said, "The question for Germany is where the greatest possible conquest can be made at least cost." (Documents from the Nuremberg Military Trial, *Nazi Conspiracy and Aggression* [Washington, D.C.: U.S. Government Printing Office, 1946], Document 386-PS, Vol. III, p. 295.)

Following my interview with Chamberlain, I invited Lord Lothian to break-fast. I had known him well as Philip Kerr, Secretary to Lloyd-George, during the first World War. He had called upon me in Palo Alto some time before to discuss American attitudes toward the European scene. I summarized to him the views which I had expressed to the Prime Minister, with which he was in full agreement. He sent to me a copy of a speech he had made in the House of Lords a year before (March 2, 1937), in confirmation of his views. In this address, he blamed the United States for not having entered into a military alliance with France, and at the same time decried the British involvement in the French system of alliances generally, and expressed non-interventionist views after my own heart. There were paragraphs in this speech which were profoundly prophetic.

> ... This new alliance system, now ennobled by the phrase "collective security," began with the military alliances between France and the Little Entente and Poland. It has now been extended to Russia by the Treaty of Mutual Assistance between France and Russia, a Treaty which has its duplicate or its parallel in the Treaty between Czechoslovakia and Russia. That is one side of the alliance system. Inevitably, as has always happened in the past and as under any system in which alliances are involved between sovereign States, always will happen in the future, that system has begun to produce an alliance system on the other side. It produced what is called the Rome-Berlin axis, it produced the Anti–Comintern Agreement between Germany and Japan....
>
> The Franco-Russian Treaty of Mutual Assistance has the inevitable effect that, if a war breaks out, it tends to make certain that the war shall be in the West and directed at the West and will not be concerned in the first instance with Eastern Europe....
>
> [...–ed.] The only possible cause we could be fighting for would be to insist on the maintenance of the anarchy of Europe; [...–ed.] I venture to think that that is not a cause for which it is worth while laying down the lives of British men....[16]

Apparently at Mr. Chamberlain's instigation, the King asked me to tea. I found him an intelligent young man greatly interested in the situation on the Continent, but he confined himself to questions and offered no views of his own. This was partially due to his difficulty of stuttering.

---

16. [*Editor's note*: Lord Lothian's speech may be found in Great Britain, Parliament, *Parliamentary Debates*, House of Lords, vol. 104, Second Volume of 1936–37 (London: His Majesty's Stationery Office, 1937), pp. 391–403.]

My old friend, Francis Hirst, formerly editor of the *London Economist,* gave a lunch for me at which one of the editorial staff of the *Times* was present with several of the younger members of Parliament. The Belgian Ambassador, Baron Cartier, gave a dinner where several other diplomatic representatives in London were present. I saw several of the American correspondents and other old London friends who called. The American Ambassador called during the last day and stayed for over an hour discussing the outlook. Altogether I was able to canvass the situation with some thirty men of intelligence and information. The British Government sent proper officials to do the courtesies of seeing us off.

My impression of England at this moment was that something, somewhere, had gone out of it. The last war wiped out its best manhood. No new man of great consequence had come up. During the last war there were twenty men who could have carried on as Prime Minister with success. It did not seem to me there were a third of that number now. When the last war came, they raised the first million by volunteers from the best they had; they were exterminated. The Germans, by conscription, spread the loss over all grades of intelligence, and by saving their officers saved even more. Anyway, new men of comparable intelligence and leadership are not coming on in England. There is no extensive group of young, virile men of brains and courage aspiring to government as it was in old England. Chamberlain was a good parliamentary politician and an honest, earnest man, but I could not feel the intellectual vigor of Asquith, Lloyd-George, Milner, Balfour, Law, Lansdowne, or Grey.

On the other hand the British are a dogged, courageous people capable of the utmost sacrifice for their Empire. They had been weakened economically by shifts in world industry. Worse, by failure to maintain a competitive system by anti-trust laws, their industrial plants had become obsolete. The pressures of their system of trusts were profits from price fixing, not on decreasing costs by plant improvement as under our American competitive system. There had been a secret parliamentary inquiry into their industrial problems. I was given their table of comparative unit output per man per hour. It showed from 1 ¼ hours to four hours, an average of 2.2 hours, to secure the same unit output as in the United States. They were also plagued by the economic weakness of the Continent. Before the war they obtained raw materials cheaply as the return cargo for outward movement of coal. They were the corner grocery store of Europe. Oil and electricity have disturbed the raw material cycle and Europe is too poor to buy their manufactures. Their basis of foreign policies is, as ever before and notwithstanding the League of Nations, to maintain a balance of power upon the Continent. They had now, however, only a weak France and an explosive Germany in their scales. They had either encouraged the re-militarization of Germany or at least acquiesced in it as an antidote to Russia.

On March 23rd we finally sailed on the fog-delayed "Normandie." On the steamer I pulled my impressions together into a speech I had agreed to deliver in New York. Many of my observations were of the type which might be misinterpreted and had to be stated with moderation. While I did not want to be an alarmist I did want my countrymen to understand some of the forces in motion that might affect us.

On the steamer at New York I was met by the reporters. Their one question was, "Will there be war in Europe?" I said that it was not immediate and strong forces were working to prevent it.[17]

The Lessons of Europe

Upon my return from Europe I delivered three nationally broadcast addresses summing up my conclusions as to the situation in Europe and its lessons to the American people.

As I have given elsewhere the portions of these addresses relating to the forces which were accumulating for explosion into war, I give here parts of those speeches relating to the march of collectivism and its analogies to the New Deal.

My first address was from New York on March 31st, continuing it at San Francisco a week later, and again at Oklahoma City on May 5th.

I said in part at New York:[18]

> . . . It is impossible for mortal man wholly to evaluate such forces, even on the ground. It is possible, however, to learn more of the furniture in men's minds. And certainly with such contacts it is possible to form impressions of elusive yet potent movements which cannot be gained from this distance. And these forces are cumulating to affect our country greatly. They are cumulating to affect the very foundations of contemporary civilization itself.
>
> Seven obvious forces or factors have come to the forefront in Europe over these nineteen years.

---

17. It did not come for seventeen months—and would not have come then but for the blunders in British diplomacy and the perfidious action by Stalin and Hitler in August, 1939.

18. For full text [of all three addresses–ed.], see [Herbert Hoover,] *Addresses upon the American Road, 1933–1938* [New York: Charles Scribner's Sons, 1938], pp. 309–354 [309–34, 343–54–ed.]. [*Editor's note*: In the quoted passages that follow, I have reproduced the quotations as printed in Hoover's *Addresses* and have corrected without comment a few minor typographical or transcription errors in Hoover's manuscript.]

The first of these is the rise of dictatorships—totalitarian, authoritarian or centralized governments, all with so-called Managed or Planned Economies. Nationalism, militarism and imperialism have certainly not diminished in nineteen years. At one moment (if we include the Kerensky regime in Russia) over 500,000,000 people in Europe embraced the forms of Democracy.

Today, if we apply the very simple tests of free speech, free press, free worship and constitutional protections to individuals and minorities, then liberty has been eclipsed amongst about 370,000,000 of these people. Today there are 30,000,000 less people living under liberal institutions than there were before the War.

The second great movement today, partly cause and partly effect, is the race to arms. Every nation in Europe—Communist, Fascist, Democratic— is now building for war or defense more feverishly than ever before in its history. In five years their expenditures have doubled from four to eight billion dollars annually. That is probably three times as much of their national substance as before the war. Europe today is a rumbling war machine, without the men yet in the trenches.

The third process in motion is increased government debts and deficits. There is hardly a balanced budget in Europe—that is, if we strip off the disguises of words. Government debts are increasing everywhere. Another inflation in some form seems inevitable.

The fourth movement is that every European nation is striving for more and more self-sufficiency in industry and food production for either military reasons or to meet the necessities of "Planned Economy." This applies not only to the Fascist and Communist areas but in some degree to even England and France. The old-fashioned barrier to imports by simple tariffs has proved inadequate to protect these policies. New and far more effective walls have been erected around each nation by quotas, exchange controls, internal price fixing, clearing agreements, and inter-government agreements on both purchases and sales.

The fifth factor is the failure of the League of Nations as a potent force for peace, and its complete replacement by the old shifting balances of power. And they are certainly shifting.

The sixth of these forces is fear—fear by nations of one another, fear by governments of their citizens, fear by citizens of their governments and the vague fear of people everywhere that general war is upon them again. And there is the fear of the promised massacre of civil populations from the air.

The seventh force is the steady increase in some nations of brutality, of terrorism, and disregard for both life and justice. Concentration camps, persecution of Jews, political trials, bombing of civil populations are but the physical expression of an underlying failure of morals terrible to contemplate.

All in all, it is an alarming and disheartening picture. There is a brighter side. Their recovery from the depression has been better than ours. They have little unemployment. Some part of employment, especially in authoritarian states, is due to a boom in armaments, nonproductive public works and subsidized self-sufficiency programs.

I then sketched the war-like forces moving, and continued:

There sounds constantly through this labyrinth the shrill note of new philosophies of government and the echoes of old orders of society disguised in new phrases. There are democracy, socialism and communism of fifty-seven varieties; there is Fascism with its variations from soft to hard; there are autocratic forms all the way from disguised democracy through authoritarianism, totalitarianism to dictatorships and unlimited monarchy. . . .

I need not recall to you that after the war the first rise of hope to this distraught humanity was democracy. [And–*ed.*] the steps by which this liberty was lost are as important to the American people as what actually happens under despotism when it arrives. They indeed need to sink into the American mind.

No country started with the intention to sacrifice liberty. Each started to solve economic problems. In broad terms the steps are always the same. The economic system of Europe before and after the war was relatively free. There were many deep abuses. The new democracies brought resolute reforms on a large scale. But with the handicap of the miserable inheritances of the war Utopia did not come.

Then came socialism hand in hand with its bloody brother communism crying immediate Utopia in a wilderness of suffering people. They took advantage of the tolerance and freedoms of liberal institutions to mislead the people. Their methods were the preaching of class hate, the exaggeration of every abuse, the besmirching of every leader, blame for every ill that swept over their borders. At the next step politicians arose by trying to compromise with these enemies of true liberalism. The result was governments constantly interfering with the proper functions of businessmen, labor and farmers. By these compromises they further weakened the initiative and enterprise of the men who really made the system work. They destroyed that confidence and energy by which free economic systems are moved to great production. Finally came vast unemployment, conflict and desperate people.

But socialism has not triumphed from its work. Socialism and its compromisers in Europe have invariably served only to demoralize democracies and open the door to reactionary forces.

Italy produced Fascism. Fascism promised a new Utopia through restored order, discipline and planned economy, jobs and future for the youth. It is worthy of emphasis that Fascism has always begun in the form of managed [planned–*ed.*] economy. And it was ushered in by the same cries and slogans that they were for the liberation of the common man.

With Managed Planning once started, each step has required another until it arrives at government dictation to business, to labor and farmers of wages, hours, production, consumption, prices, profits, finance, imports and exports. Coercion becomes a necessary instrument, and then it is but a few steps to complete dictatorship. All opposition becomes treason.

Denounce it as we may as despotism and the destroyer of liberty and abhorrent to free men, yet the Fascist form of government is today a raging power. Its acts are being rationalized into a philosophy. It has now embraced a sort of mysticism based on theories of racialism and nationalism. It is becoming a militant ideology. It does not hold within its original boundaries. Fourteen nations in Europe, with 240,000,000 people, have adopted these notions of Fascism in major part.

In Germany Fascism has had its most complete development under the iron rule of the Nazi party. In order better to understand that Nazi regime we must not overlook its *apparent accomplishments.* . . .[19]

So far as material things are concerned the average German is today better off than five years ago. Yet to a lover of human liberty there is another side to even this picture. All the remaining democracies in Europe have made sounder and greater recovery from the depression than has Germany or any of the Fascist states in the same period. And the standard of living is higher in all the Democratic states than in any of the Fascist states.

But for us there are deeper issues in all this. Under this regime the spirit of man is subordinated to the state. The individual must be developed into conformity with the national will as expressed by the leaders. Whatever is deemed by them as good for the state becomes the standard of justice, right, and morality. That has become the basis of law.

And Fascism has demonstrated a way to fool all the people all the time— by suppression of all criticism and free expression; and by drilling children and youth, stage by stage, to a governmentally prescribed mental attitude. A

---

19. [*Editor's note*: Italics added by Hoover in his *Crusade* manuscript.]

controlled press and organized propaganda have poured this new faith into the adults. It has stamped out, or controlled, every form of independent association from Trades Union to Universities. It has instituted a form of terrorism, for the fear of concentration camps is ever present. Its darkest picture is expressed in the heart-breaking persecution of helpless Jews. Intellectual sterility and deadened initiative and individuality are its inevitable results. It is becoming a gigantic spartanism. And let no one believe it is about to collapse.

Parallel with the rise of the Fascist philosophy, Marxian Socialism is a dying faith. They have something in common. They are both enemies of Liberty. The gigantic experiment in socialism in Russia is now devouring its own children and shedding rivers of blood. And it is moving steadily toward a sort of Fascism regime.

Now we must distill some conclusions as to what should be the American attitude toward all this maze of forces. We may divide our relations to them into three parts. Our relations to these forces politically; our relations to them economically; and our relationship to them socially.

I then discussed our international relations with them:

[. . .–ed.] I wish further to discuss [. . .–ed.] our American relationship to the vast ferment of new and old social philosophies which boils furiously throughout the world. The wholesale eclipse of democracy must concern us. Our national mission is to keep alight the lamp of true liberalism. But it is in the United States that we must keep it alight.

Every few centuries the world gives birth to new systems of government and life. Or it resurrects old systems under new phrases. In any event they mostly revolve around two old and diametrically opposed concepts—that the development of the individual is the prime purpose of the state or the individual is the pawn of the state. . . .

True liberalism is not a mere middle ground between Fascism and Socialism. Both Fascism and Socialism hold to the other concept—that the individual is but the pawn of an all-wise, omnipotent state. Liberalism has no compromise with either of these two forms of the same concept.

Let no man believe in either of two popular misapprehensions so widespread in this country today. This philosophy of Communism is not imposed, suddenly, new born, from the bottom up. And this thing called Fascism is not imposed, suddenly, new born, from the top down. Both grew in prepared soils. Both are the aftermath of a gradual infection of Democracy, a gradual perversion of true liberalism.

And let me again repeat that Democracies are first infected by the plausible notions of "Cure the business slump" through so-called economic planning. Every step in this direction requires another. Every step further demoralizes free economy. And step by step more force and coercion must be applied until all liberty—economic and personal and political—is lost.

Let no man mistake that we in America have until now avoided the infection of these European systems. If our own so called Planned Economy is not an infection from the original stream of Fascism it is at least a remarkable coincidence.

The leader of German Fascism in a speech last week hurled the taunt to democracies that "not a single decent nation has died for the sake of democratic formalities." To the extent that races do not actually die because they forfeit individual liberty, that may be true. But what is far more important is that when true Liberty dies, then Justice and Truth die. And intellectual progress and morality die also.

I have no doubt that Fascism will fail some time, just as Marxian Socialism has failed already. The stifling of intellectual progress, the repression of the spirit of men, the destruction of initiative and enterprise, will offset all the efficacies of planned economy. Even economic life cannot succeed where criticism has disappeared and where individual responsibility is constantly shirked for fear of the state. Even in Fascist countries liberal ideas are not dead and will not be downed. Every despotism today lives with fear of liberty at its heart—or there would be no concentration camps. [. . .–ed.]

[. . .–ed.] Though I had little need for confirmation in my faith, I pray God that this nation may keep its anchors firmly grounded in intellectual liberty and spiritual freedom. These values can be preserved only by keeping government from the first pitfall of direction or participation in economic life—except that it shall sternly repress, by due process of law but not by edict, every abuse of liberty and honesty.

The protection of Democracy is that we live it, that we revitalize it within our own borders, that we keep it clean of infections, that we wipe out its corruptions, that we incessantly fight its abuses, that we insist upon intellectual honesty, that we build its morals, that we keep out of war.

That is the greatest service that this nation can give to the future of humanity.

I continued this discussion in a nation-wide broadcast from San Francisco a week later at a public meeting, welcoming me home, and a month later from a great meeting at Oklahoma City. My purpose was to translate the forces in motion in Europe to understanding of their influence upon individual Americans.

While these two addresses are devoted in the main to the American scene, yet they reflect the European background and are therefore given here.

At San Francisco I said:

I am always glad to get back to the West. It has certain outstanding advantages. This spot is 7,200 miles from certain spots in Europe. If your imagination is lively enough to imagine California under conditions on the Continent our advantages would be even more manifest to you. [. . .–ed.]

If we had an up-to-date authoritarian state, there are still other possibilities of discomfort. Then your soul belongs generally to the state. If you carry over the old idea that perhaps it belongs to you, then you go to a concentration camp to rest your nerves. If you are a farmer you plant what the agricultural policeman tells you to plant. And you raise the pigs and cows he thinks are good for the state. If you are a worker you work where you are told. And you work the hours you are told. And you get the wages you are told. Your trade union having been dissolved you can belong to a government recreation project. You will also be taught to sing cheerful songs in the recreation hours and to march all about. You have social security if you conform. If you do not conform you get security in concentration camp. You will be secure anyway. So as not to have your doubts raised and your feelings harried by critics of this more redundant life they are just put away in the same concentration camps. Your freedom of speech is a sort of a one-way street. You do gain something by saving half the public speeches in the country by doing away with all those of the opposition. Your newspaper contains what the all-powerful thinks is good for your soul. And your books are carefully chosen that your economic and romantic feelings shall not be polluted. If you kick about the way the government does it you will be placed under protective arrest to prevent harm coming to you.

There are some forces in motion in the United States which might make California an uncomfortable place. But we will at least deliver a lot of free speech before that time arrives. [. . .–ed.]

Turning to the American Scene

And now let me return for a moment to the American scene. The real, the immediate, the pressing problem of this country is unemployment. When I went abroad we had 10 million or 11 million unemployed. I return to find they have increased by another million or two. . . .

That 12,000,000 unemployed is obviously the indication of something terribly wrong in our own economic machine. Let me say something perhaps elementary on this American economic machine and the way it starts and stops. It moves forward and employs people only when there is confidence and hope. A large part of its movement forward depends on confidence and hope. A large part of its stoppage comes from fear. When confidence breaks down fear seizes control and unemployment becomes rampant. Prosperity and depression are greatly influenced by these two emotions. There are other factors but of later years these emotions have become immensely more potent than ever before.

One reason for this is the increasing proportion of postponable goods in our standard of living. If you will look over the country you will find that about 40 percent of what the American people consume can be postponed. About 60 percent are absolute necessities and cannot be postponed. A new pair of shoes can be postponed for three months; a suit of clothes six months; an automobile for a year. What we call durable goods, such as houses, can be postponed longer than shoes. If a shiver of fear comes over the country most people postpone the purchase of something. And instantly somebody somewhere has lost a job making shoes or automobiles or houses. In turn those out of a job have to postpone the purchase of even necessities. And the fellow who has a job, seeing somebody lose his job, then also postpones something out of fear of losing his job. Then we are on a downward spiral.

This danger does not arise in those Asiatic countries where people have only the bare necessities. It existed to a much less extent in the United States fifty years ago. In other words, when we built up the American standard of living and jobs of men to include an automobile, a radio, an extra suit of clothes, and a trip to the movies, we introduced a most delicate adjustment.

In the United States today everybody has lost some confidence and everybody has some fear. It is nonsense to say that either big or little business is on a strike. It is not so. Business is yearning to sell automobiles and new suits of clothes. It is the people who are scared. Big business or little business is not scared to take on men if anybody will give them an order for goods.

With 12,000,000 people out of a job it is our business to explore the cause of these fears. I was especially interested to find if any of them were coming from abroad. One of the causes which sucked us into the whirlpool of world-wide depression in 1931 came from Europe.

There has been general recovery in Europe from that depression. There is no financial panic brewing over there to pull down our credit structure as in 1931. Their regained economic strength is even helping us now by purchasing our goods, whereas in 1931 they stopped their purchases abruptly.

In the democracies there is no unemployment at all comparable to ours. They are indeed prosperous. France is of course having trouble because she adopted the New Deal two years ago.

Even in the authoritarian states and the dictatorships there is less unemployment than we have per million of people even if we deduct those employed manufacturing arms. It is true their standard of living is less than the democracies but the people are largely employed.

. . . Certainly we have no fear of war against us. There is no threat of any one pouring fire or explosives on our cities out of the sky. There is not the remotest chance that our national independence will be challenged from abroad.

Certainly this great fear among the American people does not come from outside our borders.

We ought to explore for the sources of fear at home. Today we have no inflated bubble of gambling credit or a weak banking system that we must be afraid of as there was in 1929. The banks are full of surplus credit. There is no over-expansion in industry in America. In fact we are short of equipment. There is no consequential over-stocking of goods. There is no over-expansion of buildings and homes. In fact there are not enough good homes. There is no crop failure or threatened shortage of food or clothes. Every one of the factors and forces within our borders that ordinarily produce fear and its consequence in unemployment is absent.

Yet we are stark facing that fact of 12,000,000 people out of jobs. Every one of those families is suffering from privation and worry. And there is no anxiety on earth like that of not knowing where the next week's living for your family is to come from. Some newspaper said the other day that I must get satisfaction out of this depression. I don't. I don't get satisfaction out of human misery.

I do have a recollection of a bitter slogan used against us in the 1932 campaign. They said often and harshly that it could not be worse. But some one said that was about forty billion dollars ago. And we must live in the present.

It is the first job of America to restore genuine self-respecting jobs in productive enterprises. It transcends all other questions. It transcends all party politics. It must be met without flinching, whether it be government theories, taxes, waste, corruption, unmoral acts of men in high places.

I then reviewed the forces making for our unemployment.

If we again return to the European scene, we find seven or eight Democracies which refused to adopt these courses of Planned Economy. They are today the most prosperous nations in the world despite the dangers under which they live. One other great Democracy, France, did adopt these ideas. They are today also in deep trouble. The other gigantic fact of European experience is that some twelve or fourteen nations belonging to Western civilization, embracing nearly three hundred millions of people, have moved from the foundations of popular government and free men to the foundations of authoritarian government where personal liberty is extinguished in the state.

And at one stage in this transformation they compromised between true liberalism and socialism or with attempts at government dictation of business, farming, and labor. That is the common denominator when democracy has fallen. They tried various breeds of Planned Economy. They tried to mix social philosophies. These attempts at mixture generated their own hates and fears.

They paralyzed with fear the delicate confidence and hope of the future with which all business moves and revives in a free system. They undermined the initiative and enterprise of men which is the sole mainspring of progress to free institutions. Out of fear they produced more and more deeper depressions and panics which finally reached chaos where men surrendered all liberty to the State to save themselves. [. . .–ed.]

I was at the very seat of Fascism when one of our important government officials broadcasted over Europe an attack upon Fascism itself. It was received with great amusement. And I was compelled to listen to a relation of the uncanny parallel of steps taken in the United States under so-called Planned Economy with those which had bred the sort of chaos in Europe from which Fascism sprang.

I do not say that our economic system has been brought to this dangerous point where Fascism is its destination. But with all the solemnity I can command I do say that the direction that we are going in today is precisely that which in the end creates the demoralization from which Fascism invariably springs.

Whether our Planned Economy is an infection from Europe of creeping collectivism or whether it is a native American product is less important than its actual results upon us and where it leads to.

And where have we arrived? At a discouraged and fearful people, with 12,000,000 unemployed. Is not the very system itself making the one-third ill fed and ill clothed?

The primary objective of our system must be to eliminate poverty and the fear of it.

Men cannot be free until the minds of men are free from insecurity and want. But security and plenty can be builded only upon a release of the productive energies of men from fear and handicap. That America must have.

In the address at Oklahoma City, on May 5, 1938, I said:

I am going to speak to you on the dangerous road for democracy. I wish to speak to you not as Republicans but as citizens. For these things reach to fundamentals far deeper than party labels. At my position in life, my sole concern over political parties is that they stand up and face these fundamentals with courage and intellectual honesty. I wish to see unity among all right thinking men and women in this time of national difficulty. [. . .–ed.]

And before I go further, let me define the economic system which is inseparable from free men.

That is private enterprise regulated to prevent monopoly and exploitation. For that the government must be a vigorous umpire and not a Simon Legree. Nor is a free system a frozen system which resists reform to meet new abuses, new inventions or responsibility for the less fortunate. And our system cannot be free unless it protects the people from exploitation and calamity and unless it strives for equal opportunity among men.

We Americans are travelling a road dangerous not only to such a system but to liberty itself. We are faced with 12,000,000 of our own countrymen unemployed and in want. These things are not unrelated. [. . .–ed.]

It is cheaply superficial to say that these people become [became–ed.] despaired, tired of unemployment, of hunger, and misery, and class-conflict. That is true, but what caused all this vast unemployment, misery and conflict?[20]

Ten days ago I delivered an address upon the moral degeneration in democracies which contributes to their fall.

Tonight I propose to discuss what economic causes contributed to these miseries which ended in the suicide of liberty. And I am not interested in this as an academic student of government. I am interested because it concerns the future of liberty in our country. And I am interested because the experiences of these nations point to the causes of 12,000,000 lost jobs in our country today.

Not one of these 14 nations started with the intention to surrender liberty. They started by adopting panaceas to cure slumps or overcome economic difficulties. They all undertook New Deals under some title, usually Planned

---

20. [Editor's note: Hoover omitted three paragraphs immediately preceding this one. It is clear from the context that "these people" in this paragraph referred to fourteen nations in Europe that he said had abandoned democracy for "some form of dictatorship" since the end of World War I.]

Economy. In variable doses they undertook credit and currency manipulation, price fixing, pump priming, and spending with huge deficits and huge taxes. Step by step they sapped the vitality of free enterprise by government experiments in dictation and socialistic competition. They had the illusion that true liberalism was a middle road between Fascism on the right and Socialism on the left. They sacrificed free enterprise to pursue the Utopias of both of them.

Every succeeding step was egged on by politicians fanning class hate, exaggerating every abuse and besmirching every protesting voice. Every step was accompanied by greater corruption of the electorate, increasing intellectual and moral dishonesty in government. They did produce periods of artificial prosperity, only to collapse again.

These forces finally jammed the mainspring by which private enterprise is moved to production. That is confidence. Fear and unemployment paralyzed the consumption of goods.

It was at the end of this dangerous road that hunger came to their cities with violent labor conflict and final despair. Those desperate people willingly surrendered every liberty to some man or group of men who promised economic security, moral regeneration, discipline, and hope. [. . .–*ed.*]

Let there be no mistake; a new way of life is rising in the world. It directly challenges all our American concepts of free men. And let me tell you that upon my recent journey over and over again men of responsibility breathed to me one prayer. They did not seek military alliances. They did not seek loans. What they prayed was that we hold the fort of liberty in America. For that is the hope of the world.

Now what road have we been travelling in the United States? We followed a sign marked Planned Economy, the way to end all depressions. The subtitle was To Abundant Life. We at least know now where we have got to. It can be said in two sentences.

The New Deal started with a Government debt of $21,000,000,000 and today finds itself with a debt either direct or guaranteed of $42,000,000,000. It started with 12,000,000 unemployed; it finds itself after five years with 12,000,000 unemployed. [. . .–*ed.*]

And now let us examine the dangerous road we have been travelling.

It would startle this country if our people had a detailed list of the powers over their daily life they have surrendered to the President and his bureaucracy. More and more we have submitted to authoritarian action. A large part of these powers are invisible. But they weave together and expand within a bureaucracy. And bear in mind, power is just as powerful through subsidies and favor of political jobs as it is by coercion and jail.

And the sheep's clothing of these powers is that righteous phrase, Planned Economy. The Communists first invented it. The Fascists adopted it. It still serves to fool the people. It carries the illusion that it means forward-looking. But its reality is the wolf of bureaucratic power. And it bites the flock.

Never before except in a dictatorship have such powers been given to the head of a state. And the craving of bureaucracy for more power is never satisfied. Failure does not stop their dreams; it only multiplies their alibis.

If these are not at least the infant steps along the dangerous road that European democracies took, then they are an astonishing parallel.

We also have had credit and currency manipulation, pump priming and spending with huge deficits. We have had huge increase of taxes, government restriction of production, government price fixing. We have had artificially increased prices and genuinely stifled consumption. And these manipulations are shot through with dictation and threat. They are accompanied by forays of the government into competition with private enterprise. But why recite all the creeping collectivism?

This country was definitely on the way to recovery in 1932 with all the rest of the world. These manipulations beginning in 1933 at first retarded us. Then they produced an artificial and distorted appearance of recovery claimed in 1936–37. Like all shots in the arm, a lovely time was had by all. Except for some 5,000,000 men who never got jobs. [. . .–ed.]

And now let us analyze this whole New Deal philosophy a little more deeply in its practical aspects. We can at least discover why attempts of government to manage a system of private enterprise must have a Nemesis — or several of them — so long as there is any freedom left in it.

The first is that free private enterprise will not mix with either the dictation or the government-competition, for one stymies the other. Germany and Italy have demonstrated that complete Fascism will work for a while. Russia has demonstrated that Socialism will not work. America has demonstrated for over 160 years that a free system will work. Just as did the 14 fallen democracies of Europe, now America is demonstrating all over again that a mixture will never work.

A drop of typhoid in a barrel of water will sicken a whole village. A few drops of Socialism or Fascism is poison to private enterprise. The Federal Government goes into less than ten percent of the power business. At once the investor, fearful of government competition and seizure, fears to hazard his capital. And hundreds of thousands of men lose jobs. . . .

Under these mixtures every man must conduct his business with one eye on Washington. Every plan of action is a bet on what bureaucracy may do. Every farmer must act with an eye on an agricultural agent. Every investment of savings is a gamble on what will be done to the currency. Every future price of a commodity is not a judgment on the law of supply and demand, but another bet on Washington. Every venture into new enterprises must be calculated upon what will be left after punitive taxes.

All along the line it weakens the judgment of men. It sickens initiative and enterprise. It knocks the confidence out of men. It substitutes fear. It destroys millions of jobs. [. . .–ed.]

And let me add that there . . . will not be real recovery with full or permanent employment if we continue down this dangerous road. And we are not going to go down that road without a lot more fighting free speech.

CHAPTER 9

The Crusade against Collectivism from the Landon Defeat in 1936 to the Congressional Election in 1938 (Continued)

The 1938 Congressional Campaign

Despite the Republican debacle in 1936, I felt that the Congressional candidates, being free from the compromises of the Presidential candidate, could gain ground on the real issues. There would be about 460 Republican Congressional and Senatorial candidates in the field. I know [knew–*ed.*] that many of them would have the courage to face the major issue of our times.

I had received urgings from many persons of meagre political understanding that inasmuch as the supporters of the American system in the combined North and South comprised a majority, we should bring about a union of these forces. It was devoutly to be wished. To test out its possibilities, I arranged with former Secretary Arthur M. Hyde[1] that we make a journey of inquiry through the solid South, he taking its western parts, I the eastern ones. We arranged many "off the record" meetings with substantial Southern Republicans and Jeffersonian Democrats. Obviously, the Republicans of the North could not accept their insistence on "white ascendancy." That would be a violation of both their principles and their tradition. We could agree upon the fundamental of collectivism, but always a black apparition rose to stop any consequential action.

Either out of moral zeal or to capture the negro vote in the North, Mr. and Mrs. Roosevelt for years advocated everything with respect to the negroes that was obnoxious to the Southern Democrats, yet they still voted for the Roosevelts. The reason was obvious. By holding the Democratic Party in power in their state and county governments, they held the power over the

---

1. [*Editor's note:* Arthur M. Hyde (1877–1947) served as Hoover's secretary of agriculture from 1929 to 1933.]

negro. Some of them even liked Mrs. Roosevelt's negro agitations as it took votes from the Republicans in the North, and gave the Democratic party command of the Federal administration with its patronage. But equally important, the President spent a volume of Federal money in the South that amounted to an indemnity for the Civil War every twelve months, all of which transcended the collectivist issue and its breaking down of states' rights, etc.

Improving the Party Platform

I had never given much for party platforms—composed as they were by delegates collected from each of the states at the last moment and many of whom were little acquainted with issues outside their own areas. Their product was necessarily much by way of compromise between pressure groups and regional interests, all put together when weary under midnight oil. However, in 1937, as a life [lift?–ed.] to the Party from its depths, I thought it might be worth while to try for a real platform in advance, making exhaustive research and taking ample time in the hope that it might be more direct and might influence the next Convention. In any event, it would show that the party was not dead. To that end, I secured that the Republican National Committee set up what was in fact an advance "resolutions committee" by representatives from each of the States. Glenn Frank, President of the University of Wisconsin, was appointed Chairman. He was an able and thoughtful man. The setting up of the Committee itself and its public discussions did serve to keep interest in the party alive. But Frank found the currents of politics too complex, and too conflicting for much but eloquent generalities. The Republican Party was not yet ready to vigorously realign itself on the fundamental issue of collectivism. The statement issued certainly did not cause a national sensation.

Despite this, I continued to hammer away on . . . [sic–ed.] subject.[2] In July [September–ed.], 1937, upon request, I contributed an objective analysis of where the Republicans should stand on this issue to the *Atlantic Monthly*.[3]

Again in an address to an audience of Young Republicans, broadcast nationally from Boston on October 26, 1937, I traversed the whole issue, saying in part:[4]

---

2. [*Editor's note*: In his 1953 redraft of *The Crusade Years*, Hoover wrote: ". . . hammer away on the subject." Why he inserted an ellipsis in his 1955 version, printed here, is unknown.]

3. [*Editor's note*: See Herbert Hoover, "The Crisis and the Political Parties," *Atlantic Monthly* September 1937, pp. 257–68, reprinted in Herbert Hoover, *Addresses upon the American Road, 1933–1938* (New York: Charles Scribner's Sons, 1938), pp. 243–63.]

4. [Hoover,] *Addresses upon the American Road, 1933–1938*, pp. 265, 270–1, 274–5.

I am interested in building up the Republican Party not as a partisan but as a citizen. So let us look at it as citizens and not as politicians. We are concerned now with something greater than a game or securing public office.

The Republican Party even out of office is a national necessity as a unified opposition party to check excesses and protect minorities. But it has a mission far greater than just being against. . . .

This party must have a fighting cause; it must have an affirmative program; and it must present effective methods; it must have a forward purpose; it must have idealism, and it must be responsive to the needs and crises of the people. If a party should come into power without such definite purpose it would be of little good to the nation. It would mean only that a few people have got up to the public trough. . . .

[. . .–ed.] Our country must have emancipation from the moral degeneration of current government methods. It must have emancipation from what Walter Lippmann so aptly calls "gradual collectivism." . . . It must make possible humanitarian objectives which are otherwise wrecked by wrongful and ineffective methods. . . .

If that be so, all the wiles, the tricks, and the petty artfulness of politics are of minor moment. [. . .–ed.]

I have used the term "True Liberalism." I would prefer to use the more direct term of "Americanism." The term liberal has now become the fashionable clothing of all collectivists, whether they be New Dealers, with creeping collectivism, or frank and open Socialists, or the unconscious Fascists. [. . .–ed.]

That "gradual collectivism" is creeping upon us should be evident by this time to any understanding American. The government manipulation of money and credit, government restriction of production, government control of hours and wages, the entry of the government into competitive business on a large scale, government coercion of upright citizens—these are but part of it. The conflict of the two systems creates at once attack on constitutional government. Undermining the independence of Congress, packing the Supreme Court, the weakening of local and State government, the new proposals to invade judicial authority under the guise of administrative reorganization are but part of the centralization of government and the increase in personal government.[5]

Once economic life is started in this direction it creates its own demand for more and more personal power. And one of its results is a Frankenstein of hate

---

5. [*Editor's note*: Probably in the interest of condensation, Hoover somewhat altered the wording of the last two sentences of this quotation. I have restored the original wording.]

and national disunity. There cannot be a system part collectivist and part regulated private enterprise. The very conflict of the two systems creates one economic emergency after another. We witness that at this very hour. Do you think the confidence of men, the enterprise of men, is not today chilled to the bone?

I then discussed our present social and economic issues in detail and concluded:

And again I return to my opening.

There is a mighty service to be performed. This party must make the humanitarian objectives of the nation possible which are wrecked by wrongful and ineffective methods. It must reform destructive economic policies which undermine the standards of living of the economic middle class and thus all the people. It must emancipate the people from this creeping collectivism and restore true liberalism. It must emancipate them from the moral degeneration in government. The interest of the nation requires that the Republican Party shall provide the country with positive and affirmative principles and proposals that will meet these yearnings of the people today for a way out and forward. It is a gigantic task. But should we not make a beginning?

That is a task in which youth must join.

You have the blood and urge of your American forbears. You are as good stuff as they. You are better trained and equipped than they were. I have no doubt of your character and your resolution.

On November 8, 1937, I was asked to deliver the address in celebration of the one hundredth year commemoration of Elijah Parish Lovejoy at Colby College, Waterville, Maine. I devoted it mainly to the current corruption of freedom by lying propaganda:[6]

In an address broadcast at Chicago on December 16, 1937, I said in part:[7]

[. . .–ed.] It is currents deeper than this recession that we are discussing tonight. . . .

Whether Planned Economy is an infection from Europe of creeping collectivism or whether it is a native American product is less important than its actual results upon us. . . .

The central idea of Planned Economy which concerns me is the gigantic shift of government from the function of umpire to the function of directing, dictating and competing in our economic life. No one will deny that

---

6. *Addresses upon the American Road, 1933–1938*, pp. 276–280.
7. Ibid., pp. 287–299.

the government is today increasingly controlling prices, wages, volume of production and investment. [. . .–*ed.*]

. . . Transient political officials cannot plan the evolution of 120,000,000 people. We cannot assume that Americans are incapable of conducting their own lives and their daily affairs for their own good. We cannot increase standards of living by restricting production. We cannot spend ourselves into prosperity. We cannot hate ourselves into it either. We cannot constantly increase costs of production without increasing prices and therefore decreasing consumption and employment. We cannot place punitive taxes on industry without stifling new enterprise and jobs. [. . .–*ed.*]

Today . . . the citizen confronts an . . . unpredictable factor in conducting his affairs. That is political action. The people move hourly upon their own judgments as to supply and demand, as to prices and outlook. But today every plan in life is a bet on Washington. Every investment of savings is a gamble on the currency. Every future price is another bet on Washington. [. . .–*ed.*]

When the government expands into business then in order to protect itself it is driven irresistibly toward control of men's thoughts and the press. We see it daily in propaganda. . . .

Let me shortly sketch what I conceive to be a philosophy of government and economics which would promote this sort of living and would preserve free men and women in our modern world. It is no magic formula. It does not lend itself to oratory.

First: The main anchor of our civilization must be intellectual and spiritual liberty. Ideas, invention, initiative, enterprise and leadership spring best from free men and women. The only economic system which will not limit or destroy these forces of progress is private enterprise.

Second: In the operation of the economic system there is but one hope of increased security, of increased standards of living, and of greater opportunity. That is to drive every new invention, every machine, every improvement, every elimination of waste, unceasingly for the reduction of costs and the maximum production that can be consumed. We must work our machines heartlessly, but not our men and women.

By these means we sell goods cheaper. More people can buy. And thereby we have higher wages, more jobs and more new enterprise. New industries and new articles add again to the standards of living. That is the road to more jobs; it is the cure of temporary machine displacement. That is no robbery, it is progress.

Third: To preserve freedom and equal opportunity we must regulate business. But true regulation is as far from government-dictated business as the two poles. [. . .–*ed.*]

Our transcendent need at this moment in America is a change in direction toward this system.

A confident, alert, alive and free people, enthused with incentive and enterprise, can quickly repair losses, repay debts, and bury mistakes. It can build new opportunity and new achievement.

The year 1937 closed with some greater understanding of the real issues. But the difficulties of drilling into the public mind the philosophic ideas which lie at the base of American life were considerable to say the least. The people naturally and properly were concerned mostly with their daily tasks. Social philosophies were over the heads of most of them. As I often said, they had breathed their fundamental concepts from the air rather than formulating them into a doctrine. However, my hope was to energize the minority of thinking people into action in the confidence that the gospel would some day prevail.

The Republican Campaign Committee of the House of Representatives at last realized the importance of the collectivist issue and as there were few who could command nation-wide hearings they asked me (for the first time) to enter this arena for their members in the campaign of 1938. I spent two months in careful preparation of three nationally broadcast addresses. They were well heralded by the Committee. The first was delivered at Kansas City on September 28th on "Morals in Government"; the second at Hartford (on October 17th) on "Undermining Representative Government"; the third at Spokane (November 5th) on "The Economic Consequences of the New Deal."

It may be difficult for those who come after us to envisage our struggle to open the eyes of our countrymen to the dangers of New Deal collectivism. Perhaps the nature of our problem may be obtained from rather full quotation from these three addresses.

[1938: Three Campaign Addresses–ed.]

[First Address (Kansas City, September 28, 1938)
Morals in Government–ed.]

At Kansas City I said in part:[8]

When we come to questions of immorality in government there can be no soft and respectful argument. The only emotion appropriate to immorality is indignation. That is the time to take the gloves off. They are off.

---

8. For full text [of all three addresses–ed.], see [Hoover, Further] Addresses upon the American Road, 1938–1940 [New York: Charles Scribner's Sons, 1940], pp. 3–57.

These moral forces which affect the character and the soul of a people will control its destinies. Where they enter government they far transcend all political partisanship. The progress of mankind is in proportion to the advancement of truth and justice. Standards of truth and justice are what we usually call morals.

I have little need to define moral standards. The American people learn them at their mothers' knees. They include not only money honesty. They include telling the whole truth. They include keeping one's word. They include fidelity to public trust.

They exclude hypocrisy. They exclude creation of hate. Half-truth, hypocrisy and hate are departments in the art of demagogues. The polite phrase for all this is intellectual dishonesty.

It is moral standards in government which create sturdy self-reliance and self-respect among citizens. It is moral standards that create perceptions of what degrades the faith of people in self-government.

During the last six years the growth of the cancerous idea that there are two standards of morals in American life has been foisted on the American people. That malignant idea is that political morals are a lower code than private morals. The apology for this double standard for government has been that the end, or to use New Deal words, "the objective," justifies the means. . . . In practice it works out that government must be conducted by fooling the majority of the people all the time or buying them part of the time.

When citizens are crooked among themselves the damage falls mostly upon themselves. And it may affect their chances in the Life Eternal. But when government is immoral, it damages the morals of a whole people.

And let me say at once I do not claim that political morals have been perfect in this Republic under any political party. There have been sporadic incidents and there have been black spots which have been our shame. But during the past six years there has been systematic degeneration.

. . . It is the moral slide more even than the economic degeneration that in the last twenty years has carried nation after nation over the precipice to dictatorship.

I propose to illustrate what I mean with a few examples. In this single address I can deal only with seven or eight. If you look around you will be able to collect others.

Sample I
The foremost of the New Deal Party's alphabetical morals is the G. E. A. A.—Get Elected Anyhow Anyway.

For fifty years the American people have fought the politicians to dig out the spoils system. They fought not alone to stop corruption but to stop government employees from packing elections. [To do it]⁹ They built a great moral dike of non-political selection by merit. In six years we have lost forty years of the ground gained by that moral crusade.

At the end of my Administration 83 percent of all Federal employees had been selected upon merit by the Civil Service Commission. That is the highest figure ever attained. And if a Democratic Congress had been willing it would have been 95 percent.

During the six years of Mr. Roosevelt's Administration over 300,000 office holders have been politically appointed to the Federal government. They were without the merit requirement of the Civil Service. And that does not include some 100,000 part-time committee members. . . . Andrew Jackson's dream of spoils rose to only four or five thousands. [. . .–ed.]

If you can find any of that Roosevelt three to four hundred thousand who are not interfering with a free ballot in this campaign, it is because their bosses have slipped up. . . .

. . . This spoils system . . . degrades public life. By example it pollutes every local government. [. . .–ed.]

This New Deal army of political appointees is the American form of the Praetorian Guard of Ancient Rome. That political band had exactly similar habits in making elections foolproof. They were also active in the decline and fall of the morals of the Roman Empire. We have, however, improved the Roman practice. Our three to four hundred thousand of New Deal political employees are the officers of an army of ten million voters who receive benefits from the government.

Sample II

And this brings me to Sample No. II, concerning the activity of these officers. But it will need a moment's background.

In 1930 as President I announced that as a nation we "must prevent hunger and cold to those of our people who are in honest difficulties." And I undertook the organization of their relief. I had had some years' experience elsewhere with the moral and political dangers of relief. I determined that America should not be subjected to those calamities. To prevent this we saw to it that non-partisan committees of leading citizens were established in some 3000 communities, where relief was needed. These committees were

---

9. [*Editor's note*: Hoover's insertion.]

given [the–*ed.*] full responsibility of administration. These committees were unpaid. They had no vested interest in keeping unemployment going. At the start their money support was local. As the situation deepened, first the States and finally the Federal government gave financial aid to these committees. Parallel with this we greatly expanded useful Public Works at regular pay and full-time employment.

At this point I may wipe away a current New Deal crocodile tear. And that wells constantly out of their emotion that they were the first administration with human sympathy or to give real relief to the distressed. They admit now that when they took over the government in 1933, our relief organization was regularly providing for over 5,400,000 distressed homes of over 21,000,000 persons. . . . What the New Deal in fact did was to wreck this system of local, non-partisan administration and substitute a political administration centralized in Washington. . . . The moral consequences have been degrading to the whole people.

Under local administration there was a summoning of community sympathy, a desire to help not alone with relief but with jobs and encouragement. . . . A hierarchy of officials is being built whose jobs depend on keeping people on relief. And American youth is being poured into this mould. It is sheer madness. A class wall of hate and fear of those on relief is growing daily.

And now, national sympathy is being defied by politics. Harry Hopkins and Aubrey Williams[10] . . . have the power in this Republic to say who shall have bread and who shall not.

You will recollect the trick words by which these men this last June effectually told people on relief how to vote—or else.

Ripped of all disguises and all intellectual dishonesty, the statements of these men were a direction to these millions and their wives and relatives how to vote.

. . . A Congressional Committee has shown that nevertheless in [. . .–*ed.*] those[11] election months (1934 and 1936)[12] the number of people assisted by relief was greatly expanded. It also showed that in the same months in the off years they were greatly decreased. . . .

. . . The hideous morals of these actions in a free Republic were denounced by a few Democratic Senators whose morals rise above elections. Democratic

---

10. [*Editor's note*: Harry Hopkins (1870–1946) and Aubrey Williams (1890–1965) were prominent New Deal relief administrators in the 1930s.]

11. [*Editor's note*: Hoover removed this word from the quotation. I have restored it for clarity.]

12. [*Editor's note*: Hoover's parenthetical insertion.]

Senator Hatch[13] proposed a law in the Senate designed to stop relief officials from using relief for vote-getting purposes. The Senator said, "Those who believe that out in the counties and in the cities and in the precincts this instrumentality which we have set up is not being used for political purposes are more credulous than I am."

However, Senator Barkley[14], President Roosevelt's selected leader of the Senate, led the opposition to Senator Hatch's motion. The motion was defeated by President Roosevelt's rubber-stamp followers in the Senate.

Would this law have been defeated if President Roosevelt had breathed one whisper of approval for it? . . .

. . . Some months ago the Democratic Scripps-Howard papers courageously exposed the use of the WPA in Kentucky "as a grand political racket in which the taxpayer is the victim." Harry Hopkins as usual denounced the reporter as untruthful. Later on, even the Senate Committee, after investigation, had to stigmatize this stench. They said, "These facts should arouse the conscience of the country. They imperil the right of the people to a free and unpolluted ballot." I notice it was the conscience of the country that they summoned. They apparently did not think it worth while to call it to the conscience of the President.

Mr. Roosevelt has mastered the power to bestow bread and butter to millions of people or withhold it from them. He called upon the people specifically in Kentucky, in Oklahoma, Georgia, South Carolina, and Maryland to vote for his selections for the Senate. At about the same time relief wages in those territories were raised. Mr. Roosevelt threw in a few bridges and announced a new economic program for the South by government subsidy. . . .

Nor is this use of bait sectional. It envelops the whole nation. . . . Just before this election, this three-billion-dollar pump-priming program was enacted. The headlines daily flame with the assignment of some pork to every Congressional district. New Deal candidates proudly announce its arrival to their constituents. Cities and communities push in Washington to get their feet in the trough. Hundreds of them justify . . . by the immoral excuse that somebody else will get it. . . .

[. . .–ed.] Do you wonder that every dictator in Europe uses this exhibit to prove the failure of self-government?

---

13. [Editor's note: Carl Hatch (1889–1963), a U.S. senator from New Mexico from 1933 to 1949. Author/sponsor of the so-called Hatch Act of 1939, which prohibited partisan activity by most federal government employees.]

14. [Editor's note: Alben Barkley (1887–1956), majority leader of the U.S. Senate from 1937 to 1947 and vice president of the United States from 1949 to 1953.]

... We are today confronted with more disheartening growth of high-powered political machines in our cities than ever before in our history. Kansas City, Saint Louis, Jersey City, Philadelphia, Pittsburgh, Memphis, Chicago, and what not. It may be coincidence that these machines are supporting the New Deal. It is no coincidence that for six years the patronage and the subsidies of the New Deal have been handled by these political bosses.

We hear much Presidential urging of economic royalists to virtue. It is probably coincidence that we hear no moral urging of political royalists.

And these are but a few of the black spots. What of the stench of the primaries in Pennsylvania, New Mexico, Indiana and Tennessee? What of the indictments of high officials in Connecticut? In New York? What of the New Deal Governor of Pennsylvania who compels a legislature to suppress a Grand Jury inquiry into charges of corruption against him?

... Moral corruption by expenditure of these huge sums of public money penetrates every county and every village. The indignant citizen used to roll up his sleeves and with his neighbors hope to clean corruption in his own town. But when it floods from Washington what hope has he to stem the tide?

Do you wonder that our own people lose faith in honesty? Do they not lose faith in democracy? Does it not disintegrate the moral standards of our people?

This gigantic expenditure of public money will make its beneficiaries drunk on the basest selfishness and it will make any group drunk with power.

That seems to be one of the attractions of this New Deal Liberal Party.

Sample III

We may take up another spot where a contribution could be made to higher morals. A Republican Administration in 1925 passed a Corrupt Practices Act prohibiting corporations from contributing to political funds. That law was founded upon public morals. It seems that the New Deal considers it a reactionary measure. In a liberal spirit, something over a year ago Mr. Roosevelt personally autographed several hundred blank sheets of paper. These autographs turned up in Democratic propaganda books. These books could be produced for about 50 cents per copy. On August 12, 1937, the Congress was asked to investigate the selling of these books to corporations for $250 apiece. . . .[15] Perhaps those corporations were collecting autographs. But Mr.

---

15. [Editor's note: Here Hoover omitted an implicitly critical reference in his 1938 speech to Roosevelt's postmaster general, James Farley. By 1955, as Hoover was revising this portion of his memoirs for

Roosevelt's autograph can be bought in the bookshops for 95 percent less than $250. But no doubt the corporations needed autographed special editions of this book. And for the good of these corporations it was decided they needed not one autograph each but even ten or twenty. They no doubt could learn from it how to make nails or cement. . . .

In asking for an investigation, a mass of affidavits, original letters, and photostatic copies of correspondence and other evidence was laid before the House of Representatives. These proved that Mr. Farley's agents had sold these books to wealthy corporations for party funds under thinly disguised threats and thinly disguised promises. After the incessant and lofty urging to virtue which the corporations have received this must have been a bump. . . . No investigation could be had.

Later on, a list of hundreds of corporations to which these books [had] . . . [been–*ed.*] sold was exposed in the press. Many of them were firms having business with the government. . . .

And this immorality does not end with government officials. There are two parties to these transactions. There were some men of moral stamina who refused to buy. Their corporate morals were higher than the government's. But does this not show a breakdown . . . of the moral stamina in the men who bought these books [. . .–*ed.*]?

Sample IV

There is another department of current government morals. That has to do with financial honor in government business. We can select from a wide display of samples.

In the campaign of 1932 from information obviously since corroborated I challenged Mr. Roosevelt's intention to tinker with the currency. He denied such an idea indignantly as immoral, and he assured the country that the contract (that is the obligation written on government currency and bonds to pay in gold of present weight and fineness) was more than a contract— it was a covenant. But to make us really feel uncomfortable Mr. Roosevelt asked Senator Glass[16] also to make a reply to my charges. The Senator's reputation for veracity was impregnable. The Senator did the job with his unsurpassed vocabulary.[17] But the Senator is an honest man. Let me quote from

publication, Farley was no longer an ardent New Deal Democrat and in fact was a friend of Hoover's. This probably explains Hoover's deletion.]

16. [*Editor's note*: Carter Glass (1858–1946), a conservative Democratic senator from Virginia.]

17. [*Editor's note*: The text of Senator Glass's fiery blast at Hoover on November 1, 1932, was printed in the *New York Times*, November 2, 1932, p. 12.]

his speech only seven months later. After indicating his regret at ever having delivered that first speech, he continued: ". . . To me the suggestion that we may devalue the gold dollar 50 percent means national repudiation. To me it means dishonor. In my conception of it, it is immoral. All the legalistic arguments . . . have not dislodged from my mind the irrevocable conviction that it is immoral, and that it means not only contravention of my party's platform . . . but the promises of party spokesmen during the campaign. . . ."[18]

And the New Deal passed a law preventing the citizen from access to the courts for justice and redress.

That was the beginning of New Deal standards in Financial Morals. It has not been the end.

We may take a more recent sample. Most of us favor old age pensions. We helped establish them in the states before the New Deal was born. We do not criticize that purpose of the Social Security Act. That Act, however, developed other purposes. The country was told it was a system of contributory old age insurance. It has turned out to be concealed taxation of the poorest of our people. It is said the collections are paid into a reserve fund. The collections last year were used for current expenditures of the government. You will have to be taxed over again to make it good. That scheme also obscures the real deficit and fools the people into thinking that their budget is nearer to being balanced.

To prove my language is moderate, let me quote some phrases from an editorial in the Democratic *New York Times* of about a month ago. The *Times* supported Mr. Roosevelt's election in 1932 and 1936. They call it [the Social Security "reserve fund"–*ed*.] "pious fraud," "a fraud and a delusion," "not a reserve in the real sense of the word," "already been spent," "funds will have to be raised all over again by new taxation," "this hocus-pocus."[19]

It is an intricate piece of morals. I am reminded of a postmaster who got in the habit of taking the cash from the till and putting in his I.O.U. The Postal Inspector caught up with him and he received five years. In his application for pardon his friends urged strongly that he was a rigidly honest man, and as proof of it, they cited the fact that he put his I.O.U. in the till each time he took out the money.

This postmaster's "objectives" were no doubt good. He was no doubt building up a reserve for his old age. Certainly his confusion of objectives and morals had a modernistic flavor.

---

18. [*Editor's note*: For the text of Senator Glass's speech of April 27, 1933, quoted here by Hoover, see *New York Times*, April 28, 1933, p. 3.]

19. [*Editor's note*: See editorial in *New York Times*, August 9, 1938, p. 18. The editorial was titled "The Pious Fraud."]

This juggling of government accounts to obscure the realities goes much further. If you will examine the published statements of the Treasury, you will find that collections from government recoverable loans are being used for current expenses. And yet they claim that recoverable loans should be deducted from their increase of national debt. And the old game of obscuring accounts between Regular Expenses and the Emergency and Relief goes on and on. Mr. Roosevelt uses the expression "a layman's budget" every autumn. It serves effectively for the annual pledge of a balanced budget. And in the spring it serves to explain the deficit. . . . And that postpones the feelings of the taxpayer.

There is one certainty about this "layman's budget." The layman is a person who is ignorant of a science. But in this case the bill may teach him something.

I delivered a whole address on samples of this particular form of government by deception two years ago. It is still unanswered.[20]

Sample V

There is another large department of New Deal morals that we may also explore. We hear much of social conscience and social justice these days. That is public conscience. . . . But public conscience will wilt away unless there be the still small voice of personal conscience. For thence spring good faith, honor, and personal integrity. Here rest intellectual honesty and justice itself. . . . As personal conscience dies, social conscience becomes but a stepping stone of personal power.

. . .

As an example of personal conscience, we might examine the reasons given and the methods used by Mr. Roosevelt in his attempts to pack the Supreme Court. I am not going to enter into the demerits of packing the Court. I am concerned with the moral processes in explaining the reasons for it to the country.

Urbanity of debate limits my use of the English language. I shall therefore quote wholly from those who have supported Mr. Roosevelt. I shall not tire you with long quotations. I will merely mention some of the hard words they use.

---

20. [*Further*] *Addresses upon the American Road, 1938–1940*, p. 14. [*Editor's note*: Hoover's footnote here refers merely to the page in *Further Addresses* where this quoted passage appears—not to the "whole address" he gave two years earlier. He may have meant to refer to his speech, "Intellectual Dishonesty in Government," delivered in Philadelphia on October 1, 1936. It was reprinted in Hoover, *Addresses . . . 1933–1938*, pp. 201–15.]

Mr. Walter Lippmann's expressions include "trick," "concealed his purposes," "lack of good faith," "lawless legality," "vicious legalism," "use the letter of the law to violate the spirit," "degrading," "reactionary," "misleading," "impairs the dignity of his office," "injure the moral foundations of the Republic."

The Democratic *New York Times* uses the words, "political sharp practice," "indirectness," "adroitness."

The Democratic *Baltimore Sun* says "disingenuous," "devious," "deceptive," "an intent to deceive."

The Democratic *Richmond Times-Dispatch* says "lack of frankness."

The Democratic *New York World-Telegram* uses "too clever." Its correspondent says "trying to deceive."

Democratic Senators used about all the other anti-hypocritical phrases, "reasons that obscured its real purpose," "concealed aims," "unmoral reasons," "camouflage," "hypocrisy," and a lot of even harder words. But such un-friendly sentiments lead to purges.

I could continue indefinitely these phrases from pained Democratic supporters, who are now condemned to outer darkness. But I merely wish to illustrate what I mean when I talk of intellectual integrity in government.

Sample VI

We may sample still another area of morals where grows the fruit of Mr. Roosevelt's New Deal Party. National conscience has hitherto embraced the notion of fidelity to truth in government.

It never has taken much effort or literary skill to tell the truth about what goes on in government. Yet this administration has installed some hundreds of skilled propagandists. The deluge of free mail sent out by the Government Departments in 1937 would have required $34,000,000 in postage if they paid it. In the last year of my Administration it was $9,000,000. That increase by nearly four hundred percent does not include Congressional mail either. Surely it now takes a powerful effort to tell the truth. The increase is not devoted to unfavorable news about government activities.

But beyond all this is the radio. Every hour of the day somewhere in the country some person is painting the glories of this abundant life, or to use the more recent term, "our objectives."

The whole of this propaganda is impregnated with suppression of fact, the distortion of statistics, the creation of misleading slogans, the building of prejudice or hate.

The Democratic *New York World-Telegram* estimates the cost of these propaganda officials at over twenty million dollars a year.

You cannot have government by public opinion when opinion of the people is manufactured by paid press agents of the government.

The first weapon of dictatorship is organized propaganda. A dozen democracies in Europe have been destroyed by mass persuasion and the creation of mass prejudice. That is the stuff that dictators grow from. It is the sustenance they live by. It is the stuff the New Deal lives by.

Every dictator in Europe has proved that by propaganda you can fool enough of the people all the time.

One play in the routine game of propaganda is to steal righteous phrases and devote them to evil-doing. Thus we have Good Neighbors and Social Security, National Planning, Reform and More Abundant Life. Another department is to attach repulsive phrases to your opponents. Then we get Economic Royalists, Tories, Reactionaries, Feudalists, Wild Men and Copperheads, and Purge.

Sample VII

And there are the moral aspects of stirring ill-will, conflict and hate. Class hate is the rock upon which every republic has been wrecked. And this is the most classless nation yet born. But[21] hate is preached from the White House. . . . I shall not go further into it than to say it has set worker against employer, employer against worker, worker against worker. And I give you a statistic of only one of its consequences. In the three years of depression stress before the New Deal, the man-days lost by strikes and lock-outs averaged five million per year. In the five years of the New Deal, they have averaged eighteen million per year. That is an increase of 350 percent. Is that building good-will and cooperation?

Sample VIII

Mr. Roosevelt invites the American people to join his New Deal Party which he calls Liberal. We can explore whether it is a party of liberalism and present at the same time a sample of hypocrisy and mass propaganda by government.

. . . Are these exhibits of political morals evidences of liberalism? . . .

Many of Mr. Roosevelt's objectives are hoary with reaction. They include the destruction of the independence of the judiciary. That dates with Charles I. They include a new and avowed campaign to destroy the independence of the legislative arm. That dates with George III. It involves a centralization of

---

21. [*Editor's note*: In the original speech, Hoover had said "And" rather than "But." This is probably an example of his occasional tendency retroactively to polish his prose.]

government which invades the independence of local governments. That is one of Mr. Hitler's successful ideas.

This devaluation of currency is a trick of Roman Emperors. They were not known to be liberals. These deficit financings are as old as the French Kings. You might look up the inscription at the Feast of Belshazzar.

Mr. Roosevelt himself in discussing my increase of the debt burdens on the taxpayer of about one billion (not five billion as he implied) said that was the rock upon which liberal governments were wrecked. Surely twenty billions increase in debt is a bump to liberalism.

Are these Socialist enterprises of our government liberalism? Is this [Fascist][22] . . . dictation to labor, farmers, and business liberalism?

If this sort of stuff is liberal, then George III, Hitler, Stalin, and Boss Tweed are liberals.

Whatever the merits or demerits of such objectives may be, it is immoral to represent them as liberalism. Liberals have fought these things for centuries. What President Roosevelt is leading is not liberalism. Instead of bringing the past up to the present he is bringing the present back to the past.

These are the paving stones of the dangerous road which has wrecked liberal democracies all over the world.

Mr. Roosevelt denounces and accuses all of us who do not believe in these methods and these actions as conservatives. If being conservative on dragging America into the morass of political immorality or into the Dead Sea of reaction is Conservatism then I cheerfully join that party. And that party will yet become the hope of American life.

Whatever name we may be called, we shall hold high that lamp of morals as the guide to the American people.

But we should worry less over what is a liberal than what is honest. That is the very headlight of true Liberalism in this dark world.

And if these were successful policies for a free country why have 11,000,000 unemployed?

Conclusion

Our opponents pugnaciously demand constructive alternatives with our criticisms. I have never made an address in debate on public questions without offering a positive and constructive alternative. I do so most cheerfully upon this subject tonight.

---

22. [*Editor's note*: The word "Fascist" in brackets was Hoover's later insertion. In the original speech, as published in 1940, he had said "Nazi dictation."]

First. Be honest. Integrity lives not alone in the pocket. It lives also in the mind.

Second. Re-establish morals as the first objective of government. Give the nation leadership in moral regeneration as the road to national security. Greed and hate can be more easily cured by moral standards than by policemen. The people take their moral tone from those who occupy high office.

Third. Return the administration of Relief to non-partisan local committees even if the Federal government pays 95 percent of their expenditure. That will stop its political prostitution. It will better serve the destitute.

Fourth. Demand the whole patronage system be abolished. Demand that Congress put every single official except a few at the top under the Civil Service Merit System. Demand that every single appointee during the past six years be required to take merit examinations open to any competitor.

Fifth. Amend the Corrupt Practices Act to provide instant dismissal and jail for any of these job holders who speak out loud on politics, and take the enforcement out of partisan hands.

Sixth. Repudiate the whole idea that the end or the "objective" justifies the means. Every one of these samples I have cited is the exact practice of this grim doctrine. That doctrine is a violation of the whole Christian ethics. It is the philosophy of all dictatorship.

In conclusion may I say again that the fountains of justice alone spring from truth and honesty. There is no double standard of morals, one in public and one in private life. . . . Moral standards in the people are sullied when moral leadership in government fails. It is alone the spirit of morals that can reconcile order and freedom. A people corrupted by their government cannot remain a free people.

Second Address (Hartford, Conn., October 17, 1938)
Undermining Representative Government

The election . . . is no conflict between Republican and traditional Democratic policies. It is a conflict between two ideas of life for America. That conflict started in 1933. It is not a conflict between the old and the new in American life. It is a conflict between age-old personal government and a government of free men under the rule of law.

Mr. Roosevelt now challenges the nation to line itself into what he calls the Liberal Party. . . .

The greatest Teacher of Mankind said, "By their fruits ye shall know them. Do men gather grapes of thorns or figs of thistles?"

There are already five evil products from these years of the New Deal that have become self-evident.

The first is the degeneration of political morals to the lowest ebb in our history.

The second is the malignant growth of personal power in this Republic.

The third is heart-breaking growth of hate, class division, and disunity in the most classless country in the world.

The fourth is that underneath all this is a creeping collectivism that is steadily eating away the vitalities of free enterprise.

The fifth is that after six years of these policies we have 11,000,000 people out of jobs. Farm prices, reckoned in old gold values, are lower than ever in our history. We have before us 20 billions increase in national debt. We and the other democracies of the world in 1932 started recovery from the inevitable post-war depression. They, except France, years ago recovered employment beyond pre-depression levels—France copied the New Deal. . . .

In all the centuries of the struggle to establish liberty under the rule of law, humanity has builded stone by stone the safeguards against personal power. Every school child knows, or should know, that the reason why this Republic of free men has flourished longer than any republic in modern history is because power was divided among the three branches as check and balance each upon the other. [. . .–ed.]

Liberty never dies from direct attack. No man ever arises and says, "Down with Liberty." Liberty has died in 14 European[23] countries in a single score of years from weakening its safeguards, from demoralization of the moral stamina of the people.

Example No. 1 of Roosevelt's Attack on Freedom[24]

My first example of Mr. Roosevelt's "liberal" attack on liberty is his attempt to invade the independence of the Supreme Court. I do not need to refresh your minds much on that aggression of personal power. Nor am I here raising the question of the liberalism of the Ku Klux Klan.[25]

Some may think these assaults on the judicial bulwarks of free men are defeated and behind us. The words of the New Dealers do not confirm this hope.

---

23. [Editor's note: Hoover added this word to the manuscript reproduced here. The word was not in the original 1938 address as published in the book cited in note 8.]

24. [Editor's note: In the original text of this address as published in 1940, the caption was simply "Part II."]

25. [Editor's note: This was probably an allusion to the recent revelation that President Roosevelt's first appointee to the Supreme Court, Senator Hugo Black of Alabama, had joined the Ku Klux Klan in the 1920s.]

Example No. 2[26]

And that brings us to the second assault on the safeguards to representative government. . . .

The independence of the Congress from domination by the Executive is just as vital as the independence of the Supreme Court. The safeguards of our liberty and the rights of minorities rest as much with the Congress as they do upon the Supreme Court. And beyond all its own independent responsibility, the Congress alone can prevent Executive domination of the Judiciary. Nobody but the people can protect the Congress.

If we examine the fate of wrecked republics throughout the world we find their first symptoms in the weakening of the legislative arm. Subservience in legislative halls is the spot where liberty and political morals commit suicide.

For six years now, except for momentary gleams of independence, the country has witnessed an overwhelming majority in Congress blindly taking orders from the President.

Nobody will deny that the majority of these Congressmen have been simply rubber stamps for the Executive. They don't deny it themselves. . . .

Example No. 3[27]

The whole concept of representative government is that Senators and Congressmen should be independent-minded men chosen by the people of their districts and states. They represent the forty-eight states and not the President. They should not be chosen by the President. They should not be run by him either.

. . . Mr. Roosevelt justifies his reduction of the Congress to servitude on the ground that he must compel compliance with these mandates of his party. It would seem perplexing to a Congressman as to which are party mandates and which are Mr. Roosevelt's improvised ideas. . . .

I dislike digging up fossil bones of dead mandates. But I must take the bunk out of this mandate stuff. Their platform of 1932 had something in it about reductions of government expenditures, economy and balanced budget. From what the New Deal has left of that skeleton you cannot even make out what the animal looked like. Also I faintly remember some turgid pledges to take the government out of all fields of private enterprise. There was a blistering pledge not to tinker with the currency. And there was a

---

26. [*Editor's note*: In the original text of this address as published in 1940, the caption was simply "Part III."]

27. [*Editor's note*: In the original text of this address as published in 1940, the caption was simply "Part IV."]

resounding pledge against the use of money in politics. I would not cause pain by the recall of the death of this original list of pious mandates.

Incidentally I find that Democratic platforms in olden days demanded a non-political civil service. There is not much of that skeleton left either.

... Again in 1936 the Democratic Platform did not even intimate the packing of the Supreme Court, or the Executive control of the semi-judicial bodies or the Civil Service through the Reorganization Bill. So much for the alibi of a party mandate from the people. The so-called mandates seem to be the rubber part of the stamp. [. . .–ed.]

Destruction of Congressional Independence[28]

And now let us explore in a little detail some of the definite responsibilities of the Congress which are today in process of destruction.

1. Obviously the members are elected to formulate the laws. The President does not make the laws. He is required to call public needs to the consideration of Congress. Instead Mr. Roosevelt submitted laws fully drafted and stamped "must."

His yes-yes majority did not even protect the dignity of Congress by appearing to formulate their own bills. They took it as if they were office boys. And they often got their orders from office boys. It takes free men to make laws for free men.

2. Members of Congress are under individual oath to maintain the Constitution. They are under no oath to say yes-yes. They are the first trench of Constitutional defense. Yet this yes-yes group passed measure after measure that was unconstitutional. . . . But what is the Constitution among rubber stamps?

3. One of the highest functions of any legislative body in a democracy is sober consideration and effective debate. . . . Yet this rubber-stamp majority had permitted their responsibilities so to degenerate that they passed arrogant rules limiting debate to a few hours or even minutes. . . .

. . . The anvil of debate is the prime safety of democracy in forming its laws. That is the check on arrogance and personal power. Even the New Dealers admit that sometimes when they are trying to prove themselves Liberals.

4. When revolutionary measures are introduced to the Congress which have never been before the people in a campaign surely the people have

---

28. [*Editor's note*: In the original text of this address as published in 1940, the caption was simply "Part V."]

a right to a few days in which to express their views and show the injuries which will be done them. [...–ed.]

It is true the country was saved from two disasters—the packing of the Supreme Court and the Reorganization Bill. But that was only because a courageous minority in the Senate delayed action long enough for the people to realize their jeopardy and effectively protest.

5. The foremost purpose, from the very beginning, of all parliaments and all legislative bodies is the control of the national purse. Men died over a whole century to wrest it from the English kings. The control of executive expenditures by the people's representatives has been the battle of the people against dictatorial grasp since Edward I. That is the very root of the people's power.

And this supine majority of ours over the last six years has surrendered this vital protection of the people for the first time in our legislative history. It has voted over fifteen billions of lump sums to the President to be expended at his will. That idea goes back to Charles I.

The surrender by Congress of power over the purse through appropriation of fifteen billion dollars of lump appropriations has placed fifteen billions of personal power in the hands of the President.

Thereby they conferred upon the President the power both to cajole and to purge the individual Congressman.

The old-fashioned pork barrel has become a whole pork-packing establishment—all under the leadership of the Executive. And many members of the not-quite-yes group have been kept in line by beguilement with pieces of their own pork.

All this is a flagrant moral debauchery of their sacred function of safeguarding the money squeezed by taxes from the toil of a people.

6. The Congress is supposed to be the people's watchdog over efficiency and honesty in the bureaucracy. If ever there was a mandate from the people to the Congress it is to preserve the merit system for appointments to Federal jobs under the Civil Service Commission. It has been the battle of the people against the politicians for fifty years. Once upon a time the New Deal gave it strong lip-service. Yet this rubber-stamp majority on the President's demand specifically provided that the alphabetical agencies[29] should be politically appointed without regard to the merit system of the Civil Service Commission. It is not an imaginary idea that the yes-yes men also like the

29. [*Editor's note*: A reference to the Roosevelt administration's many new agencies such as the National Recovery Administration (NRA), the Agricultural Adjustment Administration (AAA), and the Works Progress Administration (WPA).]

notion of having some share in selecting 300,000 political appointees from their districts. These yes men have a full responsibility for this debauchery of political morals to the lowest ebb in our history.

Pollution of Elections[30]

And that brings me to the third category of these sinister aggressions of personal power in this republic. That is the Executive attempt to control elections. That alone should make the election of independent-minded men to Congress the first task of men who would be free.

We have seen Mr. Roosevelt mass this Praetorian army of political appointees to purge those men of his own party who have shown sparks of manhood, of independence, and obedience to their oath.[31]

And this is not a quarrel in the Democratic Party upon which Republicans can look with glee. If these methods be applied to members of his own party you will not expect them to be withheld from the opposition party.

But it is far more serious than any question of party. It goes to the very roots of the independence of the legislative arm. It goes to the very core of the right of the people to choose their own representatives. It goes to the whole question of the independence of the ballot itself. It goes to the foundation of personal power in this Republic.

Mr. Stalin was the founder of the political purge. Or was it Mr. Hitler?

Mr. Hitler also has a parliament. You may not know it. It was also once upon a time an independent arm of the German government. But Mr. Hitler has rearranged its function. I quote him: "Individual members may advise but never decide; that is the exclusive prerogative of the responsible president for the time being."

Mr. Roosevelt is not however proposing the German form of parliamentary practice. He only has a passion for unanimity of view. And he likes leadership with a compulsory following.

In speaking in opposition I always find myself limited in the use of hard words lest I should overstate or be lacking in courtesy. It is, I hope, permissible for me to select some words from the sackcloth wails of the Democratic newspapers who supported Mr. Roosevelt.

---

30. [*Editor's note*: In the original text of this address as published in 1940, the caption was "Part VI."]

31. [*Editor's note*: In 1938 President Roosevelt attempted to "purge" several anti–New Deal Democratic senators and members of the House of Representatives by vigorously and publicly supporting their pro–New Deal challengers in Democratic primaries. His intervention proved to be highly controversial and largely unsuccessful.]

The *New York Times* exclaims: "... How great an intellectual servitude the President now requires from his followers."

The *Atlanta Constitution* says: "He would turn the United States Senate into a gathering of 96 Charlie McCarthies with himself as Edgar Bergen."

Lynchburg (Va.) Advance: "Are the people of the forty-eight states to select their representatives in Congress or is the President of the United States to perform that duty for them and thereby become a national dictator?"

The Charlotte (Va.) [N.C.–ed.] *Observer:* "... A New Napoleon. ... Crucifixion of the inherent liberties of the people. ..."

The Norfolk (Va.) Dispatch: "... A personal ambition for unquestioned power. ..."

Baltimore Sun: "... An act of executive arrogance ... the President with more jobs and more public funds at his disposal than any other President in history. ..."

Augusta (Ga.) Chronicle: "... If the citizens of Georgia do what President Roosevelt told us ... we must forget political independence as a thing dead and reconcile ourselves to complete dictation from the Chief Executive."

Macon (Ga.) Telegraph: "The President's duplicity ... sheer malice. ..."

New Orleans States: "What right has Mr. Roosevelt to dictate to the people ... how they shall vote?"

Nashville (Tenn.) Banner: "... the power-drunk Chief Executive. ..."

Descriptive terms concerning Mr. Roosevelt as used in his own political family are certainly expressive. All Republicans are at a disadvantage for we are such polite folk. [...–ed.]

The 300,000 political appointees are only the officers of their Praetorian army. That army is the great rank and file of distressed people on relief and the other great groups receiving benefits from the government.

... Lest this appear to be biased from me, let me quote again from Democratic sources. One Senator says: "Those who believe that out in the counties and in the cities and in the precincts this instrumentality (relief) which we have set up is not being used for political purposes are more credulous than I am." Another describing conditions in certain Democratic primaries says: "These facts should arouse the conscience of the country. They imperil the right of the people to a free and unpolluted ballot."

[...–ed.] But far more important than that, what does all this mean in public and private morals? Is this liberty under the law? Or is this personal government?

New Deal Collectivism[32]

We have a fourth category of these thistles and thorns of personal power from which we have no figs and no grapes. That is the group of ideas under the euphonious title of "Planned Economy." [. . .–ed.]

Whether this compulsory economy is a creeping collectivism from Europe or whether it is a native American product, it has the same result of building intolerable personal power in this Republic. [. . .–ed.]

We have now had nearly six years' experience with these ideas. They were put forward as for an emergency. And yet every session of Congress faces further demands. Power feeds only on more power. [. . .–ed.]

You will recollect that Mr. Roosevelt in his well-known self-confession said, "In thirty-four months we have built up new instruments of public power. In the hands of the people's government this power is wholesome and proper." He concedes that in other hands "it would provide shackles for the liberties of the people." The very essence of representative government in this Republic is that no man should possess the powers to shackle the liberties of the people. I might remark that the word Liberalism comes from the word liberty and not from the word shackles. [. . .–ed.]

Power through Taxes and Spending[33]

And there is a fifth direction where this thistle of personal power is spreading. The New Deal audits itself with slogans rather than cash registers. This department of New Deal liberalism is at least consistent in one particular. It is no longer haunted by the old ghost of a balanced budget. [. . .–ed.]

Those are the implacable dangers of profligate spending. Let us not forget that increasing debts some day accumulate to where democracy cannot be brought to the agony of sufficient taxes to carry them. When that day arrives liberty dies in the gutter. It is easy to overstate the dangers. But where recklessness drives, there danger shrieks. [. . .–ed.]

Stirring Up Class Hate[34]

One of the products of this era of personal government has been the rise of bitter discord among our people. The stir of class hate in the most classless nation is but part of it. . . .

---

32. [*Editor's note*: In the original text of this address as published in 1940, the caption was simply "Part VII."]

33. [*Editor's note*: In the original text of this address as published in 1940, the caption was simply "Part VIII."]

34. [*Editor's note*: In the original text of this address as published in 1940, the caption was simply "Part IX."]

Checks on Personal Power[35]

We of the opposition have not alone the duty to call a halt to these encroachments of personal power over free men and their consequences. It is our duty also to make clear that we are not demanding a halt to the needed and progressive solutions of changing problems which arise from the changing times. It is our further duty to urge the principles and methods that will return our people to work.

We have first to clear the land of some thorns and thistles.

We must have emancipation from the threat of a controlled Judiciary. We must free Congress from its subjugation. We must have regeneration of political morals. We must end the creation of hate and group conflict. We must extirpate the whole spoils system. We must have honesty in government. We must have a free and honest ballot.

We must have expenditures controlled by Congress. . . . [36] We must have a currency convertible into gold as the only way to get it out of personal dictation. We must have a credit system independent of personal control and socialistic methods. We must have new and genuine banking reform. We must destroy exploitation and coercion of the people whether at private hands or government hands.

We must have emancipation from the creeping collectivism of dictated economy. . . . We must have reform in the Labor Act to deal equal justice to all workers and all employees. We must have the only basis of liberalism, that is the rule of law and not of men.

We must reform relief under the administration of non-partisan local committees. We must reform the old age pensions to make them just to the workers. . . .

We have need to replant the land with measures which will restore confidence among men and hope among youth. [. . .–ed.]

[Part XI–ed.]

This is no lawyer's dispute over legalisms. It is no dispute over old-time custom. It is a fundamental battle of the people.

We may sum it up. Under a screen of fair-sounding phrases we have seen the President of the United States steadily driving for more and more power over the daily lives of the people. We have seen him attempt to control the Supreme Court. We have seen his domination of Congress. We have seen personal control of expenditures. We have seen the attempt through the power of

---

35. [*Editor's note*: In the original text of this address as published in 1940, the caption was simply "Part X."]

36. [*Editor's note*: Here, for reasons unknown, Hoover deleted the sentence "We must have a balanced budget."]

government expenditures to pollute the ballot. We have seen the attempt to mix in a system of free enterprise a system of creeping collectivism. We have seen a vindictive campaign to array class against class and group against group.

[Part XII-ed.]

All this is the destruction of freedom and prosperity. If freedom is to reign on this continent the American people have to attend to it themselves. They can no longer leave it to the government.

You may ask: What can we do in the face of the formidable thing this personal power has become?

If we had an independent, courageous Congress we could find a start at solution of our ills. Therefore my first recommendation to you tonight is: Elect to Congress independent-minded men. Elect men who will stand on their own feet. Elect men of character and capacity.

Second. Defeat every man of the kind who says he is a follower of any President 100 percent or 50 percent or any other percent. Such a man is not fit to serve. Members of the Congress of the United States, if they are men, do not take orders from anybody. If you will test the New Deal candidates as to whether they will oppose every one of these five attacks on free men which I have enumerated tonight, you will find them wanting.

Never before in all American history has there been a greater need for the people to protect themselves. And it is in the power of the people to do it now. They alone can make Congress the sword and buckler of their liberties. [. . .–ed.]

The Third Address (Spokane, Wash., November 5, 1938)
The Economic Consequences of the New Deal

Last evening Mr. Roosevelt spoke highly of his success in creating economic stability, prosperity and security for the average man. Naturally he did not mention the 11,000,000 unemployed or farmers' prices, and some other instabilities and insecurities.

He probably thought I could be relied upon to supply those omissions tonight. I will do that and several others. But I shall rely upon debate and appeal to reason, not upon smearing. [. . .–ed.]

Our Economic Purpose

We have two dominant concerns in American economic life.

The first and immediate is jobs for 11,000,000 idle men and the rebuilding of agriculture.

The second is beyond this. If we stretch our vision, what is it we want the economic system to provide for all Americans? To answer we must dig deep into the whole system of life. And we must dig deep into what has happened in the last 20 years.

What do we want as a minimum standard of American living for all the people? We want American children born in health. We want them brought up with plenty of vitamins in the sunshine. We want our race physically stronger with every generation. We want our youth high in ideals and resolute in character. We want them inspired with the spirit of human brotherhood. We want them trained to make their own living, to contribute to the advancement of the nation. We want every one of them to have a job to start in life. And we want them to have constructive joy all through the process.

We want old age serene in security from poverty or the fear of it.

And we want profitable work for the great middle groups between youth and old age, for they must support the whole. The focus of their lives is the home. We want them to own their own homes. We want the gadgets that replace drudgery and give joy in these homes. We want each home to have a job or to own a farm or its own business. We want Americans to be secure in that job and get living and comfort out of it. And above all we want them to have that American personal liberty which makes the rest worth having. This is no impossible ideal. I am for whatever economic system will bring it about.

How are we to attain all this? The question is which is the right road? Which road leads to danger?

Our Economic System

In all the history of the world mankind has found only two ways of doing the work of feeding, clothing, housing and providing comforts for the people. One is the way of liberty in which every man and woman is free to plan his own life, choose his own calling, start his own adventures, secure in reward of his effort and ability. That is the system of free enterprise.

The other way is the way of compulsion by which men work for slavedrivers or governments, or as dictated by governments. The dictators of Europe have softened that rough statement by calling it Planned Economy. . . .

And let me emphasize that when I speak of free enterprise I do not mean that men can abuse or destroy the freedom of others by monopolies or any other kind of privilege or exploitation of business, farmers or labor. That destroys freedom itself. No one pretends that ours is a perfect system. There will be no perfect system until men are perfect. And economic life requires constant progressive reform and change. The reason is simple. Free men ccnstantly find new inventions and new ideas. Some of them find new varieties of wickedness. And let me interpolate that it was Old Republicans who, beginning fifty years ago with the Anti-Trust laws, established seven out of ten of the principal Federal agencies which exist today for the prevention of monopolies and business abuse. But we do not need to sink the ship just to drown the rats.

I have seen the other systems of Europe at work. I am for free enterprise not because it is a property system or a profit system or a Chamber of Commerce slogan.

I am for it because I know it is inseparable from intellectual and spiritual liberty. Because it is the only road to higher standards of living. Because it is the only system under which morals and self-respect of men can survive.

I then described the march of progress under a free economy and continued:

The major problem America confronts today is whether we shall shape our economic system on free men or whether we shall introduce into it a mixture of personal power with coerced or regimented men. That is the flaming conflict in the world today. [. . .–ed.]

No one will today doubt the enmity of many of Mr. Roosevelt's associates to free enterprise. With beguiling phrases Mr. Roosevelt has mixed some of the working parts of these coercive systems into American life.

The introduction of this power or compulsion economy into free enterprise is not always direct. It is often indirect through monetary and credit policies and spending. It is in part by beguilement of subsidies with public money and disadvantage to those who do not take it. My constant curiosity is whether it leads to complete Fascism, or to complete Socialism, or just plain economic nonsense.

In any event these children of men have erected a new Tower of Babel which they also camouflaged under the European term, Planned Economy. The true name is Coerced Economy. The headlines tell us of its bricks and mortar—Government Devalues Currency; Government Manages Currency; Government Manages Credit; Government Deficits; Government Debt Double Great War; Government Forced Monopolies in the N.R.A.; Government Dictation to Business, to Labor, to Farmers; Government Competes in Business with Citizens; Government Fixes Prices; Government Restricts Production; Government Pump Priming; Government Controls Elections; Abundant Life; Objectives.

It mixes all the stimulating drinks on the bartender's shelf. This does not make for sobriety.

You will find every one of these powers and these economic ideas some-where along the Berlin-Rome-Moscow axis.[37] And to force these ideas on America you have seen attempts to control our Courts, to control our Congress, to control our elections, to control our public opinion with mass propaganda and slogans. All that at least has a faint odor of totalitarian government.

If you do not believe something has been mixed into the American sys-tem of free men I give you a Great Mystery.

There is the mystery that if you produce less you will have more. There is the mystery of raising costs of production by government action. In that case you increase prices and then wait for the people to buy more. There is the mystery of how you fill pay envelopes while the government stimulates war between labor unions. There is the mystery of how citizens can compete in business with the government which sends its bills to the taxpayer.

There is the mystery of how money taxed from the citizen and spent by politicians will produce more employment than the citizen can give. There is the mystery of how politicians can run the specialized business of the coun-try better than the citizens can do it. There is the mystery of how farmers can use their own judgment amid orders shouted from the national capital.

There is the mystery that devaluating the dollar like shortening the yard-stick makes more cloth in the bolt. There is the mystery of how frightened men will undertake new enterprises even if the banks are jammed with printing-press credit.

And there is the mystery that Santa Claus can reign throughout the year and never pay his bills.

There is the mystery of buying all the loose gold and silver in the world, then burying it in the ground at Fort Knox and West Point. That is the old method of curing rheumatism by carrying a potato in the pocket.

There is the mystery of letting down our tariff on farm products. The for-eign farmer sells beef to us, so another foreigner will have more money to buy our surplus beef. The foreigner was grateful and complimented us highly on our good-neighbor policy.

There is the mystery of the ever-normal granary. Then surely prices were to go up. And behold, the farmer filled the granary to the roof and out into the yard. And the world saw the granary was full and they all said it was

---

37. [*Editor's note*: A reference to Nazi Germany under Adolf Hitler, Fascist Italy under Benito Mussolini, and the Communist Soviet Union under Joseph Stalin. All were in power at the time of Hoover's speech.]

good-neighbor policy. They said we do not need to buy for the present, for our good neighbor is keeping it in store for us and will always sell it at what it cost him. And the price went down. Now we propose to dump the ever-normal granary onto the foreigner at less than cost. Even Joseph did not do that. And now Mr. Wallace[38] admits it all [to be–*ed.*] a failure and says he should have some more power to perform some other mystery.

When you solve these mysteries you will know something has been mixed with free enterprise. It is probably all clear to you, now that coercive economy has been renamed Liberalism.

Mr. Roosevelt's Babel of Confused Economy certainly never reached to heaven. But like the people of Babel the speech of men is confused and their energies scattered.

The Consequences

And where have we got to now? We are six years from the beginning of the New Deal. The other democracies in the world were as deep in the wide-world depression in 1932 as we were. All of them, except France, have years ago regained employment for their people, and such degree of prosperity as new war fears or wars permit. And France adopted the New Deal. She is now trying to abandon it. We—free from those fears of war—have 11,000,000 or more unemployed. We have 30,000,000 people who are living on relief or some part of pay from the government. Our farmers are still in distress with prices lower on the old gold basis than ever before. We shall see a rise in the national debt to over 40 billions. It does not seem to have been a self-supporting prosperity. However, we are daily assured that our recovery is fully planned.

I then explored the New Deal economic results in detail:

A recent investigation and report by the New Deal itself states that poverty is increasing in the land.

With 11,000,000 unemployed after six years we did not need an elaborate report to prove it. All that it proves to me is that the New Deal slogan might be two families in every garage.

We certainly can conclude that: *The economic forces created by this mixture of European coercive systems into free enterprise have failed to bring recovery or security.*

---

38. [*Editor's note:* Henry A. Wallace (1888–1965) was President Franklin Roosevelt's secretary of agriculture from 1933 to 1940.]

I then gave figures showing failure to recover employment within six years after the New Deal started, which are stated in detail in Volume III of my *Memoirs* in a section devoted to "The Aftermath"[39] and continued:

And at this point let me explode that phantasmagoria with which the New Deal always attempts to justify its actions. They say when they came into office the people were neglected and starving. That is a lie. In various words they monotonously claim that the depression proved that free enterprise had failed. They assert the nation was bankrupt, that it was in ruins. They chatter tragically about the tramp of marching revolution. These men misled the people that they might impose a new system of life.

Certainly it is true Mr. Roosevelt's approach to the White House was greeted with a panic of bank depositors.

People were trying to remove their money from the reach of inflation or devaluation. A recent report issued by a leading group of economists confirms flatly that the incoming administration (that is the Roosevelt administration) was conclusively responsible for the panic of bank depositors and the closing of the banks.

But even a temporary bank depositor's frenzy does not bankrupt a nation. . . .

Maybe our country was bankrupt. But if so we were attending the bankruptcy proceedings in our own 20,000,000 automobiles. Nor is attendance at revolution usually by automobile. . . .

This American economic system of free enterprise depends for productivity and consequently the jobs for men on two most sensitive human emotions. Those emotions are confidence and fear. . . .

1. Six years ago the Republic Administration handed Franklin Roosevelt the Constitution intact in spirit as well as in letter. The safeguards of liberty among men were unquestioned. The independence of the courts was inviolate. Men had been appointed justices who commanded universal esteem. The Congress was respected as an independent arm of the government. The rights of the states had not been impaired.

Today not a single one of the ideals and institutions committed to Mr. Roosevelt is unqualifiedly secure.

That certainly diminishes the security of men and undermines long-view confidence.

---

39. [*Editor's note*: See Herbert Hoover, *The Memoirs of Herbert Hoover*, vol. III: *The Great Depression, 1929–1941* (New York: The Macmillan Company, 1952), pp. 349–485.]

2. There is an unmoral doctrine adopted by every government which seeks to take power from the hands of the people. That is that the end justifies the means no matter how dishonest. These exhibits all around us of wholesale political corruption undermine long-view confidence of men in the future of America.

3. A large part of the nation has been compelled or taught to depend upon the government.

The self-respect of states and local governments has been bought or sabotaged. Governments of great states and mayors of great cities stand hat in hand before the appointive nonentities in Washington, begging for a handout from moneys taken from their citizens. And these appointive nonentities act as if it were their money given as favors.

The New Deal has apparently given up all hope of returning America to full productive employment. Their relief officials tell us that the W.P.A.[40] or something like it must be permanent. That attitude toward these distressed men is the abandonment of hope for return to their productive jobs and decent wages. The attitude is wrong but certainly this does not establish confidence in the future of America.

4. And out of all this comes another evil force. That is disunity in America.

The great human objective of an economic system must be to lift the marginal substandard group into the economic middle class. But far from it today, we are on the road to the creation of a Europeanized proletariat, institutionalized by government, supported by government and voted by government.

We have workers organized against workers.[41] We see section arrayed against section. That makes for neither social justice nor social security. Nor is it America, for a house divided against itself cannot stand.

Mr. Roosevelt last night naturally mentioned the need of national unity. How about these policies of organizing workers against workers? Of section against section?

Mr. Roosevelt said: "I am proud of the fact that I have never called out the armed forces of the state or the nation except on errands of mercy." Mr. Roosevelt omitted to mention that the Governors have been compelled to call out the National Guard, which is part of the armed forces, not once but 90 times during his administration to put down conflict stirred by New Deal

---

40. [*Editor's note*: Works Progress Administration.]
41. [*Editor's note*: At the time of Hoover's speech, two labor union groups—the American Federation of Labor and the Congress of Industrial Organizations—were bitter rivals.]

policies. He neglects also to mention that in the Hoover Administration no Governor ever had to call out a single soldier to put down industrial conflict. In fact the National Guard was called only once and that was to compel the inoculation of cows in Iowa.

All this stirring of conflict does not build confidence in the future of America.

5. New Deal monetary credit and inflation policies leave every man uncertain as to what the future value of his dollar will be. His every venture, every insurance policy, even his daily business is a bet on the currency. These policies stimulate speculation in the stock market instead of creative enterprise. They constantly undermine confidence in the long-view future.

6. This trail of government spending and mounting public debt comes to one of three precipices. It must be repaid by taxes, by inflation, or by devaluation. And these taxes coming in large part from the people who toil steadily . . . [against a reduction] in the purchasing power of [money]. . . .[42]

But beyond this through ignorance or design the method of taxation discourages initiative and enterprise and confidence.

7. As to how we will pay the increasing debt, I don't know. As for tonight I accept the New Deal theory. That is, we will not have to pay for it. Our children will do that. And they will pay it with tears and bitterness toward our generation. At best it will grievously handicap their every opportunity in life. For a third of their days they will be working for the government. Certainly this constant increase in debt rots confidence in the future.

8. And there are the incessant and indiscriminate attacks upon business. Do they make for confidence in the future?

And these attacks go farther than upon business men. How about the Labor Board[43] for example? . . .

But what about the coercion of other workers by this board? What about the coercion of employers? And what of this un-American combination of powers of legislator, prosecutor, judge, jury and executioner in any group of men? That is a violation of every process of justice known to the American people. The most emphatic demand in the first constitution of Massachusetts was a government of laws and not of men. All this, however, may be merely a morning exercise in Fascism.

But does it establish confidence in the future of America?

---

42. [*Editor's note*: In the original text of this speech as printed in 1940, this sentence was as follows: "And these taxes coming in large part from the people who toil steadily reduce the purchasing power of the people." Why Hoover later changed his phraseology is unknown.]

43. [*Editor's note*: The National Labor Relations Board.]

And I am not talking about the effect of confidence or fear upon Big Business or banks or Wall Street. I am talking about John Q. Public. Big Business never leads. It is always ready to do business. It awaits on orders for goods or services or investment of savings by John Q.

John Q. sees all these mysteries and dangers about him. What does he do? If he is conservative he and his wife delay building that house. They delay buying that davenport or refrigerator. They postpone buying that piece of land. They are afraid to buy a bond for fear the government will drive or tax that industry out of business. [. . .–ed.]

From . . . John Q.'s actions business lives hectically; employment is uncertain. Because it cannot get capital, it slows down on its improvements for the future and more men are out of jobs.

And now let us explore the practical proof of all this breakdown in long-view confidence. And it is very practical. If we look back we will find that this country in the six years prior to 1932, which includes two years of the depression, spent about 45 billion 100-cent dollars on private construction work. That is homes, factories, electric power plants, machinery, etc. That is building for the future. That is the product of long-view confidence.

Now let us look at the six years subsequent to 1932. And that includes Mr. Roosevelt's "prosperity years." In that period we spent only 17 billions on private construction.

The governmental public works in the two periods shows only 2 billions increase [in construction] to offset 28 billions loss of private construction. If you search those figures you will find a large part of the reason why at the very top of Mr. Roosevelt's planned prosperity there were 11,000,000 men walking the streets looking for jobs. The New Dealers' self-justification is that their "objectives" were to help the underdog. They surely have got him under. [. . .–ed.]

Our Humanitarian Purpose

Now let us for a moment explore the economics of our larger purpose. That is the enlargement of our whole American standard of living.

We hear much of New Deal "objectives." That word has now been substituted for "the abundant life." Such words can be made to scintillate like the Aurora Borealis. And they have proved about as effective in illuminating the long and difficult highway of human progress as the Aurora itself.

Even if we assume these objectives to be sincere, certainly it is time to remember that the road to Paradise is not paved either with professions of good objectives or good resolutions. The hot spot we are now in is paved all over with "objectives."

There are a multitude of these objectives which you may surmise I do not approve of.

What of personal power, of coercive economy, of these steps toward Fascism and Socialism, this destruction of free enterprise, this weakening of the safeguards of liberty, this reckless spending, debt and unbearable taxes, of immorality in government, and others?

I have repeated elsewhere the test given us by the Greatest Teacher of mankind. "Ye shall know them by their fruits. Do men gather grapes from thorns or figs from thistles?"

The New Deal has given emphasis to humanitarian "objectives." The country needed it. . . . My criticism is that many of their other objectives destroy the hope of humanitarian progress. They cancel out any real hope of full employment and higher standards of living to all the people—labor and farmers alike. In fact the sum of these New Deal objectives cancel themselves out in poverty.

. . . Common sense is the hardest of all commodities to sell. Emotion is the easiest of all things to distribute.

Truly we wish for the abolition of sweated labor, or child labor. We want shorter hours, more leisure. We want real farm relief. We must have protection of women and children. We must have collective bargaining. We want old-age pensions, relief of the unemployed and support to war veterans. We want increasing public health services, spread of medical attention, hospitalization and education. All these and many more resolute objectives of progressive men were going concerns before the New Deal was born. The New Deal deserves credit wherever it has in reality advanced them. . . .

But when you can scan the newspaper headlines and find Grand Juries, Senatorial committees and the press charging that the administration of these humanitarian measures is impregnated with the spoils system, corruption of public officials and of elections, you at least wonder if the primary objective is not power rather than humanity.

The people grow poor in personal liberty when its officials grow rich in personal power. And you wonder if idealism can live in the same land with moral debauchery. What has a nation profited if to gain any objective it has lost its own soul? . . .

But how are we ever going to restore production under these monetary policies, these shackles on industry, this coercive economy, this discouragement of the initiative of men, this decay of confidence in the future? . . .

The greatest humanitarian objective of them all is jobs for 11,000,000 men. Another is farm stability. Another is to lift the standard of living of all the people. It would seem that these are the forgotten objectives.

[Conclusion–ed.]⁴⁴

[...–ed.]

But what should we do to restore these 11,000,000 men to productive jobs, to give real relief to the farmer and the business man and to start America on the road to progress? Mr. Roosevelt said he would not let the people down. The time has come to let them up.

I am not going into a long program. I do not suggest that the nation go backward. Progressive men never go backward. [...–ed.]

1. Resume honor to the Constitution of the United States, and thus give men confidence that the safeguards of free men will be upheld.

2. Resume common morals. Both morals in thinking and morals in governmental action.

3. Resume the American system of free enterprise. Clean out these European mixtures of coercion. Correct the faults of private enterprise, but do not destroy its productivity. Without that all else fails.

4. Trust 130,000,000 free people in the United States to have more sense than a dozen starry-eyed boys in Washington.

The first step to start us on our way is to elect independent men to Congress in the place of these yes-yes men.

To insure a free government, to maintain free enterprise we have long since learned that the Congress must be independent of the President.

Make Congress independent. That will be a sign to America that we have changed our national road from compelled men to free men. It will bring new confidence in the future that will quickly make jobs.

This must come before we can restore productive jobs for these 11,000,000 unemployed.

And this is also the first measure of farm relief, for the farmer's first market is full dinner pails at home.

Then a confident, alert, alive, and free people, enthused with incentive and enterprise, will quickly repair losses, repay debts, and bury mistakes. It will make economic security a reality for the worker and for the farmer instead of a broken-down objective.

---

44. [*Editor's note*: In his *Crusade against Collectivism in American Life* manuscript, Hoover omitted this caption, which was in the original text of the source he was quoting.]

Give us the election of a new Congress of independent men and watch America come back.

These three addresses produced an internal explosion in Mr. Roosevelt. I learned in after years they were the cause of my subsequent exclusion from any participation in war organization.

For the first time since 1932 this election of 1938 demonstrated the rising tide of opposition of the American people to the New Deal collectivism. The Republicans gained 80 seats in the House, 6 in the Senate, and 11 governorships. It was much less my addresses that made this result than the courageous meeting of the issues by our candidates. I, however, received thousands of communications and a host of editorials stating that I had made a substantial contribution to this result.

Mr. Farley's account of the election was:[45]

Election night I was at my offices in the Biltmore. [. . .–ed.] During the long night I spoke several times to the President. He was surprised at the extent of the sweep, far more surprised than I was. . . . The President said that he had expected to lose one Senator and perhaps sixteen Representatives, but he was not prepared for a deluge.

The American people seemed to be responding to the fundamental issues. . . .[46]

45. James A. Farley, *Jim Farley's Story: The Roosevelt Years* (McGraw-Hill Book Company, Inc., New York, 1948), p. 148.

46. [*Editor's note:* This sentence does not appear on page 148 of Farley's autobiography. Nor does it appear in the 1951 and 1953 versions of Hoover's *Crusade* manuscript. Most likely this sentence was Hoover's own, added by him in his 1955 revision and erroneously printed in the page proofs as part of Farley's quotation.]

CHAPTER 10

The Crusade against Collectivism from the 1938 Congressional Election to the Presidential Election of 1940

The Republican Convention and Campaign of 1940

Although much of my energies during the year 1939 (see section . . . of this memoir on *Foreign Relations*)[1] were absorbed by my crusade to keep America from becoming involved in the European war, I still tried to keep before the country our creeping collectivism of "Planned Economy" in preparation for the Presidential election of 1940.

On February 13, 1939, I delivered a Lincoln Day address from New York City. It contained a justified note of triumph from the Congressional elections. I said in part:[2]

> Eighty years ago if an observer could have looked down on this Republic from the high stratosphere he would have seen a nation sadly divided and confused. It was a nation professing liberty yet holding millions of slaves. It was furiously debating property rights, states' rights, decisions of the Courts, and secession.

> *[The Confused State of the Nation–ed.]*[3]
> . . . [But with the] renewed inspiration from Abraham Lincoln this nation marched on to a glorious progress unparalleled in the history of mankind.

---

1. [*Editor's note:* This is a reference to another segment of Hoover's memoirs: a section at one point titled *Lost Statesmanship*, at another point *Foreign Relations of the United States from 1932 to 1954*, and known informally as the "War Book" and Magnum Opus. Eventually Hoover gave it the title *Freedom Betrayed*, under which it was published posthumously. See George H. Nash, ed., *Freedom Betrayed: Herbert Hoover's Secret History of the Second World War and Its Aftermath* (Stanford, CA: Hoover Institution Press, 2011).]

2. [Herbert Hoover, *Further*] *Addresses upon the American Road, 1938–1940* [New York: Charles Scribner's Sons, 1940], pp. 58–68 [for the full text—*ed.*].

3. [*Editor's note*: In his *Crusade against Collectivism in American Life* manuscript, Hoover omitted this caption. It appears in the speech text printed in *Further Addresses*.]

Today if the observer in the high stratosphere were to look down on this Republic he would find a people more sadly divided and confused than at any time since Lincoln's time. . . .

He would find the richest and most powerful nation in the world confused by its own inventions; disordered in its own economic life; hurt by the weakening of private and public morals; arming from fear of foreign violence; discouraged by vast destitution in a land of plenty; frustrated by failure of age-old panaceas. He would find strange doctrines of class struggle, of personal power, of extravagance, of debt, and of hate. He would see our nation still professing liberty yet pursuing ideas which limit and endanger the liberty of men.

Yet none the less again today above all this din and discouragement rises that same supreme chord of all human emotions—the liberty of men.

I then sketched the progress of the Republican Party under the banner of liberty and its degeneration under the impacts of collectivism.

On June 4th I delivered, with a national broadcast, the commencement address at Lincoln University in Tennessee. I said in part:[4]

A Confused World

You are about to enter a world more confused as to its ideas and its principles of life than has been the case for a long time.

Your president has requested that I speak upon one particular confusion. That is the protection of personal liberty in the changing economic and social pressures. And the preservation of liberty is an appropriate subject to a University dedicated to the memory of Abraham Lincoln. . . .

Broadly you are in the cross rip currents from the contending forces of three revolutions in ideas which have swept over the world in recent centuries.

The first was that revolution of intellectual, spiritual and personal freedom which finally flowered into the American system of liberty. Out of these freedoms of mind and spirit were born great scientific discoveries, great inventions.

The second revolution was from the tremendous industrial and economic changes which arose with these discoveries and inventions.

The third revolution which now invades the world is a swing back to ancient ideas of compulsion now being revived as new Utopias to end the miseries of the times.

---

4. Full text in *Further Addresses . . . 1938–1940*, pp. 197–207.

There are other forces in motion but these are enough for a half hour's discussion. . . .

The Revolution of Liberty

The first revolution established your inheritance of liberties. . . .

In building protections to these liberties our forefathers were fearful mostly of the dangers of political power. They builded a government of unique checks and balances against personal power. In the youth of our national life these protections to liberty were ample except the delayed action on slavery. During this period of simpler life, economic wrong-doing could largely be dealt with under the Ten Commandments, with appropriate penalties.

The Industrial Revolution from Scientific Discovery[5]

Fifty years after the establishment of personal liberty came the real application of science. . . . From the [this–*ed.*] gigantic control of physical power we have created the huge tools of civilization. [. . .–*ed.*]

I then summarized the march of technology over the years.

About sixty years ago the economic revolution began to clash with the fundamentals of liberty.

We learned from bitter experience that these vast tools could be used for purposes of exploitation and oppression. They were sometimes so used. That defeated liberty itself.

Then we came slowly but certainly to the realization that we can no more have economic power without checks and balances than we can have political power without checks and balances. Equally they lead to tyranny.

. . . We abandoned the concept of laissez-faire half a century ago.[6] We abandoned it spiritually for its violation of liberty, and practically because we learned that it was the hindmost who threw bricks at the social edifice. We learned that the economic foremost are not always the best nor the hindmost the worst. . . . We learned that social injustice is the destruction of justice itself.

---

5. [*Editor's note*: In the quoted text as published in 1940, the word "Industrial" does not appear.]

6. [*Editor's note*: In the sentence in the original text of this address as published in 1940, Hoover declared: "The significant thing is that we began to abandon that concept of laissez-faire half a century ago." Why he later altered the wording is unknown.]

To correct these evils we began some fifty years ago to experiment with governmental regulation to protect liberty from economic abuse and economic power. Our first major step was the anti-trust laws. And we have multiplied these laws for regulation of business, of labor, and economic life every single year since. . . .

Your forefathers sought to protect liberty from political power. Your fathers sought to protect it from economic power.

A Third Revolution in the Air[7]

In the midst of these experiments with which we were bringing our economic achievements under control, there arrived a third revolution in the world. . . .

. . . The operation of all this complex mechanism of economic life is based upon the cooperation of men. . . . This cooperation can be obtained in two ways.

The one is voluntary cooperation in economic life under government as an umpire to see that liberty is not transgressed.

The other is compulsory cooperation under the dictation of government.

These do not seem far apart when stated in words, but they are the whole distance between liberty and no liberty. [. . .–ed.]

One sad fact emerges in comparing these systems. A system of liberty is the only system with humor. When you eliminate all our jokes on officials, on government or on the system under which we live, it becomes a dreary and jokeless world.

The economic system of liberty is no middle-of-the-road between Communism on the left and Fascism on the right. It is the opposite of both, for it is the opposition of coercion.

Moreover, two economic systems, of voluntary cooperation and compulsory cooperation, cannot be mixed. Voluntary cooperation moves from a delicate mainspring. That mainspring is the initiative, enterprise and confidence of men. The moment any part of compulsion or coercion is directed at free men their fears rise, their energies slacken, their productivity slows down, and the people suffer. Coercion feeds upon more coercion. . . . Those were the antecedent steps in the enslavement of free men in those dozen nations [in Europe–ed.] in 20 years.

---

7. [Editor's note: In the 1939 text of this address, this caption appeared before the preceding paragraph.]

The Danger to America

The great danger to America is not from violent invasion of these systems from abroad. The danger is not from open agitation of Socialism, Communism, or Fascism. The danger is the subtle growth of these compulsory ideas ... into our system under the subverted phrase "Planned Economy." ...

An interesting phase of this address was that over 3,000 automobiles full of people came to hear me. The College was initiating a drive to raise its deficit of $25,000 of the previous year which, being owed to the bank, had to be cleared before it could reopen. The College authorities thought it would be improper to appeal for money during my visit. I disagreed and suggested we ask for donations on the spot. The President of the University and I joined in a vigorous appeal. We collected over $23,000 in cash during the day.

In July I contributed an article to the *American Mercury* on the similarity of the New Deal to the early procedures of European collectivist revolutions. A few sentences indicate the theme:[8]

What were the impelling forces which led to this gigantic revolution in which liberty was abandoned after all this blood and suffering over two centuries? ...

The first outstanding fact was that *this stupendous revolution in ideas and government in these many nations had been taken at the will of the people themselves.* ... The proof of that is that it all happened with the initial loss of life of less than one thousand persons.

[...–ed.] *The dictatorship was established by powers conferred upon the man on horseback by Parliamentary leaders or confirmed by electoral action.* ...

The universal pattern was the general despair of the people that democracy could solve their economic and governmental problems. ...

In [an–ed.] effort to cure social and economic ills the nature of free enterprise upon which productivity depends was lost sight of. *The planners thought they could mix totalitarian economics into systems of free enterprise.* [...–ed.]

Totalitarian economics injected into free enterprise choked the productivity of the nation. The mixture is worse than either system alone.

---

8. [Herbert Hoover,] *Addresses upon the American Road, 1940–1941* [New York: Charles Scribner's Sons, 1941], pp. 165–173. [*Editor's note*: Hoover's article, titled "It Needn't Happen Here," appeared first in the July 1940 issue of the *American Mercury*. It was then reprinted in the volume of his *Addresses* cited here. The italics in the extract printed here are Hoover's.]

When democracy began to destroy free enterprise, it destroyed itself. It devoured its own child. [. . .–ed.]

Do I need point out the analogies of these pre-dictator periods to some recent years in America? The mixture of governmental dictation into free enterprise, the rise of pressure groups, of the starry-eyed, of the subversive, and at times the lapse of legislatures into impotence? . . .

But ours is not a country for despair. There is no ground for the defeatism that liberty is lost in America. On the contrary there are the sure foundations of hope and confidence. . . . The American people are realizing where it leads from bitter experience.

We can recover from that experience. For we have more fat on our bones than those nations which had been stripped by the Great War. We can stand more shocks. We have a deeper tradition of liberty and a sounder system of liberty than those nations who still carried over a class inheritance from Feudalism. We have no threat against our national independence which necessitates the devotion of so impoverishing a portion of our income to arms as European nations. We have no need to send our sons into European war. . . .

And we are not quitting the fight.

In the meantime an overshadowing issue came in American life—the issue of peace or war. With the beginning of the European War in September 1939, my major energies were devoted to keeping the United States out of it. I had been engaged in every phase of World War I, from its beginning to the attempts to make a lasting peace. From this experience with European quarrels and the forces in motion I could not do otherwise than fight against our involvement. I relate those efforts in other volumes devoted to the foreign policies of the United States from 1933.[9]

Furthermore, with the coming of the war I was appealed to by half a dozen countries to organize relief for their women and children as I had done in the First World War. My crusade on their behalf is related in another section of these memoirs.[10]

---

9. [*Editor's note*: This is a reference to the portion of his memoirs devoted to American foreign policy after 1932. This portion was known informally as the Magnum Opus and ultimately as *Freedom Betrayed*. See note 1 above.]

10. [*Editor's note*: Here Hoover refers to another portion of his memoirs, this one devoted to his humanitarian relief efforts for the civilian population of Europe during the Second World War. At one point he called this installment *The Four Horsemen in World War II*. Later he titled it *The Crusade against Famine in World War II*. In 1964 he published a considerably revised version of this manuscript as the final volume of his four-volume history of American relief work in the twentieth

Despite these preoccupations I did not abandon the collectivist issue, especially as the Presidential campaign and election of 1940 offered a possible opportunity for its defeat—and also to keep out of war.

Just to keep the issue alive, on February 12, 1940, I delivered a nationally broadcast address from Omaha at a Lincoln's Birthday celebration. I again, in different terms, reviewed the march of collectivism in the United States over the previous eight years, with remedies to be undertaken.[11]

The 1940 Democratic Convention

Roosevelt had repeatedly and flatly stated to Cordell Hull, John N. Garner, James A. Farley, and others that he would not be a candidate for a third term. He continued these assertions up to sixty days before the Democratic Convention.[12] In consequence of these assurances, all three of these gentlemen became active candidates in one fashion or another.

It seemed that as a result of these assurances of Roosevelt's retirement and the character of the three other candidates, there was the hope that we would at least have a Democratic candidate possibly opposed to collectivism or at least less enthusiastic for it. There was a large and genuine opposition to Roosevelt in the Democratic Party, not only for his collectivist drive but also on the third term issue.

The manner by which Roosevelt eliminated Farley, Hull and Garner is illuminated in the writings of the three gentlemen.

Farley[13] tells of how Roosevelt broke the news to him on July 12th that he could not be a candidate, using Cardinal Mundelein as his messenger of this bad news. Farley relates the conversation which began with the following remark from the Cardinal:

"It is my belief that he will run for a third term."

"Did he say so?" I asked eagerly.

"No," he said, slowly. "No, but I hope that you will support him if he does. . . . I am satisfied he is going to run," the Cardinal said.

"I can't believe it, and my belief is based on his own intimations and hints. . . ."

---

century. See Herbert Hoover, *An American Epic*, vol. IV: *The Guns Cease Killing and the Saving of Life from Famine Begins, 1939–1963* (Chicago: Henry Regnery Company, 1964).]

11. [*Editor's note*: Printed in Hoover, *Further Addresses . . . 1938–1940*, pp. 69–81.]

12. For specific times and dates when these statements were made see the biographies of Farley, Hull and Garner. [*Editor's note*: See the sources cited in notes 13, 14, and 19.]

13. Farley, [*Jim Farley's Story: The Roosevelt Years* (New York: McGraw-Hill Book Company, Inc., 1948),] pp. 174–177 [175–*ed.*].

Hull's description of his discard is:[14]

As late as about June 20, 1940, when I saw the President at the White House, he again referred to the statement he had made at repeated intervals since October, 1938, that he wanted me to be his successor. On this occasion he still gave me no indication that he intended to run again — in fact, just the opposite. [...—ed.]

   Then on July 3, 1940, ...

   The President had invited me to luncheon. We were alone. During the eating stage, I discussed and disposed of several Department matters. Finally the President suddenly said: "Well, now, let's talk some politics. You know, there are many people saying to me, 'You can't afford to let us down.'" ...

   The President thereupon began to speculate on how he himself might win under certain circumstances. He spoke slightly haltingly and disconnectedly. . . .

   He then started to get onto my strong and weak qualities as a candidate for President. He was extremely guarded compared to his former conversations with me, when he had forthrightly said he considered me his successor. . . .

   The President's whole tone and language during our conversation was a complete reversal of what it had been ten days before, when he was still advocating my candidacy.

Farley's[15] comment on Hull's feelings is of interest:

Late that same day [June 28, 1940], I had a long talk with Cordell Hull. He was thoroughly disgusted with the political situation. Like myself, he had taken the President at his word when the latter said he would not be a candidate and, as a result, he had not lifted a hand. . . .

   Saturday morning [end July][16] I went over to the State Department and into Hull's office [and said]:

   "You're the one I would like to see running in November. I have told everyone that, including the President, as you know. . . .

   "Thank you," he said simply. "I haven't any burning desire to be President. [...—ed.] Since the Gallup poll showed me stronger than he is (he looked significantly in the direction of the White House), every effort has been made

---

14. *The Memoirs of Cordell Hull* (The Macmillan Company, New York, 1948), Vol. I, pp. 858–9.
15. Farley, [*Jim Farley's Story,*] [p]p. 244 [, 330–31–*ed.*].
16. [*Editor's note:* Hoover's inserted date was erroneous. According to Farley, the "Saturday morning" conversation with Hull occurred on Farley's last day as U.S. postmaster-general. This was August 31, 1940.]

to destroy me. I don't understand it. If they destroy me, they destroy part of themselves, part of the country's position before the world.

... "I was treated unfairly by that fellow [Roosevelt–*ed.*] in his not ... giving me an opportunity to have my name go before the convention. ..."

Farley's[17] final conclusion was:

Deep in my heart I feel that Franklin Delano Roosevelt deprived Hull of the Presidency. I think I can say that in all honesty, having been in intimate touch with all delegations. I say this without malice or rancor. I feel that the party would be in a stronger position today had he allowed other men to follow him in the leadership, men who deserved laurels for years of faithful party service.

As to Vice President John N. Garner, Farley[18] quotes Garner a year before the Convention in which Garner says:

"I have no intention of playing poker with you, Jim, but will lay all my cards on the table," he began. "You don't have to commit yourself one way or the other. I want to let you know just where I stand and exactly how I feel. I mean on this third term business, Jim. I can't support a third term and will fight any third term bid for the good of the party. First off, I want you to believe me when I say I don't want to be President. God knows how true that is.

There were tears in his eyes and his voice was charged with conviction.

Garner's own account is given in Bascom N. Timmons' authorized biography published in *Collier's Weekly* during March 1948.

It says:[19]

... Roosevelt had told him [Garner] immediately after the 1937 inauguration he never intended to be a candidate again for any public office and had reiterated this intention at the Victory Dinner of the Democratic party on March 4, 1937. Garner took this as the final word on the matter. [. . .–*ed.*]

Actually, support for Garner for President began to manifest itself in 1938. In September of that year the Texas State Democratic convention unanimously endorsed him as Roosevelt's successor.

In December, 1938, a state-wide gathering of Texas Democrats launched a Garner-in-1940 boom at his birthplace at Detroit, Texas.

---

17. Farley, [*Jim Farley's Story,*] p. 256.
18. Ibid., p. 171.
19. [Bascom M. Timmons,] "John N. Garner's Story," *Collier's*, March 6, 1948, [pp. 24–25, 70, 72–*ed.*].

By January, 1939, Garner was getting pretty hot as a Presidential candidate. All the polls were showing him leading if Roosevelt did not run.

... Both houses of the Texas legislature unanimously endorsed Garner. [...-ed.] In March, the Gallup poll asked Democrats: "If Roosevelt is not a candidate, whom would you like to see elected President in 1940." Forty-two percent answered, "Garner."

Early in December, 1939, Garner publicly stated he would accept the nomination. In February and March, 1940, he entered his name in the Illinois, California and Oregon primaries. But Garner was destined to fall like the other two. Farley[20] describes the Convention processes of nominating Roosevelt for the Third Term:

The Hopkins-Byrnes strategy became clear that day [July 10, 1940-ed.]. Every effort was being directed at winning the nomination by acclamation, in an effort to convince the country there was a real draft. . . .

What I did not like was the hypocrisy: the effort put forth to make it appear that the President was being drafted, when everyone knew it was a forced draft fired from the White House itself. Many delegates were sincerely for the President; but I think I can truthfully make the statement that the majority were against the third term and did not want to nominate him again. . . .

Flynn[21] started to speak but I waved for silence [and said to him] . . .[22]

"Now, what they want is the few votes that have been pledged to me. Hopkins has been attempting, with White House knowledge and consent, to have those few votes taken away from me. And why? So that the outside world will think this is a 'unanimous draft.' You know as well as I that this 'draft' has been cooked up for months."

Farley's[23] description of the preparation of the "unanimous draft" during Senator Barkley's nominating speech of Roosevelt, is as follows:

Now preparations were on in earnest for a demonstration. Gradually the aisles of the convention were filled up by strangers with concealed cardboard banners. They united in the jammed aisles, shifting from foot to foot as the Barkley cadences rolled on.

---

20. Farley, [Jim Farley's Story,] pp. 260–1[, 268–ed.].

21. [Editor's note: Edward J. Flynn (1891–1953), Democratic politician, leader of the Democratic Party in the Bronx (New York City), and chairman of the Democratic National Committee from 1940 to 1943.]

22. [Editor's note: The conversation recounted here occurred in Chicago around midnight of July 14–15, 1940, on the eve of the Democratic National Convention.]

23. Farley, [Jim Farley's Story,] pp. 280–1, [282,–ed.] 288.

At length he produced what I was waiting for— . . .

". . . He [Roosevelt] wishes in all earnestness and sincerity to make it clear that all of the delegates in this convention are free to vote for any candidate. "This is the message I bear to you from the President of the United States."

Barkley gave the statement to the full of his resonant lungs. Then he turned away to await the roar of applause. There was no applause! The delegates stood pat. The strangers flashed their banners, which read "Roosevelt and Humanity," and began shuffling through the aisles. The organ pealed. But the delegates stood silent in their places, eyeing the marchers with distrust.

Suddenly, from over the loud-speakers throughout the hall came a bellow: "We want Roosevelt."

Surprise was registered on all faces. Mayor Kelly[24] beamed. The thundering voice went on at intervals for forty-five minutes chanting:

"Chicago wants Roosevelt!"

"The party wants Roosevelt!"

"New York wants Roosevelt!"

"The world needs Roosevelt!"

"Illinois wants Roosevelt!"

"America needs Roosevelt!"

"Everybody wants Roosevelt!"

Every now and then Barkley would give the voice added steam by yelling into his microphone, "We want Roosevelt!" He kissed the Kentucky banner in the parade. Few delegates, except for the most earnest New Dealers, like Senator Pepper of Florida, were in the parade. Once when the demonstration was fading, Barkley gave it new life by roaring, "Will the galleries remember they are our guests here and conduct themselves accordingly?" The laughter came from the marchers. Those in the gallery were quiet, strangely enough. Many left and there were huge gaps of empty red chairs. On the floor the Kellyites worked on and on, encouraged by smiling approval from their boss as they passed his box. One of the marchers yelled, "Hey Ed, we planned it that way!" as he filed past the box, a witticism widely quoted throughout the evening.

Those on the platform were as bewildered over the identity of the loud-speaker voice as the delegates. Reporters finally tracked it to a small basement room where the amplifier circuits were centered. There enjoying himself immensely was leather-lunged Thomas D. McGarry, Chicago's superintendent of sewers. He had been selected for the job by Kelly himself. A half dozen

---

24. [*Editor's note*: Edward Kelly (1876–1950), mayor of Chicago from 1933 to 1947.]

times he darted out of his basement cell to bask in Kelly's approval and to see the scene; then he would go back to his chant.

During the machine-made tumult, I studied the President's statement. . . . The statement itself was inconclusive. . . . Apparently no one except the President was satisfied with the statement. Everywhere it was regarded as misleading and evasive.

. . . One hour and ten minutes later, at 10:38 P.M. CDST, the third term tradition was broken. The vote was: Roosevelt 946 and one-half, Farley 72 and one-half, Garner 61, Tydings 9 and one-half.

Roosevelt put on a brilliant campaign against Willkie, the Republican candidate. It was a campaign largely devoted to the issue of war and peace. Roosevelt skillfully carried at the same time the voters that were for war by constant attack on the American non-interventionists and carried many of the non-interventionists by a score of repeated promises that we would never go to war.

There were, however, repercussions on the Democratic side. Garner, bitterly opposed to the third term, retired to private life. Farley, likewise opposed to the third term and disillusioned as to Roosevelt, quit the New Deal.

The 1940 Republican Convention

There were three important candidates before the Republican Convention: Senator Robert A. Taft, Thomas E. Dewey and Wendell Willkie.

Some months before the convention I had considered and consulted my friends as to entering the contest for the nomination on a straight platform of keeping out of both Collectivism and the European War. I finally determined not to make any such pre-convention campaign but some effort was made by my friends at the Convention. There were over a hundred friendly delegates.

Shortly before the Convention, Willkie began to show some strength. I favored my friend Robert A. Taft whose beginning in public life was on my staff in World War I.[25] I had a high respect for Dewey and when the convention assembled, I decided that whatever delegates might be for me would subtract from their strength against Willkie. I told them I preferred Taft because of his long experience in national affairs, but that if they preferred Dewey they had my blessing but, in any event, to oppose Willkie. With this action only a few votes were cast for me.

---

25. [In 1917–18 Taft served on the legal staff of the U.S. Food Administration, headed by Hoover. They became lifelong friends.]

John L. Lewis[26] created a momentary sensation by coming out for me. He had fallen out with Roosevelt. His statement about me was that he "preferred an honest conservative to a crooked left-winger." He subsequently, at great loss to himself, opposed Roosevelt in the campaign.

I was opposed to Willkie for many reasons. From years of acquaintance I had little confidence in his purposes. He was a Socialist in college, later a support of Bryan. Privately, he leaned to the left. He had been a Republican for less than twelve months; had never had a day's experience in government and I was satisfied that he was allied with the groups endeavoring to get the United States into war.

The voting record showed that Willkie had voted for Roosevelt in 1932 and 1936 and had not changed his registration from Democratic to Republican until twelve months before the Convention.

Farley,[27] commenting on Willkie, says:

On December 1, 1938, I had luncheon with Wendell Willkie. . . . In a general discussion of the political situation, *Willkie professed great admiration for the President and his program.* . . . *Willkie told me he was a firm Democrat and had cast his vote for Governor Lehman and the rest of the Democratic ticket.* [1938 election.]

Willkie's background was that of an attorney who made a good fight on behalf of certain southern power companies against the New Deal usurpation of their properties. In this he had shown great ability to handle the press. With this recommendation, the utility officials, bankers and brokers all over the country considered they had found exactly their man for President.

Among such ardent supporters was steel magnate Ernest Weir who largely financed his campaign, together with Thomas Lamont of the Morgan firm.

Also, among his ardent supporters were such leftish persons as Dorothy Thompson, Walter Lippmann and James Warburg. He was supported by many left-wing columnists who apparently thought it enterprising to get a left-wing candidate for the Republicans. They deserted him in the campaign.

Beyond all this I was well aware of his ultimate association with the promoters of intervention in the war of which Helen Reid, publisher of the New York *Herald Tribune* and Thomas Lamont were leading figures. It all made a formidable combination.

---

26. [*Editor's note:* John L. Lewis (1880–1969), an outspoken trade unionist and longtime president of the United Mine Workers of America.]

27. Farley, [*Jim Farley's Story,*] p. 157 (italics mine).

Both Senator Taft and Governor Dewey were opposed to our entry into the war and both had ardently opposed Roosevelt's collectivist measures.

Willkie was imbued with unlimited energy. He was naturally dramatic. He had a pleasing personality. He reached out a friendly grasp to everyone. His long experience as a public relations lawyer in public utility companies had given him good training in the art of pleasing people.

Willkie's investment banker and public utility supporters were very practical in their methods. They engaged certain "public relations" firms and by the nation-wide use of the public relations departments of the utility concerns, the brokerage houses and banks, laid down a barrage of telegrams to delegates demanding Willkie's nomination. Many delegates received over two thousand such telegrams. I received over six thousand. My secretary was unable to identify even a hundred of the senders.

On returning to California I placed the telegrams from several towns in the hands of friends in those localities for them to find out who the senders were and how they came to send them. In almost every case a solicitor had called and offered to send a telegram free and in many cases the sender was unknown. In Palo Alto, out of 60 telegrams to me, 20 had been signed with fictitious names, 10 by minors or non-voters; only two were Republicans. The solicitor was an employee of a utility company.

To bring further pressure in the convention, one of the Willkie managers had four thousand forged tickets printed for the galleries and distributed them to the clerks in brokerage, utility and other business concerns in Philadelphia. These employees were given a holiday, told to go to the convention in advance of the session, hold onto the gallery seats against the legitimate holders and yell, "We want Willkie." By mistake the bill for printing these fraudulent tickets was sent to the Republican National Committee. One of the managers of Willkie's convention campaign, later falling out with Willkie, informed me he had raised over $100,000 for these convention features. It was a discouraging exhibit of what can be done by artifice in a democracy.

Addressing the Republican Convention

I was urged by the Republican National Committee to deliver an address to the Convention, one whole evening session being set aside for that purpose.

Some of the columnists, including David Lawrence, announced that Willkie was opposed to my making such address. Knowing I was opposed to him, his supporters seemed to fear I might establish an ascendency in the Convention which would not be helpful to him. Naturally I took no position on candidates in this address.

An incident that occurred during the evening of my address indicated the length to which the Willkie supporters were prepared to go.

My address was the only one during that second evening of the Convention. While speaking, the loudspeaker failed to function properly. I found it to be clamped to the desk about fifteen inches below the level of my chin and I could not move it up. The address was greatly spoiled as sections of the hall were constantly yelling "louder." The photographs of the microphones on the speakers' stand before, during, and after my speech confirmed that the public address system had been tampered with. The radio network microphones were not tampered with as they were under the control of the broadcasting companies.

It happened that Boake Carter, a radio commentator, witnessed the tampering with the public address system. He later informed me that while he was broadcasting his story of the Convention from the Convention Hall prior to the evening meeting a mechanic came in and removed the normal flexible address microphone stand and substituted a gas pipe clamped to the platform. Carter had witnessed the confusion in the Hall when I spoke. He remained in the Hall after the Convention adjourned that evening to broadcast again and witnessed the same mechanic reinstall the former flexible stand. He asked the mechanic by whose orders he was doing this. The mechanic produced an order from one of Willkie's managers.

Carter dictated a sworn account of these incidents but died before he had executed it. However, Miss Dorothy Emerson, who had been cooperating with Carter in his broadcasts, executed a sworn minute-by-minute account of these events to supplement the one from Carter. She sent it to me after Carter's death.[28]

My address was another appeal to stand on three issues: Peace, defeat of New Deal collectivism, and rehabilitation of morals in government. These parts were a rephrasing of my oft expressed ideas and can be found in my published addresses.[29] That part devoted to peace and war is given in other volumes of this memoir.

---

28. [*Editor's note*: This affidavit, dated July 3, 1947, is included in a dossier of Hoover's manuscript drafts and documents pertaining to the election of 1940, in the Arthur Kemp Papers, Box 4, Hoover Institution Archives, Stanford University. Another copy is in "Campaign 1940: Candidates—Willkie," Post-Presidential Individual Correspondence File, Herbert Hoover Papers, Herbert Hoover Presidential Library.]

29. The full text appears in [Hoover,] *Addresses upon the American Road* [, *1940–1941*] (Scribners), pp. 205–223.

During the balloting Governor Dewey came to my rooms and stated that he was losing delegates and joined with me in an endeavor to throw his strength to Taft. As the convention was then balloting, we could do but little. Willkie secured the nomination.

So shrewd an old political observer as John Garner, according to his authorized biographer, Bascom N. Timmons, made some pungent observations on Willkie's nomination prior to the election:[30]

> ... The Willkie nomination at Philadelphia was another "throwaway" for the Republicans.
>
> "By all standards as political parties have applied them in this country, Willkie is the least available of any Presidential candidate nominated by either party in modern times," Garner told me. "He has no record of either elective or appointive public service and no record of high military service.
>
> "He has been elected to no office at all nor received a preference in any party primary. There is not a shred of ballot-box evidence that he has any grass-root strength for he entered no Presidential primary nor was he considered in any state convention electing delegates.
>
> "His utility background and his Wall Street law practice will be against him with many independents and progressive voters. He is an unknown quantity to the country from every standpoint insofar as public office is concerned. I know all about the telegrams, but telegrams don't come from polling booths. He is a former Democrat and can hardly expect the enthusiastic support of the Republican organization.
>
> "Any candidate considered at Philadelphia would, in my opinion, have done better than Willkie will this fall. There are twenty million Republicans and last-ditch anti-Roosevelt Democrats and I doubt if Willkie gets many more than those."

The Republican Campaign

After the nomination I was so indignant at the raid upon the convention, the forged tickets and the deliberate tampering with the loud speaker, that I at first resolved to announce my retirement from all interest in the campaign. My friends protested violently against my doing so. I finally agreed to say nothing for the moment and await clarification of Willkie's position on public questions.

---

30. [Bascom N. Timmons,] *Garner of Texas*, [New York: Harper & Brothers Publishers, 1948,] p. 272.

John and Michael Cowles, publishers of the *Des Moines Register* and great supporters of Mr. Willkie, were my guests at the Bohemian encampment[31] during the latter part of July. I pointed out to them that one of Mr. Willkie's difficulties would be to carry the Republican vote because of his Democratic and Socialist background and the conduct of his supporters at the Convention. I suggested that Willkie must build a bridge between the conservative Democrats and the conservative Republicans as his only hope of winning. The Cowles brothers asked that I write out something which could be used as a basis for a statement by Willkie to be included in his acceptance speech. The memorandum pointed up the area on which *conservative* Republicans and *conservative* Democrats were in agreement.

I insisted that if Willkie took any other line he would alienate large numbers of Republicans just as Landon had done and secure no substantial Democratic support.

I understood that Willkie took complete fright at the word "conservative," said he was a "liberal"; that he could not speak favorably of the record of the Republican party because he had been opposed to it all his life, and had spoken against the Republicans in every election for twenty years; that his strategy of the campaign was to attract the liberals; that the Republicans would necessarily go along.

Willkie urged me to meet him some place in the West. I concluded that if I could possibly influence him and contribute to bring the Roosevelt dynasty to an end, I should try it out. I suggested that he join me on a fishing expedition near Yellowstone Park where we would discuss national questions fully. He accepted and published the fact. After I arrived on the fishing grounds, however, he telephoned that he could not leave his current headquarters at Colorado Springs although it was only a few hours away by his plane. He urged me to come to see him, as he wished to consult with me on his acceptance speech. I sensed, however, from press reports, that he was embarrassed about something and I suggested that I could quite well return to California. He thought that would create adverse gossip so I agreed to go to him. I arrived in Colorado Springs on August 11th.

He wanted to know what I thought were the major issues. I stated emphatically that keeping out of war should be made his number one issue; that the No. 2 issue was the collectivism of the New Deal while the No. 3 issue was the third term which Roosevelt was seeking. He assured me he was against

---

31. [*Editor's note*: The annual encampment of the Bohemian Club in the Bohemian Grove north of San Francisco.]

"Managed Economy" root and branch; that he was from the depth of his soul against getting America into the war. I asked what he thought of the Cowles memorandum but he evaded the question. I suggested that a speech he had made at Des Moines a few days before on Agriculture was "planned economy" itself.

At the end of the conference he urged me to make three nation-wide broadcast speeches during the campaign. I concluded this would be an opportunity to freely express my views and agreed. Willkie announced this to the press.

I found that Russell Davenport, an out and out Economic Planner and interventionist, was Willkie's personal campaign manager and had drafted the acceptance speech. Willkie changed his mind after our talk and did not show the draft to me, although that was supposed to have been the purpose of my visit. Altogether it was a confused business which I was unable to explain at the time.

A few weeks later, Mrs. Hoover and I, in Palo Alto, listened to his acceptance speech over the radio. Before he was finished I passed a note on the back of an envelope to her, saying. "This fellow has lost his election right now."[32] After she passed away I found the note among her "important papers."

In the campaign, while chattering about free enterprise Willkie established a firm "me too" position on most of the New Deal collectivism, promising to do it better and cheaper. I was greatly disheartened, but despite Willkie the issue of keeping out of war and the third term presumably survived. I persuaded myself that Willkie, if elected, must have mostly a Republican Cabinet and that anything would be better than Roosevelt with the threat of war and his variety of Economic Planners. I therefore concluded to go on with the three speeches in which I would preach the gospel as I believed it.

While Willkie hesitated for nearly two months to come out sufficiently against going to war, Roosevelt shrewdly seized on his indecision and weeks ahead of Willkie began his twelve flat promises to keep out of war. Willkie never attained leadership in either of these two issues. Roosevelt complimented Willkie on his approval of New Deal policies.

My subsequent experiences with Willkie during the campaign were rather fantastic. I spent a great deal of hard work preparing the three speeches he had asked me to deliver. Early in September, with the election only sixty days away, I telephoned the Republican headquarters asking where and when I was

---

32. [*Editor's note*: Willkie's acceptance speech was delivered on August 17, 1940. Despite Hoover's disappointment with it, he immediately issued a press release praising it as "the call of a strong man . . . a call of hope for our country." The full text is in the Public Statements File, Herbert Hoover Papers, Herbert Hoover Presidential Library, West Branch, Iowa.]

to speak but received only evasions. In an effort to find out I went to Chicago, but the speakers' bureau was again evasive. Time was running short if the speeches were to have any effect as it required weeks to arrange the meetings and radio setup. It was at that moment obvious that Willkie did not want the speeches or my presence in the campaign as it might offend the "liberals" and the pro-war groups. Moreover, the opposition were carrying on their usual smear propaganda about me. And as I get no joy out of public speaking or Willkie's performances, I felt relieved.

All this attitude was pointed up about September 20th. On the approach of the Willkie train to California, some of my friends joined the train and suggested that he send a warm invitation to me to preside at his San Francisco meeting; that as I was making an address at the 200th Anniversary of the University of Pennsylvania I would not be able to be there, but they would secure a friendly telegram from me in response which would be most useful to read to the meeting. I knew nothing about this incident until I saw a story in the Press stating that I had asked Willkie to allow me to preside in San Francisco and he had refused as "he wanted no association with the reactionary Republicans." I became interested at this point and called three old friends—newspaper correspondents—who were on his train on the telephone to find what it was all about. They each informed me that Willkie had peddled this story to them himself.

His explanation was that Senator Hiram Johnson[33] objected to any such reference, and that he had been compelled to decide between offending me or Johnson. When he spoke in San Francisco to an audience of my life-long friends, he did not make a reference to me that an ex-constable or a political opponent would have merited. He made glowing references to the Senator.

Johnson had supported Roosevelt in 1932 and had attacked me bitterly. But later when the Senator discovered the real Roosevelt his naturally bitter enmities turned in that direction. As is often the case in public life, the emotions of political conflict die out with changing national issues. Johnson and I had become friendly on the common ground of keeping out of war. Upon hearing of Willkie's train statement I asked John Callan O'Laughlin, a responsible journalist and mutual friend, to see Johnson and find out what he knew about it all. O'Laughlin replied:

> I saw Senator Johnson this morning. He said he had never met Willkie, had not seen him, nor had he heard from him. He regarded Willkie's failure

---

33. [*Editor's note*: Hiram Johnson (1866–1945), a Progressive Republican senator from California (1917–45) and a frequent antagonist of Hoover.]

to mention you in California as an outrage. . . . He referred stingingly to Willkie's endorsement of every angle of the New Deal, foreign and domestic. . . . You may be sure [. . .–*ed.*] that Senator Johnson deeply regrets and resents Willkie's attitude.[34]

In these lights, I thought therefore I should have a showdown and telegraphed Willkie on September 29th, peremptorily asking him to confirm whether he wanted speeches from me or not, and if so where and when. To my astonishment, Willkie insisted he wanted all three speeches.

The explanation of all this vacillation came later from men who were on Willkie's train. They informed me that after his Mid-west and Pacific Coast appearances, he became disillusioned of the idea that the "Liberals" would flock to him. Governor Alfred Smith was the only one of even the old line Democrats of prominence who supported him. Therefore, he had concluded it was Republicans who must win the election for him and he wanted my help. However, it took a month to make the necessary arrangements as to my speeches, so they were all crowded into the last two weeks of the campaign and had little effect as the die was cast before that time.

It is of incidental interest that Russell Davenport, Willkie's personal manager, had transmitted to me a telegram at this time which read as follows:

Please[. . .–*ed.*] pour it on in praise of Willkie instead of slamming the New Deal.[35]

As my major purpose was to fight the New Deal collectivism, I did not respond enthusiastically to this idea.

The first of my speeches was on October 24th at Columbus, Ohio, upon the third term.[36] This should have been made six weeks earlier to have had any effect. I said in part:

---

34. [*Editor's note*: John C. O'Laughlin to Hoover, September 27, 1940, "Campaign 1940: Candidates—Willkie," Post-Presidential Subject File, Herbert Hoover Papers, Herbert Hoover Presidential Library.]

35. [*Editor's note*: Davenport's telegram of September 20 was addressed to Dudley White at Republican headquarters in Chicago. In this telegram Davenport first quoted an unnamed "most intelligent commentator" as advising: "Outstanding need for campaign is greater building of Willkie as the truly great leader. . . . Please urge all national speakers to pour it on in praise of Willkie instead of slamming New Deal. Please prompt Hoover [and several others–*ed.*]." Davenport then urged that all speeches for the national ticket sound a "constructive note" rather than a "destructive" one in the final two weeks of the campaign. See Russell W. Davenport telegram to Dudley White, September 20, 1940, "Campaign of 1940: Candidates—Willkie," Post-Presidential Subject File, Herbert Hoover Papers, Herbert Hoover Presidential Library.]

36. [Hoover,] *Addresses upon the American Road, 1940–1941*, pp. 224–239.

The Growth of "Power" in the Presidency

I can perhaps speak of this growth of power and its dangerous use in the hands of bureaucracy from more experience than most people.

We have no time here to catalogue the extraordinary powers that have been yielded by the Congress to the President. They number in scores. In economic powers alone they shape up into so-called Planned Economy. Therein we have been steadily building presidential control or dictation of taxation, governmental expenditures, money, credit, foreign exchange, banking, industrial production and distribution, prices, wages, hours, what the farmer can plant and reap, and who shall or shall not receive governmental relief. Regulation of business intended to prevent the abuses of minorities has been transformed into dictating the conduct of business. . . . These powers include the government in business in competition with the citizen. All this points toward an American breed of totalitarianism. And there are extraordinary powers outside the economic field.

At no time has one of these powers been voluntarily surrendered back to the people or the Congress.

In some of these cases the right of the individual even to appeal to the courts has been limited. And now Mr. Roosevelt opposes the Logan-Walter Bill, which simply restores the right of the citizen to the protection of the Courts.

Finally Mr. Roosevelt himself states: "We have built up new instruments of public power"—please note the use of that word "power"—which he says could "provide shackles for the liberties of the people." He is right. The liberties of the people have been shackled.[37]

All this in seven years represents a greater peacetime expansion of power in the office of the President than has taken place in all the previous 160 years. . . .

The third-term tradition is a direct check upon this personal power. In the face of this perilous increase of personal power, is this any time for America to surrender forever this vital check upon power?

---

37. [*Editor's note:* Hoover is alluding here to President Roosevelt's State of the Union address to Congress on January 3, 1936. In this address he denounced the "resplendent economic autocracy" that opposed his New Deal, and he declared: "They realize that in thirty-four months we have built up new instruments of public power. In the hands of a people's government this power is wholesome and proper. But in the hands of political puppets of an economic autocracy such power would provide shackles for the liberties of the people." For the complete text of President Roosevelt's message, see *New York Times,* January 4, 1936, p. 8.]

[Weakness of Power in the Congress and the Supreme Court –ed.][38]

In all the centuries of the struggle to establish liberty under the rule of law, humanity has builded stone by stone these safeguards against personal power. . . .

This rise of personal power of the President over the last seven years has been accomplished by the disastrous weakening of the legislative and judicial branches.

The sinister word "must" still rings in our ears. . . . Congress have been reduced to a rubber stamp for the Executive.[39] They don't deny it themselves.

The control of executive expenditures by the Legislative arm has been the battle of the people against dictatorial grasp since Edward I. That is the very root of the people's power. . . . And yet time after time in the last seven years we have seen that power surrendered to the President through gigantic unchecked lump appropriations. We have seen exposure after exposure of Congressional beguilement by the pork barrel and its intimidation by threat of loss of patronage.

If we examine the fate of wrecked republics through the world we find the first symptoms in the weakening of the legislative arm. Subservience in legislative halls is the spot where liberty commits suicide.

And how about weakening of the judicial arm? The majority members of the Senate Judiciary Committee, both Republicans and Democrats, . . . said among other things:

"It [Roosevelt's "court packing" bill–*ed.*] would subjugate the courts to the will . . . of the President and thereby destroy the independence of the Judiciary. . . . It points the way to invasion [evasion–*ed.*] of the Constitution. . . . [It–*ed.*] violates every sacred tradition of American democracy . . . [and would–*ed.*] make this government one of men rather than one of law. . . ."[40]

Does not that scathing denunciation breathe with the odor of grasp for personal power?

---

38. [*Editor's note*: In his *Crusade against Collectivism in American Life* manuscript Hoover omitted this caption, which appears in the text of his speech printed in his *Addresses.*]

39. [*Editor's note*: The sentence in the original text reads: "Nobody will deny that the majority of the Congress have been reduced to a rubber stamp for the Executive."]

40. [*Editor's note*: Hoover is quoting the majority report of the Senate Judiciary Committee on June 14, 1937, in opposition to President Roosevelt's "court packing" proposal. For the full text of the committee's adverse report, see *New York Times*, June 15, 1937, pp. 18–19.]

You may think the President's power dive on the Supreme Court failed. It did not. We have seen the Court weakened steadily with complaisant appointments. Who will say that the Court now is as great a check upon the personal power of the President as it has always been in the past?

Do we restore the protections of free men when we abandon the third-term check on the rise of personal power?

[What Has Been Accomplished?–ed.][41]

All these powers have been obtained on the ground of emergency. That emergency was said to be poverty, unemployment and a prostrate agriculture.

. . . After seven years we have 10 million unemployed; we have 18 million people on government relief; we have several million farmers barely keeping above water by government subsidy; . . . underneath free enterprise is paralyzed with fear of these very powers; we have a deficit without hope of balance; we have increased the public debt by 25 billion; we have a country disunited and divided by class hate.

Is it not time that these gigantic powers be reviewed lest perchance this growth of power has been either futile or actually defeating its purpose?

Will that desperately needed review of these powers be made by surrender of the third-term check?

Power Politics

Behind all these direct actions has been another and an even more sinister build-up of personal power in this Republic.

One characteristic of totalitarian government is that there is only one political party. . . .

The European "leader" has different departments for urging unanimity on his followers. They have a department of political machines made of office holders. These office holders control the loaves and fishes for everybody. They have a department of intimidation, with its final home a concentration camp. They have a purge department for those who object. They have a department of self-glorification. They have a department of hate. They have a department of emergencies. The leader must always be finding a new emergency when the old one wears out—like riding a

---

41. [*Editor's note*: In his *Crusade* manuscript Hoover omitted this caption, which appears in the version printed in the *Addresses*.]

bicycle he must keep going. The "leader" also holds to the doctrine of indispensability.

These European dictators have a department of international power politics. And the grimmest fact of all is that each one of these totalitarians eventually has ended in war. [. . .–ed.]

The New Deal has also developed a department of machine politics. They have mobilized about 1,500,000 federal and state officials who are allied with the New Deal party. And these office holders are the "power" over the great shower of manna which must or may be rained on one-third of our unfortunate homes through relief or subsidies or government contracts.

And here let me inject an example of smearing—or worse. Last night Mr. Roosevelt said:

"Back in 1932 these leaders were willing to let workers starve if they could not get a job."

He also said:

"I consider it a public duty to denounce falsifications and state the facts."

So do I—and right now. The report of Mr. Roosevelt's own officials in the *Congressional Record* shows that when he took over the Administration there were over eighteen million people receiving systematic organized relief. They were being cared for. There is not one person in all the records of the nation recorded as having died of hunger or cold. That relief was organized during my administration . . . under non-political, non-corrupt local committees. What Mr. Roosevelt did was to destroy these non-political and non-corrupt organizations of the destitute and to centralize it in a Federal Bureaucracy, thereby making a gigantic political machine of it. And after seven years of abundant life and prosperity there are still eighteen million people on relief. The United States Senate rings with denunciation and proof of the misuse of relief.

Even some Democratic Senators revolted. . . .

And do I need recall the gigantic city machines built up and reinforced by Federal expenditures?

The New Deal party has also established an intimidation department. We do not have physical concentration camps but the New Deal has erected a large number of intellectual concentration camps. You will recall one devoted to Corporations and other third-degree sweating of thousands of dollars for New Deal campaign books. You will recall the intimidations of the Labor Board. However, the most widely established intellectual concentration camp is the one to which opponents are condemned through the highly developed art of smearing. And do I need recall that the New Deal has builded power upon hate? Without a semblance of trial men have been condemned to the intellectual jail as of [being?–*ed.*] "reactionary," "Nazi," "men opposed to national welfare."

In this building of power the New Deal party also has a self-glorification department. I need only point out the 1400 ex-newspapermen who are now in every bureau and department of government and whose job it is to propagate their special bureau or department by continuous print or on the air. . . .

[Purge–ed.][42]

I mentioned that the leader of these totalitarian parties in Europe has a gentle habit of purging any opponents who may arise in his own party. The New Deal established that department also. . . .

I then recounted the history of the purge and the acrid comment of the Democratic newspapers on it.

Do you want to give another four years of building up of a single undefeatable party? After four years more, then what? Does not the surrender of the third-term tradition lead to a political machine which can elect to a fourth term or even a life term?

[The Moral Processes Used to Gain and Hold Power–ed.][43]

There is another method of building personal power in this Republic. It is an old enough phenomenon in democracies but never before has it been developed into so efficient a system.

Self-government is based on moral and spiritual concepts. The government must in itself represent the highest ideals of a people. If it fails it destroys the foundation of free government. Honesty is one of these concepts. There are three kinds of dishonesty in this world. There is money dishonesty. There is political dishonesty. There is intellectual dishonesty. The last is a term of politeness.

It was intellectual dishonesty that Lincoln referred to when he said you cannot fool all the people all the time. But it can be made into a system that will fool them long enough to bring them to disaster.

---

42. [*Editor's note:* In his *Crusade* manuscript Hoover omitted this caption, which appeared in the *Addresses.*]

43. [*Editor's note:* In his *Crusade* manuscript Hoover omitted this caption, which appeared in the *Addresses.*]

I recounted many instances.

Another intellectual dishonesty that has been put over the country is that the New Deal represents Liberalism. Mr. Roosevelt scarcely ever makes an address that he does not refer to "we liberals." He summons all liberals to join him. Earl Browder[44] and Harry Bridges[45] were joiners for a long time. . . .

And the over-all piece of intellectual dishonesty is the effort to cover up all this building up of personal power and the drift to National Socialism by ceaseless denunciation of everybody and sundry as Nazis and Fascists.

I could go on with example after example of this particular method of building personal power in the Republic, but there is not time tonight.

Money dishonesty is less destructive to democracy than intellectual dishonesty. We can put people in jail for money dishonesty. But intellectual and political dishonesty poisons the minds of the people. It degenerates every standard of truth. We cannot put people in jail for it. We have the laborious job of putting them out of public office.

Do you think we should hold to the third-term tradition as a check on the building up of this kind of power over the minds of the people?

The Draft of Mr. Roosevelt for a Third Term

Within the last 90 days we have seen the supreme demonstration of all this varied method of building personal power. You will recollect the spontaneity of the third-term nomination by the last New Deal Convention. . . . Here again the urbanity of debate leads me to leave the descriptive words to Mr. Roosevelt's one-time supporters. Surely when they exclaim in great pain they are likely to be both truthful and violent. [. . .–ed.]

But before I come to their remarks let us recall again the scene at that convention in Chicago. Beginning last March a number of states held Democratic primaries for President. The Jeffersonian Democrats wanted an open convention openly arrived at. If Mr. Roosevelt had not wanted a third term he could have withdrawn his name from those primaries with a ten-word telegram and had an open convention. He did not. Then a member of Mr. Roosevelt's cabinet went early to Chicago. He was Mr. Roosevelt's most intimate

---

44. [Editor's note: Earl Browder (1891–1973), general secretary of the Communist Party of the United States of America from 1932 to the mid-1940s.]

45. [Editor's note: Harry Bridges (1901–90), longtime president of the International Longshoremen's and Warehousemen's Union, as well as a militant leftist accused of membership in the Communist Party.]

friend. He lived actually in the White House.[46] I don't suppose they ever discussed the third term. And Mr. Hopkins sat in smoke-filled rooms, urging leaders, telephoning the White House hourly. Madame Secretary Perkins[47] describes the scene of the convention as having the air of a prayer-meeting. I rejoice to know that these office-holders were engaged in prayer. It was especially gratifying to see Mrs. Perkins, Mr. Hopkins, Mr. Wallace,[48] Mr. Kelly[49] and Mr. Hague[50] all sitting together on the stage engaged in prayer. You will recollect that down in the cellar of the Convention Hall a gentleman who held the office of Superintendent of Sewers in the Kelly-Nash machine[51] hooked in on the loud-speaker system. His job was to yell spontaneously at all times that this state or that demanded Roosevelt. Some of the state delegates were obviously surprised at the news. Once in a while he slipped in a yell that "Mayor Kelly wants Roosevelt." Here he was on truthful ground. A press dispatch observed that this deathless voice from the sewers would echo down the corridors of time. Mr. Hopkins must have been surprised by this voice of the people. Anyway they said Mr. Roosevelt was drafted.

[What Do Democrats Say?-ed.][52]

Now let us see what Mr. Roosevelt's former supporters say about this transaction.

Raymond Clapper, a most earnest New Dealer, present at the Convention, quotes Mr. Roosevelt's message to the Convention that he "has never had and has not today any desire or purpose to continue in office or to be a candidate," etc. Mr. Clapper continues, "I simply do not believe that. . . . I don't believe that statement is the truth. Up to that message I had faith in Mr. Roosevelt. I have so no longer." He moans that "something has gone out of public life."

---

46. [*Editor's note*: Hoover is referring to Harry Hopkins (1890–1946), one of Roosevelt's closest associates.]

47. [*Editor's note*: Frances Perkins (1880–1965), President Franklin Roosevelt's secretary of labor from 1933 to 1945.]

48. [*Editor's note*: Henry A. Wallace (1885–1965), President Franklin Roosevelt's secretary of agriculture (1933–1940) and his vice president (1941–1945).]

49. [*Editor's note*: See note 24 in this chapter.]

50. [*Editor's note*: Frank Hague (1876–1956), mayor of Jersey City, New Jersey, from 1917 to 1947 and a powerful political boss.]

51. [*Editor's note*: The Democratic Party political machine led by Edward Kelly and Patrick Nash dominated Chicago politics in the 1930s and 1940s.]

52. [*Editor's note*: In his *Crusade* manuscript Hoover omitted this caption, which was included in the text as printed in his *Addresses*.]

My own view is that something came into it eight years ago.

I must not take your time with a multitude of other quotations I have collected. But among the journalists who supported Mr. Roosevelt in previous elections I find such expressions as "machine politics," "a job holders' job," "debasement of party organization," "synthetic," "power draft," "spurious call," "fraud," "hypocrisy," "trend to dictatorship," "imperils the nation's free institutions and menaces democracy," "same argument equally good for life term," "they want power at the price of democracy." All of which shows that we Republicans understate the case.

After that exhibit of grasp for personal power do you want to abandon the one check upon it?

Conclusion

To sum it up—it is not only a tradition against a third term about which we are concerned. We are concerned with a vital check upon the rise of personal power in the Republic. . . .The President himself admits these powers provide shackles upon liberty which may be dangerous. . . . In building up these powers the independence of the Supreme Court, the Congress and the local government has been degraded. Methods of intellectual dishonesty have been used in creating this personal power. A political machine has been built which places all free election in jeopardy. An economic system is being created which drifts steadily away from free men and free enterprise down the suicide road of National Socialism. Under assumptions of personal power we are steadily drifting toward war. . . .

[. . .–ed.] During these last 25 years I have been an intimate witness to these forces in nations which endanger the lives, the security and the freedom of those who cannot protect themselves—the great mass of ordinary people. I have had to deal with these destructive floods in many nations. I have seen the dikes which protect the rights and security of men become soft and have seen crevasses break through the protective levies, pouring disaster and revolution before them. The homes, the savings, the jobs of workers, the farmers—all become engulfed in the flood of destitution and poverty. The ideals of nations and peoples are carried away. I do not say these things will finally overwhelm America. I believe that somewhere somehow the floods which bring these horrors will be stopped. But if they are to be stopped it must be by holding the dikes strong. Our dikes are weaker and softer today than ever before in our history. Now is the time to strengthen, not to weaken, these embankments. You can give that needed strength only by holding strong to this unwritten provision in our constitution against the rise of personal power in our Republic.

My second address in this campaign on October 31st at Lincoln, Nebraska, was flatly against joining in the war. It is given in the section of my memoirs devoted to keeping out of war.[53]

My third address in this campaign was delivered at Salt Lake City on November 1, 1940. I talked again directly on the collectivist issue.[54]

I do wish the New Dealers would get up a new speech for the use of their barnstormers in this campaign. . . . Maybe they all go back to the same ghost.

They always start with copious tears as to the state of the country in 1933. They naturally omit that the country was in a temporary depression, the price of our last war and the inevitable financial collapse of Europe. And they carefully omit that the country was on the way to recovery before the election of 1932 and the new low point they themselves created in a panic of bank-depositors. That was the result of the disclosure of Mr. Roosevelt's intention to tinker with the currency in violation of his promise only two months old. Then they quote statistics from their self-created low point as to how good and happy we have got since. Without that self-created low point they would not even be able to get these speeches started.

Then we come to that section where the New Deal has the monopoly of humanity and liberalism. They set up glorious social and human objectives with which we all agree. Then they answer our charge that they are not driving toward their claimed high objective, but over a precipice. The answer is to denounce the opposition as persons opposed to all human rights and having no belief in Heaven itself. They sorrowfully announce we are "reactionary," that we are the tools of Satan or of Wall Street. From that premise we are the enemy of all mankind.

Then they have an economic section of the speech devoted to the glories of making one blade of grass grow where two grew before. Or on how much better it is to be on the WPA than a wage slave in industry at twice the wages.

Then we come to fiscal policies and the glorious investment value of the deficit. Here they indicate that there is murder of women and children in the hearts of all those who suggest that the money has in part gone to the politicians and to get votes rather than for human compassion.

Then there is the section devoted to foreign relations by which everybody else is a Nazi, an appeaser or a Fifth-Columnist and that they themselves have had preparedness on order for a long time but kept it confidential.

---

53. [*Editor's note*: See *Freedom Betrayed*, pp. 208–9.]
54. [*Editor's note*: Printed in full in Hoover, *Addresses . . . 1940–1941*, pp. 240–55.]

And if you wait long enough you come to the peroration. It consists of many words but of one idea. That idea is that there is but one man in the United States who is indispensable. They affirm that he was spontaneously drafted for a Third Term by a Convention in prayer.

Now that we have heard this a thousand times will they please put somebody up to debate the way out of our national confusion?

How are we going to stop this steady drift to National Socialism within our own borders and substitute an economy based on faith — not upon fear?

How are we to stop the growth of dangerous personal power in this Republic by abandoning forever the great unwritten law against a third term?

How are we going to restore the dynamic forces in our country that will put 10,000,000[55] unemployed to productive jobs, build up a market for agriculture, and enable us to carry the burdens of armament?

How are we going to avoid inflation . . . with this continued spending and thereby the destruction of every social service?

How do they propose to organize this country so that it does not continue to stutter over preparedness?

How are we going to stop this continued drift toward war?

There are a lot of other questions we might discuss, such as . . . how are we going to restore morals in government?

As the standard New Deal speech naturally does not touch upon these subjects I will try to help out by dealing with some of them. . . .

The one transcendent issue[56] today is to preserve the freedom of men and women in America.

I then reviewed again the march of New Deal collectivism and some items on Roosevelt's speeches:

The Roosevelt Smears upon Me[57]

. . . Mr. Roosevelt in his various addresses this past week persists in trying to divert the third-term issues to a fight of the 1932 campaign over again. All right. I am glad to have him raise that matter. I have a better right than any one in this country to ask him a few questions about that campaign. And it

---

55. [Editor's note: The wording in Hoover's original 1940 speech text was "9,000,000." This change appears to be an instance of Hoover's tendency at times in his Crusade manuscript to sharpen or improve on the phraseology of speeches he had delivered years earlier.]

56. [Editor's note: In the 1940 text, the wording was "One transcendent issue."]

57. [Editor's note: This was a new caption introduced into the Crusade manuscript. In the 1940 text as printed in his Addresses . . . 1940–1941 (p. 245), the caption was "The Third Term."]

has an important bearing on Mr. Roosevelt's claims for an election to a third term. But that bearing does not lead us quite in the direction he intends.

Would Mr. Roosevelt have been elected in 1932 if he had frankly stated that he would spend and spend until he had increased the cost of government by 150 percent, and would have raised the national debt to over 50 billion?

Would he have been elected if he had not denied my specific charge in that campaign that he would repudiate government obligations and tinker with the currency or if he had admitted he would devalue the dollar?

Would he have been elected if he had not replied in answer to my charges with a specific promise that he would not attempt to subjugate the Supreme Court?

Would he have been elected if he had stated an intention to reduce the Congress to a pusillanimity?

Would he have been elected if he had promised to build up our modest 560,000 civil employees to a [total of–ed.] 1,100,000 by creation of new boards, bureaus and bureaucrats?

Would he have been elected if he had frankly stated that he intended to build up the most gigantic political machine in American history?

Do you think he would have been elected had the American people been promised the hard way—the only way—to recovery instead of futile white rabbits from a hat?

Would he have been elected if he had frankly admitted our charges that he intended to build up personal power in this republic until in his own words it shackled our liberties?

Would he have been elected if he had not denied the charges that he would pollute[58] American life with a mixture of fascism and Socialism?

Would he have been elected if he had proposed to abandon the whole Republican program of constructive peace to engage in foreign power politics and thereby build up not only distrust and hate for America but a gigantic military alliance against us[59] and thereby bring us steadily toward war?

Do you remember what Mr. Roosevelt actually said in 1932 and actually promised about all of these things and about many others?

Can even Mr. Roosevelt or any of his political adherents contend that the campaign of 1932 was honestly won?

---

58. [*Editor's note*: Hoover used the word "transform" in his original 1940 speech. See *Addresses ... 1940–1941*, p. 246.]

59. [*Editor's note*: Hoover was apparently alluding to a treaty signed by the governments of imperial Japan, Fascist Italy, and Nazi Germany on September 27, 1940. Each of the signatories pledged to assist one another militarily if any of them were attacked by a power not already a belligerent in the war. The pact was clearly aimed at the United States, which was still officially neutral.]

Are the promises of 1940 to be given any more credibility? For instance, to keep us out of war? . . . [60]

It is with some apology that I interrupt a discussion upon the fate of a nation to mention that part of Mr. Roosevelt's recent address in which he implied that I had talked of two chickens in a pot—I never said that. So that he can cease his anxiety over the weight of this in the future of the world.

Mr. Roosevelt also referred to my remark in 1932 about grass growing in the streets and the fields. I did say that. In his address [however–ed.][61] he omitted the context. I said it would happen if Mr. Roosevelt imposed the tariff reductions he was promising in that campaign. He did not keep that promise either. In fact he has actually increased [some–ed.][62] tariff items. He has reduced some others enough to set grass growing in the fields of the West that ought to be growing sugar beets and other crops. Also he has had the W.P.A. busy cutting down the grass. But we will let that pass. It is small stuff . . .[63] when a world is on fire and when a nation is in chaos. [. . .–ed.]

I listened the other night to an elaborate explanation of how times have changed since Jefferson's famous statement on the third term. The chief excuse was that Hitler was now around. Does it occur to you that Napoleon was around about in Jefferson's time—and was creating just as much trouble? Jefferson did not believe that a dictator in Europe necessitated one in the U.S.

But let me give emphasis to the fight we are making for a free election.

According to the Department of Labor there are about 4,500,000 persons on the Federal payroll through all its agencies. You add to this other millions receiving subsidies and contracts. . . . And in addition there are the allied armies of Hague, Flynn, Kelly and Nash. [. . .–ed.]

Do you think that in another four years you would have a chance to defeat such a presidential power for himself or his successor?

I then discussed the recovery in employment which had long since taken place in other countries, while we made no progress.

On October 20th Willkie telegraphed me flattering congratulations on the Columbus speech (Oct. 24th), including:

---

60. [*Editor's note*: In the text of this speech as printed in *Addresses . . . 1940–1941* (p. 246), this paragraph preceded the paragraph that precedes it here.]

61. [*Editor's note*: I have restored the word "however," which appears in the quoted passage. Hoover's omission of this word was probably inadvertent.]

62. [*Editor's note*: I have restored this word, which appears in the original quoted text. Why Hoover omitted the word is unknown.]

63. [*Editor's note*: Here Hoover omitted the words "for discussion by a President of the United States."]

I want you to know how much I appreciate everything you are doing to help me in the battle for the ideas for which we both stand.

November 3, 1940, a telegram from him:

Your speeches were masterpieces and a great contribution to the campaign. I am deeply grateful to you.

On November 14, 1940, he wrote to me thanking me for my work on his behalf in the campaign, adding:

I enjoyed your talks a great deal and have heard nothing but praise for them all over the country.

Such was Willkie.

Of course we were defeated.

His affront to me in California was very costly to him. He ran behind our Republican candidates for Congress in every district in the state by a total of over 400,000 votes. Senator Johnson and many of the Republican Congressmen were elected. Johnson never uttered a favorable word for him.

Willkie, like Landon, ran far behind his own ticket all over the country. That is, between one and two million persons voted for local and congressional Republican candidates and do not appear in the Democratic returns for President. Had Willkie carried all the states won by Republican governors he would have had 211 electoral votes instead of the 82 which he won. The Republican party lost seven seats in the House but gained five in the Senate because many Senators went to the heart of the issues.

After the election columnist George Sokolsky[64] apparently made some criticism of Willkie's conduct of the campaign. The following letter to me from Sokolsky is illuminating:

Wendell Willkie telephoned to me today about 2:30 o'clock on Saturday, November 9, and opened the conversation as follows:

"Your article in yesterday's *Sun* is interpreted by many of my friends as an attack on me. Why should you attack me?"

I replied: "It is not an attack on you. It is constructive criticism of a campaign, the results of which are a peril to the American people."

He replied that nobody will believe that. They will say that because of your long association with Herbert Hoover, he instructed you to do it.

---

64. [*Editor's note*: George Sokolsky (1893–1962), a newspaper correspondent, columnist, and longtime friend of Hoover.]

I replied: "That is unfair and untrue. Mr. Hoover supported you throughout the campaign in spite of very unsatisfactory treatment. [. . .–ed.]"

. . . I said that I had made twenty-eight speeches for Willkie in twenty-eight cities, traveled 9,000 miles and that my support was at the request of Mr. Hoover and at the expense of his friends. . . .

I said that two million votes more would have elected him; and that if his management had not been bungling and if disappointed and unhappy Republicans had not turned on him by doing less than their share of the work, he would have had the two million votes.[65]

Willkie had intimate and loyal friends who followed him all the way, and many of whom have always justified his conduct in the campaign on the ground that "you must first get elected." Like those surrounding all public men, there were many who hoped to rise with his star but who stood by only as the star was ascending in the early days of the campaign.

By the end of the year 1940 Willkie had gone over entirely to the War party although nothing in world affairs had changed the situation from his promises of sixty days before.

The test of Willkie's sincerity came months afterward, when before a Senate Committee under questioning on war issues, he confessed his own insincerity by a reply that these statements were "campaign oratory."

---

65. [*Editor's note*: Sokolsky's original letter of November 9, 1940, has not been found. The text of it (from which Hoover quotes partially here) is included in a dossier of Hoover's manuscript drafts and documents pertaining to the election of 1940, in the Arthur Kemp Papers, Box 4.]

CHAPTER 11

The Crusade against Collectivism from the Election of 1940 to the Presidential Campaign of 1944

The war in Europe overshadowed the crusade against collectivism. Moreover, I was compelled to devote my energies by [to?–*ed.*] the crusade against our entry into the war and a crusade for relief of European democracies.

However, I did not drop the collectivist subject. Soon after the election, on December 21, 1940, I made the Annual Address to the Pennsylvania Society in New York. Pertinent parts of it refer to the dangers of collectivism if we went to war.

> I am greatly honored to receive the gold medal of this great society. . . . I am glad to have a legal gold reserve at a time when that basis of credit is a criminal offense. . . .
>
> [. . .–*ed.*] It is [the–*ed.*] tragic jeopardy of democracy that if it would go to war it must adopt some part of the very system [Fascism] which we abhor. [. . .–*ed.*]
>
> Likewise, a democracy which goes to war must look forward to how it will come back again to full life after the war is over.
>
> It is easier to regiment a people than to unregiment them. They can be deprived of their liberties by a ukase, a command, or an administrative order. [. . .–*ed.*]
>
> [If we join in the war and after it is] over, it is certain that the forces pressing for economic dictatorship will be strong. These pressures are inevitable from the aftermath of poverty, economic disorder and suffering which we know from our last experience will haunt peace when it comes.
>
> We need to think these things through.[1]

---

1. [*Editor's note:* The full text of this address is in Herbert Hoover, *Addresses upon the American Road, 1940–1941* (New York: Charles Scribner's Sons, 1941), pp. 55–62.]

On January 6, 1941, Roosevelt announced an American crusade for the imposition of freedom "everywhere in the world," saying:

In the future days, which we seek to make secure, we look forward to a world founded upon four essential human freedoms.

The first is freedom of speech and expression—everywhere in the world.

The second is freedom of every person to worship God in his own way—everywhere in the world.

The third is freedom from want, which, translated into world terms, means economic understandings which will secure to every nation a healthy peacetime life for its inhabitants—everywhere in the world.

The fourth is freedom from fear, which, translated into world terms, means a world-wide reduction of armaments to such a point and in such a thorough fashion that no nation will be in a position to commit an act of physical aggression against any neighbor—anywhere in the world.[2]

It will be observed that economic freedom was totally omitted. Nor was this formula so convincing as to freedom because it was to the opening peal of bells summoning the American people to the second world crusade of war. We had not been successful in the First Crusade of 1917 and the odds against expanding freedom were far greater now.

Roosevelt's beginning of undeclared war after the election and the passage of the Lend-Lease Act, to my mind, implied the certainty of war and more collectivism.

At Stanford University on June 19, 1941, with the prospect of war ahead, I made an address summing up other speakers:

... In the changes with which the world is faced, many of our speakers have properly forecast the increase of governmental domination in the life of the people. It means more limitations on personal liberty. [...–ed.] It will come faster under the necessities of preparedness. And government may submerge all liberty in case of war. Then it is the Universities which must raise again the lamp of freedom.[3]

Hitler's attack on Russia on June 23 [22–ed.], 1941, and the eminence [imminence?–ed.] of Roosevelt's proposed tacit alliance with Stalin, in my

---

2. [Editor's note: See New York Times, January 7, 1941, p. 4, for the text of President Roosevelt's 1941 State of the Union message, including the portion quoted here by Hoover. I have corrected a few errors in Hoover's transcription of this quotation.]

3. [Editor's note: See Hoover, Addresses . . . 1940–1941, p. 193. For the full text, see pp. 188–95. Hoover spoke at a symposium marking the fiftieth anniversary of Stanford University.]

view endangered Communist expansion over much of the world. While this subject is a part of my memoirs in foreign policies,[4] I introduce here a few paragraphs from an address I made in Chicago on June 26 [29–ed.], 1941, in protest at such an alliance. The war situation at the time was that the British had defeated Hitler in the air battle of Britain and his design to invade across the Channel. The United States was now furnishing Britain with ample supplies and protecting them from submarines. By the diversion of the German armies, the safety of Britain was assured.

Roosevelt, a few months before, had announced his Four Freedoms for all the world. Referring to them, I said:[5]

In the last seven days that call to sacrifice American boys for an ideal has been made as a sounding brass and a tinkling cymbal. For now we find ourselves promising aid to Stalin and his militant Communist conspiracy against the whole democratic ideals of the world. Collaboration between Britain and Russia will bring them military values, but it makes the whole argument of our joining the war to bring the four freedoms to mankind a gargantuan jest. [. . .–ed.]

. . . The ideological war to bring the four freedoms to the world died spiritually when we made that promise.

If we go further and join the war and we win, then we have won for Stalin the grip of Communism on Russia and more opportunity for it to extend in the world. We should at least cease to tell our sons that they would be giving their lives to restore democracy and freedom to the world. [. . .–ed.]

Practical statesmanship leads in the same path as moral statesmanship. These two dictators—Stalin and Hitler—are in deadly combat. One of these two hideous ideologies will disappear in this fratricidal war. Both will be weakened. Statesmanship demands that the United States stand aside in watchful waiting, armed to the teeth, while these men exhaust themselves. Then the most powerful and potent nation in the world can talk to mankind with a voice that will be heard. If we get involved in this struggle we, too, will be exhausted and feeble.[6]

---

4. [*Editor's note*: See George H. Nash, ed., *Freedom Betrayed: Herbert Hoover's Secret History of the Second World War and Its Aftermath* (Stanford, CA: Hoover Institution Press, 2011), especially pp. 223–44, 581–82.]

5. *Addresses upon the American Road, 1940–1941*, pp. 87–102 [italics added here by Hoover–ed.].

6. [*Editor's note*: This paragraph does not appear in the text of Hoover's 1941 speech as printed in ibid., pp. 87–102. Nor did Hoover utter these words in his nationally broadcast address, a recording of which survives. Hoover evidently composed this paragraph but did not actually use it on June 29, 1941, because of time constraints; such was his later explanation. For more on the variant texts of this address, which Hoover considered to be the most important one of his life, see *Freedom Betrayed*, p. 231 and pp. 581–82, notes 8 and 9.]

The day will come when these nations are sufficiently exhausted to listen to the military, economic and moral powers of the United States.[7] And with these reserves unexhausted, at that moment, and that moment only, can the United States promote a just and permanent peace. . . .

Here in America today is the only remaining sanctuary of freedom, the last oasis of civilization and the last reserve of moral and economic strength. If we are wise, these values can be made to serve all mankind.

My countrymen, we have marched into the twilight of a world war. Should we not stop here and build our defense while we can still see? Shall we stumble on into the night of chaos?[8]

Speaking at Chicago on September 16, 1941, I said, in part:[9]

The first trench in the battle for the four freedoms is to maintain them in America. That rests upon fidelity not only to the letter, but to the spirit, of constitutional government. Failure of Congress to assert its responsibilities or for the Executive to take war-like steps without the approval of the Congress is a direct destruction of the safeguards of freedom itself. We are on the way to weaken these freedoms in America—not to strengthen them.

Freedom of speech and expression is being stifled by war phobia right now in the United States.

Incidentally, there is a fifth freedom. That is economic freedom. Freedom for men to choose their own callings, to accumulate property in protection of their

---

7. [*Editor's note*: Hoover's sentence here differs from the original version printed in *Addresses . . . 1940–1941*. There the sentence reads (p. 102): "When that day comes [a peace conference–*ed.*] the other nations will be sufficiently exhausted to listen to the military, economic and moral powers of the United States." Hoover appeared to be referring in 1941 to all belligerents, not just the Germans and Russians.]

8. The consequence of this alliance was to extend Communism from 200,000,000 people in Russia before the war to 800,000,000 people in Europe and Asia. Hanson Baldwin, the military editor of the *New York Times* says (*Great Mistakes of the War*, [New York: Harper & Brothers Publishers, 1949 and 1950,] p. 10):

> There is no doubt whatsoever that it would have been to the interest of Britain, the United States, and the world to have allowed—and indeed, to have encouraged—the world's two great dictatorships to fight each other to a frazzle. Such a struggle, with its resultant weakening of both Communism and Nazism, could not but have aided in the establishment of a more stable peace; it would have placed the democracies in supreme power in the world, instead of elevating one totalitarianism at the expense of another and *of the democracies* [italics are Baldwin's–*ed.*]. The great opportunity of the democracies for establishing a stable peace came on June 22, 1941, when Germany invaded Russia, but we muffed the chance.

Several other historians agreed with him.

9. Full text in *Addresses upon the American Road, 1940–1941*, pp. 103–116. [*Editor's note*: The quoted passage is found on pp. 110–11. The italics were added later by Hoover.]

children and old age, freedom of private enterprise that does not injure others. The
other four freedoms will not survive without this one.

A large number of the men administering our preparedness program do not
believe in this freedom. . . .

And listen, my countrymen, to another voice of experience. Freedom from want
was never won by a war.

With the American entry into war in December 1941, an expansion of economic and other controls was a necessity. They could be carried out by two entirely different methods: The first was to organize the largest measure of responsibility of the industries and trades to cooperate with the Government which was successfully done in the First World War. The second method was to rely wholly upon the force of law, with fines and jails for violations. The second plan with its coercions was collectivism itself. And with these methods the New Deal could realize its dreams of final and complete dictation to industry, agriculture, labor, business, government building, the operation of plants, censorships, confiscation of most incomes and most of the other gadgets of collectivism.

To many of us it appeared that the American system of freedom was lost forever. But as the war went on I gained a growing hope. The war regimentation not only proved very irksome but with it was a daily demonstration of the incapacity of bureaucracy, its arrogance, its lawlessness, and its corruption. The Economic Planners did have a heyday, but it was an overdose. The public learned the real meaning of collectivism as it crept out of its disguises.

I made an amiable address in New York on May 20, 1942, which was nationally broadcast, saying in relation to war collectivism:[10]

You asked me[11] to say something on the theory and practice of personal liberty during the war. However, when you are riding an earthquake there is a tendency to less interest in the theory of geology than to the more immediate practice.

We are in this war. The only road out of it is victory. There will be no liberty anywhere if we lose the war.

Inside America we are vibrating between two poles. We are fighting to preserve personal liberty in the world. Yet we must suspend part of it at home, in order to win. And suspension creates grave dangers because liberty

---

10. Full text in [Herbert Hoover,] *Addresses upon the American Road, 1941–1945,* [New York: D. van Nostrand Company, Inc., 1946,] pp. 160–171.

11. [*Editor's note:* In the original text as printed in Hoover's *Addresses*, this sentence began: "The Conference Board has asked me . . . ."]

rapidly atrophies from disuse. Vested interests and vested habits grow around its restrictions. It would be a vain thing to fight the war and lose our own liberties. If we would have them return we must hold furiously to these ideals. We must challenge every departure from them. [. . .–ed.]

. . . And we have no right to complain. Our soldiers and sailors are deprived of all their freedoms except the right to grouse a little. But they will expect their freedoms back when they come home.

Our Previous Experience

But at least in this war we are not on strange paths. The World War of 25 years ago was also a total war when there was total mobilization of the civilian population. It was a strange phenomenon in American experience. We had to pioneer suspensions of liberty. We had to march through strange swamps of total mobilization of civilian effort. We had to find our way in unknown and ambushed forests of peace-making and through the unrevealed and precipitous mountains of economic disorganization and restoration of liberty after the war. After that war we had to carry the burden of saving all Europe from the greatest famine of all history. No one had trod these human wildernesses before. We were lost many times. We made many mistakes. The problems of organization are today more intense as we have a larger part in the war. But there is nothing in essence of organization that differs from the last war. We then got some experience in what not to do. And we did some things successfully, including winning the war. . . . And preserving the American way of life afterwards.[12]

I then sketched our experience with freedom in World War I and discussed the problems of economic freedom and free speech during the second world war, saying:

My first suggestion is that we adjourn trying to reform freedom and to make America over anew socially and economically during the war. This war is dangerous enough to require one single undeviating purpose on the part of the Government. . . .[13]

There will be plenty of time to exercise the spirit of reform after the war is over. The world is passing into different forms and shapes which no man

---

12. [*Editor's note*: This sentence does not appear in the original address as published in 1946. Hoover apparently added it later.]

13. [*Editor's note*: Italics added later by Hoover.]

can foresee. The things to reform will be far different from what they now appear. Just now such efforts divert the energies of the government and the people, they dislocate war effort and above all they create a thousand frictions, a thousand controversies, suspicions and disintegrating currents which destroy unity in the people.

I have, however, felt that we must be philosophical on these questions, for every generation discovers the world and its tasks as being all new and strange to the human race. And it is a good thing that they do—or we would grow too old and lose our race vitality.

But I would like again to suggest that total war is not new. I venture the further idea that we generally have a little too much of the word New around about. In trying to get out of the age of misery imposed by the last world war we have somewhat overworked this word New. It has become a signpost to some easy way to escape.

We have had in the last 25 years the New Freedom, the New Day, the New Era, the New Outlook, the New Epoch, the New Economy, the New Dawn, the New Deal, the New Proposal and the New Liberty. I coined one of them myself, but a newer thing came along. Now we are fighting against Hitler's New Order and Tojo's New Asia. This war seems to revolve around the word New. The New Testament being often omitted.

That word applies better to physical things than to human forces. Indeed when the sun rises in the morning we hail it as a new day. We cheer the passing of the night. But it is a false analogy in the march of civilization. Our chores for the new day were assigned the night before. Our abilities to perform them were formed not only last year but over centuries or even geologic time. If the new day has no link with yesterday there will be chaos.

I wish sometimes we could change words once in a while. We might give some relief to the word New by substituting such ideas as advance, progress or recovery. They would not only connote forward movement but they would also connote that there were values in the past. They would connote stability instead of violence.

In any event, there is no need to take on the load of a new social and economic order in the middle of this dangerous stream. It does not help us to get across.[14] [. . .–*ed.*]

. . . Today intolerance at the hands of some self-appointed persons and organizations has already, in five months, risen to great heights. . . .

---

14. [*Editor's note*: Italics added later by Hoover.]

[. . .–*ed.*] One cult undoubtedly believes that [. . .–*ed.*] there is a great group of Americans somewhere in some dark corner who want defeat. . . .[15]

[But–*ed.*] the national gunning for this phantasmagoria has taken in too much ground. The high priests of this cult have concluded that all those who were opposed to war before Pearl Harbor cannot possibly debate. . . .[16]

[. . .–*ed.*] [Debate] must come from many sources and many places and not from the government alone. It is a safe area for vigorous speech. [. . .–*ed.*]

Today again we have a victory to win in war, in making peace and in restoration of freedom. And again as before it must be won by our united effort, by the heroism of our men in the field, and by the eternal vigilance of a free people.

During 1942, I had several calls from British Cabinet members such as Ministers Sir Oliver Lyttleton, Lord Beaverbrook and Brendan Bracken, together with Mr. Arthur [W. S.–*ed.*] Robinson,[17] Mr. Churchill's "Colonel House." I took those occasions to impress upon them the dangerous fire with which the British were playing in the character of propaganda lecturers and missionaries they were sending to the United States. They were dominantly of the Fabian Socialist Party, such as Harold Laski, H. G. Wells, J. B. Priestley, and the Red Dean of Canterbury.[18] Their purpose was to cultivate permanent collectivism in the United States. I suggested that if we in the United States went collectivist, Britain would follow. My auditors insisted that they had to send men agreeable to Roosevelt.

Despite the heart-breaking blunders in war administration, I kept quiet for a whole year until December 3, 1942, when I broke out with a gentle national broadcast from New York on the philosophy of organization which I felt some of the officials in Washington, whose work was already bogging down, might take to heart.[19]

---

15. [*Editor's note*: This was apparently a reference to pre–Pearl Harbor interventionists who now wondered whether those who had been pre–Pearl Harbor isolationists were genuinely committed to the war effort.]

16. [*Editor's note*: In the original text as published in his *Addresses*, Hoover had said ". . . cannot possibly be patriotic Americans ever." Why he changed his wording is unknown.]

17. [*Editor's note*: Hoover was undoubtedly referring to William S. Robinson (1876–1963), a prominent Australian businessman and an old friend from Hoover's mining days. Robinson visited Hoover in New York City several times during World War II, when Robinson was working closely with the Australian and British governments on war-related mining matters. Hoover considered Robinson to be a kind of "Colonel House"—that is, an informal adviser to Prime Minister Winston Churchill of Great Britain. During World War I, Colonel Edward M. House had been an intimate adviser to President Woodrow Wilson.]

18. [*Editor's note*: Hewlett Johnson (1874–1966), a noted British Anglican clergyman, known as the "Red Dean of Canterbury" because of his outspokenly pro-Soviet political views.]

19. *Addresses upon the American Road, 1941–1945*, pp. 172–178.

Some Principles of Civilian Economic Organization in Total War

[. . .–*ed.*] In total war the first necessity is to put forth the maximum military strength. The only limitation on the size and equipment of military forces is the number of men that can be spared from the two jobs of producing arms and keeping the civilian population alive and the spirit strong on the home front. Obviously the utmost work, the energy, the talents of every adult civilian are involved.

Failure in organization and strategy on the home front may be as disastrous as failure in organization and strategy on the military front. [. . .–*ed.*]

Those who participated in the sleepless nights and the sweaty days of organizing civilians in the First World War naturally look at the organization of this war somewhat through the spectacles of that experience. The organization of the last war was not perfect. It had to pioneer its problems without a previous World War to refer to. This war should be easier to organize than the last one by virtue of that experience and the lanterns it affords for dark places. [. . .–*ed.*] And each generation has to learn not to touch hot stoves and has generally to discover the world. . . . Time makes us philosophical. For democracy moves by incessant trial and error. [. . .–*ed.*]

Seventeen months after passing the Conscription Act in that war 4,400,000 men were in arms, largely trained and largely equipped. About 2,000,000 of them were transported overseas. That war was organized by increasing the Federal civilian employees by about 435,000. It is now twenty-seven months since the Conscription Act of this war was passed. The present armed forces are about six million men. Less than one million are overseas. And we have increased the Federal civilian employees by over 2,000,000 to do the job in this war. . . .

From our own experience and the experience of all other countries in the last war . . . we can distill some principles or policies of organization of civilians. . . .

(1) The first of these principles for democratic countries is that all civilian activities should be directed by civilians and within limitations laid down by the legislative body. Otherwise we shall be a military dictatorship with all its implications.

(2) The second principle is that civilian activities must be directed by single-headed administrators. In every country in the last war—and in this war—the United States, Britain, France, and for that matter Germany, all boards, committees, or commissions proved a failure except in advisory or judicial functions. . . . We can no more administer civilian activities in war with a committee than we could direct a battle with a committee.

(3) The third principle is that all functions and authority in respect to a particular activity must be concentrated into the hands of one administrator. We can no more have an administrative job divided over several independent men than we could conduct a battle with several independent generals. The problems of production, distribution, conservation, and price fixing in any particular material are interlocked. The same single head must direct all these functions. Otherwise we have infinite confusion, conflicts, and waste. . . .

(4) The head administrators of such major groups should comprise a War Council sitting directly with the President. Here alone the general economic and civilian policies should be determined, the conflicts and overlaps planed out, with the President present as the final umpire. There was a War Council or a War Cabinet in every principal nation in the last war. There is one in every principal nation in this war, except in the United States.

(5) The first civil necessity of total war is the maximum production of war essentials. Increased production is the best answer to shortage, and all the mechanisms of price and controlled distribution must be focused toward increasing production. If maximum production is to be secured, the high-cost producer must be brought into action. And, with drastic taxes on excess profits, the low-cost producer does not get away with anything consequential.

To secure maximum production there must be no rules of labor that restrict or retard effort or output beyond those which safeguard health.

(6) There are some principles or policies in assignment of manpower. We can better appraise our manpower if we calculate the male manpower available and assume that women can do the rest. There are certain jobs that only men can do. There are jobs that are beyond the physical strength of women. There are jobs that require long training and skill for which there is no time to train women. The number of males between 18 years and old age is a positive number and there is a considerable number who are unable to work. If we compute the males necessary to carry on the government, the professions, the farms, the transportation, the mines, the skilled crafts, and to fight, we shall find certain limitations on what we can do. . . .

(7) The seventh principle relates to control of inflation and justice in distribution of short commodities. That involves price fixing, wage fixing, controlled distribution, conservation, and rationing, all of which are inherent in the administration of total war.

In general there are two methods of price fixing. The one is by fixing . . . price ceilings over retail and wholesale prices. The other method is to fix prices of a given commodity or raw material at as near the source of production as possible and to regulate the subsequent percentage addition for processors and the mark-up for merchants. General price ceilings . . . were tried out by every nation in that war [World War I–*ed.*] and proved a failure. All nations came to the alternative method. Theoretically, if all prices were frozen before the economic structure was disrupted by war, they might work. But to fix them after war begins, with price and wage relations distorted, only leads to a million conflicts and confusions. [. . .–*ed.*]

Another objection to general price ceilings is that they too often stifle and delay production, and they stimulate black markets. The subsidy phase offers large opportunity for blunder and favoritism. The alternative method is just as effective in retarding price rises; it avoids stifling of production; it is a lesser burden upon conduct of the trade; it is easier to police; it requires a far less number of government officials to police and direct it.

Fixing of wages is now wholly determinable by the cost of living. There enter into it the comparative wages in other trades. Otherwise men naturally drift to the highest-paid calling and production is stifled in the lower-paid industries. To freeze men to their jobs is a violation of the constitutional freedom of men from involuntary labor.

(8) The eighth principle of war organization is to do no more regulating than is necessary to attain the major objective. Fixing of prices is necessary only upon things that the Government uses or that comprise the essentials of the cost of living. To the great mass of people 95 per cent of the cost of living lies in less than 40 staple raw materials. Price control starting near the source avoids a host of price fixing and policing of non-essentials.

(9) The ninth principle relates to the necessity to change from the normal bid and contract peace practice of Governmental purchases of commodities and services. That safeguard cannot be made universal in war. But a great measure of successful alternative was found in the system of allocations first developed in the last war. Where Government purchases or uses are from the existing industries, such as canned goods, steel, or copper, and a host of others, this system avoids a multitude of priorities and it sustains much small business.

(10) The tenth principle is to secure the enthusiastic cooperation of the civilians with the Government in order to mobilize their abilities, skill, and sacrifice with the least bureaucracy and force. A given industry will function indefinitely better with an Advisory War Board to its Federal Administrator if it be elected by the industry itself. We can have confidence that leaders of a given industry when so organized and given responsibility will serve patriotically just as we can expect of government officials. The American people respond better to a statement of the need under the words "please" and "serve" than they do under the word "verboten."

(11) The eleventh principle applies to the concentration of every governmental energy upon winning the war. Reforms or making America over, no matter how attractive, cannot but dislocate the war effort. If we lose or delay the winning of the war, social gains will be scarce for a generation. If we win it, there will be plenty of time to reform our way of life. And there will be plenty to do.

(12) And, finally, a major principle is to organize all these activities so as to assure the return to economic and personal liberty the moment the war is over. Civilian war organization is economic Fascism itself, and if Democracy is to live these measures must be dissolved. In peace times we must think in terms of preparedness for war. Likewise in war times we must think in terms of preparedness for peace—and of return to freedom.

Reconstruction and Collectivism

Holding to the hope of restored freedom after the war, I published a magazine article (*Collier's*, February 5, 1944) entitled, "A Preliminary Program of Reconstruction." The pertinent parts are as follows:[20]

> When these men, whom we fondly call boys, come back from the wars, what sort of a country will they find? What sort of a country do they want to live in?
>
> They will, under the experience in this war, have increased individual initiative, dignity and skills. They are the self-reliant. They want the security and self-respect of a job, not a dole. They want to be free to choose their own jobs and to prove their own worth. They want the rewards of their own efforts. They want to be free to plan their own lives. They want to be free to undertake their own adventures.
>
> They want the pleasure of creative work and the battle of competition. They want the joy of championing justice for the weak. They want to tell every evil person where he can go. They want a government that will keep the channels of opportunity open and equal. They want a government that keeps down economic abuse and crime. That is the social and economic climate they are looking for. . . .

I then analyzed the forces of cooperation, taxes, conversion of industry, reemployment, reducing bureaucracy and Fascist controls, and policies on

---

20. Full text in *Addresses upon the American Road, 1941–1945*, pp. 226–241. For a more extensive discussion of food problems, relief and reconstruction, see the section of these memoirs concerned with the *Crusade against Famine in World War II*. [*Editor's note*: See chapter 10, note 10.]

housing and agriculture. I especially stressed the moral and economic climate necessary for successful conversion to peace, saying:

> ... A climate of high moral standards are [*sic–ed.*] even more important to national progress than economic or social standards. Therefore, we have a job of regeneration of morals and of spirit as well as economic reconstruction. ... Also the[21] economic and social climate ... underlies the successful solution of all our problems. ...
>
> In war, the altruistic impulses rise above all others and they mainly drive the economic machine. But regrettable as it may be, the self-interest group are the dominant drive force in peace.
>
> It is this impulse that makes the difference in war. In war our people are willingly the servants of the State, but in peace they want the government to be the servant of the people.
>
> Out of all these complex instincts and impulses, we must fashion our economic life. Even the squirrels have an acquisitive nature.
>
> ... Men cannot be free in mind and spirit if government is either to operate or dictate their economic life. Nor can we have a mixture of government operation and dictation on Economic life, ... the slowing down of any one of which affects a hundred others. [...–*ed.*][22]
>
> Above all contributions to a regenerative economic and social climate is the building of a lasting peace—and confidence that it will be rightly built.

---

21. [*Editor's note:* Hoover later added these two words. As published in his *Addresses* ... *1941– 1945,* this sentence originally was as follows: "We shall explore this question of economics and social climate further for that underlies the successful solution of all our problems."]

22. [*Editor's note*: Here Hoover again altered his original wording. As published in his *Addresses*... *1941–1945,* the second sentence (and its sequel) in this paragraph read: "Nor can we have a mixture of government operation and dictation. Economic life is interlocked in a myriad of impulses and deeds, the slowing down of any of which affects a hundred others."]

CHAPTER 12

The Presidential Conventions and Campaigns of 1944

Roosevelt was nominated by the Democratic Convention for a fourth term without opposition.[1] I relate in my memoirs on Foreign Policies the promises he made to various racial groups which were subsequently repudiated.[2]

Roosevelt had campaign assistance from the usual corrupt city organizations, the Solid South and especially in a perfected hatchet group organized by the Congress of Industrial Organizations. The C.I.O. sometime before had organized the Political Action Committee under leadership of card-carrying Communists who acted under direct orders from Moscow. The C.I.O. and P.A.C. served to mobilize labor for Roosevelt, and more particularly to raise and spend money not permitted by law to the political parties.

In May, John L. Lewis called me on the telephone from Washington and warned me that, at a meeting of the P.A.C., Charles Michelson[3] had laid out their major strategy. Once again they would make me the symbol of general public wickedness. I felt flattered that I should be regarded as so important by these Communist-dominated elements.[4]

---

1. [*Editor's note*: In his *Crusade Years* version (1953) of this chapter, Hoover began: "Roosevelt insisted upon being nominated for a fourth time in 1944. He was already so physically enfeebled as to be unable to properly conduct public business and doomed to die."]

2. [*Editor's note*: Hoover was critical of President Roosevelt's behavior toward Polish-American and Jewish voters in the 1944 election campaign. See George H. Nash, ed., *Freedom Betrayed: Herbert Hoover's Secret History of the Second World War and Its Aftermath* (Stanford, CA: Hoover Institution Press, 2011), pp. 477–48, 661–65.]

3. [*Editor's note*: Charles Michelson (1869–1948), the first full-time publicity director of the Democratic National Committee and a tireless orchestrator of political attacks on President Hoover.]

4. The subversive character of the C.I.O. Political Action Committee is revealed and documented in *Report on the C.I.O. Political Action Committee*, House Report No. 1311, 78th Con[g]., 2d Sess. (Washington, 1944). [*Editor's note*: In the 1955 version of Hoover's manuscript, he included this footnote on this page but did not indicate where the note number went in his text. The 1953 version of his manuscript (*The Crusade Years*, p. 333) indicates that it belongs here.]

Lewis quickly proved correct for at once all the heavy attacks upon me were revived. It did not worry me but Dewey[5] became very concerned at their representing him as my Charles McCarthy and generally as my dummy.[6] The speeches in the Democratic Convention (which followed the Republican session) carried out the CIO program of directing the whole Democratic attack on me instead of Dewey. He was hardly mentioned. Apparently I was still as important as in 1932, 1936 and 1940. The entire tactic was completely Communist in its method—"operations smear" by creating a symbol of evil. Anyone interested in proofs can read a speech by Governor Kerr of Oklahoma at the Democratic Convention as a sample.[7] I was told Kerr had supported me in 1928 against Governor Smith. I asked my friend, Richard Lloyd Jones, publisher of the Tulsa *Tribune*, to find out why Kerr did such a foul thing as this speech. Jones reported that the whole speech was written in Washington and sent to Kerr from the White House to be delivered as it was.

As many of the statements were outrageous big lies, the California Women's Republican Committee issued a small pamphlet in answer to two score of the bolder ones. They appealed to Dewey to use this information as evidence of the intellectual dishonesty of the Democratic campaign.

The Republican Convention and Campaign

There were only two serious Republican candidates—Governor Thomas E. Dewey and Senator John Bricker.

Willkie had been a candidate for a little while. As early as 1942 he began again to make approaches to me and, in fact, said many pleasant things about me in the press. He had totally betrayed the promises he gave me during the campaign of 1940. Naturally I could not support his ambitions.

Roosevelt assisted in an effort to split the Republican party by advancing Willkie in the public mind. The President sent him around the world at

---

5. [*Editor's note*: Thomas E. Dewey (1902–71), the Republican Party's presidential nominee in 1944 and 1948.]

6. [*Editor's note*: Charlie McCarthy was the wooden dummy and sidekick of the American ventriloquist and entertainer Edgar Bergen (1903–78). The pair's comedy routines were immensely popular on radio programs from the late 1930s to the mid-1950s.]

7. [*Editor's note*: Robert Kerr (1876–1963), governor of Oklahoma (1943–47) and then a senator from Oklahoma until his death. In his keynote address at the Democratic national convention in 1944, Kerr asserted that the Republican Party had just placed "the mantle of Herbert Hoover . . . upon the shoulders of his cherished disciple, Thomas E. Dewey." Kerr vigorously denounced Hoover's response, as president from 1929 to 1933, to the Great Depression and portrayed the Republican Party as led by "modern Bourbons." The text of Kerr's address may be found in the *New York Times*, July 20, 1944, p. 11.]

government expense from all of which there was great publicity. Willkie's ideas did not find acceptance among Republicans and as a matter of fact his press activities greatly embarrassed Roosevelt. His great propaganda phrase "One World," were to become the bitter by-words to the whole human race.

He made a stupendous personal effort for the renomination by unceasing travel and speeches. He spent two or three hundred thousand dollars of his friends' money. He did not seem to realize the effect of his declaration that his attitudes in the 1940 campaign were "campaign oratory." He did not realize his hopeless standing among Republicans until his humiliating defeat in the Wisconsin primaries. With that illumination, he withdrew a very bitter man. He blamed his defeat on "conspiracies of Wall Street reactionaries" and "Republican politicians" although his financial support came again from bankers and utility men. At this very moment he was a director of the leading Wall Street bank. There was only one man in the "conspiracy" to defeat him—his name was Willkie. No observant person worried about his winning the nomination. The only real anxiety was how far his venom poured on the other Republican candidates would injure them in the next campaign.

As the pre-convention campaign progressed, it soon became evident that Dewey would be nominated. He had built a political machine throughout the country while Bricker seemed devoid of any national organization.

As usual, at the request of the National Committee, I delivered an address to the Republican Convention of Chicago on June 27, 1944. The portion dealing with Foreign Affairs appears in that section of these memoirs. One of the purposes of the address was again an appeal for Republicans to make the safeguards of free men their major issue. Also I sought to reassure Dewey by a firm announcement of my retirement from any participation in his campaign. I said:[8]

> We meet at a difficult time for a political convention. Millions of sons of both Republicans and Democrats are fighting and dying side by side. . . .
>
> You will, I am sure, permit me to claim some personal experience with these larger forces which are today dominating mankind.
>
> Like most of you coming from forebears to whom hard work was the price of existence, I worked with my hands for my daily bread. I have tasted the despair of fruitless search for a job. I have seen the problems of labor both as a workman and as a manager of industry. Long before the first world war professional work took me to many lands under many governments, both of free men and tyrannies. I dealt with the poverty and squalor of Asia and

---

8. Full text in [Herbert Hoover,] *Addresses upon the American Road, 1941–1945* [New York: D. van Nostrand Company, Inc. 1946], pp. 242–256.

the frozen class barriers of Europe. I participated on behalf of my country in the first World War. I saw the untold destruction and misery from that war. I dealt with famine among millions. I dealt with violence and revolution. I saw the degeneration and regeneration of nations. I saw intimately the making of the peace treaty of Versailles. [...–ed.]

During another twelve years I was placed by my countrymen where I had to contend with peace and war and where I had to deal with the hurricanes of social and economic destruction which were its aftermaths. I have had to deal with [the–ed.] explosion of Asiatic antagonism.... I have seen the rising tide of totalitarianism sweeping over the world.

Why do I recite all this? Because the experience that has come to me, the honors that have been given to me demand of me that I contribute whatever I can to preserve freedom in America....[9]

The 170 Years of Struggle for Freedom

Over long periods the deep-rooted forces in the world move slowly. Then from accumulated pressures have come explosive periods with wars, convulsions, violent change and a train of stupendous problems. And always a part of the complex forces in these gigantic explosions has been the quest of man to be free.

The first of these gigantic explosions which was to shake the modern world began 170 years ago with the American War of Independence and the French Revolution. After those ... wars there followed a hundred years of comparative peace in which the will to freedom spread widely over the earth.

Then came the gigantic explosion of the last World War. Again among the forces in that convulsion was the death clash of free men and dictatorship.

Men inspired by freedom were victorious twenty-five years ago and freedom spread to additional millions of mankind. But victorious men failed to lay the foundations of lasting peace. And from the destruction of that world came unemployment and poverty over the whole earth.[10] And in its wake also came instability of governments, lowering of morals, frustration of ideals and defeatism. Out of this desperate aftermath despotism rose again in the grim shapes of Fascism and Communism. By them the freedom of men was defeated over a large part of the earth.

Now we are in the midst of the greatest explosion in all the history of civilization....

---

9. [*Editor's note*: Hoover omitted here the words "and the world."]
10. [*Editor's note*: In the original text the word was "world."]

[Freedom Permits No Compromise in This War–ed.][11]

By whatever failures of statesmanship the world were [sic–ed.] brought to this ghastly second world war, the realistic fact is that we are in it. There is only one way out of war—that is, to win it. And victory will come again to our armies and fleets for the sons of America do not quit. . . .

Our Men Want Freedom When They Come Home

Recently a canvass was made among youth, both in the armed forces and on the home front, to learn what sort of a world they wanted after this war. I may tell you:

They want a home with a family, a dog and an automobile. They want the security and self-respect of a job. They want to be free to choose their own jobs and not to be ordered to them by a bureaucrat. They want to prove their own worth and have the rewards of their own efforts. They want to be free to plan their own lives. They want to be free to undertake their own adventures.

They want the pleasure of creative work. They want the joy of championing justice for the weak. They want to tell every evil person where he can go. They want a government that will keep down oppression whether from business or labor. They want a fair chance. They want peace in the world that their children never need go through the agonies and sacrifices they have themselves endured.

They want to be free Americans again. . . .

Degeneration of Freedom in the United States

At each of the great rallies of our party in 1936, in 1940 and today in 1944 I have been called to speak upon the encroachments and the dangers to freedom in our country. Each previous[12] time I knew even before I spoke that our people would not believe that the impairment of freedom could happen here. Yet each subsequent four years has shown those warnings to have been too reserved, too cautious.

The reason why these warnings have been accurate is simple. From the beginning the New Deal in a milder form has followed the tactics of European

---

11. [*Editor's note*: In his *Crusade against Collectivism in American Life* manuscript, Hoover omitted this caption, which was in the text printed in *Addresses . . . 1941–1945*.]

12. [*Editor's note*: This word was absent from the original address. This appears to be another example of Hoover's retroactively improving his text.]

revolutions which have gone before. The direction being set, the destination is not difficult to foresee.

I then again stressed the parallel march of the New Deal with European Collectivism.

[. . .–ed.] In an address on January 3, 1936, Mr. Roosevelt recounted how he had "built up new instruments of public power" which could "provide shackles for the liberties of the people" in any other hands.[13] Freedom is not promoted by shackles in anybody's hands.

We now know the peace-time shackles they provided. . . .

Can a regime which forced "shackles on the liberties of the people" in peace time be trusted to return freedom to the people from the shackles of war?

I then recounted violations of the Constitution by various Government agencies during the war and remarked:

If you happen to get into the clutches of these agencies you will find a lot of the spirit of even the Magna Charta has been forgotten, to say nothing of the Constitution. . . .

I then sketched a blueprint of how freedom should be regenerated after the war and made the following statement upon my retirement:

[Freedom, the Job of Youth][14]

[. . .–ed.] Not only life but freedom itself must find regeneration from youth. . . . Older men declare war. But it is youth that must fight and die. And it is youth who must inherit the tribulation, the sorrow and the triumphs that are the aftermath of war.

Youth Should Take Over[15]

This Convention is handing the leadership of the Republican Party to a new generation. And soon to support these younger men there will be an oncoming generation who will differ from all others. Twelve million young

---

13. [Editor's note: See chapter 10, note 37.]

14. [Editor's note: In his Crusade manuscript Hoover omitted this caption, which was in the text printed in Addresses . . . 1941–1945.]

15. [Editor's note: Hoover inserted this caption in his Crusade manuscript. It is not in the original text that he was quoting.]

men matured far beyond their years under the supreme tests of war will be coming home. To them will be added the other millions of young men and women serving in the shops, on the farms and in the offices. They also, by the responsibilities they have shared, have had their minds and understanding advanced beyond their age. From the tremendous experience in this war this new generation will have grown in responsibility, in dignity, in initiative and skills.

And these young men who are offering their lives on the beaches and in the mud, those who are fighting in the air, those who battle on the seas, will return to demand justification for their sacrifices and for the sacrifice of their buddies who have died. They will insist upon a reckoning and they will be stern and hardfaced. They will reject the easy language of politics, the straddlings and compromises, and the senseless phrases of skilled ghost-writers. And they will be watchful of political leaders lest they again be led into the giving of the blood and risking the future of their families from failures in international statesmanship. Today, more than any new generation that we have known, youth will demand a voice in its own destiny.

I rejoice that this is to be. Youth can bring the courage, the ideals and confidence which can erect a new society in America upon the debris of two world wars. We need their courage as never before.

We, the older generation, who have learned something of the great forces in the world, can advise and counsel. The issues are not new, and we can distill principles from the experience of the past. . . .

And let me say this. . . . It is through this living institution, the Republican Party, that I call upon the younger generations to take up the weapons for American liberty, to fight the good fight. . . .

And may I say this to youth: You have a great material heritage. You are receiving millions of farms and homes built by your forbears. There have been prepared for you magnificent cities, great shops and industries. But you have even a greater heritage. That is a heritage of religious faith, of morals and of liberty. . . .

You in your own manner can lead our people away from the jungle of disorderly, cynical and bitter ideas, the topsy-turvy confusions, the hopelessness and lack of faith and defeatism that have haunted this nation over these dozen years. You can lead our nation back to unity of purpose again.

We of the older generation know that you will carry forward. We wish you to carry the torch bravely and aloft. Carry it with the dauntless assurance of your forbears who faced the chill of the ocean, the dangers of the forest and desert, the loneliness of the pioneer to build upon this continent a nation dedicated to justice and liberty and the dignity of the individual man. Watch over it. Vigilantly guard it. Protect it from foes, within and without. Make for this a sanctuary and dedicate it to God and all mankind.

Youth of the Republican Party! I, representing the generation of your fathers, greet you and send you forth crusaders for freedom which alone can come under a Constitutional Republic—a Constitutional America.

We who have lived long, turn our eyes upon your generation lovingly with hope, with prayer and with confidence for our country.

Dewey was nominated. Governor Bricker was so much in the hearts of the delegates that he was nominated for Vice President by acclamation. I, of course, hoped Dewey might take up the battle for the fundamentals of freedom. I knew that Bricker would hold the lamp aloft—which he did.

Dewey's campaign strategy was again based on the fallacies of Landon and Willkie, that he could attract left-wingers and that the conservatives would vote for him anyway. Dewey asked that I take no part in the campaign as he apparently believed he could better attract the "Liberals."

The war was in fact already won and the campaign offered unexampled opportunity to challenge collectivism, the transgression of American ideals by Roosevelt, and the imperative need for their restoration—which Dewey missed. He was at times brilliant in his attacks on Roosevelt's probity, inconsistencies and administrative blundering.

A month before the election I gave the usual sealed envelope to each of two friends as to my views on the outcome, to be opened after the election. They contained nine words: "This election is lost. It could have been won."

Dewey, like Landon and Willkie, ran behind the Republican gubernatorial, senatorial and congressional candidates. Had he received these Republican votes he would have been elected.

That he could have won is also indicated by the fact that in the Congressional Campaign of 1946—only two years later—the Republican candidates not being handicapped by the compromises of this presidential candidate won handsomely.

CHAPTER 13

The Crusade against Collectivism from the Presidential Election of 1944 to the Congressional Election of 1946

Roosevelt's death on April 12, 1945 was a severe blow to the collectivists—for a while. Mr. Truman was a dual personality. On one hand he was a man of amiability and good-will, without malice or vindictiveness, with great loyalty to his friends and often with great political and moral courage. He apparently had little ideological conviction but when acting on his own instincts was more right than left.

His other personality was a Pendergast inheritance—Votes at any price, whether collectivist or freedom with the boys participating, in the good fruits of office.

Mr. Truman initially sensed the rising tide of public opposition to the Roosevelt regime and the whole collectivism of the war. Within a few months he had removed from the Cabinet Secretaries Stettinius, Stimson, Ickes, Wallace, Morgenthau, Wickard, and Perkins; Attorney General Biddle and Postmaster [General–ed.] Frank Walker departed. He brought into the Cabinet men of more conservatism, Secretary Byrnes, Patterson, Forrestal, and Anderson.

Except for a short mission to Moscow, he dropped Hopkins,[1] and for some time Thomas Corcoran, Supreme Court Justices Frankfurter, Murphy, and Black did not have the run of the White House. He even appointed a Republican—Senator Burton—to the Supreme Court.

But a political ghost soon rose by his more conservative bedside. The Democratic Party could only be held in power by the union of the solid South, Northern radicals, and City bosses. Truman, knowing the South would go along to get the loaves and fishes and to hold "white ascendancy," soon began to bring into his councils a number of the seasoned left-wingers. But he must also satisfy the Northern "liberals."

---

1. [*Editor's note*: Harry Hopkins (1890–1946), who had become Roosevelt's closest adviser.]

In his Cabinet, he appointed Senator Schwellenbach,[2] Secretary of Labor; Tom Clark as Attorney General; Julius Krug, Secretary of the Interior. He gave support or position to the old Roosevelt hands, Benjamin Cohen, Chester Bowles, Paul Porter, Clark Clifford, Leon Keyserling and Judge Rosenman.[3] In the course of time, such left-wingers as Acheson, Chapman, Brannan, and Tobin were to hold Cabinet jobs.[4]

Returning to my long crusade against Collectivism on August 11, 1945 in a nationally broadcast address on the occasion of a large celebration of my birthday, organized by the Southern California Iowa Association at Long Beach, California, I reviewed the enormous sweep of Communism and Socialism over Asia and Europe as the result of the war, and continued:[5]

The Western Hemisphere is fast becoming the last hope of free men. We do not question the right of these other nations to decide for themselves. But equally we have a right to make our own decisions. And yet we shall be besieged by the missionaries, the propaganda, the Fifth Columns of these foreign ideologies.[6] They are militant faiths that will seek to preserve themselves at home by expanding their ideas abroad, through poisoning our waters of free speech by their propaganda.

There are persons who talk of the middle of the road. The middle between what? Fascism? Communism? Socialism? Thinking American people are allergic to all of them. We should have none of them.

[The American System of Freedom–ed.][7]

Indeed the time has come when America should again proclaim our faith. We should proclaim our resolution to hold it. We should cease to apologize for it. Our first post-war purpose should be to restore it.

I then again reviewed our own system and said:

---

2. [*Editor's note*: Lewis B. Schwellenbach (1874–1948), a senator from Washington.]

3. [*Editor's note*: Samuel I. Rosenman (1896–1973), an adviser to and speechwriter for President Roosevelt.]

4. [*Editor's note*: Dean Acheson (1893–1971), secretary of state from 1949 to 1953; Oscar L. Chapman (1896–1978), secretary of the interior from 1950 to 1953; Charles F. Brannan (1903–92), secretary of agriculture from 1948 to 1953); and Maurice J. Tobin (1901–53), secretary of labor from 1949 to 1953.]

5. Full text in [Herbert Hoover,] *Addresses upon the American Road, 1941–1945* [New York: D. van Nostrand Company, Inc., 1946], pp. 257–261.

6. [*Editor's note*: In the text printed in ibid., the word was "bureaucracies."]

7. [*Editor's note*: In his *Crusade against Collectivism in American Life* manuscript, Hoover omitted this caption, which was in the source he was quoting.]

We should proclaim again and again that the road to free men and to progress and prosperity is not to be found in the spread of governmental powers and bureaucracy, but in striving to set bounds to it. For these are principles of life from which no American dare depart, whatever the exigencies or even fears of the moment.

Today fifteen million boys have joined the armed services. They have gone into battle . . . and with courage because they believed they were preserving America for free men. A million have been wounded or have died that America. . . .[8] Those who survive look to a return to the free America they have known. [. . .–ed.]

Is it not a faith? Is it not a belief for which men die? Is freedom to be defeated by slogans, or foreign propaganda, or Fifth Columns? You and I must not be marked as the generation who surrendered the heritage of America.

I made two addresses in the Fall of 1945 which attracted some attention. The first was a nationally broadcast address on "Economic Recovery from the War," at the Fiftieth Anniversary of Clarkson College of Technology at Potsdam, New York, on October 8, 1945.[9] I reviewed that the history of recovery from previous wars plainly showed that to bear the burdens of war aftermaths, we must increase the productivity of our people and the methods for doing it. I stated also that we must be free from:

Government policies which jeopardize stability of the currency and credit;

Taxes which destroy the incentives of men by taking away the reward of their efforts;

Bureaucracy which stymies productive forces by stupid meddling;

Starry-eyed Utopias which deny men reward for their efforts and thus frighten them from new adventure.

. . . Men must be free in mind, spirit and creative power so long as they do no injury to their neighbors. They must be confident of the future.[10]

On October 15 [13–ed.], 1945, I delivered a nationally broadcast address on "Moral and Spiritual Recovery from War" at the Seventy-fifth Anniversary of Wilson College at Chambersburg, Pennsylvania. Here I reviewed the war degradation of moral standards, the eclipse of truth, the increase of brutality and the degeneration in religion and the safeguards of freedom. I urged

---

8. [Editor's note: Here Hoover unaccountably omitted the words "may be free."]

9. [Editor's note: See Herbert Hoover, Addresses upon the American Road, 1945–1948 (New York: D. van Nostrand Company, Inc., 1949), pp. 29–35.]

10. [Editor's note: Ibid., p. 35.]

the obligation of our colleges to produce new leadership in the nation, and continued:[11]

> But an intangible corruption has come into our concepts of leadership during the past few years. It is dinned into us that this is the century of the common man; that he is going to do this and demand that—the idea seems to be that [the–*ed.*] common man has come into his own at last. Certainly he is a good vote-getting attachment.
>
> Thus we have developed a cult of the common man. I have not been able to find any definition of who this common man is. Most American men and especially women will fight if called common. Likewise in humility we refer to ourselves as made from common clay but we get mad when anyone says our feet are made of clay.
>
> However, whoever this political common man is, I want him to have all the unique benefits of the American way of life including full opportunity to rise to leadership. But if we are to have leadership in government, in science, in education, in the professions and in the home, we must find and train some uncommon men and women.
>
> The only seriously objectionable part of this deification of the common man is the implication that mediocrity is an ideal, that the uncommon man is to be discredited or discarded.
>
> Let us remember that the great advances have not been brought about by mediocre men and women. Rather they were brought about by distinctly uncommon men and women with vital sparks of leadership—men and women like St. Francis of Assisi, and Florence Nightingale and Abraham Lincoln. Many of these great leaders were, it is true, of humble origin, but that was not their greatness.
>
> The most gigantic experiment of this cult of all history was the dictatorship of the proletariat in Russia. It is from the fumes of this cauldron that we mostly get these ideas. But one of the humors of sociology—if there is humor in it—is that the most recent phase of the revolution in Russia is a frantic search for the uncommon man. And he is given privileges and payment relatively to other citizens far more than America offers today.
>
> There is no identity whatever between mediocrity and popular government—although that is what many of our bubble blowers are trying to put over on the American people.

---

11. Full text in [ibid.,] pp. 36–43.

The essence of our American system is that the best are to be selected for public responsibility and public service. It is also the essence of our economic life, our spiritual life, our educational institutions.

We have a recent and powerful example. In the command of our military forces and our scientific forces during the war we searched and found the uncommon men and women. . . .

[. . .–ed.] Our sure hope of recovery in the moral and spiritual world is the wealth of uncommon men and women among our people. And it is our educational institutions that will promote and train them.

To sum up (all these questions),[12] may I say that the colleges have a great obligation courageously to restore our moral and spiritual losses from the war, to renew our ideals of freedom, to regain our sensitiveness to wrong, and to provide the nation with [a–ed.] renewed supply of trained leadership. Unless we rebuild this new era on these foundations, it means the war has been lost. It means more. It means that civilization is lost. . . .

In a Lincoln Day address broadcast from New York on February 12, 1946, I struck out at the "me too" attitude of Republican candidates:[13]

Ninety years ago the great issue before the American people was free men. The Whig Party refused to accept that issue. Even worse, it sought compromises, middle courses and evasions. The young Republican Party, under Abraham Lincoln, met the issue squarely, and its strength and vitality grew from its brave and uncompromising struggle in behalf of freedom and dignity for all men. The Whig Party died.

Today the great issue before the American people is free men against the tide of Statism which is sweeping three-quarters of the world—whether it be called Communism, Fascism, Socialism or the disguised American mixture of Fascism and Socialism called "Managed Economy" now being transformed into a further ambiguity, the "Welfare State." . . .

Once more, we face a crisis in free men. As in Lincoln's time there are other issues, but again this issue dominates and underlies all others.

The question now is, will the Republican Party take this issue or will it seek to straddle, as did the Whigs 90 years ago?

---

12. [*Editor's note*: Hoover later added this phrase. It does not appear in the text as printed in *Addresses . . . 1945–1948*.]

13. Full text in *Addresses upon the American Road, 1945–1948*, pp. 49–53.

Two-party government is essential to the democratic process. But the high-purpose of two-party government is not to gain public office. The purpose is to give the people an opportunity to determine fundamental issues at the ballot box rather than elsewhere.

The American people do not have that opportunity offered to them by the political parties today. Both parties have straddled.

What the Republican Party needs, what the Nation needs from the Republican Party is a fundamental and constructive philosophy of government with the principles which flow from it. And that philosophy must reach far deeper than the froth of slogans or platform planks designed to appease every pressure group. . . .

I then sketched the history of the Party; its stand against slavery; its brave stand to end laissez-faire, a guarded economy through the Anti-Trust and regulatory laws, and over all a defiance of collectivism.

Mr. Truman, at the end of February, requested me to undertake the management of the appalling famine of 1946. On that mission, which I have described in the crusade against famine,[14] I had a unique opportunity to see personally the actual operation of Communism, Socialism, Planned Economy and Free Economy at work in 36 nations.

The processes by which Communism had triumphed in some of these countries were clear. Everywhere in the earlier stages the Socialists had cooperated with the Communists to nationalize production and distribution. In so doing, not only was the productivity of free enterprise crippled but the one substantial opposition to Communism was extinguished. They destroyed the middle-class from whom leadership in economic life must come and from whom could come the only effective opposition to Communism. The Socialists were furnishing the boarding ladders by which the Communists captured the Ship of State.

Socialism had been adopted in full scale in Britain and her productivity and living standards had dropped to the lowest levels of 70 years. France and Italy were moving to Socialism or with violent fevers of "Planned Economy." The only countries in all Europe which were making rapid recovery from the war's effects were the free enterprise countries of Belgium, Holland, Denmark, Sweden and Switzerland.

---

14. [*Editor's note*: Hoover is referring to another section of his memoirs, a segment titled at one point *The Crusade against Famine in World War II*. See chapter 10, note 10. See also George H. Nash, ed., *Freedom Betrayed: Herbert Hoover's Secret History of the Second World War and Its Aftermath* (Stanford, CA: Hoover Institution Press, 2011), pp. 576–77.]

The Tide Turns in the 1946 Congressional Election

As the 1946 Congressional election approached, it became evident that the extremes of regimentation and statism during the war had created the revulsion for which I had prayed. The 300-year old roots of freedom were not all dead.

The recoil from the war encroachments on personal liberty was evident at every hand; the exposures of the corruption and waste of the New Deal collectivism, the incapacity of bureaucracy, its arrogance, and the ruthless trampling of free men made it possible to turn the country away from collectivism. The Economic Planner had had a great spree but it was an overdose.

The turning of the people toward the right was temporarily forcing the hand of Mr. Truman. He attempted conciliation by the abolition of many of the collectivist restrictions of the war. However, his action was too little and too late for his Party. The Congressional campaign was held to the primary issue by most Republican candidates. While our Presidential candidates might hedge on the primary issue of freedom in hopes of gaining votes in the "liberals," our Congressmen and Senators from many districts had no such inhibitions. The Republican Committee having asked me to define the major issue, I stated:

> Today's major issue is between radicalism, regimentation, all-powerful bureaucracy, class exploitation, deficit spending, and machine politics as against our belief in American freedom for the individual under just laws fairly administered for all, preservation of local home rule, efficiency and pay-as-you-go economy in Government, and the protection of the American way of life against either Fascist, Communist or Socialist trends.[15]

In the Congressional elections in November, Republicans carried the control of the Senate and the House. We also elected 25 governors.

The victory was not all Republican. A solid block of anti-collectivist Democrats were returned and the totalitarian liberals and rubber stamps suffered a great defeat.

After election I made the following statement to the press:

> This has been much more than just another Congressional election. The whole world, including the United States, has been for years driving to the

---

15. [*Editor's note*: Hoover's statement has not been located in his Public Statements File at the Herbert Hoover Presidential Library. Possibly his remarks were never formally released.]

left on the totalitarian road of "planned economy," or Socialism or Communism. America is by this election the first country to repudiate this road. And it defines that the Republican Party is the party of the right. We are again moving to the goal of free men. This decision of the United States will have a profound effect on nations who have been following along the road to the left.[16]

During all these years I had received the steadfast encouragement of my friend, and a great journalist, Mark Sullivan. In this vein, he published the following statement in surveying the Republican party. He no doubt overstates my part in its resurgence, but at least it is a stimulant to one's ego.

... It is not merely that the Republicans' period out of power has been unprecedentedly long. During these twelve years the party reached a lower estate, in several respects, than any major party for generations. In one Presidential election, 1936, it carried only two states. At one time during the period, in 1937, it had the smallest representation in the House of Representatives that either party ever had—only eighty-nine Republicans out of a total of 435, approximately one out of five.

Such a low estate, of a party that had been a major one, would ordinarily have portended death. It may be said reasonably that no major political party in American history ever reached so low an estate—and survived.

The fact is, during part of the period, death of the Republican party was expected by not a few persons—some with regret, some with satisfaction. Columns of this newspaper could be filled with quotations from persons who, between 1933 and 1937, said the Republican party was dead, and waited only to be buried.

Not only did they say the Republican party was dead. With it, they said, went the thing the Republican party symbolized—the philosophy of individualism, and the so-called capitalist economic system. A phrase, "the new era," was common. President Roosevelt spoke of the "new order," rising, he said, out of the ruins of the old. It was said that President Hoover would go down in history with two distinctions, both somber—he would be known as the last Republican President and as the symbol of a dying order.

It was during those years [from 1933 to 1937—ed.][17] that Mr. Hoover, in private life, strove passionately with word and pen, in addresses, magazine

---

16. [*Editor's note*: Hoover, *Addresses . . . 1945–1948*, p. 54.]

17. [*Editor's note*: Hoover's text omitted these bracketed words, which appeared in the source he was citing.]

articles and books, to make America see the virtues of individualism, the perils of the collectivism which threatened to supplant it. That patient and laborious work of public education carried on at a time when Mr. Hoover was in the shadow of defeat, his quiet valor and steady faith—it is this, and the success that attended it, that will be Mr. Hoover's real distinction in history, rather than the somber distinctions which some assigned to him.[18]

---

18. [*Editor's note*: Mark Sullivan's column, quoted by Hoover here, appeared in the *New York Herald Tribune*, June 25, 1944, p. 2.]

CHAPTER 14

The Crusade against Collectivism from the Congressional Election of 1946 to the Presidential Election of 1948

The First Republican Congress in 17 Years

The Republican Congress (the 80th), convening January, 1947, at once began unraveling the collectivist fabric of the years before. Its major acts were:

(a) Reduction of appropriations $6,000,000,000 below the amount requested by the President. For the first time in more than 16 years, there was an operating surplus and a payment was made upon the national debt. Income taxes were reduced by $4,800,000,000 per annum. These reductions eliminated 7,000,000 workers from income tax as 71% of the reductions went to incomes under $5,000 a year.

(b) The Taft-Harley Act was passed which modified the extremely one-sided Wagner Act of 1935 and provided many protections for the individual worker.

(c) A vigorous reorganization of the Executive Branch of the Government was undertaken through a partial unification of the armed services under a single Secretary of Defense.

(d) A non-partisan commission was created by unanimous vote to examine and recommend changes in the whole executive branch of the Federal government of which I was made Chairman.

(e) A Constitutional Amendment was submitted to the States (and adopted) providing for the limitation of Presidential tenure to two terms.

(f) The Economic Cooperation Administration was established for better administration of aid and relief to foreign countries.

(g) Legislation was passed providing for a gradual step down of fabulous farm price supports.

(h) Modification was made in the tariff-making powers of the
Executive under the guise of reciprocal trade agreements.

(i) A housing program was provided under private enterprise with aid
from the government.

(j) The Congress directly or indirectly repealed or modified 76,000
rules, regulations, laws, directives and orders. The President vetoed
the Taft-Hartley Act and some other of the measures but they
were passed over his veto, with the assistance of the Conservative
Democrats. The Congress turned down many of Truman's
appointees as being inadequate for their jobs.

Taken altogether, the energies and capacities of American citizens were
released for a while from the collectivist chains which had tightened about
them for so many years.

Truman had been slow in cleaning out the Communist[s–*ed.*] and fellow-
travelers in the Government whom he had inherited from Roosevelt. The Republican Congress undertook vigorous investigation into these matters. The
President, under left-wing pressures, developed an attitude of opposition to
the Congressional efforts to get rid of them, referring to these urgings as a
"red herring." But the constant exposure by the Congressional Committees
not only of a horde of Communists in public office but their actual traitorship left him in a difficult position. Over two hundred Communists and two
hundred fellow-travelers who had filtered into the Roosevelt regime and who
held important positions, were ultimately exposed.

In the winter of 1947 I journeyed to Germany and Austria at President Truman's request to undertake what was in reality an investigation of the work of
the spirit of the Morgenthau Plan[1] in their economy. I also looked into their
recurrent food shortage which was one of the consequences of that policy. I
visited Rome, Paris and London. I give full account of the German and Austrian economy and the food question was related in that section of the memoirs on the Crusade against Famine and my report to the President, in my
memoirs on *Foreign Policies.*[2]

---

1. [*Editor's note*: In 1944 President Roosevelt's secretary of the treasury, Henry Morgenthau Jr.,
proposed a plan for the deindustrialization and "pastoralization" of Germany in order to destroy
Germany's ability to wage future wars.]

2. [*Editor's note*: This is a syntactically awkward reference to the portion of Hoover's evolving
memoirs titled *The Crusade against Famine in World War II* and to the segment on foreign policy
known informally as the Magnum Opus. See above, chapter 10, notes 1 and 10, and George H. Nash,
ed., *Freedom Betrayed: Herbert Hoover's Secret History of the Second World War and Its Aftermath* (Stanford, CA: Hoover Institution Press, 2011), pp. 769–809.]

Here I may relate that the Morgenthau idea of reducing Germany to a pastoral state was both the ultimates of vengeance and collectivism. I summed up my verbal report to the President: "You can govern Germany and Austria under the rigors of the Old Testament or can govern it under the good will of the New Testament. The difference is $1,000,000,000 a year to the American taxpayer and sowing Dragon's teeth for the Third World War."

Mr. Truman and the friends I had made in his Cabinet reversed these policies. The Germans rapidly restored free enterprise; made gigantic strides to recovery; and became a bulwark of American defense against the Communists.

On this journey I stopped in England to examine the degeneration of Britain under Socialism. I found the country on the economic down-hill slide— and already imposing drastic "austerity" to cover up decreased productivity.

To put a little more kindling under the collectivist pot, I made a Bicentennial Celebration address at Princeton University on June 16, 1947. It contained some ideological observations with an attempt at humor. I therefore give it more extensively in the hope of lightening this otherwise somber text. I said in part:[3]

I gather from other speakers that we are assembled here to celebrate the beginning of learning among the Presbyterians. Their first invitation to learning no doubt included the ideology of predestination with a fifty-fifty chance of a hot fire. Being in the neighborhood of the Quakers of Philadelphia, Princeton was naturally weaned away from [the–ed.] predestination part. Sometimes I regret the doubts which are rising about the hot fire end of that ideology. I have at times had great consolation in holding to that part of orthodoxy, because I despaired of an adequate heating place on this earth for some people. However, I will not dwell upon their names at this time.

Anyway, time has mellowed Princeton to the idea that people should be prepared to live as well as to die. [. . .–ed.]

In all professions, including my own, there is polite contempt for the ignorance and lack of real understanding of all laymen. In my youth my professors expressed it in gentle pity. I therefore agreed to take part tonight with some trepidation at fronting such a mass concentration of collegiate pity potential. However, I will never again have the chance to speak my mind to so many representatives of higher learning from all over the United States. And whatever your inward feelings are, I have you at a disadvantage. I could recall to you the beautiful citations from many of your institutions as to my wisdom

___

3. Full text in [Herbert Hoover,] *Addresses upon the American Road, 1945–1948* [New York: D. van Nostrand Company, Inc., 1949], pp. 156–162.

and knowledge with which you accompanied honorary degrees. In fact more of these citations than any one of you. With this cuttle-fish preparation, I shall list some of a layman's complaints about professors in general. [. . .–*ed.*]

Someone of your[4] profession recently announced that American colleges had degenerated into service for only the sons of rich men. Not having seen the Washington index numbers for the last hour, I do not know how many rich fathers are left. There are over 2,200,000 youth in institutions of higher learning, and if there are that many rich families in the country after taxes, then the income tax collector has missed over two-thirds of them.

But I recognize that higher education must always be in a perpetual ferment of reform. The sounds emitted, however, give the impression of mixed self-flagellation, sackcloth, ashes, determination that nothing is any good, and that the trustees are to blame. The curious part of this is that despite these no doubt minority convictions that everything in your service is wrong, 2,200,000 students insist on listening to you.

I also read that you, like all other professions—except the lawyers whom you manufacture—are greatly underpaid. I agree that you have not been carried up on our spiral of inflation. Until salvation comes, I offer you a solace. There is an idea promulgated by one wing of your faculties which implies that the full professor's salaries should be averaged down with the instructors'. I assure you that we right-wingers will support you against compulsory application of this equalitarian idea.

May I mention also an occasional attitude of a certain wing of our faculties who hold that the elders and forebears of these two million youngsters have done a wholly bad job in this land and that it must all be upset. Perhaps it could have been done better. I am sure that if I ran the place it would be better. However, the worm's eye view has its values in discovering bugs, but the bird's eye view sees the glories of the landscape.

After all, in this 200 years since the founding of Princeton, a God-fearing people under the blessing of the right-wing system of freedoms have built up quite a plant and equipment in this continent. It teems with millions of comfortable farms and homes, cattle and hogs. It is equipped with railroads, power plants, factories, highways, automobiles and death warnings. It is studded with magnificent cities and traffic jams. The terrible reactionaries have filled the land with legislatures, town councils, a free press, orchestras, bands, radios, juke-boxes and other noises. It has a full complement of stadiums, ball players and college yells. Furthermore, they have sprinkled the country

---

4. [*Editor's note*: "Our" in the original text printed in ibid., p. 157.]

with churches, laboratories, built ten thousand schools and a thousand institutions of higher learning. And somehow, these right-wing taxpayers are squeezing out the resources which maintain a million devoted teachers, a hundred thousand able professors, and the keep of these two million youngsters in colleges and universities. Possibly, another ideology could do better in the next two hundred years. But I suggest we had better continue to suffer the evils of right-wing freedoms than to die of nostalgia.

I will not dwell on worm's eye views longer. A bird's eye view shows that your profession is today doing the most amazing thing in all the history of human culture. You are providing training and the inspiration of ideals to more youth than in all the rest of the world put together. Yet we are only 6 percent of the world's population. And as a reference to my own state of California is necessary on all public occasions, I may tell you that we have more such students in higher education than in the whole United Kingdom. You have taken the burden of the G.I. flood in your stride and without complaint.

It comes my way to visit many colleges. I am confident that their two million American youth under your guidance and inspiration are the best and most promising body of future leadership this country or the world has yet seen. That they have flocked to your classrooms and laboratories is proof that they believe in you. Out of your labors there is rising a greater host of efficient, morally and patriotically inspired men and women, with a better understanding of their public responsibilities, than has any generation and any nation yet possessed. You are contributing not only to the American people but to the whole world. You are performing an exacting task requiring not only knowledge but patience, tact and vision. Yours is indeed a glorious mission, magnificently performed. You are entitled to retain your pity of all laymen.

[. . .–ed.] I will close by relating to you an incident which occurred on this campus 200 years ago. It may be an apocryphal story, and it is at least hoary with age. About this time of night a member of the new Princeton faculty rushed into the office of the sheriff of Mercer County. Excitedly he announced that he had killed a man, that he had committed murder. The sheriff told him to be calm and to tell him all about it. The professor explained that they were having a banquet on oatmeal mush to initiate this new college on its 200-year mission; there were eight speakers, just as there are tonight. And he said that when the eighth speaker had drooled a long while, "I could not stand it any longer. I fetched the college blunderbuss and shot him dead." The sheriff remarked: "You have come to the wrong place. You should go to the Scrivener's office—he pays the bounties for varmints."

With these dangers surrounding me, I close with one further remark: This University has in 200 years poured a magnificent stream of ideals and leaders into our country. The American people will gladly celebrate its birthday again 200 years hence.

Having failed to recuperate from the physical damage of my trip to Europe I went to the West for a rest. In June 1947 I was called by Speaker Joseph Martin[5] and asked if I would undertake the Chairmanship of a Commission on Organization of the Executive Branch of the Government (mentioned in "d" above). He urged that with my consent the legislation could be passed unanimously. I agreed but a month later I had an unusually severe attack of the shingles, probably as the result of my physically low state from the German winter experience. With skilled physicians I made partial recovery but had need of a trained nurse for nine months while I conducted the Commission.

I describe the work of this Commission in a separate part of this memoir entitled "The Crusade to Reorganize the Federal Government."[6]

Truman Turns Left

Mr. Truman's dual personality came up sharply to view in late 1947 and early 1948.

On October 16, 1947, he said in reply to a press question on the restoration of price and wage control, "Price and rationing controls are police-state methods. . . ." Yet only 90 days later, in his annual message to Congress, he demanded the restoration of the whole planned economy line. He had, in the meantime, become alarmed at the rise of Henry Wallace in leadership of the left-wing elements and thus a split in the Democratic Party.

As Chairman of [the–ed.] bi-partisan Commission on Organization of the Executive Branch of the Government, I engaged in no political action. However, the Republican National Committee having insisted that I appear on June 22nd [1948–ed.] before the Convention at Philadelphia, I returned to the crusade against collectivism, but formulated my speech in non-partisan terms. It was certainly non-collectivist. I said:[7]

---

5. [*Editor's note*: The Republican Speaker of the U.S. House of Representatives.]

6. [*Editor's note*: No manuscript bearing this precise title has been found. But see Hoover's manuscript "Crusade against Waste in the Federal Government: 1921 to 1955," portions of which are included in Appendix I of this volume.]

7. Full text in *Addresses upon the American Road, 1945–1948*, pp. 67–73.

This convention meets again in a continuing grave crisis.[8] And this crisis is deeper than some may think. Every important government including our own has broken its promises to mankind. [But?–*ed.*] civilization moves forward only on promises that are kept. [. . .–*ed.*] Faith has been hurt; hope has been diminished; thinking has been corrupted, and fear has been spread—all over the world.

The problems which confront us far transcend partisan action and I do not propose to speak in that sense tonight. [. . .–*ed.*]

What is done here, what *you* do here, will affect the destiny of our country beyond any estimation of this moment. For you are more than ever before the trustees of a great cause, the cause for which this party was founded, the cause of human liberty.

[The World Problem of Free Men–ed.][9]

Liberty has been defeated in a score of nations. They have revived slavery. They have revived mass guilt. They have revived government by hatred, by torture, by exile. Today the men in the Kremlin hold in their right hands the threat of military aggression against all civilization. With their left hands they work to weaken civilization by boring from within.

These tyrants have created a situation new in all human experience. We saved them from Hitler but they refuse to cooperate with us in good will or peace on earth. A powerful nation, dominated by men without conscience, finds it useful to have neither peace nor war in the world.

Whether some of us, who foresaw that danger and warned of it, were right or wrong, and whatever the terrible blunders[10] of American statesmanship that helped bring it about, we are today faced with a world situation in which there is little time for regrets.

The only obstacle to the annihilation of freedom has been the United States of America. Only as long as the United States is free and strong will human liberty survive in a world frustrated and devastated by these two wars.[11]

---

8. [*Editor's note*: This sentence does not appear in the original speech text that Hoover is quoting. There the paragraph begins: "Those who have already addressed you in this Convention have emphasized the continuing grave crisis which envelops our own country and the world." Why Hoover altered this sentence when quoting it here is unclear. Possibly he wished retroactively to improve what he had earlier written and delivered.]

9. [*Editor's note*: Hoover omitted this caption, which appears in the original speech text published in *Addresses . . . 1945–1948.*]

10. [*Editor's note*: In the original speech text, Hoover had used the word "errors."]

11. [*Editor's note*: In the original speech text, Hoover had said: "Only as long as America is free and strong will human liberty survive in the world."]

[Our Aid to Free Men Abroad—ed.][12]

It is in our interest and, above all, in the interest of liberty throughout the world, that we aid in giving strength and unity to the nations of Western Europe. It is only thus that we can restore a balance of power in the world able to resist the hordes from the Eurasian steppes who would ruin Western Civilization.

We have also the burden of increased armament to assure that no hostile force will ever reach this hemisphere.[13]

With all the good will in our hearts, our friends abroad should realize that our economy must not be exhausted or over-strained by those burdens, or the last hope of the world is lost. We should only be playing Stalin's game, for his expressed real[14] hope lies in our economic collapse for which his Fifth Columns are busily planning.

Our friends abroad should realize that we are today certainly straining our American economy to the utmost. [. . .–ed.]

Therefore, with full compassion for those nations in difficulties, certain matters in aid to them must be recognized on both sides of the world.

Our task is solely to aid their reconstruction.[15] We can provide only bare necessities. There is no room for non-essentials, profligacy, or inefficiency.

We must not create a perpetual dependence of Europe and Asia upon us. We must not soften their preparedness to meet their own dangers. Otherwise our sacrifices will only undermine their self-reliance and the contribution they must make themselves toward the saving of Western Civilization.

We must insist that reconstruction of Western Europe be as a whole. That must include the restoration of the productivity of Germany, or Europe will die. We need neither forget nor condone Nazi guilt, but a free world must not poison its concepts of life by accepting malice[16] and hatred as a guide. Otherwise, not only will our efforts fail, but the American taxpayer will be bled white supporting an idle and despairing German people.

---

12. [*Editor's note*: Hoover omitted this caption, which appears in the original speech text as printed.]

13. [*Editor's note*: In the original speech text, Hoover had written: "And we have also a huge burden . . . ."]

14. [*Editor's note*: This word does not appear in the original speech text that Hoover was quoting.]

15. [*Editor's note*: In the original speech text, Hoover had written: "The first is that our task is solely to aid their reconstruction."]

16. [*Editor's note*: In the original speech text, Hoover used the word "revenge."]

[Great Strikes Can Defeat All Freedom–ed.][17]

And if we are to carry these burdens of relief and armament, we must have uninterrupted operation of the major tools of production and distribution among all the participating nations.

We in America must face the fact that no citizen, or group of citizens, in this Republic can assume[18] the power to endanger not only the health and welfare of our own people, but freedom of the world, by halting or paralyzing the economic life of this nation. Such men have not been elected by the people to have such powers. Representative government must be master in its own house, or it will perish. We fought that battle out once with arrogant business men. We can no more have economic tyranny, if freedom is to live, than we can have political tyranny. There are other ways for determining economic justice than war on our people.

The Battle for Freedom[19] at Home

Nor does the battle for freedom all lie beyond our borders. We also have been infected with the European intermittent fever of creeping totalitarianism. It has been a mingling of germs from Karl Marx and Mussolini, with cheers from the Communists. This collectivism has slowly inserted its tentacles into our labor unions, our universities, our intelligentsia, and our Government.

Our difficulty lies not so much with obnoxious Communists in our midst as with the fuzzy-minded people who think we can have totalitarian economics in the hands of bureaucracy, and at the same time have personal liberty for the people and representative government in the nation. Their confused thinking convinces them that they are liberals—but if they are liberals, they have liberalism without liberty. Nor are they middle-of the-roaders as they claim to be; they are a half-way house to totalitarianism.

They should note that in every one of the countries of Europe where 400,000,000 people are now enslaved by the Communists, it has been the totalitarian liberals who provided the ladders upon which the Communist pirates have boarded the Ship of State.

The whole world was steadily moving along these collectivist roads until two years ago. Then in our Congressional elections, by their votes for

---

17. [*Editor's note*: In his *Crusade* manuscript Hoover omitted this caption, which appears in the original speech text printed in *Addresses . . . 1945–1948.*]

18. [*Editor's note*: In the original text, Hoover had used the word "assure."]

19. [*Editor's note*: In the original speech text, this word was "Liberty."]

both the Republican and Democratic candidates, the people showed the first turn from collectivism that has been made by any important nation in recent years.

The 300-year-old roots of freedom in America showed their resistance to the collectivist blight. The influence of our rebirth of liberty has now echoed throughout the world. But the battle is still on.

The deep soil of these 300-year-old roots is the spiritual concept that the rights of man to freedom are personal to him from the[20] Creator—not from the State. That is our point of departure from all others. This spiritual concept, whatever our faults may be, has guided our people to a life, not only of material abundance, but also a life of liberty and human dignity.[21]

Today the American people have reached an historic stage which has come to a few strong nations in their ability to contribute to moral leadership in the world. Few such nations have come upon that task with so few liabilities. In these 30 years of wars we alone have taken no people's land; we have oppressed no race of man. We have faced all the world in friendship, with compassion, with a genuine love and helpfulness for our fellow men. In war, in peace, in disaster, we have aided those whom we believed to be in the right and to require our aid. At the end of wars, we have aided foe as well as ally; and in each instance, even the children of those who would do us hurt. We have hated war; we have loved peace.

What other nation has such a record?

The Responsibilities of This Convention[22]

It is these concepts of your country that this Party must bear high as the banner of a marching army. From this hall free men and women can cheer free men and women the world over. You can say to them that the day is *not* done, that night has *not* come—that human liberty lives—and lives eternally here upon this continent, here among us.[23] [. . .–*ed.*]

Therefore, unusual responsibilities devolve upon this Convention.[24] There may be some of you who believe that you have come here only to pass upon a platform, and to select candidates for President and Vice President.

---

20. [*Editor's note*: In the original speech text, this word was "his."]

21. [*Editor's note*: In the original speech text as printed, Hoover had said: ". . . not only of material abundance, but far more glorious, to a life of human dignity."]

22. [*Editor's note*: In the original speech text in the *Addresses . . . 1945–1948*, this caption followed the next paragraph printed here.]

23. [*Editor's note*: The words "here among us" do not appear in the original speech text.]

24. [*Editor's note*: This sentence does not appear in the original speech text.]

Your greater task by far is to generate a spirit which will rekindle in every American a love not only for his country but for the American civilization.[25] You are here to feed the reviving fires of spiritual fervor which once made the word, American, a stirring description of a man who lived and died for human liberty, who knew no private interest, no personal ambition, no popular acclaim, no advantage of pride or place which overshadows the burning love for the freedom of man.

Great as your problems are, they are no greater than Americans have met before your time. You are no less able or courageous than they were.

Therefore, I repeat, what you say and do here [. . .–ed.] is of transcendent importance.

If you produce nothing but improvised platitudes, you will give no hope.

If you produce no leadership here, no virile fighter for the right, you will have done nothing of historic significance.

If you follow the counsel of those who believe that politics is only a game to be played for personal advantage, you are wasting your time and effort.

If [. . .–ed.] you calculate what will please this or that little segment of our population, and satisfy this or that pressure group or sectional interest, you will be betraying your opportunity, and tragically missing the call of your time.

If you temporize with collectivism you will stimulate its growth and the defeat of free men.[26]

If, on the other hand, [. . .–ed.] as a mature and inspired political party, you face the truth that we are in a critical battle to safeguard our nation and civilization which, under God, have brought to us a life of liberty, then you will be guided in every step[27] to restore the foundations of faith, of morals and of right thinking.[28] If you choose your leadership with full recognition that only those can lead you who believe in your ideals, who seek not only victory but the opportunity to serve in this fight, then you will issue from this hall a clarion call, in as pure a note, in as full a tone as that call to arms which your political ancestors issued at Ripon, Wisconsin, when this party was born to make all men free.

And so I bespeak to you tonight to make yourselves worthy of the victory.

---

25. [*Editor's note*: In the original speech text, Hoover had said: ". . . a love not only for his country but a devotion to American civilization."]

26. [*Editor's note*: In the original speech text, Hoover had said: "If you temporize with collectivism in any form, you will stimulate its growth and make certain the defeat of free men."]

27. [*Editor's note*: In the original speech text, Hoover had said: ". . . guided step by step."]

28. [*Editor's note*: In the original speech text, Hoover had said: "to restore the foundations of right thinking, of morals and of faith."]

The astonishing thing about this address was congratulatory telegrams and letters from President Truman and four members of his Cabinet, that is Marshall, Forrestal, Anderson, and Snyder.[29]

Mr. Truman's letter to me said:

Dear Mr. President:

Your speech to the Republican Convention was the utterance of a statesman. May I presume to congratulate you upon it.

Sincerely,

Harry S. Truman[30]

For many years I had not made an address which received such an ovation from the audience, the public and the press.

I have not encumbered these memoirs with the tens of thousands of approving (or disapproving) press comments over the years. I am, however, immodest enough to include the newspaper column of Louis Bromfield[31] on this address. Bromfield holds a light high in the American literary world and at one time was an ardent New Dealer and a bitter critic of mine.

One of the great moments in the history of American politics occurred with the great demonstration for Herbert Hoover at the Republican convention in Philadelphia. It was spontaneous, violent and long and, after the first outburst, one realized quickly that this was not merely a partisan tribute but the tribute of the thousands of American citizens seated in the great auditorium.

If there was any doubt about it one had only to look toward the press box where were seated about 1,200 of the most hard-boiled, experienced, intelligent, informed and wise citizens of the nation. Throughout the convention they had pounded typewriters, talked to each other, moved about noisily, ignoring the speakers. They all had mimeographed handouts of the speeches. They knew the speakers out of the past. They had heard the words "peepul," "constitution," "democracy" until they had become very nearly meaningless. And then on the second night of the convention there appeared at the

---

29. [Editor's note: Secretary of State George Marshall, Secretary of Defense James Forrestal, Secretary of Agriculture Clinton P. Anderson, and Secretary of the Treasury John W. Snyder.]

30. [Editor's note: Harry S. Truman to Herbert Hoover, June 23, 1948, Post-Presidential Individual Correspondence File (hereafter PPI), Herbert Hoover Papers, Herbert Hoover Presidential Library, West Branch, Iowa. Truman's letter was handwritten. Three days later, Hoover warmly thanked Truman for his "touching note." Hoover to Truman, June 26, 1948 (in the same file).]

31. [Editor's note: Louis Bromfield (1896–1956), a popular American novelist, screenwriter, farmer, and conservationist.]

back of the big speakers' platform the gray-haired figure of the only living former President of the United States.

The band struck up one of the world's most stirring and beautiful hymns — "The Battle Hymn of the Republic" — and an immense wave of emotion and even love ran through the whole auditorium. Suddenly thousands of people were on their feet singing and cheering. Some were crying for the great, honorable and able American citizen who had for years been submitted to one of the most cruel and calculated campaigns of calumny the world has [had–ed.] ever known. In the press box even the hardboiled press people cheered and pounded their hands — all but three or four known Communists and their fellow travelers.

Clearly, the demonstration was more than the vindication of one man and a tribute to him. It was the vindication at last of what was essentially the American idea.

Behind the great demonstration lay much history — years of some times haphazard experiment, some fear and hysteria, the trial of alien Marxian ideas, of arbitrary government controls and regulations, occasional encroachment of constitutional rights of government institutions and even individuals, shameful and calculated campaigns of abuse and smear and the great trials of war. Now, after all the experiments and blunders and some social gains, the sideshow was over, the alien ideas had been tried and found wanting, and the nation and the people were back again on the track of liberalism in the true indigenous American tradition.

The elderly, tired, gray man standing in the glaring lights [with tears in his eyes–ed.] was a symbol of the return to confidence and faith in the American way of doing things. Around the world the other ideologies, plus war, had produced social and economic misery, loss of liberty and human dignity and moral collapse.

The American people had come to know the man standing there on the platform — that there was no demagoguery in him, that he was an honest and straightforward man, that he was above [all–ed.] political trickery and detested the compromising and unscrupulous professional politician, that he had given much in terms of material things and even more of what was more precious, his time, his energies and his good will, not only to his own nation, but to the suffering peoples of the world. He had believed, and still believes, that his fellow citizens were intelligent enough and responsible enough to play their part in government.

Herbert Hoover is a fortunate man, for he has lived to see the confusion and rout of the men who had abused and smeared him and the failure of ideas in which he had no faith. The tribute was a great one, but the greatest and most significant tribute came from the press box, where every man and woman, save a tiny handful of Stalinites [Stalinists–ed.], were on their feet and cheering. They represented the segment of the American people who knew the inside of the Hoover story. They, the ones whose business it is to write our day-by-day history, were, more than any other group in the nation, qualified to judge.[32]

As a curious evidence of Mr. Truman's dual personality, a few weeks after sending me the congratulatory letter on my speech to the Republican Convention, he made a speech in Boston to gain Catholic votes in Massachusetts by smearing me dreadfully.[33] Again, a month after the election, he was seeking my aid and exuding good will.

The Campaign of 1948

Anxious to keep the reorganization question out of politics I took no part in the Presidential campaign.

The Republican Convention adopted a banal platform compromising all along the line. Governor Dewey was selected as its candidate. The Governor again avoided the vital issues and rested mostly on a platform of "sweetness and light," believing he was certain to be elected. He indicated a leaning to New Deal ideas but cheaper. He said little in support of the work of the Republican 80th Congress which Truman bitterly attacked. That Congress had made a real Republican program and his failure to support it alienated a host of Republicans.

Part of Truman's problem was to undermine Henry Wallace, who was now a candidate for the faction on the extreme left. The South, although growling, was bound to support him, as they wanted the loaves and fishes which could

---

32. [*Editor's note*: Bromfield's column appeared in the *Columbus (Ohio) Dispatch*, July 4, 1948. A typed copy is in "Bromfield, Louis," PPI, Herbert Hoover Papers. Hoover reproduced Bromfield's text here with insignificant variations, except where noted in brackets.]

33. [*Editor's note*: In his speech in heavily Democratic and Roman Catholic Boston on October 27, 1948, Truman recalled the campaign of 1928, "when Al Smith ran for President against that well-known engineer—Herbert Hoover. He was one engineer who really did a job of running things backward." Truman accused Republican Party leaders of basing their campaign in 1928 on "religious prejudice because of Al Smith's Catholic faith" and of signaling that "they would stop at nothing in order to gain power." Truman thundered: "I say to you people of Boston that if Al Smith—and not Herbert Hoover—had become President in 1928, we and the world would have been spared untold misery and suffering." Truman added that under Franklin Roosevelt's leadership "we licked the Hoover depression." For the text of Truman's address, see *New York Times*, October 28, 1948, p. 26.]

only be had by winning an election with the aid of the radical support in the North. The President had promulgated a radical program which outdid Bryan and Roosevelt combined. He succeeded in reducing Wallace's expected vote of 6,000,000 to under 2,000,000. He was elected by a majority of the electoral college but a minority of the popular vote. He swept in a Democratic majority of the Congress.

The light vote in Republican areas indicated that either Republicans failed to come to the polls, and when they did come, many of them either did not vote for Dewey.[34] He again ran behind the aggregate Republican vote for Congressmen or Governors and this time to an amount that would have elected him.

I Attack Collectivism Again

I did make one speech during the 1948 campaign that was not political but was surely anti-collectivist.

The Village of West Branch, Iowa,[35] urged me to attend a reception on August 10, 1948, being my seventy-fourth birthday. This little town of under a thousand people beautifully organized and conducted an audience of over 30,000 people. [Excerpts of Hoover's speech follow–ed.]

Perhaps without immodesty I can claim to have had some experience in what *American* means. I have lived many kinds of American life. After my early boyhood in an[36] Iowa village, I lived as the ward of a country doctor in Oregon. I lived among those to whom hard work was the price of existence. The opportunities of America opened up[37] to me the public schools. They carried me to the professional training of an American university. I began by working with my own hands for my daily bread. I have tasted the despair of fruitless search for a job. I know the kindly encouragement of a humble boarding-house keeper. [. . .–ed.]

I have conducted the administration of great industries with their problems of production and the well-being of their employees.

I have seen America in contrast with many nations and races. My profession took me into many foreign lands under many kinds of government. I have worked with their great spiritual leaders and their great statesmen. I

---

34. [*Editor's note*: Despite the awkward syntax (which Hoover probably would have revised), his meaning is clear.]

35. [*Editor's note*: Hoover's birthplace.]

36. [*Editor's note*: In the original speech text as later published: "this."]

37. [*Editor's note*: In the original speech text as later published: "opened out."]

have worked in governments of free men, of tyrannies, of Socialists and of Communists. I have met with princes, kings, despots and desperados.

I have seen the squalor of Asia, the frozen class barriers of Europe. [And–*ed.*] I was not a tourist. I was associated in their working lives and problems. I had to deal with their social systems and their governments. And outstanding everywhere to these great masses of people there was a hallowed word— America. To them it was the hope of the world.

Every homecoming was for me a reaffirmation of the glory of America.[38] Each time my soul was washed by the relief from the grinding poverty of other nations, by the greater kindliness and frankness which comes from acceptance of equality and the wide-open opportunity to all who want a chance. It is more than that. It is a land of self-respect born alone of free men [and women–*ed.*].

In later years I participated on behalf of America in a great war. I saw untold misery and revolution. I have seen liberty die and tyranny rise. I have seen human slavery again on the march.

I have been repeatedly placed by my countrymen where I had need to deal with the hurricanes of social and economic destruction which have swept the world. I have seen bitter famine and the worst misery that the brutality of war can produce.

I have had every honor to which any man could aspire. There is no place on the whole earth except here in America where all the sons of man could have this chance in life. [. . .–*ed.*]

The meaning of our word *America* flows from one pure source. Within the soul of America is the freedom of mind and spirit in man. Here alone are the open windows through which pours the sunlight of the human spirit. Here alone human dignity is not a dream but a major accomplishment.[39] [. . .–*ed.*]

At the time our ancestors were proclaiming that the Creator had endowed all mankind with rights of freedom as the children of God, with a free will, the German philosophers, Hegel and others, and later Karl Marx, were proclaiming[40] a satanic philosophy of agnosticism and that the rights of man came from the State. The greatness of America today comes from one philosophy, the despair of Europe from the other.

---

38. [*Editor's note*: In the original speech text as later published, Hoover said: "My every frequent homecoming has been a re-affirmation of the glory of America."]

39. [*Editor's note*: In the original speech text as later published, the wording was slightly different: "Here alone is human dignity not a dream, but an accomplishment."]

40. [*Editor's note*: In the original speech text as later published, Hoover said: ". . . with a free will, there was being proclaimed by Hegel, and later by Karl Marx . . . ."]

But there are people in our country today who would compromise in these fundamental concepts.[41] They scoff at these tested qualities in men. They never have understood and never will understand what the word *America* means. They explain that these qualities were good while there was a continent to conquer and a nation to build. They say that time has passed. No doubt the land frontier has passed. But the frontiers of science and better understanding of human welfare are barely opening.

This new land of science with all its high promise cannot and will not be conquered except by men and women inspired by these same concepts of free spirit and free mind.

And it is those moral and spiritual qualities which rise alone in free men which will fulfill the meaning of the word *American*. And with them will come centuries of further greatness to our country.[42]

---

41. [*Editor's note*: In the original speech text as later published, Hoover said: "There are today fuzzy-minded people in our country who would compromise in these fundamental concepts."]

42. [*Editor's note*: For the full text of Hoover's speech in West Branch, Iowa, on August 10, 1948, see his *Addresses . . . 1945–1948*, pp. 74–79.]

CHAPTER 15

The Crusade against Collectivism from the Presidential Election of 1948 to the Presidential Election in 1952

Truman Goes Violently Left

With the assembly of Congress in January, 1949, the President declared his "Fair Deal." If enacted it would have been a gigantic step into mixed Socialist and Fascist collectivism. It included:

1. Socialized medicine.
2. Socialized electric power.
3. Socialized manufactures (steel and other materials "in critical short supply").
4. Socialized housing.
5. Presidential powers to fix wages and prices.
6. Powers to control consumer and bank credits.
7. Expansion of rent controls.
8. Increased subsidies and control of farmers.
9. Federal Control of education through subsidies.
10. Regulation of "civil rights."
11. Repeal of the Taft-Harley labor act.
12. A gigantic program of increased foreign aid to build industrial production ("Point 4").
13. Increased taxes on business.
14. Budget recommendations (not including the increase of expenditures necessary to carry out the above program) which would produce a 6 billion dollar deficit in peace time.

I estimated that this program would add another $20 billion to the already $46 billion Federal expenditure. (The actual budget was less than this but by various devices the budget covered up some $4 billion real expenditures.)

However, the 1949 session of the Congress practically rebelled, through unity between the Republicans and Southern Conservatives. By direct defeat, delays and "bottling up in Committees" the President only succeeded in two items. They were an attenuated increase in minimum wages and some increased Federal expenditures. The inherent anti-collectivist attitudes of the country were strong enough to stem the tide despite the President.

I was confident that most of Truman's program represented his dual personality. The dominant one now was Pendergast where everything went for votes—he being now completely dependent upon the left-wing elements.

One of the sensational events of the year was the trial of Alger Hiss in May 1949 for perjury in denial of his Communist affiliations. The work of the Republican Congressional Committees in exposure of his activities had at last forced the administration to place him on trial after years of evasion. Hiss had been a most prominent State Department official, an important advisor at Yalta and the San Francisco Conference of the United Nations, and many other activities. He escaped direct trial as a traitor due to the statute of limitations, but the trial was in reality on that charge. The jury in the first trial disagreed 8 for conviction and 4 for acquittal. He was subsequently tried again and convicted. He was one as to whom Truman had declared it was all a red herring. Evidence of many other officials co-operating with the Russian spy apparatus was disclosed in the trial. The defense of him by Justice Frankfurter[1] and subsequently Secretary of State Acheson was a shock to the nation. Scores of other Communist activities in the Government were exposed.

The work of the Commission on Organization of the Executive Branch of the Government[2] was completed early in 1949 and I was thus able to take up my crusade against collectivism.

On April 25th, I was called upon by a House Committee to analyze Mr. Truman's Old Age Pension proposals.[3] I later (December 15, 1949) gave a short condensation of the previous rather elaborate report in reply to one of the Senators.[4]

The tenor of these reports was that the pensions should be increased and the area expanded, but that it must be put upon a pay-as-you-go basis instead

---

1. [Editor's note: Felix Frankfurter (1882–1965), a Supreme Court justice from 1939 to 1965. At Hiss's first trial, Frankfurter was a character witness for Hiss, who had been his protégé at Harvard Law School in the late 1920s. Frankfurter was not a character witness at the second trial.]

2. [Editor's note: Commonly known as the Hoover Commission or First Hoover Commission (1947–49). A successor, commonly called the Second Hoover Commission, worked from 1953 to 1955.]

3. [Editor's note: Herbert Hoover, Addresses upon the American Road, 1948–1950 (Stanford, CA: Stanford University Press, 1951), pp. 32–40.]

4. [Editor's note: Ibid., pp. 47–49.]

of the fraud of spending the surplus tax collections for other Government expenses, and thus in the end requiring the pensioners to pay twice through later taxes.

Arising out of the information and reports of the Reorganization Commission, I was called upon by the Chairman of the House Committee to analyze Mr. Truman's Federal educational proposals. I did so, on June 22, 1949, and presented a constructive program in opposition to "pork-barrel" "grants-in-aid." I pointed out the particular evils in this bill:[5]

> In order not to deny to children of the real backward states the opportunity they need, and also at the same time to avoid as many as possible of the evils of "grants-in-aid" and to produce economy which the nation badly needs, I suggest [. . .–ed.] there should be no general "grants-in-aid" to all states. All "grants-in-aid" should be limited in each case to the real backward states.

I suggested certain other amendments which would secure its objective and avoid its evils.

And let me add that of all the accomplishments of our Republic, the greatest has been our educational system in the strong states. It ranks above that of all other nations. It is the product of private effort, of local and state government. To place a Federal bureaucracy over the whole national system will be, in my mind, a disaster to educational progress—no matter what legal limits are put on it or what advantages are painted. [. . .–ed.]

What we need in the national interest is to bring the backward states up to the national level of educational care for children and preserve the nation from the evils inherent in the "grants-in-aid" system.

On July 11, 1949, in an address at Ohio Wesleyan University, I returned to the collectivist crusade and said in part:

This season you and a mighty host of 500,000 other American graduates are lining up to receive your college diplomas.

Once upon a time, I lined up just as you are. For me, it was a day of lowered spirit. The night before we had . . . chanted of "Working on the Railroad" and that immortal college dirge about going "Into the Cold, Cold World." . . .

I had to listen to an address made up of the standardized parts which were at that time generally sold at Commencements. It took over an hour for the speaker to put the parts together. We were warned that our diploma was

---

5. Ibid., pp. 41–46.

an entrance ticket to jungles of temptation and hard knocks. Our speaker dwelled upon the Founding Fathers, the division of powers, upon Herbert Spencer and John Stuart Mill. He said we were living in a New Era in the world. He described it as Liberalism. The idea had to do with free minds and free spirits. It included the notion that America was a land of opportunity—with the great ideal of being a land of *equal* opportunity. We were told that life was a race where society laid down rules of sportsmanship but "let the best man win." The encouraging note in his address was emphasis upon Christian in *The Pilgrim's Progress* and Horatio Alger.

I confess my attention on that occasion was distracted by a sinking realization that I had to find a job—and quick. Also, I knew a girl. Put in economic terms, I was wishing somebody with a profit motive would allow me to help him earn a profit, and thus support the girl. At the risk of seeming revolutionary and a defender of evil, I suggest that this basis of test for a job has considerable merit. It does not require qualifications either of good looks, ancestry, religion, or ability to get votes.

It is true that I had some difficulty in impressing any of the profit and loss takers with the high potentialities of my diploma. But I was without the information at that time that I was a wage slave. I was buoyed up with the notion that if I did not like any particular profit taker, I could find another one somewhere else.

And let me add, that under that particular New Era I did not find a cold, cold world. I found the profit takers a cheery and helpful lot of folks, who took an enormous interest in helping youngsters get a start and get ahead in life. And you will find that is also true today. Indeed, their helpfulness has improved, for, as technology becomes more intricate, they are searching for skills, and your diploma commands more respect.

And now voices tell us that we are in another New Era. In fact, we seem to have a newer era every little while.

Incidentally, I entered the cold, cold world in the midst of what the latest New Era calls a "disinflation." We mistakenly thought its name was "depression." But as I was not told[6] that governments could cure it, I did not have the additional worry of what the Government was going to do about it.

The new era of today seems united in the notion that they have just discovered real Liberalism and that all previous eras are reactionary. Some tell us that, in their New Era, life is still a race, but that everybody must come

---

6. [*Editor's note*: In the original text as published in ibid., p. 10, Hoover said: "But as I did not then know . . . ."]

out even at the end. Another modernistic school adds to this that life may still be a race, but that each step must be dictated by some official or unofficial bureaucrat with Stop-and-Go signals. They hold out the attraction that with this security you will finish with an old-age pension and your funeral expenses from the Government.

Whether these newest eras are right or wrong, "security," which eliminates the risks in life, also kills the joy that lies in competition, in individual adventure, new undertakings, and new achievements. These contain moral and intellectual impulses more vital than even profits. For from them alone comes national progress. At all times in history there have been many who sought escape into "security" from self-reliance.

And if you will look over the workings of these newest New Eras throughout the world, you may notice that the judgment of the Lord on Adam has not been entirely reversed, even by the Supreme Court of the United States. Moreover, governments have not been able to fix the wages of sin. Nor have they found a substitute for profit and other personal stimulants.

America has not yet embraced all these new ideas. The reactionary notion of equal opportunity with the right of everyone to go as far as his ambitions and abilities will take him, provided he does not trespass on others, still holds in the American dream.

How far he can get has been damaged by two great wars and inefficiently organized government, which we have to pay for. To pay it, you will need to work two days out of the week for the Government for a long time. The Commission upon which President Flemming[7] and I have taken part is trying to take a few hours off that penalty.

And there is something more to be said for the old reactionary notions which held to basic freedoms of mind and spirit, holding aloft the lamp of equal opportunity. . . .

I then sketched the progress of America under these ideas, and continued:

It is very sad, but did it ever occur to you that all the people who live in these houses and all those who run this complicated machine are going to die? Just as sure as death, the jobs are yours. The plant and equipment comes to you by inheritance ready to run. And there are opportunities in every inch of it. But the best of these jobs are never filled by security seekers.

---

7. [*Editor's note*: Arthur Flemming (1905–96) was president of Ohio Wesleyan University at the time Hoover gave the address. Flemming had been a member of the First Hoover Commission (1947–49).]

Moreover, there are other vast opportunities for those who are willing to take a chance. If we just hold to our reactionary ideas of free minds, free spirits, and equal opportunity, we have another glorious opening for every young man and woman. Science and invention, even during these troubled years, have given us further mighty powers of progress. New discoveries in science and their flow of new inventions will continue to create a thousand new frontiers for those who still would adventure.

You have the blood and the urge of your American forebears. You are made of as good stuff as they. I have no doubt of your character and your self-reliance. You are better trained and equipped than we were. I know you are champing at the bit to take your chance in an opening world.

Do not fear it will be cold to you.[8]

Just to keep the pot boiling, I made a response to an award on October 18th, 1949, by poking some fun at collectivist activities, which had wide circulation.

I have had some doubt about what a recipient of an award ought to say. I [have a–ed.] suspicion that inside this award there is an intellectual gadget that presses the recipient to say something that would justify his having received it.

Ruminating over this problem of what to say, it seemed to me that the real test of whether the recipient has said something justifying the award is whether his remarks make a page one, column one, double headline in the morning papers.

So I have been haunted for days with a subconscious search for subject or eloquent phrase which would land at that spot.

In that search I examined the current press for what sort of remarks from speakers got page one, double column. I found they all relate to ideas of alarm, emergency, crisis, warning, purge, execution, condemnation, or the current practice of diplomats in denouncing other governments. So I looked over those intellectual provinces to see if I could find a shot that might land.

For instance, I thought it ought to shock the world if I said something about the balancing of the Federal budget. That, however, does not seem to have clicked in the headlines for the last eighteen years.

I also considered a mordant economic discourse on why loans by our tax-payers to foreign governments physically cannot and never will be repaid. Then it occurred to me that Santa Claus is a person of far more favorable reputation than Shylock, certainly in the international field. It also occurred

---

8. [*Editor's note*: For the full text of this address, see Hoover, *Addresses . . . 1948–1950*, pp. 8–12.]

to me we could choose either reputation at exactly the same price. That idea, however, has not been news since the first World War.

I thought perhaps I might define the welfare state. But I feel it would be respectful to concede the President has a monopoly of shocks from that quarter.

It would be natural for me to talk about the reorganization of the Federal Government. Indeed, it is about the only issue in which there is complete unity of all political parties, races, religions, and government bureaus. Its merit has the same acceptance of universal merit which our grandmothers established for mustard plasters. But it has the same sort of exception—the fellow to be reorganized. The wails and miseries of its application today take all the headlines, not the reasons for reorganization.

I thought also I might appeal for more unity in world affairs—by way of discussing the United Nations or Union Now or World Federation. But there is no derivative of the Latin root of unity which would make a headline anymore. It is vitriolic international conversation that gets page 1, column 1.

I might speak of the Point 4 program, whereby American private enterprise is presumed to go abroad and fill the world with milk and honey. I surmised, however, you already know that by double taxation at home. Business now has more than it can bear without seeking to expose itself twice more to the tax mercies of two countries at the same time. To suggest a mitigation of taxes between these two stools might help but you cannot make headline stuff of double taxation in this world, to say nothing of such quadruple taxation.

For all these reasons and for the good of your digestion, I will speak on none of these subjects.[9]

As my 75th birthday was approaching,[10] the Congress passed a unique and unanimous resolution of eulogy. Mr. Truman and most of his Cabinet sent me beautiful messages.

I spoke again against collectivism at Stanford University, on August 10, 1949. I said in part:[11]

Now, as never before, we need thinking on some of these questions. If America is to be run by the people, it is the people who must think, and think

---

9. [*Editor's note*: See ibid., pp. 55–56, for the full text.]
10. [*Editor's note*: Hoover turned seventy-five on August 10, 1949.]
11. *Addresses upon the American Road, 1948–1950*, pp. 13–21.

now. And we do not need to put on sackcloth and ashes to think. Nor should our minds work like a sundial which records only sunshine. However, our thinking must square against some lessons of history, some principles of government and morals, if we would preserve the rights and dignity of men to which this nation is dedicated.

The real test of our thinking is not so much the next election as it is the next generation.

I am not going to offer you solutions to our national ills. But I shall list some items for thought. Perhaps in Japanese-English a subhead would be "Bring feet from clouds into swamp where we now are."

The Growth of Governmental Spending

We must wish to maintain a dynamic progressive people. No nation can remain static and survive. But dynamic progress is not made with dynamite. And that dynamite today is the geometrical increase of spending by our governments—Federal, state, municipal and local.

Perhaps I can visualize what this growth has been. Twenty years ago, all varieties of government, omitting Federal debt service, cost the average family less than $200 annually. Today, also omitting debt service, it costs an average family about $1300 annually.

This is bad enough. But beyond this is the alarming fact that at this moment executives and legislatures are seriously proposing projects which if enacted would add one-third more annually to our spending. Add to these the debt service and the average family may be paying $1,900 yearly taxes. They may get a little back if they live to over 65 years of age.

It does not seem very generous to set up an "acceptable" standard of living and then make it impossible by taxes.

The Growth of Bureaucracy

No doubt life was simpler about 147 years ago, when our government got well under way. At that time there was less than one government employee, Federal, state and local including the paid military, to each 120 of that population. Twenty years ago, there was one government employee to about 40 of the population. Today, there is one government employee to about every 22 of the population. Worse than this, there is today one government employee to about 8 of the working population in the United States.

The Growth of Dependency

Twenty years ago, persons directly or indirectly receiving regular monies from the government—that is, officials, soldiers, sailors, pensioners, subsidized persons and contractors' employees working exclusively for the government—represented about one person in every 40 of the population.

Today a little more than one person out of every 7 in the population is a regular recipient of government monies. If those of age are all married, they comprise about one-half the voters of the last Presidential election.

Think it over.

Working for the Government

In the long run it is the Average Working Citizen who pays by hidden and other taxes. I have made up a little table showing the number of days which this kind of citizen must work on average to pay the taxes.

Days' Work

Obligations from former wars	11
Defense and Cold War	24
Other Federal expenditures	12
State and local expenditures	14
Total thus far	61

But beyond this the seriously proposed further spending now in process will take another 20 days' work from Mr. and Mrs. Average W. Citizen.

Taking out holidays, Sundays, and average vacations, there are about 235 working days in the year. Therefore, this total of 81 days' work a year for taxes will be about one week out of every month.

You might want to work for your family instead of paying for a gigantic bureaucracy.

Think it over. [. . .–ed.]

One end result of the actual and proposed spendings and taxes to meet them is that the Government becomes the major source of credit and capital to the economic system. At best the small business man is starved in the capital he can find. Venture capital to develop new ideas tends to become confined to the large corporations and they grow bigger. There are ample signs of these results already.

Governments do not develop gadgets of improved living.

Another end result is to expose all our independent colleges and other privately supported institutions to the risk of becoming dependent upon the state. Already it is more and more difficult for these institutions to find resources.

Then through politics we will undermine their independence which gives lifting standards and stimulus to government supported institutions.

No nation grows stronger by such subtraction.

Think it over.

Government Borrowing

It is proposed that we can avoid these disasters by more government borrowing. That is a device to load our extravagance and waste on to the next generation. But increasing government debts can carry immediate punishment for that is the road to inflation. There is far more courage in reducing our gigantic national debt than in increasing it. And that is a duty to our children.

Increasing Taxes

And there is no room for this spending and taxes except to cut the standard of living of most of our people below the "acceptable" level. It is easy to say, "Increase corporation taxes." That is an illusion. The bulk of corporation taxes is passed on to the consumer—that is, to every family. It is easy to say, "Increase taxes on the higher personal income brackets." But if all incomes over $8,000 a year were confiscated, it would cover less than 10% of these actual and proposed spendings.

The real road before us is to reduce spending and waste and defer some desirable things for a while.

We Cannot Have Everything at Once

There are many absolute necessities and there are many less urgent meritorious and desirable things that every individual family in the nation would like to have but cannot afford. To spend for them, or borrow money for them, would endanger the family home and the family life. So it is with the national family. [. . .–ed.]

Think it over.

The Back Road to Collectivism

The American mind is troubled by the growth of collectivism throughout the world.

We have a few hundred thousand Communists and their fellow travelers in this country. They cannot destroy the Republic. They are a nuisance and require attention. We also have the doctrinaire socialists who peacefully dream of their utopia.

But there is a considerable group of fuzzy-minded people who are engineering a compromise between free men and these European infections. They fail to realize that our American system has grown away from the systems of Europe for 250 years. They have the foolish notion that a collectivist economy can at the same time preserve personal liberty and constitutional government. That cannot be done.

The steady lowering of the standard of living by this compromised collectivist system under the title "austerity" in England should be sufficient spectacle for the American people. It aims at an abundant life but it ends in a ration.

Most Americans do not believe in these compromises with collectivism. But they do not realize that through governmental spending and taxes, our nation is blissfully driving down the back road to it at top speed.

In the end these solutions of national problems by spending are always the same—power, more power, more centralization in the hands of the state.

Along this road of spending, the Government either takes over economic life, which is socialism, or dictates institutional and economic life, which is fascism.

We have not had a great socialization of property, but we are on the last miles of collectivism through governmental spending of the savings of the people.

Think it over. [. . .–ed.]

In Conclusion

And finally, may I say that thinking and debate on these questions must not be limited to legislative halls. We should debate them in every school. We should resort to the old cracker barrel debate in every corner grocery. In those places these phrases and slogans can be liquidated by common sense and intellectual integrity.

A splendid storehouse of integrity and freedom has been bequeathed to us by our forefathers. In this day of confusion, of world peril to free men, our high duty is to see that this storehouse is not robbed of its contents.

We dare not see the birthright of posterity to individual independence, initiative and freedom of choice bartered for a mess of collectivism.

My word to you, my fellow-citizens, on this seventy-fifth birthday is this: The Founding Fathers dedicated the structure of our government "to secure the blessings of liberty to ourselves and our posterity." A century and a half later, we of this generation still inherited this precious blessing. Yet as spend-thrifts we are on our way to rob posterity of its inheritance.

The American people have solved many great difficulties in the develop-ment of national life. The qualities of self-restraint, of integrity, of conscience and courage still live in our people. It is not too late to summon these quali-ties into action.

On April 27, 1950, two months prior to our entry into the Korean War, I made a broadcast address to the American Newspaper Publishers Associa-tion, again partly on the collectivist questions. I said:[12]

My subject on this occasion arises from my suspicion that the world in its tumults has abandoned most of its acceptance of history as a guidepost.

There are plenty of voices about but the voice of world experience seems to have become stilled.

[. . .–ed.] I propose for a few moments to add some of the voices of world experience to the present clamor. I shall explore four samples, one each from the economic, social, political, and international field.

Some Economic Experience

In the economic field there are as you well know many shrill voices proclaim-ing that our American economic system is outmoded. They say it was born of undesirable parents, such as American Individualism and a French lady named *Laissez-Faire*. They accuse the ghost of Adam Smith as having had something to do with the matter. They conclude our system is of the jungle or dog-eat-dog variety.

It might be observed that the alternative offered us is a drink mixed by three different ghosts. That is, the shade of Karl Marx with his socialism; the shade of Mussolini with his dictated and planned economy; the spook of

---

12. Ibid., pp. 59–67.

Lord John Maynard Keynes with his "operation Cuttlefish." That comprises "managed currency," peacetime inflation by "deficit spending" and perpetual endowment for bureaucrats. And we have contributed an American ideology. That is give-away programs. It might be called the New Generosity. It is not yet a ghost. However, the handiwork of the ghosts and their auxiliaries furnish you most of your Page One.

I am not going to repeat the old and valid defenses of the American Economic System; I may mention that in recent years we have taken strong drinks from the three "hants" [ghosts?–ed.] I have mentioned, and from the New Generosity, all mixed with varying amounts of pure water from the American System.

The Economic Revolution

Be all that as it may, my purpose at this moment is to call your attention to a less obvious world experience.

Sixty years ago our American System was divorced from the *Laissez-Faire* lady. We started proceedings in 1887 when we created the Interstate Commerce Commission, thereby initiating the control of natural monopolies. But far more revolutionary was the Anti-Trust Act of 1890.

Western Europe has never had effective Anti-Trust laws. To the contrary, there grew up in those countries a maze of state-favored private trade restraints, combinations, trusts and cartels. That form of economic organization sought profits by fixing prices and by control of production and distribution.

Under our revolutionized American System, competition fairly well remained the restless pillow of progress. It had to seek profits from improved technology and lowered costs of production.

In time, Western Europe, without the full pressure of competition, lost much of the impulse to improve methods and equipment. Plants became obsolete; standards of living stagnated.

In contrast, our technology with one hundred times as many inventing laboratories and a thousand times more trained technicians has steadily improved its tools. Our standards of living increased with cheaper costs and more goods. Our system was dynamic; theirs was static.

Finally, Western Europe, with its obsolete plants, its inability to compete in world trade, except at the expense of labor, was desperate. It took to hard drinking of the potions from the shades of Marx, Mussolini and Keynes — plus the New Generosity.

Our American System continues to produce despite periodic indulgence in these drinks. It does it despite two world wars, innumerable interferences with incentives, and a government take of 60 or 70 percent of its savings. It still retains the dynamic power to provide the greatest and widest spread of comfort to our people that the world has ever known. That is, if we would join Alcoholics Anonymous and quit mixed drinks.

Lest any dangerous thought flash through your minds, I am recalling this experience exclusively to you as publishers and editors.

An Experience in Sociology

Now lest someone think all this is economics without humanism, I offer an experience on the social side. It is punctuated today by the siren voices calling for "security from the cradle to the grave."

Security from the cradle to about 18 or 20 years of age, and from about 65 to the grave, has always been sacred to the American people.

The training of our children, the care of our aged and the unfortunate have been a part of our system since the founding of the Republic. It is part of our civilization. The governmental part, however, needs some repairs.

But the voice of experience which I wish to recall relates to the idea of security for the middle group—say, from 20 to 65 years of age. We have less than 70,000,000 providers in this group, and they must provide for 80,000,000 children, aged, sick, nonproductive Government employees and their wives. It is solely from the energies of this middle group, their inventions and their productivity that can come the support of the young, the old and the sick—and the Government employees.

Unless there is the constant pressure of competition on this group between 20 and 65 plus the beckoning of fairies and rewards, to stimulate incentives and work, the children and the aged will be the victims. This middle group can find its own security only in a free but tough system of risk and self-reliance. It can be destroyed by taxes and the four mixed drinks.

Experience calls sorrowful confirmation of all this. My recollection is that the Lord remarked to Adam something about sweat.

Be that as it may, there is convincing evidence from the British experience of trying to include the middle group in blessed security. Their incentives to sweat have diminished under that illusion. The needed leadership of the middle group in production and distribution is being slowly destroyed. Otherwise they would not need lean on the New Generosity.

There are also some lessons of experience to be had from Russia where the grave is close to the cradle. There, in order to get production, 15,000,000 people are compelled to work in slave camps under the whip.

An Experience in the Political Field

The voice of world experience also calls loudly as to organization of the political field. In 1938, I spent some months[13] on the Continent inquiring "how come" the failure of fifteen new democracies created after the First World War.

The downfall of these representative governments was due in part to the drinks compounded by the three ghosts. But there was another step in their arrival at chaos, which contains a potent experience for the United States.

There had grown up in their legislatures a multitude of splinter parties. There were all the way from five to fifteen of them. In consequence there was no responsible majority. Governments were driven to improvised legislative coalitions, which could only agree upon negative policies and give-away programs. In each coalition small foreign-controlled tricky groups played a part. In confusion and despair, their peoples welcomed the Man on Horseback.

Even though old-time religion, it is worth repeating that the preservation of representative government requires two major political parties.

I am not going to deliver a history of the rifts between major parties in the United States. So you may relax. I might mention that once upon a time, say for a period of about 60 years, the members of both of our major political parties were, in large majority, liberals in the 19th century sense. They quarreled mostly over the tariff but not over ideologies.

However, since Lenin's implication that the hermit crab, by seizing the shell of another animal, knew his business, the term "liberal" has lost its soul. Its cheerful spirit of less power in government and more freedom of men has passed to the world beyond.

Nor am I going to try your after-dinner souls with ideological definitions—not even the "Welfare State." The real ideological definition has already been made instinctively by the common tongue of all nations where free speech still has a part in their proceedings. That effective but perhaps unrefined definition is "right wing" and "left wing."

---

13. [*Editor's note*: It was just under two months. Hoover's account of this journey is given above in chapter 8.]

The point I am concerned with here is that from the ideological tumults stirred by the three shades and their helpers, our major American political parties have been in large degree reoriented into these new compartments of "right" and "left."

I do not charge the real Communists to the American left wing. They are agents of a foreign government.

If a Man from the Moon, who knew the essentials of representative government, came as a total stranger to the United States, he would say some obvious things within the first week or two.

He would say to the Republican Party: There is no room for you on the left. You must be the party of the right, or you will split into ineffective fragments.

And with equal emphasis he would say to the Democrats: Your die is cast. You are the party of the left, or you will likewise split into ineffective fragments.

He would say to some members of both Parties: You are not in your proper spiritual homes.

He would say that in all this ideological tumult, if there cannot be a reasonably cohesive body of opinion in each major party, you are on a blind road where there is no authority in the ballot box or in government.

He would say that if you want confirmation look at fifteen European countries where representative government was torn to shreds.

On June 16, 1950, ten days prior to our entry into the Korean War, I made a nation-wide broadcast before the Junior Chamber of Commerce at Chicago, saying in part:

Some of your officers asked me to speak on the relation of Government expenditures, deficits, and taxes to jobs and to national life.

The Five Questions

They propounded to me five questions:

1. Who pays these taxes?
2. Can taxes be sufficiently increased to meet these deficits?
3. Will deficits not lead to more inflation?
4. Can expenses be reduced?
5. What stands in the way of reductions?

It is these five questions, plus the activities of the different breeds of collectivists, which plague the American people today....

Anyone interested in the answers can find them in that address.[14]

The Presidential Campaign of 1952

After the Congressional elections of 1950, the need was to build up the background for the Presidential campaign of 1952. The problem involved both the foreign and domestic policies of the Truman Administration.

On October 19, 1950 I began a series of attacks upon the Truman-Acheson foreign policies which became known as "The Great Debate."

I deal with the foreign phases of the debate fully in another part of my Memoirs[15] but interwoven with it were the effects upon our domestic life, with all the dangers to free men at home.

I give here in their appropriate dates, among other statements, some paragraphs relating to the domestic, economic and social dangers imposed by these policies.

In my second address of December 19[20–*ed.*], 1950 on foreign policies, I pointed out:

[...–*ed.*] The 150,000,000 American people are already economically strained by government expenditures. It must not be forgotten that we are carrying huge burdens from previous wars including obligations to veterans and $260 billions of bond and currency issues from those wars. In the fiscal year 1952, federal and local expenditures are likely to exceed $90 billions. That is more than our total savings. We must finance huge deficits by further government issues. Inflation is already moving. The dollar has in six months fallen 15 or 20 percent in purchasing power. But we might with stern measures avoid the economic disintegration of such a load for a very few years. If we continue long on this road the one center of resistance in the world will collapse in economic disaster.[16]

On February 9, 1951 I again took part in the Great Debate in a nation-wide broadcast. I again gave warning of the dangers to our system of life, not only

---

14. *Addresses upon the American Road, 1948–1950*, pp. 22–31.

15. [Editor's note: So far as is known, Hoover never wrote the part of his memoirs that was to discuss the "Great Debate" of 1950–51. See, in this volume, p. 4, note 6.]

16. [*Editor's note:* See Herbert Hoover, *Addresses upon the American Road, 1950–1955* (Stanford, CA: Stanford University Press, 1955), pp. 3–10, for the full address. The quoted passage is on pp. 5–6.]

by directly involving us in a ground war in Europe but in the repercussions upon our domestic, economic and social freedom, saying:[17]

Our American Economic Capacity

The third stark realism upon which our policies must be built is our economic capacity. . . .

The new budget calls for federal spending of over $71.6 billions. This $71 billions alone, plus state and local expenditures, is about 37% of our national income.

That is beyond the long endurance of any nation and fatal to the preservation of a system of free men.

The President has asked for a large increase of taxes. We will need also to increase state and local government taxes.

This burden is going to fall on people with smaller incomes. The proof of this is easy.

If all personal incomes above the level of a United States Senator were confiscated it would yield only about $2.5 billion of additional revenues. But confiscation would stop most people earning the $2.5 billion. We must also remember that excise and corporation taxes in most part are ultimately passed on to the consumer or these milch cows would die.

Grim austerity must enter the door of every American home.

Even before these burdens are actually imposed there are stark signs of economic strain. The purchasing power of the dollar has fallen 20 percent in six months. The stock boom indicates that many people are seeking flight from inflation. Our already gigantic government debts permit little expansion without inflation of credit. Two wars prove economic controls cannot wholly stop inflation. The surest road away from inflation is to accept the President's wise proposal to "Pay-as-you-go."

But we simply cannot carry this experience [expenditure–*ed.*] or such tax load for long.

Spending, taxing and inflating ourselves into economic exhaustion are the routes by which Stalin hopes to overcome the United States.

On August 30, 1951 I made a frontal attack upon the corruption of the Truman Administration in a nation-wide broadcast at Des Moines, Iowa, in connection with the celebration of the Iowa Centennial:[18]

17.Ibid., pp. 11–22 [for the full text–*ed.*]
18. Ibid., pp. 111–118.

Concerning Honor in Public Life

I am indebted to the Governor, the Legislature and the people of my native State for a most distinguished honor at this celebration of Iowa's Centennial.

In view of our serious national situation I would like on this occasion to review a few things for you to think about. They are mainly related to honor in public life. Let me say at once that honor is not the exclusive property of any political party.

I may start with the idea that all things in government which bear the prefix "new" are not necessarily new. They may not all of them even be good. Truly every generation discovers the world all new again and knows it can improve it. It is a good thing that they do — or our race would shrink in vitality and grow senile.

Each generation also wants to find out for itself that the stove is hot. A renewal of that sort of information is valuable.

But we have overworked this word "new" in trying to get out of this age of misery from our 37 years of hot and cold wars, with intervals of hot and cold peace.

In this period we have either been cured or made over "new" about fourteen times. We have had the New Order, the New Freedom, the New Day, the New Era, the New Outlook, the New Epoch, the New Economy, the New Dawn, the New Deal, the New Religion, the New Liberalism, the New War and Several New Foreign Policies. None of these were really "new" discoveries.

And the New Treatment [Testament–*ed.*] is too often omitted. After each "new" we have a relapse and take another pill, labelled "new."

Some of these somethings "new" have value. Too many have been false signposts on the road of national progress. Some point to will-o'-wisps of security not to be had on this earth. Some lead the nation over the precipice of inflation and socialism. Some just lead to the land of make-believe. Certainly some of them are tainted with untruth and a diluted intellectual honesty.

The word "new" applies better to physical things than to human forces. Indeed when the sun rises in the morning we hail it as a new day. We cheer the passing of the night. But it is a false analogy in the march of civilization.

Most of our chores for the new day were assigned the night before. Our abilities to perform them were formed not only last year but over centuries or even geologic time. If the new day has no link with yesterday we would be without know-how and morals today. The loss of that link can bring chaos to the whole economic, the moral and the spiritual world.

An Adjournment for a While

As an aside, I suggest at least we adjourn trying to make America over into some other shape until we get out of this cold or hot war. Our present crisis is dangerous enough to require one concentrated undeviating purpose in Washington.

Many of our so-called social and economic gains will go by the board, anyway, if this hot and cold war keeps up. After all, the great social gains of the last century were a mixture of liberty, compassion, unlimited meat, automobiles and washing machines. These are at least getting scarcer.

There will be plenty of time to exercise our muscles on "new" experiments after these violent changes in international temperature are survived. And these programs of making America over add an especially destructive "new"—that is, New Taxes.

Think about it.

Let Us Use the Word "Old" Once in a While

The practical thing we can do if we really want to make the world over again is to try out the word "old" for a while. There are some "old" things that made this country.

There is the Old Virtue of religious faith.

There are the Old Virtues of integrity and the whole truth.

There is the Old Virtue of incorruptible service and honor in public office.

There are the Old Virtues of economy in government, of self-reliance, thrift and individual liberty.

There are the Old Virtues of patriotism, real love of country and willingness to sacrifice for it.

These "old" ideas are very inexpensive. They even would help win hot and cold wars.

I realize that such suggestions will raise that cuss word "reactionary." But some of these "old" things are slipping badly in American life. And if they slip too far, the lights will go out of America, even if we win these cold and hot wars.

Think about it.

The Flight from Honor

We might explore some of the things that have happened to the "old" virtues of integrity, truth, and honor in public life. During the recent past we have had a flood of exposures by Congressional committees, by State Legislatures, by Grand Juries in scores of cities, and the press.

A few days more than one hundred seventy-five years ago, the 56 members of the Continental Congress of the United States unanimously declared a program of action and certain principles of American life. The concluding words of the Declaration are a pledge of "our sacred Honor."

I sometimes wonder what the 56 Founding Fathers, from their invisible presence in our Congressional Halls, would say about the procession of men in responsible positions who have come before its committees of this day. What would they have thought of the "sacred Honor" of the five per-centers, mink coats, deep freezers and free hotel bills?[19] Or favoritism in Government loans and Government contracts? Or failures to prosecute evil-doers who spread cancerous rackets and gambling rings with their train of bribed officials?

But I am less concerned at stealing public money than with the far more destructive forms of dishonor. What would the Founding Fathers have thought of those who coquette with traitorship? Or of secret and disastrous commitments of our nation which were denied at the time? Or high officials under oath contradicting each other as to facts? Or the failure to keep promises to the people? Our civilization moves forward on promises that are kept.

We thus have a cancerous growth of intellectual dishonesty in public life which is mostly beyond the law. One of its chief instruments is corrupt propaganda. There has been such propaganda by foreign governments and our own designed to get us into war. Then we have the propaganda to keep up our pep. Then the habit continues in peace time. And some pressure groups have learned this trick to get something they ought not to have.

The mildest form of corrupt propaganda is a process of persuasive part-truths. At times it even rises to the high moral levels of selling snake oil.

But the malignant form of propaganda spreads deadly poisons. Its process is to create suspicion, hate and fear. Its purpose is less to persuade than to conceal truth and to crush opposition.

The machinery of propaganda is made of standardized gadgets by which you can detect it.

One of the standard gadgets is slogans. They freeze the real process of thought.

If you will examine the two-score loud slogans created during the last third of a century, you will find most of them, like the Apples of Sodom, have turned to bitter ashes in our national mouth. Most of them became ripe

---

19. [*Editor's note*: This was a reference to a number of scandals in the Truman administration.]

in a year or two, some lasted a little longer. Some very new ones are already turning mouldy.

One of these gadgets is to create fear by describing the horrors of invasion of the United States by foreign armies. This one always arises to its maximum decibel when pressuring legislation and elections. While aircraft can come our way no armies on earth can land on our shores.

Another gadget is to give new meaning to old, simple, and well-understood expressions until the integrity of our language is polluted. The term "liberalism" has turned pink inside. The term "welfare" never before meant the "welfare state" with its red or pink colors. The Chinese Communists were not "agrarian liberals." From that perversion of truth alone, we suffered a gigantic defeat of free men in China.

You can test malignant propaganda from another of its gadgets. That is the smear. This gadget has wide potency. When Mr. X presents an inconvenient fact or argument, the propagandists can simplify matters by pointing out that he was once a banker or was fined for speeding. With this gadget you can get your opponent either way in the international field by just suggesting he is an appeaser, or a war-monger, or an isolationist. On the issue of government spending, he can be flattened out by calling him an inflationist or he is against the underdog. If he comments on either side of ideological matters, you can defeat him going or coming by calling him a Fascist, or a reactionary, or a fellow-traveller, or just a red-herring.

There is still another of these propaganda gadgets. That is to squelch debate by cries for "Unity!" Unity! The implication is that the citizen is disloyal to his country if he disagrees with the powers that be.

I suggest that these are not operations of rugged intellectual honesty. They are attempts to coerce men into the intellectual concentration camp named fear. These gadgets have been very handy tools for making America over into fourteen new varieties of getting us into hot and cold wars.

Think about it.

Unveiling Truth by Debate

It is difficult enough to debate against the gadgets of propaganda. But there is something worse. That is the concealment of truth and commitments. I am not here discussing our foreign policies. But may I ask you a question?

Does anybody believe that the propaganda-promoted foreign policies over the past dozen years have always been right? Or that there has always been a disclosure of the whole truth?

For example, certain secret commitments were entered into at Teheran and Yalta which sold the freedom of half a billion people down the river. They were not disclosed to the Congress or to the American people. Does anyone believe that, had they been submitted to the American people for debate and to the Congress for decision, they would ever have been approved? That is where we lost the peace and wandered into the land of hot and cold wars.

Debate founded on the full disclosure of the whole truth and free of these gadgets is the stuff that can save free men.

Think about it.

Our Sacred Honor

I would like to explore this "old" virtue of truth, integrity and honor in public life a little further.

Congress can well widen the laws so as to clutch the "new" kinds of bribes and benefits they have discovered. But Congress cannot reach intellectual dishonors.

Part truth, concealment of public commitments, propaganda and its gadgets and failure to enforce the laws are but part of them. And there are group pressures "to get theirs" which smell from both the decay of integrity and the rotting of patriotism. And some persons arrive at their[20] morals with a divining rod that measures morals in terms of votes.

The Congress, from its own inquiries, is confronted with the fact that sacred Honor cannot always be tested by legality or enforced by law. In its frustration, the Congress is groping for some sort of code of ethics, which with a prefix "new" might protect the citizen from his own officials.

Might I suggest that there are already some old and tested codes of ethics? There are the Ten Commandments, the Sermon on the Mount, and the rules of the game which we learned at our Mother's knee.

Can a nation live if these are not the guides of public life?

Think it over.

Our Right to Complain

The American people have a right to bitter complaint over these disclosures of dishonor in high places. The duty of public men in this Republic is to lead in standards of integrity—both in mind and money.

---

20. [*Editor's note*: This word was "the" in the cited source (p. 116).]

Dishonor in public life has a double poison. When people are dishonorable in private business, they injure only those with whom they deal or their own chances in the next world. But when there is a lack of honor in Government, the morals of the whole people are poisoned.

The drip of such poisons may have nothing to do with dishonor in some college athletics or the occasional policemen on the beat. But the rules of the game have been loosened somewhere.

Some folks seem to think these are necessary evils in a free government. Or that it is smart politics. Those are deadly sleeping pills. No public man can be just a little crooked. There is no such thing as a no-man's-land between honesty and dishonesty. Our strength is not in politics, prices, or production, or price controls. Our strength lies in spiritual concepts. It lies in public sensitiveness to evil.

Much as the Congress has my good wishes, something stronger than a new code of ethics is needed by America. The issue is decency in public life against indecency.

Our greatest danger is not from invasion by foreign armies. Our dangers are that we may commit suicide from within by complaisance with evil. Or by public tolerance of scandalous behavior. Or by cynical acceptance of dishonor. These evils have defeated nations many times in human history.

The redemption of mankind by America will depend upon our ability to cope with these evils right here at home.

Think about it.

Conclusion

But I do not wish to leave you, the neighbors of my childhood, with any implication of pessimism. I speak to you of some of our weaknesses, not because of frustration or despair, but to urge remedy. The fact that we are vigorously washing our dirty linen in the open is a sign that moral stamina still survives.

Without bitterness in our hearts, we are raising our eyes to the Creator of man who assured us that in American soil we can find the moral and spiritual forces which make free men and women. In His guidance, we shall find the fortitude to correct our errors, to straighten our courses, to resurrect the spirit that made our America so free and bountiful a nation.

For reassurance in the future I need only to turn my thoughts to my grandparents who came to this State in the covered wagon. Here they and my parents toiled that their children might have greater opportunities than had been theirs. Here they worshipped God. Here they lived out their lives in the faith and hope of Americans. They lie buried on an Iowa hillside.

Therefore, here in this State where I was nurtured, I cannot but feel a strength that comes up from the deep roots in the very soil on which we stand. That strength is in character and truth and decent living. And it will triumph.

It will triumph because I know America is turning its face away from the maudlin left "isms" and the spread of untruth of the past two decades. We sense the frauds on men's minds and morals. Moral indignation is on the march again.

On January 27, 1952 I made another attack on the Truman foreign policies and their domestic economic effect. As to the latter, I said:[21]

The outstanding phenomenon in the United States is the dangerous over-straining of our economy by our gigantic expenditures.

The American people have not yet felt the full impact of the gigantic increase in Government spending and taxes. Yet we already suffer from the blight of inflation and confiscatory taxes.

[Inflation–ed.][22]

We are actually in a war economy except for[23] world-wide shooting. We are diverting more and more civilian production to war materials. We are placing a greater portion of our manpower under arms. All this creates scarcity in civilian goods and increased spending power; both of which fan the flames of inflation.

We are constantly told that measures are being taken by the Government to "prevent" inflation. This ignores the fact that we are in the middle of inflationary operations at this very minute. Even since the end of the Second World War the purchasing power of our money, measured in wholesale prices, has decreased 40 percent.

Controls of the type we have imposed on wages and prices cannot in the long run prevent inflation. The experience of six great commercial nations in two wars has proved that controls are, at best, a retarding device.

Under the demands of Washington we are confronted with a probable Federal deficit of $30 to $40 billions for immediate rearmament. We already

---

21. *Addresses upon the American Road, 1950–1955*, pp. 40–42. [*Editor's note*: The full text of Hoover's speech is printed on pp. 35–44.]

22. [*Editor's note*: Hoover omitted this caption, which appeared in the text as printed in his *Addresses.*]

23. [*Editor's note*: The words were "without any" in the cited source.]

have government obligations and currency of $280 billion. And private credit is dangerously over-expanded. In the brief period since the war, it has swelled by $130 billion.

The Government will need to cover part of its deficit by selling its bonds or notes, some part of which must be sold to the banks. That is direct inflation of credit and results in an addition to the currency in the form of bank check money.

The two pressures—scarcities and expanding credit or paper money—are the irresistible forces of inflation. They are already being expressed in gray markets and a sporadic spiral of higher wages and then higher prices.

Our standard of living will be reduced in millions of families. Lifetime savings will be taken from millions of other families. Rising prices are coming through the kitchen while taxes are invading our homes through the front door.

[Taxes–ed.][24]

These huge taxes are also overstraining our economy. Moreover they have probably reached the point of diminishing return. That is indicated by the fact that the various taxes on the top bracket incomes can possibly exceed 100 percent. If all remaining untaxed income above that level of the salary and expense allowance of a United States Senator were confiscated, it would bring only about $2 billions annually to the Federal Treasury. That would last less than 10 days. And that assumes that these taxpayers would continue to work for nothing which they will not do.

It is the average family who pays the bulk of taxes both income and hidden. Among them are corporation taxes. These are ultimately passed on to their customers or the corporation would quickly go bankrupt.

Families with incomes of from $3,000 to $4,000 a year will pay in total taxes an average of over $900 per year. The double effect of inflation and taxes is indicated by the fact that a family with $3,000 net annual income 10 years ago must now earn over $6,000 to maintain the same standard of living.

And this spending and taxes is not a quickie program soon over. When our great military forces are assembled, they must continue to be paid for. Due to constant new inventions in weapons, the new devices must continuously replace the old. That will cost more billions.

A man may carry a load of 300 pounds across the room, but he will break his back if he carries it around the block.

---

24. [*Editor's note*: Hoover omitted this caption, which appeared in the text as printed in his *Addresses*.]

Communism is an evil thing. It is contrary to the spiritual, moral, and material aspirations of man. These very reasons give rise to my conviction that it will decay and die of its own poisons. But that may be many years away and, in the meantime, we must be prepared for a long journey.

There are men who welcome these inflation and tax pressures because these forces drive to socialize the income of our people. That is the inevitable end, even if it were not the avowed purpose. If this form of creeping socialism continues, we may be permitted to hold the paper title to property, while bureaucracy spends our income. Along this road the erosion of our productive capital and the destruction of incentives to economic progress are inevitable.

[Some Alternative Calculations of Risk That Might be Considered by the Congress-ed.][25]

In view of this past year's experience, and these rising pressures, the Congress should again re-examine our situation.

I believe there are methods more effective to check the Communist menace in the long run and at the same time to lessen our domestic dangers.

On July 8, 1952 I again addressed the Republican National Convention and again upon the issue of free men:[26]

This is the fifth time I have had the high honor of addressing the Conventions of the Republican Party. From the inexorable course of nature, this is likely to be the last time I shall attend your conventions.

The Issue of Free Men

In our country one dominant issue overshadows all others.

That is, the freedom of men. And that today includes our relations to the rest of the world.

At each of those four-year intervals I have pointed out the inch-by-inch destruction of the ramparts of free men in the United States.

This issue far transcends in importance the transitory questions of national life. It is a matter of life itself.

---

25. [*Editor's note*: In his *Crusade against Collectivism in American Life* manuscript, Hoover omitted this caption, which appeared in the text as printed in his *Addresses*.]

26. *Addresses upon the American Road, 1950–1955*, pp. 53–65.

Throughout the centuries of history freedom has been the constant quest of men. For this the best and bravest on earth have fought and died.

The tables of free men, lost in the Dark Ages, were again handed down to the American people. Those tablets bore not only the words of the Declaration of Independence and the Constitution but they expressed the very spirit of free men.

Do you not believe the words have been distorted and their spirit violated?

Let Us Look at the Record

The genius of our Founding Fathers which preserved this Republic longer than any Republic in history was the concept of the limitation of powers within our government. One of their strong purposes was to protect free men by restriction of Presidential power.

For twenty years we have seen constant attrition of those Constitutional safeguards of free men.

I do not need recall to you the "Rubber Stamp Congress"; the packed Supreme Court; war without approval of Congress; and a score of dire secret international commitments without consent of the Senate.

And now comes, after one hundred seventy years, a new discovery in Presidential power. That is an "inherent" power to seize anything, anytime. All Republican Presidents were densely ignorant of those inherent powers.

Over these twenty years we have seen pressure groups fostered and appeased by Presidents until they intimidate and paralyze the life of the nation. No man has been elected by the people to have such powers. If freedom is to live, we can no more have economic tyranny than we can have political tyranny. Representative government has not been maintained to the mastery of its own house.

Our social order does not rest upon Constitutional safeguards alone. This Republic was founded on a pledge of sacred honor. Yet we have writhed under shocking disclosures of intellectual dishonesty and unpunished corruption in high places—greater in aggregate than all such sins in our history put together.

The grandeur of a people comes from their moral and spiritual character. Today that grandeur is corroded by this intellectual dishonesty and corruption among public officials. The drip, drip, drip from dishonor in high places plays a part in the increasing of crime among the people.

These acts do not make for free men.

Other Assassinations of Free Men

And there have been other assassins of freedom.

Within eight years since victory, we will have seen tax-and-tax—spend-and-spend reach a fantastic total greater than in all the previous one hundred seventy years of our Republic.

Behind this plush curtain of tax and spend, three sinister spooks or ghosts are mixing poison for the American people. They are the shades of Mussolini, with his bureaucratic fascism; of Karl Marx, and his socialism; and of Lord Keynes, with his perpetual government spending, deficits, and inflation. And we added a new ideology of our own. That is government give-away programs.

I will in a few moments measure for you the blight of inflation from this mixture that has poured into every American home.

By way of the bureaucracy part of this mixture, within twenty years we have seen it grow from under 600,000 Federal officials under Republican Administration to over 2,300,000 officials today—with the addition of almost a thousand of government agencies. In fascist fashion, they dictate and give orders and favors to our citizens. Still worse, they do have a real inherent power. Their inherent power is that of all bureaucracy to lay its paralyzing hand more and more heavily upon free men. They rush headlong into its phantasies of the millennium and send the bills to the Treasury.

If you want to see pure fascism mixed with give-away programs, take a look into the Brannan Plan.[27]

If you want to see pure socialism mixed with give-away programs, take a look at socialized medicine and socialized electrical power.

These things do not make for free men.

Man was created somewhat lower than the angels, but to him the Creator gave the right to plan his own life, to dare his own adventure, to earn his own reward so long as he does no harm to his fellows.

Either we shall have a society based upon ordered liberty and the creative energy of free men or we shall have a dictated society.

I have said before now that there are immutable principles which neither the rigors of depression, nor the tricks of inherent powers, nor lost statesmanship, nor wars, nor New Dealers, nor militarists can change. These immutable principles came into the universe along with the shooting stars of

---

27. [*Editor's note*: A controversial farm price support plan proposed in 1949 by President Harry Truman's secretary of agriculture, Charles F. Brannan (1903–92).]

which worlds are made, and they have always been and ever will be true. Such are the presence of God, the laws of gravitation, and the ceaseless struggle of mankind to be free.

Shall we keep that faith? Must we condemn unborn generations to fight again and to die for the right to be free?

These Foreign Policies

For nearly forty years I have had need to deal with international relations. I would be less than frank if on this, my last address to you, I did not speak from my heart and from that hard experience. And I can relieve all candidates from embarrassment by stating in their behalf at once that these are my views alone.

And if I seem to stress our foreign policies, I do so because within them lies the future of freedom of men and women in America, and because in the First World War I witnessed the Communists give rebirth to slavery on earth. One Democratic and three Republican Presidents refused to recognize their government and thus admit their official agents into our household.

Over those years I have known of a long roll of good men and women in many foreign lands, with whom I worked in intimacy to save their starving peoples, who died in Communist dungeons or dangled at the end of the hangman's rope.

For years I have protested that the lost statesmanship of dealing with them would drag the world into great calamities. However, there is no satisfaction in having been proved right by disasters to the American people.

Until twenty years ago our dedication to free men was admired and aspired to by all mankind. The undertakings of our government were trusted throughout the whole earth. Today, that respect and trust have been blemished by a hundred actions.

Twelve years ago we were led into a great war crusade on the promise of freedom to men and to nations under the banner of the Four Freedoms and the Atlantic Charter. Then at Teheran, Yalta and Potsdam we sacrificed the freedom of 650 millions of human beings on the altar of appeasement to Communism. The souls of one-quarter of mankind have been seared by the violation of that American promise. The ghosts of the Four Freedoms and the Atlantic Charter now wander amid the clanking chains of a thousand slave camps.

Where have we arrived after this war crusade for freedom? I need not remind you that we lost the peace despite the valor and the sacrifice of our manhood on a hundred battlefields. Our bewildered statesmanship has brought no return from the sacrifices and the tears of millions of mothers and wives. There is less freedom in the world today than at any time for a whole century. Have our foreign policies over those years been a success? They certainly did not make free men.

The Communists

Our opponents frequently remind me that this is all in the past. The past is the father of right now. And we have to deal with the menace they created.

Nurtured by policies participated in by our government and by Communists in the highest echelons of our Washington Administration, the Kremlin now cracks its whip over a horde of 800 million people. They are now armed with 300 divisions, 30,000 tanks and 20,000 war planes. American and British traitors have given them the atomic bomb.

Our need today is a cold and objective look at where we have got to, both abroad and within the United States, under the Truman-Acheson foreign and military policies dealing with the Communists.

Time tonight only permits me to appraise where we have got to on three major fronts. That is Korea, Western Europe, and the United States. And I shall add some constructive alternatives.

Korea

The situation in Korea was born at Yalta, and nourished by American support of so-called "agrarian liberals" in China.

We joined with more than twoscore of non-Communist members of the United Nations to defeat this Communist aggression. But we find ourselves furnishing 90 percent of the military forces sent there and taking 90 percent of the losses.

America's price so far is 120,000 dead, wounded and sick with 300,000 of our youth still fighting.

General MacArthur well said that in war there is no substitute for victory. Instead of victory, the Administration substituted appeasement on the 38th Parallel, just where we started from. After twelve months of negotiation, the Communists so far do not seem to want to be appeased. In the meantime they have so increased their forces that the military initiative is now in their hands. The end is not yet.

But can anyone say these policies in Korea have been a great success?

Continental Europe

We may also take a cold look at the second major area of the Truman-Acheson policies. That is—Western Europe.

Beginning six years ago with an unrepayable loan of over $3 billions to Britain, the Administration has poured $35 billions into Europe trying to build up their will power, their military strength, and furnishing them an American ground army.

For six years we have listened to a multitude of plans, agreements, pronouncements, and promises of great European armies. What is the net result of these efforts?

Three years ago, with the signing of the North Atlantic Pact, we were told that great ground armies would at last spring up on that continent. And to pass that treaty, a pledge was given to the Senate by the Administration that we would not contribute more ground troops to Europe. Then we shipped them 200,000 more American boys.

Three years after the Atlantic Pact, in February of this year, there was another conference at Lisbon. It was impressively announced that by the end of this year there would be, exclusive of American and British divisions, an army of about 15 battleworthy and 25 reserve divisions in Europe.

The *London Times,* commenting on the Lisbon agreement, published an editorial entitled, "A Phantom Army." The *Times* pointed out that even this small army could not possibly be ready in 1952.

Six weeks ago we witnessed the signing of a step toward freedom of Western Germany. That was a good deed. A few days later we saw the signing of the European Defense Community treaty by six Continental nations. That will be an advance in European unity provided it is ratified by six distracted parliaments. But it was announced [in the *New York Times* of May 28 that, by a secret agreement,–*ed.*][28] these six nations would by 1954 or 1955, create 55 divisions of which 15 would be reserve divisions.

Aside from American and British divisions, this European army seems determined to keep its phantom quality.

Can anyone say that this size army even three years hence is any real deterrent in a ground war to the already six times greater forces of the Communist horde? Or that it could even avert a Dunkirk of the six American divisions we have placed there?

---

28. [*Editor's note:* The words within brackets appear in Hoover's cited source. Why he deleted these words from his later manuscript is unclear.]

Compare this promised fifty-odd division army three years hence with the 160 effective divisions these same six Western European nations—comprising 160 million people—put in the field within 60 days in both World War I and World War II. Today their manpower and productive capacity is greater than in either of those wars. The potential is there, but we must by this time realize that the will is lacking.

The only other explanation of their attitude is that these six nations of Western Europe have no stirring belief in present danger. We have heard no clamor from these countries to spend their lives, their fortunes, or their sacred honor to defend their liberties. They have proclaimed no such emergencies, carried on no such propaganda of peril, nor stimulated such war psychoses as have emanated from Washington, D.C.

Can anyone honestly say that these policies of making great ground armies in Western Europe have been a great success?

The Effect of These Policies on Freedom in the United States

Now let us take a good look at the economic and social effect of these Administration policies on the United States. It is no news to you that the federal and local governments are spending about 35 percent of the national income. That is more than any nation can bear.

I have long had great sympathy for the humble decimal point. He has to jump three zeros every little while. He had to make three jumps to punctuate our present deficit.

We do not need to look far to find the blazing proof in our midst that we cannot carry this economic burden.

If you think these policies are not producing an inflation which is wrecking American lives, just recall but a few things: Already after this six years of these Washington policies the American worker must have an annual income of $4,500 today to live as well as he did on $3,000 six years ago. If this does not convince you, look about you at the necessary round of wage increases going on today which means you can buy less with your money tomorrow.

Look around and you will see millions who have earned pensions or saved to protect their old age being reduced to the tragedy of want.

Look still further and you will find not only inflation but that the intolerable taxes stifle initiative and are driving millions of our people to become more and more dependent upon the Government.

Look again and you will find this tax-and-spend used as a vehicle to mix collectivism into American life.

You can look even more deeply. No government can spend such sums of money and not corrupt the spenders. And no government can levy such taxes without breeding a horde of tax dodgers and bribers.

Do you want to go on with this spending, inflation and corruption?

If free men are to survive in America, we must reduce spending and taxes. It is true we can make some cuts in spending by stopping waste, corruption, and private privilege. But the total of all such reductions would not even reduce the prospective budget deficit by one-half. To say nothing of stopping inflation or reducing taxes.

It is not enough just to say we will balance the budget and reduce taxes. Or to say we will do it some years hence. We must face the grim reality of how and where to do it now.

The reality is that we cannot ever balance the budget and reduce taxes except by cutting into this military and foreign spending.

To find this how and where, and still do our part in the world, we must take a new look into these military policies.

The Administration and the Pentagon have been building up four gigantic military programs. First, they insist upon huge ground armies; second, naval forces; third, air forces; and fourth, munitions and cash subsidies to other nations. And now they propose to add huge numbers to these armies by compulsory universal military service. All this step-by-step building of great ground armies is the road to militarism. That is at its base a threat to all freedoms. That has brought ruin to freedom ever since Rome. That wrecked Germany and Japan.

Moreover, the military strength of America does not lie today in great ground armies.

How many mistakes do we have to make before we learn that our genius lies in the invention, production, and operation of great weapons? Our future is in these great weapons, not in bayonets. And we can furnish these great weapons to nations who have the will to defend themselves.

Lest you think the Pentagon is not determined on bayonets, I may mention their bulletin of February 1st of this year, which I quote. They say:

"The individual rifleman is the most effective and most essential weapon against the enemy. All other services exist to support the infantry soldier."

The Alternative

All Americans wish to see civilization preserved in Western Europe.

But we must recognize their lack of will in preparedness which might have been a deterrent to Communist aggression. Therefore, we must determine what real deterrent America can furnish within our economic and manpower capacities.

The effective deterrent which American resources can contribute is not bayonets against overwhelming land forces, but the expansion of air power and navies to make up a great striking force, which could destroy the Communist military potential if they started any aggression anywhere. And this striking force naturally includes strategic bases with a stretch of water in front of them over which Communist armies cannot pass our Navy.

It is asserted today that our air force is now inferior to that of Russia. Yet simply as an example we could add one-half more to our air strength and maintain it at less cost than we can recruit, train, arm, and maintain 10 divisions of ground troops. And those planes, so essential to our own safety, would be a far better defense of Europe.

The American people will start no wars. But the sure defense of New York, London, and Paris is the fear of counter-attack on Moscow by air. The Kremlin will not be much frightened over an American ground war against their overwhelming forces. In that area of menace the military initiative is on the Communist side today.

Sometime ago when, as a mere civilian, I proposed this alternative program of less armies and an overwhelming striking force at less cost, a yell went up, "Here comes the armchair strategist." But promptly this proposal was supported by seven of our most distinguished retired Army, Navy and Air officers. It was supported by six of our most seasoned diplomats.

Such a program would restore the advantage of military initiative to us.

It would extend our effectiveness to aid all menaced countries.

It would assure American youth that their lives will not be widely interrupted and that they will not be sent into the overwhelming Communist quicksands.

It would enable us to stop this creeping Fascism and Socialism.

It would balance our budget and start to cut our taxes.

It would avoid our bankruptcy which is Stalin's greatest hope.

It has been said that in these evil times peace can be preserved only through strength. That is true. But the center and final reserve of strength of the free world lies now in the Western Hemisphere. I am not ashamed to say that our first duty is to defend the United States. For if we fall, the freedom of men falls in the whole world.

What I propose is an entire reconsideration of these policies based on the realities which have today developed both in the United States and abroad.

I do not propose that we retreat into our shell like a turtle. I do propose the deadly reprisal strategy of a rattlesnake.

The way out from the perils, begotten from these twelve years of lost statesmanship, is not easy. Certainly sane policies cannot be made amid college yells of "isolationist" or "internationalist," nor by smears and slanted news which are the ugly instruments of those who would dictate.

Other Tasks before Us

The Republican Party must not blink the other many difficulties of the times and the other tasks before us. Our Party welcomes change in the social and economic order when it will produce a more fair, a more free and more satisfying civilization. But change which destroys the safeguards of free men and women will be only an apple of Sodom. Again I may say I have great sympathy for those who honestly seek for short cuts to solve our complex problems. But the structure of betterment can only be built brick by brick by men and women free in spirit and mind. The bricks must come from the mold of religious faith, of justice, of integrity, of fidelity to the spirit of the Constitution. Any other mold is distorted; any other bricks are without straw.

This Election

This election may well be the last chance for the survival of freedom in America.

In a time of confusion and crisis the action of a Republican Convention ninety years ago saved this nation for free men.

The Whig Party temporized, compromised upon the issue of freedom for the Negro. That party disappeared. It deserved to disappear. Shall the Republican Party receive or deserve any better fate if it compromises upon the issue of freedom for all men, white as well as black?

If you make free men your issue, you can again revive the call which your and my ancestors issued ninety years ago when this party was born to make all men free.

Also there was a Convention in 1776. Their Declaration stirred the world with its ringing appeal for free men, its righteous recital of transgressions and its pledge of Life, Fortune and sacred Honor.

America needs today a new Declaration that will raise the hearts of our people to their spiritual purpose and their eyes into the sunlight of freedom.

Its first sentence should read:

"The Republican Party is determined to restore free men in the United States."

That Declaration really needs nothing more to revive again hope in a frustrated people.

That is your great issue.

Yours is the task to stop this retreat; to lead the attack and recapture the citadels of liberty in the United States. Thus can America be preserved. Thus can it hold the lamp of free men aloft to a confused world. Thus can we wipe out coercion and corruption. Thus can the peace, plenty, and security be re-established and expanded. Thus can the opportunity, and the spiritual future of your children be guaranteed. And thus you will win the gratitude of posterity, and the blessing of Almighty God.

In my opening remarks I stated that from the inexorable course of nature, this is most likely the last time I will have the honor of attending your Conventions. Therefore, in closing, I wish to express my deep gratitude to this great party you represent, for the many honors you have bestowed upon me. If I have won some measure of your affections, it is a high award. But the greatest glory that can come to man is to be given the opportunity to fight for free men. And I shall continue to fight for those principles which made the United States the greatest gift of God to freedom. I pray to Him to strengthen your hands and give you courage.

The Convention nominated General Dwight D. Eisenhower. I had favored Senator Robert A. Taft for many reasons. At General Eisenhower's urgent request, I delivered an address in his support on October 18, 1952:[29]

I have tonight come out of what I had hoped was final retirement from political activities. I have done so at General Eisenhower's request. I have done so because I believe General Eisenhower and the Republican ticket should be elected. I am convinced that the fate of our country in these confused and perilous times hangs upon a change in the Administration in Washington.

A major safeguard of American freedom is two virile political parties. A great political party, despite secondary internal differences, is welded together by certain common loyalties and beliefs, certain principles, and certain ideals of government.

---

29. *Addresses upon the American Road, 1950–1955*, pp. 122–135. [*Editor's note*: In the following quoted text, as in other extended quotations in Hoover's *Crusade against Collectivism in American Life* manuscript, Hoover often made minor stylistic changes, such as deleting commas and capitalizing words that were not capitalized in the quoted source. Unless these changes were of a substantive nature, I have reverted to the text as printed in the original, cited source.]

When we elect a President, we are not electing a single person. We are electing a group of party members to take over the direction of the Government.

My major purpose tonight is to address the 40 percent—about 40 million—of our eligible voters who have come of age since there was a Republican Administration. You 40 million must choose the course, select the management of the United States in the immediate years ahead. With you rests the destiny of our country.

You 40 million new voters have known little of the Republican Party's background of principles and of its forward-looking constructive accomplishments.

Incessantly for the past twenty years, and including this campaign, the American people have been deluged by misrepresentations and false slogans aimed at the principles, the ideals, and the record of the Republican Party. Such statements do not befit the sense of fair play, of honor or of statesmanship in our national life or in either party.

No political party is perfect and I have no desire to minimize the service of the Democratic Party under such leaders as Jefferson, Cleveland, and Wilson. They as did Republican leaders believed in that true Liberalism which made this country great.

The Major Misrepresentations

The major misrepresentations and falsehoods now current today appear in seven categories.

1. That the Republican Party is the party of privilege and the tool of Wall Street or "big business."
2. That the Great Depression was caused by Republicans and they did nothing about it.
3. That the Republican Party is a reactionary party opposed to change and reforms so necessary in a progressive national life, or is not "forward-looking."
4. That the Republican Party neglected and is opposed to the conservation and development of natural resources.
5. That the Republican Administrations were corrupt.
6. That the Republican Party is incompetent to preserve peace.
7. That the growth of communism in the United States was caused by the Republican years of the Depression.

The proper reply to these misrepresentations is not counter-smear, but presentation of the facts to thinking people.

1. What about Privilege, Wall Street, Big Business?

The Republican Party is now almost 100 years old. Its dominant principle has always been the freedom of men.

Twenty-five years after Lincoln's emancipation of the slaves there was a second great revolutionary act by Republicans to free men from oppression. The gigantic economic development of our country had led to new forms of oppression of free men. These were abuses by big business, monopolies, and restraints of trade.

By the Republican Sherman Act of 1890 these doings were prohibited. It produced far deeper consequences than mere negation. It produced an economic revolution. Our whole economic system was transformed from the unrestrained laissez-faire, dog-eat-dog concepts which we had inherited from Europe. By this Act our economy was first geared to standards of conduct which preserve freedom. We call it regulation. I may say at once such regulation is not to be confused with regimentation.

By the standards in the Sherman Act we assured competition in the United States. Under competition American business has been forced to earn its profits by constantly improving its plants, by lowering its costs of production. Europe continued the system of trade monopolies, cartels, and combinations, whose profits were thus partly made from control of prices and distribution. European business lost much of the pressure for improvement of plant and method. Under the impulses of competition, American industry leads the world. Much European economy has so lost efficiency that Socialism has become their fatal answer.

"Big business" did not rejoice over the Sherman Act. Many of them have never become reconciled to it. They induced the New Dealers in 1933 to, in effect, repeal the Antitrust laws by an imitation of Mussolini's Corporate State through creating the N.R.A. Only the Supreme Court saved our competitive economy from Fascism. A Democratic President denounced this action of the Court as "reactionary."

Nor was the Sherman Antitrust law a solitary action in safeguarding free men from economic oppression. The Republican Party continued to put restraints on oppressive business up to its last moments in office in 1933. To prove that, I must recite a long list of Federal laws passed under Republican Presidents.

It was Republicans who, by successive laws from 1903 to 1910, gave the Interstate Commerce Commission its full authority to control railway rates. In 1910 came the control of the telephone and telegraph rates.

In 1906 Republicans passed the Pure Food and Drug Acts.

Returning to the office after being out for eight years, Republicans, in 1922, regulated the grain exchanges. In 1924 they secured regulation of the Federal fisheries. In 1926 came the regulation of aviation. In 1927 came the regulation of radio. In 1930 the Tariff Commission (a statistical agency) was transformed into a bipartisan body for the regulation of the tariff, in order to take the tariff out of politics.

And in 1930 came the creation of a real Federal Power Commission.

In 1932 we reformed the Bankruptcy Laws so as to prevent the flood of fraud on creditors.

I may sum up that of the eighteen major acts erecting standards of conduct for business, twelve were of Republican origin and four originated under Cleveland and Wilson.

Does this Republican record look like the tool of "big business" or privilege? It is the very essence of preserving men free from oppression.

The New Dealers have preferred creeping socialism to the establishment of proper standards of conduct among free men.

2. The Misrepresentation That the Republicans Created the Great Depression and Then Did Nothing about It

The misrepresentation that Republicans created the Great Depression, which came ten years after the First World War, is still oratory in this campaign. That nonsense has been exploded a thousand times by a multitude of economists, historians, and statesmen.

The Great Depression started elsewhere in the world before it struck the United States. Its major violence came from the inevitable bankruptcy of Europe as the aftermath of the First World War.

In this economic hurricane, the economy of one foreign country after another crumbled, panics and political revolutions took place in a score of foreign nations. In effect all but two nations in the world abandoned the gold standard. Trying to protect themselves these foreign nations imposed restrictions on their exchange and imports. They suspended payments on their obligations. Our farm and other exports to Europe practically ceased. Unemployment spread over the whole earth. Our gold standard was jeopardized. The impact of these forces spread constant fear and near panic in the United States. Our weak banking and credit system was toppling all around us.

To solve these emergencies and ameliorate the successive shocks the Republican administration created unprecedented agencies and took unprecedented actions.

Relief to the Unemployed

We organized direct relief to those in distress and indirect relief to the un-employed by huge public works. We did so with never a charge of corrup-tion. No one went hungry or cold if our system of committees knew of it. We temporarily stopped immigration to prevent loss of jobs by our workers. We sustained wages, we reduced employer-employee friction to the lowest levels in recent times.

Aids to Farmers

In 1923 Republicans had already created the Federal Intermediate Credit Banks to finance the marketing of farm products. In 1929 Republicans cre-ated the Federal Farm Board with a capital of half a billion dollars, which supported farm prices in the depression. Out of it came the present Bank for Farm Co-operatives. Republicans expanded the Farm Loan Board and created the Agricultural Credit Banks to finance famers' production. The Democrats abolished this one.

Aids to Business

We created the Reconstruction Finance Corporation with three billion dol-lars capital. We created the Home Loan Banks. We expanded the Federal Reserve Credit System. We accomplished these measures against the opposi-tion or delays of a Democratic House of Representatives.

Far from "bailing out" the rich, as one orator says, 90 percent of the loans under Republican Administrations went to saving Building and Loan As-sociations, Savings Banks, insurance companies, small country banks, and Farmers' Loan Associations. These were not the institutions of the rich. They represented the small savings of the people.

We incessantly urged reform of our obsolete banking laws so as to protect depositors. But a Democratic Congress refused.

We prevented panic in the United States until after the election of the New Deal. We secured the country from being forced off the gold standard and kept the American dollar ringing true on every counter in the entire world.

Co-operation with Foreign Nations

To protect [the–*ed.*] foreign economy from complete collapse in the Depres-sion, we created a moratorium on world governmental debts and brought about the Standstill Agreements. To restore the demoralized world mon-etary standards and to decrease trade barriers we originated the World Eco-nomic Conference. That conference was convened in London after we left office. But it was assassinated in its youth by a Democratic President. In his memoirs the then Democratic Secretary of State implies this action sowed the seeds of the second World War.

Too many young voters have been led to believe the New Deal enacted all this multitude of measures.

Most outstanding economists are agreed that Republican measures brought beginnings of the recovery in July 1932. But our recovery then in motion was reversed by a wholly unnecessary panic of bank depositors. That was created by refusal of the incoming New Deal to co-operate with us in foreign and domestic remedial measures for the whole four months after the election. It was also due to public panic over the New Deal proposals to tinker with the value of our money and thus inflation. And now the New Dealers date all their doleful statistics from the bottom of this setback, which they themselves created.

They might mention that they have continued to tinker with money, credit, debt, and inflation until an income of $3,000 per annum in 1932 would buy more than an income of $8,000 today. Your annual Federal taxes in 1932 averaged under $100. Today they are over $1,300 per family.

A dozen other nations, with free economies, within three years after the New Deal election, marched out of the Depression to higher levels of employment and production than those of the boom year of 1928.

There were about 11,000,000 unemployed at the time of Roosevelt's election in November 1932. But the New Deal violated their every election promise and attempted to mix fascism and socialism into the American system. From their actions America continued to wallow every winter in 10 to 11 million unemployed. Eight years of this New Deal unemployment only found remedy in jobs from the Second World War.

If you want more proof of these misrepresentations, I have published a whole book on the subject.[30]

3. Reactionary and Opposed to Change

A daily misrepresentation in this campaign is that the Republican Party is reactionary, opposed to change, and without courage to take action needed in a progressive country.

---

30. [*Editor's note*: This is a reference to *The Memoirs of Herbert Hoover*, vol. III: *The Great Depression, 1929–1941* (New York: The Macmillan Company, 1952).]

It would seem that what I have recounted as to Republican action on business oppression and action during the world-wide depression would be sufficient answer. But just in case you want some more evidence I will give you a few of many samples of Republican attitudes to reform and change in the fields of labor, children, farmers, veterans and homes.

Labor

As to labor, in 1903, Republicans created the Department of Labor and Commerce. Returning to office after the Wilson Administration, we secured in 1923 the abolition of the twelve-hour day in industry. A Republican administration was the first officially to establish collective bargaining when we established the Railway Mediation board in 1926. The act limiting the use of Federal Court injunctions in labor disputes was signed by a Republican President. Was this reactionary?

Children

As to the protection of children, in 1912, Republicans established the Children's Bureau in the Federal Government. Following our return to office after World War I, Republicans in 1924 submitted a Constitutional Amendment prohibiting child labor. The Amendment failed because enough State Legislatures, predominantly Democratic, refused to ratify it. In 1931 a Republican Administration proposed subsidies for Rural Child Welfare, which were passed by the House of Representatives but killed by a filibuster of a Democratic Senator. Were these actions reactionary?

Farmers

I have already given evidence of our interest in the farmers' well-being. I may point out further that for ninety-six years Republicans supported tariff protection for the farmers. Republicans in 1862 created the Agricultural Commission which subsequently became the Department of Agriculture. Republicans expanded the Department from 1902 to 1932 by creating six of its most important Bureaus. In 1932 we proposed the retirement of marginal lands from production to remedy the farmers' chronic surplus production. It was turned down by a Democratic Congress. Was this reactionary?

Housing and Homes

As to housing and homes, after the dislocations of the First World War the Republicans in 1922 established the first Bureau of Housing in the Federal

Government. By co-operative measures with the people, we secured construction of more new homes during the decade of the Twenties than the whole eight years of the New Deal. A Republican Administration in 1932 established the Home Loan Banks and the same year initiated the first Federal aid to slum clearance. Was this reactionary?

Veterans

As to veterans, in 1868, Republicans established pensions for veterans disabled in the Civil War and for their widows and orphans. They did so in 1908 for Spanish-American War veterans. They did so for World War I veterans. In 1924 Republicans enacted the Veterans' Bonus Bill. In 1932 Republicans established the Veterans' Administration as a major agency of the Government. In 1930, Republicans provided disability allowances and hospitalization to all indigent veterans, irrespective of the origins of the illness. In 1933, the New Deal repealed this service and deprived 300,000 veterans of this aid. From 1921 to 1933, Republicans built 46 hospitals with 25,260 beds for veterans. A study by The Brookings Institution says: "... The eight years ending with March 4, 1933 saw the greatest expansion and liberalization in legislation relating to Veterans ever known in this country or probably in any other country."

Federal Administration

And we may look at the organization of the Federal Government itself. In addition to establishing the Departments of Labor and Commerce, Republicans established the Patent Office, the Weather Bureau, and the Postal Savings Banks.

To take civil employees out of politics, Republicans in 1883 established the bipartisan Civil Service Commission. The act provided that all new employees with a few exceptions were to be admitted on merit by open competitive examinations and proof as to character. This meant equal rights to all irrespective of politics, religion, or race.

By 1932 all but 19 percent of the 580,000 Federal employees had entered government service through the non-partisan merit gate of the Civil Service Commission. But during the succeeding eight years of the New Deal, twenty-four acts were passed exempting groups from Civil Service requirements. The Democratic County chairmen did most of the appointing. One might also note that, in 1937, a Democratic Administration attempted to abolish the Commission and was defeated in Congress. By 1952 the bureaucracy has swelled to over 2,500,000 persons of whom I doubt one-half ever originally passed the full competitive Civil Service Commission examinations before their employment.

In 1921, Republicans established for the first time a Federal Budget and a General Accounting Office for control and audit of accounts.

If all these evidences of reform and "forward look" to meet the change in national life are not enough, I will give you some more from the record.

In 1930 and 1932 a Republican Administration reformed the Federal Criminal procedures so as to abolish much of the trick delays in criminal trials.

We reformed the whole Federal prison system, with separate prisons for hardened criminals, and special prisons for women. We established a system of probation and parole. We passed the Federal anti-kidnapping laws.

In 1926 and 1930 we established the FBI.

4. Conservation and Development of Natural Resources

The statement is made that Republicans would stifle governmental aid to conservation and development of natural resources.

Republicans originated practically the whole idea and every bureau of Federal conservation of natural resources.

In 1891, Republicans established the first National Forests and, in 1905, the Forest Service.

The National Forests comprised 161 million acres in 1932. They have been increased by only 12 percent in the last twenty years.

In 1872, Republicans established the first National Park. Of the 28 major National Parks, 23 were founded by Republicans.

In 1924, Republicans established the Oil Conservation Board and, in 1929, all oil beneath the free public lands was withdrawn from private entry. That same year a Republican administration initiated the great interstate compact for conservation of oil which has since come into being among twenty-one states.

In 1902, Republicans established and vigorously carried out Federal reclamation of arid lands. Of the 62 reclamation projects today, 41 were created by Republicans. And these included the first gigantic multiple purpose dam on the Colorado River and we nearly finished it. Furthermore we approved and were engaged in the engineering plans for the great Grand Coulee Dam and Central Valley of California developments.

In 1930, laws were recommended for the conservation of the public ranges in the west.

Other Great Public Improvements

As to purported Republican opposition to public improvements generally, I may mention that a Republican Administration in 1905 undertook and built the Panama Canal. Seven administrations of Republicans constantly expanded the development of our rivers, harbors, and canals. In 1929 we established the concept of an integrated waterway system connecting great cities 1,600 miles east and west and 1,500 miles north and south. We largely completed it. Without this system we could not have handled our traffic in World War II.

From 1927 to 1932 we rebuilt the flood control on the lower Mississippi and Sacramento rivers. We did so good a job that there have been no flood disasters on these rivers since.

The Republicans vigorously supported the States in constructing inter-state roads. By 1932 about 129,000 miles of surfaced roads had been built. In 1932 a Republican Administrations, through the RFC, established the policy of Federal loans for self-liquidating public works then financially unfeasible by private capital or State funds. The San Francisco Bay Bridge and the Colorado River water supply to the Los Angeles area were examples. And those loans made by Republican Administrations have all been repaid to the Federal Government.

In 1928, Republicans undertook the public building program which has so beautified Washington and many other cities.

In fact, in the single four years from 1929 to 1933, Republicans built more useful public works than in the entire previous thirty years.

Taking all this into account it would seem that phrase "Republicans do nothing" is somewhat overdone in this campaign.

5. Corruption

During the last fifty-two years Republicans and Democrats equally divided the time in office. The Republicans had just one bad episode of corruption. That was during the Harding Administration. Democrats do not fail to recall it even in the present campaign.

Without examining whether corruption can be absolved by pointing an accusing finger at older sins, I suggest a wide difference between the conduct of Republican and Democratic administrations in their two fields of wickedness. There were nine men involved in the Harding episode. The other members of the Administration were aghast. They determined to pursue these men implacably. Before we had finished with them, two of them had committed suicide, one died while awaiting trial, four landed in prison, and one escaped by a twice-hung jury.

Can the perpetrators of the present mess in Washington point to any such vigorous house-cleaning?

In the past twenty years of Democratic Administration, there have been over 300 cases of Congressional or administrative condemnation or public exposure of every variety of transgression of national honor. It appears that except for cases forced by Congressional Committees, so far less than twenty-five persons have landed in jail. Washington nowadays seems neither aghast nor implacable.

6. Republicans and Peace

The misrepresentation that the Republican Party is an isolationist Party is false on the record.

Republicans in 1899 established the Open Door policy in China and in 1922 brought about the Nine-Power Treaty for its protection. In 1928, Republicans initiated the Kellogg-Briand Pact against aggression. From 1921 to 1932, Republican Administrations entered into over 60 conciliation and arbitration treaties with different nations. For 12 years—from 1921 to 1933—Republican Presidents ceaselessly urged our joining the World Court. The New Deal dropped it.

In 1922, Republican Administrations brought about partial limitation in size of the major navies of the world, and, in 1930, completed that job. The ending of naval competition over the following decade contributed to peace and saved billions of taxpayers' money.

In our Western Hemisphere relations, beginning in 1890 and by 1910, Republican Secretaries of State had established the Pan-American Union. Returning again to Washington after Wilson, a Republican Administration in 1929 established the Good Neighbor Policy.

I have already related our international co-operation to alleviate the Depression.

As to ability to keep peace I may mention that during twelve years of the last Republican Administrations, nations embracing nearly 2 billion of the world's population, as a result of American policies, held the United States in high esteem and warm friendship. I doubt if there are twenty-five percent of those 2 billions remaining our friends today.

All this is scarcely an isolationist record.

Our critics are correct that most Republicans opposed our joining with Stalin in the second World War. We believed these monsters, Stalin and Hitler, should exhaust each other. We said repeatedly that by joining with Stalin in the war we would spread Communism over the earth. If this was isolationism, I am proud of it.

7. Communism

A few days ago it was said that the growth of Communism in the United States was caused by the "Republican Depression."

In the 15 years after the Communist Revolution in Russia until the end of Republican Administrations the Communist Party had grown to a meager 13,000 members. During this time we had refused to give respectability to this slave state by having any relations with it. In the ten years after the New Deal recognition of Communist Russia, the Communist Party in the United States grew to over 80,000 members.

Their front organizations cast over 500,000 votes.

Republicans tolerated no communists in the Federal Government. I leave the recital of the New Deal record to you.

In Conclusion

I could go on endlessly with this record of constructive courageous action. I have surely said enough to refute the myriad of falsehoods and misrepresentations in this campaign.

This is not ancient stuff. It is pertinent to this moment as these daily misrepresentations indicate the character of the party seeking by such means to retain their hold on Washington. Second, it is pertinent to reassure new voters from the record that the Party behind such great men as General Eisenhower and Senator Nixon is a constructive party of probity, courage, ideals, and vision, worthy to be entrusted with the administration of our country.

This address which was made over TV and radio brought one outstanding surprise. That was over 95,000 post-cards, letters or telegrams from individuals over the country. The greatest number of such communications from any of General Eisenhower's speeches was under 25,000.

General Eisenhower was elected on November 4th. I issued the following statement:

The American people have ordered a change in the administration of our Government. But the hour of victory for our cause is no time for either re-crimination or exaltation. The problems before us are more difficult than were even debated in this campaign. The majority of our people are giving their faith of solution of our problems into the hands of General Eisenhower and his friends. I am sure the whole American people pray the Almighty for his success in the great task now before him.[31]

31. [*Editor's note*: Hoover, *Addresses upon the American Road, 1950–1955*, p. 137.]

CHAPTER 16

The Continental¹ Crusade after 1952

I attended the Inauguration² with the hope this was the last incident in my crusade against collectivism. But that was not to be. Observing some hesitation in the new Administration at cleaning out the Socialist activities inherited from the Roosevelt-Truman regime, I again addressed the American people at Case Institute of Technology, Cleveland, Ohio on April 11, 1953:³

This is a celebration of the founding of a great institution dedicated to scientific research and the training of engineers and scientists. You seek to sharpen their abilities and initiative for a climate of free men. It is an appropriate time for discussion of some of the forces in our Federal government which have been destructive of such a climate.

In the field of Federal electric power we have an example of twenty years of creeping socialism with a demonstration of its results.

Three years ago the Commission on Organization of the Executive Branch of the Government, under my chairmanship, made an investigation into the Federal activities in electric power. As the Commission was not dealing with public policies, its recommendations were confined to administrative reforms. Even these have not been carried out. The highly critical reports of our staff of accountants and engineers amply illuminated the results of this socialist invasion.

---

1. [*Editor's note*: This may be a misprint in Hoover's 1955 page-proof manuscript. In the 1953 version of his *Crusade Years* manuscript, the word was "Continued."]

2. [*Editor's note*: That is, the presidential inauguration of Dwight Eisenhower on January 20, 1953.]

3. [Herbert Hoover,] *Addresses upon the American Road, 1950–1955* [Stanford, CA: Stanford University Press, 1955], pp. 141–152. [*Editor's note*: As with other extended quotations from Hoover's previously published addresses, I have used here the punctuation and stylistic form as printed in the original, cited source.]

And at once let me state that the present Administration is not responsible for this situation; they inherited it on January 20, 1953.

What Is the American Way of Life?

Before I go into more detail I wish to say something as to what the American way of free men really is.

The socialists, with their ideas imported from Europe, totally misconstrue the unique structure of American life. They envisage it in terms of European societies.

Ours is a system of free men and free enterprise in which our concepts have steadily departed from those of the Old World in two directions.

We have conceived that, to have free men, we must be free from the economic tyrannies which were nurtured in Europe's laissez-faire, dog-eat-dog system of economy.

Free men can no more permit private economic power without checks and balances than governmental power without checks and balances.

The great enterprises of production and distribution can be used for economic oppression. To prevent this oppression of free men, we originated government regulation unique in the world. We regulate rates and services of natural monopolies such as the electric power utilities. We insist upon freedom from trade monopolies and the enforcement of constructive competition. We adopted this economic philosophy seventy years ago in a revolution from European concepts and practices.

And in another departure from European social structures we have developed a far greater expansion of free co-operation between men in community interest. Its extent is without parallel in any other country. It gained force from the necessities of a pioneer people where co-operative action was vital to their existence. Today I dare say we have a million nongovernmental organizations for cooperative action in our country. They include thousands of health, educational, sports, musical, social, business, farmer, and labor organizations. They have been created without the aid of bureaucrats. In some aspects we could add to these our insurance and savings banks and our corporations in general.

And we hold 10,000 annual conventions of them and survive unending speeches and banquets.

This co-operative system is self-government of the people outside of government. It is the most powerful development among free men that has taken place in all the world.

The Old World, however, went on with its lack of effective economic safe-guards for free men and its dearth of co-operation in the American sense. One result was the rise of socialism as a protest.

I emphasize this unique structure of our American economic and social life because it is into this system, far divorced from the Old World, that our fuzzy-minded socialists are striving to inject ideas foreign to our concept of life.

And they have made progress with these adulterants. They intrude into many avenues of American life. And they threaten a new oppression of free men greater than the old dog-eat-dog economy.

Tonight I shall appraise the aspects of creeping socialism in the electric power industry by the *Federal Government only*. Rightly or wrongly the State and municipal governments do engage in electric enterprises. But at least their activities respond to the will and scrutiny of local government.

Nor do I include the Rural Electrification Administration in this discussion although it receives great government subsidies. It has worthy purpose, but that operation is so small a percent of the electric power in the country that it cannot eat up the industry.

Private Enterprise in Electricity

In the electric field there are certain transcendent facts.

First. Under the initiative of free men we developed the technology and use of electricity far beyond any other country.

Second. Stemming from private enterprise, we have created a per capita supply of electrical power for our people three times that of the combined Western European nations and eleven times the average of the whole foreign world.

Third. Private enterprise could keep in pace with demand, and could have more advantageously distributed the power from Federal water conservation projects.

Fourth. With our advancing technology and individual initiative, the average price of household electric power is sold today by our private enterprise utilities at one-third of the price of thirty years ago—and that is while most other commodities and wages have increased by 50 percent to 100 percent. There is no such parallel in any other commodity.

Despite these results from a free economy, these concepts of free men were abandoned twenty years ago when the Federal Government entered into the socialization of electric power in a big way.

The Method of Socialization

The device by which our Federal bureaucracy started to socialize this industry was through the electric power from our multiple-purpose water conservation dams. We needed these dams. And need more of them. They were built to serve navigation, flood control, irrigation and domestic water supplies and to provide electric energy. However, the central question here is not the creation of this electric power but using it to promote socialism. The first step toward socialization was taken when the Federal Government undertook itself to generate and distribute this electric power from multiple-purpose dams. And now the Federal Government has taken further socialistic leaps by building steam and hydro plants solely for the generation of electric power.

Up to twenty years ago we avoided socialism by selling the energy at the dams to private utilities and irrigation districts. The government received a return without incurring operating expenses.

Let no one misinterpret my views on water conservation. I have been for thirty years an ardent exponent of multiple-purpose dams. I can claim some credit for the first gigantic multiple-purpose dam in the United States. That one is in the Colorado River.[4]

But again on the Colorado we avoided socialism by stipulating that before construction began the energy should be leased to the private utilities and municipalities. And we contracted to sell it at a rate which provided for interest on the Government investment and the complete repayment of the investment within a period of fifty years. The consumers over these seventeen years since have found no cause for complaint from that arrangement.

The March of Socialism

Do not think these Federal electric enterprises are small business.

Twenty years ago the total generating capacity of electric power from Federal dams was about 300,000 horsepower. It was about two-thirds of one percent of the total electric generating capacity at that time.

As some people are confused by the technical terms "kilowatts" and "kilowatt hours," I have translated them into horsepower.

By the middle of 1953, the Federal Government will have a generating capacity of about 15,000,000 horsepower. That is about 12 percent of the utility

---

4. [*Editor's note*: The Hoover Dam.]

generating capacity for sale to the public. Federal power is already being sent into twenty-seven states.

But far beyond this, there are Federal generating plants in construction or authorized by the Congress, making a total of over 200 plants which will bring the total up to about 37,000,000 horsepower. If completed the Federal Government would be furnishing somewhere from 20 percent to 25 percent of the electric utility capacity of the nation. The cost in capital outlay to the taxpayer will be about $10 to $11 billions, plus some great deficits in promised interest and other returns.

But that is not all. Further projects have been recommended to Congress. And still more are contemplated in government reports. If they were all undertaken, it would bring the total to about 90,000,000 horsepower.

This bureaucracy now employs 33,000 persons and is increasing every day. And if all these dreams were realized, their employees on the Federal payroll will likely exceed 200,000.

But even this is not the whole story. Lest anyone thinks this is good for us, I may point to some of the already evident consequences of socialized electric power.

Expansion by Duress

Under the irresistible nature of bureaucracy and the backing of the socialists every one of these Federal enterprises becomes a center of encroachments upon or coercion and absorption of the private industry. For instance, by the threat of WPA gifts and low interest rates on loans to municipalities, private enterprises were absorbed at less than their worth.

Great duplicate transmission lines have been built and more are contemplated.

Some of these Government enterprises are given the power of eminent domain by which they could seize transmission lines and sub-stations of competitors and, if the owner refuses their price, he can pay lawyers for years to fight for compensation in the courts. Free enterprise never had such a privilege.

Some part of the heavy taxes on private utilities goes to build up and support their Federal competitors.

Private enterprises have been prevented from undertaking certain hydro-electric developments in favor of the Government agencies.

These manipulations and powers threaten and weaken the ability of many private concerns to finance their needed expansions.

Indeed some of them with these guns pointed at them have already thrown up their hands.

Socialization in other directions has been injected into these projects. For instance, the provision that water will not be supplied to farms of over 160 acres in some of the California Central Valley operations. Apparently all others are Kulaks. Also, some of these Federal power enterprises, with cheap Federal capital and subsidized power, are engaged in manufacturing business in competition with private enterprise.

Freedom from Taxes

These Federal enterprises and their distributing allies pay no taxes to the Federal Government and comparatively little to the local governments. In the last fiscal year the private enterprise utilities paid over $750,000,000 taxes to the Federal Government and nearly $470,000,000 to the state and local governments. The actual Federal electric enterprises paid less than $5,000,000 toward State and local taxes.

Obviously there is here a huge burden thrust onto every taxpayer throughout the nation. It will be much greater if the 37,000,000 horsepower program is completed.

Nor is this all of the burdens thrust upon the nation-wide taxpayer as I will show you in a few moments.

Unkept Representations to the Congress

In many cases the cost of constructing these projects has been woefully underestimated. For instance, the Colorado–Big Thompson project was originally estimated at about $44,000,000, but is costing over $160,000,000. The Hungry Horse project originally estimated at $39,000,000 will cost over $109,000,000. Work has been started on the Oahe project. It was originally estimated to cost about $72,000,000. It is now estimated that it will cost $293,000,000.

Some of the increased cost has been due to rising prices but such an excuse by no means explains the degree of underestimate. Some of this underestimation is possibly due to presenting the Congress with a modest project and then hugely edging it up.

Another variety of underestimation is shown in the case of the Cumberland River development where the proposals were justified to the Congress on a valuation of the power which was subsequently sold for less than one-half that amount. Whether these are devices to persuade and commit the Congress or just incompetence, I do not know.

In any event such methods would break any business except government.

Unkept Promises as to Returns

The original New Deal promises assured Congress that these enterprises would pay 3 percent interest and pay back, that is, amortize the Federal investment over fifty years. This formula has either been abandoned, sadly ignored, or juggled.

First. The cost of a multiple-purpose water project must be divided among its several functions, such as navigation, flood control, irrigation, community water supply, and hydro-electric power. The interest and amortization of the Federal electric power investment can be decreased by assigning more capital cost to flood control and navigation. The reports of the Federal Comptroller General have protested that such favors have been done.

Some of the Federal enterprises do not include interest on their capital cost during construction, which, again, decreases the payment of interest and amortization on the Federal taxpayers' capital invested. All of which thereby decreases the claimed costs.

But these practices again subsidize the rates to a minority of consumers at the expense of the nation-wide taxpayers.

Second. Taking these enterprises as a whole, comparatively little interest and amortization have been paid to the Federal Treasury on the Government investment over all the past years. There is a huge accumulation of this deficiency which should be repaid. Some of these Federal enterprises do not take into account interest and amortization in their costs and thus lower the rates they make their consumers [pay–ed.]. Some of them do not even enter such a charge in their books.

Some of them do not include the pensions to their employees which, under Civil Service, are partly loaded on the taxpayer.

Further, a question could also be raised as to the method providing for the costs of depreciation and provision for obsolescence.

Third. Our Federal Reorganization Commission employed Haskins and Sells, one of the leading accounting firms in the United States, to investigate the finances and accounting practices of a large part of these Federal electric power activities. They applied the yardstick of 3 percent interest and amortization in fifty years to the acknowledged Federal investment in power in many of these Federal enterprises. They found many of them would never be able to make the return which was at one time promised to the Congress.

Still Further Burdens and Losses to the Nation-wide Taxpayers

And there are more burdens thrust on the taxpayer from this program of socialized power. He has to furnish by taxes the huge capital being invested. Also, as these Federal enterprises have not paid the promised interest, the taxpayer has had to pay it on government bonds. And the nation-wide taxpayer will have to stand all the deficits from mistakes and underestimates.

Under these present methods and practices, this burden and losses to the nation-wide taxpayer is not small change. It will run into billions.

And from another angle, if the price of power from the Federal enterprises were placed at a level which would include tax equivalents and all the other nonincluded costs, their rates generally would be equal to, and in some cases higher than, the rates of neighboring private utilities.

The Operating Balance Sheet

We can appraise what all this means in actual figures. I have received from the Federal Budget Bureau a statement of the gross receipts and gross operating expenses of these Federal enterprises taken as a whole for the fiscal year 1952, and the estimates for the year ending June 30 of this year. This statement shows an apparent surplus over operating expenses of about $100,000,000 for each of these years. Here, however, come in several great "buts."

If the omitted interest, the omitted amortization and the refunding the accumulated deficiency of these items, and other costs I have mentioned were included, this so-called "surplus" would turn into a deficit.

And I do not include in this deficit any equivalent for taxes—another large sum.

Also, I am advised that the operating receipts for 1952 could have been $75,000,000 greater had this power been sold at the market price.

Accounting

Our Reorganization Commission accountants condemned many of the Federal power financial and accounting methods and estimates. They found the true construction and operating cost to be obscured. They proposed many reforms which have not been adopted. The Comptroller General of the United States, as late as sixty-six days ago, commented on accounting deficiencies.

The Federal power enterprises do not even keep their accounts or present their statements in the intelligible manner which the Government requires of private enterprise. They do, however, emit a host of propaganda figures in press releases.

I recommend to anyone interested in bureaucratic action to see whether he can add up the sums, past and present, involved in Federal electric enterprises from among the 4,000,000 words and sums in the Federal budget.

Other Effects on Citizens

All this affects the citizen in many ways aside from the injustice of huge losses and tax burdens which result in subsidized power to favored groups and communities.

There is a constitutional question involved in these enterprises which must concern the citizen. No one can even attempt to defend many of these activities except on the Welfare Clause in the Constitution. Under that interpretation, the Federal government could take over about everything except elections and the churches.

And there is a further important question to the citizen. There is here being erected a sort of Federal regional control in which State governments have some nominal representation but without authority. The people in these regions may get power at the expense of the nation-wide taxpayer, but they are surrendering the control of their resources and energies to a Federal bureaucracy.

Remedy

However, I do not believe in criticism without remedies.

Over twenty years ago I recommended to Congress the transformation of an ex-officio Commission into a full Federal Power Commission with regulations which had teeth in them. The purpose was to control the oppressive empires then growing in the private electric utilities. The transformation was made but without the teeth. My successors set up the Securities [and–ed.] Exchange Commission to do this de-empiring. Now, however, it is the Federal Government itself that urgently needs the same de-empiring.

The first steps should be:

1. The Congress should cease to make appropriations for more steam plants or hydroelectric plants solely for power. If they are justified, private enterprise will build them and pay taxes on them.
2. The Congress should follow the precedent of the Colorado project and make no more appropriations for new multiple-purpose projects unless the electric power is first leased on terms, the standards of which I will describe in a moment.
3. The Congress should, jointly with the President, set up a temporary Commission on reorganization of this whole Federal venture with resources to employ technical assistance.

(a) This Commission should investigate and recommend proper methods of accounting and a revision of the division of Federal investment in these projects between electric power and other purposes, and recommend proper practices for the future.

(b) The Commission should report on the actual cost of, and the prospective returns from, each of these major enterprises.

(c) The Commission should formulate the methods and standard terms for leasing generating plants, transmission lines, and the electric energy to private enterprise or to municipalities or to the States or to regional authorities that may be set and managed by the States. These standard terms should provide for payment of interest and amortization of the Federal investment, the refunding of arrears in these items, and also some contribution in lieu of taxes. The latter would not need apply in some cases of private enterprises as they pay their own taxes.

(d) The Commission should develop methods by which non-Federal agencies can share cooperatively in the cost of future capital outlays on the electrical part of multiple-purpose dams.

Working Out These Policies

Some of these projects could be disposed of so as to return these standard terms to the Federal Government. Others, due to excessive cost, may need concessions, and the Federal Government would need [to–*ed.*] cut its losses.

Others of them, pending disposal, will need [to–*ed.*] continue to be operated by the Federal Government. In these cases the Commission should recommend what rates they should charge their customers so as to make the standard returns. They should recommend methods to compel such payments to the Federal Treasury instead of their diversion to other purposes. Such action would test the value of these enterprises and, in some cases, indicate what losses may need [to–*ed.*] be cut.

The objective of the whole proceeding should be to get the Federal Government out of the business of generating and distributing power as soon as possible.

In any event, the consumer at all times can be protected by regulation of rates by the State or Federal authorities.

The Results

It is my belief that, if these proposals be carried out, the ultimate result would be a substantial return to the Treasury without consequential operating expense or bureaucracy.

Moreover, the agencies to whom these projects were leased would undertake or co-operate in their own expansions.

It is my belief that if these things be done, the Federal Government ultimately could reduce its annual investment in power enterprises by at least $600,000,000 per annum.

This program would begin the end of Federal bureaucratic regional control of the States and their people.

Above all, we would rescue free men from this variety of creeping socialism. The American people have fought off socialized medicine, but here is a hole in the dike of free men that is bringing a flood.

There are those who shy away from the use of the term "socialism," or the name of Karl Marx, in connection with what is going on in the power field. But, excepting those who *desire* socialization, they are blind to the facts. Socialism has become the world's nightmare. It is not the American dream.

The intellectuals who advocate these Federal activities carry a banner on which they falsely inscribe the world "liberalism." There is one thing I can say beyond any measure of doubt. It is a false liberalism that expresses itself by Federal operation of business in competition with the citizen. It is the road not to more liberty but to less liberty. True liberalism is found not in striving to spread bureaucracy, but in striving to set bounds to it. True liberalism seeks all legitimate freedom, in the confident belief that without freedom, all other blessings are vain. Liberalism is a force truly of the spirit coming from a realization that economic freedom cannot be sacrificed if political freedom is to be preserved.

The unanimous creation by the Congress in 1953 of the Second Commission on Organization of the Executive Branch of the Government under my Chairmanship plunged me into the very middle of the whole collectivist trends of our Government. I deal at length with these matters in another section of these memoirs under the title "The Crusade for Reorganization of the Government."[5] I may mention here that the powers of this Second Commission were far greater than those of the First Commission and included a directive to report to the Congress on the Federal business activities, competition with private enterprise and to report on policies which included a still further area of collectivist activities.

---

5. [*Editor's note*: No manuscript bearing this precise title has been found. But see Hoover's manuscript "Crusade against Waste in the Federal Government: 1921 to 1955," excerpts of which are included in Appendix I of this volume.]

Editor's Postscript to Part III

At this point the portion of Hoover's memoirs titled "The Crusade against Collectivism in American Life" came to an end. On December 20, 1955, the final page proofs of the latest version of this segment were returned to his Waldorf-Astoria suite by the printer. The section now comprised 282 printed pages; they have been reproduced here as Part III of *The Crusade Years*.

So far as is known, Hoover never again revised "The Crusade against Collectivism in American Life." Instead, even as the printer was completing the newest set of page proofs of it, the elderly former president was briskly drafting or planning to draft additional components of his memoirs depicting other political battles and "crusades."

Several of these drafts, which complement Parts I–III of this volume, have been located and are included in Appendix I. If Hoover's *Crusade Years* project was in a sense his "unfinished symphony," four of its late "movements" now appear in the pages that follow.

Other Crusades

Republican presidential
nominee, Governor Alf M.
Landon (left), with Herbert
Hoover in Topeka, Kansas,
during the campaign of 1936.

endell Willkie, Republican
presidential candidate in
940, with Herbert Hoover
in Colorado Springs,
Colorado, August 12, 1940.

Herbert Hoover and Governor
Thomas E. Dewey act as honorary
pallbearers at the funeral of Charles D.
Hilles, New York City, August 30, 1949.

Above: Speaker of the Hou⸱ Joseph Martin, Jr., Senato⸱ Robert A. Taft, and Herbe⸱ Hoover confer at the U.S. Capitol, June 24, 1953.

Left: The crusader at work Herbert Hoover addresses ⸱ Republican National Conven⸱ Chicago, June 27, 1944.

Crusading against collectivism: Herbert Hoover addresses
the Republican National Convention, July 8, 1952.

Herbert Hoover confers with President Harry Truman on the day Hoover
became chairman of the Commission on Organization of the Executive Branch
of the Government (the first Hoover Commission), September 29, 1947.

As part of his worldwide famine survey mission for President Truman, Herbert Hoover visits the devastated "Old City" of Warsaw, Poland, April 2, 1946, as Polish women collect firewood in the rubble.

Herbert Hoover visits a throng of Polish war orphans in Warsaw, April 2, 1946, during his survey of food conditions abroad.

President Harry Truman (center), meets with the first Hoover Commission, ca. 1948 (Herbert Hoover at Truman's right, Joseph Kennedy at Truman's left).

Herbert Hoover confers with resident Dwight Eisenhower at : White House, July 21, 1953, and es to chair a second Commission Organization of the Executive Branch of the Government.

President Dwight Eisenhower and Herbert Hoover broil steaks after a day vacationing together at the Byers Peak Ranch in Fraser, Colorado, September 1, 1954.

X 1.

The Library on War Peace and Revolution at Stanford University

I barely mentioned this institution in my memoirs published in 1951-52. But in view of its present importance I warrants a further account of its origins and growth.

In 1915 on one of my journeys across the North Sea — I read some remarks by Andrew D. White the great Historian of the French Revolution on the difficulty of reconstructing the life of the ordinary people in France during that period because of the large disappearance of contemporaneous documents and ...

Excerpt from the first draft of Hoover's mini-memoir in 1955 about the Hoover Institution. (The typed version is printed in Appendix I.) Hoover wrote his first drafts entirely by hand.

left three of these such as
newspapers, leaflets, and speeches
and the like, As occupied towns they
were constantly
traveling to and from the belligerent
countries on both sides that
I had an unequal opportunity to
collect such materials for future
historians. I therefore engaged
book dealers and some college
authorities to collect such material
in addition to what I and my
staff on the Belgian Commission
could secure. Established these
various collection agencies in
Germany France Britain Holland
Belgium Norway Sweden Switzerland
Spain and Britain undertaking to
after the war was over
day for this ... national key

Herbert Hoover at his office in the tower of the Hoover Institution, 1957.

EDITORIAL NOTE ON APPENDIX I

In 1955 Hoover completed his latest revisions of his *Crusade Years* memoirs, including the three parts that appear in the preceding pages of this volume. But, characteristically, he did not stop there. At some point that year, he decided to augment his memoirs by writing still more segments covering still more "crusades."

By mid-December 1955 Hoover had produced at least four additional autobiographical essays. Three were of some length: "Crusade against Waste in the Federal Government," "The Crusade for American Children," and "My Crusade against Collectivism." They were quickly set in page proofs by his printer. During the busy autumn of 1955, Hoover also composed a fresh account of the origins and significance of the Hoover Institution and made known his intent to prepare two more sections of his memoirs: one on his "Crusade for Scientific Research" and the other to be titled "The Crusade against Famine."[1]

It is uncertain how Hoover planned to integrate this material into his ever-evolving memoirs. Some of the newly completed manuscripts covered subjects he had already addressed in Parts II and III of the present volume. Why, one wonders, did he feel the need to write about these topics again? In any event, after writing the four new components mentioned above in late 1955, he appears to have abandoned further work on them in favor of two other writing projects that now took precedence in his mind. The first was his foreign policy Magnum Opus eventually known as *Freedom Betrayed*. The second

---

1. [*Editor's note*: Loretta L. Camp to Rita Campbell, August 8, 1964, Hoover Institution Records, Box 2800, Hoover Institution Archives, Stanford University. No Hoover manuscript bearing the title "Crusade for Scientific Research" has been found, although Camp (one of Hoover's secretaries) recalled that such a manuscript had been composed and set in page proofs. For "The Crusade against Famine," see below, Appendix I, Document 3, chapter 1, note 1.]

was a full-scale history of his "crusade against famine." Originally intended to be a one-volume work, it grew into a four-volume set titled *An American Epic*, which he published between 1959 and 1964.

Because the four previously unknown mini-memoirs that Hoover wrote in late 1955 are both biographically significant and closely connected to Hoover's *Crusade Years* manuscript, it seems appropriate to include them here. In a few (duly noted) places, I have condensed or omitted lengthy quoted passages that are easily accessible elsewhere.

"Crusade against Waste in the Federal Government 1921 to 1955"

November 1955

Hoover appears to have written the first draft of this essay in the late summer or early autumn of 1955. The text reproduced here is the page-proof version returned to him by the printer in November 1955. It was forty-nine pages long. It is found in the Herbert Hoover Papers, Box 94, Hoover Institution Archives, Stanford University.

Introduction

The peace-time reorganization of the Executive Branch of the Government to secure greater efficiency and economy has been a matter of concern ever since the Civil War. Every war left an aftermath of increased debt, increased expenditures and increased bureaucracy. The periods of war aftermath have been the scene of most of the attempts at improvement.

The following tables in round numbers indicate what happened in these aftermaths:

NUMBER CIVIL EMPLOYEES

	1 Year before War	Maximum in War	Two Years after War	Increment Civil Employees from the War	Peace Expenditures
Civil War	49,200	480,000	70,000	21,000	
World War I	480,000	917,000	690,000	210,000	
World War II	851,000	3,770,000	2,180,000	1,329,000	
Korea and Cold War	2,100,000	2,600,000	2,253,000	153,000	

MAXIMUM ARMED FORCES
(Federal Government)

Civil War	28,000	796,000	50,000	22,000	
World War I	180,000	4,175,000	343,000	163,000	
World War II	454,000	12,121,000	2,100,000	1,646,000	
Korea and Cold War	1,423,000	3,660,000	3,000,000	1,577,000	

EXPENDITURES
(Federal Government)

	1 Year before War	Maximum in War	Two Years after War	Increment from the War
Civil War	63,000,000	1,300,000,000	357,500,000	294,500,000
World War I	734,000,000	18,500,000,000	5,100,000,000	4,366,000,000
World War II	9,000,000,000	100,400,000,000	39,300,000,000	30,300,000,000
Korea and Cold War	40,200,000,000	74,600,000,000	63,000,000,000	23,000,000,000

The necessarily arbitrary choice of one year before the wars and 2 years after to measure increments does not always reflect the exact increments. The Civil War figures on civilian employees are approximations from indirect data. The Cold War at this writing is still in progress.

The efforts to create better organization began with the Grant Administration following the Civil War when examinations as to merit to enter the Civil Service were first initiated. During the years prior to the First World War there was some interest in widespread reorganization but nothing serious was done, no doubt because the Federal expenditures were no great burden on the taxpayers.

My connection with the subject grew out of the pressures arising in aftermaths of the First World War, the Second World War and the Korean and Cold Wars, and continues to the date of the writing of this section of my memoirs.

CHAPTER 1

The inefficient and wasteful organization of the Executive Branch of the Federal Government had been one of my preoccupations ever since I came to Washington in 1917 as Food Administrator, new in government, but experienced in administration.

In a public address in April 1920, I said:

A prime matter of government organization is in the establishment of a national budget. To minds charged with the primary necessity of advance planning, co-ordination, provision of synchronizing parts in organization, the whole notion of our hit-or-miss system is repugnant. A budget system is not the remedy for all administrative ills. It does provide a basis of organization that at least does not paralyze administrative efficiency as our system does today. Through it, the co-ordination of expenditure in government departments, the prevention of waste and overlapping in government bureaus, the exposure of the pork barrel, and the balancing of the relative importance of different national activities in the allocation of our national income can all be greatly improved. The budget system in some form is so universal in civilized governments and in competently conducted business enterprise, (it has been adopted in thirty of our States) that its absence in our Federal Government is most extraordinary. . . .[1]

In a public address in October 1920, I said:

Our federal machinery is the result of a hundred years of patchwork and has lagged lamentably behind the skill in organization and administration of our

---

1. [*Editor's note*: The "public address" to which Hoover refers has not been located. But a virtually identical passage appears in Herbert Hoover, "Economic, Social and Industrial Problems Confronting the Nation," *Trust Companies* (April 1920): 350, copy in Public Statements File, Herbert Hoover Papers, Herbert Hoover Presidential Library, West Branch, Iowa].

people. The strain of war gave daily vivid exhibitions of its weakness, its inability to cope with great emergency, and displayed the tremendous wastes that flowed from faulty organization. Some of its weaknesses have been pointed out consistently for many years. . . .

Necessary as the budget is, it is not the solution of all ills. It is, in fact, merely a limelight upon some of them.

. . . Reorganization of deeper character than setting up a budget also must be effected if we are to have capable government. For instance, we have six different departments actively engaged in engineering and construction work, spending collectively on a peace basis from $200,000,000 to $300,000,000 annually. These different departments do not cooperate, they compete for power, for material, for labor and for skill. There is profound waste by overlap. There is an infinite opportunity for log rolling, pork barrel and waste through the lack of cohesion of policies. There is no policy of public works as a whole. The cheese paring that normally goes on now in the honest effort of Congressional committees to control departmental expenditure is but a tithe of that which could be effected if there were some concentration of administration so demonstrated as necessary in the success of private business.[2]

Reorganization became a definite job when I became secretary of commerce in 1921.

As a result of the First World War, the Executive Branch of the Government settled down after demobilization with an increase from pre-war of about 200,000 civil employees and an increase in expenditures of about $4 billions per annum, with a national debt increased from pre-war by from about $1,200,000,000 to about $23,000,000,000.

Soon after becoming secretary of commerce I took part in a Cabinet Committee on better organization. As a result of this Committee's work President Harding, on April 22, 1921, recommended the creation of the Federal Budget and the Congress enacted the Budget and Accounting Act on June 10, 1921, which in addition to the establishment of the national budget also created the office and authority of the Controller General to pass upon the legality of Federal expenditures.

As recommended by the Cabinet Committee President Harding, in his message of April 22, also recommended that the Congress establish a Joint Committee to study government reorganization generally. On May 5, 1921

---

2. [*Editor's note*: Hoover address before the Columbia Club of Indianapolis, October 9, 1920, Public Statements File, Hoover Papers, Herbert Hoover Presidential Library.]

the Congress established this committee and authorized the President to appoint a personal representative upon the Committee. Walter F. Brown was designated by the President and was elected chairman. Mr. Brown cooperated with the Cabinet Committee of which I was a member. The Joint Congressional Committee, having made little progress, the Cabinet Committee, with Brown's assistance, made certain recommendations which President Harding submitted to the Congress on February 13, 1923, stating that they had the approval of the Cabinet.

These members of the Cabinet, including myself, appeared at the extensive hearings by the Committee. My testimony covers about 30 pages in the printed Committee record. No action was taken by the Congress on the recommendations of the members of the Cabinet Committee or the Joint Committee itself. Nothing came of it.

About a year later (May, 1925), with the approval of my Cabinet Colleagues, I concluded to review the whole problem in a public address nationally broadcast. My purpose was to state the need, the philosophy, the framework and the origins of opposition to accomplishment. I have many horrid examples. The address proved to be about 19 years ahead of the times. But as I believe this was the first complete statement of the problem, I give more than usual quotations from it.[3]

Reduction of Waste in Government by Reorganization of Executive Departments

From time to time I have had a good deal of cooperation from business in the elimination of waste by better organization in our economic system. . . . The business man often retorts that government might cooperate to eliminate some of the wastes it imposes upon him.[4] . . . So tonight it seems fair that I should[5] . . . talk about our governmental organization and the great wastes that result.

. . . The government is the greatest business undertaking yet submitted to the mind of man. Bad coordination among industries finally comes home to

---

3. [*Editor's note*: In the long passage that follows, Hoover quotes from an address he delivered before the Chamber of Commerce of the United States on May 21, 1925. The address was titled "Reduction of Waste in Government by Reorganization of Executive Departments." For the complete text, see Public Statements File, Hoover Papers, Herbert Hoover Presidential Library.]

4. [*Editor's note*: In the original address from which he was quoting, Hoover had written: "Whatever the businessman may feel, he does not often retort that government might cooperate to eliminate some of the wastes it imposes upon him."]

5. [*Editor's note*: Here Hoover omitted the words "take the part of a business man and."]

the people as a whole in the form of increased prices. And bad organization in government comes home in many more directions than even the taxes it wastes.

And this is another of these laborious subjects in which stimulating oratory is about as serviceable as a sermon on high voltage and it contains about the same proportion of humor and good cheer as a reminder that we have to work when the trout are rising.

Over many years our people have been striving to better the federal administration. We have succeeded in two major steps; we still have a third equally important and perhaps more difficult one to accomplish. The first step was the establishment of government employment based upon merit; the second was the establishment of adequate control of appropriations through the Budget System. There still remains the third and even more important step to relieve the taxpayer of a greater but more obscure waste — that resulting from faulty organization of administrative functions. And the first two steps will never reach the full realization without the third.

. . . For lack of legislative authority we have not been able to reach into . . . the waste which arises from the swamp of bad organization.

As is said in the maiden speech of every constitutional orator, our government is divided into the legislative, judicial and executive branches. . . . And in 150 years of the highest development of skill in organization of big industry and commerce, we have right down to today proved the soundness of this principle, namely, many minds for legislative, judicial and advisory decisions, but a single mind for executive authority. Yet in government we have been busy for the last century violating these primary principles of good organization.

. . . When Hamilton laid out the scheme of executive departments he placed the different functions of administration as nearly as might be into groups of the same general major purpose under single headed responsibility. But ever since his time we have been busy dividing responsibility by scattering services directed to substantially the same major purpose over many different executive departments and bureaus. . . .Whenever a new activity has been authorized or a new bureau created it has been thrown wherever it happened to be most convenient at the moment or wherever its sponsors thought it would have the most friendly treatment, without any thought of a sound basis of organization, and we have shunted along misfit after misfit from one generation to another.

On the executive side of the federal government we have grown to have more than 200 different bureaus, boards and commissions with a total of

550,000 employees. For the most part they have been thrown hodge podge into ten different executive departments, under Cabinet officers. But there are more than 40 independent establishments either directly under the President.[6] ...

As these 200 bureaus and agencies are now grouped and organized there are two primary streams of confusion and waste. There is a confusion of basic principles; there is a grouping of federal bureaus which divides responsibility. There consequently arises a lack of definite national policies, and direct wastes arise from overlap and conflict. Indirectly large costs are imposed upon citizens by this scattering of functions. ... There are too many floating islands in this dismal swamp. They are technically anchored to the President, but really responsible to nobody. With all this division of authority there continues and multiplies a self-propelled urge for expansion of federal activities in every direction.

Confusion of Basic Principles

It is not my purpose to deal primarily with the legislative and judicial arms of the government. I am directing my remarks to the executive side only. With the growing complexity of government problems it has been necessary for Congress to delegate to the executive side many secondary legislative functions in the making of regulations, and many secondary judicial functions in the enforcement of them. That is the so-called administrative law. And there has been the crudest mixing of these semi-legislative and semi-judicial functions with purely executive functions. These semi-judicial and semi-legislative duties are frequently entrusted to single officers, while purely administrative functions are often carried on by boards. All of this is exactly the reverse of the basic principles of sound administration. Boards and Commissions are soundly adapted to the deliberate processes necessary to semi-judicial and semi-legislative and advisory functions, but they are absolutely hopeless where decisive administrative action is necessary. And likewise most of such functions should not be entrusted to a single mind. There is not a single successful business organization in the country that confuses such functions the way we do in government.

The Shipping Board—to cite a glaring case—was originally created as a body to regulate rates and abolish discrimination in ocean-going traffic. These are semi-judicial functions that quite properly were entrusted to a

---

6. [*Editor's note*: Here Hoover omitted the words "or directly under Congress."]

board. Political jealousies and sectional jealousies, however, resulted in a bipartisan body selected from different parts of the country although it was to perform an expert judicial function. Then this structure was suddenly loaded with the most difficult of administrative jobs—the actual construction and operation of the greatest single merchant fleet in history. The losses and waste which have resulted from this blunder of assigning executive and administrative functions to the joint and equal minds of a wrongly constructed semi-judicial body have amounted to . . . hundreds of millions out of the three billion we have lost on shipping, but beyond this the impossibility of a continuous merchant marine policy has worked great losses upon our privately owned merchant marine. Nor can we properly blame the individual member of the Shipping Board. Not even two geniuses of equal authority could administer a competitive business—let alone seven. There are other breeds of this same sort of conclusion between individual and joint responsibility. . . .

Administrative Officials with Judicial and Legislative Authority

This same chaos of function is carried into other directions where administrative or executive officials are given these semi-judicial and semi-legislative authorities. The Secretary of Agriculture has been loaded with powers of a semi-legislative and judicial character in the administration of the stockyards and commodity exchanges. The Secretary of Commerce has semi-legislative and semi-judicial powers over navigation and some branches of communications, and the Secretary of Labor has certainly a judicial authority over matters of immigration. Nor do these confusing functions solely reside in Cabinet officers; many bureau heads have such powers. The responsibilities in decisions under these powers are at least as important as those of Federal Courts, with this important difference, however, that while there is theoretical appeal to the courts in most cases, yet practically most decisions are final. Worst of all there are none of the safeguards as to the right of individuals in the determination of questions submitted such as are in our courts. Duties of this semi-legislative and semi-judicial character should not be imposed upon administrative officials. In those matters where they involve semi-legislative action they should not even be conferred upon a judge, much less upon executive officials. No individual should be at the same time legislator, policeman, prosecutor, judge and jury. Yet in many instances he is. We arrive at judgments the best we can in old Kadi fashion and the culprit usually knuckles down quietly because he feels we might look for him again if he protested.

The dangers of oppression in these matters are not merely a theory—they are a fact. All these confusions of functions were perhaps of less importance in days gone by when our population was smaller and higher officials were less pressed with administrative work.

Every single department, bureau and board in the entire government should be placed upon the operating table and a cleancut separation established between semi-judicial and semi-legislative functions on the one hand, and of administration on the other. The former rightly belongs to boards or commissions, the latter to individuals. For instance, the semi-judicial and semi-legislative functions arising from the navigation laws should be transferred to a properly constituted Shipping Board, leaving matters of administration of such decisions to the Department of Commerce.

Division of Authority in Administrative Agencies

Our other greatest weakness in organization is the division of authority over services directed to the same major purpose by scattering them through unrelated groups. Needless to say some of the ten executive departments are fairly homogeneously devoted to a particular major purpose—notably the Department of Justice, the Navy Department, the State Department . . . . and the Post Office Department. But all the others, and even some of these contain functions that should be transferred elsewhere. . . .

To illustrate my point, I have made a partial collection of misfits and in so doing I have taken no account of either incidental functions or semi-legislative or semi-judicial agencies, except so far as they have administrative functions.

	Number of Bureaus or Agencies	Number of Departments or Independent Agencies in Which They Are Located
Public Works Construction	14	9
Conservation of National Resources	8	5
Direct Aids to Industry	5	2
Direct Aids to Merchant Marine	14	6
Direct Aids to Education	6	3
Direct Aids to Veterans	4	4
Government of Territories and Dependencies	4	3
Public Health	4	2
Purchase of $250,000,000 of supplies annually		In every bureau of the Government

It is not necessary that each of these groups should become a whole executive department, each under a Cabinet officer; but it is entirely feasible to place each one of them under the supervision of a special assistant secretary, and if we were truly intelligent we would class him as an expert and selection on other than political grounds.[7] It is entirely secondary what Department these groups are in. The big thing is to bring these kindred agencies together under one leadership so that their overlapping edges can be clipped and their fights stopped. No one familiar with the internal workings of the departments will deny the direct waste which comes from overlap and friction as the result of the present lack of coordination of activities.

Coordination is feasible when some one person is responsible; with divided authority among the different branches of government it is a hypothesis that evaporated soon after the perennial conferences of Cabinet officers on the subject. It all costs somebody money. One of the favorite indoor sports of our newspaper correspondents is to ventilate these conflicts.

The divided responsibility with absence of centralized authority prevents the constructive and consistent development of broad national policies in these special branches of governmental activity, for there is by necessity of this division constant conflict of view within the government itself. We have a bundle of divergent ideas without focus; lumber piled together does not make a house. The treatment of our national resources furnishes a good instance. If anything is certain, it is that the government should have a continuous, definite, and consistent policy directed to intelligent conservation and use of national resources. But it can have no such policy so long as responsibility is split up among half a dozen different departments. The recent occurrences in oil leases are a fair example of what may happen by the lack of singlehanded responsibility in such matters. No policy of real guardianship of our reserve resources will exist until we put all conservation business in the hands of an Under Secretary for Conservation, with the spotlight of public opinion continuously upon him.

The same is true of our deplorable lack of a definite and organized merchant marine policy. . . .

In our public works there has been no concept of the nation's priority needs or its needs as a whole, and enormous sums have been sunk upon many fruitless works that got nowhere. It has been a question of satisfying the demands of a given community or a particular section with little thought

---

7. [*Editor's note*: In the quoted text, Hoover had written: "as an expert and outside selection on political grounds."]

to concerted development for the good of the nation as a whole. We have the same problems in public buildings.

The scattering of our government purchasing agencies and the method of purchasing of government supplies result in such obvious losses as to require little discussion. The government agencies compete with each other for commodities of the same kind.

... A bureau or function may be conducted economically enough so far as personnel and pencils are concerned, and without overlap or friction with its neighbors, and yet owing to the unnecessary complexity of the laws or regulations which it administers and the demands it makes upon the citizen, it imposes much needless expense upon the public. I need go no further than the income tax maze. Whole new professions of tax lawyers, tax experts, tax accountants, have grown up, which cost the citizen far more than it costs the government to collect the taxes. [...–ed.]

Under existing hodge podge arrangement, the citizen is driven from pillar to post among the bureaus, seeking information he wants, settling the demands upon him or determining the regulations by which he is required to conduct his business. I have daily evidence in the Department of Commerce of all these forces. Assistance to and regulation of navigation is not by any means one of the principal functions of our government, but it must be a sore trial to the hardy mariner. The delay of ships, the time lost to masters and officers as they are shuttled from one office to another, or as one official after another operates on him from the 14 agencies in six different departments which have to do with shipping must sorely try his temper. Perhaps hardships at sea make him immune to trouble ashore. But it is a great burden on the Merchant Marine.

The Problem of Questionnaires

Again there are a great many bureaus at Washington which are given to important economic research. The boundary lines which separate these bureaus, one from another, are necessarily indeterminate. The business man who is accustomed to receive a bombardment of questionnaires from these establishments has good reason to dread the extension of federal encroachment upon business. He would have much less cause for complaining if these government activities were grouped in such fashion that these matters fell under the control of fewer superior officials. If investigation of the same general character has been concentrated, one of the recent widespread questionnaires would never have been sent out because so far as the information desired could ever be effectively collected it was already in the hands of the government. In this case if replies were complete enough to be of any value a low estimate of the cost to the citizen of making the returns would be fifty million dollars in bookkeeping alone. One firm stated that a reply would cost them $20,000, a country doctor complained it would cost him $100. This case illustrated another point. The questionnaire carried every earmark of peremptory demand, yet as a matter of fact no citizen was required by law to furnish the information asked for. Such activities are a definite form of oppression. They lend themselves to doubtful constitutional practices of search and inquiry.

The Independent Agencies

The forty governmental agencies which are now supposed to function directly under the President present another problem. . . . They are supposed to act under the direct supervision of the President. But it is preposterous to expect that with his multitude of higher obligations the President can give them anything like adequate supervision. As a matter of fact, these independent establishments conduct their activities with very little supervision or coordination. This group, the straight administrative, expend nearly half a billion a year—as much as the total of five of the departments under Cabinet officers. If for no other reason, this group should be placed directly in the departments in order that the President may exercise through his Cabinet the guidance and control of the administrative arm of the government. And the President already overworked in major policies must be relieved of detail.

The largest of the independent establishments is, of course, the Veterans Bureau. It is my belief that if this bureau had been directly responsible to a Cabinet officer there would have been, as in the case of other departmental bureaus, so many more safeguards in the management as to have prevented the frauds which have been exposed in the courts in the recent history of that bureau. . . .

Centralization of Government

No one doubts that for many years there has been a steady tide of federal encroachment into State authority—and beyond this a steady thrust of the arm of [the–ed.] federal government into our private business. Some of it has been necessary. But many of the functions now performed by the federal government would much better be left to the States. They are now so securely entrenched as to make decentralization a very difficult job.

But if we examined these encroachments we would find some considerable part of it takes root in the very lack of organization in our federal government. There is an impelling urge in most of these agencies which pushes them on to extend some fraction of their functions into all sorts of activities which the federal government should leave to other quarters.

Bureau Expansion

Every well-balanced citizen knows of something in this world that ought to be regulated that is not being regulated. Every agency of the federal government knows this also, but the difference is that every government agency is under constant pressure, or sometimes is anxious, to expand[8] its power further than was originally contemplated. When any particular theme is large in the national mind, every bureau that has any relationship to the problem or thinks it can get some appropriation for it immediately rushes in that direction. They compete with each other, tread on each other's toes, fight each other, but the net effect is expansion.[9] And it costs somebody money. The very scattering of government agencies gives impetus to this tendency. There would be far less of this if there were concentrated authority over related things.

The natural tendency of most healthy things is to grow. There are, of course, government bureaus which should grow, and as the country gets bigger and more complicated they must grow. But they should grow in directions approved by the whole people, and in line with fundamental national policies. . . .

The Proper Expansion of Federal Government

The border line around proper extension of federal authority is not theoretical. It permits of no philosophic solution. It must be handled problem by problem, with always an extreme leaning to local and private responsibility. The only justification of expansion of authority by the federal government is in the cases where constitutional inhibitions prevent State solution, or where

---

8. [*Editor's note*: In the quoted text: "to read and expand."]
9. [*Editor's note*: Here Hoover omitted the following sentence in the quoted text: "Much of it originates from worthy zeal."]

overpowering and destructive action would result to local communities but for federal control. We had better suffer from some slackness in State and local government, and even some abuse, than to undermine the foundation of self government. Among the real safeguards against continued expansion, concentration of administrative responsibility is just as important as vigilance on the part of the public and a willingness on the part of the States to assume their proper responsibilities.

There is one side of the federal government that is certainly not sufficiently expanded today—that is scientific and economic research and the promotion of public interest by voluntary cooperation with the community at large. This is never an encroachment upon the rights of individuals. It can truly be better organized but today the whole of our activities in these directions involve less than 3 per cent of our federal budget—and they bring returns to the taxpayer not in few per cent but in hundreds of per cent every year.

There is often complaint of the red tape and unnecessary motion in the government, but a certain amount of red tape is a necessary thing.[10] Unless the public is to be subjected to arbitrary action, unless the way is to be opened to manipulation and fraud, much of the government's administrative work must be completely surrounded with checks and balances. When a business man takes a wrong course he pays for it in dollars; when government officials take a wrong course the people pay for it in injustice and oppression and taxes. From this phase of the governmental situation there is no full escape so long as human beings are fallible. This very fact is the weightiest of all reasons for limiting the functions of the government to those things which only the government is in a position to do—those things which cannot be reached by private enterprise, or accomplished directly by our people.

In General

I wish to repeat that the faults of organization are not a matter of the taxpayers' small change. They form a total of waste, which, considering the indirect results, runs into high figures. [. . .–ed.]

We do not need to approach administrative reorganization with meticulous extremes of logic. [. . .–ed.] It would not be sound organization

---

10. [*Editor's note*: In the quoted text Hoover had written: ". . . but a certain amount of red tape in the public service is, as a matter fact, a necessary thing."]

to put all the stenographers, or all the engineers, or all the statisticians, or all the aeroplanes in the same department. The Tariff Commission, the Treasury Department, and the Department of Commerce, for example, all employ tariff experts, but to accomplish major purposes which are widely different.

What we need is three primary reforms; first, to group together all agencies having the same predominant major purpose under the same administrative supervision; second, to separate the semi-judicial and the semi-legislative and advisory functions from the administrative functions, placing the former under joint minds, the latter under single responsibility, and third, we should relieve the President of a vast amount of direct administrative labor.

Past Efforts of the Organization

Every President from Theodore Roosevelt to Calvin Coolidge has urged upon Congress a reorganization of the executive arm of the government, commissions have been appointed, Congressional committees have investigated, reports have been made, confirming all this. Cabinet officers express their feelings in spirited annual reports with a circulation of a few hundred copies. More than once a complete program of reorganization has been formulated, and put forward as a basis for general consideration.

But practically every single item in such a program has invariably met with opposition of some vested official, or it has disturbed some vested habit, and offended some organized minority. It has aroused the paid propagandists. All these vested officials, vested habits, organized propaganda groups, are in favor of every item of reorganization except that which affects the bureau or the activity in which they are specially interested. No proposed change is so unimportant that it is not bitterly opposed by someone. In the aggregate, these directors of vested habits surround Congress with a confusing fog of opposition. Meantime the inchoate voice of the public gets nowhere but to swear at "bureaucracy."

Nor will we ever attain reorganization until Congress will give actual authority to the president or some board, if you will, or a committee of its own members to do it. It is of no purpose to investigate again and report. We have had years of investigation and every investigation has resulted in some recommended action. [. . .–ed.][11] What is needed is the actual delegation of authority to act. Congress courageously removed the Civil Service from politics;

---

11. [*Editor's note*: Italics added by Hoover.]

it created the Budget, it established the Classification. The remaining great step is to authorize somebody to reorganize the administrative arm of the government.[12]

It is impossible for such an overworked body as Congress to study directly and act upon the overwhelming detail involved or to determine the right and wrong of a thousand clamors.[13]

I do not expect that the Federal Government will ever be a model of organization, but I have aspirations to see it improve.

---

12. It was not until 1947 that the Commission on Organization of the Executive Branch of the government seconded that such an authority be given to the President.

13. [*Editor's note*: Here Hoover again altered his quoted text. The original paragraph was: "Nor is Congress to be blamed for this situation, as it is impossible for such an overworked body to study directly and act upon the overwhelming detail involved. Nor is it possible for a great body like this to determine the right and wrong of a thousand clamors."]

CHAPTER 2

When I entered the White House in 1929 I had reorganization on my agenda. In my first message on the State of the Union on December 3, 1929 I said:

Departmental Reorganization

This subject has been under consideration for over 20 years. It was promised by both political parties in the recent campaign. It has been repeatedly examined by committees and commissions—congressional, executive, and voluntary. The conclusions of these investigations have been unanimous that reorganization is a necessity of sound administration; of economy; of more effective governmental policies and of relief to the citizen from unnecessary harassment in his relations with a multitude of scattered governmental agencies. But the presentation of any specific plan at once enlivens opposition from every official whose authority may be curtailed or who fears his position is imperiled by such a result; of bureaus and departments which wish to maintain their authority and activities; of citizens and their organizations who are selfishly interested, or who are inspired by fear that their favorite bureau may, in a new setting, be less subject to their influence or more subject to some other influence.

. . . The essential principles of reorganization are two in number. First, all administrative activities of the same major purpose should be placed in groups under single-headed responsibility; second, all executive and administrative functions should be separated from boards and commissions and placed under individual responsibility, while quasi legislative and quasi judicial and broadly advisory functions should be removed from individual authority and assigned to boards and commissions. Indeed, these are the fundamental principles upon which our government was founded, and they are the principles which have been adhered to in the whole development of our business structure, and they are the distillation of the common sense of generations.

For instance, the conservation of national resources is spread among eight agencies in five departments. They suffer from conflict and overlap. There is no proper development and adherence to broad national policies and no central point where the searchlight of public opinion may concentrate itself. These functions should be grouped under the direction of some such official as an assistant secretary of conservation. The particular department or cabinet officer under which such a group should be placed is of secondary importance to the need of concentration. The same may be said of educational services, of merchant marine aids, of public works, of public health, of veterans' services, and many others, the component parts of which are widely scattered in the various departments and independent agencies. It is desirable that we first have experience with these different groups in action before we create new departments. These may be necessary later on.

With this background of all previous experience I can see no hope for the development of a sound reorganization of the Government unless Congress be willing to delegate its authority over the problem (subject to defined principles) to the Executive, who should act upon approval of a joint committee of Congress or with the reservation of power of revision by Congress within some limited period adequate for its consideration.[1]

This was the first appearance of this formula. It was subsequently presented to Congress time and again by every President.[2]

I carried through certain consolidation of agencies but they were only a fragment of the whole problem as they reduced the number of employees by only about 10,000.

On February 17, 1932, I sent a special message to the Congress traversing the whole problem and again presenting the formula for authority in the President, subject to a veto by the Congress recommending Congress enact a law giving

... authority to redistribute executive groups in the 10 executive departments of the Government or in the independent establishments, as the President may determine, by Executive order, such Executive order to lie before the

---

1. [*Editor's note*: Italics added by Hoover.]
2. It was finally enacted into law on recommendation of the First Commission on Organization of the Executive Branch of which I was Chairman (1947–49), just 18 years later.

Congress for 60 days during sessions thereof before becoming effective at the end of such period unless the Congress shall request suspension of action.

I described the changes necessary and concluded:

In conclusion, I can not recommend too strongly that the Congress give the subject of effective organization of the executive branch of the Government its early and serious attention. It is an essential part of a sound reconstruction and economy program. A patchwork organization compels inefficiency, waste, and extravagance. Economy and efficiency can come only through modernization. A proper reorganization of our departments, commissions, and bureaus will result not only in much greater efficiency and public convenience, but in the saving of many millions of dollars now extracted annually from our overburdened taxpayers.

I repeatedly urged this idea upon the Congress. Finally the Democratic Congress pretended to respond but by passing a joker on June 30, 1932, just at the end of the session. The joker reversed the idea of Congressional veto into the form that the President could issue executive orders which were to become effective only if the Congress, by affirmative joint resolution of both Houses, confirmed them. That brought the situation back to exactly where it always had been. I publicly expressed disgust. Nevertheless, after my defeat for the Presidency, I returned to the charge in a message of December 9th, and did lay before the Congress executive orders for a complete detailed reorganization of the Executive Branch, grouping 58 different agencies which would step over later and eliminate about 15 of them. I had a hope that the election being over, Congress might want the incoming Democratic President to have a better organization. I stated:

These orders . . . undertake to group certain Executive agencies and activities in logical and orderly relation to each other as determined by their major functions and purposes, and to vest in the head of each department, subject to Executive approval, the authority and responsibility to develop and put into effect the ultimate details of better organization, elimination of overlap, duplication, and unnecessary expenditure. These results can only be worked out progressively by the Executive officers placed in charge of the different divisions. . . .

The Congress refused and I expressed regret in the Press.[3]

---

3. [*Editor's note*: For Hoover's statement of regret, see *Public Papers of the Presidents of the United States: Herbert Hoover, Containing the Public Messages, Speeches, and Statements of the President*,

The next attempt at reorganization was made by the creation of a Senate Committee (February, 1936), and a House Committee appointed a similar Committee. Following this President Franklin Roosevelt, in May, 1936, appointed a three man commission to make recommendations. He transmitted their report to Congress in January, 1937 and recommended its adoption.

This Commission made some useful suggestions, but some of them went far beyond sound government. They sought to shear from the Comptroller General his authority to disapprove of expenditures which might be contrary to law; to make the regulatory commissions subject to Presidential control. The bill including these items raised great opposition even in the wholly Democratic Congress as they would result in an increase of Presidential powers over both Congressional and Judicial branches. The bill was passed through the Senate only by great political pressures and was rejected by the House by a vote of 204 to 196, in April, 1939.[4]

I felt compelled to advise my Republican friends that no such extension of Presidential powers should be permitted. The bitterness of the debate was increased by the President's previous activities in packing the Supreme Court. An innocuous bill was passed later on which perfected no reorganization.

Nothing happened from 1933 to 1940 except reckless expansion of the Federal Administration, with a multitude of new Federal agencies. In this period the number of civil employees was increased from 566,986 at the end of my administration, of which 81% had entered through the Civil Service merit gate, to 1,002,820 of whom about 450,000 were politically appointed. Expenditures had increased from about $3,200,000,000 to about $9,000,000,000 annually (omitting recoverable loans in both cases) with an increase in the national debt of $26,000,000,000.

Over these years I, of course, made a multitude of speeches railing at the failure of any reorganization.

January 1, 1932 to March 4, 1933 (Washington, D.C.: U.S. Government Printing Office, 1977), pp. 921–23.]

4. James A. Farley, in his book "Jim Farley's Story" describes these activities in detail on pages 127–130. [Editor's note: Farley's book was published by the McGraw-Hill Book Company of New York in 1948.]

CHAPTER 3

The World War naturally suspended such activities in reorganization. With the end of the war there was again hope that something could be done to reduce wastes in the Government now greater than ever due to war expansion. The Government in 1947, after demobilization, had settled down to about 1400 different executive agencies, employing about 2,130,000 civilians, with most of the political appointees having been blanketed into the Civil Service by Executive Orders. The expenditures were at the rate of about $40 billions annually and the national debt about $370 billions, including the currency.

The Congress began to take interest in the seriousness of the situation and I was called in the spring of 1947 into conference by leading members of the House and Senate Committees for advice. They proposed to set up a bi-partisan Commission of 12 members, 2 Congressmen and 2 civilians to be appointed by the Speaker of the House, 2 Senators and 2 civilians by the President of the Senate and 4 members appointed by the President. They stated that with their multitude of other duties the Congressional Committee investigations and recommendations could only be superficial. I urged that the Commission be created and President Truman approved it.

I had gone west seeking recovery from certain infections which I had acquired during the winter trip I had made at the request of President Truman where I had instigated an attack on the survivals of the Morgenthau Plan for the Allied administration of West Germany. I was called on the telephone at the request of Congressional leaders, stating the stumbling block to the legislation was the selection of a chairman, and that if I would agree to accept it, then the project could be consummated. They stated that President Truman also wished me to undertake it. I hesitated to take the job because of disabilities, but after a night's consideration I stated that if they could not otherwise solve the problem, I would undertake it if: no report was called for until after the election of 1948 (so as to keep the subject out of campaign debate); and ample funds were provided.

The act establishing the "Commission on Organization of the Executive Branch" was enacted unanimously on July 7, 1947.

The Commissioners comprised:

Herbert Hoover, Chairman
James Forrestal, Secretary of Defense
Dean Acheson (Under Secretary and later Secretary of State)
Senator George Aiken
Senator John McClellan
Congressman Clarence J. Brown
Congressman Carter Monasco
Joseph P. Kennedy, Former Ambassador to Great Britain
George Mead (formerly in Defense Department)
Arthur S. Flemming, former Chairman of the Civil Service
    Commission
James H. Rowe, formerly on the White House Staff
James K. Pollock of the University of Michigan.

In August, no doubt as a result of debilities from the German job I had a severe attack of the shingles which paralyzed my right arm and shoulder. For nine months, I had to be accompanied by a nurse. However, in view of the reason for the Congressional set-up I continued.

I suggested that Mr. Truman call the first meeting of the Commission on September 28, 1947 at the White House. I proposed to the Commission a system of appointing what I called "Task Forces" of from 6 to 20 eminent men, experienced in government to undertake exhaustive investigation of most of the important Departments and agencies; each of the Task Forces to be furnished with expert staffs. I reserved certain investigation for direct undertaking by the Commission. I was authorized to appoint these "Task Forces" and from time to time they were set up to cover the following subjects:

Commission Reports	Teller of Task Force	Chairman of Task Force
1. General Management of the Executive Branch	Departmental Management	H. Struve Hensel and John D. Millett
2. Personnel Management	Federal Personnel	John A. Stevenson
3. Offices of General Services Supply Activities	The Federal Supply System Records Management	Russell Forbes E. J. Leahy
4. The Post Office	The Post Office	Frank Elmendorf
5. Foreign Affairs	Foreign Affairs	Harvey H. Bundy and James G. Rogers

Commission Reports	Teller of Task Force	Chairman of Task Force
6. Department of Agriculture	Agriculture Activities	H. P. Rusk
7. Budgeting and Accounting	Fiscal Budgeting and Accounting Activities	John W. Hanes
	Statistical Agencies	Frederick C. Mills and Clarence D. Long
8. The National Security Organization	National Security Organization	Ferdinand Eberstadt
9. Veterans Affairs	Veterans Administration	Franklin d'Olier
10. Department of Commerce	Regulatory Commissions	Robert R. Bowie and Owen D. Young
11. Treasury Department	(Fiscal Budgeting and Accounting Activities listed above in "Budgeting and Accounting")	John W. Hanes
12. Regulatory Commissions	(Regulatory Commissions listed with "Department of Commerce" above)	Robert R. Bowie
13. Department of Labor	Department of Labor	George W. Taylor
14. Interior Department	Natural Resources	Leslie A. Miller
	Public Works	Robert Moses
	(Agriculture Activities listed above with "Department of Agriculture")	H. P. Rusk
15. Social Security and Education Indian Affairs	Public Welfare	Lewis Meriam George Graham
16. Medical Activities	Federal Medical Services	Tracy S. Voorhees
17. Overseas Administration Federal-State Relations Federal Research		Dr. Rupert Emerson T. Jefferson Coolidge None
18. Business Enterprises	Revolving Funds and Business Enterprises	Colonel Andrew Stewart
19. Concluding Report	Lending Agencies Water Resources Projects	Paul Grady A. B. Roberts

I presided at each of the 70 Commission meetings except one, and participated in many of the "Task Force" meetings. I was greatly aided by Mr. Sidney Mitchell, who volunteered as Executive Director; by Lawrence Richey as my personal assistant; Frank Brassor,[1] whom I had borrowed from the Civil Service Commission, as Secretary of the Commission; by Robert L. L. McCormick and Herbert Miller as research directors for the Commission itself, and Charles B. Coates as Press Representative.

The "Task Forces" were uninhibited in their findings and recommendations, but we soon found that the Commission was also inhibited from dealing

---

1. [*Editor's note*: Francis P. Brassor.]

with policy questions and thus limited to recommendations for improvement of the executive structure.

It was the expressed desire of the members that political considerations be avoided, and in fact that Commission never divided on political grounds. And the Task Forces embraced members from both political parties.

As is the nature of varied experience and strong individualities, on the Commission we often differed in views but every recommendation was carried by a majority which represented members of both parties. The discussions and dissents were courteous and reasoned. The Commission did not always follow the Task Force recommendations as in itself it was a wealth of governmental experience.

Only on one subject were we unable to reach definitive findings and recommendations. Because of limitations on policy questions and ideological differences, we were unable to present effective conclusions as to Government business enterprises in competition with private enterprise.

The Commission began to crystallize its conclusions from the Task Force investigations and our own research and the public experience of our members in September 1948. We finished our last report on March 2, 1949. I personally wrote the first draft of 16 out of 19 reports containing over 280 recommendations. The net economies which could be made in the existing functions of Government were between $2 and $3 billion, with a reduction of about 300,000 Federal employees and better efficiency without them. The total expenditures of the Commission were $. . . . . . . [sic–ed.] and were saved many times over.

Knowing the inevitable bureaucratic and pressure groups' opposition attached to each agency would result in a burial of many recommendations, I was determined to keep them alive by education of the public on the government and to create an effective public opinion in demand for administrative and Congressional action.

Immediately after the Commission's legal end, I organized a Citizens' Committee of some thousands of members on a non-partisan basis to support the recommendations. It embraced most of the members of our task forces. At my request, former Vice Presidents Dawes and Garner and five former Cabinet officers from each of the Republican and Democratic sides joined in it. The Committee did a good job under President Robert L. Johnson of Temple University, as President, and Mr. Coates in charge of propaganda, with Robert McCormick representing the Committee in Washington.

Through the Citizens' Committee we organized a real crusade—not alone for more efficient organization of the Government but against the huge government spending in general.

I made public addresses or published magazine articles or gave press releases on the Commission's recommendations on April 18, 19, 20, 21 and 22, June 21, July 5, December 1 and December 12, in 1948. I appeared before open hearings of Congressional Committees on December 13, 1948, January 31, April 11, June 20, June 29, June 30 and December 12, 1949.

During the five years from 1947 to the end of 1952, our crusade influenced the adoption by the Administration and the Congress of about 71 per cent of the Commission recommendations. Among the outstanding accomplishments were the better unification of the Armed Services; a new agency called the General Services Administration; the reorganization of government accounting; improvement in budgeting; establishments of inventories; the consolidation of many agencies, and the establishment of improved White House and Departmental organization which removed a host of road blocks from internal reforms and economies. In the Armed Services a reduction of nearly 100,000 civil employees and savings of over a billion dollars a year appeared at once in a budget reduction, without decreasing the defense. The General Services Administration provided for consolidated and systemized buying of supplies for several Departments, the control of government buildings, rented space, and many other functions which serviced other agencies, with great savings.

But when all is said, a perfect organization is no better in the hands of mediocre men than a bad organization in the hands of capable men. We could [do–ed.] no more than smooth the path of competency.

Pressure groups attached to the bureaus sprang up objecting with vicious and untruthful propaganda, which stopped many needed reforms. We were the first of the many Commissions on reorganization over 40 years, which succeeded in a great measure of effective action.

I may give part of the text of one of my addresses to the Citizens' Committee as typical of our crusade. (December 12, 1949)

... You can have confidence that you are succeeding.

The last session of Congress adopted several important recommendations of the Commission and of the President. These measures have already secured large savings. In the Defense Department alone they will soon be at the rate of about $1 billion a year, and Secretary Johnson believes they will amount to fully $2 billions without impairing national defense. And other measures have been enacted into law. We are already clearing the tracks for competence in government.

[...–ed.] I want to tell you four reasons why this crusade of ours has wider implications than specific reforms.

First—Fiscal and Economic Survival

The first implication relates to our fiscal [and–*ed.*] economic survival.

During these last six months, the financial situation of our Government has become still more difficult. Federal expenditure of over $43 billions and a deficit of over $5 billions are announced for the present fiscal year. I believe it may be much greater for the next fiscal year. We may be turning two Frankensteins loose in the land. Their terrifying names are "Higher Taxes" and "Inflation." We are interested here in combating them.

When you listen to "billions" over the radio, you no doubt try to size them up in terms of your church contributions. I might remark that the decimal point leads a restless and uneasy life in the Federal Government. Those groups of three ciphers which are separated by commas are moving steadily to the left. [. . .–*ed.*]

Our economists seem to agree that taxation beyond 25 percent of our national income will bring disaster. Possibly your life has been brightened by some economists who dismiss the Federal expenditures as amounting to only 20 percent of the national income, anyway. On that subject, if you add up the actual and prospective annual expenditures of the Federal Government and the local governments, and if you truly compute the national income, you will find this warning red light no longer shines with an intensity of only 20 percent but with considerably over 30 percent. This means far more than 30 percent of the national income. It is a combustion of your savings and your possible standards of living.

Some one remarked that about the time we think we can make ends meet, somebody moves the ends. Despite this, you should not be discouraged in the work we have undertaken. Whatever we can accomplish helps confine the two Frankensteins. And we can ask our people to think it over.

Second—Education in Good Government

Second, another of the wider implications of this crusade is its by-product in public understanding. Millions of American people are receiving a lesson in the fundamentals and methods of good government. We are making some of the people economy-minded.

One of our results has been the setting up of Reorganization Commissions in 20 states and 10 municipalities for a treatment similar to that of our Commission. We are thus clearing other tracks of obstacles to competence in government.

Third—Preservation of the American Experiment

Third, in a larger sense, this is a crusade to make democracy work. There is today much apprehension lest the American experiment will fail. We have need to re-establish faith that the whole of the preamble to the Declaration of Independence and the Gettysburg Address are still related to government. If the Republic is not to be overwhelmed, the people must have such methods and systems as will enable good officials to give them good government.

Success in our crusade will help bring faith instead of cynicism and disillusionment.

Fourth—Helping in the Cold War

Fourth, success in our crusade to reduce cost of government is a necessary condition to winning the cold war. We are fighting this war at frightful cost. The way to win that war is to reduce our wastes, give competence a chance, and defer some government ventures. By these reforms and these self-denials, we can help disappoint Mr. Stalin.

I then described the critical reforms as yet uncompleted, and concluded:

These are not merely statistical assertions nor academic theories. These forces reach into every cottage in the land. They carry with them the future of our youth and of our country.

We must conserve our strength and stop wasting our heritage if we are to survive as a free people.[2]

---

2. [*Editor's note*: For the complete text of this speech, see Herbert Hoover, *Addresses upon the American Road, 1948–1950* (Stanford, CA: Stanford University Press, 1951), pp. 155–63.]

The Commission on Organization of the Executive Branch of 1953

Early in the 1953 session of Congress I was again asked for advice by Congressional leaders on setting up a second Commission on Organization of the Executive Branch.[1]

Since the first Commission the Korean War, the rearmament and defense in the cold war had increased Federal Expenditures from $42 billion to about $72 billion, the civilian personnel had increased by about 500,000, and the number of agencies had multiplied.

Again, the Committees of the Congress could not take the time from other duties to make the necessary exhaustive investigations. These leaders stated that if word could be passed that I would again take the Chairmanship the necessary law could be passed unanimously. I stated at various meetings with them that I did not feel that at my age I should undertake it but I had never refused a public service if it was insisted upon. I stated, however, that the law must give much wider authority than to the first Commission; that, in addition to previous provisions, it must include authority to investigate and report on policy as well as organization questions; that it must contain a directive to investigate and report on Government business enterprises in competition with private enterprises; and that it must give the authority to subpoena documents and persons and place such persons on oath with the usual penalties for perjury; and that my appointment should be made by the President and not by the Speaker of the House as on the previous occasion. I had no idea that we would use the subpoena authority but felt that it would be potent in securing cooperation. The purpose of the Presidential appointment was also to better influence cooperation from the Departments. To all this these leaders agreed. The bill was introduced with these new features and passed

---

1. [*Editor's note*: Commonly called the Second Hoover Commission.]

unanimously on July 10, 1953, being almost exactly six years after the creation of the First Commission.

The Commission comprised 12 members, as before; four members appointed by each the Speaker, the Vice President and the President. The appointments from the House and Senate were two members and two civilians divided between the two political parties.

The President, in addition to appointing me, wished two members of his Administration, and thus only one appointment from the Democratic Party. I had some misgivings on this point, as again it seemed to me we would be more effective with 6 members of each political party instead of five to seven. It did create some criticism later, but again both the Commission members and I wished to avoid political division and in fact we never did disagree on political lines.

The members of the Second Commission were:

Herbert Hoover, Chairman
Herbert Brownell, Jr., Attorney General
Arthur S. Flemming, Director of Office of Defense Mobilization
James A. Farley, Former Postmaster General
Senator Homer Ferguson (Resigned April 4, 1955)
Senator Styles Bridges (Succeeded Senator Ferguson April 4, 1955)
Senator John L. McClellan
Representative Clarence J. Brown
Representative Chet Holifield
Solomon C. Hollister (Dean of College of Engineering, Cornell
    University)
Robert G. Storey, President of the American Bar Association
Joseph P. Kennedy, Former Ambassador to Great Britain
Sidney A. Mitchell, Formerly served in the Departments of State and
    Navy and as Executive Director of the First Commission.

Thus there were 5 persons (Flemming, Kennedy, Brown, McClellan and Mitchell) who had served with the First Commission.

I secured that President Eisenhower call the first meeting of the Commission at the White House on September 29, 1953.

I proposed to the Commission that we proceed by Task Forces as in the First Commission; that the subjects to be undertaken, as before, should be authorized by the Commission, and that while I would be glad to have suggestions, that I should appoint the members of the Task Forces and the staff of the Commission. This was agreed to.

I determined that we should make a wholly different approach to the problem than in the First Commission. I decided upon this course because of our experience in the First Commission; because of our wider powers of investigation; because of our authority to deal with policy questions. Moreover, the First Commission's work had resulted in an organization set up for the departments by which they could carry out any needed internal reforms. The new program provided that in the main we should make our investigation functionally instead of departmentally. That is, we would examine certain activities, such as Lending and Guaranteeing agencies, Government Business Enterprises, Civil Service, Surplus Property, Paperwork Management, etc., straight across the whole Federal front and thus more fully develop their duplications, overlaps and policy weaknesses.

In the course of the work the following investigations were authorized by the Commission and I appointed the necessary Task Forces as follows (given alphabetically):

BUDGET AND ACCOUNTING, Chairman, J. Harold Stewart of
    Massachusetts
FEDERAL ACTIVITIES COMPETITIVE WITH PRIVATE
    ENTERPRISE, Chairman, Joseph B. Hall of Ohio
COMMITTEE ON BUSINESS ORGANIZATION OF THE
    DEPARTMENT OF DEFENSE, Chairman, Charles R. Hook
    of Ohio
DEPOT UTILIZATION, Chairman, Clifford E. Hicks of New York
INTELLIGENCE ACTIVITIES, Chairman, General Mark W. Clark
    of South Carolina
LEGAL SERVICES AND PROCEDURE, Chairman, Justice James M.
    Douglas of Missouri
LENDING, GUARANTEEING, AND INSURANCE ACTIVITIES,
    Chairman, Paul Grady of New York
MEDICAL SERVICES, Chairman, Chauncey McCormick of Illinois
    (deceased Sept. 8, 1954) and succeeded by Dr. Theodore G.
    Klumpp of New York
Subcommittee on Dentistry, Chairman, Dr. Otto W. Brandhorst of
    Missouri
Subcommittee on Health Insurance, Chairman, Msgr. Donald A.
    McGowan of Virginia
MILITARY PROCUREMENT, Chairman, Robert Wilson Wolcott of
    Pennsylvania

OVERSEAS ECONOMIC OPERATIONS, *Chairman,* Henning W. Prentis of Pennsylvania
PAPERWORK MANAGEMENT, *Chairman,* Emmett J. Leahy of Connecticut
PERSONNEL AND CIVIL SERVICE, *Chairman,* Harold W. Dodds of New Jersey
PERSONNEL PROBLEMS IN THE DEPARTMENT OF DEFENSE, *Chairman,* Thomas R. Reid of Michigan
REAL PROPERTY MANAGEMENT, *Chairman,* John R. Lotz of New York
RESEARCH AND DEVELOPMENT, *Chairman,* Mervin J. Kelly of New Jersey
SUBSISTENCE SERVICES, *Chairman,* Joseph P. Binns of New York
TRANSPORTATION, *Chairman,* Perry M. Shoemaker of New Jersey
USE AND DISPOSAL OF FEDERAL SURPLUS PROPERTY, *Chairman,* General Robert E. Wood of Illinois
WATER RESOURCES AND POWER, *Chairman,* Admiral Ben Moreell of Pennsylvania.

Short biographical sketches of the chairmen and members of these task forces were included in our Progress Report to the Congress as of December 31, 1954, indicating their previous experience in Government or public life.

The Task Forces were again selected for experience and ability and embraced members of both political parties. Their members mostly served without remuneration—and one of my satisfactions was that of some 300 men whom I requested to serve only two declined and for good reasons, and they served at great sacrifice to themselves.

I was greatly assisted by Former Congressman John B. Hollister as Director (succeeded by Hallam Tuck, the Deputy Director on June 7, 1955), Harold W. Metz as Director of Research and again, Francis P. Brassor as Executive Secretary of the Commission. Mr. Sidney Mitchell, with his wealth of experience on the first Commission, gave practically all his time to the work and was of immense help. Again, I had as assistant Lawrence Richey, and one of our most valuable aids was Neil MacNeil as Chief Editorial Director, who had been for 30 years a member of the *New York Times* staff.

The Commission made 314 recommendations. They fell into two categories: those requiring action by the Congress—"legislative recommendation"—and those which could be put into effect within the powers of the Departments—"Administrative recommendations."

The Task Force findings and recommendations after 20 months of exhaustive work began to appear in March 1955, and as in the first Commission, the Commission members did not always follow Task Force recommendations but drew upon their own wide experience and the work of our research staff.

Again, as before, there were dissents of minority members but every recommendation was carried by a majority and the majority included, on every occasion, members of both political parties.

There was one painful difference from the first Commission. A member of the extreme left wing organization the "Americans for Democratic Action." One member dissented from almost all reports and often in terms that reflected upon the Commission. He repeatedly stimulated pressure groups and members of the Congress to attack the Commission even before we had delivered our conclusions.[2]

Growing out of my previous experience in securing Departmental adoption of "Administration" recommendations, this time I secured that the President erect a unit in the Bureau of the Budget upon which the Citizens Committee would be represented. With the help of Mr. Tracy S. Voorhees and with the fine cooperation of the Secretary of Defense, we arranged that the representatives of that Department should be appointed to work with former members of our Task Force in that connection.

The Citizens Committee

As Dr. Johnson felt he must give his entire time to Temple University, I secured that Mr. Clarence Francis become chairman of a revitalized "Citizens Committee for the Hoover Reports," with Charles B. Coates and Robert L. L. McCormick again retained to conduct the detailed work of the Committee.

In the course of the Commission's work I made four addresses which may well be included here as indicating the problem and our hopes.[3]

---

2. [*Editor's note*: Hoover refers here to Chester ("Chet") Holifield (1903–95), an outspoken liberal Democrat and a member of the U.S. House of Representatives from California from 1943 to 1974.]

3. [*Editor's note*: At this point Hoover inserted in his manuscript extended quotations from three of his speeches and a press release concerning the work of the Second Hoover Commission. The addresses were delivered at the National Press Club on March 10, 1954; at a meeting of the American Society of Newspaper Editors on April 17, 1954; and before the U.S. Chamber of Commerce on May 4, 1955. His press statement was released on June 30, 1955.

I have omitted these four lengthy texts (which absorbed more than twenty pages in Hoover's page-proof copy of his manuscript). These documents may be found in Herbert Hoover, *Addresses upon the American Road, 1950–1955* (Stanford, CA: Stanford University Press, 1955), pp. 264–69,

[. . .-ed.]

In September [1955-ed.] a smearing article appeared in the official organ of the Democratic party about the Commission. I denounced it for what it was. The Press and many Democratic leaders took the editor to task. To settle the matter down I wrote an article for the organ as follows, which has some interest as indicating the non-political character of the Commission:[4]

163–70, and Herbert Hoover, *Addresses upon the American Road, 1955–1960* (Caldwell, ID: Caxton Printers, 1961), pp. 172–76, 186–92.]

4. [*Editor's note*: Hoover's manuscript ends at this point. Evidently he never completed it. For the "smearing article" that so offended him, see "The Second Hoover Commission Abandons Reform for Revolution," *Democratic Digest* 3 (September 1955): 25–31. The article accused the Hoover Commission of seeking "to turn the clock back" on government policy and accused Hoover himself of "flagrant abuses" of his appointment powers as the commission's chairman. It charged that Hoover had deliberately "stacked" the commission's task forces with men who shared his political philosophy and had excluded advocates of "public power" from fair representation on the panel studying the use of the nation's water resources.

The *Democratic Digest*'s attack appeared on August 15, 1955. The next day Hoover angrily denounced it as an "infamous smear." He denied stacking his task forces with ideological sympathizers and insisted that the commission had "never divided upon political grounds." See his press release of August 16, 1955, in the Public Statements File, Herbert Hoover Papers, Herbert Hoover Presidential Library.

Under pressure from Hoover and others, the editor of the *Democratic Digest* published a rejoinder by Hoover himself. See Hoover, "Reorganizing the Government: As Mr. Hoover Sees It . . . ," *Democratic Digest* 3 (November 1955): 25–27.]

"The Library on War, Revolution and Peace at Stanford University"

November 14, 1955

Hoover discussed the founding and history of the Hoover Institution in chapter 5 of the volume before you. Why he decided to return to this subject is unclear, but he did so in the autumn of 1955, in a handwritten draft that was typed for him on November 14. The typescript version, which is reproduced here, is found (along with the holograph version) in the Herbert Hoover Papers, Box 90, Hoover Institution Archives.

It is possible that Hoover contemplated substituting this essay for the earlier account given in chapter 5. In any case, his November 1955 statement has interest in its own right.

11/14/55

I barely mentioned this institution in my memoirs published in 1951–52. But in view of its present importance it warrants a further account of its origins and growth.

In 1915, on one of my frequent journeys to Belgium across the North Sea, I read some remarks by Andrew D. White, the great historian of the French Revolution, on the difficulty of reconstructing the life of the ordinary people in France during that period because of the large disappearance of contemporaneous documents and fugitive literature, such as newspapers, bulletins, speeches and the like. It occurred to me that as I was constantly traveling to and from the belligerent countries on both sides that I had a unique opportunity to collect such materials for future historians. I, therefore, engaged book dealers and some college authorities to collect such material in addition to what I and my staff on the Belgian Commission could secure. I established collection agencies in Germany, France, Britain, Holland, Belgium, Norway, Sweden, Switzerland and Spain, undertaking to pay, after the war was over, for material they had collected. Most of these agencies were very fruitful.

On my return to the United States in 1917 to take part in the War Administration, I again had opportunities to expand the collections to further countries and to more important matters than fugitive literature. When I returned
to Europe immediately after the Armistice in 1918 to direct the rehabilitation
and relief of Europe for the Allied Governments I put the work upon a more
systematic basis. I secured that E. D. Adams, Professor of History at Stanford,
come to Europe and join my staff, with the sole job of organizing these collections, and I advanced him something over $80,000 to pay our obligations
and to finance more collections. I had need to set up organizations to administer the multitude of rehabilitation and relief activities in every country in
Europe.

General Pershing took a great interest in my collection project and assigned a number of young professors of history from his then idle army to
my aid. Professor Adams attached them to some of our 28 different missions
which stretched from Helsinki to Constantinople, including the areas of Russia under anti-Communist control.

I made personal requests of the officials in many countries for their cooperation and received great assistance from those countries. We shipped large
quantities of materials by sea to San Francisco at no cost as the shipping companies gladly gave us this service free.

At the end of the war, the Library possessed complete files of our [over?–
ed.] fifty newspapers for the war period and by agreement of various authorities became the repository of the files of the Relief and Rehabilitation
Administration, including all of its special missions.

My own files included copies of the important documents of the Supreme
Economic Council, the United States Food Administration, the minutes of
the Peace Conference and its multitude of Committees. The Library at even
this point was an important institution containing a vast amount of material
and documentation covering the First World War.

Quickly social forces in motion in the world became of primary importance. We undertook to expand the collection to cover the rise of new
democracy on the embers of Empire, the emergence of Communism and
Fascism.

As secretary of commerce I was able to secure voluntary assistance from
the many employers [employees?–ed.] of that Department over the world
and they, in turn, secured the cooperation of many governments in materials
bearing on the world-wide social and political ferments.

In addition, I had the Library establish its own agents in the important
capitals of the world. One of our collections in this period proved to be of

unique importance. In 1922–23 [1921–23–*ed.*] I had undertaken the relief of the famine in South Russia at the request of the Communist Government. I dispatched Professor of History Golder of Stanford[1] as a member of this staff. Having been born and raised as a boy of American Consular parents in Russia, he spoke and read Russian perfectly. He presented his mission on historical material to the Communist leaders who, surprisingly, took a great interest in his work. He was able to obtain complete documentation on the Communist Revolution and much material as to the Russian participation in the war. As our Commerce and Library agents had instructions to specialize in the Communist conspiracy in all countries they, with the aid of many officials, brought to us the most complete materials in existence on this movement.

While I was in the White House, knowing my interest in the Library many governments and institutions over the world furnished us more materials. Soon after my term as President came the sequence of Hitler's national socialism and the revolutions in some ten former democracies to fascism.

In 1938 I made a journey to Europe, in response to invitations from many governments who wished to express their gratitude for my services during and after World War I. I visited some 14 countries, my major purpose being a study of the causes of the rise of totalitarian governments. The welcome I received enabled me to secure cooperation from many governments, unique materials bearing on political and social phenomena. This included eight countries now with totalitarian governments.

With the coming of World War II we again strengthened our collection agencies over the entire area of conflict. After the war we further expanded our collection agencies and staffs abroad and today the Library has the most important collections in the world on the Hitler regime in Germany, the Mussolini regime in Italy, and the events of the countries occupied by German, Italian and Russian armies, including their underground organizations.

In 1946, having been appointed by President Truman to coordinate the efforts of some 38 countries to overcome that greatest famine in all history, I visited each of these countries by plane and, naturally, I and my staff loaded the plane with materials for the Library.

Again in 1947, at the request of President Truman, I made a study on the ground of the allied governments of Germany and Austria. And again unique materials came to my hand.

---

1. [*Editor's note*: Frank A. Golder (1877–1929), a historian and avid collection of documents for the nascent Hoover Institution during the 1920s.]

The Library not only contains my personal archives of my public life, but the personal archives of many men, women and agencies which have had a part in public affairs over these years.

Naturally, the Library has complete files of our own and foreign governmental publications, and even continuous files of important newspapers, going back for nearly forty years.

Due to the destruction of the French and German war libraries and the partial destruction of the British collections in the Second World War, the students of history from all nations now find their only sources at Stanford.

After leaving the White House I organized more extensive finances for the Library, including the erection of the special building which was completed and dedicated on June 20, 1941. It has cost a considerable sum to build the Library, pay the cost of collection of materials and operate its services. The operations alone require about $250,000 per annum. To the end of its fiscal year on the 30th of August 1955, a total of $_____ has been collected from generous sources of which the University has contributed about $_____. Of these funds $_____ are for endowment, yielding about $35,000 per annum.

Speaking at the dedication of the new building on June 20, 1941, prior to American entry into World War II, I expressed my purposes in creating it. I stated that as the result of great mutual effort. . . .[2]

Since that address America has fought another great war. The warnings of national and world experience went unheeded. Today, the stocks and cellars bulge with the documentary output of that war.

As an answer to those who say these collections and lessons from them are of little importance I could point to two very practical uses. During the war the staff here conducted a continuous school of military officers preparing them from these materials for the problems they would meet in a world unknown to them. Here the Intelligence staffs of our Government searched for—and found—materials for the guidance of military action. One item alone saved thousands of American lives. In these archives were the military maps of North Africa. They existed nowhere else, accessible to the Allies. The landing on the African coast was guided by these maps. However, it was not to make successful war that this institution was founded but to aid in successful peace.

---

2. [*Editor's note*: Hoover's manuscript is blank at this point. He no doubt intended to fill in the quotation later. In his discussion of the Hoover Institution in chapter 5 of this volume, he quoted extensively from the same dedicatory remarks.]

And its purpose is to establish truth or to reestablish truth for these shelves contain the refutation of myriads of lies which have been told to the American people.

A cynical historian visiting the Library remarked: "Military commanders in war move upon fact and experience; political commanders move on propaganda and lies. Our soldiers always win wars; the politicians always lose wars."

Perhaps experience is a teacher. If so, this Library can teach. That hope justifies the devoted efforts of my many friends in its upbuilding.

"The Crusade for American Children"

December 1, 1955

Hoover composed this memoir-essay in the autumn of 1955. After making revisions he dispatched it, as was his custom, to a printer, who returned it to him in page-proof format on December 1. The page-proof version is reproduced here.

Along with its antecedent drafts, it is in the Herbert Hoover Papers, Box 94, Hoover Institution Archives.

Introduction

I returned to the United States in 1919, after the First World War, with a vivid experience in conducting an organization for the rehabilitation of 15,000,000 war children. While we continued that foreign service until 1923, my mind necessarily turned to the condition of American children. The draft experience in the war had brought to the surface the appalling fact that over 30 per cent of draftees had been rejected for physical and educational reasons. It seemed to me a terrible black spot on our civilization. Obviously this situation was in part due to undernourishment in childhood.

We had demonstrated by our European experiences that rehabilitation of children from undernourishment could be assured by a noonday extra meal of properly balanced food, and we had established such a system during and after the war for these millions of children.

I first addressed myself to the American problem in a speech at San Francisco, December 29, 1919, saying in part:

> If we could systematically grapple with the whole child problem in the United States, if we could insist on the proper conditions of birth, upon proper safeguarding of their general health, upon proper education, we could

then say with confidence that the problem of Americanization would be met in twenty years by its complete accomplishment, that our public health and efficiency would be enormously improved, that the sanity, morals and stability of the whole population would be advanced beyond anything that any nation has yet aspired to . . . that undernourishment problems arise not only from poverty but also ignorance of parents.[1] . . . The provision of at least one meal a day in the public schools of certain districts has a warrant, not in charity but in insurance to the whole community against distortions in body and mind in[2] our population for years to come.

The part of malnutrition due to ignorance on the part of parents can find[3] its solution in the education of parents; and, of equal importance, the education of children now in the schools as to methods by which their successors in life must be brought up. [. . .–ed.]

[. . .–ed.][4] If we could subject all the children to medical inspection, we would have entered into the province of prevention from the province of cure.[5]

The Constitutional Amendment prohibiting child labor had just been declared unconstitutional.[6] On May 28, 1920, I joined in urging a revision of the amendment by a statement saying in part:

Such a practice [child labor–ed.] results in the progressive degeneration of the race and tends to impair the human resources of the country. . . . The matter cannot wisely be left to the sole initiative of the separate states.[7]

---

1. [Editor's note: Here Hoover altered his quoted text. The original passage reads: "Any study of the nutrition problem for children in the cities quickly divides malnutrition into that due to poverty and that due to ignorance on the part of parents."]

2. [Editor's note: Here Hoover again altered his quoted text. In the original passage, he had written: "against deficiencies in the health and mind of."]

3. [Editor's note: In the original quoted passage, Hoover had written: "again finds."]

4. [Editor's note: Hoover omitted here the words "We believed that." In his 1919 speech he was referring in this passage to his experience in World War I providing food relief to the adults and children of German-occupied Belgium.]

5. [Editor's note: Hoover address to the Associated Charities of San Francisco, December 29, 1919, entry no. 40, Public Statements File, Herbert Hoover Papers, Herbert Hoover Presidential Library, West Branch, Iowa.]

6. [Editor's note: In Hammer v. Dagenhart (1918), the U.S. Supreme Court had ruled unconstitutional the Keating-Owen Act of 1916, in which Congress had banned products of child labor from interstate commerce. This was a law (not, as Hoover says here, a constitutional amendment) that the Court overturned. The decision spurred efforts in the 1920s to outlaw child labor by an amendment to the U.S. Constitution.]

7. [Editor's note: Herbert Hoover, "The Next Generation," Quaker, May 28, 1920, p. 27. Copy in entry no. 71, Public Statements File, Hoover Papers.]

I was requested to speak to a health association meeting in St. Louis on October 11, 1920. I stated in part:

... Few of our communities today can point to all its children as 100 percent sound in birth, health, education and moral surroundings. Such perfection will probably never be attained, but most communities are lamentably behind the possibilities of this ideal. [. . .–*ed.*]

If we were to take a broad survey of the children of our nation, we could say at once that probably sixty percent of them are from the homes of intelligence[8] and education. The character of their parents, and the public school system[9] need give us but little anxiety as to this great majority. It is upon the reduction of the remaining forty percent that our solicitude must concentrate itself.

I cited the community responsibility for supply of adequate and pure milk; the necessity to cure malnutrition by systematic school lunches; clinical examination of all school children, and teaching the fundamentals of health in the schools. I continued:

Some may object that medical supervision[10] by community nurses, clinical inspection of children in the schools, a supplemental meal in schools of certain sections, all tend to undue extension of government.[11] In the very creation of free schools and compulsory education itself, we have accepted the fact that we cannot as a nation rely for the upbuilding of the race upon the initiative of the parents alone. No one can deny that the physical development of child life is of equal importance with education. We every one of us pay the price in our jails, in our poorhouses, in our hospitals, in the loss of our economic efficiency, the fertile ground that we furnish for all the social patent medicines. . . . We should also have a re-submission of the Child Labor Amendment.[12]

---

8. [*Editor's note*: In the original quoted text: "high intelligence."]

9. [*Editor's note*: Here Hoover again altered his quoted text. The original quoted passage reads: "the homes of high intelligence and education, that the high character of their parents, with facilities furnished by the State in our public school system,"]

10. [*Editor's note*: In the original quoted text: "that this extension of medical supervision."]

11. [*Editor's note*: Here Hoover again altered his quoted text. In the original passage in 1920, Hoover had said: "all tend to too intimate an extension of government."]

12. [*Editor's note*: This sentence does not appear in Hoover's 1920 address. He evidently added it here as a kind of paraphrase of his 1920 remarks. In the 1920 address he forcefully advocated (as "absolutely critical") adoption of a constitutional amendment permitting the federal government to "take direct action on this question." He condemned child labor as leading to "the progressive degeneration of the race" and as tending "to impair the human resources of the country on which the coming generation must rely."]

These complex problems cannot be solved by any ironclad system of governmental action. When all public interest has expended itself, child development still rests with parents, and parents need much bringing up.[13]

On January 29, 1922, I joined in a public statement on Child Labor, saying:

It is infinitely better to prevent child labor and to compel and support education of our children today than to look after untrained, inefficient, unhealthy citizens tomorrow.[14]

In the meantime I had conducted a survey of the voluntary associations devoted to these problems to see where I could help. As a result, I undertook several activities in the course of years, principally the American Child Health Association, the American Children's Fund, the Boys' Clubs of America, and the Belgian-American Educational Foundation. I served also as an official for several other institutions such as the Boy Scouts, the Girl Scouts, and secured aid to other activities.

I have devoted a few paragraphs in my published memoirs to these subjects, but they warrant a much more extensive account. These activities at times paralleled each other, but for clarity I shall discuss them topically rather than chronologically.

13. [*Editor's note*: Hoover address to the annual meeting of the American Child Hygiene Association, October 11, 1920, entry no. 93, Public Statements File, Hoover Papers.]

14. [*Editor's note*: Hoover to Owen R. Lovejoy (general secretary of the National Child Labor Committee), December 8, 1921; released to the public on January 22, 1922. Copy in entry no. 187-A, Public Statements File, Hoover Papers.]

CHAPTER 1

The American Children's Fund

After the completion in 1923, under my chairmanship, of the American Relief Administration's postwar activities in Europe,[1] which were devoted to the rehabilitation of war and famine children, there were certain residue funds in the hands of that organization. These residue funds had been raised largely by State Committees in a drive set up for those purposes. There were also certain assets arising from ship insurance claims and the sale of former equipment in Europe. In November, 1923, I proposed to the Directors and to the State Committees that for the future we should devote these residue funds to activities relating to American children. The proposal was unanimously agreed to.

On December 1, 1923, we incorporated the "American Children's Fund" as a nonprofit institution, with "membership" from the Directors of the American Relief Administration and the Chairmen of the State Committees. These "members," about thirty-five in number, embraced such persons as Robert A. Taft and Alexander Smith, later United States Senators: Hugh Gibson, later Ambassador to Poland, Switzerland, Brazil and Belgium; Harvey A. Bundy, later Assistant Secretary of State; Christian A. Herter, later Governor of Massachusetts; Lewis L. Strauss, later Chairman of the Atomic Energy Commission; H. L. Spaulding, former Governor of New Hampshire; Edgar Rickard, former Assistant Food Administrator of the United States; President Ray Lyman Wilbur, President of Stanford University; Professor Charles M.

---

1. The history of these activities will be found in that section of these memoirs dedicated to *The Crusade against Famine*. [*Editor's note*: "The Crusade against Famine in World War II" was the title, as of 1955, of the portion of Hoover's memoirs devoted to his relief efforts during and just after the Second World War. (An earlier title for this segment was "The Crusade against the Four Horsemen in World War II.") In this footnote Hoover signaled a new conceptualization of this part of his memoirs: a decision to expand its scope to encompass his relief work in Europe during and after the *First* World War. In the late 1950s he moved in precisely this direction, composing what became a four-volume series titled *An American Epic*, which he published between 1959 and 1964.]

Bakewell of Yale University; Judge Edwin F. Shattuck, and other leading professional and business executives interested in these problems. The "members" chose the officers annually and acted as a board of directors.

The first officers were:

Herbert Hoover, Chairman
Edgar Rickard, President
Perrin Galpin, Vice President
Raymond Sawtelle, Treasurer
Hugo Meier, Secretary

Over its twenty years of service the Fund received:

From the American Relief Organization. $5,358,114.16
Profit on sale of securities, sundry donations, interest
    and dividends 2,408,082.60
Total . . . . $7,756,202.76[2]

The growth of the fund was due to the devoted service of its Finance Committee, comprising at various times over the years of Edgar Rickard, Lewis Strauss, Hallam Tuck, Sidney Mitchell, John Simpson, Raymond Sawtelle and Scott Turner.

Our activities were mostly directed to grants to various organizations directly or indirectly devoted to the welfare of children and youth. The grants made over the years indicate our policies. The following are the more important of them:

The American Child Health Association $3,360,325.00
    (described later on)
The Girl Scouts of America 858,000.00
The Boy Scouts of America 725,902.00
The Boys' Clubs of America. 311,420.00
To various schools and colleges. 281,000.00
The President's Conference on Housing, Home
    Ownership and Slum Improvements 501,371.00
    (largely for publications)
The Puerto Rican Relief Committee for the relief of
    Puerto Rican Children 213,773.00

---

2. [*Editor's note*: Hoover's total here seems to be in error. On the basis of the figures given, the total should be $7,766,196.76.]

The Friends Service Committee for the Relief of Children	
in Coal Regions	225,000.00
The American Red Cross for Child Health	500,000.00
The National Committee on Food for Children in	
World War II	52,516.00
The Allied Jewish Committee for Children	50,000.00
Sundry Appropriations under $50,000	143,904.00
Total.	$7,223,211.00

As the Fund had no paid officials and secured its quarters and staff by participation in office work of other organizations, there was very little overhead. Having expended the Fund, we placed it in liquidation on April 12, 1950. After liquidation of the minor liabilities, the small residue of the Fund was granted to the Belgian-American Educational Foundation.

I may mention in this connection that in 1922 Mrs. Hoover and Mrs. Edgar Rickard took over the management of the Girl Scouts as Chairman and Treasurer. They started with 100,000 girls and ended up with more than 1,500,000 some years later. They raised by one method or another over $1,500,000 in addition to the contribution of the American Children's Fund.

CHAPTER 2

The American Child Health Association

Of the various organizations interested in children's problems, I concluded from my survey that the strongest of these was the "American Child Hygiene Association," conducted by public spirited doctors under the leadership of Dr. Philip Van Ingen. I met with these leaders in late 1921 to offer our aid to their efforts, and they promptly urged that I accept the Presidency of the Association. I did so. At once I sought to strengthen the Association by consolidating it with the other associations in the field. They were mainly the Child Health Organization, under the leadership of Sally Lucas Jean; the National Child Health Council; the Child Health section of the American Red Cross, under the leadership of Dr. Livingston Farrand, and the Children's Division of the National Public Health Nursing Association. We first effected consolidation with the Child Health Organization of America.

In a Presidential address to the Child Hygiene Association on October 12, 1922, I said:

> I have the honor to announce two most important events in the history of voluntary effort to advance child health in our country.
>
> First, the practical completion of the consolidation of the two great national voluntary societies devoted to this object—your association and the Child Health Organization of America. These two great societies have for years carried the burden of voluntary effort on behalf of child health, each in its own field. These two associations include 340 local voluntary associations, concerned with the problems of childhood from school age forward.[1] By the

---

1. [*Editor's note*: Here Hoover truncated and altered the quoted text. The original passage reads: "... each in its own field, your association comprised as it is of 340 voluntary associations, concerned with the problems of child health up to the school age, and its companion society concerned with the problems of children from school age forward."]

consolidation of these two societies we shall now attain a great national institution coordinating all voluntary effort on behalf of child health. . . .

The purpose [*sic–ed.*] of the proposed new association are educational; the stimulation of public interest in these problems; provision of scientific guidance; to be built upon community action, not on the shifting sands of overcentralization. It does not purport to train individual children or parents. It proposes to inspire all the agencies to those ends and to assist them in its accomplishment.[2]

Proceeding from this point, we secured consolidation with the National Health Council, the Child Health section of the American Red Cross, and the Children's Division and [of?–*ed.*] the National Public Health Nursing Association. These negotiations were tedious, but my assurance of more ample resources finally forged them into a great team.

We launched the consolidated organization under the title of The American Child Health Association early in 1923.

The initial officers were:

Herbert Hoover, President
Dr. L. Emmett Holt, 1st Vice President
Dr. Livingston Farrand, 2d Vice President
Dr. Thomas D. Wood, 3d Vice President
Dr. Philip Van Ingen, Secretary.

The Executive Committee in addition to the officers included:

---

2. [*Editor's note*: This paragraph does not match the actual text of Hoover's speech held in his papers. What Hoover actually said in 1922 was as follows:

"The objects of these associations are:

"First. That we stipulate appreciation of the service that can be done for children and the nation in the matter of health.

"Second. That the enormous activity in America for the welfare of children and mothers shall be directed in a scientific manner and by scientifically trained men and women.

"Third. That these applications of science shall reach every corner of the country and every child in it.

Fourth. That these efforts on behalf of children shall be built upon the solid rock of inspiration in the local community to its responsibility, and not built upon the shifting sands of over centralization.

"This association is thus an educational institution. It does not purport to train the individual, the child, or the parent. It proposes to inspire all the agencies to those ends and to assist them in their labor through its branches of research, its branches of instruction as to community organization, and its branches of demonstration."

The typewritten text of Hoover's address to the American Child Hygiene Association on October 12, 1922, is entry no. 262-A in the Public Statements File, Hoover Papers.]

Mrs. William B. Meloney
Miss Grace Abbott[3]
Dr. Samuel Hamill
Clinton Crane[4]
Mrs. Aida de Acosta Root.[5]

The initial Executive Staff was:

Courtenay Dinwiddie
Dr. Richard A. Bolt
Sally Lucas Jean.

The Board of Directors comprised about eighty eminent citizens of whom about one-half were doctors and public health officials, the others being representative of public interest in this field.

Changes of officers took place over the years. Mr. Dinwiddie was succeeded in 1925 by Dr. S. J. Crumbine, one-time Dean of the School of Medicine, Kansas University, and Director of the Kansas State Board of Health. Edgar Rickard succeeded me as President, and I became Chairman. During my time in the White House, from 1929 to 1933, I became Honorary Chairman and Dr. Ray Lyman Wilbur became the active Chairman.

As I served in the Cabinet and in the White House from 1920 [1921–ed.] to 1933, I was able to secure the complete cooperation with the Association, of the National Public Health Service and most state and municipal health officials.

When we first consolidated these organizations, their combined annual resources (all from gifts) were under $75,000 per annum. I at once stiffened the organization up from the American Children's Fund from whence, as stated previously, we contributed over the years a total of $3,360,325. In addition, during the life of the Association we collected somewhat over $1,500,000 in donations. Our budget ranged from $150,000 to $500,000 per annum.

In reply to a press query as to our program, I said on February [date not given–ed.], 1923:

That there should be no child in America who:

Is not born under proper conditions.
Does not live in hygienic surroundings.

---

3. [*Editor's note*: In his 1955 manuscript Hoover mistakenly listed Grace Abbott as "Mrs."]
4. [*Editor's note*: In his 1955 manuscript Hoover mistakenly gave Crane's first name as Clayton.]
5. [*Editor's note*: In his 1955 manuscript Hoover misspelled Mrs. Root's full name, which has been rendered correctly here and elsewhere.]

Ever suffers from malnutrition.

Does not have prompt and efficient medical inspection and attention.

Does not receive primary instruction in the elements of hygiene and good health.

Does not express in the fullest measure the spirit which is the endowment of each human being.[6]

This statement was gradually developed into a positive "Bill of Rights for Children," having its fullest expression at the White House Conference of 1930, which is referred to later on.

We held the first national convention of the Association in Detroit on October 15, 1923, attended by a thousand delegates from official and unofficial organizations. I said in addressing them:

... The Association is devoted to one primary proposition, which is the organization of the moral force in each community for the better protection of children[7] as the foundation of progress. There are many functions which cannot be served by individual action. The prevention of infection, the provision of a better water supply, sufficient quantities of pure milk, and a score of items, can only be perfected and improved by the action of the community as a whole. Governments and city authorities cannot go further than public understanding, public spirit, and public demand, and it is, therefore, the function of this Association to bring about that understanding in the community which leads to better and more efficient community action. Good community action must be based upon full realization of sound and practical measures. Idealism in these problems of social progress must have its root in ruthless realism and in scientific research. Practical experience must precede action and ... the experience of one community may be applied in another. [...–ed.]

We are realizing more and more, as time goes on, that force, compulsion, autocratic action of government, of bureaucracy, are no solution for our social problems. We know that a community nurse is better than a dozen policemen. We know now, if we can build our children in sound health and in

---

6. [*Editor's note*: See Hoover, "A Bill of Rights," February 1923, entry no. 283-B, Public Statements File, Hoover Papers. This document does not contain the final sentence that Hoover included here. Around 1927, he revised his "Children's Bill of Rights" by adding, among other things, a line that there should be no child in America who "has not the encouragement to express in fullest measure the spirit within which is the final endowment of each human being." The document was widely publicized in 1927 and 1928. The version printed here seems to reflect further editing by Hoover in 1955.]

7. [*Editor's note*: In the original quoted passage: "child health."]

sound mind, if we can summon the moral forces of the community for complete action in these directions, we can give protection not only to health, but to the spiritual forces among our children; that if we could secure these results in their perfection of[8] a period of only a score of years, we could speed civilization a century.[9]

Over the ten years of its active existence, the work of the Association embraced seven major programs.

First The preparation and continuous distribution of brochures and pamphlets. They were designed for parents and teachers and even for the children themselves. Also, I participated in this educational work by scores of press statements, magazine articles and my Presidential addresses at most of the annual meetings of the Association.

We carried on many radio programs and for many years we supported a radio program, "Cheerio," by Charles K. Field, for the benefit of shut-ins and to popularize the work of the Association.

Second The Association was entrusted, by one of the great foundations, and a gift of $300,000 to conduct a complete program of ideal organizations for children in three typical counties. The counties chosen were in North Dakota, Tennessee, and Georgia. We secured further funds for the project, and we had the full cooperation of state and local authorities. The experiment lasted for three years. My own appraisal of results was that while we had effected lasting progress in school facilities, teaching and promoting health and in other directions, the full program we installed was beyond the economic strength of the counties to carry on. We prepared modified programs and urged more state aid.

Third A much more ambitious and more effective program was "the test of eighty-six cities." I announced the program on October 15, 1923. We had determined to make a scientific appraisal of the standards maintained by these cities for child health and protection. The standards involved volume and purity of milk supply; clinical examination of school children; hospitalization facilities for maternity and children; infant mortality; birth registration; public health inspection service guaranteeing facilities for contagious diseases; purity of water supply; school attendance; midday school meals and other conditions relating to children.

In announcing the program I stated:

---

8. [*Editor's note*: In the original quoted passage: "for."]
9. [*Editor's note*: Hoover address at a public meeting of the annual session of the American Child Health Association, October 15, 1923, entry no. 330-A, Public Statements File, Hoover Papers.]

. . . We propose to examine as many communities as our resources will permit and to grade them as to their relative perfection in these protective measures. We have hopes that we can bring stimulation to many of them; indication of their delinquencies will be helpful in remedy.[10]

We began the work in 1924 with our own efficient staff and cooperation from the public health officers. We completed it in 1926. The eighty-six cities varied from 40,000 to 90,000 population. They were in thirty-one states. The survey showed that forty-one of the cities had no full-time health official and that half of the part-time officials they had were without a medical degree. Sixteen cities had not even a nominal board of health, and forty-one had fewer than three sanitary inspectors. Half of the cities had no reliable birth or death records on children. Twenty-eight different procedures were in use for quarantine of diphtheria and scarlet fever patients. Thirty-seven cities' vaccination was not compulsory, and 44 per cent of the children were not protected against smallpox. Eighteen cities had no facilities to hospitalize contagious diseases. Twenty-one did not even have clinics for diagnosis and treatment of venereal disease. Fifteen were without clinics to diagnose tuberculosis. A large majority had no maternity hospitals. Seventeen had no medical inspection in the schools, and in thirty-five the inspectors devoted less than two minutes to each child. Scarcely any of the cities had a "follow-up" system to correct defects. In twenty-one there was no health instruction in the schools. Four had an unsafe water supply. Only eight cities pasteurized their whole milk supply. Forty-seven pasteurized less than half of it. Four cities had no playgrounds outside the school yards. In forty others the play facilities were wholly inadequate. Of 35,000 fifth grade children examined, nearly a quarter had no milk. A pint of milk a day having been set by our specialists as the minimum, we found 42 per cent of them had less than this. There were eighteen preventable epidemics among children in these cities in a period of four years.

We set up standards for city conduct based upon the best work in the eighty-six cities. We published in the press the ratings and defaults of each city. The report produced an explosion. There were heated mayors and town councilmen, and many of them met defeat in elections at the hands of embittered mothers and the press.

Fourth Our fourth effective program was to appropriate May Day away from its degeneration toward a propaganda day by the Communists and turn

---

10. [*Editor's note*: Hoover address at the first annual session of the American Child Health Association, October 15, 1923, entry no. 330, Public Statements File, Hoover Papers.]

it into Child Health Day. On February 26, 1924, I addressed a note to President Coolidge, which read in part:

> May Day is traditionally and peculiarly a children's day. It is the desire of many organizations devoted to children[11] to establish the first of May 1924 as a day for constructive, concentrated thought and demonstration on behalf of community action for the American child. It is thought that on that day, if you approve, the governors of states, commissioners of health and education, mayors of cities, and various organizations working for child health and welfare, the press, motion picture industry, radio broadcasting stations, and other agencies might be asked to join in stimulating consideration throughout the country to these problems. I, therefore, would be glad to know if you could give your approval to such an effort.[12]

The President made the necessary declaration. We organized demonstrations in hundreds of towns and cities, and we continued them each year for ten years. The masses of marching, chattering children with gay banners, May-poles, teachers and bands, including their banners of protest against bad milk and child labor and other evils, made a deep emotional impression on the country.

As President of the Association, I usually issued a statement for each May Day, of which this of 1928 is typical:

> ... In this day, which for the past five years has been set aside as a day for concentration of interest upon the health of children, we have an instance of what can be accomplished by bringing together many forces in a single interest. Remarkable things have been accomplished all over the country through the influence[13] of May Day. Clinics have been opened to guard the health of children, many thousand children have been immunized against certain communicable diseases. Many thousand more [have been–ed.] examined and defects corrected. Central councils have been formed in many states which unite all the groups interested in the health and welfare of children. Yet these things—significant as they are—tell only a small part of the story. The largest accomplishment cannot be reckoned concretely—it is the stirring of the public conscience to the obligations of children.[14]

---

11. [*Editor's note*: The words "devoted to children" do not appear in the text that Hoover is quoting.]

12. [*Editor's note*: Hoover to Calvin Coolidge, February 26, 1924, entry no. 330, Public Statements File, Hoover Papers.]

13. [*Editor's note*: In Hoover's original text of 1928 he used the word "stimulus."]

14. [*Editor's note*: Hoover statement/radio address about child health and May Day, May 1, 1928, entry no. 853, Public Statements File, Hoover Papers.]

In congratulating Mrs. Aida de Acosta Root, who managed these demonstrations for us, I said:

... It was a great achievement, and I am proud to be President of the American Child Health Association, which initiated the idea, and whose personnel is responsible for the inspiration which carried it to success.

Health officers of the various communities; governors of states; mayors of cities; teachers in our schools; many individual welfare workers and organizations; not to mention the clergy; a veritable army, all united in an effort to do the utmost within their power in a permanent American movement toward accruing[15] to our children their most elemental rights; —to be born well; to have a healthy childhood and to reach maturity in the happiness that comes in its fullness only to those whose physical heritage has been safe-guarded.[16]

Fifth The Association carried on an active campaign for abolition of child labor, a constitutional amendment to that end having been declared invalid by the Supreme Court. After this defeat, we supported another version of the amendment introduced by Senator Lenroot and passed by the Congress for submission to the states. We, however, warned the Senator and the committees of Congress that placing the age limit at eighteen was so high that states would reject it, which happened. We then turned our attention to legislation by the states. Most of the northern states had limited child labor before 1932.

Sixth On July 2, 1929, as President, I announced a conference on Child Health and Protection, to be held at the White House in November of 1930. I placed Secretary of the Interior Ray Lyman Wilbur, who was chairman of the Child Health Association, in charge with the assistance of Dr. Crumbine, its director. In the meantime we prepared for the conference by eleven months of work by special committees on the multiple phases of the problem, so that the conference could start effective action.

The conference included one thousand delegates from interested national associations—governors, mayors and public health authorities.

My address opening the conference is too long for reproduction, but a few of its paragraphs re-echoed for years. They were:

We approach all problems of childhood with affection. Theirs is the province of joy and good humor. They are the most wholesome part of the race, the sweetest, for they are fresher from the hands of God. Whimsical, ingenious, mischievous,

---

15. [*Editor's note*: In the original quoted text: "securing."]
16. [*Editor's note*: Hoover to Aida de Acosta Root, May 1, 1925, entry no. 478, Public Statements File, Hoover Papers.]

we live a life of apprehension as to what their opinion may be of us; a life of defense against their terrifying energy; we put them to bed with a sense of relief and a lingering of devotion. We envy them the freshness of adventures and discovery of life; we mourn over the disappointments they will meet. [. . .–ed.]

I have the classification of the 45,000,000 American children furnished to me by the research committees as follows:

35,000,000 are reasonably normal.

6,000,000 are improperly nourished.

1,000,000 have defective speech.

1,000,000 have weak or damaged hearts.

675,000 present behavior problems.

450,000 are mentally retarded.

382,000 are tubercular.

342,000 have impaired hearing.

18,000 are totally deaf.

300,000 are crippled.

50,000 are partially blind.

14,000 are wholly blind.

200,000 are delinquent.

500,000 are dependent.

And so on, to a total of at least 10 millions of deficients, more than 80 per cent of whom are not receiving the necessary attention, though our knowledge and experience show that these deficiencies can be prevented and remedied to a high degree. The reports you have before you are not only replete with information upon each of these groups, they are also vivid with recommendation for remedy. And if we do not perform our duty to these children, we leave them dependent, or we provide from them the major recruiting ground for the army of ne'er-do-wells and criminals.

But that we be not discouraged let us bear in mind that there are 35,000,000 reasonably normal, cheerful human electrons radiating joy and mischief and hope and faith. Their faces are turned toward the light—theirs is the life of great adventure. These are the vivid, romping, everyday children, our own and our neighbors' with all their strongly marked differences—and the more differences the better. The more they charge us with their separate problems the more we know they are vitally and humanly alive.[17]

---

17. [*Editor's note*: Hoover address to the White House Conference on Child Health and Protection, November 19, 1930. For the complete text, see *Papers of the Presidents of the United States:*

I had from time to time revised and elaborated my "Bill of Rights of Children." I proposed it to the Conference and it was unanimously adopted. As it was reproduced in millions of copies, I give the full text here:

For every child spiritual and moral training to help him to stand firm under the pressure of life.

For every child understanding and the guarding of his personality as his most precious right.

For every child a home and that love and security which a home provides, a dwelling place safe, sanitary and wholesome, a home environment harmonious and enriching.

For every child full preparation for his birth, his mother receiving prenatal, natal, and postnatal care.

For every child health protection from birth, promotion of health, health instruction and physical and mental recreation.

For every child a school which is safe from hazards, sanitary, properly equipped, lighted and ventilated; an education which prepares him for life and prepares him for a living.

For every child a community which recognizes and plans for his needs, protects him against physical dangers, moral hazards, and disease; provides him with safe and wholesome places for play and recreation, and education for safety and protection against accidents.

For every child who is blind, deaf, crippled or otherwise handicapped, care and treatment, and such training that he may become an asset to society.

For every child who is in conflict with society the right to be dealt with intelligently as society's charge, not society's outcast.

For every child the right to grow up in a family with an adequate standard of living and the security of a stable income.

For every child protection against labor that stunts growth, that limits education, that deprives children of the right of comradeship, of play, and of joy.

For every rural child as satisfactory schooling and health services as for the city child.

Every stimulation and encouragement to the voluntary youth organizations.

Everywhere a district, county, or community organization for health, education and welfare, with full-time officials, coordinating with a statewide

Herbert Hoover: Containing the Public Messages, Speeches, and Statements of the President, January 1 to December 31, 1930 (Washington: U.S. Government Printing Office, 1976), pp. 489–96. This text varies insignificantly in a few places from the version quoted here by Hoover in his 1955 manuscript.]

program, which will be responsive to a nation-wide service of general information, statistics, and scientific research.

For every child these rights, regardless of race, or color, or situation, wherever he may live under the protection of the American flag.[18]

The work of the Conference did not end with its adjournment. The conference committees subsequently formulated their research and findings in a series of monographs which were not only circulated free to all of the delegates, but to interested persons all over the country. A permanent staff was set up to establish state conferences, many of which were held.

As one of the conference recommendations, I proposed to the Congress in 1929 a Federal subsidy to backward counties willing to undertake certain requirements. The legislation was passed by the House in 1930 and killed by a filibuster in the Senate. I repeated the recommendation of this legislation in 1931 and 1932 sessions, but it was held up by [an–ed.] antagonistic Congress.

During my administration I did secure a law authorizing Federal authorities to turn juvenile Federal offenders over to the State juvenile courts and the stringent laws on the kidnapping which had terrorized the country following the kidnapping of the Lindbergh baby.

Eight[19] During the depression we had set up local committees everywhere to administer relief to the unemployed. Wherever possible, we secured that Child Health Association members join these committees and give especial emphasis to the care of children. The result of the work of these committees serves both as proof that there was no starvation during the period and also the devotion of these committees to children. The test and proof lie in the public health statistics as to infant mortality.

The numbers were as follows:

---

18. [*Editor's note*: Hoover's "Bill of Rights of Children," as printed here, differs in many places from the document known as the "Children's Charter," adopted by the White House Conference on Child Health and Protection, which met in Washington, D.C., in November 1930. Hoover appears to have reproduced here his own draft, not the final version as amended and revised by the conference. According to two of Hoover's cabinet secretaries, Hoover drafted the "first outline" of the "Children's Charter," which was then "put in final form" by the conference.

For the full text of the final version, which Hoover endorsed and commended to the nation, see *Public Papers of the Presidents of the United States: Herbert Hoover: Containing the Public Messages, Speeches, and Statements of the President, January 1 to December 31, 1931* (Washington: U.S. Government Printing Office, 1976), pp. 171–73. See also Ray Lyman Wilbur and Arthur Mastick Hyde, *The Hoover Policies* (New York: Charles Scribner's Sons, 1937), pp. 64–67.]

19. [*Editor's note*: This should probably be "Seven." No item marked "Seven" appears earlier in Hoover's manuscript.]

1928   6880 deaths per 100,000

1929   6700 deaths per 100,000

1930   6400 deaths per 100,000

1931   6170 deaths per 100,000

1932   5700 deaths per 100,000.

On leaving the White House in 1933, I again took a more active managerial part in the association and carried on its work for two years. However, funds in my control and public donations so diminished that we could not work effectively—that being one of the results of my diminished public influence during that period.

I believe it will be confirmed that this Association played a part in the awakening of the American people to the problems of childhood.

CHAPTER 3

Boys' Clubs of America

In 1929 an old friend of the First World War, William Edwin Hall, President of the national organization of "the Boys' Clubs of America," sought me as President of the United States to become their Honorary Chairman. This national organization dated from 1908, although there were operating clubs in several cities, some going back to 1894, Mr. Hall becoming President in 1916. I had observed his service over the years and was glad to add to the credibility of the movement. After I left the White House in 1933, Mr. Hall and the Directors of the Club urged that I continue as Honorary Chairman. I did so. As the organization badly needed both funds and expansion Mr. Hall and the Directors in 1936 urged that I take a major responsibility in its administration policies by becoming the active Chairman of the Board, and we dropped the "Honorary" title. Mr. Hall continued as President until 1954, when he was compelled to resign because of ill health after thirty-eight years of service. He was one of the most dedicated men I have known, and we worked closely together. At my suggestion the Board elected Mr. Albert L. Cole as President.

The fundamental purpose of the Boys' Clubs is service in the congested districts (slums) of our cities. Here with only the pavements for outdoors after school and nights, Saturdays and holidays, is the breeding ground of delinquency and gangsterism.

Each club is established by its community or city and is conducted by its own Board of Directors. The clubs are admitted into the National Association and to receive its services and aid upon attaining certain standards of equipment and management.

After I became Chairman we increased the Board of Directors by adding twenty prominent and devoted citizens from all over the country. We established National Associate Directors in the leading cities, now numbering 216. We established a training college for Boys' Club leaders recruited from the graduates of our universities; we established a unit of architectural guidance for construction of new clubs; we spread a system of skilled advisors on management over the country; and we conducted a systematic nationwide action inspiring, developing and aiding in securing financial support for more clubs. We greatly stiffened the central organization under the Directorship of Sanford Bates, and upon his resignation to accept a high state position in 1940, we secured the unique service of Mr. David W. Armstrong, who long had been the director of the finely developed boys club in Worcester, Massachusetts.

The association had carried many activities for boys of secondary character on its rolls. In 1941 we vigorously revised the standards for the admission as members of the Boys' Clubs of America. We did not cease our services to the substandard activities but used the "full membership" as a goal for development. In 1943 we established a special fund for development of new clubs.

Omitting the substandard activities we, during the period from 1934 until 1955, expanded full standard membership from about 160 Clubs to over 425 and the boy membership from under 200,000 to over 400,000. The staff of the Clubs in 1955 include 1,630 trained workers, 3,132 part-time trained workers and 3,740 volunteers. In addition, the Board of Directors of the local Clubs exceed 7,500 members, or a total of about 16,000 persons continuously interested.

We established a method of systematic solicitation of contributions of from $10 to $20 through our Directors and our affiliate Directors, and a systematic appeal to corporations and charitable foundations for support.

In 1936, at the time I became Chairman, the entire operating budget of the National Organization was $85,169.73. In 1955 it was $688,496.76, and in addition, our Extension Fund for that year was $76,112, or a total budget of $764,608.76.

The total operating expenditures of the Boys' Clubs of America from 1936 to 1956 were over $7,000,000, and the funds raised by the individual clubs for operation purposes, mostly from Community Chests, in this period probably exceeded $10,000,000. In addition, huge sums were raised for construction and improvement of the clubs, the cost of a Club building ranging from $250,000 to $500,000. The amounts raised for new construction and improvements of the clubs during the period 1936–1956 is indicated by the fact that the replacement cost of the clubs in 1936 was estimated at $20,000,000 and, in 1956, at over $120,000,000. I claim no credit for these sums, but these figures serve to illuminate the devotion of a great body of men and women.

I gave much time to the work of the clubs. I traveled to many cities to take part in public meetings to raise money for their construction and maintenance. I visited many clubs and I dedicated a host of new ones. I presided over every meeting of the Directors for twenty years except one while absent on famine work.

I made in these years a multitude of public addresses from which I give a few extracts as they interpret the progress and spirit of the movement.

In an address at the National Convention of the Clubs in New York on May 13, 1937, I said:

> This convention is dealing with the Public Relations of boys. We do not exclude their sisters—if anything, our sentiment for them is even more tender. But we are here engaged with the business of boys.
>
> This evening I wish to examine the nature of the animal.
>
> To explore what civilization has done to some of them.
>
> To relate an experiment.
>
> To lay before you a proposition which involves $15,000,000.
>
> To give the reasons for it all.
>
> And finally to wind up with the peroration. And to do it all in fifteen minutes.
>
> Together with his sister, the boy is our most precious possession. But he presents not only joys and hopes, but also paradoxes. He strains our nerves, yet he is a complex of cells teeming with affections. He is a periodic nuisance, yet he is a joy forever. He is a part-time incarnation of destruction, yet he radiates sunlight to all the world. He gives evidence of being the child of iniquity, yet he makes a great nation. He is filled with curiosity as to every mortal thing, he is an illuminated interrogation point, yet he is the most entertaining animal that is.
>
> The whole world is new to him. Therefore his should be a life of adventure, of discovery, of great undertakings. He must spend much time, if he is to expand, in the land of make-believe. One of the sad things in the world is that he must grow up into the land of realities.
>
> He is endowed with a dynamic energy and an impelling desire to take exercise on all occasions. His primary instinct is to hunt in a pack and that multiplies his devices. He is a complete self-starter, and therefore wisdom in dealing with him consists mostly in what to do with him next.
>
> The Constitution provides him, or at least at one time it did, with the inalienable right of liberty, and the pursuit of happiness. We are not so much concerned at the moment with his liberties as guaranteed by the Bill of Rights as we are with his processes for the pursuit of happiness. He will find the tragedies of both liberty and happiness when he becomes a tax-payer.

He and his pack can go on this hunt for happiness either constructively or destructively. Our first problem is to find him constructive joy, instead of destructive glee.

To complicate this problem, this civilization has gone and built up great cities. We have increased the number of boys per acre. We have paved all this part of the land with cement and cobblestones. There are about twenty million of these human organisms in the country. Of these perhaps three million are crowded into the poorer sections and slums of our cities. They have to spend their spare time on these pavements, surrounded by brick walls. That boy has a life of stairs, light switches, alleys, fire escapes, bells and cobblestones, and a chance to get run over by a truck. Thus these boys are today separated from Mother Earth and all her works, except the weather. The outlet of curiosity in exploring the streams and the fields is closed to him. The mysteries of the birds and bees and fish are denied to him.

The normal boy is a primitive animal and takes to competition and battle. In the days before our civilization became so perfect, he matched his wits with the birds, the bees and the fish. He cannot find[1] battle with animals or plants in zoos or parks. If he doesn't contend with nature, he is likely to take on contention with a policeman. And yet we cannot restore many of these constructive joys in a land of cement and bricks.

This is a marginal problem. It concerns only a minority of boys. And I may state generally that if the American people would only realize that our national problems are all marginal problems of eliminating evil, correcting abuse and building up the weak, rather than the legerdemain of Utopia, we would make more progress. And I dislike to refer to these boys as "underprivileged." That is only a half-truth. The government provides even the marginal city boys with better facilities for education and better protection of health than any other government in the world. And we are today doing a better job of these things than ever before in our history. Far less than his grandfather does he suffer from mumps and measles; more quickly do we heal his fractures. Far less does he have to endure stench and filth. And the electric light has banished the former curse of all boys, of cleaning lamps and everlastingly carrying them about. The light switch has driven away the goblins that lived in dark corners and under the bed. It clothes drab streets with gaiety and cheer by night. And it is the attraction of these bright lights that increases our problem.

---

1. [*Editor's note*: In the original address as printed in Hoover's *Addresses upon the American Road, 1933–1938*, Hoover said: "At least he found."]

There are other privileges that the most lowly of them have. It is a privilege to have been born in America. They live under a democracy where they have more opportunity of becoming a mayor or a policeman or an editor or even a banker than in any other country. So they have some privileges.

But we are concerned with the privileges which this civilization has taken away; and the particular ones with which we are concerned bear on his character and moral stature. Now this brick and cement foundation of life is a hard soil for these growths. Somebody will say morals are the job of parents. The better the parents are, the better the morals; the worse they are, the greater our problem. But the best of parents cannot keep him indoors all the time. And the world in the streets is a distorted and dangerous world, which the parents cannot make or unmake. So it becomes a job of public relations.

But there is more than that. The fine qualities of loyalty to the pack, competition with violent zeal yet without bitterness, the restraints that cover the rights of others—these are the spirit of sportsmanship. They are not so good on the pavements. For here the pack turns to the gang, where his superabundant vitality leads him to depredation. And here we make gangsters and feed jails.

And let no one tell you that crime is decreasing in the United States. Nor is that due to lack of vigilance on the part of public authorities. I recollect that during my administration we doubled the population of Federal jails. Crime increases despite all this repression. And with all the wave of beneficent prison reforms of the past ten years, and all the expensive attempt to make good men out of criminals, we have not decreased crime. The way to stop crime is to stop the manufacture of criminals.

And there is far more to our purpose than stopping crime at its source or to let off the boy's physical violence without getting into the police court. If there is such a thing as rights in the world, there are also rights that belong to pavement boys. There are, of course, the rights to proper homes, there are rights to education and health. But there are still other rights, and these other rights are where we come in. That is, the right to play games—the right to glimpse into the constructive joys—the right to develop an occupation fitted to his inclination and talents—and the right to develop his personality.

There is more to this than even exercise and morals. There is the job of stretching his vision of life. The priceless treasure of boyhood is his endless enthusiasm, his high store of idealism, his affections, and his hopes. When we preserve these, we have made men. We have made citizens, and we have made Americans. But the hard pavements do not reek with these things. . . .

... Over these years, the clubs and the parent organization have trained a staff of skill and devotion. Some of these clubs have as many as 5000[2] boys causing the premises to throb with their devices. Their total annual cost of operation is near $2,000,000, contributed by their own towns and cities. That is, about $10 per boy. And that $10 saves many hundred times as much to society. The boys pay dues of mostly 1 cent per month.[3]

In these clubs the pavement boy had opportunity for organization of the pack for its proper constructive joys, instead of the gang. Here they could find outlet for their superlative energy in play and the land of make-believe. These opportunities stretch all the way from checkers to sandlot baseball. There are gymnasiums and swimming pools. And here also they are given glimpses of the opportunities of a greater America. They are encouraged to music, to manufacture, to make and to construct. Their faculties and qualities are tested to find their occupational direction. They are given preliminary training in the arts and in the trades. And, above all, they are taught the spirit of sportsmanship, which is the second highest moral code in the world.

They are taught the rules of health—they are each examined and each repaired for his physical weaknesses. And the repair of boys to keep them physically fit is of the largest importance in their moral and spiritual development.

The police cases and juvenile delinquencies in the areas where these clubs work regularly show striking decreases. They have produced men of leadership in their communities. There are great editors, sculptors and actors who came from this boys' mill. And they have produced two players in major league baseball. The feet of thousands have been set on the road of American opportunity.

That is an experiment, but it is an experiment that has gone so far as to become an answer.

This movement is in no sense a competitor with the magnificent work of the Boy Scouts. There are in fact many troops in the clubs. They provide an entirely different set of influences.

I could stop at length to pay tribute to the men who have builded all this effort. They are legion. To none of them do we owe more than to Mr. W. E. Hall, for twenty-one years the President of this Association....

---

2. [*Editor's note*: In the original address as printed in *Addresses... 1933–1938*, Hoover said: "7000."]

3. [*Editor's note*: In the original address as printed in *Addresses... 1933–1938*, Hoover worded these lines differently: "Their annual cost is near $2,000,000 to supplement the boys' own payments; that is, about $10 per boy. And that $10 saves many hundred times as much to society." The earlier text had no reference to the boys' paying monthly dues.]

Now, as to the proposition of which I warned you. There are in fact two propositions. The first is to establish buildings and equipment for two or three million more boys. That means we must expand by ten times. That takes money, that takes devotion, and that takes service. It can be done, although we cannot do it all at once. Our second proposition is to find their skilled direction and to find their annual support. That is difficult but between good folks and community chests and the energies of the managers, that is kept up pretty well by the local communities where they are started. And upon this side, I want to mention the Union League Club of Chicago. This great men's club has adopted two boys' clubs. Every great social club in the United States would be a better place if it also had such adopted children.

The most difficult job is to find land and pay for buildings and equipment. As somebody said some four hundred years ago, "There's the rub." Over a term of years we need $15,000,000 for that job. We ought to start 100 new clubs in 50 cities during the next three years.

And what do I say for a peroration? But little. You picture that pavement boy entering the door of that house of constructive joy. The light of his face—the gleam of honest devilment in his eye—the feeling of trust and security in his heart.

And here is the sense of safety and gratitude which warms his mother's heart also.[4]

---

4. [*Editor's note*: The complete text of this address is printed in Herbert Hoover, *Addresses upon the American Road, 1933–1938* (New York: Charles Scribner's Sons, 1938), pp. 237–42.

The remainder of Hoover's memoir-essay (comprising about sixteen single-spaced pages in his 1955 page-proof set) is omitted. It consists of the verbatim texts and extended extracts of eight more Hoover speeches concerning the Boys Club movement. The speeches were delivered on April 29, 1940; June 5, 1941; May 7, 1942; May 6, 1943; May 4, 1944; June 6, 1945; June 24, 1954; and August 8, 1955. In the last-mentioned address, given shortly before Hoover composed this mini-memoir, he discussed the rising national problem of juvenile delinquency and hailed the Boys Clubs as "the greatest cure for delinquency in our country."

Readers interested in these speeches may find them in Herbert Hoover, *Further Addresses upon the American Road, 1938–1940* (New York: Charles Scribner's Sons, 1940), pp. 219–23; Herbert Hoover, *Addresses upon the American Road, 1940–1941* (New York: Charles Scribner's Sons, 1941), pp. 174–77; Herbert Hoover, *Addresses upon the American Road, 1941–1945* (New York: D. van Nostrand Company, Inc., 1946), pp. 375–77, 389–91, 407–9, 410–17; Herbert Hoover, *Addresses upon the American Road, 1950–1955* (Stanford, CA: Stanford University Press, 1955), pp. 171–74; Herbert Hoover, *Addresses upon the American Road, 1955–1960* (Caldwell, ID: The Caxton Printers, Ltd., 1961), pp. 333–35.]

"My Crusade against Collectivism"

December 23, 1955

Although Hoover had written literally hundreds of pages about his "crusade against collectivism" by 1955 (including the twice-revised manuscript printed as part III of this book), he nevertheless felt compelled to return to the subject that autumn. He did so by drafting a brand new essay titled "My Crusade against Collectivism." When it came back to him from the printer in page-proof form on December 23, it comprised twenty-nine printed pages.

But there was a difference. In the lengthy memoir reproduced in part III, Hoover recounted his "crusade against collectivism in American life" after March 4, 1933—that is, after he left the presidency. In the document before you, he essentially began his story in the year 1919 and ended it with his departure from the White House in early 1933. In this respect, it resembles Document 3, above, which traces the origins of Hoover's crusade for American child welfare to the same year: 1919.

Hoover never indicated where, precisely, he planned to incorporate "My Crusade against Collectivism" into his elaborate memoirs. But it may best be read as a prologue to part III of the present volume.

The page-proof text reproduced here is in the Herbert Hoover Papers, Box 94, Hoover Institution Archives.

Introduction

My opposition to totalitarianism, whether dictator, monarch, oligarchy, Communist, Socialist or Fascist, began long before the New Deal and the Fair Deal. Those American manifestations were merely attempts to mix these old European shapes into American freedoms.

In practicing my profession prior to the First World War, I lived in many of the countries of Asia, Europe, Australia and Latin America. I was not a tourist. I worked with their people and I had to deal with their governments.

During the Czarist regime I had for some years a part in the administration of industrial enterprises in Russia employing over 150,000 men. They brought me not only in contact with Czarist officials but also with political exiles in Siberia.

In China and Japan I lived under complete governmental absolutism, but with a business and industrial economy based generally on free enterprise, and an agricultural economy based on varying degrees of landlordism.

In Australia I had to deal with governments tainted with Socialism and had to endure such incompetently conducted government enterprises as their railways.

In South Africa I had to deal with business tyranny over helpless natives.

All over Europe, including Britain, where there were great areas of freedom with its protections, there were frozen class stratifications, which greatly impeded the equal opportunity of men to rise in the social mass.

By necessity I was interested in the governmental and ideological phenomena in the work. During eighteen years of such occupation, I was compelled to take long journeys by ship, by rail and by pack train. I filled literally months of idle hours of travel in reading. In the course of time I had digested Engels, Karl Marx, Mills,[1] Herbert Spencer, John Morley, Adam Smith, Voltaire and even Plato as well as many others.

My opposition to and acute experience with Socialism and Communism (then called Bolshevism) began after the First World War when I was appointed in 1918 Director of Relief and Rehabilitation of Europe. The Socialists of Europe were of two breeds. Those who advocated a creeping Socialism under legal procedures, and those who advocated its imposition by violence—Communism. History has fully demonstrated that creeping Socialism reaches a point where it undermines private enterprise, and on this recession of the opposition becomes the bordering [boarding–*ed.*][2] ladder to Communist seizure.

---

1. [*Editor's note*: Presumably John Stuart Mill.]
2. [*Editor's note*: In his handwritten first draft, Hoover wrote: "bording." His typist interpreted this as "bordering."

Hoover expressed a similar thought in his address at the Republican national convention in 1948. See, in this volume, p. 270.]

CHAPTER 1

Socialism and Communism

In my official capacity [in Europe in 1918–19–*ed.*] I had to deal with famine, the breakdown of coal supplies and railway transportation, and to provide advisors on government economics and finance to the host of new democracies which emerged from the ruins of the old empires.

The Communists and Socialists, under their Internationale prior to the war, had accomplished some infiltration in continental countries.

The Communist Revolution had Socialism in Russia in 1917 under Lenin's leadership with all of its hideous and bloody deeds. With the coming of the Russian revolution, the Communists' wing of Socialism was equipped with the gold reserve of Russia. Immediately after the Armistice, they began using this money to stimulate their previous cells into motion, and for this purpose they spread agents over the continent.

With nations prostrated and frustrated from defeat and starvation, the scene was fertile for action. Their conspiracies in Germany and their gorgeous promises of Utopia succeeded in their seizure of the municipal governments of Hamburg, Stettin and Munich.

These catastrophes were indeed partly to be blamed upon the British who had maintained the food blockade on Germany four and one half months after the Armistice.[1] One of the reasons for Germany's surrender were [*sic–ed.*] hunger and the consequent breakdown of morale. Food was promised by the Armistice agreement, and I had piled up hundreds of thousands of tons of it in continental ports, while we Americans were fighting to get the British to take down their blockade. The whole matter came to a head when the British General commanding their occupation troops came to Prime Minister Lloyd George in Paris

---

1. *The Blockade of Germany after the Armistice, 1918–1919,* Suda Bane and Ralph Lutz, [eds.,] Stanford University Press, 1942.

with the alarm that not only were German children starving and his troops losing morale witnessing their disintegration, but that the whole feeble government of Germany was in danger of immediate collapse. Lloyd George sought to blame it on me for not sending in food. I gave him an attack on British and French policies, which he took amiably and made many notes. With that flexibility characteristic of him, he asked that I appear before the Supreme Council and say it over again with emphasis. I did so. I give Lloyd George's statement from the record, because it indicates the seriousness of the Communist threat at the time. It also represents Lloyd George's agility in finding the French to blame, although the blockade was being enforced at that very moment by the British Fleet.[2]

... He wished to urge with all his might that steps should at once be taken to revictual Germany. The honour of the Allies was involved. Under the terms of the armistice the Allies did imply that they meant to let food into Germany. The Germans had accepted our armistice conditions, which were sufficiently severe, and they had complied with the majority of those conditions. But so far, not a single ton of food had been sent into Germany. The fishing fleet had even been prevented from going out to catch a few herrings. The Allies were now on top, but the memories of starvation might one day turn against them. The Germans were being allowed to starve whilst at the same time hundreds of thousands of tons of foods were lying at Rotterdam, waiting to be taken up the waterways into Germany. These incidents constituted far more formidable weapons for use against the Allies than any of the armaments it was sought to limit. The Allies were sowing hatred for the future: they were piling up agony, not for the Germans but for themselves. The British troops were indignant about our refusal to revictual Germany. General Plumer had said that he could not be responsible for his troops if children were allowed to wander about the streets, half starving. The British soldiers would not stand that, they were beginning to make complaints, and the most urgent demands were being received from them. Furthermore, British Officers who had been in Germany said that Bolshevism was being created, and the determining factor was going to be food. As long as the people were starving they would listen to the arguments of the Spartacists, and the Allies by their action were simply encouraging elements of disruption and anarchism. It was like stirring up an influenza puddle, just next door to one's self.

---

2. *Years of Adventure.* [*Editor's note*: Hoover's reference here is to the first published volume of his *Memoirs*, subtitled *Years of Adventure, 1874–1920* (New York: The Macmillan Company, 1951), pp. 343–44. Hoover was quoting the official record of a meeting of the Supreme War Council at the Paris peace conference on March 8, 1919. The quoted passage is reproduced in Bane and Lutz, eds., *Blockade of Germany*, pp. 208–9, 216, 218.]

The condition of Russia was well known, and it might be possible to look on at a muddle which had there been created. But, now, if Germany went, and Spain: who would feel safe? As long as order was maintained in Germany, a breakwater would exist between the countries of the Allies and the waters of Revolution beyond. But once that breakwater was swept away, he could not speak for France, but trembled for his own country. The situation was particularly serious in Munich. Bavaria, which once had been thought to represent the most solid and conservative part of Germany, had already gone. He was there that afternoon to reinforce the appeal which had come to him from the men who had helped the Allies to conquer the Germans, the soldiers, who said that they refused to continue to occupy a territory in order to maintain the population in a state of starvation. Meanwhile the Conference continued to haggle. Six weeks ago the same arguments about gold and foreign securities had been raised, and it had then been decided that Germany should be given food. He begged the Conference to reaffirm that decision in the most unequivocal terms, unless this people were fed, if as a result of a process of starvation enforced by the Allies, the people of Germany were allowed to run riot, a state of revolution among the working classes of all countries would ensue with which it would be impossible to cope. . . . On January 13th exactly the same speeches had been made by M. Klotz [the French Minister of Finance] and he had then been overruled by the Supreme War Council. M. Klotz should . . . submit to the decisions then given by the Supreme War Council. [. . .–ed.]

Nothing had, however, been done during those two months, and now the question had been brought up for discussion with all the old arguments. He would not have raised the matter, but for the fact that during the past two months, in spite of the decision reached by the Supreme War Council in January last, obstacles had continually been put in [Mr. Hoover's] way, with the result that nothing had been done. *He appealed to M. Clemenceau to put a stop to these obstructive tactics, otherwise M. Klotz would rank with Lenin and Trotsky among those who had spread Bolshevism in Europe.*[3]

Within forty-eight hours after getting permission, I had moved huge quantities of food into the hands of the new democratic government of Germany, and with this weapon they were able to stop the march of Communism.

The Communists succeeded in a revolution in Hungary in March, 1919, placing a Lenin-indoctrinated Communist, Bela Kuhn,[4] as dictator. All of the

---

3. [*Editor's note*: Italics added by Hoover.]
4. [*Editor's note*: Usually spelled Bela Kun.]

bloody methods of Lenin were repeated. This regime was thrown out by a counter-revolution of the Trades Unions who had the promise of food supplies. During this period my interest in the whole Communist movement was necessarily stimulated. At this time I secured all the writings of Lenin and other Communist leaders which were available. I now became fully acquainted with the utter lack of integrity, humanity and international unreliability of Moscow.

During the peace negotiations President Wilson frequently called upon me for advice on Russian matters because my men were distributed all along the borders of the Communist area and thus as well informed as it was possible to be, and because of my familiarity with Russia during the Czarist regime.

I give some extracts from memoranda furnished to him at various times. On March 28, 1919, in the face of the Allies urging America to join the French and British military activities against the Communists, he asked for a comprehensive statement covering the whole Communist question. It is too long for reproduction here, but some sentences will indicate the tenor:

> ... These views at least have the merit of being an analysis of information and thought gleaned from my own experience and the independent sources which I now have over the whole of Europe, through our widespread relief organization.
>
> It simply cannot be denied that this swinging of the pendulum from the tyranny of the extreme right to the tyranny of the extreme left is based on a foundation of real grievance. . . . The suffering of their common people is but a commonplace to every social student. . . . The famine [. . .–ed.] has further illuminated [emphasized–ed.] the gulf. [. . .–ed.]
>
> It is not necessary for any American to debate the utter foolishness of these economic tenets. . . .
>
> Politically, the Bolsheviki most certainly represent a minority in every country where they are in control, and as such they constitute a tyranny that is the negation of democracy. . . . The Bolshevik has resorted to terror, bloodshed and murder to a degree long since abandoned even amongst reactionary tyrannies. [Lenin][5] has even to a greater degree relied upon criminal instinct to support his doctrines than even autocracy did.
>
> ... An important point to be examined ... is[6] ... whether the Bolshevik centers now stirred by great emotional hopes will not at once[7] undertake large

---

5. [*Editor's note*: Here Hoover, in 1955, inserted the word "Lenin" in brackets in place of the word "He." In the quoted text, "He" referred to "the Bolshevik" as an archetype.]

6. [*Editor's note*: Here Hoover again altered his quoted text. The original sentence began: "There remains in my mind one more point to be examined, that is as to whether . . . ."]

7. [*Editor's note*: In 1955 Hoover added the words "at once." They do not appear here in his 1919 letter.]

military crusades in an attempt to impose their doctrines on other defenseless people . . . [and it seems–*ed.*] to me [that–*ed.*] the whole treatment of the problem must resolve on this [one–*ed.*] question. If this spirit is inherent in their doctrine, it appears to me that we must . . . be prepared to fight, (sooner or later).[8] . . . If this is not the case, (immediately),[9] then it appears to me that . . . we should not involve ourselves in what may be a ten year military entanglement in Europe. The American people cannot say that we are going to insist that any given population must work out its internal social problems according to our particular concepts.[10] . . . In [the–*ed.*] event, I have the most serious doubt that outside forces entering upon such an enterprise can do other than infinite harm, for any great wave of emotion must ferment and spread under repression . . . (and we could awaken a stupendous materialism.)[11]

. . . We also have to contemplate what would actually happen if we undertook military intervention. . . . We should probably be involved in years of police duty, and our first act would probably in the nature of things make us a party to re-establishing the (old regime).[12] . . . This is against our fundamental national spirit. . . . The problem[13] also requires consideration as to whether or not our people at home, on . . . enlightenment as to the social wrongs[14] . . . in these countries, would stand for our providing military forces for such action.[15]

. . . [By joining the Allies][16] we become . . . one of four mandatories, each with a different political and social outlook. . . . Furthermore, in our present engagements with France, England and Italy, we become a junior in this partnership of four. It is therefore inevitable that in these matters, where our views and principles are at variance with the European Allies, we would find ourselves subordinated and even committed to policies against our convictions. . . .

. . . [Nor can we][17] even remotely recognize this murderous tyranny without stimulating actionist radicalism in every country in Europe and without transgressing on every National ideal on our own.[18]

---

8. [*Editor's note*: Hoover added the parenthetical expression "(sooner or later)" in 1955. It does not appear in his 1919 letter.]

9. [*Editor's note*: Hoover added this word, which is not in the quoted text.]

10. [*Editor's note*: In his 1919 letter, Hoover had written: "conception of democracy."]

11. [*Editor's note*: This parenthetical phrase does not appear in Hoover's quoted text.]

12. [*Editor's note*: In the quoted document Hoover had written: "reactionary classes."]

13. [*Editor's note*: In the quoted text: "It." The words "The problem" do not appear.]

14. [*Editor's note*: Here Hoover omitted the words "of the lower classes."]

15. [*Editor's note*: In the original letter Hoover had written: "would stand for our providing power by which such reactionaries held their position."]

16. [*Editor's note*: Parenthetical phrase added by Hoover.]

17. [*Editor's note*: Parenthetical phrase added by Hoover.]

18. [*Editor's note*: Hoover's letter (memorandum) to President Wilson, March 28, 1919, quoted here, is printed in Arthur S. Link et al., eds., *The Papers of Woodrow Wilson*, vol. 56 (Princeton, NJ:

In a further memorandum at the request of the President, I said on April 11, 1919:

I have the feeling that revolution in Europe is by no means over. The social wrongs in these countries are far from solution and the tempest must blow itself out, probably with enormous violence. Our people are not prepared for us to undertake the military policing of Europe while it boils out its social wrongs. I have no doubt that if we could undertake to police the world and had the wisdom of statesmanship to see its gradual social evolution, that we would be making a great contribution to civilization, but I am certain that the American people are not prepared for any such a measure and I am also sure that if we remain in Europe with military force, tied in an alliance which we have never undertaken, we should be forced into this storm of repression of revolution, and forced in under terms of co-ordination with other people that would make our independence of action wholly impossible.[19]

In reply to a press request on April 25, 1919, I included some of the material in the previous memorandum and said in part:

... The prime objective of the United States in undertaking the fight against famine in Europe is to save the lives of starving people.

The secondary object, however, and of hardly less importance, was to defeat anarchy, which is the handmaiden of Hunger. The United States Food Administration in Europe therefore necessarily has to take into account all of the political and social currents that are in motion in each country where it operates. . . .

Practically the whole territory involved in the war from the old western front is in a state of political and social revolution—330,000,000 people. . . . Out of four great States, eighteen new States have already emerged. In none of them is there visible scarcely a single political leader of six months' experience.[20] . . .

These are not merely political revolutions, as a reaction from failure of their politicians in war, they are infinitely deeper seated. . . . The basis of these revolutions, while superficially political, is basically economic. Populations engulfed in starvation and misery are easily misled. . . .

Princeton University Press, 1987), pp. 375–78. I have found no evidence that the President asked Hoover for this statement of views.]

19. [*Editor's note*: Hoover to Woodrow Wilson, April 11, 1919, printed in Arthur S. Link et al., eds., *The Papers of Woodrow Wilson*, vol. 57 (Princeton, NJ: Princeton University Press, 1987), pp. 271–74. I have found no evidence that President Wilson solicited this letter.]

20. [*Editor's note*: In the original (1919) text: "of six months ago."]

Bolshevism is a theory or practice of Socialism by which economic equality is to be obtained by destruction of the organization and processes of production and distribution in order that all men may restart the race level and then be held level during the race. . . . It is hardly necessary for any American to debate the utter foolishness of these economic tenets. . . .[21]

Confronted with the breakdown in production and distribution, Lenin had begun his "new-economic policy," which was apparently a turn to a free economy.[22] During this period, until Lenin's death in . . . [1924–ed.] and the rise of Stalin, I expressed great hopes that the Communist revolution was emerging into some sort of sanity, but it soon proved an illusion.

In 1922 [1921–ed.], there was a great famine in South Russia. A representative of the Communist government appealed to me to organize help for them. I was not only moved by the appeal of starving people but also felt that generous action on our part might further the Lenin economic retreat. I deal with this matter in that part of the memoirs of the Crusade against Famine,[23] but I may mention here that we expended some $75,000,000, and on the statement of the Russians themselves saved some five million lives. The Communist Ministry sent me a great scroll expressing gratitude. But three years after the completion of this work the Communists asserted that our American administrators had been spies, and they arrested, imprisoned or exiled many Russians whom we had employed in the distribution of relief. I denounced their action with some vigor but have no belief it did any good.

President Wilson had established the policy of adamant opposition to the recognition of Russia. The formal statement of his Secretary of State was in part:

. . . The Bolsheviki . . . an inconsiderable minority of the people, by force and cunning seized the powers and machinery of Government [from the democratic state] and have continued to use them with savage oppression. . . . The responsible statesmen . . . have declared . . . the very existence of Bolshevism

---

21. [*Editor's note*: Hoover statement prepared for the press, April 25, 1919, printed in Francis William O'Brien, ed., *Two Peacemakers in Paris: The Hoover-Wilson Post-Armistice Letters, 1918–1920* (College Station: Texas A& M University Press, 1978), pp. 135–41.]

22. [*Editor's note*: Lenin's New Economic Policy was launched in 1921.]

23. [*Editor's note*: See Herbert Hoover, *An American Epic*, vol. III: *Famine in Forty-five Nations: The Battle on the Front Lines, 1914–1923* (Chicago: Henry Regnery Company, 1961), pp. 423–521. Two more recent and excellent accounts are Benjamin M. Weissman, *Herbert Hoover and Famine Relief to Soviet Russia, 1921–23* (Stanford, CA: Hoover Institution Press, 1974), and Bertrand M. Patenaude, *The Big Show in Bololand: The American Relief Expedition to Soviet Russia in the Famine of 1921* (Stanford, CA: Stanford University Press, 2002).]

... depends ... upon the occurrence of revolution in all other great nations, including the United States. ... The Third Internationale, ... heavily subsidized by the Bolshevist Government from the public revenues of Russia, has for its openly avowed aim the promotion of Bolshevist revolutions throughout the world. ... There can be no mutual confidence ... if pledges are to be given ... with cynical repudiation ... already in the mind of one of the parties. We cannot recognize ... a Government which is determined and bound to conspire against our institutions. ... .[24]

Continuously over 16 years four Presidents and six Secretaries of State were adamant against the recognition of Russia for these continuing reasons and the determination not to establish the moral position of this conspiracy among nations. Our philosophy was that while we would undertake no violence to an evil neighbor, we would not give him a color of respectability in the community by inviting him into our homes.

When I became secretary of commerce, there was immediate pressure from some of the business world for recognition of Communist Russia and the resumption of trade. It also had the support of many intellectuals.

As secretary of commerce, I merely pointed out that there were neither consequential exports possible from Russia nor purchasing power for our goods; and I had to point it out periodically. A typical statement was:

> ... As a matter of trade, the first thing to be determined about Russia is if and when they change their economic system. If they so change its basis as to accept the rights of private property, freedom of labor, provide for the safety of human life, and so forth, there is hope of their recovery ... in production and the upbuilding of trade.
>
> Nothing is more important to the whole commercial world than the recovery of productivity in Russia. However, without a fundamental change in their whole economic system, there will be no consequential trade or production and no stoppage of continuous degeneration.[25]

---

24. [*Editor's note*: Hoover was quoting Secretary of State Bainbridge Colby's diplomatic note of August 10, 1920, on U.S. foreign policy toward Soviet Russia and Poland. Hoover's transcription contained a number of errors, which have been corrected. The quotation now conforms to Colby's note as printed in the *New York Times*, August 11, 1920, pp. 1–2.]

25. [*Editor's note*: Hoover statement on trade with Soviet Russia, March 25, 1921, entry no. 138-A, Public Statements File, Herbert Hoover Papers, Herbert Hoover Presidential Library, West Branch, Iowa. Hoover's statement was quoted in the *New York Times*, March 26, 1921, pp. 1–2.]

CHAPTER 2

Fascism

Mussolini brought this form of collectivism to Italy in 1922. He had invented nothing new. Its economic system was simply an expansion of the methods used to some extent by all governments in World War I, including our own. It comprised government control of labor, production, distribution, prices, and income with some latitudes of initiative, private enterprise and property ownership. The government was of the pattern of all dictatorships under which there were no constitutions, protection or individual rights.

From an economic point of view it bore no relation to Marxian socialism for the government itself conducted little actual production and distribution. They did continue operation of the railways by the government which had been long established and the advance in Italian civilization that I could observe was that Mussolini ran the trains on time and swept out the cars.

(Later in this narrative I recount from personal observation the sweep of Fascism over most of Europe.)[1]

---

1. [*Editor's note*: See chapter 8 in this volume and Hoover's similar account in George H. Nash, ed., *Freedom Betrayed: Herbert Hoover's Secret History of the Second World War and Its Aftermath* (Stanford CA: Hoover Institution Press, 2011), pp. 55–105.]

CHAPTER 3

American Collectivism in World War I

During World War I we of necessity adopted pieces of what later became known as Fascism, as we partially adopted government control of production, distribution and prices. We touched on Socialism by government operation of railways, some ships and other minor enterprises.

In the Food Administration[1] I dissolved most of these activities within sixty days after the Armistice, some activities continuing a few months further to comply with contracts.

President Wilson, in March 1919, sent me a bundle of telegrams and letters from officials, manufacturers, business houses, farm organizations and others urging the continuation of certain production, distribution and price controls, requesting my views. They enjoyed guaranteed prices and apportioned production better than competition. I drafted a telegram for him directing their immediate dissolution which he warmly approved.

But some of these activities on the socialist fringe lingered on, particularly the government operation of railways and ships. I made many speeches in 1920 and 1921 urging the government to get out of these fields and ultimately the railways and ships were returned to private enterprise. But even with the Republican Administration some government business competitive with private enterprise continued on. These agencies had been set up to perform a war task; had completed their task, but in the meantime had built up a bureaucracy anxious to hold its jobs and it was supported by a pressure group which benefited from it. The classical case was a Mississippi barge concern which held on for 33 years with the aid of Chamber of Commerce type of pressure groups and lost money nearly every year. A special committee of the

---

1. [*Editor's note*: Hoover served in President Woodrow Wilson's administration as head of the U.S. Food Administration (a wartime agency) from 1917 to 1919.]

House of Representatives in 1933 made an exhaustive investigation and found several minor government business enterprises still hanging on 14 years after the war was over.

During the economic emergency of the Great Depression, created by the breakdown of the credit structure and the European collapse in purchasing our commodities, I was compelled to adopt some such direct government action and they, too, lived on and on in succeeding administrations long after their task was completed.

As President I had to meet the urge of socialists for government operation of electrical power. Here arose a most difficult problem because conservation of our water resources required the building of great dams for the multiple purpose of flood control, irrigation and navigation. They also created electrical power. The "liberal" urge was for Federal distribution of the power in competition with private enterprise. I set up certain principles in connection with the Hoover Dam on the Colorado which I hoped would clear the issue for all future cases. In that case the Government sold the power at the Dam to private utilities and the municipalities on a contract for 50 years, which would repay the Federal investment with interest during that period. This did not satisfy the socialists and I had to veto legislation creating such enterprises without this provision. This safeguard was abandoned under later administrations because of socialistic pressures and the Government got deep in [the–ed.] competitive power business.

The American System

It is unnecessary for me to quote here from the multitude of statements and addresses which I have made over the years in exposition of what I believed the governmental economy or social structure of the American people should be. Any researcher will find they are true to 19th century liberalism—a word now distorted to include various colors of collectivism. It can be simply stated without ideological verbiage that our way of life is founded upon spiritual and moral rights of man which are the gift of the Creator, not of governments. Ours is a constitutional expression of these rights. It is a representative government of laws—not of men. Our economic system is founded on private enterprise and initiative regulated to prevent monopolies and unfair competition. The Government should only intervene where the people cannot do it for themselves.

And those aids by government include such matters as education, care of the aged, care of the sick, prevention of contagions, conservation of natural resources and punishment of crime.

CHAPTER 5

Collectivism Comes to America

The character of the Roosevelt New Deal as a mixture of Socialism and Fascism into American freedom unfolded itself during the 1932 campaign. My first comprehensive attack upon it was made in an address on October 31st in New York City:[1]

> This campaign is more than a contest between two men. It is more than a contest between two parties. It is a contest between two philosophies of government.
>
> We are told by the opposition that we must have a change, that we must have a new deal. It is not the change that comes from normal development of national life to which I object, but the proposal to alter the whole foundations of our national life which have been builded through generations of testing and struggle, and of the principles upon which we have builded the nation. The expressions our opponents use must refer to important changes in our economic and social system and our system of government, otherwise they are nothing but vacuous words. . . .
>
> This question is the basis upon which our opponents are appealing to the people in their fears and distress. They are proposing changes and so-called new deals which would destroy the very foundations of our American system.
>
> Our people should consider the primary facts before they come to the judgment—not merely through political agitation, the glitter of promise, and the discouragement of temporary hardships[2] . . . which radically affect

---

1. [Herbert Hoover,] *Addresses upon the American Road, 1933–1938* [New York: Charles Scribner's Sons, 1938], pp. 1–19. [*Editor's note*: Hoover frequently quoted from and alluded to this address in later years. He considered it prophetic.]

2. [*Editor's note*: Here Hoover omitted the phrase "—whether they will support changes."]

the whole system which has been builded up by a hundred and fifty years of the toil of our fathers. . . .

Our economic system has received abnormal shocks during the last three years, which temporarily dislocated its normal functioning. These shocks have in a large sense come from without our borders, but I say to you that our system of government has enabled us to take such strong action as to prevent the disaster which would otherwise have come to our Nation. It has enabled us further to develop measures and programs which are now demonstrating their ability to bring about restoration and progress.

. . . We can find what our opponents would do after searching the record of their appeals to discontent, group and sectional interest. We must search for them in the legislative acts which they sponsored. . . .

And we must look still further than this as to what revolutionary changes have been proposed by the candidates themselves.

We must look into the type of leaders [. . .–ed.] whose philosophies have been well known all their lives. [. . .–ed.] I can respect the sincerity of these men in their desire to change our form of government and our social and economic system, though I shall do my best tonight to prove they are wrong. . . .

I may say at once that the changes proposed . . . are of the most profound.[3] . . .

Let us pause for a moment and examine the American system of government, of social and economic life, which it is now proposed that we should alter. Our system is the product of our race and of our experience in building a nation to heights unparalleled in the whole history of the world. It is a system peculiar to the American people. It differs essentially from all others in the world. It is an American system.

It is founded on the conception that only through ordered liberty, through freedom to the individual, and equal opportunity to the individual will his initiative and enterprise be summoned to spur the march of progress.

It is by the maintenance of equality of opportunity and therefore of a society absolutely fluid in freedom of the movement of its human particles that our individualism departs from the individualism of Europe. We resent class distinction because there can be no rise for the individual through the frozen strata of classes and no stratification of classes can take place in a mass livened by the free rise of its particles. Thus in our ideals the able and ambitious are able to rise constantly from the bottom to leadership in the community.

---

3. [*Editor's note*: Here Hoover omitted the words "and penetrating character. If they are brought about this will not be the America which we have known in the past."]

This freedom of the individual creates of itself the necessity and the cheerful willingness of men to act co-operatively in a thousand ways. . . . It permits such voluntary co-operations to be dissolved as soon as they have served their purpose. . . .

There has thus grown within us, to gigantic importance, a new conception. That is, this voluntary co-operation within the community. Co-operation to perfect the social organizations; co-operation for the care of those in distress; co-operation for the advancement of knowledge, of scientific research, of education; for co-operative action in the advancement of many phases of economic life. This is self-government by the people outside of Government; it is the most powerful development of individual freedom . . . that has taken place in the century and a half since our fundamental institutions were founded.

. . . The greatest function of government is to build up that co-operation, and its most resolute action should be to deny the extension of bureaucracy. We have developed great agencies of co-operation by the assistance of the Government which promote and protect the interests of individuals. . . . The Federal Reserve System, in its strengthening and support of the smaller banks; the Farm Board, in its strengthening and support of the farm co-operatives; the Home Loan banks, in the mobilizing of building and loan associations and savings banks; the Federal land banks, in giving independence and strength to land mortgage associations; the great mobilization of relief to distress, the mobilization of business and industry in measures of recovery, and a score of other activities are not socialism—they are the essence of protection to the development of free men.

The primary conception of this whole American system is not the regimentation of men but the co-operation of free men. . . .

. . . The centralization of government will undermine responsibilities and will destroy the system.

Our Government differs from all previous conceptions, not only in this decentralization, but also in the separation of functions between the legislative, executive, and judicial arms of government, in which the independence of the judicial arm is the keystone of the whole structure.

It is founded on a conception that in times of emergency, when forces are running beyond control of individuals or . . . co-operative action, . . . then the great reserve powers of the Federal Government shall be brought into action to protect the community. But when these forces have ceased there must be a return of . . . individual responsibility.

The implacable march of scientific discovery with its train of new inventions presents every year new problems to government and new problems to the social order. Questions often arise whether, in the face of the growth of these new and gigantic tools, democracy can remain master in its own house, can preserve the fundamentals of our American system. I contend that it can; and I contend that this American system of ours has demonstrated its validity and superiority over any system yet invented by [the–*ed.*] human mind.

It has demonstrated it in the face of the greatest test of our history—that is the emergency which we have faced in the last three years.

When the political and economic weakness of many nations of Europe, the result of the World War and its aftermath, finally culminated in collapse of their institutions, the delicate adjustments of our economic and social life received a shock unparalleled in our history....

Yet these forces were overcome....

In spite of all these obstructions we did succeed. Our form of government did prove itself equal to the task. We saved this Nation from a quarter of a century of chaos and degeneration, and we preserved the savings, the insurance policies, gave a fighting chance to men to hold their homes. We saved the integrity of our Government and the honesty of the American dollar. And we installed measures which today are bringing back recovery. Employment, agriculture, business—all of these show the steady, if slow, healing of our enormous wound.

... To enter upon a series of deep changes to embark upon this inchoate new deal which has been propounded in this campaign would be to undermine and destroy our American system.

Before we enter upon such courses, I would like you to consider what the results of this American system have been during the last thirty years—that is, one single generation....

Now, if we look back over the last generation we find that the number of our families and, therefore, our homes, has increased from sixteen to twenty-five million, or 62 per cent. In that time we have builded for them 15,000,000 new and better homes. We have equipped 20,000,000 homes with electricity; thereby we have lifted infinite drudgery from women and men. The barriers of time and space have been swept away. Life has been made freer, the intellectual vision of every individual has been expanded by the installation of 20,000,000 telephones, 12,000,000 radios, and the service of 20,000,000 automobiles. Our cities have been made magnificent with beautiful buildings, parks, and playgrounds. Our countryside has been knit together with splendid roads. We have increased by twelve times the use of electrical power and thereby taken sweat from the backs of men. In this broad sweep real wages and purchasing power of men and women have steadily increased. New comforts have steadily come to them. The hours of labor have decreased, the 12-hour day has disappeared, even the 9-hour day has almost gone. We are now advancing the 5-day week. The portals of opportunity to our children have ever widened. While our population grew by but 62 per cent, we have increased the number of children in high schools by 700 per cent, those in institutions of higher learning by 300 per cent. With all our spending, we multiplied by six times the savings in our banks and in our building and loan associations. We multiplied by 1,200 per cent the amount of our life insurance. With the enlargement of our leisure we have come to a fuller life; we gained new visions of hope, we more nearly realize our national aspirations and give increasing scope to the creative power of every individual and expansion of every man's mind.

Our people in these thirty years grew in the sense of social responsibility. There is profound progress in the relation of the employer and employed. We have more nearly met with a full hand the most sacred obligation of man, that is, the responsibility of a man to his neighbor. Support to our schools, hospitals, and institutions for the care of the afflicted surpassed in totals of billions the proportionate service in any period of history in any nation in the world.

Three years ago there came a break in this progress. A break of the same type we have met fifteen times in a century and yet we have overcome them. But eighteen months later came a further blow by shocks transmitted to us by the earthquakes of the collapse in nations throughout the world as the aftermath of the World War. . . . I do not seek to minimize the depth of it. We may thank God that in view of this storm 30,000,000 still have their jobs; yet this must not distract our thoughts from the suffering of the other 10,000,000.

. . . This thirty years of incomparable improvement in the scale of living, the advance of comfort and intellectual life, inspiration and ideals did not arise without right principles animating the American system which produced them. Shall that system be discarded because vote-seeking men appeal to distress and say that the machinery is all wrong and that it must be abandoned or tampered with? Is it not more sensible to realize the simple fact that some extraordinary force has been thrown into the mechanism, temporarily deranging its operation? Is it not wiser to believe that the difficulty is not with the principles upon which our American system is founded and designed through all these generations of inheritance? Should not our purpose be to restore the normal working of that system which has brought to us such immeasurable benefits, and not destroy it?

[. . .–ed.] I propose to analyze a few of the proposals of our opponents in their relation to these fundamentals.

First: A proposal of our opponents which would break down the American system is the expansion of Government expenditure by yielding to sectional and group raids on the Public Treasury. The extension of Government expenditures beyond the minimum limit necessary to conduct the proper functions of the Government enslaves men to work for the Government. . . .

[. . .–*ed.*] I only need recall to you that the Democratic House of Representatives passed bills in the last session that would have increased our expenditures by $3,500,000,000, or 87 per cent. Expressed in days' labor, this would have meant the conscription of sixteen days' additional work from every citizen for the Government. This I stopped. [Furthermore,–*ed.*] they refused to accept recommendations from the Administration in respect to [. . .–*ed.*] reductions in [. . .–*ed.*] expenditures, and finally they forced upon us increasing expenditure. [. . .–*ed.*] In spite of this, the ordinary expenses of the Government have been reduced. . . . Those who pay are [. . .–*ed.*] the man who works at the bench, the desk, and on the farm. [. . .–*ed.*]

Second: Another proposal of our opponents which would destroy the American system is[. . .–*ed.*] inflation of the currency. The bill which passed the last session of the Democratic House called upon the Treasury of the United States to issue $2,300,000,000 in paper currency that would be unconvertible into solid values. Call it what you will, greenbacks or fiat money. It was that nightmare which overhung our own country for years after the Civil War. . . .

Third: In the last session the Congress, under the personal leadership of the Democratic Vice-Presidential candidate, and their allies in the Senate, enacted a law to extend the Government into [the–*ed.*] personal banking business. This I was compelled to veto, out of fidelity to the whole American system of life and government. . . .

Fourth: Another proposal of our opponents which would wholly alter our American system of life is to reduce the protective tariff to a competitive tariff for revenue. The protective tariff . . . has become gradually embedded into our economic life since the first protective tariff act passed by the American Congress under the Administration of George Washington. . . .

Fifth: Another proposal is that the Government go into the power business. Three years ago, in view of the extension of the use of transmission of power over State borders and the difficulties of State regulatory bodies in the face of this interstate action, I recommended to the Congress that such interstate power should be placed under regulation by the Federal Government in co-operation with the state authorities.

That recommendation was in accord with the principles . . . to provide regulation where public interest had developed in tools of industry which was beyond control and regulation of the States.

I succeeded in creating an independent Power Commission to handle such matters, but this Democratic House declined to approve the further powers to this commission necessary for such regulation.

I have stated unceasingly that I am opposed to the Federal Government going into the power business. I have insisted upon rigid regulation. The Democratic candidate has declared . . . to put the Federal Government into the power business. He is being actively supported [by–ed.] . . . [those] who are pledged to Federal operation of electrical power.

[. . .–ed.] In fact thirty-one Democratic Senators, being all except three, voted to override that veto. In that bill was the flat issue of the Federal Government permanently in competition in competitive business. I vetoed it because of principle and not because it was especially the power business. In that veto I stated . . . [In vetoing one of these bills], I said:

"There are national emergencies which require that the Government should temporarily enter the field of business but that they must be emergency actions and in matters where the cost of the project is secondary to much higher consideration. There are many localities where the Federal Government is justified in the construction of great dams and reservoirs, where navigation, flood control, reclamation, or stream regulation are of dominant importance, and where they are beyond the capacity or purpose of private or local government capital to construct. In these cases, power is often a by-product and should be disposed of by contract or lease. But for the Federal Government to deliberately go out to build up and expand such an occasion to the major purpose of a power and manufacturing business is to break down the initiative and enterprise of the American people. . . . It is the negation of the ideals upon which our civilization has been based.

"This bill raises one of the important issues confronting our people. That is squarely the issue of Federal Government ownership and operation of power and manufacturing business not as a minor byproduct but as a major purpose. Involved in this question is the agitation against the conduct of the power industry. . . . The remedy for abuses in the conduct of that industry lies in regulation and not by the Federal Government entering upon the business. . . . I have recommended to the Congress on various occasions that action should be taken to establish Federal regulation of interstate power in co-operation with State authorities. This bill would launch the Federal Government upon a policy of ownership of power utilities . . . instead of by the proper Government function of regulation for the protection of all the people. I hesitate to contemplate the future of our institutions, of our Government, and of our country, if the preoccupation of its officials is to be no longer the promotion of justice and equal opportunity but is to be devoted to barter in the markets. That is not liberalism; it is degeneration."

... Our opponents propose to put the Federal Government in the power business with all its additions to Federal bureaucracy, its tyranny over State and local governments, its undermining of State and local responsibilities and initiative.

Sixth: I may cite another instance of absolutely destructive proposals to our American system by our opponents.

Recently there was circulated through the unemployed in this country a letter from the Democratic candidate in which he stated that he "... would support measures for the inauguration of self-liquidating public works such as the utilization of water resources, flood control, land reclamation, to provide employment *for all surplus labor at all times*."[4]

I especially emphasize that promise to promote "employment for all surplus labor at all times." At first I could not believe that any one would be so cruel as to hold out a hope so absolutely impossible of realization to those 10,000,000 who are unemployed.... It is easily demonstrable that no such employment can be found.... It is another mark of the character of the new deal.... If it were possible to give this employment to 10,000,000 people by the Government, it would cost upwards of $9,000,000,000 a year....

[...–*ed.*] The only method by which we can stop the suffering and unemployment is by returning our people to their normal jobs in their normal homes, carrying on their normal functions of living. This can be done only by sound processes of protecting and stimulating recovery of the ... economic system upon which we have builded our progress thus far—preventing distress ... in the meantime.

Seventh: Recently, at Indianapolis, I called attention to the statement made by Governor Roosevelt in his address on October 25th with respect to the Supreme Court of the United States. He said:

"After March 4, 1929, the Republican Party was in complete control of all branches of the Government—Executive, Senate, and House, and I may add, for good measure, in order to make it complete, the Supreme Court as well." [The count is 3 Republicans and 4 Democrats.][5]

---

4. [*Editor's note*: Italics added by Hoover.]
5. [*Editor's note*: Bracketed sentence added here by Hoover. It was not in the 1932 speech.]

I am not called upon to defend the Supreme Court of the United States from this slurring reflection. Fortunately that court has jealously maintained over the years its high standard of integrity, impartiality, . . . so that the confidence of the people is sound and unshaken.

But is the Democratic candidate . . . proposing the most revolutionary new deal, . . . the most destructive undermining of the very safeguard of our form of government yet proposed by a Presidential candidate?[6]

Eighth: In order that we may get at the philosophical background of the mind which pronounces the necessity for profound change in our American system and a new deal, I would call your attention to an address delivered by the Democratic candidate in San Francisco, early in October.

He said:

"Our industrial plant is built. The problem just now is whether under existing conditions it is not overbuilt. Our last frontier has long since been reached. There is practically no more free land. There is no safety valve in the Western prairies where we can go for a new start. . . . The mere building of more industrial plants, the organization of more corporations is as likely to be as much a danger as a help. . . . Our task now is not the discovery of natural resources or necessarily the production of more goods, it is the sober, less dramatic business of administering the resources and plants already in hand. . . ."

[. . .–*ed.*] I do challenge the whole idea that we have ended the advance of America, that this country has reached the zenith of its power, the height of its development. That is the counsel of despair. . . . That is not the spirit by which we shall emerge from this depression. That is not the spirit that made this country. . . . I deny that the promise of American life has been fulfilled, for that means we have begun the decline and fall. No nation can cease to move forward without degeneration of spirit. . . .

If these measures, these promises . . . or . . . this attitude of mind, mean anything, they mean the enormous expansion of the Federal Government; they mean the growth of bureaucracy such as we have never seen in our history. No man who has not occupied my position in Washington can fully realize the constant battle which must be carried on against incompetence, corruption, [and] tyranny of government. . . . [This is] the most gigantic increase in expenditure ever known in history. That alone would break down the savings, the wages . . . among our people. These measures would transfer

---

6. [*Editor's note*: By his omissions, Hoover converted a declarative sentence in his 1932 text to a question here.]

vast responsibilities to the Federal Government from the States, the local governments, and the individuals. But that is not all; they would break down our form of government. Our legislative bodies cannot delegate their authority to any dictator. . . .

. . . At once when these extensions take place by the Federal Government, the authority and responsibility of State governments and institutions [will be] . . . undermined. Every enterprise of private business is at once halted to know what Federal action is going to be. It destroys initiative and courage. We can do no better than quote that great statesman of labor, the late Samuel Gompers, in speaking of a similar situation:

"It is a question of whether it shall be government ownership or private ownership under control. If I were a minority of one in this convention, I would want to cast my vote so that the men of labor shall not willingly enslave themselves to government in their industrial effort."

We have heard a great deal in this campaign about reactionaries, conservatives, progressives, liberals, and radicals. I have not yet heard an attempt by any one of the orators who mouth these phrases to define the principles upon which they base these classifications. There is one thing I can say without any question of doubt—that is, that the spirit of liberalism is to create free men; it is not the regimentation of men. It is not the extension of bureaucracy. . . . You cannot extend the mastery of government over the daily life of a people without somewhere making it master of people's souls and thoughts. Expansion of government [into free enterprise] . . . means that the government, in order to protect itself from the political consequences of its errors, is driven irresistibly without peace to greater and greater control of the Nation's press and platform. Free speech does not live many hours after free industry and free commerce die. It is a false liberalism that interprets itself into Government operation of business. Every step in that direction poisons the very roots of liberalism. It poisons political equality, free speech, free press, and equality of opportunity: It is the road not to liberty but to less liberty. *True liberalism is found not in striving to spread bureaucracy, but in striving to set bounds to it. True liberalism seeks all legitimate freedom first in the confident belief that without such freedom the pursuit of other blessings is in vain. Liberalism is a force truly of the spirit proceeding from the deep realization that economic freedom cannot be sacrificed if political freedom is to be preserved.*[7]

Even if the Government conduct of business could give us the maximum efficiency instead of least efficiency, it would be purchased at the cost of freedom.

---

7. [*Editor's note*: Italics added here by Hoover.]

It would increase rather than decrease abuse and corruption, stifle initiative and invention, undermine development of leadership, cripple mental and spiritual energies of our people, extinguish equality of opportunity, and dry up the spirit of liberty and progress. Men who are going about this country announcing that they are liberals because of their promises to extend the Government in business are not liberals, they are reactionaries of the United States.

And I do not wish to be misquoted or misunderstood. I do not mean that our Government is to part with one iota of its national resources without complete protection to the public interest. I have already stated that democracy must remain master in its own house. I have stated that abuse and wrongdoing must be punished and controlled. Nor do I wish to be misinterpreted as stating that the United States is a free-for-all and devil-take-the-hindermost society.

The very essence of equality of opportunity of our American system is that there shall be no monopoly or domination by any group or section in this country, whether it be business, sectional, or a group interest. On the contrary, our American system demands economic justice as well as political and social justice; it is not a system of *laissez faire*.

I am not setting up the contention that our American system is perfect. No human ideal has ever been perfectly attained, since humanity itself is not perfect. But the wisdom of our forefathers and the wisdom of the thirty men who have preceded me in this office . . . have held unalterably to these principles. [. . .–*ed.*]

In my acceptance speech four years ago at Palo Alto I stated that—"One of the oldest aspirations of the human race was the abolition of poverty. By poverty I mean the grinding by under-nourishment, cold, ignorance, fear of old age to those who have the will to work."

I stated that—

"In America today we are nearer a final triumph over poverty than in any land. The poorhouse has vanished from among us; we have not reached that goal, but given a chance to go forward, we shall, with the help of God, be in sight of the day when poverty will be banished from this Nation."[8]

---

8. [*Editor's note*: In his 1932 speech Hoover misquoted this passage from his 1928 speech accepting his party's presidential nomination. On that occasion he had said: "We in America today are nearer to the final triumph over poverty than ever before in the history of any land. The poorhouse is vanishing from among us. We have not yet reached the goal, but, given a chance to go forward with the policies of the last 8 years, we shall soon with the help of God be in sight of the day when poverty will be banished from this Nation." In 1932 Hoover did not quote the phrase "with the policies of the last 8 years" (a reference to the Harding–Coolidge era of 1921–28). He probably did not want to associate himself in 1932 with policies that his opponents considered to be flawed and leading to the stock market crash of 1929.]

. . .

My countrymen, the proposals of our opponents represent a profound change in American life. . . . This election is not a mere shift from the ins to the outs. It means deciding the direction our Nation will take over a century to come.

My conception of America is a land where men and women may walk in ordered liberty, where they may enjoy the advantages of wealth not concentrated in the hands of a few but diffused through the lives of all, where they build and safeguard their homes, give to their children full opportunities of American life, where every man shall be respected in the faith that his conscience and his heart direct him to follow, where people secure in their liberty shall have leisure and impulse to seek a fuller life. That leads to the release of the energies of men and women, to the wider vision and higher hope; it leads to opportunity for greater and greater service not alone of man to man in our country but from our country to the world. It leads to health in body and a spirit unfettered, youthful, eager with a vision stretching beyond the farthest horizons with an open mind, sympathetic and generous. But that must be builded upon . . . the foundations which have made our country great. . . .

My last statement from the White House on the American system was a letter in reply to an inquiry from an important citizen.[9] It is of some importance here because it outlined the constructive measures needed by the country:

I have your request that I should state in writing what I said to you a few days ago as to the broad conclusions I have formed from experience of the last four years as to the functioning of our economic system. It is, of course, impossible in the time I have left at my disposal or within the reach of a short statement, to cover all phases of the problem.

Our whole economic system naturally divides itself into production, distribution, and finance. By finance I mean every phase of investment, banking and credit. And at once I may say that the major fault in the system as it stands is in the financial system.

As to production, our system of stimulated individual effort, by its creation of enterprise, development of skill and discoveries in science and invention, has resulted in production of the greatest quantity of commodities

---

9. *Addresses . . . 1933–1938*, p. 20[–p.25]. [*Editor's note*: Hoover addressed this letter to his friend Arch W. Shaw of Chicago.]

and services of the most infinite variety that were ever known in the history of man. Our production in 1924–28, for instance, in the flow of commodities, service and leisure, resulted in the highest standard of living of any group of humanity in the history of the world. Even in these years, without machinery and equipment and labor and business organizations, we could have produced more and could have enjoyed an even higher standard of living if all the adjustments of economic mechanism had been more perfect. We can say, however, without qualification, that the motivation of production based on private initiative has proved the very mother of plenty. It has faults, for humanity is not without faults. Difficulties arise from overexpansion and adjustment to the march of labor-saving devices, but in broad result it stands in sharp contrast with the failure of the system of production as in its greater exemplar—Russia—where after fifteen years of trial in a land of as great natural resources as ours, that system has never produced in a single year an adequate supply of even the barest necessities in food and clothing for its people.

In the larger sense our system of distribution in normal times is sufficient and effective. Our transportation and communication is rapid and universal. The trades distribute the necessities of life at profits which represent a remarkably small percentage of their value.

The system moves supplies of everything into remotest villages and crossroads; it feeds and clothes great cities each day with the regularity and assurance which causes never a thought or anxiety. The diffusion of commodities and services in a social sense has faults. In normal times out of our 120,000,000 people there are a few millions who conscientiously work and strive, yet do not receive that minimum of commodities and services to which they have a just right as earnest members of the community. The system does not give to them that assurance of security and living which frees them from fear for the future.

There is another fringe of a few hundred thousand who receive more than they deserve for the effort they make. But taxes are furnishing rapid correction in this quarter. The great mass of people enjoy in normal times a broader diffusion of our wealth, commodities and services than ever before in history. The enlarging social sense of our people is furnishing the impulse to correction of faults. That correction is to be brought about by diffusion of property through constructive development within the system itself, with social vision as well as economic vision. It is not to be brought about by destruction of the system.

The last four years have shown unquestionably that it is mainly the third element of our system—that is, finance—which has failed and produced by far the largest part of the demoralization of our systems of production and distribution with its thousand tragedies which wring the heart of the nation. I am not insensible to the disturbing war inheritances, of our expansion of production in certain branches, nor to the effect of increased labor-saving devices on employment, but these are minor notes of discord compared to that arising from failure of the financial system. This failure has been evidenced in two directions: That is, the lack of organization for domestic purposes and the weakness presented by a disintegrated front to the world through which we have been infinitely more demoralized by repeated shocks from abroad.

The credit system in all its phases should be merely a lubricant to the systems of production and distribution. It is not its function to control these systems. That it should be so badly organized, that the volume of currency and credit, whether long or short term, should expand and shrink irrespective of the needs of production and distribution; that its stability should be the particular creature of emotional fear or optimism; that it should be insecure; that it should dominate and not be subordinate to production and distribution—all this is intolerable if we are to maintain our civilization. Yet these things have happened on a gigantic scale. We could have weathered through these failures with some losses and could have secured reorganization as we went along, planing out failures in the fundamental organization of the financial system. The rain of blows from abroad, however, on the system of such weakness has wholly prostrated us by a second phase of this depression which came from a collapse of the financial systems in Europe.

In this system I am not referring to individual banks or financial institutions. Many of them have shown distinguished courage and ability. On the contrary I am referring to the system itself, which is so organized, or so lacking in organization, that it fails in its primary function of stable and steady service to the production and distribution system. In an emergency its very mechanism increases the jeopardy and paralyzes action of the community.

Clearly we must secure sound organization of our financial system as a prerequisite of the functioning of the whole economic system. The first steps in that system are sound currency, economy in government, balanced governmental budgets, whether national or local. The second step is an adequate separation of commercial banking from investment banking, whether in mortgages, bonds or other forms of long-term securities. The next step is to secure effective co-ordination between national and state systems. We cannot endure 49 separate regulatory systems which are both conflicting and weakening. We must accept the large view that the mismanagement, instability and bad functioning of any single institution affects the stability of some part of production and distribution and a multitude of other financial institutions. Therefore there must be co-operation within the financial system enforced by control and regulation by the Government, that will assure that this segment of our economic system does not, through faulty organization and action, bring our people again to these tragedies of unemployment and loss of homes which are today a stigma upon national life. We cannot endure that enormous sums of the people's savings shall be poured out either at home or abroad without making the promoter responsible for his every statement. We cannot endure that men will either manipulate the savings of the people so abundantly evidenced in recent exposures.

That it has been necessary for the Government, through emergency action, to protect us while holding a wealth of gold from being taken off the gold standard, to erect gigantic credit institutions with the full pledge of Government credit to save the nation from chaos through this failure of the financial system, that it is necessary for us to devise schemes of clearing-house protections and to install such temporary devices throughout the nation, is full proof of all I have said. That is the big question. If we can solve this, then we must take in hand the faults of the production and distribution systems — and many problems in the social and political system. But this financial system simply must be made to function first.

There is a phase of all this that must cause anxiety to every American. Democracy cannot survive unless it is master in its own house. The economic system cannot survive unless there are real restraints upon unbridled greed or dishonest reach for power. Greed and dishonesty are not attributes solely of our system — they are human and will infect Socialism or any ism. But if our production and distribution systems are to function we must have effective restraints on manipulation, greed and dishonesty. Our Democracy has proved its ability to put its unruly occupants under control but never until their conduct has been a public scandal and a stench. For instance, you will recollect my own opposition to Government operation of electric power, for that is a violation of the very fundamentals of our system; but parallel with it I asked and preached for regulation of it to protect the public from its financial manipulation. We gained the Power Commission but Congress refused it the regulatory authority we asked. I have time and again warned, asked and urged the reorganization of the banking system. The inertia of the Democracy is never more marked than in promotion of what seem abstract or indirect ideas. The recent scandals are the result. Democracy, always lagging, will no doubt now act and may act destructively to the system, for it is mad. It is this lag, the failure to act in time for prevention which I fear most in the sane advancement of economic life. For an outraged people may destroy the whole economic system rather than reconstruct and control the segment which has failed in its function. I trust the new Administration will recognize the difference between crime and economic functioning; between constructive prevention and organization as contrasted with destruction.

During these four years I have been fighting to preserve this fundamental system of production and distribution from destruction through collapse and bad functioning of the financial system. Time can only tell if we have succeeded. Success means higher and higher standards of living, greater comfort, more opportunity for intellectual, moral and spiritual development. Failure means a new form of the Middle Ages.

If we succeed in the job of preservation, certainly the next effort before the country is to reorganize the financial system so that all this will not happen again. We must organize for advance in the other directions, but that is another subject.

Yours faithfully,

Herbert Hoover[10]

---

10. [*Editor's note*: Hoover wrote this letter on February 17, 1933. Sixteen days later, his presidency ended.]

APPENDIX II

Selected Documents Pertaining to Hoover's Crusade Book Project

EDITORIAL NOTE ON APPENDIX II

Hoover's *Crusade Years* manuscript and related autobiographical writings did not contain an appendix. But it seems appropriate to create one as an aid to understanding the origins, development, and purposes of this previously unknown volume of his memoirs.

During Hoover's long and hyperactive ex-presidency (1933–1964), he generated and amassed literally hundreds of boxes of correspondence, memoranda, research material, manuscript drafts, and other records. These papers are housed today in two repositories: the Herbert Hoover Presidential Library in West Branch, Iowa, and the Hoover Institution on War, Revolution and Peace on the campus of Stanford University in Palo Alto, California. The relevant papers include, among other holdings, the Post-Presidential Individual Correspondence File, the Post-Presidential General Correspondence File, and the Post-Presidential Subject File in Iowa, and parts of the Herbert Hoover Subject Collection in California. In addition, the Hoover Institution Archives possesses the recently opened Herbert Hoover Papers (173 boxes) and Arthur Kemp Papers (59 boxes). These related primarily to Hoover's preparation in his later years of his monumental foreign policy memoir and history of World War II known as the Magnum Opus, which was published posthumously in 2011 under the title *Freedom Betrayed*. Both collections also contain a substantial array of documents and manuscripts pertaining to Hoover's *Crusade Years* volume. In all, Hoover's own papers bearing on his ex-presidency comprise more than one thousand boxes.

From this lode of documentation I have selected a few nuggets for inclusion here. Several of these items are scattered in files that have been open for research for some years. But a number have been available only since 2011, and a few are being made public here for the first time. Together, they help to illuminate Hoover's postpresidential "years as crusader," as well as the process by which he recorded and then recounted his contribution to American history.

The documents are presented in chronological order.

Memorandum of a Conversation with Wendell Willkie

November 16, 1940

During the postpresidential years (1933–55) covered by this volume, Hoover was in the thick of Republican Party politics, as he sought to repulse Franklin Roosevelt's New Deal. Never was his activism more intense than in the tumultuous year 1940, when Hoover himself covertly sought the Republican presidential nomination, only to be overtaken by a boisterous newcomer named Wendell Willkie.

Although Hoover campaigned for Willkie's election that autumn, relations between the two men were never smooth, as Hoover's memoirs vividly attest. His distrust of what he perceived as Willkie's unsteady temperament and ideological shallowness, however, did not prevent the former president from inviting Willkie to lunch in mid-November 1940, just days after the Republican nominee's loss of the presidential election to Franklin Roosevelt. From the notes that Hoover dictated after this luncheon conversation, it appears that he was especially anxious to tutor Willkie on the need to stay resolute in opposition to American entry into World War II.

Document 1 keenly illustrates Hoover's attitude toward the spreading war in late 1940, as well as his antipathy toward President Roosevelt and his "mass of smearing liars." It also discloses Hoover's concern that pro-Willkie clubs might become a disruptive force in the Republican Party. Hoover may also have feared that these bands of enthusiasts would become a base for another presidential run by Willkie—something Hoover was soon determined to prevent.

This document is noteworthy in another respect: it exemplifies a practice that Hoover cultivated during his later years. After an important meeting with a distinguished guest, the former president would often dictate or draft an account of the conversation for his files. A number of these memoranda survive today in Hoover's papers. For historians, they shed valuable light on Hoover's actions and mindset at the time. For Hoover himself they provided aide-mémoires upon which he could draw when preparing his *Crusade Years* book and other writings some years later.

The typescript document reproduced here is found in the Arthur Kemp Papers, Box 4, Hoover Institution Archives.

November 16 [1940–*ed.*]
(Note dictated at the time)

Yesterday Larry[1] invited Wendell Willkie to have lunch with me today.

I introduced three principal subjects of discussion. The first was the necessity to concentrate all efforts on keeping this country out of war.

The second was that in these measures short of war we ought to get a definition quickly to what *was* short of war so as to stop these continuous steps.

We had a long conversation about the inevitable collapse of democracy if we ever got into war, and I told him about the Fascist steps we had taken during the last war and the dissolution of them which took place as a result of an interview that took place between myself and Wilson during the Armistice. We entirely agreed that if this country should go to war it was the end of this civilization. We agreed that we wanted to give such financial help as we could to the British but we do not intend to enter into this war.

I was very emphatic on the statement that the British ought to know how far we were willing to go, because this war had arrived, at worst, at a stalemate, and the reason why the British kept on was because of their confidence that the Americans were coming into the war and would take over the burden of it at some time. I mentioned the prospect that Hitler would attack Russia (his fundamental enemy). I told him the only discussion going on in England was the date; that even the British were not anxious for us to come into the war until after we had industry tuned up to where it could support not only them but ourselves, but that they confidently expect for us to come in later. Therefore, it was vitally necessary that they should know that we were not coming in. That my own feeling was that if they could get that through their thick heads, they probably could produce a peace that would preserve the British Empire.

He said that Roosevelt was trying to get him to come down to Washington; that Stimson[2] and Knox[3] had sent word to him that he should come down and discuss matters with them and Hull,[4] and intimated that Roosevelt probably could be brought into the conversations a little later. I told him that I

---

1. [*Editor's note*: Probably Lawrence Richey (1885–1959), Hoover's longtime confidential secretary and troubleshooter.]
2. [*Editor's note*: Henry L. Stimson (1867–1950), secretary of war from 1940 to 1945.]
3. [*Editor's note*: Frank Knox (1874–1944), secretary of the navy from 1940 to 1944.]
4. [*Editor's note*: Cordell Hull (1871–1955), secretary of state from 1933 to 1944.]

never would discuss things with No. 2 men in any event, and that I would not discuss things with Roosevelt unless such discussions could have two or three honest men present with him who knew the subject well in order that he should have protection for himself against a mass of smearing liars, and that the subject should be discussed by men who had a larger background in foreign affairs than he could expect to command. He seemed to agree with this.

In view of his announcement that the Willkie Clubs woulf nr krpy slibr,[5] I told him that I wanted to make him a recommendation. These clubs were a thorn in the side of the regular Republican organization; they were zealous young men who might be made of use but if we were to be a real constructive party that we must have a consolidated front; that I realized it was impossible to say to them overnight that they were to join with the Republican Party or its local organizations, but that unless something was done to indicate to the regular Republicans that these were a Republican auxiliary and not a new political party that there was going to be a fight in every district all over the country. I thought the graceful way and the effective way to bring about a consolidation of fronts would be for him to say to these clubs: that the job is to save the country and to elect the Congress in 1942 and they had better go to work right away preparing for the congressional election; that this would not be a command for them to get inside the Republican Party overnight but automatically they would be supporting Republican candidates and that would bring them in; that such a motion as this on his part would be welcomed by all the Republicans as being a move towards a consolidated front; that it would not destroy the zeal and effectiveness of these young groups. He said this was extremely wise and that it was the best suggestion he had had and that he would take it up and do it in the course of time.

We discussed the election shortly. I pointed out that the mysterious thing about the election was the fact that obviously the regular Republicans went into the ballot boxes and voted local Republican tickets, and therefore they must have been Republicans, and yet at the same time did not vote for him. He asserted that it was because they wanted to go to war and they believed Roosevelt was a liar in his public assertions and would take them to war, and that therefore they preferred Roosevelt as being the more likely avenue to get in the war than himself. I did not dispute this with him as my only object was to call his attention to the fact that he had run far behind the regular Republican ticket.

---

5. [Editor's note: This was apparently a typographical error or possibly a code phrase.]

Memorandum of a Conversation with Governor Thomas E. Dewey

March 29, 1944

After failing to receive the Republican presidential nomination in 1940, Hoover commenced in earnest to write his memoirs. By 1944 he had produced voluminous drafts covering his life up through his presidency. Nevertheless, he continued to be acutely interested in current politics and was determined to remain a figure of influence on the national stage.

One sign of Hoover's enduring prestige among his fellow Republicans was his dinner meeting on March 28, 1944, with Governor Thomas E. Dewey of New York. At this time Dewey was the front runner for the 1944 Republican Party nomination, which he eventually received. Although evidently eager to secure Hoover's goodwill, Dewey—it later transpired—considered the former president to be a political albatross. Hoover, for his part, had reservations about the governor, as Hoover's memorandum of their conversation reveals.

A copy of this document is in the folder "Dewey, Thomas E.: 1944–48," Post-Presidential Individual Correspondence File, Herbert Hoover Papers, Herbert Hoover Presidential Library. Another copy is in the Arthur Kemp Papers, Box 4, Hoover Institution Archives.

New York, New York
Wednesday, March 29, 1944

Governor Dewey dined with me last night. We canvassed the Republican presidential set-up in the country. I found he had agents in practically every state who were actively working for his nomination and keeping him in touch with the situation throughout the country. His friends were also providing some funds. He did not state he would accept the nomination but he was able to summate his strength in each state. He seemed to cling to the idea that he must be drafted but I got the impression that he was going to see that the draft machinery was in high gear. We had a long discussion on what should be the tactics prior to the Convention and those afterward. He approached everything we touched upon from the obvious mental point of view that he was going to [be–*ed.*] the Republican candidate. His figures gave Mr. Willkie[1] about 170 delegates, Mr. Bricker[2] about 150 delegates, and Mr. Stassen[3] about 50 delegates. He credited MacArthur[4] with only 10 or 12. It was obvious that he had in mind that he would probably be nominated on the first ballot. He thought that Warren[5] was the only man to be nominated for the vice-presidency. He agreed with my idea that Stassen was really a candidate for Secretary of the Navy[6] and the [that–*ed.*] he ought to be brought back to take part in the campaign.

Dewey told me that he was making a speech on foreign affairs on April 27th and was anxious to have my views. It developed during the conversation that John Foster Dulles[7] had written a draft of a speech for him. I told him that John Foster Dulles was filled with a lot of fuzzy ideas; that he was living in a dream-land which had been completely knocked into a cocked hat by Joe Stalin; that the outlook for the world had been changed; that there would be nothing in the nature of a "world government" and that there would be no surrendering of sovereignty; that irrespective of what might be the attitude of the United States, neither Russia nor Britain would accept any such fuzzy ideas.

The Governor and I discussed the conduct of the war. At one point I suggested that if he were elected he would have to create a special bureau of 600 lawyers and 2000 detectives to expose at least one case per day of the corruption of the present regime; that this would be the only method of preventing the New Dealers from undermining him during the next four years and thus defeat him for a second term. Dewey said that he thought I was wrong, that we should have 6000 lawyers and 20,000 detectives and some new jails.

---

1. [*Editor's note*: Wendell Willkie (1892–1944), the Republican Party's presidential nominee in 1940.]

2. [*Editor's note*: John W. Bricker (1893–1980), governor of Ohio from 1939 to 1945. In 1944 he was the Republican Party's vice-presidential nominee.]

3. [*Editor's note*: Harold Stassen (1907–2001), the Republican governor of Minnesota from 1939 to 1943.]

4. [*Editor's note*: General Douglas MacArthur (1880–1964), supreme commander of U.S. Army forces in the South West Pacific Area from 1942 to 1945.]

5. [*Editor's note*: Earl Warren (1891–1974), the Republican governor of California from 1943 to 1953. Later chief justice of the U.S. Supreme Court.]

6. [*Editor's note*: At the time of the Hoover-Dewey dinner meeting, Stassen was in uniform, serving on the staff of Admiral William L. Halsey Jr., commander of U.S. naval forces in the South Pacific.]

7. [*Editor's note*: John Foster Dulles (1888–1959), an international lawyer and foreign policy advisor to Governor Dewey in 1944. Later U.S. secretary of state under President Dwight Eisenhower.]

He agreed with me that the present administration had been left completely without any foreign policy as a result of the Teheran conferences and Stalin's attitude. That we could make a great issue of this during the campaign. That the other great issue could be the domestic situation.

Further, if the war drifted along as it looked now as if it would, we could make serious charges as to the conduct of the war.

Dewey did not take to my suggestion that MacArthur might be the vice-presidential candidate. He told me that Patrick Hurly [Hurley–ed.][8] had spent five hours with him at Quaker Hill by very special appointment; that Pat had not suggested it, but that it was obvious that Pat wanted to be nominated the vice-president on the Republican ticket. (Pat had told me the day before that the Democrats had approached him to find out whether he would accept the vice-presidency on the Democratic ticket, and he asked me for my views on it.)

I came out of the long discussion with confirmation of my high esteem for Dewey's intellectual capacities, his energy, and his political ability, but in some way I have a reservation as to his character. Nevertheless, at the moment, he seems to be the inevitable candidate, and the spiritual winds that blow through the White House may strengthen any of the deficiencies on the character side. He has fewer of the human qualities than Bricker has. Whatever humanitarism [sic–ed.] he has is coldly calculated in the terms of votes. He is seemingly convinced of his own intellectual superiority and abilities. His mannerism of constantly interrupting conversation with unctious [sic–ed.] contradictory statements has softened a good deal. In this respect he will make a better candidate now than he would have four years ago. The great contrast between Bricker and Dewey as candidates can be seen in the political management Dewey has already set up around himself whereas Bricker has none of importance.

---

8. [Editor's note: Patrick Hurley (1883–1963), secretary of war under President Hoover from 1929 to 1933. During World War II he undertook a number of missions as a representative of President Roosevelt, including service as U.S. ambassador to China from late 1944 to 1945.]

The Origins of Hoover's "Crusade against Collectivism"

September 30, 1944

This document appears to be the earliest extant fragment of Hoover's memoirs relating to his postpresidential years. He probably composed it by hand in late September 1944. The typescript version printed here bears the date "9/30/44": probably the day one of his secretaries typed it.

In this brief essay Hoover identified the poisonous "philosophical error" that had come to dominate American politics during the New Deal years, an error he deemed it his moral duty to combat. Although his document was initially untitled, at some point he scribbled across the top of the first page the words "Crusade against Collectivism." It was probably his way of indicating for his files that this typescript belonged to the segment of his memoirs that he eventually titled "The Crusade against Collectivism in American Life" (part III of the book in your hands).

Hoover ultimately incorporated the final paragraph of this little essay (in slightly revised form) into his *Crusade Years* manuscript. (See pp. 57 and 60 of the present volume.) But the other paragraphs for some reason eventually fell by the wayside. The full document is reproduced here. It provides a valuable glimpse of Hoover's thinking and self-image as he launched the postpresidential phase of his memoirs.

Document 3 is in the Herbert Hoover Papers, Box 3, folder 7, Hoover Institution Archives.

9/30/44

The period from 1933 to 1938 in America was dominated by a clash in philosophical ideas to which I felt it was my duty to apply every bit of strength I possessed. I was convinced that a great error had come into liberal thinking, which threatened to destroy the magnificent civilization which intellectual and spiritual freedom had builded and which was its impulse to progress.

The rise of personal liberty and its expression in the American and French Revolutions, and to a less extent in the Reform Period in England, had been produced rather in an intellectual and political climate than in an economic one.

With the stimulation to scientific discovery and invention came the industrial revolution some fifty to seventy-five years later. Its result was not only the greatest lift to standards of living and comfort in the history of the world, but also the most serious encroachments upon individual liberty and individual opportunity. The great instruments of production and distribution could be, and were, used to oppress fellowmen; great disparities in living were created by the lift of a huge middle class from the levels of primitive living with which people had at one time been content. Particularly in America were we struggling, and in fact, making progress, in defending personal liberty and encroachments upon it by the manipulation of these great economic instrumentalities. We had developed legal standards of conduct for corporations, railroads, utilities and manufacturing concerns with effective enforcement agencies. They were not always perfect, and sometimes slow in enactment, but we had demonstrated that this threat from the industrial revolution could be overcome. We had developed taxation which reduced excessive wealth and with free education, public health, and a hundred community services, we were indirectly providing a great contribution to the living of the less fortunate and successful. The sense of community responsibility had developed to a conscious responsibility that none should go hungry and cold from honest misfortune. We had discarded the philosophy of laissez-faire or dog-eat-dog economics. We were on the way to preserve the imperative impulses of progress which came alone from intellectual, spiritual and political liberty, and at the same time to give security and increasing standards of living to our people.

The error in ideas came first in the form of Socialism but had made little progress prior to the first World War. The root of the error was that government operation of economic instrumentalities, or government direction of their operation other than establishment of rules of conduct, could short-cut all human ills and produce immediate Utopia. This gigantic poison of liberty received a great impulse from the government agencies created to mobilize the whole energies of peoples in total war. Here the impulses of patriotism to produce and labor and the fear of the enemy were substituted for free will. After the war the inevitable flood of misery, of impoverishment and frustration furnished the hotbed for the growth of this gigantic error. It developed over Europe in various forms—all from the same root. Communism, Fascism, and the milder forms of Statism, were heralded by well-meaning and generous-minded men as to the new road to life. They were joined by demagogs and seekers-for-power. The ultimate end was slavery, whether in Communistic or Fascist form. This philosophic error had spread mildly in American thinking, but attained no dangerous proportions until the world-wide depression struck us with all its violence, misery and exposure of wrong-doing.

It was certain in my mind that the New Deal was but one form of this same error in ideas and that it was my job to fight it. But fighting a philosophic idea among a people who had never thought in these channels was not only a difficult thing in itself, but one must contend with demagogic promises of Utopia to a suffering people and the obvious needs of reform in the system itself.

The American people at large had scarcely heard the word *ideology*. They had developed and they had lived and breathed a way of life without defining it as an "ideology."

On arriving at Stanford I asked Professor Robinson[1] to send me the list of books required to be read by all students in a course of "Citizenship." I found about one hundred books listed, of which some twenty were bare descriptives of the machinery of our civil government and nearly eighty which were devoted, directly or indirectly, to the favorable discussion of the ideologies of Socialism, Communism, Fascism, or attacks upon true Liberalism. I determined I would contribute a book, and in 1934 I published "The Challenge to Liberty." The book had a reasonable circulation (135,000), but it was too early. The left-wingers, however, were quick to appreciate its import and their reviews were vociferous in denunciation of the book. As the sales of all books are greatly dominated by the book reviewers in New York, the violence of their efforts should have destroyed it. I soon learned that the reviewers of the *New York Times*, the New York *Herald Tribune*, and of journals of review met regularly to determine in what manner they should destroy books which were not to their ideological liking. They did their best. A man named Chamberlain on the *Times* was particularly dishonest in his review, but I had the satisfaction of seeing him, some years later, a disillusioned person, trying to imitate a true liberal.[2]

---

1. [*Editor's note*: Edgar Eugene Robinson (1887–1977), a professor of history at Stanford University for many years. After leaving the White House in March 1933, Hoover returned to the Stanford campus, where he had built a home in 1919–20.]

2. [*Editor's note*: John Chamberlain (1903–95), an American author and journalist, was the daily book reviewer for the *New York Times* for several years in the 1930s. At that time his politics were well to the left of center. Later he moved right, became a libertarian conservative, and wrote for William F. Buckley Jr.'s conservative magazine *National Review* for nearly forty years.

Chamberlain's critical review of *The Challenge to Liberty* (a review written in his left-wing phase) appeared in the *New York Times*, September 28, 1934, p. 21.]

Hoover's Appraisal of Wendell Willkie

October 18, 1944

After the election of 1940, Wendell Willkie became a fast friend of Franklin Roosevelt, a vocal supporter of Roosevelt's interventionist foreign policy, and an ardent internationalist. His best-selling 1943 book *One World* was seen by some as a prelude to another presidential run. All these developments worried and antagonized Hoover, who spent considerable energy between 1941 and 1944 in efforts to curb Willkie's influence among Republicans and to block Willkie's presidential ambitions. Hoover was delighted when, on April 4, 1944, Willkie fared poorly in the Wisconsin Republican presidential primary, effectively ending his hopes of a political comeback as a Republican.

On October 8, 1944, Willkie died in New York City. Within days Hoover composed the document printed here. It is among the earliest surviving fragments of what became the portion of his memoirs devoted to his postpresidential involvement in American politics.

Hoover eventually incorporated most of this account, in somewhat altered form, into successive drafts of his *Crusade Years* manuscript, including the 1955 version published in this volume. Document 4 is in the Herbert Hoover Papers, Box 3, folder 6, Hoover Institution Archives.

10/18/44

Willkie was a genuinely patriotic man. He possessed a warm personality, unlimited energy and an effective training at influencing people. His real occupation had long been that of a public relations lawyer in public utility companies. He was naturally dramatic, but, beyond a superficial views [*sic–ed.*] of public questions, his mind was greatly confused. He relied wholly upon ghost writers for his more serious public utterances.

For the nomination he had the support of two diametrically opposed groups. He had made a good public fight against the New Deal usurpation on behalf of southern power companies and shown great ability to handle the press. From this action the utility officials, bankers and brokers all over the country considered they had found exactly the man for President. They did not, however, realize Willkie's life-long personal associations were with the left wing. He had been a socialist in college, a follower of Bryan and La-Follette.[1] Those of us who knew his personal associations knew they comprised such individuals as Walter Davenport[2] of Time publications, Dorothy Thompson, Walter Lippmann, Hugh Johnson—all columnists—and other active "Economic Planners." Some of these, like Johnson, had quarreled with Roosevelt, having made a mess of things, had blamed Roosevelt and had been thrown overboard with Roosevelt's private hate. Thus, Willkie had the support of a group of left-wing publicists who thought it an enterprising idea to nominate a left winger for the Republican Party. All of the left wingers, including the New Deal press, applauded this idea. But most of the left wingers deserted Willkie after the nomination.

Thus at the convention we saw such personages as Thomas Lamont of J. P. Morgan's, alongside Dorothy Thompson, button-holing delegates. The bankers, brokers and public utility men had engaged certain "public relations" firms and by their nation-wide use of the public relations departments of the utility concerns and of the brokerage houses, banks etc., they put on a rain of telegrams to delegates demanding Willkie's nomination. Many delegates received over two thousand such telegrams. I received over nine thousand.[3] My secretary was unable to identify half a dozen of the senders. On returning to California I placed the telegrams from several towns in the hands of friends in those localities to find out who the senders were. In almost every case a solicitor had called and offered to send a telegram free, and in many cases the sender was unknown. In Palo Alto, out of 60 telegrams to me, 20 had been signed by fictitious names, 10 by minors or non-voters; only two were Republicans. The solicitor was an employee of the Pacific Gas and Electric Company. To bring further pressure in the convention, the Willkie managers printed four thousand duplicate tickets to the galleries and distributed them to the clerks in brokerage and utility and other business concerns in Philadelphia. They were given a holiday to go early to the convention, hold

---

1. [*Editor's note*: That is, William Jennings Bryan and Robert LaFollette.]

2. [*Editor's note*: Hoover almost certainly meant Russell W. Davenport (1899–1954), who left his position as managing editor of *Fortune* in 1940 to become Wendell Willkie's principal campaign strategist and speechwriter. Like Willkie, Davenport was an internationalist and critic of isolationism. He later became the chief editorial writer for *Life* magazine.]

3. [*Editor's note*: In the version printed on p. 211 of this volume, Hoover wrote: "over six thousand."]

onto the seats and yell, "We want Willkie." Tolbert,[4] one of the managers of Willkie's convention campaign, later falling out with Willkie, informed me he had raised over $100,000 for this program. It was a discouraging exhibit of what can be done with mob pressures in a democracy.

Knowing Willkie's background, I naturally opposed his nomination and supported Taft. I was so indignant that I at first resolved to announce my retirement from all political life. At his urgent request I talked with Willkie at Colorado Springs. He assured me he was against "Economic Planning" and bureaucracy root and branch; that he was for "private enterprise" against all things and all comers; that he was from the depth of his soul against getting America in war. I did not believe him but concluded that if this was his public program, I would go along and upon his urging agreed to make three nation-wide broadcasts during the campaign. All of which was announced [in–*ed.*] the press.

---

4. [*Editor's note*: No Willkie associate of this name has been identified. Hoover was probably referring to Harold E. Talbott (1888–1957), a pioneer in the aviation industry and a leading fundraiser for Willkie's campaign. Talbott later served as secretary of the air force from 1953 to 1955 during the Eisenhower administration.]

The "Greatest Lie" of the 1944 Election Campaign

November 3, 1944

One of the animating impulses driving Hoover after 1933 was a desire to vindicate his conduct as president during the early years of the Great Depression. He deeply resented what he called the "smears" perpetuated by Franklin Roosevelt and other New Dealers, as well as the failure of Republican leaders like Alf Landon, Wendell Willkie, and Thomas Dewey to defend the Hoover administration's record with what Hoover considered sufficient zeal.

In the presidential contest of 1944, Hoover's indignation boiled over. Democratic Party leaders and pro-Roosevelt campaigners repeatedly sought to discredit the Republican presidential nominee, Thomas Dewey, by portraying him as an intellectual lightweight who would be a puppet and "mouthpiece" for Hoover and reactionary "Hooverism" if elected. Unwilling to countenance any longer the Democrats' attacks upon his record, Hoover composed the scathing rejoinder printed here as Document 5.

On November 3, 1944, Hoover sent a copy of his rebuttal to a number of friends, along with a single-sentence cover letter: "Herewith for your personal information one of the lies in this campaign that meets the Hitler prescription of being big enough." One of those who received Hoover's apologia was his good friend Frank R. Kent, a syndicated newspaper columnist associated with the *Baltimore Sun*. So pleased was Kent that he lightly edited Hoover's manuscript and published it under his own name as a column that circulated nationwide in mid-November.

So far as is known, neither Hoover nor Kent ever acknowledged that Hoover had largely written Kent's column. Nor did Hoover appear to object to what his journalist friend had done. After Kent's piece was inserted in the *Congressional Record*, Hoover ordered four thousand reprints at his own expense. The former president eventually quoted it approvingly in his *Crusade Years* memoirs. It appears on pp. 110–11 of this volume.

Document 5 is significant as a revelation of Hoover's state of mind in the autumn of 1944 as he turned to the postpresidential sections of his memoirs. This simple, six-paragraph memorandum is also a succinct and trenchant formulation of a "history lesson" that he expounded and elaborated upon repeatedly in his memoirs and other writings after he left the White House.

A copy of Hoover's memorandum is attached to his letter of November 3, 1944, to Robert G. Simmons, in the Robert G. Simmons Papers, Herbert Hoover Presidential Library. Another copy is in the Mark Sullivan file in the Post-Presidential Individual Correspondence File, Herbert Hoover Papers, at the same repository. The same terse letter that Hoover addressed to Simmons he also addressed to Frank R. Kent and William Henry Chamberlin. Copies of these are in their respective files in Hoover's Post-Presidential Individual Correspondence File.

The greatest lie told in this whole campaign has been that the Depression of 1930–32 was caused by the Republican Party; that the Republicans did nothing about it; that the people were allowed to starve and were compelled to sell apples; that the country was in ruins; and that Roosevelt rescued it from complete wreck.

This lie has been promulgated in a thousand speeches, in millions of scurrilous pamphlets and circulars. Mr. Roosevelt has himself given currency to it and constantly refers to apple selling. Before stating the facts, it may be mentioned that Mr. Roosevelt, then a candidate for President, was Governor of New York, the richest state in the Union, that the Democratic Party was in control of the richest city in the world, and that he could have met any relief needed and could have stopped apple dealers from exploiting people's sympathy by marketing their wares in this fashion.

The broader facts are and history will record that the depression was world-wide; that its major origins were in Europe; that it swept in on the United States like a hurricane; that it originated from the aftermaths of World War I, including the Treaty of Versailles; that by action of the Republican Administration 18,000,000 people were under organized relief and that any consequential hunger and cold were prevented; that the Republican Administration took drastic measures to protect the peoples' savings from the storm by creating the R.F.C., the Home Loan Banks and by expanding agricultural credit institutions. There were failures mostly in State Banks not under Federal control.

History will also record that the depression was turned world-wide in June and July of 1932; that we were on our way out with employment increasing but that recovery was halted when business confidence was shaken by the impending election of the New Deal; that with the election the whole country further hesitated awaiting the new policies; that rumors quickly spread that Mr. Roosevelt would devalue the currency; that in consequence, people tried to get their money from the banks and that speculators tried to ship it out of the country; that Mr. Roosevelt upon Mr. Hoover's request refused to reaffirm the promises he had made the night before election not to tinker with the currency; that Mr. Roosevelt refused to cooperate in other directions with Mr. Hoover to stem the tide of fear—fear of what? It was of the New Deal, not of a retiring administration. It was a panic of bank depositors induced by the New Deal and Mr. Roosevelt. After the banks were reopened it was found that 98% of their deposits were good.

History will also record that the rest of the world, not having a "new deal," went straight out of the depression and recovered its employment by 1934–35; that unemployment here in the United States continued on a vast scale for six years of the New Deal; and that it took a war to get us out of it.

The whole of the story put over by the New Deal orators is the most gigantic dishonesty ever known in American politics.

Hoover Assesses Governor Dewey's Campaign on the Eve of the 1944 Presidential Election

November 5, 1944

Although "passionately anxious" that Thomas Dewey defeat Franklin Roosevelt in the presidential election of 1944, Hoover was perturbed by what he saw as weaknesses in Dewey's campaign as the election approached. Two nights before the voting, the veteran foreign correspondent and commentator Henry J. Taylor came to dinner at Hoover's residence in New York, where Hoover read aloud a critique he had written of Dewey's campaign "failures." It adumbrated themes to which Hoover returned in the memoirs he was just beginning to prepare about his life after 1932.

Hoover's typescript memorandum is in the Arthur Kemp Papers, Box 4, Hoover Institution Archives. A handwritten note by Hoover at the top of the first page indicates that he gave a copy of his remarks to Taylor and his wife.

Statement read to Henry Taylor[1] and His Wife Sunday Evening, November Fifth. 1944

I am passionately anxious that Dewey shall win this campaign; it marks the final turning point on whether the country goes right or left. The campaign could be won. It will be won or lost by narrow margins unless there is a "silent vote" which is not disclosed to the usual estimators of public sentiment. If Dewey loses, it will be because of certain failures in the conduct of the campaign. These failures are:

1. Too much "me too" on fundamental New Deal policies and too much endorsement of them, i.e., not enough philosophic differentiation which must

---

1. [*Editor's note*: Henry J. Taylor (1902–84), an author, foreign correspondent, political commentator, and U.S. ambassador to Switzerland (1957–61). Taylor became a good friend of Hoover and a frequent visitor to Hoover's New York City home during and after World War II.]

form the basis of division between political parties. He seems very ignorant of the fundamental conflict that lies in many of these policies between true liberalism and collectivism. For instance, liberalism calls for regulation to prevent abuse defined in statutory law. The New Deal has used regulation as an instrumentality of centralized power for dictation and control of business, farmers and labor. All this could be stated simply and could have been made to commend itself to labor and farmers as well as business and professions. One consequence of this failure is that anti–New Deal Democrats who approve Roosevelt's war and peace policies but hate his home-front policies are not coming into our side as was indicated two months ago. Also a good many Republicans are saying that if we have to have the New Deal, let the Democrats stay in office till it blows up.

2. This ignorance or unwillingness resulted in a still wider failure—that is to establish that the fundamental ideological issue of our time in [is–ed.] the movement toward collectivism inherent in the "planned economy" vs. true liberalism. Dewey's claim that Roosevelt sold out to the Communists is too extreme for the people to accept. The real issue is a creeping collectivism vs. liberalism—not Communism vs. "American way of life." The former could have been proved; the latter is regarded by most folks as a campaign bogy. One effect was to dull public conviction as to the importance of the Hillman-Browder issue.[2] The latter would have had more force if it had been set as one element in the proof of the collectivist characteristics of the New Deal "planned economy" with the background of its progress toward centralized government, bureaucratic governmental domination of economic life, of stimulated class conflict, of internal hates, of one-party government, of purge, of smear, of intellectual dishonesty, of unbalanced budgets and evident step by step destruction of the American system; these could all have been easily established. And the danger of our totalitarian liberals and fellow travelers in governmental positions should have been expounded. Such a line could have been made to serve as proof that Dewey could provide employment instead of just promising it. It could have been used to prove the falsity of Roosevelt's promises of free enterprise and employment. It was the way to prove that Roosevelt had himself continued the depression. For this collectivist drift of

2. [*Editor's note*: Sidney Hillman (1887–1946) was the longtime head of the Amalgamated Clothing Workers of America and one of Franklin Roosevelt's most important political allies in the election campaign of 1944. Earl Browder (1891–1973) was the leader of the Communist Party USA from the early 1930s to 1945. During 1944 Hillman's political action committee skillfully mobilized its followers to reelect Roosevelt. The influence of left-wing labor unions and Communists in Roosevelt's coalition became a Republican campaign issue.]

the New Deal had paralyzed initiative and continued unemployment up to the war.

3. Failure to courageously answer the No. 1 big lie of the New Dealers that the Republicans were responsible for the depression and that Roosevelt saved the country in 1933.

4. Instead of concentrating the attack on the New Deal record into salvos of a speech devoted to one subject at a time so that the statement would have sunk in, there was too much scattering birdshot. After the general attack at Oklahoma City, this phase should have been amplified by single speeches devoted, say, to "incapacity and bungling," "unpreparedness," "Roosevelt's isolation," "dishonesty—intellectual and financial," "profligacy and waste," "bureaucracy," and other single subjects. There were too many generalized blasts.

5. By excluding Senators, Congressmen and others from important nationwide broadcasts in the campaign, there has been little emphasis upon Dewey's qualifications which he could not himself express and thus the campaign drifted almost wholly into "Against Roosevelt" with little pro-Dewey build up. In excluding all the older members of the party even from a confidential consultation he lost much valuable material and strategy.

6. Dewey lifted the new League of Nations[3] to the forefront of foreign policies then agreed with Roosevelt upon it. It is but a minor part of our foreign policies. We have to make peace before we can preserve it. Dewey made no broad analysis of Roosevelt's failures in foreign policies which will make or break peace. He did not point out the vital affect [sic–ed.] of Roosevelt's miscalculations which led to Japan's actions against us, the appeasement which has made domination of Russia over the peace and the failure of the Atlantic Charter idea—all of which will defeat any league. The public thinks Dewey approves Roosevelt's foreign policies.

If Dewey wins, it will have been upon the level of "hate Roosevelt" and Dewey's abundant promises, given with the vigor of youth, and his sincerity of determination. As it is at this moment, the limitation of the campaign to these levels may not be enough to overweigh the Roosevelt assertions of preparedness, victory, peace, free enterprise intentions and general disinclination to change in the midst of a crisis.

---

3. [*Editor's note*: The proposed United Nations, which was created at an international conference in San Francisco in 1945.]

Hoover Criticizes the Recent Election Campaign

November 9, 1944

Two days after Franklin Roosevelt was elected president for the fourth time, Hoover wrote a memorandum lamenting the superficiality, "smearing," and evasion of the "real issues" by both political parties during the just-completed campaign. The seventy-year-old former president was not in a cheerful mood as he contemplated the postwar world and soldiered on with his ever-expanding memoirs.

Hoover's typewritten memorandum is in the Arthur Kemp Papers, Box 4, Hoover Institution Archives. A handwritten marginal note by Hoover on the first page says: "Note by HH on the campaign sent to friends Nov 9, 1944."

11/9/44

This last Presidential campaign should cause Americans to pause a moment on the methods by which we are conducting the democratic process. As usual, when the fight is over all Americans accept the verdict, wish success to the administration and the more especially in this case do we close our ranks to win the war.

I have sat upon the side lines of this campaign watching matters. What policies are proposed for solution of the world's gigantic problems? What policies are being proposed for our gigantic American problems? What mandate is being given to the winner to do what? Post mortems in campaigns are only justified to discover if there is something damaging to American life and of danger to the Republic. In this I do not propose to discuss either the merits of the verdict or the merits and demerits of the candidates or the issues but solely the method.

The real issues before the American people were either only superficially treated, many unreal issues were raised to imaginative heights, and the whole was obscured by an unparalleled slugging match and a volume of smearing was resorted to such as we have not seen in a generation. And this applies to both sides. We may accept that the candidates were worthy representatives of the two great political parties and that they would both make able presidents; yet, no matter which was elected, it would be upon the many false issues and the scant presentation of the real issues and no mandate on any of them.

I suppose smearing is an accepted art in American politics, but, nevertheless, it is not particularly elevating morally or spiritually. The line where necessary exposure of truth ends and downright libel, slander, misrepresentation and lying begins is impossible to define in rules. No thoughtful person can fail to recognize the difference in the bold brush with which campaigns are fought. If our libel and slander laws were tightened up to the British standard, we would have far less of it—particularly if the Federal laws and enforcement of criminal libel were revised so as to protect the citizen. It has wider implications than the injury to contestants and bystanders. Thousands of needed men and women who would be great additions to public service refuse to go into "politics" because they regard it as a dirty experience and one from which the respect of their neighbors or even their families are jeopardized.

An inspection of the literature of this campaign quickly discloses that it is not so much the official organization of the parties which does the worst of this as it is the host of outside activities with which these organizations surround themselves. We can sample two instances. The whispering campaign emanating from Republican ranks as to the [sic–ed.] President Roosevelt's health and the consequent necessity for him to stay in the rain for six hours to the real danger of his health will serve for one. And the flood of despicable literature about Governor Dewey which flooded the country from the P.A.C.[1] and Communist organs is a counterpart, and it was less easy to overcome for it penetrated those ranks who paid little attention to the major speeches. But these degrading methods are not as important as the failures of the campaign to reach the real issues. Aside from war and peace the issue before the whole world today is the drift away from true liberalism toward collectivism. Colloquially, that has become the movement toward the "left" or to the "right." These

---

1. [*Editor's note*: In July 1943 the militant federation of labor unions known as the Congress of Industrial Organization (CIO) established a political action committee called the CIO-PAC. Its chairman was the left-wing labor leader Sidney Hillman (1887–1946), a close ally of the Roosevelt administration (see Document 6, note 2). In the campaign of 1944 the high-powered CIO-PAC energetically mobilized voters and got them to the polls in great numbers. Its efforts may well have made the difference for Roosevelt's reelection. To Hoover and many other Republicans, the CIO-PAC's propaganda and tactics were "despicable" and dangerous.]

left movements have different terms—Socialism, Communism, National Socialism, Fascism and Planned Economy. They have one common denominator and that is greater or less government operation or dictation to the economic system. No one will deny that this movement is in progress in the United States, Britain and all of the remaining democracies. In this campaign we have had no real debate of this issue. Mr. Roosevelt has expressed his great devotion to a nebular "private enterprise" but has given no assurance of stoppage to these drifts in a dozen government activities. On the other hand Mr. Dewey has contented himself with the statement that the Democratic Party has been sold on the auction block to the Communists. No one believes either assertion. And there has been no clarification of the real issues as applied to what is going on in the United States.

Another of our great problems is reconstruction after the war. We have been solemnly promised by both sides abundant prosperity with no depressions, with full employment of 60,000,000 workers at high wages and shorter hours after the war. No one stood up and told the American people the plain truth—that the aftermath of every war is impoverishment, inflation and that the one and only remedy will be longer hours and harder work and more economical living. No one mentioned that after the war in order to care for our debt, our returning soldiers, the relief to civilians and the other expenses of the Federal Government, we shall need to spend twenty billions a year and that that money comes out of somebody, somehow. No one suggested how we will lay such taxes with the least paralysis of production. We were, of course, promised that taxes would be lowered from war levels of fifty billions which is obvious, but the problem which we face was dodged.

On the question of foreign affairs, the machinery to preserve peace was lifted to such dimensions as to obscure the whole sky on foreign relations. The real issue of how we are going to first make a peace that can be preserved was not really mentioned. The Atlantic Charter may have been such a foreign policy, but the American people were not told that it is dead. We were not told that we are faced with an era of Communist expansion in Europe and that through Russian spheres of influence, annexations, ideological penetrations such as the world has never seen. We were not given any idea as to what we were going to do about any of them.

We were not told that the ferment of Asia for Asiatics had reached a volume that portends continuous clash between Western and Eastern civilizations as a dominant note in war aftermaths, and no suggestion was made as to what we are going to do about it.

These are the real foreign issues, and until some stability is reached upon them, the results of Dumbarton Oaks[2] stand little chance of being more than fine ideals and little purpose.

Obviously, this world will have to disarm from its present military strength, but the question of what and how much of a burden of arms we are to carry after the war was not mentioned.

When the war is over the world [will–*ed.*] be impoverished and intensely socialistic in its struggle to give employment. Already the rest of the world is planning vast self-containments (much of it at our expense). We heard not a word on what our policies were to be with regard to it.

---

2. [*Editor's note*: At the Dumbarton Oaks Conference, held in Washington, D.C., between August 21 and October 7, 1944, leading diplomats from the United States, the Soviet Union, Great Britain, and China formulated plans for a postwar world organization that became the United Nations.]

Hoover's First Months as an Ex-President

n.d.

[circa 1945–1947–ed.]

In the autumn of 1944 Hoover began systematically to organize the volume of his memoirs devoted to his battle against collectivism after he left the White House. He gave this installment the working title *Twelve Years 1932-1944*. By mid-December he had drafted chapter 1. It began: "American democracy is not a polite employer."

Hoover later used this opening passage on pp. 344–45 of the third volume of his *Memoirs*, published in 1952. The passage also appears on page 8 of the present volume. But as was his wont, he rarely left his memoirs' drafts alone. At some point after composing chapter 1 of *Twelve Years 1932-1944*, he rewrote it, adding several pages concerning his adjustment to private life during his first months as a former president. This new material became the opening pages in an undated set of page proofs of chapters 1 and 2 of *Twelve Years 1932-1944*.

For reasons unknown, Hoover never used most of this new material. Because of its intrinsic interest, it is reproduced here.

Document 8, consisting of pp. 1–4 of the undated, page-proof edition, is in "The Aftermath: Twelve Years 1932-1944 Edition Undated," *Memoirs of Herbert Hoover* Book Manuscript File, Box 13, Herbert Hoover Presidential Library. Two antecedent, typewritten drafts of chapter 1 (dated 12/19/44 and Dec. 24–28, 1944) are in the same collection, Box 13, in a folder labeled "The Aftermath: Twelve Years 1932-1944 Edition, Incomplete Drafts, December 1944."

Twelve Years 1932-1944

Chapter 1

I spent a few days at the Waldorf Astoria in New York to look after my sadly demoralized investments.[1] Old friends who had been caught in the holocaust

---

1. [*Editor's note*: After Franklin Roosevelt was inaugurated as president on March 4, 1933, Hoover took a train from Washington, D.C., to New York City, where he stayed for a couple of weeks before going home to California.]

had, from time to time, during the past two years, appealed to me for financial help which, given to friends, was naturally without security. I had extended it far beyond my means and in addition had violated a life-long rule by endorsing notes for some of them. It was evident that I should need take large losses on their account. I had made it a rule during my entire public service to have no interests except bonds of the trustee type. I had not, for fourteen years, held shares or other interests in any sort of business enterprise and therefore had no consequential losses on my own account.

I abstained from any comment on Mr. Roosevelt's actions, although in the general acclaim at his closing of the banks, I could have justifiably exposed the fact that had he been willing to cooperate with me and to keep his campaign promises, there need never have been a panic of depositors at all.

As for myself, I took but little interest in the urging of many to return to my profession, being incessantly concerned with public matters. When my own affairs were somewhat straightened out and we could see sufficient income with some drafts on capital savings to see Mrs. Hoover and me through life but on a much reduced scale of living which was no hardship.[2] Incidental receipts from writing were considerable and welcome. I had never accepted payment or even expenses for public speaking as I had always felt I owed that service to the country. I did not feel the same way as to requiring publishers who operated for a profit to pay something to me. The very considerable contributions to charity and public organizations which we had been able to make by dividing my official salaries among them proved an embarrassment. All of these agencies seemed to think such sums should be continued, but we simply did not have the resources to do so.

As soon as I could get some order into my private affairs, I returned to Palo Alto. Mrs. Hoover had preceded me to get the house in order for living after nearly twenty years of absence. I was given a hearty welcome home by the Governor of the State, the Mayor and a host of friends at the railway stations. At Palo Alto the students staged a vociferous reception. I found an accumulation of some twenty thousand letters, breathing devotion and loyalty; a third of them were hand written on the blue-lined paper of lowly home [*sic–ed.*]. We quickly organized a stenographic staff and gave to each of the latter a signed acknowledgement of their friendship. Signing these notes indeed was a tiresome task, but it seemed so little to do for so great an outpouring of affection.

---

2. [*Editor's note*: This sentence, though ungrammatical, is left as Hoover wrote it.]

I have read much editorializing on what to do with ex-Presidents. I realized they were a kind of menace chiefly because people had to listen to them. But my own recipe is to leave them alone and they will find plenty to do.

I resumed active participation in the management of a number of institutions to which I had paid little attention while in the White House. In various capacities as trustee, director or chairman, I took part in the work of Stanford University, the Huntington Library, Mills College, the Carnegie Institute, the Boys' Clubs of America, the American Children's Fund, the Belgian-American Educational Foundation and other committees.

In those cases where there were substantial endowments (a total of $100,000,000) my first effort was to secure the investment of part of such funds in common stocks instead of all in bonds and prior lien securities. I was confident that sooner or later the inevitable consequence of "Planned Economy" and management of money and credit would be the decreasing purchasing value of fixed incomes. While common stocks were no guarantee that income would keep pace, yet they at least had a chance. In the case of Stanford University it was necessary to secure an amendment to the trust deed through the courts before we could acquire other than prior lien securities. The institutions with which I was connected converted from 25% to 40% of their funds into equities. In every single case both their income and capital profited by the conversion.

I was asked to join the Board of the New York Life Insurance Company, several former Presidents having sat upon the Board of that great mutual trust. I found, however, that I could not, with partial residence in California, give it the attention which it seemed to me to devolve upon a director and I therefore resigned in order that a member who lived more constantly on the job might be elected.

Of these associations I gave probably the most attention to and derived the most satisfaction from being Chairman of the Boys' Clubs of America. Some indication of the importance and character of its work is indicated by one of my addresses to an annual meeting.[3]

◆ ◆ ◆

It was necessary for me to devote a good deal of time to the raising of funds for these scientific, educational, public welfare and relief institutions. Directly

---

3. [*Editor's note*: Hoover did not include any of his Boys Clubs addresses at this place in the document printed here. But he spoke at Boys Clubs gatherings on many occasions. See Appendix I, Document 2, chapter 3, especially note 4.]

and indirectly I must have raised from the public 15 to 20 millions for such purposes over the twelve years.

I was particularly interested in securing material for the Library on War, Peace and Revolution[4] at Stanford University and, further, in securing a building and endowment for it. With the help of nearly 1,000 old friends, including Edgar Rickard, Perrin Galpin and Jeremiah Milbank who organized it, we raised nearly $2,000,000 for this purpose. It has become an institution unique in the whole world. It has at least contributed to winning World War II by its being America's major source of vital material from World War I. Whether it will contribute to winning the peace is more problematical. Military men are avid for the lessons of experience. Politicians want to create the impression of inventing something "new."

I was soon to realize at least one great gain from leaving administrative office. It was the emancipation from a sort of peonage—a revolution back to personal freedom.[5]

---

4. [*Editor's note*: From 1938 to 1946, the enterprise that Hoover founded in 1919 was known officially as the Hoover Library on War, Revolution and Peace. In 1946, with Hoover's approval, the name was officially changed to the Hoover Institute and Library on War, Revolution and Peace. Since 1957, it has been known officially as the Hoover Institution on War, Revolution and Peace.]

5. [*Editor's note*: The next paragraph in Hoover's manuscript begins: "Democracy is not a polite employer." In somewhat revised form the ensuing passage made its way into Hoover's published *Memoirs*, as mentioned above.]

More Thoughts on Wendell Willkie and the Republican National Convention of 1940

1947

While Hoover was working on the manuscript that evolved into *The Crusade Years*, he was simultaneously preparing other sections of his memoirs, notably the "War Book" or Magnum Opus, which focused on World War II. By mid-1947 the War Book comprised 1,099 pages in page proofs, arranged chronologically in the form of chapters for each year between 1938 and 1946.

In his chapter for 1940 (a whopping 131 pages), Hoover penned a candid account of the Republican national convention that year, in the context of his impassioned campaign against American intervention in the war raging in Europe. Much of what he wrote there found its way in time (after revision) into his separate *Crusade Years* manuscript. But the passage printed as Document 9 did not. Most likely it fell victim to Hoover's urge to condense. In any case, because of its historical interest it is included here.

The text of Document 9 is taken from Hoover's "War Book," "1940" chapter, pp. 91–93, in the Herbert Hoover Papers, Box 6, folder 7, Hoover Institution Archives.

He [Wendell Willkie–*ed.*] believed he could talk any enemy into a friend any time. He spent hours talking to people on the telephone who had criticized him. It was all a kind of intellectual "kissing babies." But also it left a trail of people who were convinced that he was uninformed as to the issues, that his word was no good, that he was insincere.

He had intimate and loyal friends who followed him all the way, and many of whom have always justified his conduct on the ground that "you must first get elected." Like those surrounding all public men, there were many who hoped to rise with his star but who stood by only as the star was ascending. Probably the most bitter moment that comes to all men in public life is when this sort of intimate departs carrying away confidences, the favors he has received and begins to justify his action by mean statements. Willkie had so little time in public life before he became popular and powerful that his mind had not become calloused to such people. He suffered much more than the seasoned public animal who admits people to the inner sanctum much more carefully.

Knowing Willkie's private assurances to some of his supporters, I had little more faith in his promises to keep us out of war than in those of Roosevelt. However, he moved with the popular tide against war in his public utterances.

In a statement (June 18, 1940), a week before the Convention, which was widely distributed among the delegates, Willkie said:

> I want to repeat what I have said on several previous occasions. . . . We do not intend to send men from the shores of this continent to fight in any war. . . . We shall not serve the cause of democracy and human freedom by becoming involved in the present war; we shall serve that cause only by keeping out of war.
>
> . . . It is the duty of the President of the United States to recognize the determination of the people to stay out of war and to do nothing by word or deed that will undermine that determination.
>
> No man has the right to use the great powers of the Presidency to lead the people, indirectly, into war; only the people through their elected representatives can make that awful decision, and there is no question as to their education.

I was totally unable to reconcile this statement with a coincident circumstance. Two days before the Convention Mrs. Helen Reid, who in reality directed the policies of the *New York Herald Tribune*, called upon me to urge my support of Mr. Willkie. I informed her that Willkie could never be elected. Mrs. Reid, whose father-in-law had been Whitelaw Reid, Ambassador to the Court of St. James, was always more British than American and had often taken me savagely to task in her paper for my opposition to involving the United States in the war. On this occasion she violently opposed my suggestion of Senator Taft as a preferable candidate and told me that some days before she had given a lunch at which Senator Taft, Wendell Willkie, and interventionists Thomas Lamont, Lewis Douglas, Dorothy Thompson, Lord Lothian, the British Ambassador,[1] and others were present. Various views

---

1. [*Editor's note:* Thomas Lamont (1870–1948), an influential banker and longtime partner at J. P. Morgan and Company; Lewis Douglas (1894–1994), a politician, businessman, director of the U.S. Bureau of the Budget (1933–34), and active internationalist in 1939–41; Dorothy Thompson (1893–1961), an influential journalist and newspaper columnist, acclaimed by admirers as "the First Lady of American Journalism"; Philip Kerr (1882–1940), Marquess of Lothian, the British ambassador to the United States from September 1939 to December 1940.]

had been expressed that there must be "all-out" aid to Britain. Willkie had pledged himself in full but Taft had said that such a proposal was a subterfuge in phrases and that they really meant war. He would, therefore, not go along with such weasel words. Mrs. Reid told me he had been "very rude." The following day I confirmed her account from Senator Taft who admitted that his remarks might be construed as rude because he wanted no misunderstanding of his position. He told me that Willkie refused and evaded his demand to know if he included naval or land war in the "all-out" aid. There could be no doubt that in their hearts this "all-out" aid pledge meant war. Certainly the interventionists present considered Willkie as "safe." Knowing his background, I naturally opposed his nomination and supported Taft.

Preface to *Collectivism Comes to America*

1950

By early 1950 Hoover's manuscript *Twelve Years 1932–1944* had morphed into a massive two-volume tome titled *Collectivism Comes to America*. The first volume was subtitled *Roosevelt's First Term, 1933–1936*; the second, *Roosevelt's Second Term, 1936–1940*. In page-proof form, the work totaled 538 pages.

In its preface, Hoover bluntly explained the guiding purposes of the parts of his memoirs dealing with his postpresidential years, including his *Collectivism* segment. Plainly he was writing no leisurely chronicle of gentle reminiscences.

The page proofs of the first volume of *Collectivism Comes to America* were returned to Hoover by the printer on April 7, 1950. The preface, printed here, appears on pp. 1–3 of this set of proofs, which is filed in "The Aftermath: Collectivism Comes to America—Roosevelt's First Term, 1933–1936" (two folders), *Memoirs of Herbert Hoover* Book Manuscript File, Box 13, Herbert Hoover Presidential Library.

Preface

From leaving the White House in 1933 to 1950, my purpose and my occupation was to aid the American people in their multitude of problems.

Transcending all recreation and other kinds of occupations was the compelling conscience that comes from a duty to a people by one who has been honored by their highest trust—especially when they are misguided.

I have prepared these memoirs for several purposes. First, to prove the follies of our departure from the American system we have steadily builded over 300 years. Second, to strip polluted history of its falsehoods. That is necessary if a people are to be guided by experience and truth. Third, to give the views I held on these questions at the time.

During the years after the presidency, I conducted or participated in four major crusades on public questions. To give a chronological account of these activities would be most confusing. I have therefore divided these memoirs after 1933 into three series.

The first series is entitled, "The Crusade against Collectivism in America." It began with Roosevelt's New Deal. My activities contributed something to check its march.

The second series is entitled, "Memoirs upon the Foreign Policies of the United States, 1933–1947."[1] It embraces my crusade to keep America out of World War II and an analysis of Roosevelt's foreign policies from 1933 to 1945 and their consequences.

This crusade failed at Pearl Harbor in 1941 through Roosevelt's provocative and unconstitutional actions. However, it contributed something to keep the great majority of the people steadfast against the war until that time. In this series I have included a third crusade that is my effort to establish certain principles vital to a lasting peace. They were defeated by Roosevelt's and Truman's foreign policies.

The third series of these memoirs is entitled, "Food and Economics in the Second World War."[2] In this crusade, I had some successes.

I make no pretense that I was the only or even the most important crusader. There were thousands or even millions of Americans of the same views.

Thus, from 1933 on, these memoirs consist of three series, parallel as to dates in certain periods.

In preparing each particular series, I have proceeded by topics, roughly in chronological order. While topical treatment in this way requires some retracing of the time over short periods, yet if the whole were put in chronological diary form, the particular movements which it is my object to trace would be utterly confusing to the reader.

The crusade against "Collectivism" runs from 1933 to 1950. Although during the four years of the Second World War I was necessarily less active on this subject, yet during this 17 years, I delivered over 60 national addresses on related subjects of which 50 were nationwide broadcasts. I wrote articles

---

1. [*Editor's note*: This was the "War Book" or Magnum Opus, as Hoover and his intimates called it. It had several working titles. In 1962 Hoover settled on the title *Freedom Betrayed*, under which it was published posthumously by the Hoover Institution Press in 2011.]

2. [*Editor's note*: This segment focused primarily on Hoover's humanitarian relief efforts for war-ravaged nations during and immediately after World War II. He later titled it *The Four Horsemen in World War II* and *The Crusade against Famine in World War II*. In much revised form it was published in 1964 as volume IV of Hoover's *An American Epic* (Chicago: Henry Regnery Company.)]

for magazines, published 8 books,[3] gave out a host of press releases, and made literally thousands of talks before local audiences, associations and Congressional committees.

In preparing this series I have included my own statements at the time, to establish that there is not rationalization by retrospective comment. Where criticism otherwise than from myself of the New Deal collectivism is introduced, I have restricted it to individuals and representatives of the press who were at one time or another supporters or associates of President Roosevelt. To quote Republicans would carry less conviction.

This segment of my memoirs is in no sense a history of the Roosevelt and Truman administrations with all their vagaries and extravagances. It is limited to those activities which undermine the American System of life.

Some of these crusades brought me considerable defamation and some of them were, perhaps, lost causes at the time. But with the faith of a crusader to himself, his cause is never lost.

The world has survived error in ideas and confusion before. And men have grown in soul and safety because some groups of them have stood solid. They stood fast not because they knew the solutions to all the confusions, not even because they had the power to find the solution. They stood firm and they held up the light until the furies passed because they held certain sacred principles of life, of morals, and of spiritual values. I could at least do that.

---

3. A friend in Battle Creek, Michigan, considered it important to preserve my speeches and writings and therefore paid for their publication in periodic volumes under the title, *Addresses upon the American Road*. Five volumes have been issued over the years: (1) 1933–1938; (2) 1938–1940; (3) 1940–1941 (Charles Scribner's Sons, New York, 1938, 1940, 1941); (4) 1941–1945 (D. Van Nostrand Company, Inc., New York, 1946). [*Editor's note*: Hoover's benefactor was the breakfast cereals magnate W. K. Kellogg.]

Hoover Seeks Advice about Publishing His Memoirs

May 21, 1950

By the spring of 1950 Hoover's gargantuan memoirs had grown to include eight separate components. The accumulated page proofs probably exceeded three thousand printed pages.

Since the eight units (especially those for 1933 onward) were not strictly chronological, the former president faced a puzzling question: in what order should he publish them? How should he combine these independent but sometimes overlapping parts? In the letter printed here, he turned to his intimate friend Lewis L. Strauss for advice.

Document 11 is contained in "Strauss, Lewis L.," Post-Presidential Individual Correspondence File, Herbert Hoover Papers, Herbert Hoover Presidential Library.

The Waldorf Astoria Towers
New York, New York
May 21, 1950

Mr. Lewis Strauss
Brandy
Virginia

My dear Lewis:

You are doing me a good turn by looking over that Mss. I am not asking you to correct grammer [*sic–ed.*] or diction. But I need advice in a wider field. These memoirs are now in an advanced stage covering:

1. 1874–1914 — Private Life (which you have)
2. 1914–1919 — Food and Reconstruction in World War I (which you have)
3. 1919–1929 — Reconstruction in the United States (being my eight years in the Department of Commerce)

4. 1929–1933—Policies, Development and Reform (in one volume)
5. 1929–1933—The Great Depression and the Campaign of 1932 (in one volume)[1]
6. 1933–1940—Collectivism Comes to the United States (in two volumes)
7. 1938–1947—Foreign Policies of the United States (in three volumes)[2]
8. Food and Relief in World War II (or The Four Horsemen in World War II) (in one volume).[3]

In the manuscript you have there is Private Life and World War II.

Bud Kelland[4] thinks I should take the Private Life section, abstract the interesting and human incidents from World War II, plus a continuation of the same process of extraction from other Memoirs, all to make a purely personal volume. He says, and I agree, that the jump from a personal to an official account at 1914 is not good, and that it does not make a complete personal history. He wants to issue the reconstructed personal history at once.

I have great doubts over that method. If I extract the interesting incidents and the personal parts from the volumes from 1914 to 1933, it leaves the other volumes of that period very flat, and I am afraid robs them of public interest.

I had hoped to have sent to you No. 3 (The Secretary of Commerce), but it is not back from the printer. I believe it is of some importance in history as showing the reconstruction of the United States after the war.

My present thought is to combine No. 2 and No. 3 into one volume and entitle it The Four Horsemen in World War I, and for the present not to issue the private life section. As a second dose I would then follow with No. 4 and No. 5, covering my period in the White House. Then, having established these backgrounds, to follow with the private life account. The volumes No. 6, No. 7, and No. 8 should not be issued for some years in any event.

---

1. [Editor's note: The first five units listed here were published in The Memoirs of Herbert Hoover (1951–52) (three volumes). See editor's introduction to Appendix II, Document 12.]

2. [Editor's note: This is a reference to Hoover's foreign policy Magnum Opus, ultimately published in 2011 as Freedom Betrayed.]

3. [Editor's note: Later revised and published as volume IV of Hoover's An American Epic. See Appendix II, Document 10, note 2.]

4. [Editor's note: Clarence Budington Kelland (1881–1964), was a prolific novelist and author of short stories, and from the mid-1930s an anti–New Deal, Republican activist living in Arizona. For many years he was a good friend and informal literary advisor to Hoover.]

I have experimented along Bud Kelland's line by recasting the private life section and the interesting incidents up to 1929. But it certainly leaves the full text from 1914 to 1929 very flat and just a recitation of details of organization, of personnel, and statistical results which I cannot believe would command much reading, and at the same time it does not give a full picture of 1914–1929.

What do you think?

Yours faithfully,
[Herbert Hoover–*ed.*]

Introduction to *The Years as Crusader*

April 26, 1951

In 1951–52 the Macmillan Company in New York published the first three volumes of *The Memoirs of Herbert Hoover*. They included the first five segments that he mentioned in Document 11. The final section of the third published volume consisted of a substantial portion of volume I of his manuscript *Collectivism Comes to America*.

Meanwhile, Hoover had been reworking the rest of *Collectivism Comes to America* into a new text called *The Crusade against Collectivism*. Hoover now intended to incorporate it—and several other unpublished units of his memoirs—into a single, enormous volume that he titled *The Years as Crusader*.

Document 12 clarifies Hoover's reconceptualization of his writing task as the first installments of his multivolume memoirs headed toward publication. His introduction to *The Years as Crusader* printed here is the first page of a 280-page set of page proofs containing Parts 1 and 2 of the segments listed in the Introduction. The full document is filed in the Herbert Hoover Papers, Box 88, folder 1, Hoover Institution Archives. The date of the document—April 26, 1951—was penciled in (as "4/26/51") on the first page. It probably denoted the date that the page proofs came back from the printer.

The Years as Crusader

Introduction

This volume is a summary of many activities.

Part 1. Some Incidents of Family Life and Some Activities of an Ex-President.

Part 2. Seventeen Years' Crusade against Collectivism in America. This necessarily includes a discussion of the political campaigns and political personages of the times.

Part 3. Three Years of Crusade against Joining in World War II and My Crusade against Entry into Possible World War III. The account of these activities is not to be published for some years.[1]

Part 4. The Four Horsemen in World War II. This is an account of my crusades on behalf of starving peoples and my relief activities.

As in previous memoirs, I have treated various subjects topically, but roughly chronologically, rather than the confusion of strict chronological recitation.

---

1. [*Editor's note*: No memoirs drafts of "Part 3" have been found, unless Hoover was referring obliquely to his foreign policy volume known as the "War Book" or Magnum Opus, which he was concurrently writing. The reference to his "crusade" against entry into a possible World War III was probably an allusion to his recent, very public participation in the so-called Great Debate of 1950–51 over American military strategy and foreign policy vis-à-vis Europe. Hoover evidently intended to cover this topic in his memoirs but appears not to have done so.]

Introduction to *The Four Horsemen in World War II*

May 2, 1951

Document 13 is the first page of a lengthy account of Hoover's humanitarian relief efforts during and after World War II. The entire manuscript (215 pages in page proofs) is in the Herbert Hoover Papers, Box 88, folder 2, Hoover Institution Archives.

As mentioned earlier, in the spring of 1951 Hoover intended this narrative to be part 4 of *The Years as Crusader*. Thirteen years later, a much revised version of it was published separately as volume IV in Hoover's series *An American Epic*.

Hoover's brief introductory statement of purpose offers a glimpse of some of the other subjects on his mind as he juggled the writing of his multivolume memoirs.

The Four Horsemen in World War II

Introduction

With my experience in World War I and my natural sympathies for the women, children and civilian men in war-torn countries, I naturally took some part in combating the work of the Four Horsemen in World War II and in an endeavor for their proper organization.

I shall relate elsewhere in my memoirs my views on the Foreign Policies in World War II. This volume is confined to my participation in the problems of Food and Reconstruction.

Four separate problems of relief, food, famine and reconstruction appeared in World War II and its aftermath.

The first was the relief during the war to the women and children of the German-occupied democracies.

The second was our economic and food organization on the Home Front.

The third was the preparation for reconstruction and the inevitable postwar famine.

The fourth was the Great World Famine of 1946 and its aftermath in 1947.

For clarity, this memoir has been divided into four parts under the topics listed above, rather than in chronological order. Within each topic, however, the treatment is as far as possible chronological.

In this text, wherever possible, I have condensed documents and statements to eliminate repetitions and immaterial matter. My public addresses during this period were published in a series of volumes entitled "Addresses upon the American Road." The full texts of other documents referred to are in the War Library at Stanford University.

A Hoover Memorandum on Dwight Eisenhower and Robert Taft

May 6, 1952

Even as Hoover was writing and revising his colossal memoirs, focusing on his past achievements and crusades, he was also immersed in crusades in the stormy present, as this document reminds us. In the spring of 1952, as Dwight Eisenhower and Robert Taft battled for the Republican presidential nomination, Hoover covertly but energetically supported Taft. In the unsigned memorandum reproduced here, Hoover bluntly gave his reasons.

In this document Hoover at one point referred to himself in the third person—a sign that he probably intended to circulate his analysis anonymously, since he had not yet publicly endorsed any candidate. It is also possible that he contemplated giving this memo to someone else to promulgate under that person's name. Although Hoover often poked fun at ghostwriters (as readers of this volume will have noticed), over the years he frequently drafted letters and other documents for friends and associates to sign as their own. The Chief (as his intimates called him) enjoyed political wire-pulling while carefully staying out of view. It was a form of self-protection for a man increasingly acclaimed as an elder statesman. The essay printed here is an example of what one might call Hoover's "hidden hand" ex-presidency.

Document 14 is found among a number of Hoover-generated typescripts in a folder labeled "Campaign 1952: Taft—Pre-convention Struggle," Post-Presidential Subject File, Herbert Hoover Papers, Herbert Hoover Presidential Library. The handwritten date ("5/6/52 II") on the first page may indicate that it was a second draft or a second copy of the document.

5/6/52

What Are the Differences between the Stand of Eisenhower and Taft on Foreign Relations?

Eisenhower stands for the Truman-Acheson policies in Western Europe which he has repeatedly advocated in speeches and before Congressional committees.

These comprise:

(a) The building up of great American ground armies in Western Europe (4 divisions of American boys have already been shipped at Eisenhower's direct demand on Congress).

The Europeans are supposed to join in this ground-army venture. Despite direct or indirect American subsidies of 50 billions over 5 years, Western European nations have, up to date, contributed only 10 or 15 divisions with which to meet 300 Russian divisions. They have no belief in a Russian danger. They have made repeated promises to supply their own ground armies. As recently as February 15, 1952, they again signed an agreement—at Lisbon—by which they were to have, according to General Eisenhower, 50 divisions (including American and British) by the end of 1952. This agreement provided for 12 German divisions. Neither the German or French Parliaments have ratified the agreement. It is very unlikely that they will do so. Even so, the *London Times* (February 22, 1952) states that Eisenhower's Army is a Phantom Army.

As a matter of fact the whole scheme has failed and our 250,000 American boys in Europe are left "holding the Bag," against 3,500,000 Russians.

This Western European scheme is the cause of our huge budget, our huge taxes and our increasing inflation. Eisenhower advocates that we continue all of these things.

Furthermore, Eisenhower, in order to support this building of ground armies in the United States, now demands universal compulsory military training—a nation in uniform—(with, in his view, a military President).

Eisenhower has been part of the Roosevelt-Truman administration ever since 1940. He can hardly criticize any of their terrible mistakes and must in any campaign support these Truman-Acheson policies as he has been in large degree their maker.

Taft's views are as follows:

Taft adopted former President Hoover's proposal that we cannot support great ground armies, air and naval forces, and munitions and subsidies to Europe all at the same time. He advocated that we reduce ground armies, have no universal compulsory military training, but confine our great productivity to the building up of an overwhelming air and naval force, and the supplying of munitions to such European countries as are willing to really arm in their own defense. This overwhelming air and naval force is not only the real deterrent to Russian aggression, but could destroy their war potential if they started a war.[1]

---

1. [*Editor's note*: Hoover was summarizing his foreign policy address of January 27, 1952, printed in the *New York Times*, January 28, 1952, p. 6.]

This plan is supported by leading army and naval officers who have stated that by doing so we can far better deter Russian aggression and can do it without this destructive burden of spending, taxes, and inflation. Among those supporting this policy are Generals: MacArthur, Wedemeyer, Groves, George, Knerr, Disque; Admirals: Standley, Pratt, Yarnell and many other high military authorities.[2]

The Eisenhower policy means continued gigantic spending, taxes, inflation. (This very spending is the origin of great corruption in Washington.)

The Taft policy assures the absolute defense of the United States, our doing a reasonable service to foreign nations and doing it without destroying our American life.

Taft can go into the campaign in full criticism of the Truman-Acheson policies, past and present.

As General Wedemeyer has said[:–ed.] "Taft is neither an isolationist, nor an internationalist, he is a realist"—and will put up a fighting campaign, not again the Republican "me-too" campaign as in 1940–1944 and 1948.

---

2. [*Editor's note*: Hoover was evidently referring to retired Generals Douglas MacArthur, Albert Wedemeyer, Leslie R. Groves, Harold L. George, Hugh Knerr, and Brice P. Disque and to retired Admirals William H. Standley, William V. Pratt, and Harry E. Yarnell. Most of them had applauded a major foreign policy address by Hoover on January 27, 1952. See *New York Times*, February 8, 1952, p. 8, and Herbert Hoover, *Addresses upon the American Road, 1950–1955* (Stanford, CA: Stanford University Press, 1955), pp. 45–52.]

Introduction to *The Crusade Years*

May 29, 1953

Sometime in 1952 or early 1953 Hoover revised and revamped his 1951 manuscript *The Years as Crusader*. He gave the new version a new title: *The Crusade Years*. Gone now was any mention of part III of the 1951 draft, which was to have chronicled his crusades against America's entering World War II and a possible World War III. (See Document 12.) In its place, he inserted a short memoir-essay on his "Crusades for Benevolent Institutions."

As thus reconfigured, *The Crusade Years* (1953 edition) comprised 564 pages in page proofs. At this point Hoover still intended to include "The Crusade against the Four Horsemen in World War II" in this volume. A couple of years later he changed his mind.

The introduction reproduced here is the first page of the 1953, page-proof edition of *The Crusade Years*. A faint, handwritten notation indicates that the initial batch of page proofs (including the introduction) was returned to Hoover from the printer on May 29, 1953.

Hoover's master copy of *The Crusade Years* (1953 version), including the extract printed here, is located in the Herbert Hoover Papers, Box 89, folders 2 and 3, Hoover Institution Archives.

Introduction

This volume recounts my activities, apart from problems of foreign relations, during the 20-year period after leaving the White House in 1932 until the establishment of a Republican Administration in January 1953.

The material in this volume was put together incidentally during the work on the three volumes of *Memoirs*, published in 1951–1952,[1] and on the two

---

1. *The Memoirs of Herbert Hoover: The Years of Adventure* (Vol. I); *The Cabinet and the Presidency* (Vol. II); *The Great Depression* (Vol. III). All three volumes were published by The Macmillan Company in 1951–1952.

volumes of *Memoirs* entitled *Lost Statesmanship*, which cover American Foreign Relations from 1932 to 1953.[2] Its purpose is to provide material for future historical use, and its composition has served to fill in many lonesome hours between public service and occasional periods of recreation.

I have divided this volume into four sections, treating the subjects topically rather than chronologically. Within the sections I have also followed the topical pattern. Although there is, as a result, an overlap in time, much confusion of the various subjects is avoided.

The Sections are:

Section I   Some Notes on Private Life
Section II   Crusades for Benevolent Institutions
Section III   The Crusade against the Four Horsemen in World War II
Section IV   The Crusade against Collectivism in American Life

In this text, wherever possible, I have condensed documents and statements to eliminate repetitions and subordinate matter. My public addresses during this period were published in a series of volumes entitled *Addresses upon the American Road*. The full texts of all other documents referred to are in the War Library at Stanford University.

---

2. [*Editor's note*: Hoover is referring here to his vast foreign policy manuscript known as the Magnum Opus, to which he gave the title *Lost Statesmanship* in 1950. As mentioned earlier, he changed its title more than once. Its final title was *Freedom Betrayed*.]

DOCUMENT 16

"The Incident of Justice Hughes"

n.d.

[circa 1953?–ed.]

From 1946 to 1953 Arthur Kemp assisted Hoover in the preparation of his memoirs. In Kemp's papers (opened to researchers in 2011) there is a batch of documents originally contained in an envelope marked "The campaign of 1940 With Notes on Wendle [*sic–ed.*] Willkie." This dossier contains Hoover's revision of chapter 10 of his page-proof manuscript, dated 1951, of *The Years as Crusader*. Chapter 10 was titled "The Presidential Campaign of 1940." The rewritten and amplified chapter consists of marked-up page proofs intermingled with typewritten copies of Hoover's relevant correspondence and memoranda of 1940, all assembled in chronological order with connective, narrative comments by Hoover.

Among the many gems of political history in this dossier is a three-page typewritten memorandum titled "The Incident of Justice Hughes." Therein Hoover recounted his remarkable attempt to persuade Chief Justice Charles Evans Hughes to resign from the Supreme Court at the height of the 1940 election campaign and call for the nation to repudiate Franklin Roosevelt at the polls.

Hoover's written appeal to Chief Justice Hughes on October 17, 1940, has long been known. Hughes's biographer, Merlo J. Pusey, had access to Hoover's letter and quoted it in a biography of Hughes published in 1951. But no complete text of Hoover's letter appears to have survived, other than in the document made public here for the first time. Nor has the background of Hoover's letter been disclosed before now. Document 16, therefore, is of more than ordinary interest. It is Hoover's account of the episode in his own words.

It is not known precisely when Hoover composed this document, but it was obviously sometime after he prepared the page proofs of *The Years as Crusader* in 1951.

The document and the full dossier are filed in the Arthur Kemp Papers, Box 4, Hoover Institution Archives.

The Incident of Justice Hughes

October 15, 1940—Memorandum

Will Hays[1] a few days ago asked if I would not send a letter to Chief Justice Hughes, suggesting to him that he resign his position and come out for Willkie. I informed Hays that I would not do so unless it came to me as a request from Willkie. In the course of time he secured the attached telegram from Willkie.

I wrote the letter and it was delivered by Larry[2] at five o'clock this afternoon. The Chief Justice said he had already been approached on the subject by Mr. Willkie or from Mr. Willkie. He had already made up his mind that he would not do so.

October 16, 1940—Telegram to HH from Mr. [Wendell–ed.] Willkie

"I have heard of the suggestion. If you believe the request is consistent with the proprieties I hope that you may see fit to make it. The seriousness of the national situation seems to warrant the action. My best wishes to you."

October 17, 1940—Letter to Chief Justice Hughes from HH

"I am about to make a suggestion that may impress you as fantastic. I would not do so if I did not believe that the whole future of the American people hangs upon the decision of this election. The growth of personal power in the Republic; the gradual subjugation of the Congress and the Supreme Court; the steady drawing of this country into European war; the constant undermining of free enterprise and the inevitable downfall of civil liberty that goes with it; the degeneration of manhood and womanhood under the impact of government subsidy; and a thousand other forces in motion mean the defeat of this civilization if Mr. Roosevelt is continued in office. And it seems to me the only hope of the world lies in this Republic.

"You and I are getting far along in life. We have little further to contribute. Public office can have no attraction for either of us. Our only hope is to preserve something of the ideals of this country for our children and other children.

"Mr. Willkie is making some progress under the most difficult of campaigns. No matter whether in details he believes as you and I may believe, yet

---

1. [*Editor's note*: Will H. Hays (1879–1954), postmaster-general of the United States from 1921 to 1922 and president of the Motion Picture Producers and Distributors of American from 1927 to 1945. He and Hoover met and corresponded frequently over many years. Hoover's calendar at the Herbert Hoover Presidential Library shows that they met on October 4, 10, and 16, 1940.]

2. [*Editor's note*: Lawrence Richey (1885–1959), Hoover's longtime confidential secretary and troubleshooter.]

I assure you he is a man of intellectual integrity and devoted to the historic liberalism of this country. These fundamental qualities are the only thing that can now save the American Republic. At the present moment he will not be elected. We have another two or three weeks of the battle. It is doubtful whether without some extraordinary and dramatic action we can pull him over. And that brings me to the fantastic suggestion I have to make.

"That is whether you feel that in this extraordinary crisis of the nation you could resign from your high office with a declaration to the country of the complete necessity for a change in Administration. There is no man in the whole country who enjoys so complete a confidence from the American people as yourself and in whose word they would repose more belief. Your voice has not been worn out by controversy. I have been fighting against Mr. Roosevelt and his New Deal for eight years. My effect is worn thin. But such as I have in me is going into this campaign.

"Somewhere, somehow a new voice needs to appear to give guidance to our people. They are confused, frustrated and fearful. And under all the various machinations and impacts of this monstrous machine in Washington they are today most likely to be misguided.

"I am sending this to you by a trusted secretary, and either way that you may decide shall remain as between you and me."

◆ ◆ ◆

(Larry presented this letter to Hughes on the 19th. His reply was "I have already been approached and I have had to decline to entertain it."[3]

Thus the effort was spoiled for obviously with all the world butting in he could not protect his position otherwise.)

◆ ◆ ◆

(I subsequently regretted having sent the letter because of my certification of Willkie's intellectual integrity. As an alternative to Roosevelt the letter was correct.)

---

3. [*Editor's note*: To his biographer Hughes later gave a different explanation. Hughes said he told Hoover's courier that he could not consider what Hoover asked him to do; that he (the chief justice) had always tried to keep the Supreme Court out of politics; and that he could not change this policy for the sake of a political campaign. Hughes added that he did not think that his resigning from the court would be effective. President Roosevelt would simply nominate a new chief justice, and Hughes himself would lose his prestige of office if he entered the political fray. See Merlo J. Pusey memorandum of interview with Charles Evans Hughes, June 4, 1946, in Merle J. Pusey Papers, L. Tom Perry Special Collections Library, Harold B. Lee Library, Brigham Young University, Provo, Utah. See also Merlo J. Pusey, *Charles Evans Hughes* (New York: The Macmillan Company, 1951), pp. 785–86.]

Hoover's Role in the Election of 1952

n.d.

[circa 1953?–ed.]

In the *Crusade against Collectivism* section of Hoover's *Crusade Years* manuscript, the former president barely mentioned his role in the presidential election campaign of 1952, other than his nationally broadcast radio and television address on behalf of the Republican ticket on October 18. On page 315 in the present volume, he noted tersely in a single sentence that he had "favored" Senator Robert A. Taft over General Dwight D. Eisenhower for the Republican Party's presidential nomination.

In fact, Hoover had strenuously opposed Eisenhower and just as strenuously supported the more conservative Taft, whom he publicly endorsed during the Republican national convention. But more than that, for many months before the convention Hoover maneuvered constantly behind the scenes to promote Taft's candidacy—as partly disclosed in the memorandum printed here.

This undated, memoirish document appears to have been a product of Hoover's updating of his *Crusade* manuscript in 1953 or 1955. Why he did not complete the document and put it into page proofs is unknown, but two factors most likely provide the explanation. First, between 1953 and 1961 Dwight Eisenhower was president of the United States, and during part of this period (1953 to 1955) Hoover was chairman of the Commission on Organization of the Executive Branch of the Government (the Second Hoover Commission). To wield influence, he needed to be on good terms with Eisenhower, the first Republican president in twenty years. Second, from 1954 to 1957 Hoover's older son served as undersecretary of state in Eisenhower's administration. Under these circumstances, one could not expect the former president to disclose to the world that in 1952 he had harbored deep reservations about Eisenhower's suitability for the White House.

Nevertheless, Hoover did, at some later point, record his concerns about Eisenhower in the candid memoir fragment reproduced here. This document helps to fill a noticeable void in Hoover's *Crusade Years* reminiscences. Perhaps because Document 17 is unfinished, it does not fully spell out the lengths to which Hoover went to advance Taft's candidacy and thwart Eisenhower's in the rancorous political campaign of 1952.

Document 17 is filed in "Campaign 1952: Taft, Pre-Convention Struggle," Post-Presidential Subject File, Herbert Hoover Papers, Herbert Hoover Presidential Library.

When General Eisenhower indicated in the fall of 1951 that he was willing to be drafted, I felt that Senator Taft, a civilian with long experience in public administration and with his integrity and courage, would be of much greater service to the Republican Party and to the country. I greatly opposed a professional soldier for President, not only because of his lack of experience in civil live [*sic–ed.*] but also because the policies of the country were steadily drifting toward militarism, as witness the building of great ground armies and the further proposal, supported by General Eisenhower, of compulsory/universal/military training. General Eisenhower had himself in 1948 declared that no professional soldier should be President in a statement in the *New York Times*.

General Eisenhower, on January 22, 1948, stated:

. . . I am not available for and could not accept nomination to high political office. . . .

It is my conviction that the necessary and wise subordination of the military to civil power will be best sustained and our people will have greater confidence that it is so sustained when lifelong professional soldiers in the absence of some obvious and overriding reasons, abstain from seeking high political office. This truth has a possible inverse application. I would regard it as unalloyed tragedy for our country if ever should come the day when military commanders might be selected with an eye to their future potentialities in the political field rather than exclusively upon judgment as to their military abilities.

Politics is a profession; a serious, complicated and, in its true sense, a noble one.

In the American scene I see no dearth of men fitted by training, talent and integrity for national leadership. On the other hand, nothing in the international or domestic situation especially qualifies for the most important office in the world a man whose adult years have been spent in the country's military forces. At least this is true in my case.[4]

Moreover, I was reminded of the statement of General Sherman when in 1884 he said he would not seek the nomination if nominated, he would

---

4. [*Editor's note*: *New York Times*, January 24, 1948, p. 2. I have corrected a few minor transcription errors in Hoover's quotation of Eisenhower's statement.]

refuse it if he were nominated, and if elected, he would not serve. But more pertinent was his statement in reply again to an urging from James G. Blaine that his name be allowed to be put in nomination. On May 25, 1884, James G. Baline [Blaine–*ed.*] wrote to General William J.[T.–*ed.*] Sherman, the great Civil War general, urging him to become a candidate for President. To which General Sherman replied:

> I will not in any event entertain or accept a nomination as a candidate for President by the Chicago Republican convention, or any other convention, for reasons personal to myself. I claim that the Civil War, in which I simply did a man's fair share of work, so perfectly accomplished peace that military men have an absolute right to rest, and to demand that the men who have been schooled in the arts and practice of peace shall now do their work equally well. *Any Senator can step from his chair at the Capitol into the White House and fulfill the office of President with more skill and success than a Grant, Sherman or Sheridan, who were soldiers by education and nature, who filled well their office when the country was in danger, but were not schooled in the practice by which civil communities are and should be governed.* I claim that our experience since 1865 demonstrates the truth of this my proposition. Therefore I say that patriotism does not demand of me what I construe as a sacrifice of judgment, of inclination, and of self-interest.[5]

General Sherman was no doubt referring to the Grant Administration from 1869 to 1876.

The Eisenhower supporters contended we had had many professional soldiers in the Presidency. Only one of them was a professional soldier—General Ulysses S. Grant—and his inabilities to contend with civilian problems was one of the dark pages of our history. Even George Washington had worn a uniform less than ten years of his 67 years of life. All the others were men who had served only a few years in war or insurrections and were in fact civilians. Except for Grant, none of them had spent the major years of their adult life on active military duty.

General Eisenhower had other liabilities. He was the symbole [*sic–ed.*] of Truman's foreign policies with its unbearable spending and taxation, which were breaking the economic back of the United States. Having been associated with the Democratic leaders over ten years of war and with the gigantic

---

5. [Editor's note: Italics are Hoover's. General William Tecumseh Sherman's letter to Senator James G. Blaine was dated May 28, 1884. It is printed in W. T. Sherman, "Hon. James G. Blaine," *North American Review* 147 (December 1888): 622–23. I have slightly modified Hoover's punctuation to conform to Sherman's.]

failure to make peace, he was in no position to take up vigorous and effective opposition to the Democratic position.

Eisenhower, like Willkie, was not a Republican who could command the zeal of real Republicans. He had voted for Roosevelt and, after leaving the military service in 1948, he registered as an Independent for the 1949 election. No doubt he looked upon the Republican label as a liability.

Under these circumstances I determined to do what I properly could to aid Senator Robert Taft. Taft and his managers considered my public support as a liability as witness my proposal to issue a statement during the New Hampshire primaries on March 11, 1952, which they requested me not to do. The statement I offered to them was as follows:

(The following statement was offered to Taft and Hamilton for use in the New Hampshire Primaries but they decided not to use it.)

I have your request on behalf of my New Hampshire friends that I give my conclusions as to the Republican Presidential candidates.

I have not done so for many years, but in this election we will determine whether or not we shall preserve the freedoms of American life. I, therefore, give my views on our major candidates without reserve.

I have known Senator Taft for thirty-five years since he joined my organization during the First World War. At that time he assumed an important administrative position in which he demonstrated high executive abilities. Most of his mature life has been one of continuous experience in every phase of our government.

In the ensuing years he has continually demonstrated a forthright, courageous character of complete intellectual and financial integrity. His has been a high statesmanship with an unfailing devotion to the fundamental principles of American life.

We may differ on secondary issues, but in these sober and dangerous times, it is these qualities above all others that we need in a Presidential Candidate.

If the Republican Party is to survive, it must repudiate me-too-ism and resume its role as the true champion of American principles. Senator Taft is a fighter for those principles. This is a fight to save America.[6]

Taft was not a good organizer of a campaign. On _____ I had a session with some of his managers, Ben Tate[7] and _____ and _____, where

---

6. [*Editor's note*: The date of this proffered endorsement was February 26, 1952. See copy in "Campaign 1952: Taft—Pre-convention Struggle," Post-Presidential Subject File, Herbert Hoover Papers, Herbert Hoover Presidential Library.]

7. [*Editor's note*: Ben E. Tate was the national treasurer of Senator Robert A. Taft's presidential campaign committee in 1952.]

I proposed the immediate and widespread organization of Taft Clubs at the grass roots, which would work for Taft delegates in the caucuses, state conventions, and primaries. They, however, considered the strategy to be used was Taft's great debating powers plus the usual political manipulation.

On January 16, 1952, John Colman [Colmar–*ed.*] of Chicago,[8] who had on his own motion started such clubs, came in to see me to tell me that the Taft managers had asked him to stop. The same word came to me on January 30, 1952 from Mr. Reilly and Mr. Porteous [Portious–*ed.*] of Westchester County, New York, who had started Taft Clubs. But Taft's managers objected, and the plan was laid aside.

When Taft's campaign began to slump at the grass roots as witness much failure in primaries and conventions, such as New Hampshire (March 11), Minnesota (March 18) I again on [date not given–*ed.*] proposed the Wedemeyer Committee.[9] Although _____ months late, that Committee put a shot in the arm of the campaign which saved it. I selected Jim Selvage[10] as its director and secured that my friends furnish the modest finance which it needed. I took an active part in setting up their committees in[11]

---

8. [*Editor's note*: John L. Colmar was the national chairman of the Taft Clubs of America in early 1952.]

9. [*Editor's note*: The Citizens for Taft committee was officially launched on May 5, 1952. General Albert Wedemeyer (1897–1989), a friend of Taft and Hoover, was its chairman.]

10. [*Editor's note*: James P. Selvage (1902–75) was a New York public relations executive and an active Republican. In 1940 he assisted Hoover's quest for the Republican Party's presidential nomination.]

11. [*Editor's note*: Hoover's memorandum ends at this point.]

INDEX

Britioth, Barge, 136
Bromfield, Louis, 273–75
brotherhood, gospel of, 103
Browder, Earl, 223, 461, 461n2
Brown, Clarence J., 368, 375
Brown, Walter F., 351
Brownell, Herbert, Jr., 375
Bruhn, Bruno, 127
Brussels World Fair (1958), xxxii
Bryan, William Jennings, 455
Bucknell, Howard, 117
budget
    Bureau of, 378
    Layman's, 173
    See also balanced budget
Budget and Accounting Act, 350
Bundy, Harvey A., 389
Bureau of the Budget, 378
bureaucracy
    character and, 39
    electric power and, 332
    growth of, 286, 352–53, 366
    increased, 347, 359
    political, 76–77, 286
business
    aids to, 319
    big, 316–18
    government as, 351
    government questionnaires and, 357–58
    regulation of, 83–84, 164, 329, 434–35

Cajander, Kaarlo, 135
California Women's Republican Committee, 246
Canterbury Tales, 23–24
Carnegie Institute, 469
Carr, Wilbur C., 122
Carter, Boake, 212
Carter, Jimmy, xxxii
Cartier, Baron, 145
Case Institute of Technology, 328
centralization
    of government, 358–59, 426, 461
    regulation and, 461
    of relief, 92
    waste in federal government and, 358–59
The Challenge to Liberty (Hoover, H.), xvii–
        xxii, xxxiii, xln39, 57–60, 453
    book reviews of, xix–xxii, 60, 453, 453n2
Chamberlain, John, xxi, 453, 453n2
Chamberlain, Neville, 117, 121, 142–45
Chamberlin, William Henry, 458
chaos, as prelude to Fascism, 132–33
charitable contributions by the Hoovers, 10, 468
charity, 39
Charlotte (N.C.) Observer, 183
Chautemps, Camille, 117
"Cheerio," 396

Chicago
    Junior Chamber of Commerce, 294
    Union League Club, 410
Child Health Day, 398
child labor
    abolition of, 89, 195, 321, 386–87, 386n6, 399
    crusade by Hoover for American children
        and, 386–88, 386n6
    Hammer v. Dagenhart and, 386n6
children
    Bill of Rights of, 395, 395n6, 401–2, 402n18
    classification of, 400
    in family life, 12–16
    food relief and, 385–87, 413–14
    juvenile offenders, 402, 409, 410n4
    Republican policy toward, 321
    undernourishment and, 385–87
    See also American children, crusade for; boys
Children's Bureau, 321
China
    Communism in, 300
    Hoover, Herbert, living in, 412
    Open Door policy in, 325
Churchill, Winston, xxvi, xxxiv, 31, 141, 239n17
CIO. See Congress of Industrial Organizations
Citizens Committee for the Hoover Reports
    First Hoover Commission and, 370–73
    Second Hoover Commission and, 378–79
"Citizenship" (course at Stanford University),
        57, 453
Civil Service Commission, 322
Civil War, U.S., 347–48, 430
civilian economic organization, in war, 240–43
civilian employees, number of, in federal gov-
        ernment, 68, 347, 366
civilization
    liberty and, 164
    newspapers and, 72
Clapper, Raymond, 224
class
    hate, 103, 175, 184
    stratification in Europe, 412
Clemenceau, Georges, 415
Cleveland, Grover, 19, 101n12, 316, 318
Coates, Charles B., 369–70, 378
codes of ethics, in government, 301–2
coerced economy, 188, 196
Colby, Bainbridge, 419–20, 420n24
Colby College, 163
Cold War
    Great Debate and (1950–51), xxix
    ground armies and, 312
    militarism and, 312
    waste in federal government and, 347–48, 373
    winning, Hoover's prescription for, 373
Cole, Albert L., 404
collective bargaining, 84

democracy
experiment of, preserved, 373
inertia of, 439–40
as living force, 108
prosperity and, 122
protection of, 151
two-party government in, 258
Democratic Party
Congress controlled by, 365
conventions, 94–100, 204–9, 245–46
corruption in, 324–25
New Deal imprisoning of, 88
as party of the left, 294
philosophical differentiation of, from Republicans, 460–61
platforms, 179–80
service of, under past leaders, 316
Southern Democrats in, 160–61
true liberalism and, 316
Department of Agriculture, 321
Department of Commerce, 357
departmental reorganization, 363–66
dependency, growth of, 287
Des Moines Register, 214
devaluation of currency, 69, 71, 176
Dewey, Thomas
assessment of, by Hoover, xxiv, 460–62
memorandum of Hoover's conversation with, 448–50
in 1944 presidential election, 109–11, 246–47, 252, 448–50, 457, 460–62, 464–65
in 1948 presidential election, 275–76
nomination of, 110, 209, 246–47, 252, 275, 448–50
Senate appointment by, 13
Taft and, 213
unemployment and, 461
WW II and, 211, 449
dictatorships
military, 240
of proletariat, 256
propaganda used by, 175
rise of, 147
Dinwiddie, Courtenay, 394
disarmament, 466
dishonesty
greatest lie of 1944 presidential campaign, 110–11, 457–59
honesty and, 177, 181, 222, 302
intellectual, 222–23, 225, 299, 306
money, 222–23
political, 222–23
restraints on, 439
disinflation, 282
Disque, Brice P., 486, 486n2
distribution
of commodities, 241–42

industrial revolution and, 452
in U.S. economic system, 436–40
Dollfuss, Engelbert, 122
Do-Nothing policies, attributed to Republicans, 100
draft (WW I), 385
dry-fly fishermen, 21, 24
dude ranch, visited by Hoover, 23
Dulles, John Foster, 449
Dumbarton Oaks, 466, 466n2

Ebert, Friedrich, 49
"The Economic Consequences of the New Deal" address, 186–97
Economic Cooperation Administration, 262
economic experience, Hoover's crusade against collectivism and, 290–91
economic freedom, 235–37
"Economic Recovery from the War" address, 255
economic revolution, 291–92
economic system
of liberty, 201
U.S., 187–90, 291–92, 424–26, 436–40
economy
capacity of, in U.S., 296
civilian organization of, in war, 240–43
coerced, 188, 196
German, 127
government-dictated, 83, 85–87, 164
laissez-faire, 200, 291, 317, 329, 435, 452
Lenin's New Economic Policy and, 419
purpose of, 186–87
research on, 357–58
of scarcity, 63, 65
survival of, 372
war, 65, 240
See also planned economy
education
in good government, 372
higher, reform and, 265–66
Eisenhower, Dwight
fishing by, 19
foreign policy views of, 484–86
Hoover, Herbert, and, xxix, xxxii, 19, 315–28, 375, 484–86, 492–95
liabilities of, 494–95
memorandum by Hoover on, 484–86
New York Times and, 493
in 1952 presidential election, 315–27, 492–95
nomination of, 315
reorganization of executive branch and, 375
Roosevelt, Franklin, and, 485
Socialism and, 328
Truman and, 484–85, 494
Willkie and, 495
elections, pollution of, 182–83
See also specific elections

health (Hoover's), xxxii–xxxiii, 267, 367–68
  gall bladder operation, xxxii
  shingles and, xxxii, 267, 368
Henry, Lou. *See* Hoover, Lou
Herbert Hoover Foundation, xxxi
Herbert Hoover Papers, xliii–xliv
Herbert Hoover Presidential Library, ix, 443
Herter, Christian A., 389
hidden hand ex-presidency (Hoover's), 484
higher education, reform and, 265–66
highways, Hoover's travels on, 22–25
Hillman, Sidney, 461, 461n2
Hirst, Francis, 145
Hiss, Alger, 61, 280
hitchhikers, 23–24
"Historic Liberalism," xxii
Hitler, Adolf
  Communism and, 125
  Germany and, 113–14, 121–22, 124–25, 128,
    143n15, 176, 182, 233–34, 268, 326, 382, 446
  meeting of Hoover with, 124–25
  Treaty of Versailles repudiated by, 114, 128
  WW II and, 233–34, 268, 326, 446
Hodza, Milan, 123
Holifield, Chet, 375, 378, 378n2
Hollister, John B., 377
Hollister, Solomon C., 375
Holsti, Rudolf, 135
Holt, L. Emmett, 393
home (Hoover's)
  in London, 15–16
  in Palo Alto, xv, xx, xxiv, xlin55, 7, 7n3, 11n9,
    12, 34, 468
  at Waldorf-Astoria, xxiv, xxviii, xxxi, xxxiii, 11,
    11n9, 341, 467
honesty, 177, 181, 222, 302
honor
  of Allies, 414–15
  of Constitution, 196
  of ex-presidency, 8
  flight from, 298–300
  in public life, 90–91, 297–302
  sacred, 301, 306
Hoover, Allan (son), 34
  family life with, 12–16
  on motor trip, 24
Hoover, Herbert. *See specific topics*
Hoover, Herbert, Jr. (son), 12–16, 34, 492
Hoover, Lou (wife)
  death of, xlin55, 31–34
  family life with, 7–9, 11, 15
  Girl Scouts and, 391
  marriage of Hoover to, 7–9, 11, 15, 18, 24–25,
    31–32, 34, 215, 468
  recreation and, 18, 24–25
  at Stanford University, 31–32, 34
  on Willkie, 215

Hoover, Theodore (brother), xxxv
The Hoover Administration (Newton and
  Myers), 60
Hoover Commission. *See* Commission on Or-
  ganization of the Executive Branch of the
  Government
"Hoover farm," 11
Hoover Institution on War, Revolution and
  Peace
  Adams and, 46, 381
  as benevolent institution, 45–49, 380–84
  finances, 383, 470
  Hoover, Herbert, and, xxiv, xxxi, xliii–xliv,
    45–49, 380–84, 443, 470, 470n4, 483, 488
  name of, 470n4
  1938 European visit by Hoover and, 382
  peace and, 47, 383–84
  uses of, 383–84, 470
  WW II and, 48, 383
The Hoover Policies (Wilbur and Hyde), 60–61
Hoovervilles, xviii
Hopkins, Harry, 99, 168, 224, 253
House, Edward M., 239n17
housing
  New Deal and, 89
  Republican Party and, 321–22
Hughes, Charles Evans, 489–91, 491n3
Hull, Cordell, 204–5, 446
humanitarianism
  of Hoover, Herbert, xii–xiii, xxxiv, 31, 31n1,
    167–68, 203, 475, 475n2, 482–83
  purpose of, in U.S., 194–96
  See also relief
Hungary, 122, 415
Huntington Library, 469
Hurley, Patrick, 450
Hyde, Arthur M., 60–61, 80, 160

Ickes, Harold, xix, xxi, 253
idealism, xxxiv–xxxvi, 47, 80, 195
ideology, 453
"The Incident of Justice Hughes," 489–91
independent agencies, of federal government,
  358
indirect regulation, 84
individualism
  American, xiii, xvi, 82, 290
  Ickes and, xix
  as social security, 63, 65–66
  in Stanford University commencement ad-
    dress by Hoover, 63–66
  in Sweden, 136
Industrial Revolution
  distribution and, 452
  oppression in, 200, 452
  production and, 452
  from scientific discovery, 200–201

infant mortality, in U.S. during Great Depression, 93, 402–3
inflation
   crusade by Hoover against collectivism and, 303–5
   currency, 241, 303–5, 430
integrity
   in mind, 177
   of Supreme Court, 432–33, 491n3
intellectual dishonesty, 222–23, 225, 299, 306
international relations
   cooperation in, 319–20
   foreign policy and, 308–13
   peace in, 465
   unity in, 285
Interstate Commerce Commission, 317
interstate roads, 324
investment banking, 438
Iowa Centennial, 296–97
Iran, 14
Irwin, Will, xxxii, 26, 29
Italy
   Fascism in, 149, 421
   Mussolini in, 134, 290–91, 307, 317, 382, 421
   revolution in, 139
   Socialism and, 258

Jackson, Andrew, 68
Janson, Paul, 113
Jean, Sally Lucas, 394
Jefferson, Thomas, 229, 316
Johnson, Hewlett, 239, 239n18
Johnson, Hiram, xxxiv, 216, 230
Johnson, Hugh, 455
Johnson, Robert L., 370, 378
Jones, Richard Lloyd, 246
judicial authority, of administrators, 354–55
Junior Chamber of Commerce, at Chicago, 294
juvenile offenders, 402, 409, 410n4

Kallio, Kyosti, 135
Karin Hall, 125
Keating-Owen Act of 1916, 386n6
Kelland, Clarence Budington, 29–30, 478–79, 478n4
Kellogg, Vernon L., 49, 49n12
Kellogg, W. K., xxiii, 475n3
Kelly, Edward, 208, 208n23, 224
Kemmerer, Edwin W., 90, 90n41
Kemp, Arthur
   assistance from, xxvii, xlin60, 489
   papers of, 443, 446, 448, 460, 463, 489
Kennedy, Joseph P., 141–42, 368, 375
Kennedy, Thomas, 97
Kent, Frank, 110–11, 111n22, 457
Kerr, Philip, 144, 472, 472n1
Kerr, Robert, 246, 246n7

Keynes, John Maynard, 291, 307
kidnapping laws, 402
Kienbock, Viktor, 119
Klotz, Louis-Lucien, 415
Knerr, Hugh, 486, 486n2
Knox, Frank, 105, 446
Korean War, 290, 294, 309, 347–48
Kover, Edgar, 134
Krofta, Kamil, 122–23
Ku Klux Klan, 178, 178n25
Kun, Bela, 415
Kwapiszewski, Michael, 129

Labor unions
   CIO, 245–46, 464, 464n1
   collective bargaining by, 84
   Communism and, 98
   disunity in, 192, 192n41
   Republican Party and, 321
   secretary of, 354
   UMW and, 97–98
   See also child labor
LaFollette, Robert, 455
laissez-faire, xix, 82, 200, 291, 317, 329, 435, 452
Lamont, Thomas, 210, 455, 472, 472n1
Landon, Alf
   crusade by Hoover against collectivism after defeat of, 112–97
   Hoover, Herbert, and, xxiv, 100, 101n12, 105–7, 109, 457
   in 1936 presidential campaign, 97, 100, 101n12, 105–7, 109, 214, 230, 252
Lane, Gertrude, xvii–xviii
Laski, Harold, 239
Latvia
   Fascism in, 132
   liberty in, 133
   1938 visit by Hoover to, 131–34
Lawrence, David, 211
layman's budget, 173
leadership
   concepts, corruption in, 256
   intellectual, of Republican Party, xxiii
League of Nations
   foreign policy and, 117–21, 123, 147, 462
   1938 European visit by Hoover and, 117–21
Lebrun, Albert, 116
left wing, 293–94, 464–65
left wingers, xxiv, 105
legislative authority, of administrators, 354–55
Lenin, Vladimir
   New Economic Policy of, 419
   in Soviet Russia, 137–38, 293, 413, 415–16, 419
Leonard, Walter, 134
Leopold III (king), 113–14, 113n4
Lewald, Theodor, 127
Lewis, John L., 97, 210, 245–46

Lewis, Sinclair, xxxii
libel, in politics, 464
liberalism
  false, xx, xxii, 103, 338, 434
  Hoover, Herbert, and, xvi, xix–xx, xxii,
    58n4, 86–88, 103, 117, 120, 162, 190, 223, 270,
    281–82, 293, 300, 338, 434, 460–61
  meaning of, 86–88, 162, 190, 293, 300, 338
  philosophical differentiation of, from New
    Deal, 460–61
  spirit of, 434
  totalitarianism and, 117, 120, 270, 461
  See also true liberalism
liberty
  aid abroad for, 269
  as anchor of civilization, 164
  under attack, 57–60, 82, 104, 108, 142, 147–48,
    178–80, 236–37, 270–71, 315, 452
  The Challenge to Liberty and, xix–xxii, xxxiii,
    xln39, 57–60, 453
  decadence of, abroad, 102
  economic system of, 201
  government-regulated business preserving,
    83–84
  in Latvia, 133
  political power and, 201
  revolution of, 200
  right to, 57
  rise of, 451–52
  war and, 236–37, 243, 259
  world problem of, 268–69
  See also freedom
Library on War, Revolution and Peace. See
  Hoover Institution on War, Revolution and
  Peace
Lincoln, Abraham, 90, 198–99, 222, 257, 317
Lincoln Day addresses (Hoover's), 198–99, 257–58
Lincoln University commencement address
  (Hoover's), 199–202
Lindbergh, Charles, 128
Lippmann, Walter, 162, 174, 455
Lisbon agreement, 310
Lloyd George, David, 413–14
local self-government, 76
Lochner, Louis, 128
Logan-Walter Bill, 218
London, Hoover family life in, 15–17
London Times, 310, 485
longevity of Hoover, xxxii
Lorimer, George Horace, 60
Lost Statesmanship (Hoover, H.), xxviii, 488
Lynchburg (Va.) Advance, 183
Lyttleton, Oliver, 239

MacArthur, Douglas, 309, 449–50, 486, 486n2
machine politics, 221
MacNeil, Neil, 377

Macon (Ga.) Telegraph, 183
Magnum Opus. See Freedom Betrayed
managed currency, 70–71, 105, 171–72, 176, 193,
  459
management style (Hoover's), xxxiv
manpower, assignment of, 241
manuscript sources, for The Crusade Years,
  xliii–xliv
Marshall, George, 273
Martin, Joseph, 267
Marx, Karl, 277, 290–91, 307, 338, 412
May Day, 397–98
McClellan, John, 368, 375
McCormick, Robert L. L., 369–70, 378
McGarry, Thomas D., 208
"me too" attitude, in Republican Party, 257,
  460–61, 486
Mead, George, 368
Meier, Hugo, 390
Meloney, Mrs. William B., 394
Memoirs (Hoover, H.), 3, 53, 191
  advice about publishing, 477–78
  book manuscript file, xliii–xliv
  footnotes of, xlv
  making of, xiv, xxv–xxxii, xliii–xliv, 341,
    345–46, 443–44, 451, 467, 480
  New Deal and, xxvii–xxviii, 53–54
  purpose of, 474
memoranda (Hoover's)
  assessment of Dewey's 1944 presidential cam-
    paign, 460–62
  of conversation with Dewey, 448–50
  of conversation with Willkie, 445–47
  on Eisenhower and Taft, 484–86
  greatest lie of 1944 presidential campaign,
    110–11, 457–59
  habit of making, 445
  on Hughes, 489–91
Metz, Harold W., 377
Michelson, Charles, 245
migrant workers, in California, 14–15
Miklas, Wilhelm, 122
Milbank, Jeremiah, 48, 48n10, 470
military
  air force, 313
  dictatorships, 240
  disarmament of, 466
  ground armies, 312, 485
  maximum armed forces, 347
  naval competition, 325
  politics and, 493
  race to arms and, 147
  reorganization of, 371
  of Soviet Russia, 313, 485
  strength, 240, 312–13, 466
Miller, Douglas, 128
Miller, Herbert, 369

politics, 220–22
  in presidency, 218–19, 366
  of Supreme Court, 219–20
  through taxes and spending, 184
Power Commission. *See* Federal Power
  Commission
power companies. *See* electric power, private
  enterprise in
practical achievement, exalted by Hoover, xxxv
Praetorian Guard, 167, 182
Pratt, William V., 486, 486n2
"A Preliminary Program of Reconstruction"
  (Hoover, H.), 243–44
president (U.S.)
  pension for, xliin81, 8–10, 8n5, 10n8
  power of, 218–19, 366
  professional soldiers as, 494–95
  two-term limit of, 262
  war council of, 241
  See also executive branch; ex-presidency
presidential elections. *See* nomination, presidential; party conventions; *specific elections*
Pressman, Lee, 61
price fixing, 241–42
Priestley, J. B., 239
primary source, *The Crusade Years* as, xlv
prime minister (British), pension of, 8, 8n5
Princeton University, 264–67
prison reform, 323
production
  industrial revolution and, 452
  oppression from, 329
  in U.S. economic system, 436–40
  of war essentials, 241
productivity
  increased, 64, 164
  as social security, 65
professional soldiers, 494–95
proletariat, dictatorship of, 256
propaganda
  dictatorships using, 175
  gadgets of, 299–300
  May Day, 397
  In New Deal, 164, 174–75
  radio, 174
  reorganization of executive branch and, 361
public improvements, 324
public life, honor in, 90–91, 297–302
public works
  agencies, 355, 364
  expenditures, 71, 76, 93, 194, 356
  policy, 350, 356
  Republicans and, 324
  Task Force, 369
  unemployment and, 120, 140, 148, 168, 194,
    319, 432
Pure Food and Drug Acts, 318

pursuit of happiness, 41, 406
Pusey, Merlo J., 489

Quakers. *See* Society of Friends

race to arms, in Europe, 147
Radical, definitions of, 86–87
radio
  "Cheerio" program, 396
  highways and, 22
  used for New Deal propaganda, 174
reactionary
  defined, 86–87
  Hoover, Herbert, and, 82, 86–87, 94, 106, 175,
    216, 222, 226, 265, 282–84, 298, 300, 316–17,
    320–23
  "old" and, 298
  Republican Party misrepresented as, 82, 216,
    316, 320–23
  Supreme Court accused by Roosevelt, Frank-
    lin, of being, 317
Reagan, Ronald, xxxvii
reconstruction
  collectivism and, 243–44
  of Europe, 269
  in "A Preliminary Program of Reconstruc-
    tion," 243–44
  WW II and, 243–44, 269, 465, 482
recovery
  from Great Depression, 94, 148, 153–54, 158,
    320, 458
  New Deal and, 458
  from war, 255–58
recreation (Hoover's)
  fishing, 18–21, 23–24
  Hoover, Lou, and, 18, 24–25
  motor trips, 22–25
Red House, 15–16
Red Imperialism, 137
red tape, and government, 360
reform
  higher education and, 265
  waste in federal government and, 361
regimentation, New Deal as, xix
regulation
  banking, 84, 319
  business, 83–84, 164, 329, 434–35
  centralization and, 461
  indirect, 84
Reid, Helen, 210, 472–73
Reid, Whitelaw, 472
relief
  American Relief Administration and, xii,
    389
  CRB, xi, xxx, 44, 46, 380
  decentralization of, 92, 177
  farm, 77–78, 262, 319, 321

Taft, Robert
  aid to Britain and, 473
  American Children's Fund and, 389
  Dewey and, 213
  fishing by, 19
  foreign policy views of, 484–86
  Hoover, Herbert, and, xxix, xxxiv, 19, 209, 211,
    213, 315, 389, 456, 472–73, 492–96
  memorandum by Hoover on, 484–86
Taft Clubs, 496
Taft-Harley Act, 262–63
Talbott, Harold E., 456, 456n4
Tammany Hall, 91, 100
tariffs, xvii, 263, 318, 361, 430
Task Forces
  of First Hoover Commission, 368–70
  of Second Hoover Commission, 375–78
Tate, Ben, 495
Tatter, Albert, 134
taxes, 84, 437
  as assassin of freedom, 307
  corporation, 288
  crusade by Hoover against collectivism and,
    304–5
  days' work to pay, 287
  debt paid with, 193
  development of, 452
  income tax maze, 357
  increased, 288
  new, 298
  power amassed through, 184
  private enterprise in electric power and, 333
  after WW II, 465
  waste in federal government and, 372
Taylor, Henry J., 460–62, 460n1
technological advances, 64, 291, 427–28
telegrams
  Hoover, Herbert, and, 11, 87, 211, 213, 216–17,
    217n35, 230, 273, 422, 455, 490
  received in Palo Alto (1940), 211, 455
Thompson, Dorothy, 210, 455, 472, 472n1
Tientsin, siege of, 32–33, 33n3
Timmons, Bascom N., 206, 213
Tory, defined, 86–87
totalitarian economics, 202
totalitarian liberals, 120, 259, 270, 461
totalitarianism
  Communism and, 270
  liberalism and, 117, 120, 270
  opposition of Hoover to, 411–12
Treaty of Versailles
  consequences of, 116, 118–21, 132, 140
  Europe and, 114, 116, 118–21, 128, 132, 140, 248,
    458
  Hitler repudiation of, 114, 128
true liberalism
  drift away from, 464

Hoover, Herbert, and, xx, 150, 155, 162–63,
    282, 338, 424, 434, 453, 461, 464
  spirit of, 434
  See also liberalism
Truman, Harry
  Acheson and, 254, 280, 295, 309–10, 484–86
  appointees of, 263
  attacks on, 295–305
  crusade by Hoover against collectivism and,
    253–54, 263, 267, 273
  dual personality of, 253, 267, 275, 280
  Eisenhower and, 484–85, 494
  Fair Deal of, 279–80
  fishing and, 20
  foreign policy of, 303, 475, 484–85
  Hoover, Herbert, and, xxiv, xxviii, 253–54,
    258–59, 263–64, 273, 285, 295–327, 367–68,
    382
  left turn of, 267, 279–81
  in 1948 presidential election, 275–76
  North and, 253
  Old Age Pension proposals of, 280–81
  planned economy and, 267
  reorganization of executive branch and, 367–68
  smears by, 275, 275n33
  South and, 253
  Supreme Court and, 253
truth
  in government, 174
  unveiled by debate, 300–301
Tuck, Hallam, 377, 390
Turner, Scott, 390
"Twelve Years 1932–1944" (Hoover, H.), 467–70
two-party government, 258, 315
two-term limit, of president, 262

Ulmanis, Karlis, 131–34, 131n11, 134n12
UMW. See United Mine Workers
uncommon man, 256. See also common man,
  cult of
"Undermining Representative Government,"
  177–86
undernourishment of American children, 385–87
underprivileged boys, 42, 407–8
unemployment
  Dewey and, 461
  in Fascism, 85
  humanitarianism and, 196
  insurance, 85
  pressing problem of (1938), 152–54, 156, 186
  public works and, 120, 140, 148, 168, 194, 319, 432
  relief, 76, 92, 319, 402
  Republican Party and, 76
  Roosevelt, Franklin, and, 461–62
  in Socialism, 85
  after WW II, 465–66
Union League Club, 410

United Kingdom. *See* Britain
United Mine Workers (UMW), 97–98
United States (U.S.)
  air force, 178
  balanced budget in, 67–68, 173, 284, 312
  benevolence of, xi
  Civil War, 347–48, 430
  collectivism in, 422–23, 425–40
  Communism in, 61, 289, 294
  confused state of (1939), 198–99
  credit system, 438
  danger to (1939), 202
  Declaration of Independence of, 314–15, 373
  disunity in (1938), 192–93
  economic capacity of, 296
  economic purpose in (1938), 186–87
  economic system of, 187–90, 291–92, 424–26,
    436–40
  Europe's relationship with, 115, 150–51
  experiment of, preserved, 373
  fear in, 153–54, 459
  Founding Fathers of, 41, 282, 290, 299, 306
  freedom destroyed in, 186, 249–50
  government system of, 425–26
  greatness of, 276–77
  humanitarian purpose of, 194–96
  individualism in, xiii, xvi, 82, 290
  national debt of, 67, 69, 367, 372
  securities, 140
  social responsibility, growth of in, 429
  system of freedom in, 254–58, 311–12, 426–27
  Ulmanis and, 131–34, 131n11
  at war, 203, 228, 228n59, 347–48, 416–17, 430
  See also American system; American way of
    life; Constitution, U.S.
universe, moral purpose of, 102
U.S. *See* United States

Van Ingen, Philip, 392–93
Vandenburg, Arthur H., 105
veterans, Republican policy toward, 322
Veterans Bureau, 358
vindication, Hoover's desire for, xxiii, xxix,
    xxxiv–xxxv, 274, 457
virtues, "old," 298, 301
Voltaire, 412
voluntary cooperation, 38, 201, 427
Voorhees, Tracy S., 378

wage fixing, 241–42
Wagner, Robert F., 13
Wagner Act of 1935, 262
Waldorf-Astoria
  death of Hoover at, xxxi
  Hoover, Herbert, at, xxiv, xxviii, xxxi, xxxiii,
    11, 11n9, 341, 467
Wall Street, 316–18

Wallace, Henry A., 190, 224, 253
  New Frontiers by, xviii, xx–xxi
  in 1948 presidential election, 275–76
war
  administrators during, 240–41
  Civil, 347–48, 430
  civilian economic organization in, 240–43
  collectivism and, 236–37
  economy, 65, 303
  essentials, production of, 241
  focus on victory after, 243
  Korean, 290, 294, 309, 347–48
  liberty and, 236–37, 243, 259
  Napoleonic, 64, 78
  reconstruction and, 243–44, 269, 465, 482
  Roosevelt, Franklin, and, 215, 233–34, 462, 472
  U.S. at, 203, 228, 228n59, 347–48, 416–17, 430
  veterans, 322
  waste in federal government and, 347–48,
    360, 373–74
  See also Cold War; Hoover Institution on
    War, Revolution and Peace; World War I;
    World War II
Warburg, James, 210
Ware cell, 61
Warren, Earl, 449
Washington, George, 27, 103, 430, 494
waste in federal government, Hoover's crusade
    against
  address on, 351–62
  centralization and, 358–59
  Cold War and, 347–48, 373
  confusion of basic principles in, 353–54
  Congress and, 353, 361–62, 364–68, 374, 378
  division of authority and, 355–57
  education in good government from, 372
  growth of bureaucracy and, 286, 352–53, 366
  independent agencies in, 358
  introduction to, 347–48
  from 1921-1955, 347–79
  preoccupation with, 349–50
  proper expansion of government in, 359–60
  questionnaires in, 357–58
  reforms, 361
  reorganization of executive branch in, 347–48,
    351–79, 360
  Shipping Board in, 353–55
  taxes and, 372
  war and, 347–48, 360, 373–74
Wedemeyer, Albert, 486, 486n2
Wedemeyer Committee, 496
welfare state, 300
Welfare Clause (of U.S. Constitution), 336
Wells, H. G., 239
West Branch, IA, 276, 443
West Germany, 310, 367
wet-fly fishermen, 21

518 • *Index*

Whig Party, 104, 257, 314
White, Andrew D., 380
White, Harry Dexter, 61
White, William Allen, xix, xxi, 87–88, 88n38
"white ascendancy," in Southern politics, 160, 253
White House Conference on Child Health and
    Protection, 395, 399–402
Wickett, Fred A., 48, 48n10
Wiedmann, Fritz, 124
Wilbur, Ray Lyman, 26, 31–32, 46
    American Child Health Association and,
        394, 399
    American Children's Fund and, 389
    The Hoover Policies by, 60–61
Wiley, John C., 119
Williams, Aubrey, 168
Willkie, Wendell
    aid to Britain and, 473
    appraisal of, by Hoover, 454–56, 471–73
    death of, 454
    Eisenhower and, 495
    electricity and, 454–55
    Hoover, Lou, on, 215
    Hughes and, 490–91
    memorandum of Hoover's conversation with,
        445–47
    in 1940 presidential election, xxiii–xxiv, 11n9,
        209–17, 229–31, 252, 445, 471–73
    1944 presidential election and, 246–47, 449, 457
    nomination of, xxiii, 209–13, 445, 454–55
    One World by, 454
    planned economy and, 456
    Roosevelt, Franklin, and, 209–10, 246–47,
        446–47, 454
    sincerity of, 231
    WW II and, 215, 445–46, 472–73
Willkie Clubs, 447
Wilson, Hugh, 124
Wilson, Woodrow
    Hoover, Herbert, and, xii, xxii, xxx, 20, 316,
        318, 416, 419, 422
    Soviet Russia and, 416, 419
Wilson College, 255
women, as consumers, 89–90
Wood, Thomas D., 393
World Court, 325
World Economic Conference, 61, 319–20
World War I (WW I)
    agriculture and, 78
    civilian economic organization in, 240, 242

collectivism in, 422–23
draft, 385
Fascism and, 421–22, 446
Great Depression and, 318
Hoover, Herbert, and, xi, xxx, 33, 48, 203, 209,
    236–38, 240, 242, 413–20, 422–23, 482
institutions collapsing after, 428–29
progress following, 428–29
Socialism in, 422
waste in federal government and, 347–48
World War II (WW II)
    alliances, 233–35, 235n8, 326, 414–17
    Asia's future after, 465
    Britain in, 234, 239, 413–14, 446
    cause of, 115–16, 142–43
    crusade by Hoover against collectivism and,
        232–43
    Dewey and, 211, 449
    famine after, 482–83
    and freedom, 248–52
    Hitler and, 233–34, 268, 326, 446
    Hoover Institution on War, Revolution and
        Peace and, 48, 383
    reconstruction after, 243–44, 269, 465,
        482
    recovery from, 255–57
    relief during, xii, xxx, 203
    reorganization of executive branch and,
        367
    taxes after, 465
    unemployment after, 465–66
    U.S. in, 203, 228, 228n58, 416–17
    waste in federal government and, 347–48
    Willkie and, 215, 445–46, 472–73
    See also European visit by Hoover (1938)
writing practices (Hoover's), xxxiii
WW I. *See* World War I
WW II. *See* World War II
Wyoming, 23

Yarnell, Harry E., 486, 486n2
The Years as a Crusader (Hoover, H.), 480–82,
    487, 489
Young Republicans
    1936 presidential election and, 82–87
    1938 Congressional election and, 161–65
youth
    freedom and, 250–52
    and Republican Party, 82–87, 161–65,
        250–52

Illustration Sources/Credits

Frontispiece photo on page ii:
© Bettmann/CORBIS/AP Images (no. U1196267/5908061210).

Photo Section I:
PAGE 1: Herbert Hoover Presidential Library (image #1933-62).
PAGE 2: *(TOP)* Herbert Hoover Presidential Library (image #1935-48), © Bettmann/CORBIS/Acme Newspictures, Inc.; *(BOTTOM)* Herbert Hoover Presidential Library (image #1937-34).
PAGE 3: Herbert Hoover Presidential Library (image #1935-22), © Bettmann/CORBIS/AP Images.
PAGE 4: Herbert Hoover Presidential Library (image #1953-12A), © Bettmann/CORBIS/AP Images.
PAGE 5: Herbert Hoover Presidential Library (from Fred Clark Papers, FGC–Sm–Album 01, 1948), Fred Clark, photographer.
PAGE 6: *(TOP)* Herbert Hoover Presidential Library (image #1940-36A); *(BOTTOM)* Herbert Hoover Presidential Library (image #1958-11A)
PAGE 7: Herbert Hoover Presidential Library (from Fred Clark Papers, FGC–Sm–Album 01, 1953), Fred Clark, photographer.
PAGE 8: Herbert Hoover Presidential Library (image #1941-24).

Photo Section II:
PAGE 1: *(TOP)* Herbert Hoover Presidential Library (image #1936-20A), © CORBIS/Acme Newspictures, Inc.; *(MIDDLE)* Herbert Hoover Presidential Library (image #1940-41), © CORBIS/Acme Newspictures, Inc.; *(BOTTOM)* Herbert Hoover Presidential Library (image #1949-44), *New York World-Telegram* photo [public domain].
PAGE 2: *(TOP)* Herbert Hoover Presidential Library (image #1953-23), © CORBIS/International News Photos; *(BOTTOM)* Herbert Hoover Presidential Library (image #1944-12), © CORBIS/International News Photos.
PAGE 3: *(TOP)* Herbert Hoover Presidential Library (image #1952-17), © Bettmann/CORBIS/United Press Telephoto; *(BOTTOM)* Herbert Hoover Presidential Library (image #1947-35), United States Information Agency.
PAGE 4: *(TOP)* Herbert Hoover Presidential Library (image #1946-77), © CORBIS/Acme Newspictures, Inc.; *(BOTTOM)* Herbert Hoover Presidential Library (image #1946-51), © CORBIS/Acme Newspictures, Inc.
PAGE 5: *(TOP)* Herbert Hoover Presidential Library (image #1948-60); *(MIDDLE)* Herbert Hoover Presidential Library (in Lawrence Richey Collection, HH DDE 1953), National Park Service—Abbie Rowe, photographer; *(BOTTOM)* Herbert Hoover Presidential Library (image #1954-7A), © Bettmann/CORBIS/AP Images.
PAGES 6 AND 7: Hoover Institution Archives, Stanford University (manuscript draft in Herbert Hoover's Papers, Box 90, folder 2), © Herbert Hoover Foundation.
PAGE 8: Herbert Hoover Presidential Library (image #1957-97).